Global America

GLOBAL AMERICA

THE UNITED STATES IN THE TWENTIETH CENTURY

Robert C. McGreevey
Christopher T. Fisher
Alan Dawley

New York   *Oxford*
OXFORD UNIVERSITY PRESS

Oxford University Press is a department of the University of Oxford. It furthers
the University's objective of excellence in research, scholarship, and education
by publishing worldwide. Oxford is a registered trademark of Oxford University
Press in the UK and certain other countries.

Published in the United States of America by Oxford University Press
198 Madison Avenue, New York, NY 10016, United States of America.

Library of Congress Cataloging-in-Publication Data

Names: McGreevey, Robert, author. | Fisher, Christopher, (Historian), author.
 | Dawley, Alan, 1943-2008, author.
Title: Global America : the United States in the twentieth century / Robert
 McGreevey, Christopher Fisher, Alan Dawley.
Description: New York, NY : Oxford University Press, 2018. | Includes index.
Identifiers: LCCN 2017025524 | ISBN 9780190279905 (pbk.)
Subjects: LCSH: United States—Foreign relations—20th century. |
 Globalization—History—20th century.
Classification: LCC E744 .M4165 2018 | DDC 327.73009/04—dc23
LC record available at https://lccn.loc.gov/2017025524

9 8 7 6 5 4 3 2 1
Printed by LSC Communications, Inc., United States of America

For Alan Charles Dawley, mentor, colleague, and friend,
who thought and lived with purpose.

Brief
CONTENTS

Part 1: INDUSTRY AND EMPIRE, 1893–1945

Part 2: BURDENS OF THE COLOSSUS, 1945–2012

CONTENTS

List of
MAPS

List of
GRAPHS

PREFACE

Global America tells the story of how Americans were swept up in the swift-moving currents of twentieth-century world history. Starting with U.S. expansion in the late nineteenth century, the book situates American developments within the context of major political and economic events, explores key developments in culture and society, and ends with the rise and partial decline of American power in recent years. Written as a synthesis of some of the latest research on the history of the United States in the world, *Global America* clearly demonstrates how global interactions and developments transformed both America and the world.

Scholars began to internationalize the history of the United States two decades ago. From 1997 to 2000, a group of historians led by Thomas Bender, Linda Kerber, and David Thelen organized meetings at La Pietra, New York University's off-campus site in Florence, Italy, for the purpose of reconceptualizing American history in the wider global arena. As a group, these historians were frustrated with the separation between American historians and historians who studied the rest of the world, particularly in an age of globalization. Wanting to write the United States back into world history, those meetings produced the "La Pietra Report," which launched a new approach to American history known as U.S. in the World. With this approach, historians sought to push beyond the limits of national history to explore the connections that tied different parts of the world together, while still respecting the distinctions between peoples and states.

Shaped by the La Pietra meetings, U.S. in the World scholars sought a balance between the world out there and the nation here at home. Following the example of earlier transnational histories, such as Paul Gilroy's important study of the black Atlantic in the 1990s and Olive Banks's examination of transatlantic feminism, this new generation of historians began to track the flows of people, ideas, money, and goods across national boundaries. American historians devoted increased attention to networks and nonstate actors, as well as to the unanticipated domestic effects of U.S. involvement overseas. In the give and take between the United States and the world, these scholars hoped to convey a dynamic America.

Global America is written in the spirit of La Pietra and the ongoing effort to trace a globalized U.S. history. It grew out of the life work and scholarship of the late historian Alan Dawley, one of the early leaders of the U.S. in the World approach. Alan began working on *Global America* as he shifted his focus from labor history to the history of the U.S. in the world. Christopher T. Fisher, a scholar of U.S. Cold War relations, and Robert C. McGreevey, a historian of America in the Gilded Age and Progressive Era, took over the completion of the textbook after Alan's sudden passing in 2008. *Global America* has evolved to reflect changes in the field of U.S. social, diplomatic, political, cultural, and economic history.

Drawing on published scholarship on topics as varied as labor resistance to U.S. corporate expansion in Latin America, the role of Hollywood in the post-war reconstruction of Japan, and the links between American foreign policy and immigration, *Global America* highlights America's effect on the wider world and the reciprocal impact of global developments on the United States. The text pays particular attention to themes of race, class, and gender and how each has shaped—and been shaped by—U.S. engagement with the world. The book explores a system of feedback loops, or reciprocating chain reactions between America and the world, that became a constitutive part of the larger globalization dynamic in the twentieth century. *Global America* argues that the more America sought to change the world, the more the world changed America.

In exploring these themes, this book offers a synthesis accessible to undergraduates. The chapters are organized chronologically, beginning with the 1890s and ending in 2013. To enliven connections between American and world history, each chapter begins with a vividly written vignette that offers a microcosm of the larger developments discussed throughout the chapter. For example, Chapter 2, on the War of 1898, begins with U.S. colonialism in Puerto Rico and then moves to the role colonial migrants played in shaping new immigration laws in Washington. Similarly, Chapter 9 on civil rights begins with Martin Luther King Jr. at the celebration of Ghana's independence and then shows how race relations in the United States and the changing fate of colonial peoples intersected in a larger history of race, power, and difference. To ground the reader in time, place, and meaning and as a way of connecting the story to the book's overarching themes, a clear delineation of the chapter's key concepts follows each vignette. In the case of the War of 1898, Chapter 2 examines migration, labor, and the building of the U.S. empire, whereas Chapter 9 examines the global contours of race and social reform during the Cold War. Maps and illustrations are closely tied to the narrative throughout. Suggestions for further reading are included after the conclusion of each chapter for students looking to expand their knowledge further.

Global America could not have been completed without the kind support of the Dawley family. *Global America* began with Alan's probing questions about social justice in the modern world, but it was Katy Dawley, his wife, who brought it to a conclusion through the force of her will alone. Through the process of writing and revising this book, we have had the privilege of continuing warm conversations begun on cold fall evenings at small dinner parties many years ago and sharing the growth of our families as we came together to celebrate Alan's life. Like the nation, we were shaken by the tragedy of 9/11, and Alan channeled that anxiety into efforts that seeded this examination of the United States in the world.

This book has benefited from the generosity of many people. We thank Evan Dawley, a historian of East Asia, whose expertise and careful editing rescued relevant sections of the text from error, sharpened interpretations, and improved the writing. For reading individual chapters, we thank Art Schmidt (Chapters 1 and 2), Roman Kovalev (Chapter 8), David Farber (Chapter 11), Marianna Sullivan and Michael Sullivan (Chapter 14), Jeremy Suri (prospectus), David Watt (prospectus), and Katy Dawley (for responses to many queries about her field of twentieth-century health care). We thank our colleagues who have supported this project and helped us think through various connections between U.S. and global histories: Mekala Audain, Matthew Bender, William Carter, Celia Chazelle, Daniel Crofts, Jo-Ann Gross, Craig Hollander, Alejandra Irigoin, John Karras, Roman Kovalev, Adam Knobler, Xinru Liu, Michael Marino, Ann Marie Nicolosi, Cynthia Paces, Qin Shao, and Jodi Weinstein. We also thank Jamie Bischoff as well as our students who have read drafts of chapters, especially Justine Thomas and Kathryn Wertheimer, who played a pivotal role in preparing the photos and maps for production.

We thank the humanities librarian at the College of New Jersey, David Murray, as well as our director of faculty–student collaborative activity, Jarret Crawford, and our deans, Jane Wong and Benjamin Rifkin. We thank our colleagues who keep the spirit of Alan's life work alive through the Alan Dawley Center for the Study of Social Justice. We thank the history department of the University of Pennsylvania for granting Alan Dawley the privileges of a visiting scholar, as well as the staff of the Van Pelt Library. Likewise, we extend our deepest appreciation to the many scholars whose work informs this book. Although partial lists of names are included in the Further Reading sections at the end of each chapter, this book draws on the work of many others as well. Our sincerest thanks go to the panels of anonymous readers who offered corrections and suggestions that are critical to the success of this book. Thanks to Jamie Bischoff for supporting this project from the beginning. We also thank our editor, Charles Cavaliere, and our editorial assistant Rowan Wixted, from Oxford University Press, and our former editors, Ann West and Brian Wheel, for their support of this book. We also owe a special thanks to Tee Williams and Miriam Shakow, who have supported us in more ways than we can count. Finally, we thank Benjamin A. Coates, Wake Forest University; Jeffrey D. Gonda, Syracuse University; Tracy K'Meyer, University of Louisville; Michelle Wick Patterson, Mount St. Mary's University; Bradley D. Snow, Montana State University; Sean P. Cunningham,

Texas Tech University; Nancy Beck Young, University of Houston; David E. Hamilton, University of Kentucky; and Chris Dietrich, Fordham University, who shared their helpful feedback with us.

As this book goes to press, Americans face such pressing societal concerns as international terrorism, global migration, climate change, national rivalries, economic turmoil, the costs of technological innovation, and a backlash against democratic government, among others. This book aims to open conversations about the complex past and present of America's relationship with the wider world in an effort to promote global understanding and citizenship.

ABOUT THE AUTHORS

ROBERT C. MCGREEVEY is an associate professor of history at the College of New Jersey. He holds a BA in history from Swarthmore College and a PhD in history from Brandeis University. A specialist in the political, social, and cultural history of United States from 1877 to 1945, he teaches courses on the Gilded Age and Progressive Era, America in the twentieth century, and the history of U.S. in the World. His research focuses on the intersection of foreign policy and migration in the twentieth century and has been supported by the Society for Historians of American Foreign Relations, the Immigration and Ethnic History Society, and the Organization of American Historians. His first book is *Borderline Citizens: The United States, Puerto Rico, and the Politics of Colonial Migration* (Cornell, 2018). His articles, book chapters, and reviews have been published in the *Journal of the Gilded Age and Progressive Era*, the *Journal of American History*, the *Journal of American Ethnic History*, and the *Blackwell Companion* series.

CHRISTOPHER T. FISHER, associate professor of history at the College of New Jersey in Ewing, New Jersey, earned a BA in history and political science from Rutgers College in 1993 and his PhD in history, with a focus on U.S. diplomacy, from Rutgers University in 2001. He has published in *Pacific Historical Review* and *International History Review*. Fisher is currently writing a book on the consequences of Cold War culture in the 1970s. His areas of expertise are the United States in the twentieth century, Cold War culture and diplomacy, U.S. in the World, American empire and imperialism, African American history, and racism and race relations in the United States.

ALAN DAWLEY died suddenly in 2008. He was a professor of history at the College of New Jersey, in Ewing, New Jersey. He founded TCNJ's Center for the Study of Social Justice as well as the U.S. in the World program. He was a participant in the La Pietra conference and a national leader in the movement for U.S. in the World scholarship. He earned a BA from Oberlin College in 1965 and his PhD in history at Harvard University in 1971. His areas of expertise included labor history, late nineteenth- and twentieth-century social history, and U.S. foreign relations, but his field of vision extended further to include questions of civil, gender, and human rights. He won the prestigious Bancroft Prize for his first book, *Class and Community: The Industrial Revolution in Lynn (Harvard, 1976)*. His subsequent books include: *Working for Democracy: American Workers from the Revolution to the Present (Illinois, 1985)*, *Struggles for Justice: Social Responsibility and the Liberal State (Harvard, 1993)*, and *Changing the World: American Progressives in War and Revolution (Princeton, 2005)*.

Part 1

INDUSTRY AND EMPIRE, 1893–1945

CHAPTER 1

THE UNITED STATES IN THE WORLD ECONOMY AT THE DAWN OF THE TWENTIETH CENTURY

The grand edifices of the Chicago World's Fair, known as the White City, incorporated neoclassical architecture and electric lights to convey Western ideals of civilization and progress. Frances Benjamin Johnston Collection, Library of Congress, Washington, DC.

1893: WORLD'S COLUMBIAN EXPOSITION

There was only one place for an American tourist to be in the summer of 1893: the World's Columbian Exposition in Chicago. Timed to commemorate the four hundredth anniversary of Christopher Columbus's historic voyage, the Chicago World's Fair showcased advances in science and industry while celebrating America's ascent to the front rank of human progress.

3

Since few tourists of the day could travel the world over, the world came to them through world's fairs. In Chicago, exhibits from Britain, Brazil, and dozens of other countries were on display in grand pavilions whose overall theme was progress. The story of progress was told through new telephone switchboards in the Electricity Building, new machines in the Hall of Manufactures, and the many accomplishments of women in the Women's Pavilion. Even a casual tourist could see the lesson of progress in the contrast between primitive Amazonian villages erected on the fairgrounds and the high civilization of the White City, a fantasyland of neoclassical sculptures and Greek temples illuminated by thousands of electric lights.

In highlighting such contrasts, the exposition reflected the late nineteenth-century penchant for understanding northern industrializing societies as more "civilized" than southern agricultural ones. As a writer for the Chicago Tribune *remarked while surveying the White City, "What an opportunity was here afforded to the scientific mind to descend the spiral of evolution, tracing humanity in its highest phases down almost to its animalistic origins." Such evolutionist thinking would shape Americans' hierarchical view of the world's people, with white Europeans and Americans at the very top and nonwhite peoples far below.*

When it was time to leave the White City, tourists passed through the city of Chicago. Like all industrial cities of the age, Chicago was a study in contrasts. It was a spectacle of industrial development with vast rail yards, steel mills, and meat-packing plants. Chicago's ten-story Home Insurance Building, completed in 1885, was the world's first skyscraper made with a steel frame. But Chicago was also home to urban squalor. An unwary tourist who strayed from the appointed path might wind up on streets begrimed with coal dust in the back-of-the-yards, enveloped by the nauseating stench of slaughtered cattle. Unlike the fair's fantasy world, flesh-and-blood Chicago seethed with labor discontent, which erupted in violent strikes against the very captains of industry whose generous donations had helped build the White City.

PROGRESS AND POVERTY IN THE WORLD ECONOMY

The stark contrast between the White City and the city of Chicago points to a defining feature of the late nineteenth century: the coexistence of progress and poverty. To be sure, new technologies of industrialization and ever-thickening transportation networks led to spectacular feats of production and distribution. On a world scale, increasing interdependence of the various parts of the world economy boosted the fortunes of the whole.

But the world economy was increasingly unequal. Great misery coexisted with great wealth. Slums disfigured booming cities. Agricultural distress accompanied industrial growth. Alongside these internal inequalities within industrial societies were growing gaps between them. Instead of uniform growth, this period was marked by patterns of uneven development in which the three tiers of the world economy—the industrial North, the middle tier of developing countries, and the agrarian South—reaped increasingly unequal rewards.

To thinkers of the day, these contradictions were something of a riddle. Puzzling over what he called "the enigma of our times," Henry George, a self-taught economist and philosopher, published a best-selling book in 1879 that captured the contradiction in its title, *Progress and Poverty*.

The Rise of Capitalism

Inequality and uneven development were, in part, a consequence of the way capitalism had evolved over the previous two centuries. Capitalism is a system of political economy in which economic surplus—what is left over after consumption—is used for private gain. Whether individuals or corporations, private owners engaged in the making of profits rather than the making of things. Whereas private control of the economic surplus can be found in any society with a money economy from biblical times through the Middle Ages, economic activity for most of human history had been subject to strict social controls. Decisions were in the hands of kin, village, and tribe, especially when it came to the life-or-death matter of allocating the economic surplus. Even in societies with kings and emperors, profit was normally subject to stringent social regulations, hence the Christian prohibition on usury (excessive interest) and the Islamic ban on interest altogether.

Beginning in the European Renaissance, however, social controls began to be cast aside as surplus was increasingly held in private hands. Capitalist practices spread in the seventeenth century to Holland and Britain and then in the eighteenth and nineteenth centuries more widely in Europe and North America. As the profit motive cut through the local web of social obligation, the result was what has been called the overthrow of society by the market.

Unlike the economic systems of ancient times, the inner spring of profit drove capitalism toward relentless expansion. The drive to accumulate wealth led to a search for riches in the furthest reaches of the globe. Beginning in the sixteenth century, growing demand for silver, sugar, and other New World products led to the enslavement of generations of indigenous people and Africans from Brazil to Virginia. Slavery and all that went with it—the horrors of the slave trade, the legacy of racial inequality, the mixture of African and European cultures—wove a common thread through New World societies, the United States included. But slavery proved both inefficient and morally objectionable in an economy where most people were free. The movement to end slavery gradually spread around the globe. Britain's early abolition of slavery in the Atlantic world, for example, began to change American public opinion and shape the conditions for the coming of the American Civil War. Slave labor was replaced by free labor everywhere in the middle decades of the nineteenth century. The principal of free labor, however, was repeatedly violated in practice. Chinese laborers who came to the United States in the period after the Civil War, for example, were labeled *coolies* (i.e., indentured laborers) because they were bound to work for employers until they paid off their debts for the long journey to America.

The First Industrial Revolution

Meanwhile, an increasing share of capital was finding its way into industry to launch the first in a series of industrial revolutions. Starting in Britain in the late eighteenth century and spreading to northern Europe and the United States by the middle of the nineteenth, the first industrial revolution was based on the technologies of the steam engine, the mechanized factory, and the railroad.

When free labor was linked to these new technologies, the secret of rising productivity was discovered. As an ever-larger segment of the world's population came to be employed as wage laborers in industry, the foundation was laid for ever-expanding production of goods and services. As the first industrial revolution gained momentum, the sinews of transportation and communication spread to all but the most remote reaches of every continent. In the short span of little more than a generation between 1870 and 1910, the world's merchant shipping fleet doubled, while the world's railway network expanded fivefold to around six hundred thousand miles spanning the North American continent in 1869 and Asia by 1916. As railroads were built across the North American prairie, Latin American hinterlands, and African mining areas, distant frontiers were linked to the metropolitan centers of London, Paris, and Berlin. Rude mining camps and rough rail junctions populated by hardscrabble miners, cattle drivers, and prostitutes may have been located far from the civilized capitals of taste and refinement, but they were outposts of capitalist development all the same.

These far-flung regions became increasingly integrated in a single, interdependent network. Growth in one sector stimulated growth in another through what are known as *feedback loops*. In one such loop, more than five hundred British companies were set up between 1860 and 1901 to mine American ore, mostly in the frontier districts of the Rocky Mountains. In turn, cheap imports of iron ore and copper stimulated industrial growth in Britain, which generated profits that could be turned into mining investments in the Rockies, thus closing the loop. Combining cheap raw materials and new refining technologies helped industrial output register spectacular increases. In the case of steel, global tonnage multiplied twentyfold between 1870 and 1890, whereas iron output more than doubled in the five main producing countries.

In the context of the industrial revolution, national economies were no longer islands unto themselves; rather, they were nodes within the larger network of a world economy marked by a high degree of interdependence. Nation-states affected the structure of the world economy insofar as each had its own currency, laws, and markets, and each competed with the others for what Adam Smith, the father of classical economic theory, called "the wealth of nations." But by the end of the nineteenth century, it was possible to speak of an integrated world economy, a whole greater than the sum of its parts.

Growth and Inequality

Although the world economy became more interdependent, development throughout the system was highly unequal. Combining human labor and the profit motive led to prodigious feats of production. The overall size of the economic pie grew at the fastest rate in human history. For the world economy as a whole, gross domestic product per capita—that is, the value per person of all goods and services produced—skyrocketed from an estimated $651 in 1820 to $5,145 in 1992.

This growth is especially impressive given the expansion of the world population. In 1820, the world population totaled approximately 1 billion people. The population grew to almost 1.6 billion by 1900, then to 5.4 billion in 1992, and it passed 6 billion around 2000. In the same period (1820–1992) that saw the world population multiply about five times, the goods and services available per capita multiplied more than eight times.

In that regard, industrial capitalism was a boon to humanity. Even in the late nineteenth century, it was already clear that the industrial revolution, with its capacity for continuous expansion of industrial output, promised to raise mass living standards to the point where dreamers could reasonably contemplate visions of universal abundance. That was the vision of the future in Edward Bellamy's best-selling utopian novel *Looking Backward* (1887).

But writers such as Bellamy and Henry George also observed widespread inequality. As the overall economic pie expanded, some groups received substantially more than others. Although precise numbers are not available, informed estimates suggest a trend toward inequality. In 1820, the income ratio between the richest fifth and the poorest fifth of the world is estimated to have stood at about three to one. Fifty years later, after the Industrial Revolution in the United States and Western Europe, the ratio had risen to seven to one. By 1913, it had jumped to eleven to one. And it did not stop there. In 1960, it was up to thirty to one and in 1990 it was sixty to one. Growth was unequal and getting more so as time went on.

THE WORLD ECONOMY IN THREE TIERS

Although the boundaries blurred, three tiers in the world economy emerged by 1900, as depicted in Map 1.1: first, a rapidly developing industrial core in the upper tier of northern Europe, North America, and Japan; second, a middle tier of modest development in countries such as Russia and Mexico on the fringes of the industrial North; and third, a vast, impoverished, agrarian South encompassing most of Asia, Africa, and Latin America.

The upper tier was the heartland of industrial capitalism. It contained the major centers of capital accumulation, including London, Paris, and New York, and the biggest engines of the Industrial Revolution in cities like Birmingham, Berlin, and Chicago. Developing at breakneck speed, the industrializing upper tier was beginning to pass from the first into the second

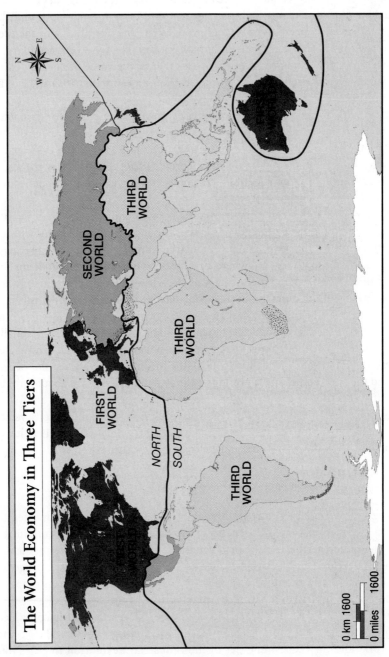

The World Economy in Three Tiers

FIRST WORLD

SECOND WORLD

THIRD WORLD

THIRD WORLD

THIRD WORLD

THIRD WORLD

FIRST WORLD

FIRST WORLD

NORTH

SOUTH

N
W—E
S

0 km 1600
0 miles 1600

MAP 1.1

8

industrial revolution of electric power, science-based technologies, and efficient work discipline. Thomas Edison, the Wizard of Menlo Park, was churning out wondrous new inventions, from the incandescent light to the moving picture, and it would not be long before Henry Ford's famous assembly line revolutionized production and the auto industry. Scottish immigrant Alexander Graham Bell invented the telephone in 1876 and steam heaters came to be widespread in the 1880s. In addition, Frederick Taylor pioneered *scientific management*, a set of incentive pay schemes and close supervision of labor intended to raise labor productivity still further. The evidence of material progress was abundant.

At the same time, dynamic development also brought discontent. Distressed farmers and impoverished urban workers in the upper tier rebelled against harsh economic conditions, while bitter labor conflicts in which strikers were sometimes killed provided the backdrop for Marxist and Populist ideologies of social revolution. The fact remained that the same dynamism absorbed enough anger to ward off lower-class revolt. Even where industrial violence was widespread, as in the United States, and where revolutionary ideas were strong, as in Germany, the upper tier averted revolution.

Class and Race in the Agrarian South

For different reasons, the agrarian South also avoided revolution. The vast belt of agricultural societies stretching across Asia, Africa, and Latin America contained a majority of the world's 1.6 billion people in 1900. Using age-old methods of tilling the soil, peasant populations were mostly confined to subsistence farming, while commerce and industry were conducted on an antiquated basis. Nonetheless, increasing numbers of workers were being drawn into production of raw materials for world markets as Indonesian rubber, South African gold, and Honduran bananas were shipped to the industrial heartland. As a result, countries in the agrarian South became economic tributaries of the industrial North.

Nowhere were the advantages of those who enriched themselves on the labor of others more apparent than in the plantation regions of the Americas and Africa. On the sugar plantations of the West Indies and the cotton plantations of the American South, classes were starkly polarized. In places only a generation or two removed from slavery, the division between landowners and degraded laborers was deepened by the cultural gulf between descendants of European settlers on one side and African slaves on the other.

The cultural contrast between Europeans and Africans had long been construed as a biological difference between races. At a time when slavery and other forms of labor coercion were giving way to free labor, racist attitudes were an especially important means of subordinating labor. For example, during the construction of the Panama Canal (1904–14), U.S. authorities put white labor on one payroll and relegated West Indians to another, with lower pay and no benefits.

Likewise, in the West Indies any white man could be called *boss*, and in both Mexico and the United States employers used racial stereotyping of *greasers* to justify inferior pay for Mexican workers.

The same was true in the southern United States, a region in many ways part of the agrarian South of the world economy. After the abolition of slavery, southern planters used the myth of white supremacy and black inferiority to keep black sharecroppers in a subordinate position to white landlords. Share-cropping contracts routinely barred blacks from raising their own livestock or cultivating their own gardens on the assumption that such activities would interfere with working the fields of the landlord. William Holtzclaw, a black sharecropper's son born in 1874 in Alabama, recalled, "I was hungry nearly all the time. . . . We were emaciated, underfed little creatures." To help supplement their meager diet, William and his siblings learned at a young age to forage for berries and nuts and later, as teenagers, to hunt for possum. Starting in 1880, the Holtzclaw family tried for four years to run their own farm. But when a flash flood and other misfortunes left the family indebted to creditors, they were forced to abandon their dream of self-sufficiency. The Holtzclaws returned to the oppressive system of sharecropping, a system that would later be duplicated in other parts of the world where landlords sought cheap labor to pick cotton, wheat, and other crops.

Backed by the Democratic Party, southern planters also disenfranchised African Americans through such legal devices as the Mississippi Plan of 1890, which imposed literacy and other tests on black voters, while allowing illiterate whites to retain the franchise if their Confederate grandfathers had voted. As a result, less than 9,000 of the 147,000 blacks of voting age in Mississippi remained registered to vote after 1890. This practice of legal discrimination against blacks came to be known as the Jim Crow system and resulted in steep internal inequality within the larger pattern of global inequality.

Such Jim Crow practices sometimes took root abroad. In Guatemala, for example, U.S. railroad contractors imported African American labor to construct lines connecting interior coffee farms to Caribbean ports. When black workers organized a strike in protest of antiblack violence, the Guatemalan government built on its own tradition of labor coercion of nonwhites, namely that of the indigenous Mayan population, and enacted vagrancy laws to force blacks back to work. The U.S. railroad contractors readily approved of such laws, recognizing them as similar to laws in the Jim Crow South.

Uneven Development in the Middle Tier

Revolution did break out in the developing nations of the middle tier. The middle tier was characterized by the uneven development of the large agrarian sector and the small but growing enclaves of modern commerce and industry. Countries such as Mexico and Russia developed enough railroads, mines, market farms, and commercial cities to lift themselves out of the

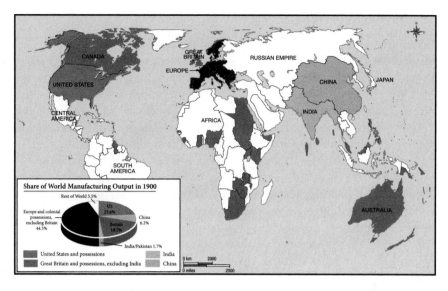

MAP 1.2

agrarian belt. At the same time, they remained dependent on outside capital and technology and thus stood halfway between underdevelopment and development.

Uneven development caused social dislocation throughout the middle tier. Among elites, there was tension between rising classes of educated business owners and older elites of landlords, aristocrats, and church leaders whose high positions rested on outmoded patriarchal forms of authority (literally rule by the father). The frustrated expectations of the new middle classes in the growing commercial cities fueled resentment, as did the anger of disaffected wage earners crowding city streets.

But economic pressures were not the only causes of revolution. In some nations, uprisings stemmed from the failure of older elites to enact political reforms. Revolutions challenged antiquated structures of power in Mexico, Russia, and Turkey early in the century and then later in China, Vietnam, and Iran. Most of the great social revolutions of the twentieth century took place not in highly developed societies, as predicted by Marxist theories of revolution, but in middle-range societies.

In the United States, industrial conflict raged throughout the late nineteenth century, from the 1877 Railroad Strike to the 1894 Pullman Strike, and served as a defining feature of the Gilded Age. Although such conflict did not develop into a full-scale revolution, America's destiny would be bound with revolutions abroad. As subsequent chapters will show, in place after place, from Mexico to Russia to Iran, Americans were drawn into the maelstrom of revolutionary upheavals.

Britain: Capitalist Headquarters

In the last quarter of the nineteenth century, the world was relatively quiet. Certainly, that was the case in Britain, the effective headquarters of world capitalism. Britain was the prime site of capital accumulation in this period. (Only after the First World War would the world's financial center move to New York.) British primacy rested, first, on the fact that the City, London's high-toned financial district, was the world's prime lender. Indeed, Britain's share of foreign investment was almost as large as the rest of the world's investments put together. In addition, Britain was the place where international accounts were balanced.

Britain's role was unique in other ways, too. For one, Britain was the world's self-appointed policeman. Its outward-looking ruling classes, educated at Oxford and Cambridge Universities, aspired to "rule the waves" of the entire planet. Furthermore, Britain won cultural prestige for its much-admired parliamentary form of government and for Victorian values, named after the long-reigning British Queen Victoria, the royal personification of virtue, duty, and high-mindedness.

Taken together, these British functions—finance capital, world policeman, cultural paragon—added up to British predominance in world affairs. This was one reason it was said the sun never sets on the British Empire.

THE PLACE OF THE UNITED STATES

By 1890, however, Britain was losing ground to its swift-moving rivals, Germany and the United States. While England's share of world steel production was declining from 31 to 10 percent between 1880 and 1913, Germany's share was rising from 15 to 24 percent, and the U.S. share was growing even faster, to 42 percent. In fact, the United States replaced Britain as the world's premiere industrial producer in the last decade of the nineteenth century. Continuing to pull ahead in the early twentieth century, the United States accounted for almost as much industrial, mining, and construction activity as the next three largest producers combined by the start of the First World War.

Watching the United States race ahead, British observers ruefully foresaw a future of U.S. world leadership. Contemplating "the Americanization of the World," W. T. Stead, a popular journalist, imagined an Englishman of 1900 sitting down to breakfast: "he eats bread made from prairie flour . . . tinned oysters from Baltimore, and a little Kansas City bacon, while his wife plays with a slice of Chicago ox-tongue." As it turned out, that vision was realized after the cataclysmic events of a world depression and two world wars between 1914 and 1945. Yet Americans were not particularly eager to shoulder the burdens of world leadership. With a huge domestic market, most of their energies focused on development within North America itself.

All the same, Americans were inextricably tied to the world economy. The North (from New England to the Midwest) was in the vanguard of global development. This rapidly urbanizing region contained upward of 70 percent of U.S. manufacturing capacity and some of the most advanced technologies and highest concentrations of wealth to be found anywhere in the industries of Chicago and Pittsburgh and the financial houses of New York.

As the U.S. North made the leap from an agrarian producer of raw materials to a highly developed manufacturer, other sections of the nation lagged behind. The West (from the Mississippi to the Pacific Ocean) was dependent on outside capital, while some parts of the South (from the Atlantic to east Texas) shared similarities with the underdeveloped world. Despite the abolition of slavery in 1865 and the beginnings of textile and steel industries, the South remained in 1900 largely a plantation-based exporter of cotton and other raw materials to the developed regions.

Corporate Capitalism

The U.S. North was at the forefront of the shift to corporate capitalism. The trend toward concentration of wealth in giant corporations was the ironic consequence of competition itself. Whereas competition is built into a market economy, persistent deflation in the late nineteenth century fostered especially harsh cutthroat practices. Deflation is the tendency of the price of things to go down while the value of money goes up. Deflation was a prime feature of what later came to be called the long depression of 1873–97, with the most severe phases coming in 1873–77 and again in 1893–97. Deflation resulted in a marketplace with competition over prices. After a particularly bruising battle for control of a railroad, one American captain of industry was heard to mutter, "Nothing is lost, save honor."

In this highly competitive environment, the ideas of Herbert Spencer, a theorist of social Darwinism, were in vogue. Applying (critics said misapplying) Charles Darwin's theory of evolution to human society, Spencer depicted an environment in which individuals and groups engaged in a struggle for survival of the fittest. Ultimately, Spencer believed that society as a whole stood to benefit from this kind of competition.

Faced with declining prices, commodity producers resorted to various survival strategies. One was to cut costs through mechanization, wage reductions, and efficiencies of scale (that is, high-volume output). Another strategy was aimed at remaking the marketplace in ways that eliminated nasty competition in the first place. One approach was to buy out or merge with all the competitors in a process called *horizontal* integration. That is what John D. Rockefeller did in creating the mammoth Standard Oil Corporation. The photograph on the next page depicts the scale of Standard Oil's operations in just one of its locations in California. Rockefeller was a devout Baptist from Cleveland, Ohio, who put religious scruples aside in ruthless acquisition of competitors to assemble a corporate empire that made him the richest man in the world.

In another strategy known as *vertical* integration, captains of industry sought control over the entire production process. This was Andrew Carnegie's strategy in

Standard Oil workers stand in front of a vast field of oil tanks in Bakersfield, California, in 1910. In this moment of transition to an oil-based economy, workers relied on horse-drawn carriages to work the oil fields that would eventually fuel motorized cars. Library of Congress Prints and Photographs Division, Washington, DC.

creating the foundation for what became the United States Steel Corporation, the largest steel company in America. Carnegie bought the ore mines in Michigan as well as the railroads that shipped the ore to the steel plants in Pittsburgh. He was an ambitious Scottish immigrant and disciple of Spencer who was determined to be a survivor regardless of the cost to competitors or employees.

Some industries, such as the beef trade in Chicago, relied on elements of both strategies to win new markets. In the 1880s, Chicago stockyards began shipping butchered cuts of meat, known as dressed beef, in refrigerated train cars along the Grand Trunk Railroad that connected Chicago to Boston and New York. Butchers in New York and other cities banded together to form the Butchers' National Protective Association in an effort to protect their interests. Despite such resistance, Chicago meat packers managed to quickly expand their market by opening refrigerated warehouses, known as branch houses, throughout the East Coast and selling meat below market prices. By 1888, one New York butcher lamented that in much of the East Coast "the slaughtering of cattle by [local] butchers is a thing of the past."

Ironically, the very intensity of a competitive market led to its opposite: the concentration of wealth, horizontal and vertical, in giant enterprises. The emergence of this handful of Goliaths was a burden on the legions of little Davids—suppliers, retailers, workers, consumers—left behind in a competitive world to face off against the giants.

Finance Capitalism

Conditions at the end of the nineteenth century were especially favorable to what contemporaries called *capitalists*, a term used to distinguish those who traded in intangible money values from those who produced coal, shoes, and other useful objects. In a system whose purpose was the making of money and not the making of things, and in an environment where sprawling rail networks and giant steel complexes required massive sums of capital, capitalists flourished and ushered in a new era of *finance capitalism.*

Early finance capitalism was based in gold. Under the international gold standard, money values were pegged to gold, and central banks were expected to keep enough gold bullion in the vaults to redeem any paper currency. Gold, as the Plains Indians said, was "the yellow metal that drives white men crazy"; as if to prove it, there were mad gold rushes in South Dakota and South Africa in the 1870s and in the Alaskan Klondike in 1898. Given their status as prime lenders, British investors had the most at stake, but French and German bankers also relied on the gold standard to sustain the value of their foreign holdings. Capitalists of each nation looked to their respective central banks to maintain a tight money supply to reduce the prospect of the economy stalling because of currency fluctuations.

On the surface, the United States seemed to be out of step. Because of democratic distrust of centralized power, there was no central bank in the United States. Yet America did come to rely on the gold standard. In the 1870s, the federal government stopped coining silver, took the popular Civil War greenback dollars out of circulation, and put the country on the gold standard. By constricting the money supply, the gold standard reinforced a general decline in prices. This downward pressure on prices was a boon to bankers, investors, and other creditors, who were able to collect interest payments in money that grew more valuable year by year.

Playing the role of financial titan to the hilt, the cigar-chomping, iron-willed J. P. Morgan was a one-man central bank. He single-handedly rescued the U.S. Treasury in the midst of the depression of the 1890s and then stepped in to end the Wall Street panic of 1907. Morgan furnished the paper securities that consolidated more than 60 percent of the nation's steel capacity to form the huge United States Steel Corporation in 1901, the first-ever business capitalized at more than $1 billion.

United States Steel was but one of thousands of business mergers that took place in the wake of the long depression at the turn of the nineteenth century. The concentration of wealth in giant industrial and financial corporations centered in New York's Wall Street altered the American social order and divided public opinion. The mighty financiers and industrialists of the day were hailed by some as captains of industry but condemned by others as robber barons.

Laissez-Faire

The rise of finance capitalism was tied to the political concept of laissez-faire liberalism. At its most basic, liberalism is the philosophy of limited government, whereas laissez-faire specifically applies limited government to the economy. Under the prevailing doctrine of laissez-faire liberalism, the role of the state was limited to guaranteeing property rights, contracts, and public order; otherwise, it was supposed to leave private individuals free to make the best deal they could.

The theory of laissez-faire represented the endpoint of the long effort of capitalists and their ideological supporters to liberate the market from social controls.

Freed from kinship ties, moral obligation, and communal decision making, property owners would be guided by what Adam Smith called the invisible hand of the market under the so-called law of supply and demand. Only Britain, Smith's homeland, came close to putting laissez-faire into practice. In the late nineteenth century, Britain had free trade, little government regulation, and few labor laws.

Although American leaders preached laissez-faire, they practiced a good deal of state intervention on behalf of business in the form of tariffs to protect domestic industry, land grants to railroads, and troops to suppress strikes. The one area where laissez-faire ruled in the United States was labor. Despite the high incidence of unemployment, industrial accidents, overwork, and poverty wages, working people were without social protection. Laissez-faire was upheld by a series of U.S. Supreme Court decisions, notably *Lochner v. New York* (1905), which threw out a maximum-work-hours law on the grounds that it violated the Fourteenth Amendment to the Constitution, which required *due process* before depriving a person of property, in this case the right of employers to conduct business as they saw fit. Laissez-faire reinforced the social Darwinist idea of survival of the fittest, leaving plenty of intelligent, hardworking, and otherwise fit people to fend for themselves, sometimes against large entities such as corporations or the state.

FROM COUNTRY TO CITY

One of the most significant consequences of economic development was to undermine age-old agrarian ways of life. At one level, economic development had many positive consequences for agriculture. Through several feedback loops stretching back and forth across the Atlantic Ocean, the food supply grew by leaps and bounds. The introduction of modern machinery on the fertile soils of the Great Plains increased grain production. Grain moved to markets in swift railcars and fast-moving transatlantic steamships. The international transportation network was financed in significant part by British capital, thus completing the loop that linked the farms of the Great Plains to banks in the city of London.

Another positive consequence was a healthier, better-fed population. The availability of cheap grain along with the spread of corn and white potatoes eliminated the scourge of famine in the developed regions. Meanwhile, improved sanitation and better health practices brought about the decline of deadly diseases such as plague and cholera. The combination of more food and less disease resulted in the doubling of the world population in the half century preceding the First World War.

In an earlier epoch, population growth of this magnitude might have led to the sort of demographic catastrophe predicted in the "dismal science" of Thomas Malthus, a British philosopher of the late eighteenth century who argued that when the population expands faster than the food supply, the result is a "dismal peak" of mass starvation. Yet, no such starvation occurred because of economic development.

At another level, economic development posed a challenge to notions of health and nutrition in agrarian societies. New tools for measuring the nutritional value of food—and the perceived value of different national diets—helped justify large-scale exports, which often undermined local agricultural production. Europeans first invented the calorie as a unit of food value in the late nineteenth century. But it was the invention of the calorimeter in turn-of-the century America that allowed U.S. scientists and government officials to rank the energy value of certain foods, with meat, milk, and wheat at the top and fruits and spices at the bottom. In this context, C. F. Langworthy, chief nutrition researcher at the U.S. Department of Agriculture, declared in 1911 that the United States had the "finest food supply of any country in the world." Convinced of the superiority of the American diet, reformers hoped to both improve the diets of immigrants in the United States and export food the world over.

The arrival of millions of bushels of cheap American grain on European loading docks led to economic dislocation in the countryside. Especially in Southern and Eastern Europe, overworked estates could not withstand the competition of cheap American grain, and landlords began to exact higher rents or convert peasant holdings to commercial estates worked by wage laborers. By the end of the nineteenth century, most rural folk in Europe were freed from oppressive economic obligations to work for landlords, but landlords were also freed from the obligation to provide social protection for the poor. Dowries vanished, marriage prospects declined, and millions of people were set adrift. The impact of American food exports on rural Europe illustrates the way gains and losses, progress and poverty, were bound together.

Mass Migrations

Driven by the breakdown of the traditional way of life, masses of erstwhile peasants in eastern and southern Europe streamed out of the countryside. Their first stop was typically a European city, but it was not long before they booked passage in steerage on a transatlantic steamer heading for the New World. Upon arrival, most found work in the railroads and factories of industrial America producing the machinery that raised agricultural productivity and sent cheap grain across the Atlantic. Thus did former peasant migrants inadvertently contribute to the very forces that had uprooted them from the soil by making cheap exports that upset the traditional way of life. Another feedback loop was closed.

Migrants did not necessarily stay in one place. Italian laborers were called *birds of passage* because their migratory habits might bring them to Buenos Aires one year and to Boston the next. Shuttling back and forth across the Atlantic in a relentless search for work, labor traveled in the same Atlantic circuit as capital and was every bit as mobile.

Nor did migrants only come from Europe. In the American West, migrants from China and Mexico arrived in large numbers in the late nineteenth century. In the 1880s and 1890s, decades before the U.S. Border Patrol was established

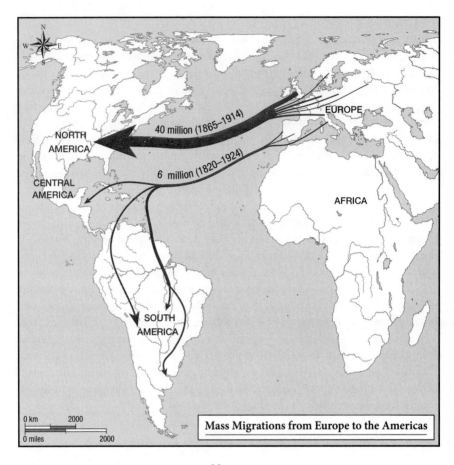

Mass Migrations from Europe to the Americas

MAP 1.3

to patrol the U.S.–Mexico border, Mexicans entering the United States did not face the same level of discrimination as the Chinese. By the terms of the Treaty of Guadalupe Hidalgo between the United States and Mexico, Mexicans in the United States were legally defined as white and eligible for citizenship. Chinese migrants, in contrast, were defined as nonwhite and ineligible for citizenship. Anti-Chinese activists such as Denis Kearney, head of the Workingmen's Party in San Francisco, led the national effort to pass the first Chinese exclusion law in 1882, which banned all but the most elite Chinese from entering the United States. Thus, the Chinese—and not Mexicans—were defined as the first "illegal" immigrants in the United States.

The United States was but one of several destinations for immigrants seeking a better life. Latin America, for instance, received six million Europeans between 1820 and 1924, including almost as many Italians as North America. Additional masses went to Australia. Although the largest number of Italians, Greeks, Poles, and other Europeans arrived in the United States—an estimated forty million immigrants came to the United States between 1865 and 1914—the percentage of foreign-born individuals was higher in Canada. As these swirling patterns suggest, the United States was an important confluence in the global flows of migrant labor. But the "huddled masses" sought out "golden doors" (the famous phrase in the poem by Emma Lazarus affixed to the Statue of Liberty) wherever they could be found, not just in the United States.

All in all, migration plus natural increase brought the U.S. population from fifty million in 1880 to seventy-six million in 1900. As the twentieth century began, the combined population of North America (the United States, Canada, and Mexico) accounted for about 5 percent of the world's total, approximately the same percentage it would claim when the century ended. A small number, it seemed, for a place of such swiftly growing importance.

Working-Class Gains and Losses

Many trends pointed toward progress, especially for skilled workers in the United States. The expanding economy created legions of new job opportunities, and overall living standards followed an upward curve. Indeed, wage earners benefited from the era's deflation because real wages (that is, wages after price changes were taken into account) tended to go up, whereas the price of food and other consumer goods went down. Italian immigrants, for example, found they could eat better in America and invented a new twist on an old favorite: spaghetti *with meatballs*. Few in Italy could afford to eat meat more than three times a year, whereas Italians in America found they could afford the luxury on a weekly basis. As one Italian American restaurant owner in New York remarked, "Someone in Italy should invent spaghetti with meatballs for the Italians over there."

New national policies governing international trade made possible the decline in food prices. In the 1870s, Congress placed coffee on the free list as part of a series of tariff bills aimed at lowering the cost of the "poor man's breakfast." This meant that imported coffee from countries such as Brazil would now be more affordable for American workers. Because of these laws, a typical American worker in the late 1800s paid about one-third of a cent per cup of coffee, a small fraction of a typical nine-cent breakfast that included pork, beans, bread with butter, and coffee with milk and sugar.

Yet even as American workers benefited from declining food prices and increasing wages, the industrializing economy also presented a series of new challenges. Workers were subjected to overcrowded tenements, a high incidence of industrial accidents, and unhealthy work environments. Millions suffered bouts of unemployment during downturns in the business cycle.

Workers also faced discrimination at the hands of employers who relied on racial ideologies to justify low pay and poor working conditions. Here, the case of Italian immigrants is particularly instructive. Although legally "white on arrival," as historian Thomas Guglielmo has observed, Italians routinely endured workplace discrimination. In the copper mines of Arizona, for instance, employers established a hierarchical system of wages where white workers were paid the highest wages, Mexicans the lowest, and Italians something in the middle.

As challenging as it was for men in the workforce, it was in some ways worse for women. Factory "girls" could expect to be paid at little more than half the rate of their male counterparts for the same hours of work. Women working unskilled jobs in factories typically worked ten hours a day, six days a week, from seven o'clock in the morning to five thirty in the evening, with thirty minutes off for lunch each day. In a memoir published in 1903, *The Woman Who Toils*, Mrs. John Van Vorst wrote that she earned a daily wage of fifty cents while working in a Chicago frame shop affixing tin moldings to two hundred gilt picture frames a day. Although few married women worked for wages, many wives took in boarders while also performing the drudgery of their own housework. Single women often found work as domestics—the largest occupational group among women—but were paid even less than female factory workers.

Increasing numbers of single women found work in the retail sector, especially in new department stores opening in major cities. Wanamaker's in Philadelphia hired so many women by 1887 that it built a residence hotel for their female clerks. At Macy's New York store, women comprised 80 percent of the employees by 1890. From 1880 to 1890, the number of women working in retail nationally jumped from eight thousand to fifty-eight thousand. As more and more women entered the workforce, some argued they deserved the same pay as male workers. But because of the large supply of female labor relative to the number of positions available and long-held paternalist ideas of male superiority, women workers continued to earn much less than their male counterparts. Such examples suggest the ways market forces could both challenge and reinforce societal views of work and gender.

Changing notions of women's place in society—along with persistent paternalist attitudes—spread beyond American borders when American missionaries traveled overseas. In China, for example, American women missionaries set up schools to educate Chinese women. But even as they challenged racial prejudices about the inferiority of the Chinese by producing students who could rival the best of America and Europe, they left intact paternalist ideas about women's role in society. As one missionary noted, "Our greatest hope is that they be made model homemakers."

Labor Unrest

In the cutthroat environment of the Gilded Age, employers engaged in a Darwinian struggle with their competitors by cutting wages, one of their largest single expenses. Despite the long-term trend toward improvement in real wages, employers frequently cut wages and payrolls at the first sign of flagging sales, especially during the worst phases of the long depression in 1873–77 and 1893–97.

The result was a series of great strikes. Largely forgotten in later years, the stories of class warfare filled the pages of daily newspapers at the time. The great railroad strikes of 1877, for example, saw pitched battles between strikers and militia against the backdrop of burning rail depots. The violence in Pittsburgh was said to have "caused more apprehension in the North than anything since General Lee's advance into Pennsylvania" during the Civil War. Indeed, the analogy between class war and civil war came easily in these years because of nearly constant battles in the coalfields, endemic violence in western mining districts, and frequent disturbances in other industries.

It was not only labor militancy that made these conflicts so ferocious. Even more important was the adamant opposition of business owners to union recognition. Instead of negotiating with unions, employers often preferred to bring in troops, which was typically the trigger for violence, as it was in 1877. Such was also the case in the infamous Homestead Strike of 1892, when the Carnegie Company relied on a private army from the Pinkerton detective agency to suppress striking workers outside Pittsburgh, resulting in a violent upheaval, killing nine workers and three detectives. Similarly, in the 1886 Bay View riot, the Wisconsin state militia killed seven unarmed Milwaukee workers marching for an eight-hour day. Compared to Europe, the United States was the site of the most violent industrial conflicts of the era.

Chicago: Crossroads of Capital and Labor

Chicago, home of the White City, was one such cauldron of conflict. Located at the tip of Lake Michigan in the heart of the North American continent, Chicago was truly one of the main crossroads of the world economy. Not for nothing did poet Carl Sandburg later call it "hog butcher to the world."

As the main rail hub of North America, the midwestern boomtown was an international shipping center where wheat and corn from the nation's breadbasket stopped briefly before heading eastward. It was also one of the key places where international capital (mostly British) and international labor (a mélange of European immigrants) met in bustling factories that sent forth a stream of tractors, clothes, and canned hams to faraway destinations.

Chicago was the setting for one of the first great events of the international labor movement. The Haymarket affair arose out of a nationwide general strike for the eight-hour day on May 1, 1886. Three days after police killed peaceful protesters at the McCormick reaper factory, workers led a demonstration in Haymarket Square. An unknown assailant threw a bomb that killed several police and the police took immediate revenge by shooting into the crowd and killing several demonstrators.

Authorities put eight radical leaders on trial, of whom several were immigrants, including the German anarchist August Spies. Neither Spies nor the homegrown radical Albert Parsons had been present at the bomb scene, but that did not prevent them from being hanged, along with two others. During the trial, there were widespread protests in America and Europe, and the deaths of Spies and Parson made them into martyrs for the growing international labor movement. In commemoration, the international Socialists Party at an 1889 meeting in Switzerland adopted May First as the international workers' holiday. When workers of the world parade on May Day, it is in commemoration of what was originally an American event.

Just a few years later, Chicago was also the center of one of the greatest strikes in the nineteenth century. The Pullman strike of 1894 grew out of a labor dispute in the nearby company town of Pullman where workers manufactured Pullman palace cars, the pinnacle of luxurious rail travel in the Gilded Age. When railway management responded to the economic downturn of 1893 by cutting wages and payrolls, Eugene V. Debs, of the American Railway Union, led fifteen thousand union members to join Pullman employees in a massive, nonviolent walkout.

Antilabor media at the time blamed the disruption on foreigners and criminals and called for stern measures, in the words of one Chicago editor, that would "whip these Slavic wolves back to the dens from which they came." The owners appealed to President Grover Cleveland (1885–89 and 1893–97). Cleveland was a former Democratic governor of New York, a conservative supporter of the gold standard, and a friend of business. He agreed to send in the U.S. cavalry, whose bayonets effectively broke the strike.

Responses to Class Conflict

Conflicts of this sort convinced many on both sides of the Atlantic that economic progress had turned sour. Fear of lower-class revolt was rife among the upper classes. European conservatives, such as German chancellor Otto von Bismarck, tried to stamp out discontent by making the German Socialist Party into an outlaw organization. Even in egalitarian America, feelings of dread filled the sermons, editorials, and books of the time. Conservatives such as Protestant churchman Josiah Strong, secretary of the American Home Missionary Society, regarded the submerged strata as the source of "anarchy and destruction," whereas liberal reformers such as Jacob Riis portrayed the squalid urban slum as a cesspool of pestilence and crime, exaggerating its pathological elements. Such reformers downplayed the sense of community and cooperation that abounded in such neighborhoods.

Many who lamented the conditions of the urban poor and called for reform also served to reinforce hierarchical ideas of the world's peoples made plain in the Columbian Exposition. Riis's exposé of tenement life, *How the Other Half Lives*, was first published in 1890. In it, he called for reform of urban housing in New York and other U.S. cities: "Think ye that building shall endure / Which shelters the noble and crushes the poor?" But Riis's writing also revealed a fascination with what he found to be exotic among the lives of immigrants and the poor. In describing an unlicensed bar on the Lower East Side, he wrote, "Grouped about a beer-keg that was propped on the wreck of a broken chair, a foul and ragged host of men and women on boxes, benches, and stools. . . . In the center of the group a sallow, wrinkled hag, evidently the ruler of the feast, dealt out the hideous stuff." Just as the White City highlighted stark differences between cultures of the industrial North and the agrarian South in the name of demonstrating American progress, Riis's writings implied an evolutionary scale with white middle-class reformers looking down on the "foreign" immigrant poor.

Contemporaries were well aware that inequality was one of the consequences of the expanding world economy. Noted author Mark Twain coined the name the Gilded Age for an age of such pronounced disparities in wealth. In a famous essay titled "Wealth," none other than Andrew Carnegie wrote, "Inequality is the price society pays for the law of competition." As one of the richest men in the world and a disciple of Herbert Spencer, Carnegie enjoyed all the benefits a laissez-faire economy could offer. He relied on hardball tactics to exploit his workers, particularly in the Homestead Strike of 1892, when he slashed wages and cut off negotiations with the union. But he also believed something had to be done to ameliorate the effects of a highly unequal economy. In his "Gospel of Wealth" (1889), Carnegie argued for the power of philanthropy. Carnegie's return of some of his proceeds to society in the form of schools and libraries set the example for corporate philanthropy of the sort practiced by the Carnegie, Rockefeller, and other giant foundations of the twentieth century.

Others more orthodox than Carnegie were content to leave well enough alone. In the view of William Graham Sumner, another American disciple of Spencer, inequality, far from being a social evil, was actually a boon to social progress. Sumner posed the question of "What the Social Classes Owe to One Another" and decided that the answer was simple: nothing. In a collection entitled *Earth-Hunger, and Other Essays*, published in 1913, Sumner wrote in stark terms: "Before the tribunal of nature a man has no more right to life than a rattlesnake; he has no more right to liberty than any wild beast; his right to pursuit of happiness is nothing but a license to maintain the struggle for existence." With such writings, Sumner argued inequality was a natural phenomenon.

Social critics did not share this complacency. Ida Tarbell's muckraking journalism exposed the injustices of monopoly capitalism that drove smaller producers out of business. In *The History of the Standard Oil Company* (1904), she demonstrated that "a community of interests exists between railroads and the Standard Oil Company sufficiently strong for the latter to get any help it wants in making it hard for rivals to do business." Her study established the standards for modern investigative journalism based in documentary records and helped lay the foundation for regulation of U.S. businesses in the early twentieth century.

In a treatise widely read on both sides of the Atlantic, Henry George argued that progress and poverty somehow developed together. George's solution—the Single Tax on rising land values—failed to address the extent of the problem. But

Ida Tarbell (1857–1944) published *The History of the Standard Oil Company,* as a series of articles in McClure's magazine in 1902–4. A scathing critique of Rockefeller's unethical business practices, Tarbell's exposé set new standards for investigative journalism. Copyright by Keystone View Co. Inc. of N.Y., New York World–Telegram and Sun Collection, Library of Congress, Washington, DC.

others stepped in to propose more thoroughgoing solutions. Under the banner of nationalism, Edward Bellamy's *Looking Backward* held out the cooperative commonwealth as an alternative to the strife-ridden reality of the times. In Bellamy's vision of the future, property would be collectively owned and everyone would have an equal share of the social product.

Such collectivist ideas ran up against American individualism. By comparison, Europeans were more inclined to embrace Socialism. Lingering traditions of *noblesse oblige* (upper-class obligation to the poor) combined with working-class solidarity to put collective ideas at the forefront. Especially in Germany, Socialist ideas flourished despite Bismarck's best efforts to suppress them. Socialists such as August Bebel called for the abolition of capitalist property, and anarchists such as Johann Most went a step further and called for the abolition of the state. When German authorities tried to stifle Most, he joined the immigrant stream to the United States, just as Spies and countless others had done before him. In fact, German immigration was second only to British as a source of the U.S. population in this period.

FARM DISTRESS IN NORTH AMERICA

As cities were being torn by industrial conflict, rural areas were also experiencing distress. Although the European countryside experienced the most severe stress, rural America also saw dramatic change. Expanding railroad connections between rural farms and urban markets shortened shipping times and increased agricultural productivity in the late nineteenth century. Farmers outside Chicago, who had spent one week or more traveling to market by wagons and teams of horses over rutted roads, now shipped their harvest to the city in one day by rail. As one Chicago writer observed, trains saved "the farmers at every stopping place from their long and tedious journeys by team, enabling them to utilize their own labor, and the services of their teams, in improving their farms."

But faster shipping times and increasing productivity created new challenges for many American farmers. The first was in the market. Under Adam Smith's law of supply and demand, increased production of agricultural goods brought declining prices. In the words of an American folk song, "Ten cent cotton and forty cent wheat; / How in the world can a poor man eat?" The price of American grain was set not in Kansas, but on the grain exchange in Liverpool, England, because Liverpool was the largest transshipment center. That meant American farms, like their European counterparts, were subject to the competitive pressures of world markets. As a result, farm ownership declined in relation to farm tenancy in the corn and wheat belt of the Midwest and Great Plains. The situation was even more severe in the cotton belt of the South, where plantation sharecroppers and landless laborers, both black and white, were caught in a vicious cycle of poverty and debt that amounted to a kind of economic servitude long after slavery was abolished in 1865.

To make matters worse, farmers were squeezed a second time at the bank. Trying to offset declining prices, they took on the costly burden of expensive equipment and supplies necessary to increase crop yields so they could sell yet more wheat and cotton. Lacking capital of their own, they had to borrow. As a classic debtor class, their position was made even worse by the deflationary times, which favored the makers of money over the producers of things. Having taken a loan in today's dollars, a debtor had to repay it in tomorrow's more expensive currency. A Kansas wheat farmer, for instance, could pay the 8 percent interest on a $2,000 mortgage with 174 bushels of wheat in 1888, but by 1890 it took over 300 bushels. With goods getting cheaper and money getting more costly, the banker's paradise was a debtor's hell.

Small farmers found it much harder than bankers or industrialists to band together to beat the competition. Instead, the Davids had to go up against the Goliaths of big business at every turn, buying equipment from giant manufacturers such as International Harvester, shipping their goods through giant railroad corporations owned by the likes of J. P. Morgan, and selling to huge agribusinesses such as General Foods.

Populist Revolt

The mounting pressure on rural producers led to a Populist outcry. Populist protest took many forms, but all were aimed at overturning laissez-faire and the gold standard. In fact, the Populist revolt in the United States was the first in a series of major reform efforts aimed at bringing the state into the market on the side of rural producers and urban wage earners. Agrarian Populism began as a protest of the hardworking rural producer against international bankers and grain speculators. "Raise less corn and more hell," shouted Mary Elizabeth Lease, a fiery Populist agitator. Populists put forward a variety of solutions to the farmer's plight. One was cooperation. As one Kansas farmer put it, "We are emerging from a period of intense individualism, supreme selfishness, and ungodly greed to a period of cooperative effort." The idea behind cooperation was to ease the pressure in the market by eliminating the middleman and instead buying directly from the wholesaler and marketing directly to the consumer. The key organization behind these ideas was the Farmers' Alliance, which grew rapidly in the late 1880s, reaching a peak of some forty thousand units nationwide.

When cooperation proved inadequate, Populists turned to the state. Organized in 1892, the Populist Party took aim at laissez-faire in a set of demands for government intervention in the market. The party's platform called for state ownership, or *nationalization*, of railroads and mines and a subtreasury system of government-owned granaries where farmers would deposit their crops and receive certificates that could be used as credit toward planting next year's crop. For good measure, Populists sought to attract urban workers with the demand for a national eight-hour day, which had been on labor's agenda ever since the 1886 general strike.

Populists also demanded state intervention to solve the "money question." Rebelling against the gold standard, they campaigned to replace it either with *fiat money*, government-issued paper dollars, or by what came to be known as *free silver*, the virtually unlimited coinage of silver. The aim was cheaper money, every debtor's dream. Inflation was supposed to bring higher prices for farm products and easier repayment of debts, thus easing the squeeze at the bank. They hoped inflation would turn the current situation upside down, creating a debtor's paradise and a banker's hell.

The revolt against gold culminated in the election of 1896. By the time William Jennings Bryan captured the Democratic nomination for president, "cheap money" had elbowed aside cooperation and nationalization. Bryan was a bible-quoting, Nebraska congressman known as the Great Commoner, and he inspired a political crusade against the *cross of gold*, a symbol of the northeastern banking and industrial establishment.

Although Bryan ran well in the agrarian regions of the South and West, he failed to capture urban workers and others in the North, who voted in large numbers for his Republican opponent, William McKinley. McKinley's election decided the money question in favor of gold, at least for the time being. Despite their defeat, Populists opened the door for more successful assaults on laissez-faire.

Varieties of Rural Protest

Comparing Populism in Europe and North America, there were many kinds of rural protest. On the Canadian prairie, farmers espoused an agrarian form of Socialism that called for the nationalization of big business. In Scandinavia and Hungary, where small farmers faced growing competition, they banded together in co-ops to market their crops.

Yet Populism proved vulnerable to demagoguery. In eastern Germany, for example, peasants threatened by declining prices in world markets seethed with resentment against big landlords, grain speculators, and moneychangers. Worried about possible peasant uprisings, German conservatives set up the Agrarian League, which was more or less successful in diverting peasant resentment away from landlords and directing it toward all manner of outsiders—Slavs, Jews, urban workers, and foreigners in general—who were said to be threats to family values and the chastity of women.

Something similar happened in the southern United States, where white planters responded to the Populist threat of a biracial lower-class rebellion with demagogic appeals to close ranks behind the lily-white Democratic Party. Senator Thomas E. Watson of Georgia exemplified this trend as he journeyed from Populist advocate for small farmers of all races to white supremacist and anti-Semite toward the end of his political career. As in Germany, demagoguery had some success in uniting upper and lower classes against common enemies, real or imagined.

In the end, none of the proposed solutions was effective in offsetting the dominant trends in the world economy toward industrialization and urbanization. Ultimately, more and more hard-pressed farmers were forced to leave the land altogether and move to the city, which helped make both Germany and the United States majority urban nations by 1920.

PROGRESS AT THE WORLD'S FAIR

Against the backdrop of social conflict, American leaders clung to an optimistic faith in progress. Nowhere was the progressive faith more clearly displayed than at the World's Columbian Exposition. Opening on May 1, 1893, the Chicago World's Fair drew several million visitors to dozens of exhibit halls whose purpose, according to the official guidebook, was "to illustrate American progress." At a time when the U.S. economy was fast becoming the world's largest, Americans wanted the world to see the United States at the forefront of human achievement.

The theme of progress was everywhere. In the Anthropology Building, an attentive fairgoer could trace the development of ever more complex tools, from simple stone arrowheads to the latest inventions on display in the immense Hall of Manufactures. An entire wing of the Manufacturing Building was devoted to the fledgling electrical industry, the prime symbol of the second industrial revolution. It showcased dynamos (generators) and other new machinery from General Electric and Westinghouse, two new corporations on their way to joining the ranks of the world's most powerful economic institutions. The exhibits also featured the largest gun ever made, a one-hundred-ton artillery piece brought from the Krupp foundry in Germany. Comparing arrowheads with modern weapons, fairgoers were invited to conclude that the change from primitive past to civilized present was exactly what progress was all about.

Perhaps the most spectacular demonstration of technical progress came in the Electricity Building. Displays included such astounding inventions as burglar alarms, telephone switchboards, and something called a kinetograph, an early version of Thomas Edison's movie projector. Ironically, Hollywood movies eventually revolutionized popular entertainment in ways that helped make world's fairs obsolete. At a time when electric lighting was still very much a novelty, the

A street in the Cairo section in the Midway Plaisance, a one-mile avenue leading to the White City at the World's Columbian Exposition in Chicago, 1893. Under the direction of Harvard anthropologist Frederic Ward Putnam, the Midway was an open-air museum of "primitive" cultures designed to stand in contrast to the grandeur of the White City. Library of Congress Prints and Photographs Division, Washington, DC.

fairgrounds sparkled at night under no fewer than 130,000 incandescent lamps electrified by dynamos powered by a giant steam engine.

In contrast to the glorification of business, labor was conspicuous by its absence. Betraying their anxiety over industrial disorder, fair organizers gave no space to show off the various labor processes that lay behind the marvelous machinery or the deplorable conditions of the poor. The lone exception was a model workingman's home set up by New York State in a forlorn plot, a faint tribute to the more than thirty workers who had died during the fair's construction.

Further testimony to progress came in the Women's Pavilion. The fact that Queen Victoria and several other women were current rulers was presented as evidence that women now competed with men in almost every department of human activity, although women lacked the right to vote in all Western societies in 1893. Likewise, at a congress of scholars devoted to assessing the status of the Negro in America, Booker T. Washington, president of the Tuskegee Institute, won applause for calling attention to the progress made by African Americans in climbing *Up from Slavery*, the title of his best-selling 1900 book.

The wedding-cake architecture of the White City was intended to project progress into an idealized future. Designed by a team of architects that included Daniel Burnham, prophet of the City Beautiful movement that brought the Beaux-Arts style of Paris to the United States, the White City turned the rough-and-tumble reality of Chicago inside out. Burnham's idea of beauty was a collection of imitation Greek temples, gleaming white columns, monumental sculptures, and glimmering reflecting pools intended to project an image of harmonious order. All in all, the White City was a kind of neoclassical forerunner of Walt Disney's world showcase at Epcot Center.

The grandeur of the White City contrasted with the humble dwellings of the ethnological exhibits. As students of human groups, ethnologists sought to portray the lives of so-called primitive peoples. They hired a group of Inuit from Canada to entertain visitors by performing dances and parading in the hot Chicago summer in native furs. Ethnologists also imported a group of "natives" in loincloths from Dahomey on the west coast of Africa to go through the motions of daily life in thatched huts. They presented American Indians and Africans as the primitive baseline against which all subsequent movement toward civilization was measured.

CONCLUSION

The world economy at the dawn of the twentieth century was highly interdependent. Bushels of wheat, investment dollars, economic ideas, and migrant laborers circulated around the globe, tying far-flung regions together in a complex network of feedback loops. The economic gains arising from international cooperation, new technologies, and rapidly rising labor productivity were so striking that visionaries dared dream that universal abundance was within reach.

But interdependence did not yield equality. To the contrary, class inequality was apparent in the spread of sometimes-violent labor disputes and in agrarian revolts against big business. Regional disparities were evident in the growing gap between the industrialized North, where wealth was concentrated, and the agrarian South, where poverty prevailed. Visitors to Chicago who stepped beyond the White City could glimpse such inequalities. Mable Treseder, an eighteen-year-old girl visiting the fair from the rural town of Viola, Wisconsin, wrote, "Our eyes witnessed some of the contrasting sights of the great city where want, misery, and crime hold sway and where poverty deals out a full measure to all. It would fairly make one's heart sick to see the distress manifested on some of those wretched alleys and lanes." Although the late nineteenth century saw spectacular gains, those gains were unequally distributed along lines of class, race, gender, and region.

Yet the exposition elevated the idea of progress to the level of myth. Myth is ideology in story form, whether it is the Indian myth of the ghost dance messiah or the Western myth of human progress. Myths performed similar functions in different societies. The myth of a new day coming for Indian people could restore a measure of hope to the hopeless. Among modern Americans, the myth of progress could override the reality of conflict, inequality, and poverty in an effort to restore confidence in a harmonious future.

FURTHER READING

Beckert, Sven. *Empire of Cotton: A Global History.* New York: Knopf, 2014.

Beckert, Sven. *The Monied Metropolis: New York City and the Consolidation of the American Bourgeoisie, 1850–1896.* Cambridge: Cambridge University Press, 2003.

Cannato, Vincent J. *American Passage: The History of Ellis Island.* New York: Harper, 2009.

Curtin, Philip D. *The World and the West: The European Challenge and the Overseas Response in the Age of Empire.* Cambridge: Cambridge University Press, 2000.

Greene, Julie. *Pure and Simple Politics: The American Federation of Labor and Political Activism, 1881–1917.* Cambridge: Cambridge University Press, 1998.

Guglielmo, Thomas. *White on Arrival: Italians, Race, Color, and Power in Chicago, 1890–1945.* Oxford: Oxford University Press, 2004.

Hobsbawm, Eric. *The Age of Empire, 1875–1914.* New York: Pantheon, 1987.

Huyssen, David. *Progressive Inequality: Rich and Poor in New York, 1890–1920.* Cambridge, MA: Harvard University Press, 2014.

Lears, Jackson. *Rebirth of a Nation: The Making of Modern America, 1877–1920.* New York: HarperPerennial, 2009.

White, Richard. *"It's Your Misfortune and None of My Own:" A History of the American West.* Norman: University of Oklahoma Press, 1991.

CHAPTER 2

THE NEW IMPERIALISM

The S.S. *Philadelphia* carried Isabel González and other migrants from San Juan, Puerto Rico, to New York City in the early 1900s. Library of Congress Prints and Photographs Division, Washington, DC.

COLONIAL MIGRATIONS

It was early August 1902 when Isabel González, a twenty-year-old pregnant widow, arrived in New York on the S.S. Philadelphia from Puerto Rico. Having paid her own passage and with only a few dollars in hand, she entered New York Harbor eager to be reunited with her brother, Louis, who had arrived six months earlier to work in a linoleum factory on Staten Island. But when entering Ellis Island, immigration agents detained González and alleged that she was "likely to become a public charge," a designation of dependency on the state that was considered common grounds for detention during this period. Such a charge was routinely leveled against foreign immigrants, especially unmarried women. Together with the Coudert brothers, a pair of young lawyers from Manhattan who specialized in international law, González contested the charge before the U.S. District Court in New York. In their petition for González they wrote,

"Your petitioner denies that she is an alien and asserts her right to entry into the U.S." By arguing that residents of U.S. colonial territories such as Puerto Rico were not foreigners and therefore not subject to immigration restrictions, they challenged the legal boundaries of the United States at a time of U.S. imperial expansion.

Isabel González's legal case was one in a series of confrontations in the early twentieth century between colonial migrants who sought entrance to the U.S. mainland and the Bureau of Immigration agents who policed U.S. borders. Although the United States had ruled Puerto Rico as a colony since the end of the War of 1898, immigration laws governing the entrance of Puerto Ricans to the U.S. mainland continued to consider Puerto Rico a foreign nation. Isabel González took her case all the way to the U.S. Supreme Court and won. In the decision Gonzales v. Williams (1904), the Court defined González as a U.S. National, a new legal category between citizen and alien. As nationals, González and other residents of U.S. territories, including Puerto Rico and the Philippines, could enter the U.S. mainland free from immigration restrictions. At the same time, however, they were denied the most basic citizenship rights, including the right to vote for president or representatives in Congress. Migrants from Puerto Rico and the Philippines entered the U.S. mainland in growing numbers in the years after the Gonzales ruling.

The streams of migrants from colonies to the mainland were tied to the dynamics of imperial rule. From the 1880s to the start of World War I, legions of soldiers, capitalists, and adventurers poured out of the United States (as well as Europe and Japan) in search of wealth, power, and adventure on foreign shores. Because they were driven by the new forces of the Industrial Revolution and because they often pushed older empires aside, the sum total of their deeds came to be called the new imperialism. Although imperial rule brought new roads, bridges, and schools to the colonies, it also brought economic dislocation such as the concentration of land and the displacement of small farmers that led many colonial subjects to leave their homelands. Yet, as the Gonzales case suggests, the history of this new imperialism is not simply one of colonial power; it is also a history of agency, resistance, and contestation. Nor is it only a history of foreign relations. Imperialism abroad had dramatic effects at home, including new migration streams from the Caribbean and Pacific. The more America went out into the world to try and change it, the more America was changed by the world.

THE NEW IMPERIALISM

In the late nineteenth century, imperialism grew, together with industry, in a cycle of expansion. As the Industrial Revolution swept successively across Western Europe, the United States, and later Japan, it supplied both the motive and the means for overseas expansion. Motives included the search for raw materials, new markets, and profitable investments, and the means included gunboats, railroads, and machine guns. In turn, overseas conquests fueled economic growth and ensured domestic peace, at least so it was commonly thought. Especially during the so-called long depression from 1873 to 1896, business leaders came to believe in the necessity of finding overseas outlets for domestic "overproduction."

By 1900, the new imperialism had divided much of the world along an axis that ran between the centers of imperial power, or metropoles, on one side and colonial dependencies on the other, as depicted in Map 2.1. In the new geography of world power, the metropoles were located in Europe, North America, and Japan, whereas colonial regions were found for the most part in Asia, Africa, and Latin America.

Along with political and economic motives, ideological impulses also drove Western expansion. Faith in progress provided a major impetus. At a time when the idea of progress captivated Western minds, the triumph of industrial over agrarian societies was seen as the advance of civilization over barbarism. Under the set of ideas known as social Darwinism, progress seemed to be the result of competition among "races" for survival of the fittest. In the language of the late nineteenth century, race was not just about color or physical differences; it was also a common term for any ethnic, linguistic, or national group. Thus, Italians, Jews, and Filipinos (inhabitants of the Philippine Islands) were all seen as competing with Anglo-Saxons and Teutons (Germans) for a place at the top of the racial hierarchy.

American expansionists partook of all these impulses. The spirit of social Darwinism was perhaps best captured by Albert Beveridge, a Republican senator from Indiana and a leading proponent of U.S. expansion. Beveridge summoned his fellow Americans to a duty of conquest in saying, "God has not been preparing the English-speaking and Teutonic peoples for a thousand years for nothing but vain and idle self-contemplation and self-admiration. No!" According to Beveridge, "superior races" had a duty to rule over races incapable of self-government. "They are not a self-governing race," he said of Filipinos; "They are Orientals, Malays, instructed by Spaniards in the latter's worst estate."

Gender also played a role. At a time when industrialization and changing relations between the sexes generated new challenges to masculine authority, war and expansion were put forward as the means of restoring lost manhood. Theodore Roosevelt, for example, championed the rigors of martial combat as a means of regenerating manly virtues in an industrial society gone soft from material comforts. Roosevelt became the most famous member of the Rough Riders, an all-volunteer brigade of American soldiers that fought against the Spanish in Cuba during the War of 1898. Seeking to turn military heroics to political advantage, he won media attention by publishing blow-by-blow accounts of his experiences, and the press obligingly turned the future president into the Hero of San Juan Hill.

Roosevelt, like other war supporters known as *jingoists*, claimed war could strengthen American democracy by building manly character. With the U.S.

western frontier officially closed to new settlement, jingoists highlighted how combat overseas provided a new way to cultivate masculine strength and independence. Women suffrage activists sometimes supported imperialism out of their own strategic interests in raising the question of women's voting rights in new territories and at the federal level. At the same time, other women activists argued for diplomacy and became leading voices in the cause of arbitration. Frances Willard, the leader of the Woman's Christian Temperance Union—the largest women's association in the United States in this period—argued that men must be taught some of the same values as women, that "true glory consists not in physical feats of warfare, but in mental and moral ability." Although American arbitrationists successfully used diplomacy to avoid war with Britain in the 1897 border dispute known as the Venezuela crisis, they lost out to the jingoists one year later in the War of 1898.

Paternalism was an important component of the gender ideology of the day. Supporters defended empire as the benevolent rule of wise authorities over unruly children. They even went so far as to claim that the main beneficiaries of foreign rule were the colonized themselves. In his landmark poem "The White Man's Burden," Rudyard Kipling appealed to his American cousins to follow the British lead, wage "savage wars of peace," and annex the Philippines for the sake of the people he denigrated as "your new-caught, sullen peoples, Half-devil and half-child." With such attitudes, Western imperialists infantilized foreign peoples of color.

National and religious beliefs were no less important. Myths of national destiny inspired empire builders of the various powers to tout the virtues of their own national cause, whether it was the French *mission civilisatrice*, German *Kultur*, or *Pax Britannica*. In the case of the United States, strong Protestant traditions imparted moralistic fervor to the belief that the United States had a divine mission to spread the blessings of liberty. Christian missionaries themselves typically linked the conversion of the heathen to Western expansion. Senator Beveridge brought together religion and nationalism in an eloquent invocation of an American mission to save the world. "And of all our race," Beveridge said, God "has marked the American people as His chosen nation to finally lead in the regeneration of the world."

Even the so-called realists of the day were swept along in the idea of national destiny. Alfred Thayer Mahan, a naval officer, promoted the importance of American sea power in language typical of the economic orthodoxy of the day by equating national interests with commercial interests. In *The Influence of Sea Power upon History*, which appeared in 1890, Mahan put it bluntly: "Navies exist for the protection of commerce." Mahan's model was Great Britain, but the day was fast approaching, Mahan believed, when the United States would require its own sea power. Writing at a time when a canal across the isthmus of Panama was still an unrealized dream, Mahan envisioned a future in which goods passed freely between the Atlantic and the Pacific under the protection of a significantly enlarged U.S. Navy.

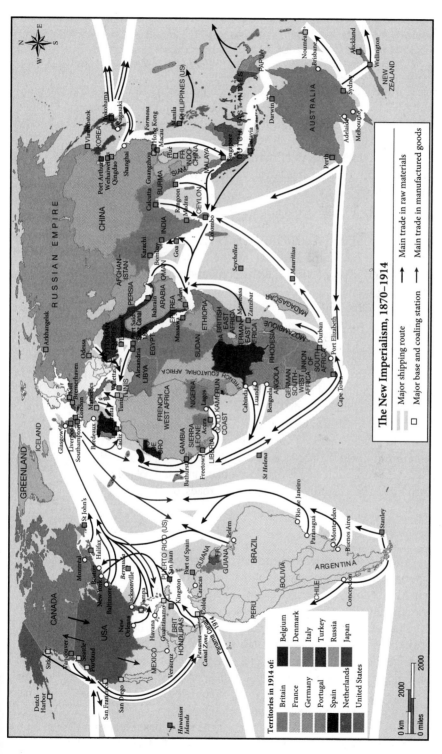

The New Imperialism, 1870–1914

Territories in 1914 of:

Britain	Belgium
France	Denmark
Germany	Italy
Portugal	Turkey
Spain	Russia
Netherlands	Japan
United States	

〰〰 Major shipping route
▢ Major base and coaling station

→ Main trade in raw materials
→ Main trade in manufactured goods

0 km ___ 2000
0 miles ___ 2000

MAP 2.1

THE NEW IMPERIALISM
AND THE WORLD ECONOMY

Along with ideas of national destiny, racial superiority, and masculinity, economic imperatives also shaped the new imperialism. The drive to accumulate wealth led to a search for raw materials, markets, and investment opportunities in the furthest reaches of the globe. With improved transportation and communication, the world economy reached deeper into every continent. By 1900, a rapidly thickening network of railroads linked distant frontier regions of North America, Latin America, and Africa to the metropolitan centers of London, New York, and Berlin.

At a time when finance capital was in the ascendancy, imperial rank was closely tied to overseas investment. The fact that Britain was the world's prime investor allowed it to remain the premier imperial power, even as its industrial sector slipped into third place behind the United States and Germany. An exceptionally large proportion of British capital—nearly 50 percent—was invested outside the home economy. The share was smaller for Germany, at roughly 15 percent, and for the United States, 10 percent. The lion's share of foreign capital circulated within the upper tier of the world economy in the industrial belt stretching from Berlin in the east to Chicago in the west. Britain, for example, directed the largest portion of its funds into North America, knowing that was where the most money was to be made from industrial customers, paid-up debtors, and growing numbers of middle-class consumers.

But investors increasingly looked beyond the industrial North. They regarded the vast, impoverished agrarian region that belted the earth from Beijing to Cairo to Mexico City as an untapped reservoir of opportunity. Investors in the United States, for example, placed the largest share of their overseas capital in Latin America. Elsewhere, investors hunted for profits in the diamonds and gold of South Africa, cattle ranching on the Argentine pampas, and railroads, ore, and oil in Mexico.

The Tribute of the Market

The flow of commodities to the industrial North amounted to a modern form of imperial tribute. In the empires of old, tribute moved from the provinces to the center in the form of taxes, exactions, and outright plunder. The Spanish crown, for example, laid claim to "the royal fifth" of all the gold and silver pouring out of the mines of the Americas. Under the new imperialism, however, tribute arrived, for the most part, through the market. The flow of cheap goods produced by cheap labor enriched the commercial classes and boosted the living standards of consumers in the modern metropole. Thus, proponents of expansion promoted visions of bountiful harvests of tropical commodities—rice, coffee, sugar, bananas, coconuts—delivered to American kitchens.

To be sure, some sectors of agrarian regions also benefited from foreign capital. To peasants barely eking out an existence on the land, the roads, railroads, and other fruits of the Industrial Revolution were the precondition for economic development. Even more welcome were life-saving advances in Western medicine and the expanded opportunity of mass education. In addition, whole new classes arose in the colonial regions to mediate between outside capital and local society. Local business people were in a better position than outsiders to manage Philippine contractors, Cuban cane cutters, and Mexican railroad workers. Members of these new business strata entered marriage alliances with the old landlord classes and the upper echelons of the military to create a new layer of elites at the top of the social pyramid.

At the same time, market tribute deepened the division in the world economy between laboring classes, who produced wealth, and capitalists, who accumulated it. Cheap labor in the agricultural regions underwrote capital accumulation and rising living standards in industrial metropoles. Foreign ownership of export-oriented copper mines, railroads, and sugar plantations meant that the products and profits from these enterprises left the country where they were produced and headed north. Even when the dependent regions shook off outside political control after World War II, they were typically unable to break free of these economic bonds, a situation that came to be known as *neocolonialism*.

Imperial Cola

Tropical commodities provide an illustration of the way market tribute worked. For two centuries, Caribbean sugar had been shipped to dining tables in Western Europe and North America—white sugar for the rich, molasses and brown sugar for everyone else. Now, as the world economy shifted toward big business and mass consumption, new opportunities arose for exploiting consumers' sweet tooths. Between 1880 and 1915, the per capita consumption of sugar doubled in the United States, while bananas, cocoa, and coffee transitioned from rare luxuries to everyday necessities.

Coca-Cola became the world's most widely recognized brand name shortly after it started out in the 1880s as just another patent medicine marketed as a cure-all for "sick head-ache, neuralgia, hysteria, melancholy." The key ingredients of the exotic concoction came from several sites of Western imperialism. Coca leaves came from the Peruvian Andes under the protection of the British and U.S. navies. The leaves were then treated through a lengthy industrial process to manufacture small amounts of cocaine, an ingredient in Coca-Cola until 1903 (a decocainized form was included thereafter). Cola nuts, the source of the caffeine, came mostly from European colonies in West Africa. The main ingredient, sugar, arrived from the Caribbean under the protection of the U.S. Navy. The tie between Coke and empire was recognized by Latin American critics who later complained about *coca-colonization*.

Coke sales took wing after the turn of the century on a mass advertising campaign that featured alluring but wholesome calendar girls cooing about giving the customer satisfaction. When temperance crusaders raised objections, the corporation responded by removing cocaine from the secret formula and by touting Coke as a refreshing "soft" drink, as opposed to "hard" liquor. Soon the all-American pick-me-up was conquering markets overseas, and by the end of the twentieth century, most of the profits of the Atlanta-based corporation came from foreign sales.

The rise of Coke exemplifies the unequal relation between the global rich and the global poor. Coke was cheap because sugar was cheap, and sugar was cheap because much of it came from Caribbean plantations worked by underpaid cane cutters who had to endure the notoriously brutal conditions that gave sugar cane its reputation as a "killer crop." In linking South American, Caribbean, and African producers to American consumers through a modern U.S. corporation, Coke flowed freely through the channels of the new imperialism.

CONFLICT IN THE CARIBBEAN

During the first age of European expansion from 1500 to 1800, Latin America had been a battleground of world power at least as important as East Asia or the Middle East. Control of the Americas had decided the fate of European kings and empires. Britain's triumph over both France and Spain by 1763 set Britain on a course that would lead it to rule the waves of much of the world. At the same time, wealth generated by trade in sugar, cotton, and slaves helped make Britain the cradle of the Industrial Revolution.

Since 1823, however, the United States sought control over the Western Hemisphere through the Monroe Doctrine. Issued as a string of Latin American republics gained independence, the doctrine named after President James Monroe decreed that the Western and Eastern Hemispheres were "separate spheres" of diplomacy and that the United States would protect Latin republics from any new colonization. For much of the nineteenth century, the United States lacked the military strength to police the Atlantic and deferred to Britain. But by the end of the nineteenth century, newfound industrial might and military prowess enabled the United States to enforce the Monroe Doctrine on its own.

For Americans, the new imperialism arrived with the War of 1898 (known variously as the Spanish–American War or the Spanish–Cuban–American War). This war was actually three wars in one: an imperial war between the United States and Spain; a colonial war in Cuba; and another colonial war in the Philippines. By the late nineteenth century, Cuba and Puerto Rico were all that was left of what had once been the vast Spanish domain in the Americas. Early in the nineteenth century, Spain had lost Mexico, Bolivia, Venezuela, and its other possessions in Latin American to independence movements that were the Spanish American counterpart of the American Revolution against Britain. When Cuban patriots raised the call for independence in 1868, they were following in the footsteps of New World revolutionaries from George Washington to Simón Bolívar.

They were also following in the footsteps of Abraham Lincoln in seeking the abolition of slavery. Cuba was the last stand of legalized slavery in the world (along with Brazil). Finally bowing to the tides of history, Spain gradually abolished slavery in the island between 1878 and 1886. Legal emancipation only whetted Cuban appetites for additional social change. By the time the fight for independence resumed in earnest in 1895, the call for *Cuba libre!* included new ideas about land reform and social justice aimed at overturning the oppressions of class and race.

The key figure in developing these new ideas was José Martí. The founder of the Cuban Revolutionary Party, Martí had settled among the Cuban expatriate community in New York at a time when some 10 percent of Cubans lived abroad. Like so many European exiles who found safe haven in the United States, Martí plotted revolution in the cafes and printing shops of New York's multiethnic metropolis. In remarkably prophetic writings, Martí warned of the growing expansionist impulse of the colossus of the North and urged fellow Latin Americans to join forces to stop "the USA from spreading over the West Indies and falling with added weight upon other lands of Our America."

Although Martí was killed in battle in 1895, his ideas helped inspire Cuban insurgents to undertake land reform. The prospect of owning their own plot of ground attracted sufficient support from the peasants to lay the basis for guerrilla war. More and more peasants took to the hills to join insurgent forces, especially in the fabled Sierra Maestra Mountains that ringed Santiago de Cuba in Oriente Province. Insurgents also attracted significant numbers of ex-slaves, free blacks, and mulattos, personified by Antonio Maceo, the brilliant black general known as the Bronze Titan, who rose to be second in command of revolutionary forces. Waging economic warfare with tactics reminiscent of the French and Haitian Revolutions, insurgents burned the haciendas and sugar fields of planters who refused to suspend the sugar cane harvest, or *zafra*. The *Cuba libre!* movement won widespread support in the United States, with both the Republican and the Democratic parties supporting the Cuban revolutionaries in their campaign platforms of 1896.

Spain did not stand idly by. The Spanish colonial office sent in General Valeriano Weyler to crush the revolt. Seeking to cut off guerrilla war at the source, Weyler began driving peasants off the land into barbed-wire concentration camps, where they could be easily controlled by Spanish soldiers. This infamous *reconcentrada* policy earned Weyler the epithet the Butcher and turned American public opinion against Spain. Despite such brutal repression, the Cuban revolutionaries seemed poised for victory over Spain by the spring of 1898.

The War of 1898

The United States had long held interests in Cuba, with northerners in the late nineteenth century seeking tropical exports from the island and southerners earlier in the century dreaming of annexing Cuba as a slave territory. Before his death in 1895, José Martí worried about the long-term effects should the United States enter the war and asked prophetically, "Once the United States is in Cuba, who will drive them out?"

The arrival of U.S. forces in April 1898 changed what had been a Spanish–Cuban war into a Spanish–Cuban–American war. The specific sequence of events that brought U.S. forces to Cuba began with a mysterious explosion that sent the USS *Maine* to the bottom of Havana Harbor on February 15 of that year. Although there was no evidence of Spanish culpability, a patriotic frenzy burst forth in the American media demanding revenge against Spain.

Although not immune to the exaggerated claims often made in the press, which became known as *yellow journalism*, President William McKinley was more responsive to the large-policy imperialists in the Republican Party, such as Theodore Roosevelt and Cushman Davis, chair of the Senate Foreign Relations Committee. As avid followers of Alfred Thayer Mahan's grandiose ideas, Roosevelt and Davis shared a romantic vision that it was U.S. national destiny to develop from a continental land power to a global sea power.

Suspicious of the intentions of the expansionists, anti-imperialists in Congress won passage of the Teller Amendment, a self-denying ordinance that swore off any intention of making Cuba a U.S. colony. After Spanish diplomatic fumbling and a U.S. ultimatum, the two countries began a collision course that led to war in late April 1898.

What Secretary of State John Hay called "a splendid little war" ended quickly. Cuban fighters had already wrested control from Spanish forces in most of the countryside. It remained for U.S. forces under General Leonard Wood, aided by Teddy Roosevelt and the Rough Riders, to win control of urban areas, such as Santiago de Cuba. What sealed Spain's fate was not U.S. victory at San Juan Hill, but the sinking of the Spanish fleet. In one of the greatest blunders in the annals of naval warfare, Spanish ships steamed out of Santiago Harbor into the waiting guns of U.S. warships and were forced aground. With no hope of resupply, Spain surrendered to the United States at an August ceremony under an ancient ceiba tree near San Juan Hill. Yet, despite the previous thirty years of fighting for independence, no Cuban was invited to the signing ceremony.

Cubans were excluded in part because of U.S. racist and paternalist attitudes. Cuban troops were frequently commanded by black officers, of whom Antonio Maceo was the prime example. For Roosevelt, black officers such as Maceo represented an unacceptable challenge to ideas of white superiority, especially in light of U.S. Army practice where white officers commanded segregated black units. At one point in the thick of battle, Roosevelt came across African American soldiers in segregated units of the U.S. Army who seemed to have lost their white officers. He immediately asserted command himself and, in case there were doubts about who was in charge, he threatened to shoot anyone who did not obey.

The U.S. invasion of Cuba helped end the war and saved the lives of countless Cubans. Yet despite widespread support in the United States for *Cuba Libre!*, including hundreds of popular American songs such as "Make Cuba Free" and "Cuba Shall Be Free," U.S. officials undermined Cubans' quest for independence after the war by questioning their fitness for self-rule. Instead of gaining

In this stereoscopic print, a segregated African American unit of the U.S. Army known as the Gallant 25th preparing to embark for Cuba in 1898. Library of Congress Prints and Photographs Division, Washington, DC.

immediate independence, Cuba was subject to a four-year U.S. occupation. Moreover, when the occupation ended in 1902, independence was compromised in ways that made the island a U.S. *protectorate*. In adopting the Platt Amendment in 1901, Congress claimed the right of the United States to send troops into Cuba whenever the U.S. government deemed it necessary "to protect Cuban independence," to exercise U.S. veto power over Cuban foreign policy, and to maintain a permanent U.S. naval station at Guantánamo. Further weakening the Cuban state, Congress insisted that the Platt Amendment be incorporated in the new Cuban constitution before the island could go its own way. The bitter irony of a foreign invasion to "protect independence" was not lost on Cubans, many of whom remember 1898 not as the first chapter in the struggle for *Cuba libre!* but as a betrayal.

Formal and Informal Empire

The U.S. intervention in Cuba pointed toward expanding U.S. influence in the Caribbean and Latin America over the next three decades. The preferred method was informal empire in the form of protectorates and open door policies promoting business expansion. As long as client regimes kept the door open to American business, they were free to go their own way, subject to U.S. oversight. When hostile forces threatened economic or strategic interests, U.S. Marines arrived to protect American interests.

In exceptional cases, the United States adopted formal methods of empire through military takeover, the installation of U.S. colonial governments, and the possession of territory. Such was the case in Puerto Rico, which Spain ceded to the United States after the War of 1898. Under the Foraker Act of 1900, Puerto Rico came under the rule of a governor appointed by the U.S. president, a practice that persisted until 1948 when the island was made a commonwealth. The Jones Act of 1917 conferred a form of second-class U.S. citizenship on island residents and established a two-house legislature whose acts were, nonetheless, subject to veto by the U.S. president and Congress. Thus did Puerto Rico acquire its peculiar status, half inside, half outside the United States.

War in the Philippines

To the empire builders who came to power in Washington with the election of President William McKinley in 1896, the path to national greatness lay in projecting power overseas. That required a large navy, coaling stations, and naval bases. American expansionists had already begun angling for Hawaii and other Pacific islands when, in 1898, their attention turned to a larger set of islands. The Philippine archipelago seemed like a perfect base of naval operations in East Asia as well as a steppingstone to the China market, as depicted in Map 2.2.

As a leading expansionist, Theodore Roosevelt played a key role not just in Cuba but also in the Philippines. During preparations for war with Spain over Cuba, the brash assistant secretary of the navy took advantage of the brief absence of his superior and issued one of the most important orders in U.S. history. He instructed Commodore George Dewey, commander of America's Pacific fleet, to leave his berth in China and attack the Spanish fleet in Manila Harbor immediately on the outbreak of war with Spain. On May 1, 1898, Dewey's guns proceeded to sink the entire Spanish fleet. News of the victory was sensationalized by the ultranationalist *jingo press* as revenge for the sinking of the *Maine*, instantly making Dewey one of America's most famous war heroes.

Yet things were not going as well in the Philippines as they were in the jingo press. Without a land army at his disposal, Dewey had to rely on Philippine nationalists who, as in Cuba, had begun a struggle for independence before the arrival of U.S. soldiers. Organized through a secret society known as the Katipunan, the ranks of Philippine patriots had swelled under Spanish repression. Under a revolutionary government-in-waiting led by Emilio Aguinaldo, a local mayor and landowner, guerrilla fighters drove the Spanish from much of the countryside. Again, as in Cuba, guerrilla war could not topple Spanish rule, and the revolt was a stalemate in 1898 with Aguinaldo in exile in Hong Kong. When Dewey arrived, he arranged for Aguinaldo to be brought back on a U.S. warship, and Aguinaldo was only too happy to cooperate with the Americans in what he expected would be a joint liberation of his country. He rallied his forces to the point where they had a stranglehold on the capital of Manila by August.

But Aguinaldo was quickly disappointed. Having relied on Filipino fighters to defeat Spanish forces, Dewey proceeded to end the war without them. At a signing ceremony in mid-August, American officials reached armistice agreements with Spanish commanders from which representatives of the Philippine people were excluded, just as the Cubans had been at San Juan Hill.

The Philippine Insurrection

Determined to be the lead actors in their own historical drama, Aguinaldo and his followers proceeded to declare independence. Following the path of nationalist revolutionaries since 1776, they elected a constituent assembly that drafted a constitution embodying universal principles of national sovereignty, representative government, individual liberty, and separation of church and state. Capping their work, they proclaimed the Republic of the Philippines on January 23, 1899. As Filipinos saw it, the United States had played a role in defeating Spain similar to the French role in helping Americans win their own revolutionary war against the British. Now it was time for the Americans to go.

Instead, the Americans stayed for almost half a century. To be sure, many Filipinos were happy to salute the American flag. The arrival of American investors opened new opportunities for local business in the booming sugar trade and the provisioning of American bases. Even Aguinaldo, who was captured in 1901, eventually became reconciled to the U.S. presence. But others—Tagalog speakers, Spanish-educated middle classes, and Muslim *Moros*—took up arms against the U.S. occupation in what soon became America's most violent conflict since the Civil War.

From mountain hideaways and jungle camps, Philippine *insurrectos* waged a guerrilla war that began almost immediately after the proclamation of the republic and dragged on for seven years. Fighting broke out on February 4, 1899, when Americans patrolling a water pipe running from a hinterland reservoir into the city of Manila exchanged fire with Filipino insurgents occupying a nearby village. This was not the first scuffle between forces on the islands, and Filipino and American historians disagree about which side initiated the conflict that night. But with the signing of the Treaty of Paris marking the close of diplomatic negotiations, both sides recognized the frustration of Filipino *insurrectos* and readied for war.

Despite the superiority of Gatling guns (an early version of the machine gun) over *bolos* (a long knife for cutting cane), the *insurrectos* inflicted heavy casualties. More than 4,000 American soldiers died in the Philippine War, compared to fewer than 400 U.S. soldiers who died from wounds or disease in the war with Spain. The cost to Filipinos was even higher. Some 20,000 were killed in the fighting, plus an estimated 250,000 civilians, perhaps one-fifth of the entire population, died from hunger and disease.

If the quick defeat of Spain merited Secretary John Hay's description of a splendid little war, the ensuing violence in the Philippines was closer to what Rudyard Kipling called savage war. "I want no prisoners," commanded U.S. General Jacob Smith; "I wish you to kill and burn: the more you kill and burn the better you will please me." Soldiers wrote home that they were fighting a race war against what they commonly referred to as *goo-goos* and *niggers*. "I am probably growing hard-hearted," one soldier admitted, "for I am in my glory when I can sight my gun on some dark skin and pull the trigger." Although racism alone does not explain U.S. expansion in the Asia–Pacific region, ideologies of racial superiority made it possible for men to kill and burn while believing they were agents of progress and enlightenment.

Yet U.S. colonialists did not simply export fixed ideas of white superiority from America to the Pacific. Instead, the conditions of empire gave rise to new racial ideologies that changed in different historical moments. During the Philippine–American War, U.S. soldiers justified mass killing with racism. But after the war, a different racial ideology was needed to legitimate the period of civilian rule when the U.S. Philippine Commission relied on support from Filipino elites to administer the islands. In the postwar period, the governor held elaborate colonial balls in which U.S. officials danced with the wives of leading Filipino elites, known as *illustrados*, as a way of proving that Filipinos were "brothers and not serfs." This represented not only a shift from wartime racial politics, but also a departure from racial ideologies of white superiority prevailing in the U.S. South. In an effort to consolidate colonial rule in the Philippines, then, U.S. officials found themselves challenging ideas of a strict racial hierarchy, ideas that were still dominant in the U.S. mainland.

Debate over Empire: The United States

The Philippine–American War led to one of the greatest foreign policy debates in American history. The debate was about not only the annexation of the Philippines but also the larger question of whether the American republic should become an empire. Because of their own anti-imperial origins and democratic traditions, Americans denied any connection to *imperialism*. Even Roosevelt, the most unabashed empire-builder ever to occupy the White House, was uncomfortable with the term, preferring *expansion* instead.

Critics objected that colonial rule violated the sacred principle of democratic self-government. Mark Twain, one of America's most beloved writers and an astute observer of American politics, mused on the riddle of imperial democracy. Commenting on America's conquest of the Philippines, Twain suggested sardonically, "There must be two Americas: one that sets the captive free, and one that takes a once-captive's new freedom away from him."

Critics also condemned jingoism. William James, a Harvard philosopher and a founder of modern psychology, disparaged the worship of what he called the "idol of a national destiny." Scorning the notion that the United States could do no wrong, James insisted, "Angelic impulses and predatory lusts divide our heart exactly as they divide the heart of other countries." There were also objections of a different sort. Some of the most ardent white supremacists, such as South Carolina's "Pitchfork" Ben Tillman, railed against Philippine annexation on the grounds that it would further threaten America's already endangered race purity.

From these different impulses came a strong anti-imperialist movement. Democrat William Jennings Bryan made another run for the presidency in 1900, basing his anti-imperialist campaign, in part, on the simple point that "a republic can have no subjects." Opposition was also evident in the Teller Amendment, the bill precluding annexation of Cuba, and in the fact that Philippine annexation only passed the Senate by a razor-thin margin.

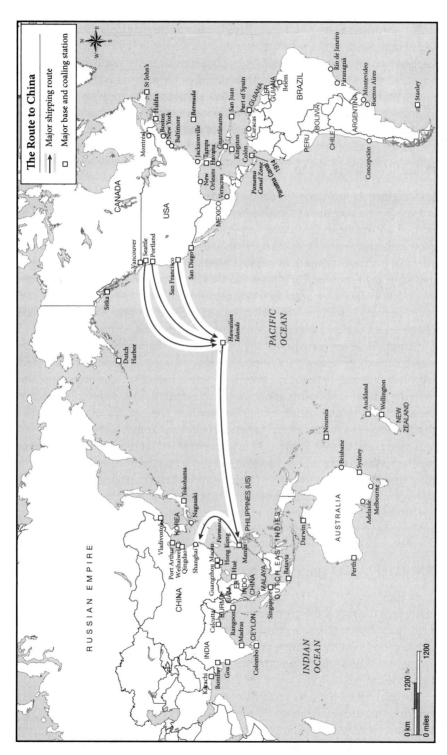

The Route to China

— Major shipping route
□ Major base and coaling station

RUSSIAN EMPIRE

CANADA

USA

Sitka

Dutch Harbor

Vancouver
Seattle
Portland
San Francisco
San Diego

Montreal
St John's
Halifax
Boston
New York
Baltimore
Bermuda
Jacksonville
New Orleans
Tampa
Havana
Veracruz
Guantanamo
San Juan
Port of Spain
Kingston
Colón
Caracas
Panama Canal Zone
Panama Canal 1914

MEXICO

PERU
BOLIVIA
BRAZIL
Belem
Rio de Janeiro
Paranaguá
Montevideo
Buenos Aires
CHILE
ARGENTINA
Concepción
Stanley

UK GUIANA
GUIANA

PACIFIC OCEAN

Hawaiian Islands

Nouméa
Auckland
Wellington
NEW ZEALAND

Brisbane
Sydney
Adelaide
Melbourne
AUSTRALIA
Darwin
Perth

Vladivostok
Port Arthur
Weihaiwei
Qingdao
KOREA
Nagasaki
Yokohama
Shanghai
Guangzhou
Macao
Formosa
Hong Kong
Hué
PHILIPPINES (US)
Manila
CHINA
INDO-CHINA
SIAM
BURMA
MALAYA
Batavia
DUTCH EAST INDIES
Singapore
Rangoon
Calcutta
Madras
CEYLON
Colombo
Goa
Bombay
Karachi
INDIA

INDIAN OCEAN

0 km   1200
0 miles   1200

MAP 2.2

But expansionists prevailed. Republican empire-builders proclaimed a sacred obligation, in the words of President McKinley, to "uplift and civilize and Christianize" backward peoples. The U.S. business interests hailed expansion as a way to solve the surplus problem while the jingo press clamored for annexation. Roosevelt and other large-policy advocates called for annexation on the grounds of strategic interests, commercial opportunity, and messianic mission. McKinley handily won the 1900 election, and his victory sent anti-imperialism into retreat.

Debate over Empire: Europe

Such arguments were part of a larger debate about empire in the Western world. Public opinion was divided everywhere. British and other European defenders minced no words in supporting imperialism, which they praised as a positive good for both colonizer and colonized. Some in Britain saw the United States as a potential partner in empire. Alongside Kipling's famous appeal to help shoulder the "white man's burden," English writer W. T. Stead in *The Americanization of the World* (1901) called for nothing less than the re-union of the "English-speaking races" so that 121 million "self-governing white citizens" of the United States and Britain could hold sway over the 353 million "Asiatics and Africans."

Critics, however, raised a variety of objections. Representatives of different social interests protested that empire fostered militarism, undermined democracy, and undercut domestic producers. A more coherent critique of empire came from the left. Most Socialists and some liberals attributed the new imperialism to the search for profit. English social reformer J. A. Hobson, for example, argued that low wages in the industrial societies shrank the home market, causing surplus capital and unsold goods to go overseas in search of more profitable outlets. Where business went, naval forces would not be far behind. In a similar vein, Russian revolutionary Vladimir Lenin argued that imperialism was itself the latest phase of capitalist development, what he called *monopoly capitalism*. To Lenin, the only way to end imperialism was through revolution that would sweep away capitalism itself.

EMPIRE AND RESISTANCE IN EAST ASIA

Over vocal opposition, Western expansion continued apace. Lured by potential markets in China, all the great powers, the United States included, sought influence there. They sent missionaries to convert Confucians and Buddhists to Christianity. They vied for railway concessions and, ultimately, millions of Chinese customers. While France took over the ancient Chinese tributary of Indochina, Japan took over Korea.

For centuries, imperial China had been one of the world's major power centers, draining off silver from the West (defined as Western Europe and the United States) while keeping foreign traders and missionaries at bay. In the nineteenth century, however, the Industrial Revolution tipped the balance against China.

Western powers used gunboats and "unequal treaties" to force open the gates of the debilitated Qing dynasty. Although China remained nominally independent, German bankers won railroad concessions and Japanese armies camped out in the countryside. American diplomats promoted the principle of the *open door*, or equal access to markets in China, as a defense against Japanese and European encroachments. In practice, however, the Open Door Notes, a set of communications issued by Secretary of State John Hay beginning in 1899, proved a unilateral policy—one not agreed to by China—that sought to bolster U.S. exports. While nationalist Chinese protested foreign influence in the Boxer Uprising of 1900, the United States sought a steppingstone to China by fighting to secure the Philippines as a U.S. colony.

Yet, China had its own imperial tradition for more than two thousand years. In the Middle Ages when Europe was comparatively insignificant, China was a great center of civilization ruled by what was already the longest succession of imperial dynasties in history. The preeminence of Chinese civilization was widely recognized throughout East Asia, as Chinese migrants fanned out to bring Chinese writing, Confucian ideology, and mercantile activity to Vietnam, the Malay peninsula, Indonesia, and the Philippines. As recently as 1800, China was the largest economy in the world, and its silk, porcelain, and a wide array of other goods moved along a vast interior network of trade routes, of which the Silk Road was only the most famous.

In the mid to late nineteenth century, however, imperial China faced new challenges. Defeated by the British in the Opium Wars (1839–42), the Qing dynasty (1644–1911) suffered a protracted civil war in the 1850s called the Taiping Rebellion in which millions died, far more than in any other conflict in the nineteenth century, including the U.S. Civil War. These internal upheavals combined with the abolition of slavery in the West to propel Chinese migrants across the Pacific, where they arrived to cut sugar cane in the West Indies, dig copper in Mexico, pan for gold in California, and build railroads through the Rocky Mountains.

While migrants headed west, foreign powers sought greater influence in the East. European powers acquired railroad concessions and sometimes conducted business tax free. Chinese law protected foreigners working in China from the byzantine legal system by granting them exemptions from prosecution under the principle of *extraterritoriality*.

The Open Door in China

With the struggle for East Asia unfolding on the far side of the Pacific, U.S. leaders sought to gain influence in China. American contacts in East Asia went back to the days of the China clippers early in the nineteenth century when New England merchant vessels returned from the Orient loaded with the porcelain, silk, and spices that had always been the staples of East–West trade. With the onset of depression in 1893, American businesses searched for new markets. "Where shall we turn for consumers of our surplus?" asked Senator Albert

Beveridge. "Geography answers the question. China is our natural customer." The U.S. leaders pursued the strategy of keeping the China market open. An exchange of diplomatic notes with their British counterparts in 1899–1900 formalized the Open Door policy.

Understanding the Open Door policy is critical to understanding U.S. participation in world affairs in the 1890s and after. As a foreign policy, support for free trade was a strategy of informal empire. Although planting the flag and establishing formal imperial rule through colonial governments were important parts of the new imperialism, especially in Puerto Rico and the Philippines, it was even more important to make economies the world over open for business with the United States. Where local elites could not provide outside capital with stable access to labor and resources, military intervention and/or formal empire were the norm. Otherwise, Americans were content to expand into overseas economies and let other governments keep order.

As the world's prime lender, Britain supported the open door, confident that it would best its economic rivals and dominate its debtors. Likewise, as a rising economic power, the United States looked forward to the time when it would do the same. As many noted at the time, the similarity of aims and interests between the two Anglo-Saxon powers pointed to a future passing of the torch of world leadership from Great Britain, the leading imperial power of the day, to the United States, which emerged as the preeminent power after the Second World War.

Americans took the liberal idea of the open door much further than their British tutors. More than a foreign policy, the open door was a worldview built around the open society and the free market. Believing they were an open-minded, freedom-loving people, Americans assumed that, given the choice, other people would embrace their idea of freedom. Accordingly, they embarked on a long-term mission of opening closed societies: Japan in the 1850s, autocratic Germany in the First World War, militarist Japan in Second World War, and the Soviet Union during the Cold War. Despite mounting resistance, they conducted a series of interventions to open the poorer countries of Latin America, southeast Asia, and the Middle East throughout the twentieth century.

The Boxer Rebellion

Decades of concessions to foreigners had not dampened Chinese nationalism. Chinese saw themselves as denizens of the "Middle Kingdom" proudly located midway between heaven and earth. Although they admired Western advances, they also looked disdainfully on Westerners as barbarians who knew nothing of Confucian traditions and claimed to be above Chinese laws.

Nationalist resistance in China sometimes took the reactionary form of nativism, the rejection of all things foreign. Chinese nativism found violent expression in the Boxer Rebellion. Based among the peasantry of the northern countryside, the movement grew out of secret societies, such as the Fists of Righteous

Harmony, or Boxers, who sought the restoration of traditional ways. Suffering from economic hardship and a punishing drought, Boxers blamed Western railroads for desecrating the land and disturbing the graves of the ancestors. Seeking retribution, they vowed, "When we have slaughtered them all, we shall tear up the railways, cut down the telegraphs, and then finish off by burning their steamboats."

The Boxers attacked foreign influence, including Western merchants and Christian missionaries. Marching from village to village, Boxers put to death Western Christians by the score, along with hundreds of Chinese converts, driving the terrorized foreigners into their Beijing legations where they anxiously awaited the relief column that finally arrived in August 1900. The composition of the relief force was a roster of the new imperialists—the Japanese contributed the largest contingent, followed by the British, French, Germans, and Russians. In addition, no fewer than five thousand Americans took part. The composition of this relief force anticipated later coalitions such as NATO in the Balkans in the early 1990s and the 1991 Gulf War coalition that consolidated Western and imperialist power.

The Rise of Japan

To Americans seeking influence in Asia, Japan presented a significant challenge. After the restoration of the Meiji emperor in 1868, Japanese elites began to import Western advances. In contrast to China, nativism played only a small role in Japan. In setting up a centralized constitutional monarchy, they borrowed Western ideas of nationalism and constitutionalism. To shore up the position of the emperor at the apex of power, they rushed to acquire Western technology for military modernization and overseas expansion, which eventually led to the same cycle of capitalist and imperial expansion found in the West.

Especially in comparison to China, the Japanese proved that the best way to resist Western domination was through imitation. The key to success was not westernization per se, but the incorporation of selected Western ideas and practices within what remained a closed Japanese society. As successive generations of Westerners would discover, that system of tight family and business alliances was extremely hard to penetrate.

The first target of Japan's new rulers was Korea. Since the Hermit Kingdom traditionally fell under Chinese protection, Japan and China were on a collision course. In the Sino-Japanese war of 1894–95, the Japanese navy surprised everyone by quickly sending the Chinese fleet to the bottom. Capitalizing on victory, Japan annexed the Chinese island of Taiwan. On top of defeat, the Chinese were forced to pay a huge indemnity, which the Japanese used to build a modern iron and steel mill, creating new demands for raw materials that could only be found outside the homeland. By 1914, the Japanese economy was characterized by a cycle of industrial growth and imperial expansion.

Japan versus the West

The rise of imperial Japan would eventually lead to conflict with the West. For now, however, Japanese expansion came at the expense of other powers, notably Russia. During the long reign of the Romanov dynasty (1613–1917), Russia had moved eastward from its European base to colonize the Caucasus, Siberia, and central Asia, much as the United States had moved westward across the North American continent. Both nations built a huge transcontinental railway system to facilitate their vast expansion. Russia under the tsars (emperors) was one of the three great land empires that remained on the Asian continent at the start of the twentieth century. Like that of imperial China and the Ottomans, the other two land empires, the days of the tsars were numbered.

Even so, no one expected Russia to suffer a humiliating defeat at the hands of the Japanese. Conflicting imperial aims in Manchuria and in islands of the north Pacific led to fighting in the Russo-Japanese War (1904–5). Once again, Japan's land and naval forces won a decisive victory, strengthening the hand of military and imperial sectors within Japanese society. Watching these events unfold, President Roosevelt grew concerned that rapid Japanese ascent might threaten U.S. access to the Far East. He offered to mediate a peace settlement at an out-of-the-way location in New Hampshire. In the resulting Treaty of Portsmouth (1905), Japan secured Russian territory and other concessions, although not as much as the Japanese imperialists thought they deserved.

Japan's victory marked a historic departure. Much like the earlier victory of African revolutionaries over white French colonial armies in the Haitian Revolution (1791–1804), a white imperialist power had been defeated. In the racial language of the day, a yellow race overcame a white one, not at all the outcome predicted by social Darwinist ideology. Indeed, for the first time since the onrush of the Ottomans into Europe in the seventeenth century, an Asian power had triumphed over a Eurasian one. All over Asia, however, the outcome was celebrated as revenge for past humiliation and as a promise of future independence.

The advent of Japan as a world power reshaped the international balance of power, especially in the Asia–Pacific region. Dubbed the Great Britain of the East, Japan would no longer defer to the West. Instead, it insisted on equal treatment in the abrogation of unequal treaties and demands for naval parity and racial equality. Then, in the 1930s, it embarked on a campaign of conquest that displaced Western empires.

Meanwhile, the United States was also expanding in Asia. Although Americans undertook only limited economic projects, their political involvement was extensive. Because East Asia was one of the world's great power centers, the decision to colonize the Philippines, protect open access to markets in China, and attempt to check Japanese expansion helped transform the United States from a hemispheric to a world power. Although it would be a mistake to assume the inevitability of war between the United States and Japan, the simultaneous advent of the two new imperial powers helped set in motion a series of events that eventually drew them both into the Second World War.

THE U.S. SPHERE OF INFLUENCE
IN LATIN AMERICA

The main bastion of U.S. power overseas in this period and for decades to come lay not in Asia, but in Latin America. From pre-Columbian times, Latin Americans and U.S. have been linked through extensive trade and migration networks. Once a major crossroads of world history, Latin America (including Mexico, Central America, South America, and the Caribbean) receded in importance as Europeans retreated from the Americas, and the region increasingly came under the sway of the United States. "Poor Mexico," lamented Mexican dictator Porfirio Díaz, "so far from God, so close to the United States." For the tiny island republics of the Caribbean it was even harder to maintain autonomy. There was little they could do to stop the Caribbean from turning into what U.S. Americans called *Mare Nostrum* (Our Sea).

Relations with El Norte

Like the Spanish before them, American capitalists turned a long history of inequality in Latin America to their advantage. Businesses in the United States retained local managers to maintain work discipline through the patriarchal authority of the *patron* (boss), and they looked to repressive regimes, such as Porfirio Díaz in Mexico (1876–80; 1884–1910) and Juan Vicente Gómez in Venezuela (1908–35) to underwrite the political stability so important to outside investors. Díaz, in particular, opened the veins of his country's copper and silver mines to foreign investors and did not hesitate to send in the infamous *rurales*, military police, to put down labor disturbances, such as the 1906 strike at the Cananea copper mines, where many strikers were killed. American capital and technology made possible the excavation of $21,664,467.89 worth of silver from the Batopilas mines between 1880 and 1909, much of which was shipped to the bank accounts of investors in New York. Mexicans critics of Díaz complained bitterly that most of the benefits of this new industrialization went to American financiers and a small number of Mexican elites.

To be sure, there were many benefits to be had from foreign investment. As in Africa and Asia, foreign capital built basic Latin American infrastructure of roads, railroads, and telephone lines, which promoted technological advance and helped break down local isolation. There were also great strides in public health and education in Cuba and Panama under American occupation. President Taft, for instance, touted the achievements of U.S. Army surgeons in lowering the incidence of infectious diseases, including smallpox, as evidence of America's capacity for bringing progress and modernity to other parts of the world.

So long as they were treated as equals, Latin Americans were glad to acknowledge the contributions of their North American brethren. Beginning at the Chicago World's Fair in 1893, the Latin America republics proudly sent their wares to the string of great exhibitions in the United States that showcased the progress of civilization. At the 1915 San Francisco Panama–Pacific Exhibition, for example, many Latin countries joined in celebrating the opening of the Panama Canal, which they hoped would foster their own economic development.

Despite the looming presence of the Colossus of the North, U.S.–Latin American relations remained a two-way exchange. Latin Americans exercised great economic and cultural influence in *El Norte* (literally, "the North"). For example, Latin labor boosted U.S. living standards. Poorly paid workers put cheap sugar into soft drinks, copper into electric lines, and oil into automobile engines. Cultural influences included Spanish language, Catholic religion, traditional customs, and delicious foods already present in the vast swath of Mexican territory between Texas and the Pacific Coast that had been annexed to the United States. The steady stream of cultural influences accelerated in the 1920s when Latin American migrants increasingly came to the United States, even as new immigration laws restricted immigration from southern and Eastern Europe. Although the depression of the 1930s temporarily reduced that flow, migration resumed after World War II, eventually reaching the point shortly after 2000 when Latinos (13 percent) overtook African Americans (12 percent) as the largest ethnic minority in the United States.

Building the Panama Canal

As the United States moved into the ranks of world powers, American statesmen adjusted their strategy. The acquisition of colonial possessions in both the Atlantic and the Pacific made a naval and commercial passage between the two oceans all the more urgent. After decades of talk about building a canal across Central America, President Roosevelt took action. He lent U.S. support to secessionists in Panama, which brought Panama independence from Colombia in 1901. The new Panamanian leaders promptly complied with U.S. wishes and granted a strip of land across the isthmus suitable for digging an interoceanic canal.

In an effort to create a highly efficient and orderly construction project, U.S. officials in the Canal Zone, led by chief engineer George Washington Goethals, relied on police spies, vagrancy laws, and race- and skill-based segregation to impede labor organizing. Under the terms of the U.S. military occupation of the Canal Zone, U.S. officials could even deport workers, including white Americans citizens, who threatened to strike. Laboring under these constraints, skilled white Americans working the steam shovels and cranes in the Canal Zone turned to their unions in the mainland United States to assert their workplace demands in Washington.

As white American workers pressed for better pay and benefits, canal officials began recruiting West Indians and other alien workers. Although officials established a two-tiered workforce—with *gold roll* workers mostly white and skilled and *silver roll* workers mostly nonwhite and unskilled—alien workers increasingly replaced white workers on the silver roll. Unlike white American canal workers, West Indians and other noncitizens lacked the power of U.S. domestic unions to press their cause. Yet they still managed to attain a measure of agency

West Indian laborers at work on the Panama Canal. Labor on the canal was strictly segregated, with white U.S. citizens working as skilled machine operators and foreign migrant laborers relegated to unskilled work. Keystone–Mast Collection, UCR/California Museum of Photography, University of California at Riverside.

in the Canal Zone by voting with their feet. Quitting, changing jobs, and refusing to show up for work proved effective strategies for these workers to win more tolerable working conditions. By refusing to work every day, for example, West Indians forced foremen to maintain a much larger labor pool than was needed on any given day, thereby affording laborers an occasional respite from the grueling pace of construction work.

African Americans, as nonwhite American citizens, challenged the strict segregation of the gold and silver rolls by claiming full citizenship rights. For reasons of foreign relations with the newly formed Republic of Panama, the United States had included "Negro" Panamanian workers on the gold roll. African Americans, however, were restricted to the silver roll, despite being skilled riveters, blacksmiths, and firemen. In 1909, six African American blacksmiths protested such restrictions, claiming their American citizenship entitled them to gold roll status. After investigating the matter, Goethals agreed to pay the workers in gold, but insisted on keeping the official designation of silver roll in their contracts. As American practices of Jim Crow segregation collided with imperialism in the Canal Zone, Republican Party officials worried that the mistreatment of black workers in the Canal Zone could compromise President Taft's standing among African American voters in the north.

At the same time, others in the United States found much to celebrate in the project. Business leaders hailed the dramatic savings in costs and time for global shipping. Progressive reformers also took great interest in the canal, seeing it as a grand experiment in state intervention. Reformers such as Gertrude Beeks and Arthur Bullard hailed the collectivist approach to government that seemed to benefit white American workers. Yet, these same reformers paid little attention to the West Indian laborers also working in the zone or to the Panamanians whose sovereignty Americans flagrantly compromised.

Business and Empire

While U.S. capital and manufactured goods traveled southward, Latin American minerals, foodstuffs, and profits headed north. By 1920, the huge U.S. market was absorbing 90 percent of all exports from Mexico, notably, oil and copper, plus nearly 80 percent of all Caribbean exports, including once-exotic tropical foods such as bananas that were fast becoming everyday items on U.S. break- fast tables. Although Latin America maintained strong ties of many sorts with Western Europe, by the end of the First World War in 1918, the United States had replaced Britain as Latin America's chief creditor and customer.

The power exercised by U.S. corporations in Latin America was evident in the derogatory term *banana republic* used to describe countries such as Costa Rica, Honduras, Guatemala, and Nicaragua. Yet Latin Americans often resisted the at- tempts of U.S. corporations to exploit their labor. In a leading example, the United Fruit Company, formed in 1899, began importing English-speaking West Indians to work in a plantation system that came to resemble the Jim Crow South. When laborers organized a strike in 1909, the company hired Spanish-speaking Hispanic workers to divide the workforce along racial lines. The strategy succeeded for a time and the company sent steady profits back to its headquarters in Boston. But local resistance among Hispanic workers eventually forced United Fruit to end its racist and divisive labor practices. The result was an economy that was shaped by the conflict between U.S. corporations and Latin American workers.

In the years after the strike, United Fruit sought to consolidate white authority and minimize turnover by encouraging their white managers to bring their fami- lies to Central America to live with them. Percy Sealey of New Jersey had served in the U.S. Army in the Panama Canal before joining United Fruit's operations in Guatemala. In 1912, his wife, Charlotte Potter Sealey, and son Philip, then just one year old, traveled to Quirigua, Guatemala, to live with him. Charlotte, who was seven months pregnant during the journey, gave birth to their second son, Robert, soon after arriving. The world they and other white families inhabited in the Banana Zone was strictly segregated from nonwhites with the exception of ser- vants. The U.S. travel writer Arthur Ruhl highlighted the experience of such seg- regation when he described United Fruit's operations in Guatemala as "a detached bit of the United States, with its 'colonial' ruling class as remote, psychologically, from the land it lives in, as are the Canal Zone Americans at Panama."

Dollar Diplomacy

The U.S. military played an active role in opening Latin America to U.S. corpora- tions. In this period of *dollar diplomacy*, when the United States sought greater access to foreign markets, American military commanders were sometimes blunt about their role in protecting the dollar. After a long career of leading marines ashore, Major General Smedley Butler shocked the establishment by stating, "I spent most of my time being a high class muscle-man for Big Business, for Wall Street, and for the Bankers. In short, I was a racketeer, a gangster for capitalism."

Whatever the truth in Butler's confession, many U.S. leaders preferred to couch military intervention in decidedly different terms. For most, the key was a stable environment favorable to U.S. interests. General Leonard Wood, commander of the initial U.S. military occupation of Cuba, explained, "When money can be borrowed at a reasonable rate of interest and when capital is willing to invest in the Island, a condition of stability will have been reached." The preference was for local regimes to do the job, but when local elites failed, the United States was ready to intervene. When the Cuban president Tomás Estrada was deposed in 1906, U.S. troops installed a Minnesota judge named Charles Magoon at the point of a bayonet to run the Cuban government. In fact, under the authority of the Platt Amendment, U.S. forces went into Cuba in 1906–9, 1912, and 1917–22. The situation was similar in the Dominican Republic. Frustrated by factional fighting, President Roosevelt announced in 1904 that the United States would henceforth exercise "an international police power" in situations of "chronic wrongdoing." Under the Roosevelt Corollary to the Monroe Doctrine, U.S. forces arrived in 1916 and remained for eight years.

The search for stability abroad, often through a regime favorable to the United States, was one thing Republicans like Roosevelt and Democrats like President Woodrow Wilson (1913–21) could agree on. Wilson's secretary of state, William Jennings Bryan, believed that military intervention should promote U.S. commercial interests, not through vulgar dollar diplomacy but through the more enlightened open door: "we believe that this can be better done by contributing to stability and order than by favoring special concessions to Americans."

The Reach of the Monroe Doctrine

When construction of the canal was finally completed in 1914, the long search for a sea route to Asia begun by Columbus five centuries earlier finally came to an end. Just as control of the Suez Canal marked Britain's global dominance, so U.S. control of this vital military and commercial highway across Panama helped to realize the aims of the Roosevelt Corollary and move the United States into the front rank of the global powers.

In the same month that the canal was opened to shipping traffic, August 1914, the guns of the Great War started firing in Europe. The war led to the decline of British imperial power in Latin America as the British transferred naval assets from the Caribbean and south Atlantic to the North Sea and the English Channel to face the rising naval power of Germany. At the same time, World War I spurred the growth of U.S. imperialism in Latin America. On heightened alert for any disturbance that might invite European interference in the Western

Hemisphere, the Wilson administration dispatched troops to the Caribbean at almost any provocation. Thus, U.S. interventions followed a contested election in Haiti in 1915, factional fighting in the Dominican Republic in 1916, a border raid by Mexican rebel general Pancho Villa that killed several Americans in 1916, and disorder in Cuba in 1917.

By this time, American elites had stretched the Monroe Doctrine to take in nearly all of Latin America as an informal U.S. protectorate. In Nicaragua, U.S. officials collected customs, U.S. administrators operated the Panama Canal, and U.S. Marines occupied Haiti and Santo Domingo and otherwise roamed freely in the Gulf of Mexico. While the British sold many of their assets in Latin America to finance the staggering costs of the First World War, the United States expanded its influence in the Western Hemisphere to the point where it exercised preponderant power in the region by the time the war ended in 1918.

In the longer term, Latin America became the workshop of U.S. empire. American trade skyrocketed in the region as the United States used its might to secure access to markets. After the War of 1898, Cuba consumed $26 million of American exports, more than twice the value of exports to China at the time. Puerto Rican consumption accelerated in this same period, with the island moving from being the twenty-seventh largest U.S. export market in 1900 to the eleventh in 1910. In a pattern that would be duplicated elsewhere, the United States brokered its first major international loan in 1899 to Mexico in partnership with J. P. Morgan. Such public–private partnerships would help catapult America to becoming a creditor nation. Seeking to replicate such success in other regions of the world, future U.S. administrations and U.S. businesses would intervene in Southeast Asia, central Africa, and the Middle East with the intention of spreading U.S. influence to the world at large.

DOMESTIC CONSEQUENCES OF EMPIRE

American efforts to influence nations overseas had important consequences at home. Americans did not assemble a massive colonial bureaucracy or embrace the ideology of imperialism the way upper-class Europeans did. For the most part, they preferred to keep their empire informal so as not to upset cherished republican traditions.

Nonetheless, American society was increasingly bound up with empire. One important aspect was the effect of empire on elite class formation in the United States. Overseas investments and interventions helped consolidate a national upper class out of often-discordant regional elites. Many of the corporate leaders with the greatest overseas interests, such as the Morgans, Rockefellers, and Guggenheims, were also the same dynasties that were taking command of the domestic economy.

Equally important in the formation of a national upper class were changes in culture associated with imperial conquest. Monumental architecture, for example, reflected an imperial style in the design of such buildings as Union Station in

Washington, DC (1907), as seen in the photograph to the right, and Pennsylvania Station in New York (1910). Both were consciously modeled on the grand edifices of the Roman empire with their arched ceilings, soaring columns, and neoclassical sculpture.

Much like the architecture of the Chicago's World Fair in 1893, the design of Union Station in Washington, DC., completed in 1907, was inspired by the neoclassical tradition. Library of Congress Prints and Photographs Division, Washington, DC.

Empire also strengthened the institutions of the state, such as the greatly expanding U.S. Navy, which grew from a total of 72 active ships in 1897 to 175 in 1903. In addition, a new group of imperial adventurers and administrators played leading roles in domestic politics. The most prominent was the Hero of San Juan Hill himself, Theodore Roosevelt, who parlayed his military service in Cuba into a vice presidential nomination and then, after McKinley's assassination, into the presidency (1901–9). The roster of former colonial administrators also included President William Howard Taft (1909–13), who had been civil commissioner of the Philippines, plus a string of cabinet members, including Secretary of War Elihu Root and Secretary of State Philander Knox.

Meanwhile, ordinary Americans increasingly saw the effects of empire in their daily lives. American consumers expected to see the fruits of Latin labor in their coffee cups and soft drinks. They depended on foreign copper for their telephone conversations. And although they rarely stopped to consider the conditions under which sugar or copper were produced, they came to appreciate the Coca-Cola Company, the American Smelting and Refining Company, and the other corporations that provided such things.

The emerging U.S. imperial society also confronted increasing numbers of migrants from America's new colonies. Much like Puerto Ricans who sailed on steamships to New York, Filipinos traveled to Seattle, San Francisco, and other points along the West Coast. Some came as students, as in the *pensionado* scholarship program of 1903–10 where the U.S. government sponsored students of relatively privileged backgrounds to attend U.S. high schools in Southern California. But most of those who came to the United States were laborers seeking a better life in the canneries, fruit orchards, and vegetable farms of the American West. Defined as U.S. Nationals after the *Gonzales* ruling of 1904, these workers were allowed to enter the United States even when other groups were excluded. Between 1907 and 1929, some seventy thousand Filipinos migrated to Hawaii as contract laborers to replace Japanese workers barred from migrating after the Gentlemen's Agreement of 1907. Such colonial migrations would prove frustrating to nativists and organized labor, which increasingly sought ways to restrict immigration.

Uncle Sam and Jim Crow

Perhaps nothing better illustrates the reciprocal impact of American empire and American society than the reshaping of relations among ethnic groups. As white men North and South united behind the domination of darker peoples overseas, they also closed ranks against African Americans, Asians, and Latinos within U.S. borders.

Social Darwinist ideas of racial competition helped propel white Americans to distant lands in the first place while myths of white, Anglo-Saxon superiority helped justify control over others. Prejudice against "Orientals" was a prime example. Although Asian immigrants amounted to a tiny percentage of the U.S. population, Orientals were held up as a symbol of an alien way of life, a cultural enemy against which otherwise fractious Americans could unite. Virulent anti-Chinese sentiment had driven Chinese immigrants into ghettoes called Chinatown, and since 1882, Chinese immigration had been prohibited by federal statute. In the domain of foreign policy, racial ideologies allowed Americans to see the defeat of the Boxers and the suppression of Philippine independence as signs of the superiority of white Anglo-Saxons over yellow Chinese and brown Filipinos.

The sense of triumph overseas, in turn, reinforced ideas of white supremacy at home. Renewed efforts to exclude all Asian races from entering the United States led to the informal Gentlemen's Agreement of 1907 barring Japanese from entering the United States, as well as formal revisions of immigration policy reaffirming Chinese exclusion. In fact, a succession of laws and court decisions culminating in the National Origins Act of 1924 lumped all Asians together as aliens ineligible for citizenship.

In one respect, African Americans had a different experience. No one any longer took seriously the idea of excluding them from citizenship, but instead consigned them to second-class citizenship. In other respects, however, empire and racism reinforced one another. When American cartoonists wanted to justify U.S. intervention in Latin America, they gave Latins black skins, a coded visual message intended to convey the idea of incapacity for self-government. This represented a triumph of racial ideology over reality, since the actual palette of colors in Latin America did not match the assumed black–white polarity in the United States. Instead, there were many gradations ranging from black, mestizo (Indian European), *zambo* (Indian African), and mulatto (African European) to white.

The more the United States embraced racial justifications for rule over others abroad, the more entrenched Jim Crow became at home. Northern elites had begun

Political cartoons of this period highlighted the skin color of foreign subjects, with Cubans depicted here as darker skinned than Puerto Ricans, to justify the exercise of imperial power. Uncle Sam to Puerto Rico: "And to think that bad boy came near being your brother!" *Chicago Inter Ocean*, 1905.

moving toward reconciliation with southern elites at the end of Reconstruction in 1877, and by 1896 most northern justices on the Supreme Court had come to accept racial segregation in public accommodations as national policy in their landmark decision in *Plessy v. Ferguson*. A few years later, American whites' growing sense of regret over extending the Fifteenth Amendment to Southern blacks shaped the decision of Congress to withhold U.S. citizenship from Puerto Ricans in the Foraker Act of 1900.

The new imperialism played an important role in further mobilizing Northern and Southern whites against ideas of racial equality. As the United States extended its rule over dark-skinned peoples in the Caribbean and the Philippines, the northeastern establishment became ever more sympathetic to the argument of Southern white supremacists that African Americans were also unfit for self-government. In the 1890s and early 1900s, growing numbers of African Americans were disenfranchised in the U.S. South.

The link between imperialism and segregation had significant implications for the quest for racial equality. One of the first to recognize its importance was W. E. B. Du Bois, a leading African American intellectual. In *Souls of Black Folk* (1903), a masterpiece of American thought and literature, Du Bois prophesied, "The problem of the twentieth century is the problem of the color line—of the relation between the lighter and darker races of mankind in America, Africa, Asia, and the islands of the sea." The implication of Du Bois's prophecy was that desegregation and decolonization would only arrive together. And so it turned out some sixty years later, in the simultaneous achievement of African independence and the first significant U.S. civil rights legislation since Reconstruction.

CONCLUSION

By the time of the outbreak of the First World War in 1914, the new imperialism had begun to redraw the map of the world. Vast swaths of territory, especially in Africa, now owed allegiance to one European monarch or another, and other stretches in many agrarian societies of Asia and Latin America were subject to the informal empire of bank loans and gunboats. Empire brought benefits for both sides, although in unequal proportion. The colonized saw some of the fruits of modern society, whereas the new imperialists received the bountiful tribute of the market and the satisfactions of world power.

But it was an unequal relationship that would bedevil the twentieth century with a host of problems. One was what Du Bois called "the problem of the color line." Having built racial inequality into the structure of empire, the new imperialists bequeathed a legacy of injustice that would be the cause of great conflict. Another was the contradiction between empire and democracy. How could Americans be champions of democracy while they deprived others of the right to rule? Every generation since has had to wrestle with Twain's two Americas, one that seeks to expand democratic freedoms and another that seeks to limit them.

America would soon face the perils of being a world power. Swelled with pride at their newfound power, Americans looked to the likes of Theodore Roosevelt, Smedley Butler, and Admiral Dewey to lead the country to new heights. But it was not long before tensions with Germany in the Caribbean helped draw Americans out of the relative safety of the Western Hemisphere and into the battlegrounds of the First World War.

FURTHER READING

Ayala, Cesar. *American Sugar Kingdom*. Chapel Hill: University of North Carolina Press, 1999.

Bederman, Gail. *Manliness and Civilization: A Cultural History of Gender and Race in the United States, 1880–1917*. Chicago: University of Chicago Press, 1995.

Colby, Jason. *The Business of Empire: United Fruit, Race, and US Expansion in Central America*. Ithaca, NY: Cornell University Press, 2011.

Fujita-Rony, Dorothy. *American Workers, Colonial Power: Philippine Seattle and the Transpacific West, 1919–1941.* Berkeley: University of California Press, 2003.

Grandin, Greg. *Empire's Workshop: Latin America, the United States, and the Rise of the New Imperialism.* New York: Holt, 2006.

Grandin, Greg. *Fordlandia: The Rise and Fall of Henry Ford's Forgotten Jungle City.* New York: Metropolitan, 2009.

Greene, Julie. *The Canal Builders: Making America's Empire at the Panama Canal.* New York: Penguin, 2009.

Hoganson, Kristen. *Fighting for American Manhood.* New Haven, CT: Yale University Press, 1998.

Kramer, Paul A. *The Blood of Government: Race, Empire, the United States and the Philippines.* Chapel Hill: University of North Carolina Press, 2006.

LaFeber, Walter. *The New Empire.* Ithaca, NY: Cornell University Press, 1998.

Perez, Louis, Jr. *The War of 1898: The United States and Cuba in History and Historiography.* Chapel Hill: University of North Carolina Press, 1998.

Silbey, David J. *A War of Frontier and Empire: The Philippine–American War, 1899–1902.* New York: Hill and Wang, 2007.

Sneider, Allison. *Suffragists in an Imperial Age: US Expansion and the Woman Question, 1870–1929.* Oxford: Oxford University Press, 2008.

Suarez Findlay, Eileen J. *Imposing Decency: The Politics of Sexuality and Race in Puerto Rico, 1870–1920.* Durham, NC: Duke University Press, 1999.

Willrich, Michael. *Pox: An American History.* New York: Penguin Books, 2011.

Zimmerman, Andrew. *Alabama in Africa: Booker T. Washington, the German Empire, and the Globalization of the New South.* Princeton, NJ: Princeton University Press, 2012.

CHAPTER 3

REFORMING MODERN SOCIETY

Alice Paul, head of the Woman's Party, was inspired by radical suffragettes in England to apply increased pressure on Washington in the 1910s. Pictured here (seated, center left) sewing a star on the Woman's Party ratification flag in 1920, Paul celebrated the ratification of the Nineteenth Amendment by another state. National Photo Company Collection, Library of Congress Prints and Photographs Division, Washington, DC.

TRANSATLANTIC REFORM: ALICE PAUL AND THE WOMEN'S SUFFRAGE MOVEMENT

In 1913, in the midst of Woodrow Wilson's presidential inauguration, more than five thousand women wearing Greek robes and riding white horses paraded along Pennsylvania Avenue calling for women's suffrage. With large numbers, strategic timing, and a flair for spectacle, these women brought national attention to the cause of women's suffrage, capturing headlines across the country. The leader of this parade was a twenty-eight-year-old New Jersey native named Alice Paul. *Born into a Quaker family, Paul moved to New York after graduating college in 1905 to work with newly arrived immigrants in the city's settlement houses. She then traveled to Birmingham, England, to study social work, and while there came to know Christabel Pankhurst and her mother, Emmeline Pankhurst, two of the most radical suffragettes in England. Inspired by their motto "Deeds not words," Paul returned to the United States in 1910 and quickly became a leading voice in support of women's right to vote.*

As head of the Woman's Party, Paul built on the long struggle for women's suffrage, which took early form in the Seneca Falls Convention of 1848, to organize protests in Washington calling for a national female suffrage amendment. From the 1913 parade on, Paul criticized President Wilson's failure to support a national amendment. In 1916, Woman's Party members interrupted Wilson during a speech before Congress by unfurling a banner from the balcony that asked, "Mr. President, What Will You Do for Woman Suffrage?" Their protest was deliberately timed to coincide with the section of Wilson's speech in which he lent support to granting male colonial subjects in Puerto Rico the right to vote. Alice Paul, and the Woman's Party seized on the question of expanded suffrage in American colonies to highlight continued congressional inaction on a female suffrage amendment in the mainland United States. To the extent that Paul was both inspired by militant British suffrage tactics, including those of the radical Emily Davison who threw herself under the king's horse in protest, and strategically engaged with U.S. imperial politics, she reached beyond U.S. continental borders to build a powerful reform movement in the United States.

REFORMING MODERN SOCIETY

As this history of suffrage suggests, Progressive reform movements in America unfolded within the larger context of the Western world. Stretching from St. Petersburg in the East to San Francisco in the West, Western society contained pivotal sites of world power as well as the largest engines of the world economy. In the period from the 1880s to the First World War, Western society changed from an agrarian-commercial to an urban-industrial way of life, a process that saw deep disturbances in family, gender, and class relations. Partly because of these social and economic dislocations, there were also great scientific and artistic breakthroughs such as Einstein's theory of relativity and Picasso's cubism that announced a new modernity.

In response to these disturbances, Progressive reformers on both sides of the Atlantic undertook two great waves of reform. One rose against patriarchy (literally, rule by the father), and another opposed the unwanted consequences of industrial capitalism. Attempting to regain the balance lost with the coming of modern society, Progressives of this era sought to put gender roles and class relations on a new footing and restore a measure of social control over the unregulated marketplace.

Despite overarching connections, modern society took different forms in different countries. With its booming industries, high living standards, and can-do spirit, the United States was seen by many as the model of modern society. Some European admirers beheld the future in America and looked to the New World as the model for the reform of the Old World. At the same time, a growing number of Americans recognized the need for reforming America itself. Determined to accord women a more equal place in public life and to bring a measure of equality to the ranks of the poor, social reformers and Progressive political leaders began the long task of subjecting the unregulated marketplace to social controls.

Economic Foundations for Transatlantic Reform

In the turn of the century period known as *la belle époque* (beautiful epoch), the thriving industrial economies of the West were increasingly tied together through the movement of people, goods, inventions, and ideas. After the long depression from 1873 to 1897, the economy was booming all around the industrial heartland. Beginning in the 1880s, the application of science to industry in the second industrial revolution brought a host of new products in chemistry, metallurgy, and electricity. By speeding up communication and transportation, the new technologies of this second industrial revolution had the effect of compressing both time and space.

Brilliant new inventions such as Alexander Graham Bell's telephone and, by the 1920s, Guglielmo Marconi's wireless radio, stitched together the developed world. News traveled much further and faster than ever before through undersea cables that crossed the Atlantic (1866) and Pacific (1903) and then fanned out through the proliferating web of domestic telephone lines to knit together ever more distant places. It was not long before transatlantic wireless radio communication (1906) took a giant step in the direction of the information age that eventually arrived late in the century with the Internet.

People traveled faster, too. In this age of the sleek ocean liner, the time between New York and Southampton, England, was compressed to one week, compared to a month on a sailing ship. Although the fledgling network of muddy roads did not yet permit speedy intercity travel by car, it was clear, especially after Henry Ford introduced the mass-produced Model T in 1909, that it would not be long before horseless carriages would be zooming around faster than any horse.

Recognizing the new ease of transatlantic communication and transportation, reformers cultivated a new spirit of internationalism and dared to revive the age-old dream of perpetual peace. Pointing to growing economic interdependence among nations, Norman Angell, a respected English author, argued in *The Great Illusion* (1910) that war had, in fact, become obsolete. Indeed, prior to the outbreak of the First World War in 1914, there had been no extended, large-scale international conflict since the end of the Napoleonic Wars a century earlier, and enlightened opinion expected peace to continue in Europe and under *Pax Britannica* around the globe.

INTELLECTUAL FOUNDATIONS FOR REFORM: THEORIZING MODERNITY AND ITS DISCONTENTS

Even as they embraced the new industrial economy, innovations in communication and transportation, and a period of global peace, denizens of la belle époque worried about losing their traditional moorings in family, church, and community. Much of this anxiety derived from the very changes that inspired progress. Material progress and urbanization brought social dislocation, psychological alienation, and what pioneer French sociologist Emile Durkheim called *anomie*, the sense of being without meaningful connections to other people. With relations between the sexes thrown into confusion and tensions between classes sometimes erupting in violence, many feared social chaos.

That was the underlying message of Sigmund Freud's analysis in *Civilization and Its Discontents*, which summarized much of his life's work. As one of the fathers of modern psychology (along with American William James and others), Freud probed beneath the surface to explore the instinctual drives of the unconscious mind. He uncovered sex drives (which he called *libido*) that he believed were powerful enough to tear society apart. Freud himself had come of age in an era of Victorian repression, and he concluded that repressing libido was necessary for the order of civilization. The price individuals had to pay for repression was psychic anxiety. The irony was that the whole scientific discussion of sexuality undermined the very repression it analyzed. It assaulted Victorian ears, challenged Christian morality, and opened a Pandora's box of sexual secrets, which all served to deepen anxieties in the modern age.

When Freud first brought his ideas to the United States in 1909, he found a younger generation of intellectuals already at work exploring the anxieties of modern civilization. Walter Lippmann, who would become one of America's prime journalists and social critics, wrote in *Drift and Mastery* (1914) that the pace and diversity of modern life undermined religious certainty, blasting apart the old rock of ages. Echoing the German philosopher Friedrich Nietzsche's late nineteenth-century claim that God is dead, Lippmann wondered, what was the source of ultimate meaning? Without a universal moral code, he asked, what would be the basis for sexual morality? In summarizing the situation, he wrote, "the chaos is our problem."

Social Foundations for Reform: Changes in Property and Family

The sense of moral disorder grew out of the ways modern society was undermining traditional authority. In traditional society, property ownership was fused with patriarchal authority. The dominant male in each household was expected to take responsibility for his dependents, including laborers, women, and children. In return, dependents were expected to defer to the lord and master, whether landlord, merchant, or *paterfamilias* (father). Property and patriarchy combined to make for privileged access to political power. Throughout Europe right down to the First World War, there were property tests for office holding and voting, and women were excluded from both. Hereditary aristocrats and monarchs ruled from on high. State power was the private preserve of gentlemen of property and standing.

Modern society undercut this traditional social formation. The rise of the propertied elite and the bourgeoisie (the middle class) increasingly took social leadership away from the aristocracy. Modern industrialists rested their claim to political power on property ownership, not family pedigree, "iron," or "blood." Despite lingering paternalist attitudes, modern industrialists increasingly dropped the practice of treating employees like their dependent children. As factories grew larger, owners abdicated responsibility to protect wage earners, and the underpaid man at the head of a working-class household was in no position to provide reliable subsistence in periods of injury, unemployment, or old age. In these changing conditions, the stern paterfamilias came to be seen as "the relic of a patriarchal age," in the stinging words of American feminist Charlotte Perkins Gilman.

In comparison to Europe, the United States had already moved far along the road toward modern society. As a land of commoners where blood aristocracy never took hold, the industrial and commercial elites and middle classes (as the bourgeoisie was called in North America) took virtually unchallenged leadership once the slave master class was eliminated during the Civil War. Under the Constitution of 1787, the country was ruled not by kings and princes but by elected representatives of the people. Although narrow at first, the circle of citizen-voters widened in the course of the nineteenth century to include propertyless workingmen and ex-slaves. It even began to include women at the state level when Wyoming became the first to enfranchise women as early as 1869. In this sense, modern America itself represented the overthrow of tradition.

All the same, patriarchy and property retained their privileges even in democratic America. Most political leaders held to the conservative conviction that a woman's place was in the home subordinate to her husband. Although he came to support women's suffrage, Theodore Roosevelt, for example, believed woman's primary duty to civilization was to breed offspring in what he called the war of the cradle between superior and inferior races. Some suffrage leaders, in fact, made strategic appeals to these conservative racial and gender ideals in the early stages of their campaign for a national suffrage amendment. Elizabeth Cady Stanton, for example, asked in her famous 1878 speech before the National Woman Suffrage Association why legislators in Washington would choose to leave their "mothers, wives, and daughters to the unwashed, unlettered, unthinking masses that carry our State elections." In posing this question, Stanton implied that a national vote for women would immediately double the political influence of "old immigrant" Anglo-Saxons and serve as a counterweight to the growing political power of "new immigrant" Catholics.

By the same token, the new crop of Gilded Age industrialists and financiers asserted their power and privilege by claiming ties to the Old World. The richest among them sought the trappings of aristocratic privilege by marrying into the bloodlines of French dukes and Italian counts and becoming voracious consumers of Old World culture. Engaging in what economist Thorstein Veblen called *conspicuous consumption*, they made the annual Grand Tour of European capitals, ransacked castles on the Loire for art treasure, and lined the walls of their baronial palaces on New York's Fifth Avenue with costly medieval tapestries.

Such privilege spurred resentment among those further down the social ladder. Whereas small shopkeepers and aspiring executives might have felt envy, the rising group of urban professionals tended to recoil at the excesses of great wealth. More telling, urban workers no longer received the patronage of the privileged, while the massing of strangers in the impersonal environment of the city further cut the ties of human sympathy. Nor was private charity able to meet the needs of impoverished families packed into overcrowded tenements. Their unmet needs were a standing rebuke to the status quo. Progressives argued that America was in need of reform.

Transatlantic Reform

Progressive reformers on both sides of the Atlantic worked toward economic and social justice in a variety of ways, including campaigns to reduce overcrowding in cities, improve public health, expand educational opportunities for the poor, limit the power of monopolies, and secure suffrage for women. Although historians have debated how best to define the Progressive impulse, much of the reform movement can be understood as an effort to use government and expertise to benefit society or the *public good*. Riding a wave of optimism, Progressive reformers convinced themselves that every social problem had a solution and that the sum of those solutions was progress.

Much of this work was inspired by earlier reform efforts, notably the Populist movement in the 1880s and 1890s. Populists mobilized millions of American farmers, including large numbers of women in the rural South who joined the Farmer's Alliance. Populist coalitions were comprised of working-class Americans, including farmers, coal miners, and railroad workers. Much like the Progressives who followed, Populists sought to attain a measure of fairness in an economy that was increasingly dominated by a corporate and wealthy minority. By the early twentieth century, as the Populist movement was eclipsed by Progressivism, some ex-Populists would find the new Socialist Party more in step with their politics than Progressives who tended to be well-educated members of the middle class.

Progressives lost no opportunity to call attention to the plight of the poor through social surveys of housing conditions in London and Pittsburgh as well as muckraking literature, such as *The Jungle*, the 1906 bestseller by Upton Sinclair. Artists of the Ashcan School made their contribution by depicting the harsh realities of urban-industrial life in works by George Bellows and John Sloan. Reformers gathered at international conferences on tenement reform and improving sanitation, while designers of international expositions made sure to include exhibits on "the social market," such as that at the Paris World's Fair of 1900.

American reform campaigns were part of an international critique of the unregulated market. Robert La Follette was one of America's leading voices in the Progressive Era, winning a raft of reforms in his home state of Wisconsin, including the direct primary, workmen's compensation, and working hours limitations. La Follette was hailed among reformers for helping spread the *Wisconsin idea*, the practice of using academic research in public universities to inform government policy, and later used his seat in the U.S. Senate to champion Progressive causes. Other powerful figures in Washington pursued the public interest through antitrust campaigns. Theodore Roosevelt became known as the trust-buster when his administration successfully prosecuted monopolies, including the Northern Securities Company and the "beef trust," under the Sherman Anti-Trust Act of 1890. William Howard Taft brought forward even more antitrust suits than Roosevelt, prosecuting United States Steel, among others. Yet antitrust campaigns showed the successes as well as the limitations of Progressive reform. Despite the initial success of the Sherman Act, the Clayton Act, which was passed by Congress in 1914 to strengthen the hand of the federal government in antitrust cases, proved to be full of too many loopholes to be effective.

Jane Addams is pictured here as part of a group of American delegates who traveled to the International Congress of Women in The Hague, Netherlands, in 1915. Bain Collection, Library of Congress Prints and Photographs Division, Washington, DC.

Although most reformers were men, women gained special prominence in the ranks of American reformers. A generation of college-educated women began to practice what was called *social housekeeping*. No one better personifies the middle-class social housekeeper than Jane Addams, pictured on the previous page. Raised in the richest family in a small town in Illinois, Addams braved the clucking tongues of society dames and turned her modest privilege toward the service of others. After an inspiring visit to London's Toynbee Hall, she returned to Chicago, moved into a rough-and-tumble immigrant neighborhood, and established Hull House in 1889, the first of many settlement houses where wealthy philanthropists joined with middle-class reformers to ameliorate the plight of the poor. Even as critics claimed Addams sought to strip immigrants and the poor of their culture and autonomy, her effort to bridge the gulf between upper and lower classes made her an example of American-style cross-class reform.

But Addams did not stop there. She had a hand in almost every major reform of the day, from the abolition of child labor to women's suffrage. Especially disturbed by the plight of working women, Addams believed that social progress depended on women's advancement in the form of protections for women workers and support for mothers and children. Toward that end, she also supported women's suffrage, believing that women voters would lend their weight to reform.

Addams was also among the many American reformers who identified the cause of social justice with world peace. In the face of a naval arms race between Britain and Germany in the early 1900s, she promoted international law and arbitration to settle disputes before they became violent. Hoping to halt the slaughter of the First World War, she was instrumental in organizing an international conference at The Hague in 1915. For her tireless work on behalf of social justice and world peace, she became the first American woman to be awarded the Nobel Peace Prize in 1931. Yet, even as she advanced these various reform campaigns, Addams subscribed to the latest in eugenics thinking and understood Anglo-Saxons to be at the top of a strict racial hierarchy, thus illustrating an important limitation of the Progressive vision.

Reform or Revolution?

Watching the pace of change quicken, many observers believed they were caught up in a race between reform and revolution. As traditional authority waned, revolutionaries came forward to call for the demolition of all existing structures of power and privilege. Drawing strength from the growing militancy of both the women's rights and the labor movements, revolutionaries embraced a range of radical causes from promoting free love in place of the oppressive patriarchal family to mobilizing the *general strike* against exploitative bosses and developing new vanguard parties to seize state power.

Underlying the revolutionary impulse was a vision of radical change. Imitating the religious faith it was intended to replace, revolutionary Socialism reworked the biblical message that the first shall be last and the last shall be first into the prophetic message: "we have been naught, we shall be all." In place of the alienation and exploitation of modern society, they vowed to forge a higher form of human solidarity. In the words of the "*Internationale*," an 1888 song that spread outward from France to become the premiere anthem of international Socialism, "the international working class shall be the human race."

Anarchists also mobilized in this period, founding the International Working People's Association in London. Led by Socialists who had grown disillusioned with electoral politics as an effective means of social change, members of what became known as the Black International argued that more militant action was needed. Anarchists gained members on both sides of the Atlantic, most notably in Chicago, where disaffected Socialists August Spies and Albert Parsons led a branch of the anarchist movement more focused on militant unions than on individual acts of violence. Western governments increasingly feared anarchism, especially after the assassination of President McKinley in 1901 by Leon Czolgosz, who had claimed to be an anarchist.

Such radicalism caused reformers to quicken their pace. Taking the parliamentary road to reform in such countries as Britain, Australia, and Austria, reformers pressed with some success for government regulation of the labor market in the form of minimum-wage laws and the abolition of child labor. They also crusaded, again with some success, for social protections, such as old-age pensions and health insurance. They were less successful before the First World War in winning over male officials to the cause of women's suffrage and gender equality in all legal matters.

In these years, the distance between reform and revolution was not as great as it would become after the 1917 Bolshevik revolution in Russia. Across the vast agrarian belt, Sun Yat-sen in China, Emiliano Zapata in Mexico, and other revolutionaries plotting the overthrow of emperors and dictators tried to put constitutions, representative assemblies, and other liberal institutions in their place. Moreover, the border between liberalism and Socialism was an open one, allowing people and ideas to cross freely back and forth.

REVOLT AGAINST PATRIARCHY

Reformers and revolutionaries alike rode two overlapping waves of social change in this era. One wave rose against patriarchy and the other rose against the undesirable consequences of modern capitalism. The assault on traditional forms of male dominance was the product of social changes that had been underway for decades. Especially for the urban middle classes, family life was being radically transformed by the *demographic transition*, the decades-long shift from high birth and death rates to low ones. The consequence of fewer children opened an opportunity for women to move from lifelong motherhood to other options, including a professional career.

Rising levels of education pointed in the same direction. With the United States in the forefront, there was a steady increase in mass education, and since the training of the young was thought to be a woman's profession, there was an accompanying increase in the employment of women teachers. Women also broke into the ranks of higher education. The transition to a highly educated populace was slow—not until after the Second World War did the majority of eighteen- to twenty-year-olds in the United States complete high school, let alone college. Nonetheless, by the turn of the century, the first generation of college-educated women was coming of age and was looking to make useful contributions outside the home.

All this fostered a conscious revolt against patriarchy. Building on decades of struggle for women's rights, the revolt was led by a social type called the *New Woman*. The New Woman was born of parents from around the Atlantic. From the pen of Norwegian playwright Henrik Ibsen came the fictional Nora, who shocked bourgeois respectability by walking out on her dissolute husband, an act that implied emancipation from wifely duty. From England came Emmeline Pankhurst, Emily Davison, and their sister suffragists who displayed a new militancy in the struggle for women's rights by braving force-feeding in jail. And from the United States came Florence Kelley, a redoubtable crusader for working women, Lillian Wald, the head of New York's Henry Street Settlement, and a host of other peers of Alice Paul and Jane Addams in the quest for social justice.

While many women reformers, including the never-married Addams, revered motherhood as the highest of women's callings, others called bourgeois marriage into question. Objecting that Victorian women were too much defined by their sex, Charlotte Perkins Gilman protested the exclusion of women from professional careers, voting rights, and political leadership. In the widely read tract *Women and Economics* (1898), Gilman rejected bourgeois marriage with its stay-at-home housewife as an outmoded imposition on women. Setting one foot outside the home, the new woman proudly claimed her place in the public sphere, in higher education, in the voting booth, and everywhere else the work of social progress went forward.

The revolt against patriarchy was for the most part a Western affair, but glimmerings could be detected elsewhere. Internal social upheaval in the agrarian societies of Asia and Africa disturbed traditional assumptions about the respective roles of the sexes, which were thrown into further disorder by the arrival of Westerners. A single European woman on a safari could throw traditional African notions of gender order into confusion. Female Christian missionaries and Western moralists campaigned against traditional forms of women's oppression, such as Chinese foot binding, east African genital mutilation, and Indian suttee (the immolation of the widow), perhaps unintentionally spreading Western ideas of women' rights.

New Sexual Morality

A minority of radical feminists took a step further toward sexual liberation. Aghast at the sexual repression built into Victorian morality, an intrepid band of radicals campaigned for what English sexologist Havelock Ellis called "the love rights of women." Radical feminists—including men like Ellis—sought to liberate the pleasures of sexual intercourse from the burdens of procreation. When Margaret Sanger, a pioneer crusader for birth control, faced prosecution under the 1873 Comstock Act's ban on the distribution of birth control information through the U.S. mail, she left home and husband and headed straight to Britain for the waiting arms of Ellis.

No one was more important to the sexual liberation movement than Emma Goldman. Born in Russia, Goldman moved with her family to upstate New York, where the young rebel began to fuse revolution against the tsar, the "patriarch of all the Russians," with rebellion against her domineering father, the patriarch of the home. A brilliant thinker and galvanizing speaker, Goldman was in wide demand on the lecture circuit for talks on everything from the anarchism of Peter Kropotkin to Ibsen's modern drama. She was also a great admirer of Freud. Defying all manner of authority—patriarchal, capitalist, political, literary—she courted frequent arrest by preaching free love, free speech, collective ownership, anarchism, and opposition to war. Goldman was arrested by U.S. authorities numerous times before she was eventually deported to Russia in 1919.

International Women's Suffrage Movement

While Goldman and other radical feminists sought sexual liberation, the international movement for women's suffrage mounted an even more sustained assault on patriarchal authority. The international movement owed a great deal to American women's rights advocates. Having forged links with their British sisters in the middle decades of the nineteenth century, American women now took the lead in a series of international gatherings that spawned the International Women's Suffrage Alliance, founded in Berlin in 1904. The International Alliance was a clearinghouse through which suffragists kept informed about developments around the world. In recognition of the pioneering work and abundant resources of their American sisters, members chose Carrie Chapman Catt, a prominent U.S. suffragist, as their perennial president. During a round-the-world speaking tour for the Alliance in 1911–13, Catt believed she uncovered a universal yearning to escape the confines of tradition: "Behind the purdah in India, in the harems of Mohammedanism, behind the veils and barred doors and closed sedan chairs, there has been rebellion in the hearts of women all down the centuries."

International momentum gave a boost to local campaigns for suffrage. Despite American pioneering, the first actual victories came in New Zealand (1893) and Australia (1901), with Finland (1906) and Norway (1907) close behind. As American women campaigned state by state, they used these overseas victories as leverage to persuade male legislators and male referendum voters that equal suffrage was inevitable and that its coming would not spell the end of civilization. Against strong opposition—not all of it from men—American women gained the vote in many states of the union by 1914, as illustrated in Map 3.1.

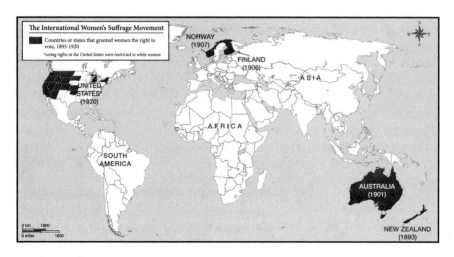

The International Women's Suffrage Movement

Countries or states that granted women the right to vote, 1893-1920

*voting rights in the United States were restricted to white women

NORWAY (1907)

FINLAND (1906)

ASIA

UNITED STATES* (1920)

AFRICA

SOUTH AMERICA

AUSTRALIA (1901)

NEW ZEALAND (1893)

0 km 1600
0 miles 1600

MAP 3.1

Many factors account for this outcome: the belief that women voters would help moralize and stabilize a disordered society; partisan political maneuvering; democratic ideals; nativism; and the relentless pressure of the women's movement itself. The fact that this mix of factors could be found in varying proportions throughout the Western world suggests that the advent of equal suffrage and the decline of patriarchy it represents were central parts of the making of modern society.

Yet timing points to the crucial impact of international influences. It was no coincidence that the greatest wave of suffrage victories came at the end of the First World War. The war was the decisive factor in countries that underwent wartime revolution, namely, Germany and the newfound Soviet Union, whose leaders sought with mixed success to mobilize the huge block of women citizens in support of the new regime. Similar motives were at work in the stable regimes of Britain and the United States, where suffrage was granted as a reward for extensive public service and in fulfillment of wartime promises to make the world safe for democracy.

For the United States, imperial politics also played a role in the development of a national amendment for female suffrage. After the Civil War, much of the struggle for women's suffrage took place at the state level. But with the advent of U.S. colonial rule in Puerto Rico and the Philippines, territories under the jurisdiction of Congress, federal officials began to take up the question of female suffrage. Debates in Congress in the 1910s regarding how to rule U.S. colonial possessions included discussion of female suffrage. Suffrage leaders such as Alice Paul and Carrie Chapman Catt seized the opportunity to push for a federal woman suffrage amendment, recognizing the chance to lift discussion of suffrage out of the states' rights framework that their opponents had long relied on to scuttle attempts at national reform. Their efforts helped bring about female suffrage in the United States. With eventual passage of the Nineteenth Amendment, all American women over the age of twenty-one (except, ironically, those living in American colonies) became eligible to vote in the 1920 presidential election. In Western society, Americans were neither the first nor the last to win that right.

Race and Reform

Just as the changing status of women was bound up with international forces, so, too, was the fate of African Americans dependent on world affairs. Although white women made significant progress in the early twentieth century, conditions worsened for nonwhite peoples, from colonial lands in Africa and Asia to the American South. After great strides in abolishing slavery in the nineteenth century, the long march against racial oppression slowed to a crawl. This is puzzling, particularly in view of the historically close parallel between the nineteenth-century movements for women's rights and slave emancipation. Why did the condition of African Americans worsen in this time of reform?

Part of the explanation relates to the new imperialism (see Chapter 2). As Westerners expanded their sway over Africans and Asians, they drew on ideas of social Darwinism to justify their subjugation of what the British poet Rudyard Kipling called "lesser breeds without the law." Anthropology emerged as a distinct field in this period, in part, to explain so-called primitive peoples to their supposedly civilized conquerors. Anthropological exhibits at the world's fairs depicted human progress in racial terms from primitive to modern as if it were scientific fact. Barriers to nonwhite advancement rose higher everywhere from South Africa to south Asia as the doctrine of white supremacy solidified its reign in the Atlantic countries and their colonies around the world.

The United States was very much a part of this trend as U.S. invasions and occupations not only brought Jim Crow segregation to Cuba, Haiti, Panama, and other countries with dark-skinned populations but also forged a transatlantic bond of white supremacy among Western colonial powers. Although Jim Crow laws had conservative origins, some white reformers, especially in the South, embraced these measures. There was also a certain aura of reform about the movement for eugenics, the effort to improve the human race through selective breeding. Eugenics was the product of race thinking combined with the new science of genetics, developed out of Gregor Mendel's experiments in plant breeding. The movement of eugenics, led on both sides of the Atlantic by intellectuals such as Madison Grant, Lothrop Stoddard, and Houston Stewart Chamberlain, rose and fell with the new imperialism.

Many did not accept this ideology of racial hierarchy. Marcus Garvey, for example, rose to prominence in the 1910s as the leader of the largest pan-African movement in the world. Born a British subject in Jamaica, Garvey traveled around the Atlantic world to promote racial uplift. In a trip to Panama after the United States began construction of the canal there in 1906, Garvey observed a two-class

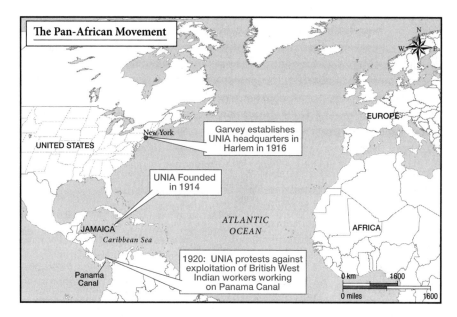

The Pan-African Movement

EUROPE

UNITED STATES

New York

Garvey establishes
UNIA headquarters in
Harlem in 1916

UNIA Founded
in 1914

ATLANTIC
OCEAN

AFRICA

JAMAICA

Caribbean Sea

1920: UNIA protests against
exploitation of British West
Indian workers working
on Panama Canal

Panama
Canal

0 km   1600

0 miles   1600

MAP 3.2

system of labor whereby the United States had instituted a gold payroll restricted to white skilled workers and a silver payroll for West Indian workers. In response, Garvey established a newspaper to give voice to the silver-roll workers who faced racial discrimination. And as a British subject, he called on officials in London to protect West Indian workers in the U.S. Canal Zone. Garvey went on to found the Universal Negro Improvement Association in Jamaica in 1914 and, two years later, moved his headquarters to Harlem, exhorting people of African descent in the United States, the Caribbean, and the world over: "Up, you mighty race, you can accomplish what you will!"

Garvey was not the only one to reject the doctrine of white supremacy. Franz Boas, a leading anthropologist, devoted much of his career to disproving theories of racial determinism and eugenics. In South Africa, Mohandas Gandhi, a young immigrant from India, challenged the tightening of racist restrictions. African subjects of European colonialism joined with a handful of African Americans, including the brilliant scholar W. E. B. Du Bois, to convene the world's first Pan-African Congress at the time of the 1900 Paris World's Fair. In addition, American Progressives formed the National Association for the Advancement of Colored People (NAACP) in 1909, with Du Bois as their leader. Claiming that "armies and navies are at bottom the tinsel and braggadocio of oppression and wrong," Du Bois decried U.S. colonialism abroad and argued instead for domestic reforms, particularly a significant new investment in African American education in the South. The NAACP went on to become the most important civil rights organization in the United States, but it was not until the early Cold War of the 1950s that Jim Crow came under serious attack in Washington, DC.

CAPITALISM AND THE SOCIAL QUESTION

The second wave of reform rose against the undesirable consequences of modern capitalism. In another example of the two-sided character of modern society, the very forces of industrial development that had boosted living standards and lengthened life spans also brought poverty, overcrowding, poor health, and other forms of social misery. Unlike the old household economy, where dependent laborers received some help from landlord or master, the industrial economy cut off wage earners from the protections of the past without creating new ones to take their place. Completely dependent on inadequate wages, working-class families had to rely on their own devices, plus whatever charity and political patronage might come their way. Especially now in the second industrial revolution, the increasing scale of production, the concentration of wealth, and the urbanization of the population only intensified these problems. In short, modern society posed what contemporaries called the social question.

The first to raise this question were working people themselves. In 1913, for instance, coal miners near Ludlow, Colorado, organized a strike for union recognition. Mother Jones, a radical leader of the labor movement, traveled to Ludlow and urged the workers to stand their ground: "You have allowed a few men to boss you, to starve you . . . to make peons of you." The owner of the mine, John D. Rockefeller Jr., declared in a congressional hearing that he would rather lose his entire fortune than recognize organized labor. The conflict escalated the following year when the Colorado state militia and company-hired guards fired machine guns at the strikers and their families encamped by the mine, killing a total of sixty-six. What is now known as the Ludlow Massacre was one of the most pitched battles between capital and labor in the twentieth century.

Through strikes, demonstrations, and union organizing, the growing mass of urban workers made known their often-desperate plight in the Darwinian struggle for the survival of the fittest. In addition, every Western nation had a mix of political movements by the turn of the century that spoke for laboring people. Among the most prominent was the Socialist International. Founded in 1889, the Socialist International adopted a Marxist program that called for the overthrow of capitalism from its main base in Germany. Another was the British Labour Party, founded in 1890, which had a more modest program of reform. Meanwhile, countries in the middle tier of the world economy, such as Russia, Italy, and Spain, were home to a good many anarchists who sought nothing less than the abolition of the state and syndicalists who sought workers' control over the means of production. Reflecting the international spirit of the prewar period, each of these movements of the left adopted the language of international solidarity.

The United States partook of these various forces in its own way. Although much weaker than in Europe, Socialism was in its heyday in the United States in the early twentieth century. In 1901 a number of small Socialist sects coalesced in the Socialist Party behind the widely loved—and widely feared—Eugene Debs.

In 1906, the Socialist writer Upton Sinclair published his novel *The Jungle*, which exposed the exploitation of immigrant workers in Chicago's meat-packing industry. Yet, in a reflection of the limits of Socialism in the United States, the novel helped spur Congress to pass the Pure Food and Drug Act (1906), a reform aimed at protecting consumers, not workers.

Adjusting to the ethnic diversity of the American work force, the U.S. branch of the Socialist International set up English and foreign language sections by 1912 and was strongly internationalist in outlook. If anything, the Industrial Workers of the World, known as the Wobblies, was even more internationally minded. Founded in 1905 under the slogan "One Big Union," the one hundred thousand members (at the peak) of the anarchosyndicalist Industrial Workers of the World aimed at getting rid of all bosses, capitalist and political, alike, so that workers could run things themselves.

Overshadowing these left influences, the largest wing of the U.S. labor movement—the American Federation of Labor under lifelong president Samuel Gompers—rejected any identification with Socialist internationalism. Founded in 1886, the American Federation of Labor reached a peak of membership 2.5 million in 1919, more than 10 percent of the total U.S. labor force. Even so, American trade unions fought as hard as any other to improve wages and working conditions, and the militant battles of America's often violent labor wars demonstrated more than any Socialist tract that the needs of America's wage earners were unmet under the existing economic system.

Challenged by this mobilization of working people, some elements of the middle classes responded with solutions of their own. In the United States, the struggle against industrial capitalism fused in distinctive ways with the revolt against patriarchy, bringing New Women such as Jane Addams, Florence Kelley, and Helen Keller to the forefront of the fight for social justice. They proposed a range of social supports to improve the conditions of work and urban life in hopes of making wage earners pillars of modern society. Florence Kelley, for example, as head of the National Consumers' League from 1898 to 1932, led campaigns in the United States for protective labor legislation such as child labor laws and the ten-hour day for women. Helen Keller, a noted Socialist and supporter of women's rights, learned to compensate for her blindness at a young age and graduated with honors from Radcliffe College in 1904. Her many books and lectures brought attention to the need for state supports of the disabled.

In Britain, Fabian Socialists (Fabius was known for his strategy of avoiding pitched battles and gradually wearing down his opponents with smaller raids and ambushes) pursued *social control*. The goal was to move from the chaos of laissez-faire to a more stable social order under the control of enlightened technical experts, or *technocrats*, like themselves. Their American counterparts—activist intellectuals such as the Sociologist E. A. Ross and Progressive writer Herbert Croly—proposed a watered-down version of social control for the United States.

The Progressives' emphasis on expertise, bureaucracy, and *enlightened tecnhocrats* could also lead to reforms that would be later decried as racist.

President Wilson's policy of segregating civil servants in Washington by race in 1913, for example, came as a shock to members of the black middle class who had doggedly pursued upward mobility in the three decades since Reconstruction. Thousands of blacks led middle-class lives in Washington with decent-paying jobs in the Census Bureau, the Treasury Department, and other offices of the federal government. When Wilson's segregationist policy went into effect, however, these workers were forced to the margins of the federal government and denied opportunities for advancement. Yet this policy choice was justified by Progressive reformers intent on rationalizing the federal bureaucracy.

Religion and Reform

The churches also played a major role in addressing the social question. As the age-old guardians of social order, they were often opposed to modern innovations. Yet some Catholic traditions were fully consistent with the quest for justice, and reformers took special encouragement from the 1890 papal encyclical *Rerum Novarum*, which called for ameliorating the conditions of labor. In the main, however, the Catholic Church was on the side of the status quo on both sides of the Atlantic. Steeped in patriarchal values, the church hierarchy combined conservative social teachings with a visceral fear of Socialism as a rival faith. As a result, especially where there were Catholic establishments, as in Italy, Austria, and parts of Germany, movements for social change often took an anticlerical position.

Protestantism was divided in a different way. On the one hand, Protestant individualism—the saving of humanity one soul at a time—militated against the salvation of society as a whole. That was especially true in the United States, where three-quarters of the total population and almost the entire elite were Protestants of one sort or another. The Lutheran church was a major bastion of conservative social teaching from the days of Martin Luther onward. In addition, conservative evangelical churches, many calling themselves fundamentalist after the 1909 publication of *The Fundamentals*, continued to stress the heroic rescue of "fallen women," the inner reform of the drunkard, and other appeals to individual conscience. Blaming poverty on the moral breakdown of the nuclear family, their remedy was for male heads of households to stop spending the family's disposable income at the corner saloon.

On the other hand, many liberal Protestants in countries around the Atlantic rim were joining the growing chorus for reform. That was certainly the case in the United States, where liberal churches were shifting from the gospel of sin to the Social Gospel. Instead of rescuing the individual sinner, leaders such as the Baptist minister Walter Rauschenbusch set out to change the social and economic conditions that gave rise to social evils in the first place. A new social conscience took its place alongside the individual conscience of old. Indeed, there was a growing realization throughout the Western world that reform at the level of individuals was not enough. There had to be social progress, too.

SOCIAL PROTECTION IN COMPARATIVE PERSPECTIVE

In attempting to address social problems, each nation developed its distinctive mix of social protections. Efforts to mitigate the sufferings of the urban working classes included everything from national health insurance to Prohibition. Although many factors were involved, in general, the extent of social protection varied with the influence of the market. Where the market held sway, as in the United States, social protections were less extensive than in places like Great Britain and Scandinavia, where social movements of civil society were influential.

Germany was the pioneer of social protection. As early as 1885, Chancellor Otto von Bismarck had instituted the world's first system of national health insurance in an effort to bridge the deep gulf between the classes in urban-industrial society. Worried about the rise of Marxian Socialism among industrial workers, the archconservative Bismarck sought to bring disaffected workers into support of the still-young German state. Although he failed to suppress radicalism— Germany became the center of gravity of international Socialism—his top-down effort to strengthen the state set the country on a path that led to the most extensive social welfare system in the world by 1914.

Other European nations and their overseas territories were moving more slowly in a similar direction. Because of the strength of the labor movement and its supporters in Britain, the world's first industrial society was gradually abandoning laissez-faire to adopt reforms such as unemployment insurance in 1911. With strong labor movements of their own, British settler societies in Australia and New Zealand were at the forefront of the social protection movement, enacting laws for minimum wages and maximum hours before anyone else.

Before World War I, there was little in the United States to compare with the social legislation of Germany or Britain. Instead, national policy was geared to the market. Faith that the market would provide a decent livelihood in the land of opportunity combined with distrust of centralized power to keep social protection at bay. The meager legislation that existed on the eve of the First World War, such as accident insurance (workman's compensation), was enacted on a state-by-state basis with the intention of shoring up the nuclear family by replacing the male breadwinner's lost income. In fact, restoring the traditional family was the aim of most of the leading reform campaigns of the day, including the abolition of child labor, protective legislation for women, and the demand for a *family wage* for the husband so that women and children did not have to enter the labor market in the first place. In these respects, social protections against the vagaries of industrial capitalism and the revolt against patriarchy were at cross-purposes.

The strength of market-based rather than state-based solutions was related to the cross-class character of American reform. Unlike Europe, where class lines were much more prominent, America's democracy of manners and faith in upward mobility tended to blur the boundary lines between social ranks and promote bridge-building between rich and poor. Cross-class organizations like the National Consumers' League, founded in 1899, and the National Women's Trade Union League, founded in 1903, had no counterpart in Europe, just as middle-class reformers like Jane Addams were not as prominent there.

Given American suspicions of state power, it is not surprising that corporate philanthropy was pioneered in the United States. A small stream of corporate wealth was diverted to social improvement through newfound private foundations with names like Rockefeller and Carnegie. Many centers of reform, including settlement houses like Hull House, depended on these wealthy benefactors to stay in business. The new philanthropic foundations also supported good works overseas. The Rockefeller Foundation, for example, funded research on tropical diseases, promoted medical education in China, and otherwise launched international humanitarian efforts.

Aeromarine Airways ran flights from Miami to Havana, Cuba, in the 1920s. During the prohibition period, Cuba became a vacation destination for Americans of means. Library of Congress Prints and Photographs Division, Washington, DC.

Yet some of the reforms of this period that were promoted by grass-roots movements and later instituted by the state ultimately proved a failure. Prohibition was one example. Temperance, or abstinence from drinking alcohol, excited much enthusiasm around the turn of the century and led to the growth of the Woman's Christian Temperance Union, the Anti-Saloon League, and other organizations that crusaded against the "demon rum." But after the failure of the U.S. experiment with national Prohibition (1918–33), authorities abandoned the goal of total abstinence in favor of more moderate regulations of tavern closing hours and liquor sales. Never again would curtailing the consumption of alcohol be put forward as a solution to social problems. The prohibition of narcotics, however, endured. In an effort to comply with an international convention to suppress opium traffic, the Congress adopted the Harrison Narcotics Act in 1914, which laid the foundation for law enforcement against all manner of narcotic drugs.

COMPARATIVE POLITICAL ECONOMY

The emergence of modern society called into question existing forms of the state. While the process unfolded in different ways depending on national circumstances, the entire Western world was caught up in twin efforts of social reform and the revolt against patriarchy. In a larger sense, both movements were part of the process of restoring social controls over private property that had been removed under laissez-faire. In long-term perspective, the twentieth-century effort to bring the state back into the business of regulating private enterprise harked back to the mercantilism of the eighteenth century, which is why modern regulation of the market is sometimes called neomercantilism, corporate liberalism, or simply corporatism. Whatever the name, extensive state regulation of the market marks a major change in political economy from nineteenth-century laissez-faire to the regulated capitalism of the middle decades of the twentieth century.

Much can be learned about this crucial change through comparison of leading countries caught up in the process. Because industrial capitalism evolved in societies with different histories and traditions, it was inevitable that political arrangements would vary from one country to the next. Placing the four largest economies along a spectrum ranging from strong market to strong state on the eve of the First World War demonstrates that the United States had the strongest market; Britain leaned toward the market; Germany leaned toward the state; and Russia, at the opposite end, had the most authoritarian state. Each of these countries entered into the destinies of the others as currents in world history.

Revolution and Reform in Russia, Germany, and Britain

Beginning at the state end, tsarist Russia was a study in contrasts between old and new. The three-hundred-year Romanov dynasty claimed to rule by divine right, while relying on ruthless secret police and fearsome Cossacks (skilled fighters from southern Russia, Ukraine, and Serbia) to club restive elements into submission. Yet modernizing forces were also at work bringing railroads, factories, and urban growth to St. Petersburg and Moscow and lifting Russia into the middle tier of the world economy.

The result was typical of other places where old and new were highly polarized. Russia became a candidate for revolution. Nihilists and other violent anarchist groups that purported to speak for oppressed peasants and workers assassinated high officials and otherwise practiced *propaganda of the deed* in an attempt to shatter the mystique of tsarist authority. Although terrorism failed to mobilize either peasants or workers, the regime enjoyed little support in modernizing sectors. George Kennan, an American journalist and lecturer, lent support to the emerging antitsarist movements by arguing that Russians were capable of self-government and as "fit for free institutions" as those in the West. When the tsar's navy was defeated in the Russo-Japanese War (1904–5), it was a signal for an uprising against a regime that was as ineffectual as it was repressive. The 1905 revolution failed. The next time, in 1917, it would succeed. When it did, Americans could not help being affected. American Socialists William English Walling, Ernest Poole, and Arthur Bullard, in fact, drew inspiration from the Russian uprisings to develop a critique of American efforts to remold other peoples, whether through settlement houses or through foreign policy.

Revolution like that in Russia was not confined to Europe. Wherever old regimes clung to antiquated forms of authority—patriarchal, aristocratic, imperial—in the face of modernizing forces, they were vulnerable to violent overthrow. In fact, a wave of twentieth-century revolutions swept through these highly polarized, semideveloped societies, the first of them in Mexico, where the dictator Porfirio Díaz was ousted in 1910. Turkey followed a decade later, and subsequently revolution came to Vietnam in Southeast Asia and Iran in the Middle East. In the case of China, modernizing forces and foreign meddling caused the ancient system of imperial rule to collapse in 1911. Two decades of chaotic warlord rule and civil war ensued. Not until the 1940s did a more developed China undergo a more decisive revolution. In these cases, old ruling classes gave way because they could not or would not accommodate modern society.

Germany, too, was torn between old and new, although not as much as Russia. The strong authoritarian state that emerged after 1870 was dominated by the kaiser (emperor) at the top and rested on two sectors of the economy. One was heavy industry, exemplified by the enormous Krupp steel empire; the other was cash-crop agriculture, dominated by the Junkers, aristocratic owners of large estates in East Prussia. Because their narrow economic interests were opposed, it was the great achievement of Bismarck to bring these two groups together in an alliance of "blood and iron."

One basis for this alliance was economic protectionism. Junkers were steadily losing their market to wheat imports from the U.S. breadbasket, and they turned to the German state for tariff protection. They were joined in this effort by big industrialists, who wanted their own products protected from foreign competition. The resulting tariff of 1879 became a cornerstone of the delicate balancing act called *Sammlungspolitik* (the politics of togetherness) that dominated German politics in an off again–on again fashion until the overthrow of the kaiser at the end of the First World War.

Another basis for alliance among the German elites was a common enemy. Ruling elites looked down on the subordinate groups of dispossessed peasants and the growing body of urban workers with a mixture of fear and contempt, tempered only by a lingering paternalism carried over from the days of aristocratic noblesse oblige. Urban workers, for their part, were increasingly angry over their exclusion from power and gravitated toward the Social Democratic Party, which grew rapidly in the decades after German unification. As we have seen, one unexpected consequence of class polarization was the world's first national health system. This pioneering measure harked back to the mercantilism of the eighteenth century, and it pointed toward a future of expanding neomercantilist regulation throughout the West. Again, Americans were affected by what happened overseas, in this case by going to war with Germany twice in the twentieth century.

Britain followed a different path to reform. As the first country to industrialize, it was the first to bring industrialists and financiers into significant roles in the state. Unlike Germany, it put landlords out to pasture with the repeal of the Corn Laws (tariffs on grain imports) as early as the 1840s and adopted, instead, free trade and laissez-faire. But Britain was also the first to feel the impact of social movements of industrial workers. As the Victorian era (1839–1901) wore on, British workers experienced gradual improvement in living standards and increasingly channeled their resistance to capital through stable trade unions, which became the base for the Labour Party. As the franchise expanded, the Labour Party posed a threat to the two-party reign of liberals and conservatives. Not long after Queen Victoria died in 1901, so-called Tory Socialists (conservatives who supported social legislation) and New Liberals, such as the future prime minister David Lloyd George, began to abandon laissez-faire and support social legislation.

The Road to Reform in the United States

In comparative terms, the United States represented yet another variation in adapting the state to modern society. At the opposite end of the spectrum from Russia, the United States had the weakest state. It was the place where the market philosophy of laissez-faire held the upper hand.

The reason laissez-faire was even stronger in the United States than in its homeland of Victorian Britain was because of the character of American class relations. There were no true lords and peasants as in eastern Germany and Russia and no privileged landed gentry as in England. The closest counterpart was the class of southern slave masters, but their defeat in the Civil War transformed them into business-minded planters. Because the planters depended on the export of cotton, they had no desire for tariff protection. Indeed, they fought against the protectionist aims of northern industrialists. Dispute over the tariff worked against anything like the German alliance between agrarian and industrial elites, blood and iron.

Moreover, northern industrialists and financiers, for their part, were resolutely opposed to state interference in the market on behalf of workers, although these propertied groups made a big exception to laissez-faire when it came to the tariff and railroad subsidies. Henry James, the noted author and Anglophile who knew England as well as he knew his native United States, satirized America's weak state when he described liberal America as a place where there was "no State, in the European sense of the word, and indeed barely a specific national name."

With a strong market, a vital civil society, and a weak state, the United States was not deeply polarized between old and new. Having gone through their own violent conflicts during the Revolution and the Civil War, Americans had already abandoned their most antiquated institutions—the monarchy, the established church, and the landlord class. Moreover, they had already achieved many of the democratic rights that Europeans were still fighting for, notably, universal male suffrage. Because its form of government was more in line with leading sectors of society, it had the most stable political system. Observers in the early twentieth century agreed that of all the Western powers, the United States was least likely to explode in revolution.

Another factor promoting stability was prosperity. A parade of European visitors came to praise higher wage levels and the prominence of small farmers and small businessmen. That was the view, for example, of H. G. Wells, one of the most popular authors of all time with a string of best-selling works of science-fantasy, notably, *The Time Machine* (1895) and *The War of the Worlds* (1898). After a 1905 visit to the United States, Wells portrayed American society as dominated by a bulging middle class, bracketed by the richest families on earth above such as the Carnegies and Rockefellers, and a sunken multitude of "new immigrants" and Negroes below.

His German contemporary, Werner Sombart, a Socialist economist, took a similar view. The idea of Marxist class struggle did not apply in the United States, Sombart argued, because widespread distribution of property and some measure of social mobility reduced class conflict. In short, American Socialism foundered on the "shoals of roast beef and apple pie." These views receive statistical confirmation in data showing the United States with the highest per capita income and highest per capita gross domestic product in the world on the eve of the First World War. Even so, American prosperity was unevenly distributed in this period, with two-thirds of Americans owning only 2 percent of the material wealth produced in the United States and the richest 2 percent of the population owning 60 percent of the wealth.

A Special Path?

For such reasons, some believed, then and now, that the United States was on a path of its own. They point to a host of differences from Europe that supposedly made America exceptional, including an unusually high degree of ethnic diversity, deep racial polarization, the early gift of the ballot, and strong Protestant individualism. There were also ideological differences: strong egalitarian beliefs, messianic Americanism (the belief that the United States has a mission to save humanity), and the myth of America as a Promised Land.

In addition, the efforts to reform capitalism and patriarchy took different forms in different countries. In Europe, on the one hand, the women's movement was often subsumed within the class struggle, the feminist movement was comparatively small, and collective solutions to social problems were the norm. In the United States, on the other hand, feminism in its broadest sense exerted a stronger independent influence on social reform. Some of the demands for change that were carried by labor and Socialist movements in Europe were shouldered, instead, by women's rights activists in the United States.

It is certainly true that American politics displayed many distinctive features. Middle-class reformers played a larger role than in Europe. When the middle classes joined forces with urban workers, they helped found a succession of cross-class political reform movements aimed at taking away power from wealthy plutocrats. Starting with Populism in the 1890s, these cross-class reform movements included Progressivism before the First World War, farmer-laborism in its wake, and the left wing of the New Deal in the 1930s. When the middle classes turned against the lower classes, they empowered the contrary political movements of nativism, immigration restriction, antiunionism, and the red scare, which came to dominate politics in Washington in the 1920s. Either way, middle elements were more politically significant than in Europe.

Another difference was the strength of political machines. Although local politicians could win the loyalty of immigrants and the poor by offering jobs, loans, and food, many were also corrupt in their use of illegal bribes and kickbacks. La Follette first cut his teeth in American reform movements by fighting corrupt political bosses. As one of America's leading Progressive voices, he argued against the "encroachment of the powerful few upon the rights of the many." Beneath highly visible struggles over reform, American politics was a free-for-all of influence peddling and cultural warfare. Unlike the class-based parties of Europe with programs closely tied to economic interests, America's two major parties—Republican and Democratic—were shifting coalitions of sometimes contradictory economic interests and conflicting cultural styles. Southern Democrats, for example, were strongly in favor of Prohibition and immigration restriction, whereas Democrats in the urban North, who were dependent on blue-collar immigrant votes, were strongly opposed to both measures.

Moreover, cultural politics were more intense. Given the proverbial diversity of American society, voters were divided by a host of moral and religious values—temperance, Sunday closing laws, ethnic identity—which weakened efforts to unify the people against the upper classes. Under these conditions, politics often came down to a matter of influence peddling by urban machines of the two major parties in which the big interests won the biggest share. In formal terms, the United States was easily the most democratic of the four societies compared here. In practice, however, the people were often overruled by powerful elites.

Similarities between the United States and Other Western Nations

Although these distinctive features exist, it is clear that American history unfolded within the bounds of Western society. That is evident in the fact that Americans were joining the wider Atlantic critique of laissez-faire. In the 1900s, political leaders who called themselves Progressive sought to bring the market under social control. Like their European counterparts, American cities at the turn of the century developed public water and sewer utilities. American reformers led efforts to build public schools and parks and invented the municipal playground, an idea later exported to Europe. This movement toward expanding public services culminated in the New Deal of the 1930s.

In the 1912 election, one of the most significant in American history, all the presidential candidates supported reform to one degree or another. Even the sitting president, William Howard Taft, a Republican who had tangled with corporate interests, became the conservative candidate only because all the others were more progressive. That was certainly the case with ex-president Theodore Roosevelt, who turned his back on conservatism to run as the candidate of the newfound Progressive Party. Under the slogan of the New Nationalism, Roosevelt demonstrated why he was the closest thing to a Tory Socialist by going further than any major party candidate thus far in proposing federal protections for women workers, the abolition of child labor, social insurance, and other reforms. A conservative at heart, Roosevelt consciously adopted reform as a means of forestalling more radical change, which earned him the title the American Bismarck.

In fact, Roosevelt did have something to fear from radicalism. The Socialist Party candidate Eugene Debs made the best showing of any leftist candidate in American history with his call for nationalization of railroads and mines, minimum wages, and maximum hours for all workers, not just women. The presence of homegrown revolutionary forces, such as the Industrial Workers of the World and left-wing Socialists, suggested that the United States was at one end of a spectrum, not off by itself.

Woodrow Wilson, the winner of the 1912 presidential election, continued many of Roosevelt's reform efforts. As a Democrat, Wilson also called for an expanded government role in the economy—a program he dubbed the New Freedom—much along the lines of Lloyd George and the British New Liberals.

Young boys waiting in line to be paid at a meat-packing house in Indianapolis, 1908. Lewis Hine child labor photos, Library of Congress Prints and Photographs Division, Washington, DC.

In fact, once in office, Wilson presided over numerous reforms. He began with tariff reduction to please the southern agrarians in the Democratic party and went on to support the creation of the Federal Reserve System, a network of national banks presided over by a presidentially appointed chairman. His first term also witnessed the strengthening of antitrust statutes in the Clayton Act and a national child labor law.

It is true that these reforms could be watered down or reversed. Indeed, that was the fate of the child labor law in the Supreme Court's 1918 decision of *Hammer v. Dagenhart*. In this case, the Court held that because child labor was not engaged directly in the commerce of goods (but rather in their manufacture), the federal regulation of child labor exceeded the commerce power of Congress and was therefore unconstitutional. It was also true that legal restraints on corporations were as weak as burdens on trade unions were strong. Nonetheless, the United States was now joining other Western nations on their way toward neomercantilist regulation of corporate capitalism.

The United States in Western Society

In other words, the United States was one nation among the larger group of nations comprising modern Western society. It was a part of the whole, not a whole unto itself. Caught up in the same basic processes, the nations of the West entered deeply into each other's histories. Certainly, the upper-tier nations of the world economy—the United States, Britain, and Germany, in that order— were part of the same circuits of capital and commodity flows, a fact that would receive harsh confirmation in the international character of the Great Depression in the 1930s. Moreover, they were part of the same international balance of power, which would see American troops drawn into the vortex of war and revolution in the 1910s.

Even in their internal workings, Western societies were immersed in transnational processes. In a multitude of transatlantic exchanges, American pioneering in the areas of women's rights, democracy, mass education, and a fast-paced way of life presaged Europe's future after the Second World War. By the same token, Europe's pioneering social welfare programs prefigured what America would become after the New Deal of the 1930s.

In that regard, European admirers saw in the United States a model of their own future. America was not exceptional, in the sense of being off on its own path; it was exemplary, in the sense of leading the rest of the world on the path of progress. That was the view of H. G. Wells. To his own surprise, Wells came away from his 1906 visit to the New World convinced that the United States held the key to the future. To be sure, he took note of many problems: extremes of wealth and poverty, political corruption, and cultural dissonance. But after a visit to the White House where he was thoroughly charmed by the energetic Theodore Roosevelt, he decided that America's can-do spirit would solve them.

CONCLUSION

In confronting social problems, the United States moved in the same currents as other Western nations. Although American mass education and American feminism were far ahead of that in Europe, American social legislation and the Socialist movement lagged behind. Whereas Americans played prominent roles in transatlantic reform movements, American revolutionaries took a back seat. When it came to government regulation of the market, Americans moved at a slower pace, but they moved in the same direction as everyone else.

As with social reforms, Americans played an increasingly important part in the balance of power among Western nations. Recognition of the United States as a world power, if not yet a great power, heralded the future shift from European to Western dominance in world affairs, in which the United States, far from being an outlier, would be at the center. In sum, the United States was an increasingly important part of the Western world: ahead in some ways, behind in others, but moving down the same path. In 1914, that path led to the First World War.

FURTHER READING

Dawley, Alan. *Changing the World: American Progressives in War and Revolution.* Princeton, NJ: Princeton University Press, 2005.

Flanagan, Maureen. *America Reformed: Progressives and Progressivisms, 1890s–1920s.* New York: Oxford University Press, 2007.

McGerr, Michael. *A Fierce Discontent: The Rise and Fall of the Progressive Movement in America, 1870–1920.* New York: Oxford University Press, 2003.

Ninkovich, Frank. *Global Dawn.* Cambridge, MA: Harvard University Press, 2009.

Pendergrast, Mark. *For God, Country, and Coca-Cola.* New York: Basic Books, 2000.

Rodgers, Daniel. *Atlantic Crossings: Social Politics in a Progressive Age.* Cambridge, MA: Harvard University Press, 1998.

Rosenberg, Emily. *Financial Missionaries to the World: The Politics and Culture of Dollar Diplomacy, 1900-1930.* Durham, NC: Duke University Press, 2004.

Spence, Jonathan. *The Search for Modern China.* New York: Norton, 1991.

Yellin, Eric S. *Racism in the Nation's Service: Government Workers and the Color Line in Woodrow Wilson's America.* Chapel Hill: University of North Carolina Press, 2013.

CHAPTER 4

GLOBAL SHIFTS AND THE FIRST WORLD WAR, 1914–18

THE AMERICAN RED CROSS IN EUROPE

Soon after the United States entered World War I, tens of thousands of Americans volunteered to serve in the American Red Cross as ambulance drivers, nurses, doctors, and other kinds of relief workers in Europe. Service in Europe offered women, in particular, the chance to contribute to the Allied effort while also attaining a measure of respect for service thought to be just as demanding and important as that of men fighting in the trenches. Clelia Duel Mosher, a physician from California, wrote that even after seven years

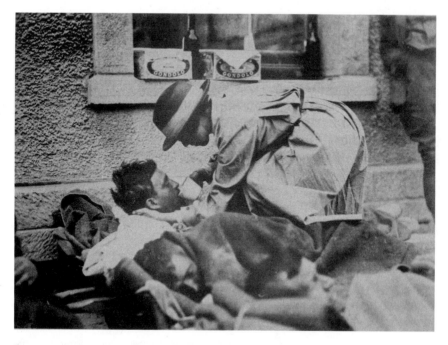

An American Red Cross volunteer serves water to a fallen British soldier at the railroad station at Montmirail, France (1918). Library of Congress Prints and Photographs Division, Washington, DC.

of practicing medicine, "every bit of experience, judgment and knowledge was called upon" in her work in war-torn France. When Alice W. Wellington of Massachusetts helped the Red Cross organize volunteers, she declared that because "our men must help drive out the invader," it was up to American women to "help restore the humble lives so ruthlessly shattered." Whether motivated by professional ambitions, patriotic duty, humanitarian impulses, or wanderlust, these women and thousands of other volunteers joined the Allied fight in Europe.

From the beginning of the war effort, the Wilson administration understood that large-scale humanitarian relief programs for easing civilian suffering in Europe would be essential to achieving its stated goal to "make the world safe for democracy." The same day that Congress voted to enter the World War, April 6, 1917, Wilson declared he had chosen the American Red Cross, a private organization that relied on volunteers, to coordinate relief efforts. As food shortages and limited access to medical care gave rise to strikes and riots in Europe, Wilson recognized the need for relief programs to stabilize war-ravaged Europe and lay a foundation for rebuilding democratic societies after the war. The success of the Red Cross's humanitarian aid program helped forge a new approach to U.S. foreign affairs as foreign aid came to play a significant role in American diplomacy. Notably, this was a development that was shaped not only by political elites but also by everyday Americans who found their own meaning in engaging with the world.

AMERICA AND THE GREAT WAR

From 1914 to 1917, as the war in Europe convulsed the international system and soon became the worst war in human history, Americans remained officially neutral. But as time went on, the United States became less and less neutral in practice. As a key trading partner of Britain and France and as an imperial power concerned about German ambitions in the Western Hemisphere, America increasingly viewed its own economy as intertwined with that of Europe. The irony was that in expanding power—economic, political, cultural—beyond their borders, Americans were affected by events beyond their control. Although the decision to go to war in April 1917 was not inevitable, America was forced to make a choice between war and peace.

The cataclysmic event that contemporaries called the Great War almost as soon as it broke out opened an age of modern warfare. This chapter focuses on the origins and impact of the war and U.S. involvement. The following chapter focuses on the period of revolution and reform that followed in its wake.

PREWAR INTERNATIONALISM

Prior to World War I, many expected increasing cooperation among nations. In *The Great Illusion*, a widely read book published in 1910, the British writer Norman Angell argued that economic and social interdependence had rendered war between states obsolete. Likewise, the American social reformer Jane Addams believed that human destiny was being shaped by what she called a growing *world consciousness*. Although reformers recognized that great powers pursued national interests, they believed that rulers would be compelled by social and economic forces to keep the peace.

Indeed, major trends confirmed these optimistic views. The world economy was more international than at any time before the late twentieth century. Money, people, and information circulated across national boundaries with minimal restrictions. European elites were knit together by blood ties—the German kaiser and the king of England were first cousins—and bonds of culture that, for example, made French the common language of diplomacy. The middle classes who read books by authors such as Angell and Addams kept in touch through international professional and scientific conferences where German was often the common language, and they looked to international law and international movements for suffrage, temperance, and the elimination of the "white slave trade" (prostitution) to improve the human race.

Among the most international segments of society were the working classes. Large numbers of workers migrated overseas or across internal European national boundaries in search of better opportunities. Certainly, those who spoke for the working class had been strongly internationalist since 1848 when the *Communist Manifesto* of Karl Marx and Frederick Engels called out, "workers of the world unite, you have nothing to lose but your chains." Answering the call, the First International (founded in 1864) and the Socialist Second International (founded in 1889) sought to convert the everyday experience of wageworkers around the world into a conscious class struggle.

Although less internationalist than their European counterparts, Americans engaged with the rest of the world in a variety of ways. Americans depended for their prosperity on the import of British capital and the export of cotton, wheat, and manufactured goods to Europe. American elites imitated Old World cultural styles, as gilded heiresses intermarried with counts and dukes. New York's leading financier, J. P. Morgan, made legendary expeditions across the Atlantic to acquire medieval tapestries and classical sculptures from the chateaus of Europe.

Among the middle classes, reformers like Addams traveled frequently to European conferences, while American Protestant missionaries spread over the globe. American workers also held connections overseas, with an average of almost one million immigrants coming to the United States each year between 1900 and 1914. At any given moment, nearly 15 percent of the population were immigrants; together with their U.S.-born descendants, they formed large immigrant enclaves in virtually every American city north of the Mason–Dixon line. Moreover, American radicals, although smaller in number than their European counterparts, were every bit as internationalist, including anarchosyndicalists such as the Industrial Workers of the World. Many would have agreed with the credo of the Socialist Eugene Debs, "My country is the world."

Underlying Causes of the War: Nationalist Ethnic Tensions and Imperial Rivalries

Because internationalist expectations ran high, many were caught off guard by the outbreak of war. As the great powers declared war on each other in rapid succession between July 28 and August 4, 1914, they brought to a close the century-long period of peace in Europe that followed the Napoleonic Wars.

There is no universal agreement among historians on the causes of this violent turn in the balance of power. But it is clear in retrospect that well before 1914, major conflicts were raging just below the surface. One set of conflicts arose out of an imbalance between state and society, as the emergence of modern, industrial society in the late nineteenth century undermined the existing structures of political power. Although the growing ranks of educated middle classes and discontented industrial workers made Western society more democratic, ruling structures remained mired in the hierarchal past. Certain states with universal male suffrage and representative assemblies did not allow elected representatives any real power. Germany, for example, had an elected assembly, the Reichstag, but was ruled, in practice, by a kaiser (emperor) and his appointed advisors.

Even where the government supposedly ruled in the name of the people, such as France, suffrage was restricted to men, and even states with representative parliaments, such as Britain, restricted suffrage still further to men of property. Under such conditions, the gap between the existing state and modern society was a source of political instability. With various groups demanding fundamental change—including suffragists, Socialists, laborites, and anarchists—rulers rightly felt threatened by their own subjects.

Many peoples without states, such as the Poles, and even many smaller ethnic groups, such as Lithuanians and Czechs, saw themselves as states-in-waiting and posed a considerable threat to state governments that did not acknowledge them. For that reason, nationalism posed a revolutionary threat to the three great Continental empires: Germany, where Kaiser Wilhelm II thwarted the aspirations of his Polish subjects; Austria-Hungary, where Emperor Franz Joseph ruled over Poles, Czechs, Croats, and others; and Russia, where the nationalist demands of Poles, Lithuanians, and Ukrainians, among others, challenged the rule of Tsar Nicholas II. Because so many nationalities aspired to greater autonomy, if not full independence, European empires struggled to maintain order. Many European leaders believed they could instill unity and discipline among their restive subjects by fighting a foreign foe. In the end, World War I would have the opposite effect.

Another set of conflicts at the center of World War I was the power struggle between empires. The handful of great powers—Britain, France, Germany, Austria-Hungary, and Russia—were empires, as were the would-be great powers of Japan and the United States. In the late nineteenth century the balance of power among them had come to rest on two great alliance systems, the Triple Alliance of Germany, Austria-Hungary, and Italy, which dated back to 1883, and the Triple Entente, formed in 1890 by Britain, France, and Russia. Within Europe there were points of imperial friction between France and Germany over the border zone of Alsace-Lorraine and between Austria-Hungary and Russia over the Balkans, especially in 1912–13 during a series of Balkan wars. Tensions were equally high overseas. Conflict between Germany and France in Morocco produced the 1911 Agadir crisis, which almost led to war. A similar incident at Fashoda in the Sudan nearly touched off war between England and France in 1898.

Overseas tensions were an outgrowth of what historians have named the *new imperialism*. As the great powers pushed ever deeper into Africa and Asia beginning in the late nineteenth century, their interests conflicted. Although understandings of imperialism ranged from Lenin's conception of empire as the latest stage of capitalism to Alfred Thayer Mahan's focus on power politics, one of the most defining aspects was a naval arms race. Indeed, Germany's adversaries had reason to tremble as the country's internal political parties united after 1897 around *Weltpolitik*, a policy of overseas expansion keyed to naval expansion. Germany's military buildup, in turn, provoked an arms race with the British and the French. In raising the stakes of colonial competition, the arms race contributed to the coming of the Great War.

Outbreak of War in Europe

These two sets of conflicts—nationalist ethnic tensions and imperial rivalries—converged in the Balkan crisis of 1914. The crisis was triggered by the assassination of the heir to the Austrian throne, Archduke Franz Ferdinand, and his wife in the Bosnian city of Sarajevo, then part of a region annexed by Austria but disputed by Serbia, on June 28. Because the perpetrator was a Serbian nationalist, the Austro-Hungarian emperor Franz Josef blamed the Serbian government for stirring up Serbs living under Austrian rule. He issued a diplomatic ultimatum demanding Serbia bow to Austrian will. Serbia's refusal triggered an Austrian declaration of war. Austria's action, in turn, caused Russia, the traditional protector of the Slavic peoples in the Balkans, to mobilize its military. Facing war with each other, Austria and Russia immediately called on their respective allies in the Triple Alliance and the Triple Entente.

Germany then became the focal point. Germany honored its alliance with Austria in surprise fashion, not by attacking Russia on the east, but by attacking its own long-time adversary, France, on the west. Under international rules of war, a country facing imminent attack is authorized to launch a preemptive war. Such was not the case here. The fact that no French attack was imminent made Germany's invasion a war of aggression (a fact that later gave France, Britain, and the United States the evidence needed to pin war guilt on Germany in the Versailles Treaty at the end of the war). But Russia's full mobilization in support of Serbia forced the Germans, in their view, to mobilize and attack France to avoid being caught in a two-front war. Germany had hoped to defeat France first before turning to its larger adversary, Russia. After Germany attacked France, Britain declared war on Germany on August 4, 1914, and the great powers embarked on the first general war in one hundred years.

Early Years of War in Europe

At the outset, everyone expected a short war. With the generals promising to hand things back to the diplomats in a matter of months, political leaders of both the Allies (Triple Entente) and the Central Powers (Triple Alliance, minus Italy) promised their respective soldiers they would be home by Christmas. Widespread popular enthusiasm also marked the early weeks of the war on all sides.

But four Christmases would come and go before all the soldiers would come home. It soon became clear that ending the fighting would be harder than starting it. Operating under the Schlieffen Plan, the Germans moved fast-marching divisions and cavalry units through the plains of Belgium into northern France with the intention of overwhelming French defenses and seizing Paris. But in a do-or-die defense of their capital, the French, with support from British troops, thwarted German intentions at the Battle of the Marne just sixty two miles from the goal. By mid-October, both sides had dug trenches along the western front running from the Swiss border to the English Channel, as seen in Map 4.1. There they remained in stalemate for the duration of the war.

Meanwhile, Britain and Germany battled at sea for control of the North Atlantic. It was an uneven contest. Although Germany had tried to match the number of big British battleships, known as dreadnaughts, by 1914 it had lost the naval arms race, producing only eighteen battleships compared to Britain's thirty-one (the United States had ten battleships). Instead of direct confrontation, each side tried to blockade the enemy's ports. Britain's naval supremacy enabled it to prevent food and other war supplies from reaching the enemy. Although the impact on German war production was minimal, by the third year the blockade had the effect, intended or not, of starving the civilian population. Unable to challenge Britain with battleships, Germany developed submarines known as U-boats (*Unterseeboots*) to prowl shipping lanes and launch torpedoes. But early German success at sinking merchant ships brought sharp protests from the United States and other neutral countries.

A different kind of war unfolded on the eastern front. Here, along the broad plains of eastern Europe, German and Russian armies fought a war of maneuver. Unlike the trenches in the west, front lines moved back and forth, as the Germans drove Russian forces out of East Prussia in the battle of Tannenburg in late August of 1914, while two weeks later Russians answered by defeating an Austro-Hungarian army at Lemberg. Not until 1917 did the high level of German organization pay off with a string of victories against the disintegrating armies of the Russian tsar.

United States Neutrality

The initial U.S. response to war was a policy of strict neutrality. Within two weeks of the outbreak, Wilson called on Americans to remain "neutral in fact as well as in deed." Safely positioned on the other side of the Atlantic Ocean, Americans looked aghast at the unfolding disaster.

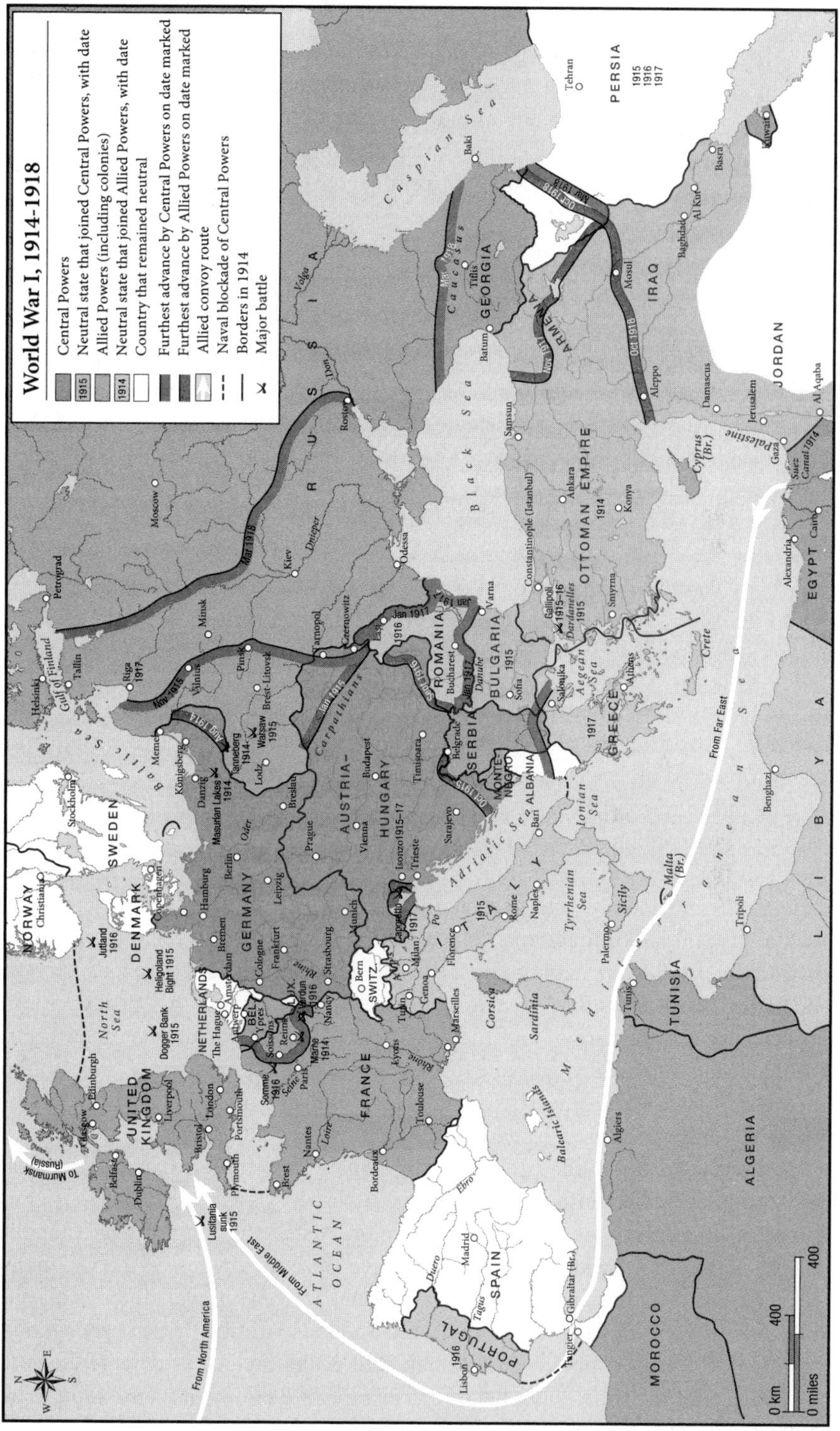

World War I, 1914-1918
Central Powers
1915
Neutral state that joined Central Powers, with date
Allied Powers (including colonies)
1914
Neutral state that joined Allied Powers, with date
Country that remained neutral
Furthest advance by Central Powers on date marked
Furthest advance by Allied Powers on date marked
Allied convoy route
Naval blockade of Central Powers
Borders in 1914
Major battle
NORWAY
Christiania
SWEDEN
Stockholm
DENMARK
Copenhagen
UNITED KINGDOM
Glasgow
Edinburgh
Belfast
Dublin
Liverpool
London
Bristol
Portsmouth
Plymouth
To Murmansk (Russia)
Lusitania sunk 1915
From North America
From Middle East
From Far East
North Sea
Jutland 1916
Heligoland Bight 1915
Dogger Bank 1915
NETHERLANDS
The Hague
Amsterdam
Antwerp
BEL.
Ypres
LUX.
Soissons
Reims
Verdun 1916
Somme 1916
Marne 1914
Paris
Seine
Nancy
FRANCE
Brest
Nantes
Loire
Bordeaux
Toulouse
Lyons
Rhône
Marseilles
GERMANY
Hamburg
Bremen
Berlin
Cologne
Frankfurt
Leipzig
Strasbourg
Munich
Rhine
Oder
Danzig
Königsberg
Memel
Masurian Lakes 1914
Tannenberg 1914
Aug 1914
Baltic Sea
SWITZ.
Bern
Alps
Turin
Milan
Genoa
Florence
Caporetto 1917
Isonzo 1915–17
Trieste
ITALY
1915
Po
Rome
Naples
Bari
Corsica
Sardinia
Sicily
Palermo
Tyrrhenian Sea
Adriatic Sea
Ionian Sea
Malta (Br.)
AUSTRIA-HUNGARY
Vienna
Prague
Budapest
Breslau
Lodz
Warsaw 1915
Carpathians
Jan 1915
Timisoara
Sarajevo
Belgrade
SERBIA
MONTENEGRO
ALBANIA
Oct 1915
Sept 1916
Jan 1917
ROMANIA
Bucharest
Danube
Iasi
1916
Czernowitz
Tarnopol
Jan 1917
BULGARIA
1915
Sofia
Varna
GREECE
1917
Salonika
Athens
Aegean Sea
Crete
Gallipoli 1915–16
Dardanelles 1915
Constantinople (Istanbul)
OTTOMAN EMPIRE
1914
Smyrna
Ankara
Konya
Samsun
Cyprus (Br.)
Black Sea
Odessa
Helsinki
Gulf of Finland
Tallin
Petrograd
Riga 1917
Nov 1915
Vilnius
Pinsk
Brest-Litovsk
Minsk
Kiev
Dnieper
Moscow
Mar 1918
RUSSIA
Rostov
Don
Volga
Caspian Sea
Caucasus
Mar 1918
Batum
Tiflis
GEORGIA
Baku
ARMENIA
Nov 1917
Oct 1918
Mar 1918
Mosul
IRAQ
Baghdad
Al Kut
Basra
Kuwait
Tehran
PERSIA
1915
1916
1917
Aleppo
Damascus
Jerusalem
Palestine
Gaza
JORDAN
Al Aqaba
Suez Canal 1914
Alexandria
Cairo
EGYPT
LIBYA
Benghazi
Tripoli
Mediterranean Sea
TUNISIA
Tunis
ALGERIA
Algiers
Balearic Islands
MOROCCO
Tangier
Gibraltar (Br.)
SPAIN
Madrid
Ebro
Duero
Tagus
PORTUGAL
1916
Lisbon
ATLANTIC OCEAN
0 km 400
0 miles 400
N
E
S
W

MAP 4.1

Yet Americans could not long stand apart from the conflict. Indeed, immigrant ties shaped American attitudes toward the war. In the roughly 45 percent of the population of British ancestry (English, Scotch, Welsh), hearts went out to embattled Britain, especially among the Anglophile elite. At the same time, there was sympathy for the Central Powers in other segments of the population, first among Americans of German descent (roughly 10 percent of the total), but also among those of Irish descent who had long opposed the British (also about 10 percent). The "new" immigrants from southern and Eastern Europe offered the most complicated response. A few sympathized with the Central Powers but many Serbs, Croats, and other southern Slavs prayed for defeat of the hated Austro-Hungarian empire, just as Russian Jews began to count the days until the overthrow of the tsar.

Wherever their sympathies lay, virtually no one in the United States was calling for a declaration of war in 1914. Few could imagine that American soldiers would ever fight on European soil. Although the United States stayed officially neutral in 1914 and 1915, that would change with the advent of total war.

TOTAL WAR AND PEOPLE'S WAR

By 1916, Europeans were fighting what the German commander Erich Ludendorff called *total war*. Unlike wars of the past fought by professional armies, workers in the factories contributed as much to the First World War as soldiers in the trenches. Governments promoted patriotic service, geared the economy to war production, and otherwise mobilized civilians as well as soldiers.

One of the most striking aspects of total war was government use of propaganda to sway public opinion. One motive for going to war in the first place was the desire of rulers to direct internal discontent against foreign enemies. Wartime governments tended to portray the struggle as a people's war. It was time, they argued, for all inhabitants to put aside criticism of the regime and unite behind the patriotic struggle against the hated enemy. In Germany, for instance, the kaiser called for a *Burgfrieden*, or "fortress truce," to end political division, and German conservatives used nationalism to intimidate Socialist deputies in the Reichstag into accepting a vote to raise war funds. National unity was also the theme in France's *union sacre* (sacred union), and the same was true in Britain, where dissent was deemed unpatriotic.

Sometimes propaganda promised a reasonable reward for patriotic service. For example, British authorities promised a "land fit for heroes" at war's end. But more often, the appeal was to raw emotion. Just as the Germans were taught to sing a "Hymn of Hate," the British people were taught to see the Germans in racist terms as barbaric Huns. In crude but effective ways, all sides played on gender themes of patriotic motherhood and masculinity. British propaganda posters, for example, portrayed German soldiers as rapists, as depicted on the next page, and the invasion of Belgium as a rape of Belgium, a theme soon to be developed in U.S. propaganda.

In the early stages of World War I, nationalist passion seemed to overwhelm everything that stood in its way—internationalism, Socialism, tolerance, even reason itself. Years after the war there was widespread retrospective criticism of the excesses of wartime propaganda, but only a few were brave enough to rise above the swelling tide of mass emotion and condemn it at the time. Jane Addams traveled to Europe in 1915 to promote peace through the International Congress of Women and Robert La Follette later voted in the U.S. Senate against entry into the war.

War Economies

The total war footing of World War I required mobilizing in the factories as well as in the trenches. Mass production techniques of the sort pioneered in Henry Ford's auto assembly line made it possible to manufacture innumerable machine guns for transport by trucks powered by the recently invented internal combustion engine. Mass production and distribution of the machine gun enabled soldiers to engage in the mass killing of opposing armies. In the 1916 Battle of the Somme, for instance,

"Once a German, always a German." This anti-German poster published in Britain in 1918 appealed to racial ideologies of German inferiority. Library of Congress Prints and Photographs Division, Washington, DC.

British commanders ordered an attack on German forces dug in along the River Somme northeast of Paris. Climbing out of their trenches and going over the top, British soldiers suffered sixty thousand casualties on the first day of battle. It was the single worst day of the entire war and, indeed, in the whole history of warfare to that point. By the time it was over, four months later, the British had gained five miles of ground at a cost on both sides of more than one million casualties.

By 1916, all the warring nations recognized the requirement for full-scale economic mobilization under government control. Governments allocated resources to munitions production and war transport, imposed food rationing, and treated workers as soldiers of production.

Often the "man behind the man behind the gun" was a woman. With so many men in arms, industry was forced to turn to female labor. By the end of the war, women accounted for about 55 percent of industrial workers in Germany, up from 35 percent in 1914, and some 36 percent in Britain and France, up from 28 percent.

Germany went furthest in subjecting the economy to state control. Adopting war Socialism under Walther Rathenau, the chief executive officer of Germany's giant General Electric Company, Germany mobilized industry from the top down.

Although nominally under a civilian government led by Chancellor Bethmann-Hollweg, by 1916, real power in Germany rested in the hands of the top military commanders Paul von Hindenburg and Erich Ludendorff, who dominated the increasingly irrelevant kaiser.

Yet putting the economy on a war footing caused considerable suffering among the civilian population. In Germany, which was isolated from the rest of Europe by the British blockade, food production and distribution declined to the point where starvation stalked the urban population in the "turnip winter" of 1916–17. British and French populations generally fared better. Although they had to scrimp and save, they continued to dine on food imports from the United States, Latin America, and their colonial sources overseas.

Total war also required massive capital outlays. Britain paid a good part of the bill from its own coffers. It was, after all, the world's premiere financier. But even that was not enough to meet the unprecedented expenses of mechanized warfare, so the government also sold war bonds to its citizens and, along with France, borrowed heavily overseas from U.S. banks.

War for Empire

The total war in Europe soon engulfed much of the world through imperial conflict overseas. Imperial rivalry, which had played such a crucial role in the origins of the war, now continued from the Middle East to Africa and East Asia as all the major powers sought to expand their empires and ward off threats from the nearby colonial holdings of their rivals. The widening circle of imperial rivalry eventually reached out to include the United States.

Although oil was just beginning to be the main energy source for modern society, the Middle East was a modern imperial battleground. In anticipation of victory over the Ottoman Empire, which had allied itself with the Central Powers, the Allies secretly agreed in the 1916 Sykes–Picot treaty to carve up the increasingly enfeebled "sick man" of the Middle East.

Africa had been an arena of conflict ever since the scramble for Africa in the late nineteenth century. In the World War I period, skirmishes were fought throughout the continent. For example, British Kenya and German East Africa (the future Tanzania) sparred with one another across Lake Victoria. Germany lost its colony of German South West Africa to South African forces in 1915.

In East Asia, Japan became the preeminent power in the region. At the outbreak of war, Japan declared war on Germany and immediately seized German concessions on China's Shandong Peninsula. Japan also took over German islands in the Pacific. Seeking to consolidate these conquests, in 1915 Japan won additional rights by imposing what was known as the Twenty-One Demands on revolution-torn China. Japan's expansion in the First World War foretold a future of Japanese attacks on China in the 1930s and then of bloody battles with the United States for the control of Pacific islands in the 1940s.

INCREASING U.S. INVOLVEMENT

The pull of total war and imperial conflict increasingly drew the United States into the war. For three years, neutral America responded to the economic demands of total war by feeding and clothing Allied soldiers and civilians. Booming sales of American wheat, cotton, and meat made war a golden age for U.S. farmers. It brought good economic times for business and workers as well. Demand for uniforms, transport vehicles, and all the other supplies needed by modern armies produced profits for manufacturers and the best labor market workers had ever known. Unemployment all but disappeared in 1917.

Above all, the war was a bonanza for U.S. banks. Increasingly desperate for capital to finance their war effort, Britain and France came knocking on their doors. Trading on its close ties to London finance, New York's House of Morgan threw open its coffers to the tune of $1.5 billion, a huge sum at the time, as was Morgan's profit of perhaps $500 million. Eventually, U.S. loans amounted to more than $2 billion, a massive sum that American banks were determined to see repaid. By war's end, American finance was on the road to becoming the world's biggest creditor, a fact that signaled a historic role reversal. Formerly, the Old World had been the banker to the New. Now it was the other way around. As a result of these growing economic ties to the Allies, the United States, although neutral in name, became less and less neutral in fact.

The Preparedness Movement

By mid-1915, several American conservatives were organizing a movement for war preparedness. Led by Republican leaders of the East Coast establishment, such as Elihu Root and Theodore Roosevelt, the movement focused on building battleships and expanding the standing army, while shoring up the power of ruling elites. One-time New Nationalists such as General Leonard Wood, commander of the Rough Riders in Cuba in 1898, believed that a patriotic campaign for national unity and military buildup would help elites maintain their political power over a diverse populace. Facing intense pressures from below for labor reform, women's suffrage, and social justice, conservatives sought to impose discipline from the top. Although far removed from the kind of revolutionary threats faced by European ruling classes, many conservative leaders held the same belief in the beneficial effects of bellicose nationalism.

The preparedness movement built on earlier efforts to Americanize immigrants. Under the battle cry of "100 percent Americanism," conservatives had played a leading role in the Americanization movement, aiming in Roosevelt's words to "yank the hyphen out of America." But now they grew impatient with the meager results of Americanization and increasingly pushed for total exclusion of immigrant groups they deemed undesirable. Under prevailing ideas of racial hierarchy, *undesirable* translated into Jews, Italians, Slavs, and other nationalities from southern and Eastern Europe. Although actual immigration had slowed to a trickle after 1914, the Immigration Restriction League and other nativist organizations worked closely with preparedness advocates such as Henry Cabot Lodge, a Republican senator from Massachusetts, for restrictions of immigration that eventually passed Congress in 1917. In its larger implications, the linking of military preparedness and patriotic nativism proved a key moment in the birth of the modern political right.

The Testing of Neutrality

German U-boats severely tested U.S. neutrality. The battery of U-boats blockading Allied ports took aim at any ship heading into the declared war zone around the British Isles. The sinking of the British ship the *Lusitania* in 1915, which killed 1,198 people, including 128 Americans, was an early test. The next test came with the loss of Americans aboard the *Sussex* on March 24, 1916, and this time Wilson issued an ultimatum to the Germans, who responded with the *Sussex* pledge promising not to sink passenger ships or merchant ships without warning.

Even with these provocations, the majority of Americans held fast to neutrality. To counter the preparedness movement, Jane Addams and other prominent reformers established the American Union against Militarism in keeping with the spirit of prewar internationalism. Although Wilson's military budget for 1916 included naval expansion, antiwar forces supported the president on the grounds that "he kept us out of war," the key slogan in his November reelection campaign.

For the time being, Wilson did not disappoint the peace movement. Feeling the undertow of war, he set out to make peace. Working first through diplomatic channels, in December 1916 he offered to mediate between the warring parties. Although neither side rejected the offer out of hand, both sides feared unfavorable peace terms more than they feared continuation of the war, and nothing came of the effort.

Wilson tried one last time in an appeal to the warring parties for "peace without victory." In one of the most eloquent state papers in the annals of U.S. diplomacy, Wilson's speech to the Senate on January 22, 1917, reached out to the people of the world. His message contained the germs of his subsequent Fourteen Points, including a *concert of nations*, rather than entangling alliances, freedom of the seas, arms reduction, and self-determination of nations, which he associated with the Monroe Doctrine. "These are American principles, American policies," he proclaimed. And then, evoking the messianic belief in an American mission to save the world, Wilson continued, "And they are also the principles and policies of forward-looking men and women everywhere, of every modern nation, of every enlightened community. They are the principles of mankind and must prevail."

Wilson's antiwar message made him both a hero to war-weary peoples in Europe and a villain to the American preparedness movement. Never one to mince words, the former Rough Rider Theodore Roosevelt attacked Wilson's stance. Responding to Wilson's idealistic words, Roosevelt retorted, "Peace without victory is the natural ideal of the man who is too proud to fight." Proud of his nickname, the Bull Moose, Roosevelt fit the description offered by former president William Howard Taft: "He loves war. He thinks it is essential to develop the highest traits in manhood, and he believes in forcible rather than peaceful methods."

Nonetheless, at the beginning of the year of decision of 1917, only a few Americans had any intention of going to war. The call for preparedness from elites had failed to excite the mass of the population. Many American workers, in fact, called for peace. In February of that year, for instance, the State Federation of Labor in Wisconsin petitioned the government to halt commercial trade with European powers to avoid being drawn into the conflict. Even those who sympathized with the Allies mostly held fast to the Monroe Doctrine's ideology of separation between the Old World and the New, and significant numbers either sympathized with Germany or, like many Irish, despised Britain.

Economic calculations cut in opposite directions. Although war loans to the Allies gave American financiers a big stake in Allied victory, neutrality had provided profits, lucrative export markets, and plentiful jobs without sending a single American overseas to die. Finally, the typical justifications for war were simply absent. No one had invaded the United States, nor was there any remote possibility of an amphibious invasion across the Atlantic. Although American citizens had died on the high seas and American goods had been confiscated, these infractions of freedom of the seas and neutral rights did not rise to the level of a major *causus belli* (justification of war). Americans held their fire regarding the war in Europe.

The United States in Latin America

But this was not the case in Latin America. During the period of U.S. neutrality in World War I (1914–17), U.S. gunboats and marines were on patrol in nearly a dozen Latin American countries. Although sometimes overlooked in explanations of why the United States went to war, U.S. empire in Latin America provided a key link in the causal chain of events. To understand why, it is necessary to examine U.S.–Latin American relations prior to the outbreak of the war.

Between 1900 and 1914, U.S. intervention in Latin America had become commonplace, as can be seen in Map 4.2. American naval action was instrumental in securing the Panama Canal Zone as U.S. troops intervened seven times in Panama between 1904 and 1925. The United States sent soldiers into Cuba (1906–9; 1912), Nicaragua (1912), and Mexico (April 1914). In these interventions, the overriding motive was to establish an environment favorable to U.S. economic and strategic interests. But especially after Woodrow Wilson became president in 1913, American expansion took on the added cause of promoting democracy. Wilson declared he was determined "to teach the South American Republics to elect good men."

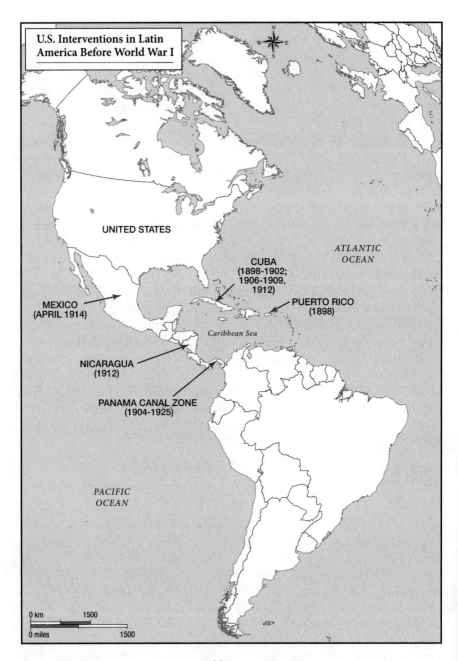

MAP 4.2

His ambassador in London, Walter Hines Page, surprised the British foreign secretary in 1913 by telling him that the United States was prepared to go on shooting for two hundred years, "till they learn to vote and to rule themselves." The use of democratic ideals to justify military intervention set the pattern for future intervention in Europe, as Wilson would soon declare, to "make the world safe for democracy."

Latin Americans themselves were divided over Uncle Sam's presence. The dynamism and personal freedoms of U.S. society found many admirers in the ranks of Latin American liberals. In addition, some of the many factions contending for power believed they could use foreign forces to their own advantage. Panamanians had relied on U.S. warships to defend their secession from Colombia in 1903, opponents of Nicaraguan President Zelaya invited in U.S. forces to overthrow him, and some Cubans were happy to invoke the Platt Amendment to bring in U.S. Marines.

Intervention, however, also provoked strong resistance against the Colossus of the North. Intellectuals such as Uruguayan-born José Enrique Rodó decried American materialism for its "inability to satisfy even a middling concept of human destiny," while Argentine writer Manuel Ugarte, a passionate partisan of Latin American unity, wrote to the newly elected President Wilson in 1913 to demand that "the stars and stripes cease to be a symbol of oppression in the New World." Such critics pointed out that democracy can only grow out of local soil and cannot be implanted by foreign troops.

United States Interventions in Latin America during World War I

Fighting in Europe gave the United States both the motive and the opportunity to greatly expand its economic and strategic position in Latin America. In economic terms, the war allowed American capitalists to acquire properties from British and German investors looking for cash to finance their own war production. Between 1914 and 1929, U.S. investments tripled in Central America, quadrupled in Cuba, and skyrocketed eightfold in South America, reaching a total of $5.4 billion. By 1929, investments in Latin America amounted to 35 percent of all U.S. foreign investments.

It was true that the war also boosted Latin American fortunes. Prices of tropical produce, coffee, sugar, tobacco, and cocoa all rose during the war years. And with the war causing a decline in imports of European manufactured goods, Latin American countries were forced to develop their own industries. Indeed, the war years were boom years for Argentina, Brazil, and other countries with capital to invest in domestic manufacturing and agriculture.

Nonetheless, the steep rise in U.S. investments in Latin America at the same time as the British were pulling out hastened the transition from British to U.S. preeminence. The same was true in the diplomatic arena. The United States forced Britain to cede ground, ending what the British had seen as joint Anglo-American supervision in the region. With the completion of the Panama Canal in August 1914, the same month as the war began, the United States increasingly sought to protect sea lanes to the Panama Canal.

For all these reasons, the Wilson administration embarked on several military interventions in Latin America during the World War I period. Just as the European powers pursued their own imperial agendas, so the U.S. military occupied Cuba (1917–22) and remained in Nicaragua (1912–25, 1927–34). Wilson drew on exaggerated German designs on the Caribbean to justify the U.S. occupations of Haiti (1915–33) and the Dominican Republic (1916–24). These occupations came on top of formal U.S. rule in the Panama Canal Zone, Puerto Rico, the Philippines, and the Virgin Islands (purchased from Denmark in 1917).

The United States also intervened in Mexico during this period. In April 1914, Wilson sent marines to Mexico in an effort to undermine the power of the current leader, General Huerta. It was not only Huerta's independence that worried Wilson. Huerta was also engaged in trade with the Germans. The pretext for invasion was the impending arrival of a shipment of arms from Germany. The outbreak of war in Europe four months later only heightened Wilson's anxiety about "German intrigues" in Mexico.

In fact, Germany was engaged in an ongoing duel with Britain to gain Mexican favor, which provided the diplomatic context for the Punitive Expedition. The Mexican general Pancho Villa crossed the border in March 1916, angered over Wilson siding with President Carranza in the Mexican civil war and his ban on arms sales to Villa's forces. The popular general attacked an army garrison in Columbus, New Mexico, killing eighteen U.S. citizens. In retaliation, Wilson ordered the U.S. military to capture Villa. Frustration mounted as the Punitive Expedition failed to catch Villa. At the same time, German foreign minister Arthur Zimmerman proposed a military alliance with Mexico. Zimmerman offered Mexico the chance to win back territory lost to the United States half a century earlier in the Mexican–American War in exchange for support of the German war effort. Intercepted by British intelligence, the Zimmerman telegram was forwarded to the Wilson administration in March 1917. Since the Monroe Doctrine of 1823, U.S. elites had kept a close watch for any new European imperial ventures in the New World, adding a series of corollaries to the doctrine designed to keep Europeans at bay. Now the Zimmerman telegram arrived as proof positive of a German threat to the U.S. sphere of influence in the Western Hemisphere. In response, the U.S. government increased security along the U.S.–Mexico border. Although the proposed German–Mexican alliance seemed unlikely in early 1917, many Americans worried what would happen if Germany won the war.

Open Door Policy and U.S. Involvement in the World War

Another important cause of U.S. involvement in World War I was concern about threats to a basic principle of U.S. foreign policy: the open door for commerce. American banks, farms, and factories had built up a booming trade with the Allies during the neutrality period. Loans were especially important because they gave the United States—or at least U.S. banks—a compelling stake in Allied victory. In just the first few months of 1917, for instance, the British government borrowed $400 million in loans from J. P. Morgan in New York to finance the purchase of war materiel. Many in U.S. finance worried they would not collect their debts if the Allies lost.

In an effort to strengthen the Allies, American leaders deemed it vital to keep open Atlantic shipping lanes. Twice in the past two and a half years, Germany had been pressured to reign in its U-boats. But now, desperate to cut off the flow of munitions and supplies, the German government decided to resume unrestricted submarine warfare beginning February 1, 1917. Even as Wilson was calling for peace without victory, Germany abandoned the *Sussex* pledge and announced that all vessels entering the blockade zone around Britain would be fair game. Although the general staff knew they risked provoking the United States into a declaration of war, they gambled that they could sink enough ships to cause Britain to surrender before the United States could mobilize effectively. Indeed, the U-boats were initially a stunning success until the Allies enforced a comprehensive convoy system in response. They sent two million tons of cargo ships to the bottom of the ocean in the first three months of the campaign. But the decision was a strategic disaster. Even more than the Zimmerman telegram, Germany's decision to escalate submarine warfare triggered U.S. intervention.

Other factors also contributed to U.S. involvement. Elites aspired to exercise power in world affairs commensurate with the premier rank of the U.S. economy, and Wilson knew he would not be able to influence the shape of the postwar world unless there were American soldiers on the ground when the shooting stopped. In addition, in March 1917 the Russian people overthrew the tsar, removing any possible embarrassment of having an autocracy on America's side in a war, as Wilson promised, to fight for democracy. Responding to the president's request for a declaration of war, Congress assumed its constitutional responsibility of deciding the question of war and peace and gave Wilson what he asked for on April 6, 1917.

On the Home Front

The American public, however, was divided about going to war. Indeed, critics of the war effort argued that a national referendum in April might have reversed the congressional declaration. Given widespread popular opposition, it was necessary to mount a campaign to drum up support. Moving quickly, the Wilson administration set up the Committee on Public Information (CPI) to orchestrate the campaign. Led by the journalist George Creel, the CPI worked closely with organizations associated with the preparedness movement to mobilize artists, writers, and historians in an effort to provide "information" (a euphemism then used for the term *propaganda*) intended to win over a reluctant public.

Tensions escalated, however, as the CPI campaign increasingly targeted for-eigners and dissidents. Taking their cue from British propaganda, the CPI and other arms of the government began preaching racial hatred of "the Hun." German Americans were quickly transformed from desirable immigrants to devious traitors. In the fervid atmosphere of hypernationalism, sauerkraut was renamed *liberty cabbage*, dachshunds were hung from telephone poles, and German language instruction was prohibited in thousands of local schools.

As part of President Wilson's Proclamation of War of April 6, 1917, all male German citizens in the United States age fourteen and older were officially clas-sified as *enemy aliens*. Under the terms of Wilson's proclamation, the U.S. gov-ernment prohibited aliens from criticizing the U.S. government in print and from living or traveling within a half-mile radius of military installations, in-cluding seaports and munitions factories. Aliens could be apprehended, their property could be seized, and they could be deported. The 1910 U.S. Census counted 8.6 million people of German birth or parentage within a total popula-tion of ninety-two million. Although the majority of German Americans were American citizens, either through naturalization or birth in the United States, many also held German citizenship under the terms of a 1913 German law that stipulated that citizenship extended to those who were also citizens by birth of another country. In this context, many German Americans who were American citizens were also German citizens and therefore subject to the enemy alien classification.

The effects of this classification could be seen in German communities throughout America. Hoboken, New Jersey, for instance, was a port of call for the Hamburg-American steamship line and home to a large German immi-grant community with several German churches. On Good Friday, 1917, the day Wilson issued his proclamation, some five hundred members of St. Matthew's German Lutheran Church waited in the pews for the start of services, but their pastor never arrived. Reverend Herman Brückner had been apprehended at his home that morning and taken to Ellis Island under allegations that his work with a charity, the German Seamen's House in Hoboken, placed him in contact with German naval personnel.

The intolerant spirit of 100 percent Americanism was not aimed only at Germans. Anyone with foreign ties became suspect. During the neutrality period, Wilson had denounced hyphenated Americans "who have poured the poison of disloyalty into our national life" and declared that "such creatures of passion, disloyalty, and anarchy must be crushed out." Perhaps unintentionally, the presi-dent's words spurred increased antiforeign sentiment, as exemplified in the 1917 congressional passage (over Wilson's veto) of the literacy test intended to prohibit illiterate immigrants from entering the country. Ellison Smith of South Caro-lina, chair of the Senate Immigration Committee in 1917, argued American sov-ereignty required the maintenance of a "pure, homogeneous American people."

Anti-immigrant sentiment also contributed to the enactment of Prohibition. The century-old temperance movement finally achieved its goal in two stages, first with the wartime Volstead Act, which suppressed public drinking near military encampments, and then with the Eighteenth "Prohibition" Amendment, which forbade the production and distribution of alcoholic beverages. Prohibition followed a wave of anti-German hostility that emerged in the war period. Shortly after the *Lusitania* bombing in 1915, a U.S. Senate investigation revealed that the National German–American Alliance, an organization funded largely by brewers, supported the publication of pro-German propaganda in American newspapers. In response, the Senate forced the alliance to disband and built support for passing Prohibition. The effort to stamp out German beer—and the power of German brewers—largely succeeded. By 1919, the brewing industry was out of business and nearly every saloon in the country was shut down. But that did not mean the end of drinking. Behind the closed doors of the speakeasy and the private home, alcohol continued to flow.

The intolerant spirit was also evident in the most extensive assault on civil liberties in U.S. history. Equating dissent with disloyalty, Congress passed the Espionage and Sedition Acts, which defined disloyalty in such broad terms that almost any criticism of authority could run afoul of the law. The Justice Department enforced the acts by conducting raids in August 1917 on offices of the antiwar Industrial Workers of the World, arresting war critics such as Victor Berger and Emma Goldman, incarcerating some six thousand enemy aliens, and setting up an amateur spy agency called the American Protective League.

In one of the most publicized cases of 1918, Mollie Steimer, a twenty-one-year-old immigrant from Russia, was arrested for violating the Sedition Act. While working in a factory in New York's garment district, she was exposed to a circle of political activists and soon joined a group of Jewish radicals known as Frayhayt (Liberty). Steimer opposed U.S. intervention in the Russian Revolution, arguing the government of her homeland was moving out of czarist control to worker control and should be allowed to find its own way. Together with Jacob Abrams and other activists, she dropped leaflets protesting U.S. foreign policy from rooftops in East Harlem. She was quickly arrested and sentenced to fifteen years in prison. Similarly, Eugene V. Debs, the Socialist candidate who ran against Woodrow Wilson for the White House in 1912, was sentenced to ten years under the Espionage Act for speaking out against U.S. entry into the war. The Supreme Court's 1919 *Schenck* decision upheld convictions of Socialist Party leaders for condemning the war. Even the liberal justice Oliver Wendell Holmes supported the acts, equating criticism of government policy in wartime with the clear and present danger of falsely shouting "Fire!" in a crowded theater.

Although such restrictions on civil liberties were not as severe as in Europe, the difference was that the United States prided itself on being the land of liberty. Although other countries had also adopted democratic practices, the U.S. Bill of Rights had set the global standard for freedoms of speech, assembly, and religion. With the passage of the Espionage and Sedition Acts, the standard-bearer violated its own liberal principles. The loss of civil liberties to wartime nationalism set the stage for the postwar red scare and a new round of more stringent immigration restrictions. It would be years—in some cases decades—before these liberties could be won back.

World War I and the Social Contract

Although the Wilson administration curtailed civil liberties during the war, it also allowed for the expanded rights of particular groups, especially workers and women, as well as a new administrative state to regulate the economy. Responding to calls for social justice from the Progressive reform movement, Congress abolished child labor in the 1916 Keating–Owen Act and granted the long-sought eight-hour day for railroad workers. To maintain labor peace after U.S. intervention, the administration heeded the call of reformers for social compromise between labor and capital and set up the National War Labor Board to mediate industrial disputes before they resulted in strikes. Together, these steps marked a significant expansion of the social contract.

At the same time, wartime conditions allowed for the advance of women's rights. With women workers taking new jobs in industry (temporarily in most cases), reformers and business leaders agreed on the need for a new federal agency, which became the permanent Women's Bureau. Housewives were enlisted in campaigns to conserve food, and elite women won a host of new advisory positions in wartime agencies, such as the Council of National Defense. Most important, in recognition of women's patriotic service and as an effort to placate the increasingly militant suffrage movement, Congress adopted the Nineteenth Amendment. As Carrie Chapman Catt, president of the National American Woman Suffrage Association, argued in the context of widespread fears of immigrant disloyalty, "It is a . . . danger to a country like ours to send 1,000,000 men out of the country who are loyal and not replace those men by the loyal votes of the women they have left at home."

The war shaped immigration patterns as well. Although wartime conditions slowed the flow of European immigrants to America, Mexican migration increased. When Congress passed the 1917 Immigration Act requiring a new literacy test for immigrants, the U.S. secretary of labor made immigrants from Mexico exempt to satisfy the labor needs of U.S. agribusiness in the southwest. The Passport Control Act in 1918, which required that aliens acquire visas to enter the United States during the war years, temporarily slowed Mexican immigration, with long lines of people applying for visas. As the U.S. Consul at Nogales, a town along the Arizona–Mexico border, complained, "I have had to put on three typists, girls, to take care of the applications. I have not been to bed a night this week before midnight and more than one time have still been in the office at one in the morning. I am sure that there are ten or twelve thousand 'crossings' daily." In response to such delays and the pressing need for wartime labor, immigration officials made an exception for Mexicans by issuing special border-crossing cards so they could more easily enter the United States.

The war also shaped African Americans' struggle for full citizenship rights. With wartime labor demand increasing in northern factories, more than half a million African Americans moved out of the South to cities such as Philadelphia, Chicago, and New York in what became known as the Great Migration. The booming steel and meat-packing industries of Chicago, for instance, hired black men to work in unskilled positions. Illinois Steel saw a spike in black employees from 35 in 1916 to 1,209 in 1919. Black workers entered the stockyards in even larger numbers and participated in efforts of the Stockyard Labor Council to organize unions with their white ethnic coworkers. As Jack Johnstone, secretary of the council, stated at a labor rally in 1919, "It does me good to see such a checkerboard crowd. . . . You are all standing shoulder to shoulder as men, regardless of whether your face is white or black." Although this union drive ultimately failed, it suggested how the Great Migration brought black and white workers into closer proximity. There were also opportunities for black women in service work in hotels, restaurants, and laundries. Although they were consigned to the lowest rungs of the economic ladder and subject to ongoing racial discrimination, some blacks also found new freedoms, including the opportunity to earn higher wages and send their children to better schools.

At the same time, the U.S. Army continued to maintain a largely segregated army. Because of concern that racial clashes would serve as a distraction from the war effort, U.S. officials relegated black soldiers to noncombatant positions. Still, some black soldiers drew inspiration from their experience overseas. The tendency of U.S. Army officials in France to punish blacks more than whites led blacks to avoid conflicts that would attract the attention of the U.S. military police. In this context, African Americans cultivated amicable relationships with merchants and townspeople. Black soldiers in France were surprised to find that the French people did not treat them with the same level of distrust and discrimination so common in America. Scores even married white French women. As one report of French military intelligence officials stated, "many of the inhabitants of villages in which they [black troops] are stationed declare they like them better than whites." For many African Americans, the war experience encouraged greater activism back home. Seeking to channel such activism among retuning soldiers, W. E. B. Du Bois wrote in *The Crisis*, a publication of the NAACP, "By the God of Heaven, we are cowards and jackasses if now that the war is over, we do not marshal every ounce of our brain and brawn to fight a sterner, longer, more unbending battle against the forces of hell in our own land."

Although the war shaped the struggles of these different groups for full citizenship, it also spawned a new administrative state to regulate private enterprise. Following the election of 1912 when all the major candidates were in some sense progressive, the Wilson administration had expanded the corporate-regulatory complex by creating the Federal Reserve System to oversee banks and the Federal Trade Commission to regulate private enterprise. In the World War I period, this administrative state expanded further in ways that fit the aims of Progressive Era reformers. The War Industries Board coordinated the manufacturing sector of the economy while the War Labor Board mediated conflicts between workers and employers.

Among the most significant of these new agencies was the U.S. Food Administration, which shipped food to millions of people in the Allied nations. Approximately 70 percent of U.S. families participated by rationing their food so that part of the U.S. harvest could be shipped overseas. Food Administration posters asked Americans to limit meat and wheat, in particular, by observing meatless Tuesdays, wheatless Mondays, and porkless Saturdays. Above and beyond U.S. national interest in supporting the Allies, many Americans understood their sacrifice as a sign of American greatness. As one journalist wrote in a Kansas newspaper, "Possibly no other nation in all the world would do what America proposes to do—refrain from using the food that is so plentiful for all our needs, in order that people we have never seen may have some of our stores." Although most people thought of the food program as simply a humanitarian effort, few recognized that it was also an economic exchange that benefited American businesses. The Allies paid for this food with loans from American banks, thus contributing to America's emerging role as a creditor nation. Herbert Hoover ran the program as a business looking to make a profit. This meant developing elaborate propaganda campaigns to convince Americans of the health benefits of eating less meat even as meat was sold to European markets.

Insofar as these agencies represented an unprecedented intervention of the state into the market, the administrative state was similar to war Socialism in Europe. The difference was that Americans preferred voluntary methods. In regulating consumption, for example, Herbert Hoover's Food Administration was able to oversee the vast outpouring of food from the American breadbasket through exhortations to housewives to modify their family's diet. Similarly, the Treasury Department relied on the volunteerism of private citizens—including that of the Boy Scouts and Hollywood stars such as Mary Pickford and Douglas Fairbanks—in selling Liberty Bonds to finance the war effort.

Despite the suppression of dissent and the growth of intolerant Americanism, the light of democracy was not extinguished entirely during the war period. To the contrary, democratic forces won concessions from elites in the form of an expanded social contract, women's suffrage, and state regulation of the market. Despite its repressive aspects, the war emergency provided opportunities for subordinate groups to win a greater share of power (see also Chapter 5).

The U.S. Contribution to Allied Victory

The U.S. decision to form the American Expeditionary Forces (AEF) and enter the war had a major effect on the war's outcome. Especially as the eastern front disintegrated over the summer and fall of 1917, the AEF helped compensate for the withdrawal of Russian troops. In the war of attrition on the western front, U.S. entry brought a seemingly unlimited supply of men and materiel to the Allied cause. Having already served as the Allies' grocer, clothier, and general quartermaster during the neutrality period, now all these contributions were expanded in addition to the new role of fighting soldier. Above all, the flow of American dollars increased, enabling the French and British governments to pay for imports of food and supplies while also funding their own war production. Acknowledging the decisive role of the United States in the war effort, the French premier Clemenceau later remarked, "If this help had not been forthcoming, our army could not have held."

Along with men and supplies, U.S. entry made possible a boost to the morale of Allied forces. By 1917, war weariness was spreading, so much so that Allied leaders expressed the need to overcome general exhaustion and offset the movement for a people's peace. Mutinies even erupted among some French units that same year. Thus, Europeans gave the Americans a huge welcome. Even before American soldiers had seen any fighting, Parisians turned out en masse to give General John "Black Jack" Pershing, commander of the AEF, a hero's welcome as he led his troops in a triumphant parade through the city in 1917 on U.S. Independence Day. Recalling the French Alliance at the time of the American Revolution, Colonel Charles E. Stanton, one of Pershing's aides, announced, "Lafayette, we are here."

The United States made another contribution six months later in the form of Wilson's Fourteen Points. Having been embarrassed by Bolshevik publication of the sordid Middle East land grab embodied in the secret Sykes–Picot treaty, Allied leaders badly needed an uplifting revision of their war aims. With his April promise to "make the world safe for democracy," Wilson had already captured the imagination of war-weary peoples, and on January 8, 1918, he lifted spirits yet again in proposing a set of liberal ideas and territorial settlements that inspired people the world over, even on the German side.

The actual U.S. military contribution to the war effort was less significant. Unlike the Second World War when America proved the *arsenal of democracy*, munitions from the United States did not weigh heavily enough in the scales to tip the balance. Although some two million America soldiers of a total of four million in uniform made their way to Europe, delays in timing and confusion in command structure limited their effectiveness. Not until the spring of 1918 were they ready in large numbers, just in time to help repel the last great German offensive that began in March. Only at Chateau-Thierry, just fifty miles from Paris, in June 1918, at St. Mihiel near Verdun

"Food Will Win the War." The U.S. Food Administration appealed to recent immigrants from eastern and southern Europe. This poster was translated into Yiddish: "You came here seeking freedom, now you must help to preserve it—Wheat is needed for the allies—Waste nothing" (1917). Library of Congress Prints and Photographs Division, Washington, DC.

in September, and the Meuse-Argonne Forest from September to November did U.S. forces make a significant contribution to winning key battles.

Over the course of the war, 128,000 U.S. soldiers died and were later honored in the dozens of cemeteries of northern France. Included in this number were large numbers of AEF fatalities from the influenza epidemic of 1918. First contracted in U.S. Army camps in Kansas and Georgia, this virulent strain infected large numbers on crowded troop ships traveling to Europe. Spreading quickly in the trenches of European battlegrounds, influenza struck the Allied and German armies with equal force and became a global pandemic.

Throughout the period of U.S. involvement, AEF soldiers fought valiantly and played a critical role as fresh reserves. British and French armies also played a crucial role on the battlefield when they defeated the Germans in what was known as the Hundred Days' Campaign. When the 1918 German offensive failed to succeed, the general staff looked at the seemingly inexhaustible supply of American replacements and drew the conclusion that victory was impossible. Contacting the Allies through President Wilson, the Germans agreed to accept an armistice—not to surrender—on the basis of the Fourteen Points. On November 11, 1918, in a rail car in Compiegne near Paris, the armistice was signed. The worst war in history, the war to end all wars, was over.

American Ascendance

World War I dramatically changed the global balance of power. A series of upheavals had destroyed four great continental empires. Tsarist Russia crumbled in March 1917, and by November, Russia was in the hands of the first avowedly anticapitalist regime in history. With German defeat in November 1918, a revolution overthrew Kaiser Wilhelm and the Hohenzollern dynasty, which had been a key force in Europe since the eighteenth century. At the same time, the subject nationalities of the Austro-Hungarian Empire overthrew the House of Habsburg, ending a rein that extended back to the sixteenth century. In its stead, a new family of nations appeared. In the case of the Ottoman Empire, young Turks who had sided with Germany in World War I blamed Armenians for supporting Russia and unleashed a wave of mass killing, resulting in the death of 1.5 million Armenians. Having allied with the losing side in the war, the Ottoman Empire soon fell victim to a nationalist revolution that created modern Turkey in 1923 and gave rise to several new Arab nations that had formerly been part of the Ottoman dominion. Ironically, European elites who had gone to war in 1914 to shore up their thrones eventually lost the whole structure of royal and aristocratic authority. Never again would ordinary peoples defer to dynastic kings and princes the way they had before the war.

Yet it was not just Germany and Austria-Hungry that lost out at the end of the war. Although the victorious British and French did not know it at the time, they, too, were gazing into a future of decline. After four centuries of ascent, four years of internecine warfare weakened the European center to the point where

Photograph of Armenians holding a Red Cross flag used to signal for help when organizing resistance to the Armenian genocide in 1915. Library of Congress Prints and Photographs Division, Washington, DC.

world power began to shift toward the Asian and American peripheries. On the east stood the Soviet Union, gathering itself for a leap into the industrial era, and further to the east was Japan, the rising power in Asia. On the west there was the United States, which played an increased role in the 1920s and eventually filled the gap left by the end of European hegemony.

It would take a second world war for these changes to be confirmed. In a sense, the First and the Second World Wars were two phases of the same war interrupted by a fitful truce. In both phases, an alliance of France, Britain, Russia, and the United States resisted Germany's bid for dominance on the European continent. Both were total wars fought not only by soldiers, but also by whole societies. Together, the two wars brought about epochal changes in world affairs, including the end of European hegemony and the rise of the United States and the Soviet Union.

Antiwar Sentiment

In its immediate impact, the First World War left the greatest trail of destruction in Western history. As many as 10 million dead and an estimated 6.5 million civilian deaths, including 1.5 million Armenians, bore testimony to the mass destruction that came when scientific rationality combined with the passions of nationalist ideologies. And these figures do not include the millions more dead from the influenza epidemic at the end of the conflict brought on partly by wartime rationing, dislocation, and exhaustion. It was no easy task to find meaning in the immense slaughter.

The first emotional need was to mourn the dead in ceremonies of remembrance. During the war, makeshift cemeteries were laid out as hallowed grounds for bereavement, described in a soldier's poem: "in Flanders field the poppies blow / Between the crosses, row on row." Soon after it was over, all the combatant nations began construction on monuments to commemorate the sacrifice, some of which grew to immense proportions, as with the huge arch built in remembrance of British losses at the Somme.

Unlike the solemn piety of these official monuments, literary reflections often expressed revulsion over the gruesome facts of trench warfare. British poet Wilfred Owen's *Dulce et Decorum Est* mocked the idea that it was "sweet and fitting" to die for one's country. Likewise, in *All Quiet on the Western Front* (1929), the German novelist Erich Maria Remarque wrote from the point of view of soldiers in the trenches, portraying the war as a grisly exercise in futility. American writers contributed to the same spirit of renunciation in such novels as Ernest Hemingway's *A Farewell to Arms* (1929), in which the protagonist simply abandons the battlefield and flees to Switzerland with a beautiful English nurse.

The same was true of the visual arts. A new breed of expressionist artists, such as George Grosz in Germany, depicted crippled and mutilated bodies as the grotesque consequences of mechanized warfare. Senseless killing helped inspire artists in the Dada movement to plumb the inner depths of the irrational mind. If ordinary reality was too grotesque, a new group of surrealist artists were ready to transcend it.

Repudiation of the war could also be heard in postwar music. American jazz became enormously popular in Europe, in part because its freewheeling improvisation and swinging trumpet riffs sounded a radical alternative to the march tempo of the military bugle. Moreover, the inventiveness of New Orleans jazz also signaled the possibility of hope for a different future.

Not everyone was revolted by the war. Some combat veterans reveled in the camaraderie of the trenches, and a few, including Adolf Hitler, turned their wartime experience into a cult of violence (a theme to be taken up in the next chapter). Nonetheless, the widespread feeling of revulsion fueled the strongest peace movement of the twentieth century in the 1920s. Vowing "never again," groups reached across national boundaries to join in broad campaigns for disarmament or the "outlawry of war."

CONCLUSION

Celebrating their victory, Americans felt buoyant at the end of the war. They had played a major role in the triumph of democracy over autocracy, expanded their empire in Latin America, increased prosperity at home, and taken their place among the ranks of the great powers—in fact, superseded them. Even reformers of the day could point to wartime advances in women's suffrage and the social contract (although not in racial justice).

The cost had been high—128,000 American lives and the loss of civil liberty to a frenzy of patriotism. But at least the sacrifices did not seem to be in vain. With their prestige riding at an all-time high, Americans exulted in the feeling of freedom. The unacknowledged irony of American power was that going out to change the world simultaneously curbed American freedom. The more the United States entered into the international balance of power, the more Americans were subject to the will of others—to Mexican revolutionaries, German U-boat captains, British generals, and French diplomats.

Americans could not have it both ways. They could not be a major force in world affairs without at the same time being constrained by events beyond their control. Most Americans reveled in the freedom that came with power. Precious few had the wisdom to recognize its limits. For much of the twentieth century, Americans would be caught in the same paradox. The more they went out to change the world, the more the world changed them.

FURTHER READING

Benton-Cohen, Katherine. *Borderline Americans: Racial Division and Labor War in the Arizona Borderlands*. Cambridge, MA: Harvard University Press, 2009.

Byerly, Carol R. *Fever of War: The Influenza Epidemic in the U.S. Army during World War I*. New York: New York University Press, 2005.

Capozzola, Christopher. *Uncle Sam Wants You: World War I and the Making of the Modern American Citizen*. Oxford: Oxford University Press, 2008.

Fussel, Paul. *The Great War and Modern Memory*. Oxford: Oxford University Press, 1975.

Hardach, Gerd. *The First World War, 1914–1918*. Berkeley: University of California Press, 1977.

Irwin, Julia F. *Making the World Safe: The American Red Cross and a Nation's Humanitarian Awakening/* Oxford: Oxford University Press, 2013.

Keegan, John. *The First World War*. New York: Random House, 1999.

Keene, Jennifer. *Doughboys, the Great War, and the Remaking of America*. Baltimore: Johns Hopkins University Press, 2003.

Kennedy, David. *Over Here: The First World War and American Society*. Oxford: Oxford University Press, 2004.

St. John, Rachel. *Line in the Sand: A History of the Western–U.S. Mexico Border*. Princeton, NJ: Princeton University Press, 2011.

Veit, Helen Zoe. *Modern Food, Moral Food: Self-Control, Science, and the Rise of Modern American Eating in the Early Twentieth Century*. Chapel Hill: University of North Carolina Press, 2013.

Winter, Jay. *The Experience of World War I*. New York: Oxford University Press, 1989.

CHAPTER 5

REVOLUTION AND REACTION, 1917–24

Russian soldiers pictured in the streets of St. Petersburg, 1917. John Reed's *Ten Days That Shook the World* told the story of the Bolshevik Revolution for Americans back home. Library of Congress Prints and Photographs Division, Washington, DC.

1917: JOHN REED AND LOUISE BRYANT IN RUSSIA

On August 17, 1917, John Reed and Louise Bryant left New York aboard the Danish steamer United States and headed into the European war zone. The two journalists were determined to witness firsthand the earthshaking events taking place in revolutionary Russia. As opponents of the First World War who sympathized with revolution, they hoped to bring back to the United States the story of a new Socialist society arising out of the ashes of world war.

Reed and Bryant had fallen in love at first sight in their hometown of Portland, Oregon, and since moved to New York's Greenwich Village, a mecca for bohemians and reformers of all stripes. Reed was a darling of the Left who had gained attention for his daring on-the-scene reporting of the Mexican revolution and his sympathetic account of striking textile workers in Patterson, New Jersey. Bryant was a radical version of the much talked about New Woman, an independent freethinker in revolt against patriarchal authority who had left her husband for Reed. It was her commission as a freelance journalist that financed much of their journey to Russia.

Skirting the German blockade, the United States carried the couple to neutral Sweden, after which they made their way by train to Russia, arriving in St. Petersburg just in time to be swept up in the Bolshevik Revolution. On November 7, they witnessed the seizure of the Winter Palace, the central act in the revolutionary drama. Over the next few weeks, they rushed from one event to the next, ducking bullets and furiously recording everything they saw, enabling Reed to write up their notes in what became the classic book, Ten Days That Shook the World. As American leftists, Reed and Bryant made the long journey from middle-class Portland to revolutionary St. Petersburg to see up close the possibilities for broad societal and political change.

AMERICAN RESPONSES TO REVOLUTION

Although Americans did not experience revolutionary change at home, many could not escape being caught up in disorders abroad. Already divided along lines of class, gender, and race, Americans divided again over how to respond to revolution. Whereas a handful joined with Reed and Bryant in embracing Socialism and some on the right saw Wilson as inclined toward Bolshevism, many more followed President Wilson in championing liberal democracy as the best alternative to revolution. With these divergent outlooks, Americans responded to upheavals near and far, including revolts in Mexico and the West Indies and a series of revolutions in Europe.

This chapter explores the different ways Americans responded to revolutions erupting around the globe in the 1910s. This was a period of ongoing peasant revolutions in China and Mexico, an anticapitalist revolution in Russia, liberal nationalist revolutions in central Europe, and anticolonial resistance movements in the Caribbean, Ireland, and India. These were not mere scuffles among elites. In every case, these revolts challenged fundamental structures of society, including inherited forms of family, property, and power. Even where social upheaval stopped well short of revolution, as in the United States, social movements took advantage of division among elites to win victories for the causes of women's suffrage, labor standards, and social justice. Especially under the destabilizing influence of the First World War, no established authority was safe and secure.

REVOLUTIONS IN THE AGRICULTURAL BELT

Americans first confronted social revolution in a place where it was least expected: the world's vast agricultural belt. Peasants comprised the great bulk of humanity almost everywhere outside Europe, where the peasantry was in steep decline, and the United States, where peasants never really existed as a class except for southern sharecroppers. Tied to the land and bound to tradition generation after generation, tillers of the soil scratched out a bare existence under the authority of landlords, village headmen, and priests.

The arrival of modern forces threw peasant societies out of balance. In what is called *uneven development*, a series of changes took place in the early twentieth century that undermined the position of traditional elites, including the rise of new commercial and industrial classes, the expansion of discontented urban wage earners, and the growth of cities at the expense of the countryside. In the same process, modern technology and scientific ideas undermined age-old religious faith while Western ideas of constitutional rights and representative government subverted political authority.

So it was with the Republican Revolution in China. The coming of railroads and trade with the West quickened the pace of economic development and gave rise to groups eager to uplift China by adopting Western technology and political institutions. But, unlike the Meiji rulers of Japan, the Qing dynasty was unwilling or unable to make the turn to modernity. After the humiliating Western invasion to suppress the Boxer Rebellion in 1900, the Qing dynasty finally lost *the mandate of heaven* (the sacred right to rule) and gave way almost without a fight in 1911, thus bringing down the curtain on the five-thousand-year-old imperial order.

Modernizing trends were personified by Sun Yat-sen, an exiled opponent of the Qing dynasty who was influenced by Christianity during a long stay in Hawaii and who first read about the collapse of the Qing while aboard a train crossing the U.S. Great Plains. Quickly returning home, he helped found the Guomindang, or Nationalist Party, around a liberal program of constitutional rights and representative government. But events in China refused to be contained within the framework of constitutional law. Soon local warlords were sending private armies to fight one another in an increasingly violent struggle for power. With the countryside in turmoil and central authority in disarray, it would be decades before China regained political stability.

To most Americans, the rumblings of revolution in China seemed far away. Apart from missionary ties and merchant voyages, there were few direct links between the two societies. Racial prejudice and fears of job competition had resulted in passage of the Chinese Exclusion Act of 1882, which had curtailed Chinese immigration to the United States. Nonetheless, as a rising power in the Pacific, the United States was a growing force in the Asian balance of power. Americans were seen by many Chinese as distant friends who might be called on for help against the nearby enemy, imperial Japan. Chinese hopes for American help became more urgent after Japan took advantage of the First World War in Europe to seize German concessions in the Shandong Peninsula and to impose a list of Twenty-One Demands in 1915.

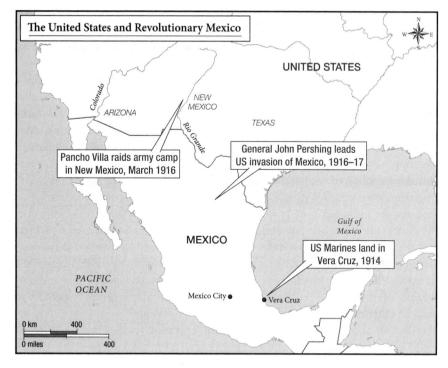

The United States and Revolutionary Mexico

UNITED STATES

NEW MEXICO

ARIZONA

TEXAS

Rio Grande

Pancho Villa raids army camp in New Mexico, March 1916

General John Pershing leads US invasion of Mexico, 1916–17

Gulf of Mexico

MEXICO

US Marines land in Vera Cruz, 1914

PACIFIC OCEAN

Mexico City ●

● Vera Cruz

0 km   400
0 miles   400

MAP 5.1

The United States and Revolutionary Mexico

If China was far away, revolution in Mexico was closer to home. The origins of the Mexican Revolution lay in rising conflict among Mexican elites, but events rapidly evolved into the first great social revolution of the twentieth century. Like other agrarian societies undergoing uneven development, Mexico was thrown into turmoil by foreign capital that came in to build railroads, extract minerals, and modernize agriculture. This produced conflicts between older landed and clerical elites and newer urban-industrial classes pushing their way to the top. Unlike narrow factional rivalries in other Latin American republics, Mexican power struggles represented conflicts among deeper social forces of landowners and peasants, indigenous communities, fledgling industrialists, and industrial workers.

During the long dictatorship of Porfirio Díaz (1876–1910), Mexican elites had welcomed outside investment. The British had invested heavily in Mexico, but increasingly, Germany and the United States challenged British dominance in Mexico. American capital poured into the Mexican industries of oil, railroads, and copper, helping to lift Mexico out of the bottom tier of the world economy.

But economic development did not bring political stability. To the contrary, it led to the overthrow of Díaz in 1910 by local landowners and business leaders such as Francisco Madero who resented outside investors. In the revolution that ensued, elites overthrew Díaz and made Madero the first president of the new regime. But conservatives and militarists soon toppled and executed Madero, who had unleashed social forces that even he failed to appreciate.

By 1915, the middle classes were looking to Venustiano Carranza to bring a new order that would be less corrupt and more democratic than the old Díaz dictatorship or the brief military rule of Victoriano Huerta (1913–14). At the same time, lower classes were lining up behind more radical leaders. Peasants in Morelos, south of Mexico City, followed the charismatic figure Emiliano Zapata in burning *haciendas* (estates), while in Chihuahua and Sonora in the north, peasant armies followed the flamboyant Pancho Villa, roaming the countryside and shutting down mines. Unlike Chinese warlords, these "men on horseback" were not just seeking their own power, but also were trying to harness social forces to change the Mexican political system. Middle classes sought constitutional government, peasants wanted their own land, and industrial workers demanded better working conditions and a share of wealth. From these conflicts came the Constitution of 1917, which contained some of the most advanced social and economic ideals of the day, including the eight-hour day and national ownership of oil and other natural resources.

It was impossible for Americans to ignore the tumult south of the border. With millions invested in Mexico and a large Mexican population in the southwestern states, some kind of U.S. response was all but inevitable. Although U.S. Marines landed at Vera Cruz in April 1914, border skirmishes continued. In March 1916, for example, the Mexican general Pancho Villa staged a cross-border raid on an army camp in southern New Mexico in an effort to embarrass the Carranza government in Mexico City by baiting Wilson to intervene.

After eighteen Americans were killed, along with over seventy Villa supporters, Wilson took the bait and sent in General John J. Pershing to track down Villa and otherwise influence the Mexican Revolution. Pershing had acquired the nickname Black Jack while leading African American troops in Cuba, and within a few months he would be commander of the American Expeditionary Forces in Europe. For the time being, Pershing led a search for Villa that took U.S. troops ever deeper into Mexican territory. But clashes with troops loyal to Carranza only raised a storm of patriotic objection to Yankee imperialism. In the end, Wilson withdrew U.S. troops from Mexico, turning his attention toward much bigger conflicts raging across the Atlantic.

WAR AND REVOLUTION IN EUROPE

If revolution was unexpected in peasant societies, it was widely anticipated in the developed societies of Europe. For decades, self-conscious revolutionaries of many stripes had plotted the overthrow of established authority. East European nationalists sought national independence. Marxist parties organized to end the reign of emperors and capitalists. Anarchosyndicalists and sexual radicals dreamed of abolishing bourgeois property and patriarchal authority in one fell swoop. These revolutionary movements had been waylaid by nationalist fervor in the beginning of the First World War, but by 1917 war weariness was opening the door to renewed social conflict.

People's Peace and the Bolshevik Revolution

The door burst open in Russia with the overthrow in March 1917 of the tsar, Emperor Nicholas II. With the ouster of Tsar Nicholas, the once mighty Romanov dynasty that earlier generations of revolutionaries had failed to topple and a generation of liberals had failed to reform collapsed overnight. The fundamental causes of the revolution in Russia lay in social and economic tensions between the privileged aristocracy of the old regime and rising groups of urban merchants, militant industrial workers, and discontented peasants. On top of these tensions of uneven development, defeat in World War I by German armies, food shortages, and demoralization among soldiers and civilians alike left the tsar with precious little support.

After the abdication of Tsar Nicholas, liberals and moderate socialists quickly formed the Provisional Government. As a symbol of the effort to bring Russia into the modern world, the old Julian calendar was dropped in favor of the Gregorian calendar that had been used elsewhere in the Western world for over three centuries, moving the date of the revolution from February to March.

The March Revolution inspired renewed demands for social and political justice elsewhere in Europe. The clearest sign of rising discontent was the movement for a people's peace to end World War I. Beginning in the spring of 1917, radical groups on both sides of the battle lines began reaching out to one another. If governments refused to make peace, then the people would have to do it themselves. The movement for a people's peace took inspiration from the St. Petersburg Soviet (council), which called for a peace settlement "without annexations or indemnities." In Britain, leftists and reformers formed the Union of Democratic Control to push for a revision of war aims along these lines. France had a similar movement and major mutinies by its own troops that amounted to a virtual strike by the French Army following the disastrous 1917 Nivelle Offensive. Even in Germany, the left wing of the Social Democratic Party led by Rosa Luxemburg and Karl Liebknecht showed support by calling for immediate peace negotiations.

These antiwar efforts coalesced around a proposed people's peace conference to be held in neutral Stockholm, Sweden, in September 1917. But the warring governments, which by this time included the United States, vigorously opposed the plans and the conference never took place. Among the disappointed were Louise Bryant and John Reed, who had traveled to Stockholm to attend.

Governments may have been able to block grass-roots peacemaking, but they could not stifle popular desires for radical change. As earlier enthusiasm for war turned sullen, there was renewed interest in social and political transformation. Leaders of the oppressed nations of Eastern Europe, such as the frequently imprisoned Polish militiaman Josef Pilsudski and the eloquent Czech spokesperson Jan Masaryk, made the rounds of Western capitals to line up support for postwar independence. In Britain and the United States, organized labor won unprecedented influence in the national government through such innovations as the U.S. National War Labor Board, which mediated labor disputes, often to the benefit of trade unions. Division among elites normally presents subordinate groups with an opportunity to advance their various causes, and the world war was no exception.

In Russia, the Bolshevik wing of the Russian Social Democratic Party embraced popular demands with the slogan "peace, land, bread." The slogan captured the hopes of the masses as Bolsheviks won support among workers and soldiers. Indeed, many Russian soldiers defied their officers by throwing down their weapons and deserting the battlefield in droves. Despite the best efforts of Kerensky's Provisional Government to bolster fighting spirits, the shrinking of Russian armies meant the collapse of the eastern front. Sensing another revolution in the East and hoping to facilitate the process, German military authorities gave Bolshevik leader Vladimir Lenin safe passage in a sealed rail car from his exile in Switzerland to a tumultuous Russia.

Bolsheviks continued to gain power in the fall of 1917. Strikes and demonstrations rocked St. Petersburg and Moscow, while peasants seized land in the countryside. With the central government losing the ability to command its own armies, the situation was ripe for insurrection by a disciplined group of political warriors. As if on cue, on November 7, 1917, Bolsheviks stormed the Winter Palace in St. Petersburg, the headquarters of the Provisional Government, and seized the reins of power. What would later turn into a terribly bloody struggle for power began as a coup d'etat.

The next day, November 8, at the assembly of the All-Russian Congress of Soviets, V. I. Lenin told the cheering throng, "Let us proceed to the construction of the new socialist order." In its first formal act, the new Bolshevik government issued a Decree on Peace vowing to end Russia's participation in World War I. Before long, the fledgling government issued a Decree on Land granting peasants title to land (only temporarily, as it turned out) and other decrees benefiting wageworkers. Three weeks later, the Bolsheviks embarrassed the Allies by publishing the secret treaties uncovered in the tsar's archives, which laid out the proposed division of imperial spoils. Those on hand to witness these events, including John Reed and Louise Bryant, knew they had seen a remarkable series of events that, in Reed's words, "shook the world."

Wilson versus Lenin

The revolution in Russia attracted international attention. European leftists rejoiced at the first successful revolution in a major European society since the liberal revolutions of 1848 and drew comparisons to the great French Revolution of 1789. Although Communism (the term came into common usage in 1919) would soon become a highly polarizing ideology in world politics, for the time being most leftists, including the American Socialist Eugene Debs and even many Progressive reformers, welcomed the Bolshevik Revolution as a harbinger of world peace and economic democracy.

To counter the appeal of Communist revolution, Western liberals such as Woodrow Wilson dusted off the idea of *liberal* revolution. His manifesto of change was the Fourteen Points. Seeking to beat Lenin at his own game, Wilson proposed peace terms on January 8, 1918, as a counter to the Bolshevik Decree on Peace of the previous November in which Lenin and other Bolshevik leaders, including Leon Trotsky, called for peace through self-determination. Wilson's aim was to define Allied war aims in a way that would win over the forces behind the peoples' peace movement and bolster the Allied will to go on fighting.

The actual terms of the Fourteen Points were surprisingly measured. There was no battle cry of freedom for oppressed peoples, no summons to social justice, no vision of human community. Instead, there was a proposal for "freedom of the seas," a call for open markets, a vague appeal for arms reduction, and a detailed proposal for boundary lines for the nations and would-be nations of Europe. Although Wilson stopped short of calling for self-determination (this phrase appeared in a later speech known as the Four Points address), he did raise the rights of colonial subjects. In point five of the fourteen, Wilson declared that in settling questions of colonial sovereignty, "the interests of the populations concerned must have equal weight with the equitable claims of the government." In addition, Wilson proposed a new concert of nations to replace the old balance of power, the only one of the Fourteen Points that truly promised what Wilson later called a new world order.

Yet despite such measured language, the Fourteen Points captured the imagination of people around the world yearning to believe that wartime sacrifice might somehow produce a better world. Oppressed nations, exploited classes, and even colonial subjects saw their own fondest hopes reflected in Wilson's Fourteen Points. Anticolonial activists in colonial capitals from Cairo to Seoul drew strategically on Wilson's rhetoric to advance their own nationalist movements. Although both Lenin and Wilson supported the principle of self-determination, many in the colonial world gravitated toward Wilson's vision, especially as Lenin was weakened by a developing civil war in Russia between revolutionaries and counterrevolutionaries. With Wilson's Fourteen Points, the Western media proclaimed that the exhausted public had received nothing less than a charter of liberation. In response, wartime morale improved and the fighting went on. In that sense, the Fourteen Points had an immediate effect.

Over the ensuing two years, Wilson and Lenin became rivals on the world stage. The two leaders had much in common because both were intellectuals in politics driven by ideological fervor: for Wilson, it was a faith in humanity's democratic destiny; for Lenin, it was a belief in the inevitable triumph of Socialism. The fact that they believed so fervidly in their respective missions to redeem humanity served them well for the world-historical role they were being called on to play.

Separate Peace and Allied Intervention

Political differences between Russia and the Allies eventually led them to part ways. Under the direction of Leon Trotsky, the Russian foreign minister and Red Army chief, the Bolsheviks were negotiating a separate peace with the Germans. Beset by myriad enemies at home, they put the defeat of Russian counterrevolutionaries, known as the White Russians, ahead of defeating German autocracy. In the Treaty of Brest–Litovsk concluded in March 1918, Trotsky was forced to cede huge swaths of the tsar's empire in Eastern Europe to the Germans, while also recognizing the independence of Ukraine and Poland.

To the Allies, Russia's separate peace was an unforgivable betrayal. As they feared, Germany immediately shifted armies from the east to the western front and began their last great offensive in March. But the Germans soon discovered that many of their troops slated for transfer from the Russian front to the Western forces had become "infected" by Bolshevik propaganda. The revolutionary virus unleashed by their shipment of Lenin to the east was now striking close to home. In response to Russia quitting the war, the Allies sent joint forces into the vast Russian landscape with the intention of reopening the eastern front starting with British and U.S. troops at Archangel and Murmansk near the Arctic Circle in the north.

What began as an Allied war measure aimed at weakening the German armies, however, soon turned into an attempt to reverse the Bolshevik Revolution. When the Armistice of November 1918 removed the original justification for intervention, Winston Churchill, the future British prime minister, simply called for a shift in the mission to "strangle the Bolshevik infant in its cradle." But as outsiders, the Allied forces garnered little support from the Russian people, and the whole counterrevolutionary enterprise collapsed because the White Russians proved incapable of defeating the Reds.

Just as the United States was concerned about growing Russian power in this period, it was also alarmed by the rising power of Japan. Since its victory over China in 1895 and Russia in 1904–5, Japan had been on a path of expansion on the Asian mainland. Now, seeking to exploit the weakness that had forced the Bolsheviks to sign the Treaty of Brest–Litovsk, Japan sent seventy-five thousand troops to take over the eastern terminus of the Trans-Siberian Railway and the warm-water port of Vladivostok. There they met a much smaller contingent of eight thousand U.S. troops, which were in eastern Russia as much to keep an eye on the Japanese as to check the Red Army.

The Allied intervention in the Far East recalled the effort in 1900 of essentially the same powers—the United States, Japan, Britain, and France—to suppress the Chinese Boxers. But unlike the Boxer Rebellion, the Russian Revolution was no nativist affair. It was a vast mobilization of forces against both antiquated supporters of the tsar and foreign invaders. Eventually, Americans went home in 1920 and the Japanese two years later.

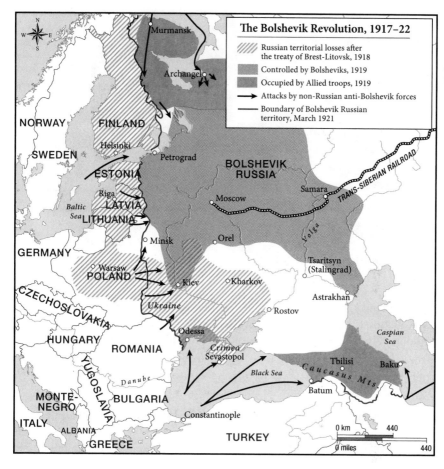

The Bolshevik Revolution, 1917–22

///// Russian territorial losses after
the treaty of Brest-Litovsk, 1918

Controlled by Bolsheviks, 1919

Occupied by Allied troops, 1919

→ Attacks by non-Russian anti-Bolshevik forces

— Boundary of Bolshevik Russian
territory, March 1921

MAP 5.2

1919: Millennial Moment

The end of the war in November 1918 began a period of hope for a new day. Oppressive empires had been toppled in Germany, Austria-Hungary, and Russia, although a new Soviet empire was in the making. A year earlier, the Bolsheviks had begun distributing land to peasants and power to the Soviets. In 1919, the Bolshevik ideas spread westward in the form of short-lived Communist regimes in Hungary and the German state of Bavaria. Meanwhile, British leaders had promised a "land fit for heroes" and a "war to end all wars." Even President Wilson stated, on his way to the Versailles Peace Conference, "liberalism must be more liberal than ever before, it must even be radical, if civilization is to escape the typhoon."

Real changes inspired millennial dreams of abolishing all forms of oppression, whether of class, gender, race, or nation, and bringing about a utopia where,

The "Big Four" in Paris at the World War I Peace Conference, May 27, 1919. Picture left to right: Prime Minister David Lloyd George, Premier Vittorio Orlando, Premier Georges Clemenceau, and President Woodrow Wilson.
Photo by Edward Jackson, Bain Collection. Library of Congress Prints and Photographs Division, Washington, DC.

in the language of the Bible, "the first shall be last and the last shall be first." Under the battle cry "No bosses in the factory, no masters in the home," radicals envisioned with Emma Goldman the simultaneous crumbling of capitalism and patriarchy. When leftists rose to sing the "*Internationale*," the anthem of international socialism, they struck a tone of radical change in singing, "the earth shall rise on new foundations, we have been naught we shall be all."

But it was not only leftists who held millennial dreams. Long-suffering peoples looked for final deliverance in one Promised Land or another. Jewish Zionists dared to hope for a return to the Holy Land on the strength of the Balfour Declaration, a promise by the British government to convert Palestine into a Jewish homeland. The fact that the British promised the same territory to Arabs prompted the witticism that Palestine was "a much promised land." Meanwhile, colonial peoples were inspired by Wilson's promises of self-determination. Nationalist movements gained strength in the British colonies of Egypt and India, as well as in Ireland, where the rebel group Sinn Fein combined the goal of national independence with plans for the reconstruction of society on a more equal foundation.

In this fervid atmosphere New Negro activists, artists, and intellectuals refused to accept second-class treatment. Marcus Garvey, the Jamaican-born prophet of the back-to-Africa movement, prophesied the advent of a new day when Africa would be for Africans, not for white colonialists. Dreams of a black empire in Africa and of fair treatment in home communities in the Americas attracted a broad variety of followers from Panama to New York who made the Universal Negro Improvement Association's estimated two million followers the largest mass movement in the history of the African diaspora. And the young leaders of color Mohandas Ghandi and Ho Chi Minh called on Wilson to support independence for their peoples in India and Indochina still held captive by Western imperialism.

Love and Revolution

The millennial atmosphere of 1919 rekindled the long-simmering revolt against patriarchal authority. Sexual rebels attacked conventional morality in the cabarets of Berlin and the freethinking parlors of St. Petersburg. Communists were at the forefront of this movement. The Russians adopted feminist policies in the form of equal suffrage, the right to sue for divorce, communal kitchens, and state-sponsored children's nurseries. Many of these measures were associated with Alexandra Kollontai, the first woman to be elected commissar (government minister), who espoused a new morality of free marital unions based on love freely given rather than on the property bond of bourgeois marriage. Never before in any country had the idea of free love received the sanction of a government ministry.

Kollontai's bold ideas about free love, state-run nurseries, and social justice were a Communist version of the fully emancipated New Woman that attracted radicals far and wide. The search for freer forms of love through revolution brought romantic revolutionaries such as John Reed and Louise Bryant to the Soviet Union. More moderate reformers in the West were also spurred by Communist experiments to renew their demands for *mothers' pensions* (state aid to single mothers), birth control, and the repeal of obscenity statutes. In a phrase that captured the intertwining of class and gender, as well as the overthrow of capitalism and the revolt against Victorian morality, the U.S. writer Max Eastman entitled his autobiography *Love and Revolution.*

In another sign of the assault on patriarchal authority, women's suffrage became law in Communist Russia as well as capitalist Britain and the United States. Although the United States boasted the oldest movement for women's suffrage in the world going back to the Seneca Falls Convention of 1848, suffrage did not arrive throughout the country until a grateful nation acknowledged women's wartime public service. During the war, Congress had adopted the Nineteenth Amendment, named the Anthony Amendment in tribute to the crusader for women's rights, Susan B. Anthony. With final acceptance in the Tennessee legislature, three-quarters of the states ratified the amendment just in time to permit women to vote in the federal election of 1920.

SEARCH FOR ORDER

The story of revolutionary change would not be complete without looking at opposing, counterrevolutionary efforts to reestablish order. Western leaders felt besieged by a host of challenges, including discontent in Germany, disorders in Eastern Europe, factory occupations in Italy, mass strikes and race riots in the United States, and the ongoing revolution in Russia. Seeking to quell these disturbances, they resorted to a combination of reform and repression.

Versailles Peace Conference

The victors of the First World War knew that reestablishing order depended on a successful peace settlement. As diplomats gathered outside Paris in January 1919 at the Versailles Palace, the resplendent home of the old Bourbon kings of France, they felt they were in a race against time to put the world back together before disorder became endemic.

Standing out among the Allied nations represented at Versailles were the so-called Big Three. The first was British Prime Minister David Lloyd George, who hoped to negotiate a balance of power on the European continent while enhancing British imperialism overseas. The second was Georges Clemenceau, known as the Tiger, the aging French premiere who symbolized the old diplomacy of power politics and who left no doubt about his desire to extract the maximum penalty from the vanquished foe. The third was Woodrow Wilson, symbol of an opposing new diplomacy who arrived almost as a messiah bearing the hopes of millions around the world for what he called a new world order based on democracy, open diplomacy, and self-determination. Despite their differences, these three men were expected to come up with a settlement that would restore peace and tame the revolutionary impulse.

The first order of business was Germany. When the Germans signed the armistice, they expected to have a seat at the peace table, but in a fateful decision even before the conference began, the victors chose to exclude Germany from the deliberations. Contrary to Wilson's earlier proposal for a magnanimous peace without victory, the Versailles Treaty as completed in June 1919 turned out to be a peace dictated by the victors. Pinning war guilt entirely on Germany, the treaty imposed hefty reparations payments, returned Alsace-Lorraine to France, demilitarized the Rhineland (the military zone from which Germany launched invasions of Belgium and France), and capped the German army at one hundred thousand troops. Rather than build a people's peace, Versailles imposed both annexations and indemnities and thereby sowed the seeds of future German resentment.

A second task was to deal with the ongoing threat of revolution, which had done so much to bring about the war in the first place. As good bourgeois gentlemen, the Big Three were as fearful of social upheaval as they were faithful to the principle of nationalism. Confronted with what Wilson called the typhoon blowing out of Bolshevik Russia, Wilson joined with Lloyd George and Clemenceau to put down revolution. In addition to sending troops into Russia until June 1920 to weaken the infant Communist regime, the Big Three sponsored the creation of half a dozen new nations in Eastern Europe as a *cordon sanitaire* (safety belt) stretching from the Baltic republics in the north through Poland and Czechoslovakia to Yugoslavia in the south. The idea was to erect a barrier against the westward spread of Communism. Nationalism had overcome Socialist internationalism at the start of World War I. After the war, the Big Three made good on Wilson's promise of self-determination and turned the passions of nationalism against the threat of Socialism.

A third major task was to create a new international framework to keep the peace. Here, too, nationalism was the guiding principle behind the establishment of the League of Nations. In Wilson's view, the league was supposed to represent the concert of nations, that is, the general interest of the international community, as against the narrow self-interest of any single nation. When an aggressor disturbed the peace, Wilson asserted, the world community should band together in *collective security*. Yet using nation-states as the basic building blocks created a league where national interests prevailed over common interests.

One major item missing from the Big Three's agenda was colonial independence. In contrast to the disappearance of the empires of the vanquished, the empires of the victors took on new life. At the Paris Peace Conference, colonial independence movements in Egypt, India, and the world over seized on the idea of self-determination and appealed to Wilson for support. The Chinese scholar and reformer Kang Youwei echoed the hopes of many when he wrote that the League of Nations could end foreign meddling and "support the weak and small countries."

Yet many anticolonial movements had their hopes dashed when the victors reasserted control in the colonies with Wilson's tacit support. Under the Mandate System of the League of Nations, Britain and France divided up the Middle East, much as they had planned to do in the Sykes–Picot treaty. With the Balfour Declaration, they promised a Jewish homeland on territory that local Arabs had lived on for centuries, a fateful decision with portentous consequences. Britain and France also occupied all the German colonial holdings in Africa. Something similar happened in Asia. After seeming to back China's plaintive calls for Western help in repelling the Japanese, the Big Three instead acceded to Japan's seizure of China's Shandong Peninsula. Such frustrations in the struggle for self-determination after the First World War laid the groundwork for future liberation movements, as in China under Mao Zedong. If there was an exception to this pattern, it was Ireland, where all but the northern counties of Ulster won independence from Britain in 1922.

POSTWAR DISORDERS

The diplomats left Versailles in June 1919 believing they had put things back in order, but events proved otherwise. Violent disorders persisted. In Central Europe, for example, the new Weimar Republic got off to a shaky start. Resting on a coalition of liberals and socialists brought to power by the German Revolution at the end of the war, the Weimar Republic was opposed from the start by right-wing groups who concocted the story of a civilian stab in the back to account for Germany's defeat. One of these groups was the *Freikorps*, former soldiers devoted to a cult of violence. Another was the National Socialist Workers Party (Nazi Party) led by a young Adolf Hitler, a disgruntled Austrian veteran of the German Army. In November 1923, Hitler attempted to seize power in what was dubbed the Beer Hall Putsch in Munich, only to land in jail, where he spent his time writing the Fascist manifesto *Mein Kampf* (my struggle).

Italy, too, found itself divided between leftist workers who organized a series of factory occupations in 1919 and bellicose Fascists on the right. Benito Mussolini, a one-time Socialist newspaper editor turned right-wing agitator, directed his Blackshirt brigades to beat up opponents and in 1922 led a paramilitary March on Rome that overthrew the Italian government. It was the first successful Fascist coup d'etat. It would not be the last.

There was also a rightward turn among Western European intellectuals. For example, conservative pessimism informed Oswald Spengler's influential *The Decline of the West*, published in 1918 just as his native Germany was undergoing defeat. In France, Charles Maurras's work exemplified much of the French right's infatuation with anti-Semitism and early-stage Fascism. In addition, books like *The Revolt of the Masses* (1930) by the Spanish philosopher Ortega y Gasset exemplified the spread of antidemocratic ideas.

Unsettled as things were in Central Europe, there was even greater turmoil in the East. Having seized power, the Bolsheviks faced mounting opposition and could only hold on to power through violent means. On top of civil war between Red revolutionaries and White counterrevolutionaries, Russia fought a brutal war with Poland over territory lost at Brest–Litovsk. More Russians died in these conflicts that in the First World War itself. Added millions perished in the famine growing out of ongoing economic disaster.

Responding to these terrible circumstances, Lenin abandoned the central controls of war Communism and instituted the more flexible New Economic Policy in 1921, which allowed for more private ownership and market competition. He also sought famine relief from the West through Herbert Hoover, the U.S. secretary of commerce who had won an international reputation as a great humanitarian for organizing Belgian relief. Now Hoover bolstered that reputation by arranging food deliveries to starving Russians.

In Asia, the Versailles Treaty itself was a source of discord. In acceding to the Japanese seizure of Shandong, the Big Three set off an explosion of Chinese nationalism. Outrage over the Japanese occupation of Chinese territory boosted the fortunes of the Guomindang, or Nationalist Party, which had been established in the early stages of the Republican Revolution and which would become the major political party in the country in the 1920s. Meanwhile, patriotic students organized the May 4th movement in 1919 to protest mistreatment, and anger over Western betrayal led some to turn toward the Soviet Union and form the Chinese Communist Party in 1923. Chinese reactions to Versailles helped open a new phase of the ongoing Republican revolution where two main forces—nationalists and Communists—would contend for power until the Communists finally won out in 1949.

Disorder in the United States

Although revolution did not come to the United States, Americans were rattled by these postwar developments. A set of epic clashes along class and ethnic lines left the country divided between capital and labor, native and immigrant, Right and Left, Euro-American and African American. These conflicts grew even more intense in the context of turmoil overseas. Sending "doughboys" to fight in Europe had opened up U.S. borders in unsettling ways, and now as postwar events spun out of control, many Americans felt they had won the war but lost the peace. Instead of producing American-style democracies overseas, the war had given birth to political disorder, civil war, and Bolshevism. As a result, the call went out to seal the borders, purge the country of foreign influences, and suppress radical dissent.

A major fault line ran between labor and capital in the postwar period. Seeking union recognition and improved conditions, workers in 1919 mounted the largest strikes in U.S. history. The number of strikers rivaled the size of wartime armies—365,000 steelworkers, 400,000 coal miners—and in some cases, notably, the Socialist-led garment workers and the Seattle General Strike, labor actions were infused with radical ideas. For their part, corporate leaders forcibly opposed workers' demands, blamed foreign radical influences, whether present or not, and brought in a battery of police, militia, and U.S. soldiers to put down the strikes.

Overlapping the class divide, another fault line opened between ethnic groups. Whereas many workers had roots in Italy, Poland, or Russia, most business leaders descended from Britain or other north European countries. Especially where a British pedigree was in the company of old money, ethnic prejudice and class snobbery took aim at Catholic and Jewish newcomers. Under the nativist banner of 100 percent Americanism, patrician elites supported stringent forms of Americanization and immigration restriction. In addition, many poor and working-class Anglo-Saxon Protestants concerned about dilution of their cultural identity in a nation of immigrants flocked to the Ku Klux Klan. Branching out from its southern origins, the Ku Klux Klan grew in the North and Midwest to claim four million members by 1924 in a crusade against Jews, Catholics, African Americans, and radicals.

Although America had its own long history of ethnic conflict and assimilation, 100 percent Americanism accorded with right-wing movements in Europe. Although the American Legion, newly formed by army veterans, was by no means as vicious as European Fascists, it acted in a similar way, agitating against labor and radicals. Like Europe's ultranationalists, American nativists were hostile to foreigners abroad and foreigners at home. Likewise, the Ku Klux Klan was a homegrown paramilitary organization, which terrorized its enemies in ways similar to Mussolini's Blackshirts and Hitler's Brownshirts.

Clashes along the Color Line

Perhaps the deepest ethnic division was the color line. The bipolar division between black and white had long set the United States apart from Europe. No

African Americans march with their hands up on Main Street in Tulsa,
Oklahoma during the Tulsa race riots of 1921. McFarlin Library, University of Tulsa.

period in U.S. history was more disfigured by violent race riots than the years
around the First World War. White mobs went on a rampage in a host of places,
including East St. Louis in 1917, Washington, DC, and Chicago in 1919, and Tulsa
in 1921, where they burned neighborhoods, terrorized residents, and left scores of
African Americans dead, more than one hundred in Tulsa alone.

Although the causal roots of the rioting were buried deep in the history of
American racism, the immediate origins lay in the sense that white privileges
were threatened by conditions arising out of the war. In the Great Migration, half
a million African Americans moved out of the South to northern cities with the
hope of securing a better life. Northern industries sought new sources of labor
as the war made the Atlantic increasingly treacherous to cross and immigration
from Europe sharply declined. Although blacks continued to face discrimination in the North, they could earn higher wages in wartime factories, access
better schools for their children, and vote. Working-class whites confronted with
competition for jobs and housing from newly arriving African Americans often
turned to violence. Resentment against the pride of returning African American
veterans fueled a psychological need in many white Southerners to put these men
"back in their place." This sense of white privilege under assault was the subject
of one of the best-selling books of the postwar period, *The Rising Tide of Color*,
by Lothrop Stoddard.

Blacks in the North responded with an assertiveness embodied in a social
type dubbed the New Negro. The New Negro could be seen in the swelling

membership rolls of the interracial NAACP. The New Negro could also be seen in the growing ranks of the Universal Negro Improvement Association, the black nationalist movement led by Marcus Garvey, which claimed two million members at its peak in 1920–22. Filled with a new spirit of defiance, the New Negro was also evident in the willingness of African Americans to fight back against white mobs. Although most of those who died in the era's race riots were black victims of white gangs or of police and militia called in to restore order, the high death tolls included a significant number of whites.

There were also cultural and ideological challenges to white supremacy. The wartime rhetoric of making the world safe for democracy encouraged the idea of making America itself safe for democracy by removing the stain of racism. Reflecting the spirit of the Harlem Renaissance in the 1920s, Langston Hughes wrote his famous poem, "I, Too, Sing America." A few brave thinkers, such as Franz Boas, had even begun to challenge the very idea that race was a legitimate way to think about divisions in humanity. Finally, there were stirrings of anticolonialism in Africa and Asia that challenged complacent assumptions that rule over dark-skinned peoples was the birthright of light-skinned ones.

Red Scare

Amid the turmoil of strikes and riots after World War I, many Americans feared that the country was about to plunge into revolution. It was true that a tiny number of left-wing Socialists such as John Reed and Louise Bryant had signed up with the Communist International, and a much larger number—perhaps in the millions—called for overturning the patriarchal, capitalist social order. Eugene Debs, for example, garnered 3.4 percent of the popular vote when he ran for president as a Socialist candidate in 1920. But revolutions in complex societies usually require the existing state to lose authority and a new power to arise out of oppressed sectors of society with significant military support. In the absence of such a revolutionary environment in the United States, it was not homegrown radicalism per se that was so disturbing, but the sense that disorder at home was but a local expression of world revolution. Unable to control subordinate groups such as striking workers, Jewish immigrants, and African Americans, dominant groups in the United States often blamed foreign influences.

During the red scare in late 1919 and early 1920, public officials took the lead in fomenting fear of the *red menace*. Instead of following Wilson's prescription for liberalism to become radical, many liberals whipped up the antiradical mob. Faced with a general strike, the mayor of Seattle, Washington, portrayed it as the first act of Bolshevik insurrection in the United States. Warning of red revolution just around the corner, Attorney General A. Mitchell Palmer authorized a series of raids on radical organizations in November 1919, followed by a nationwide crackdown in January 1920 after a second mail bomb sent to his home by anarchists exploded. Palmer ordered the deportation to Russia of a boatload of immigrant radicals, including the anarchist Emma Goldman. Whatever other motives were involved, Palmer hoped to ride the wave of fear into the Democratic presidential nomination. With the same goal on the Republican side, General Leonard Wood led army troops into the streets of striking steel towns in October 1919, making false charges of Communist influence. In the context of the red scare, these and other demagogues used fear for their own political gain.

Inspired by national political leaders, local groups such as the American Legion went on witch-hunts to uncover Communists, real or imagined, in unions and Progressive organizations. Like nativist efforts to relieve economic stress by barring immigrants, the legion sought to restore a pure America by purging the country of the contaminating foreign influence of Bolshevism. The red scare was not aimed so much at actual Communists as at the entire panoply of Progressive reform ideas. Ultraconservatives portrayed the network of women's rights organizations, hardly a hotbed of Bolshevism, as a giant web of Communist conspiracy. They also blamed the race riots on their victims—African Americans. Perhaps the main target were reforms associated with gaining a greater share of wealth and power for working people. The Right denounced minimum-wage legislation, collective bargaining, and even a proposed constitutional amendment to ban child labor as the entering wedge of Communism.

Sacco and Vanzetti

Nothing illustrates the polarization between upper-class Anglo-Saxons and immigrant radicals better than the case of Sacco and Vanzetti. Nicola Sacco and Bartolomeo Vanzetti were Italian-born anarchists living in the Boston area working, respectively, as a shoemaker and fish-peddler. The pair joined a long list of European and Latin American radicals who had found refuge in the United States, including such illustrious figures as Guiseppe Garibaldi from Italy, Johann Most from Germany, José Martí from Cuba, the Flores Magón brothers from Mexico, and Leon Trotsky from Russia. The two Italians were arrested in 1920, convicted of the murder of a payroll guard, and sentenced to die in the electric chair.

However, leftists and legal experts, including the future Supreme Court Justice Felix Frankfurter, raised compelling questions about the fairness of the proceedings. There was ample evidence of antiradical and anti-Italian prejudice in the courtroom of Judge Webster Thayer, a Boston patrician, and the case soon became an international cause célèbre with mass protests from Buenos Aires to Paris, pictured on the following page. Despite appeals from foreign governments and even the Pope, the Anglo-Saxon elite of Massachusetts closed ranks to deny all appeals and the two were executed in 1927. Outraged at the executions, leading novelist John Dos Passos wrote in a bitter epitaph, "All right, we are two nations."

The Resurgence of Patriarchy

Cutting across polarities of class and culture were divisions over gender roles. After a period when women's emancipation made great strides, above all in

Protest in Paris of the Sacco and Vanzetti ruling. Tulsa Race Riot Archive, 1989.004, Department of Special Collections and University Archives, McFarlin Library, The University of Tulsa. Tulsa, Oklahoma.

the right to vote, a patriarchal reaction gained steam in the early 1920s putting feminism on the defensive everywhere in the world. Patriarchy had always been strong in much of southern Europe and the whole of Asia and Africa, where the fledgling women's movement made few advances against customary male privilege in the family, workplace, and public life. Likewise, in Latin America the cultural traditions of *machismo* (honor-bound masculinity) and *marianismo* (glorification of motherhood) left little room for gender equality. As a consequence, women's suffrage came late to Latin America. Not until the 1930s did women gain the right to vote in a few Latin American countries, and most had to wait until the 1940s and 1950s to win equal political rights.

Patriarchal reaction was even more severe where the trauma of war gave rise to virulent forms of masculinity. Italy's Benito Mussolini, for example, asserted an aggressive kind of masculinity, demanding that Italian women confine themselves to motherhood and leave public affairs to men. In a message to a Fascist women's organization, he instructed its agents, "Go home and tell the women I need births, many births." Masculine swagger was even more integral to German Fascism. Extreme in its misogynist hatred of independent women, the Nazis sought to eliminate women from all positions of authority and confine them to the realm of *kinder, kuchen, und kirche* (children, kitchen, and church) where they would be back under the thumb of male authority.

Against this backdrop, supporters of gender equality the world over looked to the bright light of American feminism. Women in America made significant advances in the early twentieth century. After the Nineteenth Amendment went into effect in 1920, feminists called for expanded equality, debating the merits of a possible Equal Rights Amendment to the Constitution. And, over the course of the first three decades of the twentieth century, women increasingly secured white-collar jobs, with 44 percent of women workers employed in the sales, clerical, managerial, and professional fields by 1930. Yet prejudice against "the weaker sex" continued to keep women out of most positions of authority at work and in public life. Meanwhile, split images of women as either nurturing mothers or sexual vixens limited the range of role models, while commercial advertising served to reinforce confining stereotypes of the dutiful housewife. Although women in the United States made significant gains in this period, they were also restricted by the reassertion of traditional male authority.

RETREAT FROM REFORM

Under the combined assaults of nativism, racism, and the red scare, American reformers struggled to advance their causes. This period saw several retreats from reform along class and ethnic lines. With respect to labor legislation, the end of the war emergency reduced the need for labor peace, and key federal agencies such as the National War Labor Board were dismantled. As a result, instead of sending in government mediators during the series of major strikes from 1919 through 1922, the federal government reverted to strikebreaking and sent in the army. In addition, the Supreme Court overturned one piece of progressive social legislation after another, including laws for the abolition of child labor, maximum hours, and minimum wages for women workers. Reflecting the conservative turn in American politics, Warren G. Harding proclaimed during his campaign for the White House in 1920, "America's present need is not heroics, but healing; not nostrums, but normalcy; not revolution, but restoration."

There was a similar rollback of reform in immigration policy. In contrast to the optimism of the prewar period when Progressives had championed immigrant contributions to American life, nativism now dominated. Nativist hostility to foreigners and panic over the red menace reached a fever pitch in 1921 with congressional passage of a bill intended to stop the flow of so-called undesirable races from southern and Eastern Europe. The bill established a quota system that set a maximum number of immigrants allowed in from each country based on the percentage of the group counted in the 1910 census. When that failed to halt the tide of immigration, Congress tightened the restrictions in the 1924 National Origins Act, first by moving the census date back to 1890 before most of the new immigrants had arrived and then by directing the Census Bureau to determine the national origins of the current U.S. population and apportion quotas accordingly. In an added expression of racial hierarchies, the National Origins Act also excluded all who were "ineligible to citizenship," a measure that effectively prohibited all immigration from Asia.

Racial ideologies in this period were supported by the "science" of eugenics. Originally dating back to the 1880s, the pseudoscience of human breeding gained prominence on both sides of the Atlantic in the 1920s. Negative eugenics involved suppressing the births of the supposedly undesirable through sterilization and education, whereas positive eugenics involved promoting the births of the desirable. The aim was to find what Helene Stocker, the leftist German leader of the Federation for the Protection of Mothers, called "means of preventing the incurably ill or degenerate from reproducing." By no means were all of the proponents of selective breeding on the political right. Along with Stocker, many other prominent reformers embraced eugenics, including Sidney and Beatrice Webb, British Fabian Socialists, and Margaret Sanger, a one-time member of the radical Industrial Workers of the World.

One especially complicated reform measure was Prohibition. To the likes of the Woman's Christian Temperance Union and reformers such as Jane Addams, passage of the Eighteenth Amendment in 1919 prohibiting the production and distribution of alcoholic beverages was worth celebrating. To others, however, such as Samuel Gompers, the head of the American Federation of Labor, Prohibition was oppressive class legislation aimed at keeping the workers from enjoying their leisure as they saw fit. Irish, German, and Italian workers felt especially aggrieved by this policy, which seemed to target their cultural affinity toward whiskey, beer, and wine. In this sense, Prohibition was of a piece with other worker exclusions.

The early 1920s witnessed a retreat from Progressive labor and immigration reform in the United States. The relatively limited social contract that had been put in place during the years of Progressivism and war was all but abrogated. The retreat put the United States somewhat out of step with Europe, where reform hung on. Germany's fledgling Weimar Republic, for example, maintained regulations for women workers, family support payments, unemployment compensation, and a host of other social protections. Britain and France also retained more advanced social legislation, leaving the United States with the most meager package of social protections of any major industrial country.

RETREAT FROM INTERNATIONALISM

Internationalism was also in retreat in the United States. Between the Armistice of November 1918 and the early stages of the Versailles Peace conference in the spring of 1919, the spirit of internationalism had spread around the globe. In the millennial moment when popular imagination was fired by visions of self-determination, social justice, labor rights, and world peace, a host of new organizations advanced international collaboration, including the Women's International League for Peace and Freedom and the International Labour Organization. But, during the summer of 1919, government leaders fell back on the underlying institution of the nation-state. National self-interest, after all, was what elite versions of *inter*nationalism had been based on all along.

Although Wilson had initially envisioned the League of Nations as a harmonious concert of nations, he had subverted his own vision by joining with his diplomatic counterparts to exclude two potential rivals: Germany and the Soviet

Union. Moreover, in supporting the creation of a host of new nations in Eastern Europe, the Big Three were hard-pressed to explain how the prescription of increased nationalism could act as the cure for the disease of national ambition that had done so much to bring about the war in the first place. In short, the pursuit of national self-interest crippled the league from the outset.

Even so, the league might have been more of an international forum with the United States aboard. Immigrant groups in the United States with ties to colonized nations, such as Irish Americans, lent their support to the league. But after bitter debate in the U.S. Senate, American membership was rejected. Debate over ratification of the Versailles Treaty came down to an argument over whether Article 10 committing member states to collective security compromised American sovereignty. While Wilson's defenders insisted the United States would retain freedom of action, critics such as Henry Cabot Lodge, the Republican head of the Senate Foreign Relations Committee, claimed other countries would be deciding whether Americans went to war. The sense that their fate was already too much in the hands of foreigners—the same sentiment that lay behind immigration restriction and the red scare—doomed the treaty to defeat. Facing a disorderly world, American elites retreated to the familiar ground of a strongly nationalist foreign policy.

Partisan politics also played a role in this debate. Woodrow Wilson and Henry Cabot Lodge represented opposing parties and took opposing stands on the league. Wilson was incapacitated by a stroke at the height of the controversy and refused any compromise. At the same time, Lodge and his fellow Republicans intended to use the treaty against the Democrats in the presidential election of 1920. In that aim, they were successful. Refusing to embrace the League of Nations, Republican Warren G. Harding defeated the Democratic candidate in a landslide. Harding's popular campaign slogan, "America first," encapsulated a new conservative politics of isolationism and immigration restriction.

A World Safe for Empire

For different reasons, a group of Progressives also opposed the League of Nations on the grounds that it made the world safe for empire. Progressive internationalists, such as Robert La Follette, a senator from Wisconsin, pointed out that under official mandates of the league, Britain and France actually strengthened their rule over peoples in the Middle East and Africa. These same Progressives did not hesitate to condemn the imperialism of their own country, pointing to the tight grip of the United States on the Caribbean. During the period of revolutionary danger, 1917–21, the United States maintained different forms of military occupation in Cuba, the Dominican Republic, Nicaragua, Panama, and Haiti, while claiming ownership of the Panama Canal Zone and the Virgin Islands and also ruling Puerto Rico (and the Philippines) as colonies. Under the protective watch of marines, U.S. bankers were put in charge of collecting customs and otherwise managing the finances of most of these lands. Seeing secure investment opportunities, U.S. capital poured into the sugar plantations, rail lines, and port facilities of the region. American firms also took advantage of the British government's need to sell many of its Latin American holdings to defray the cost of World War I by acquiring these investments.

Opponents of U.S. empire called for Wilson and his successors to realize the ideal of self-determination. Opposition was violent in the case of Haiti, where *cacos* fought a protracted guerrilla war against U.S. Marines until America withdrew in 1934. Political opponents in the colonies were jailed or sent into exile, and the same was true of certain radical critics with large followings in the United States. Perhaps the most important was Marcus Garvey, whose Pan-African ideas, large Caribbean following, and uncompromising opposition to British and U.S. empires earned him arrest and deportation in 1922. Garvey joined a small group who were not to be trusted with their constitutional rights, including the jailed Socialist Eugene Debs and deported anarchist Emma Goldman.

From the early days of the new imperialism, overseas rule was bound up with ideas of white superiority. Often at odds on other issues, Republicans and Democrats increasingly found common ground when it came to America's empire in the tropics. The otherwise feuding Henry Cabot Lodge and Woodrow Wilson, for instance, agreed on intervention in the Caribbean in the World War I period. The bond of white solidarity extended across the Atlantic to ruling circles in Britain and France, which shared assumptions about the white man's burden of ruling over the world's darker races. Such racial ideologies shaped a double standard of self-determination: European peoples were entitled to it, whereas African, Asian, and Latin American peoples were not.

In the years during after World War I, unity among white elites—both internationally and domestically—kept various civil rights movements from making much progress. Not until after the Second World War would Western elites divide over racism and colonialism, enabling the civil rights movements of that era to drive a wedge between white liberals and white supremacists.

Washington Naval Conference

In this period of war and revolution, the United States remained very much engaged outside its own borders. But instead of pursuing an internationalist path as laid out by Progressive and Socialist reformers, it engaged in the unilateral pursuit of national interests as defined by Washington elites. So it was with U.S. participation in the Washington Naval Conference of 1921–22. Putting aside the Wilsonian idea of a concert of nations, leaders of the major powers brought back the old balance of power. They attempted to stabilize relations among the great powers in a series of treaties with special reference to Asia. Most important was the Five Power Treaty, which carefully calculated the balance of naval warships at the ratio of five to five to three for Britain, the United States, and Japan, respectively, with France and Italy added in at the ratio of one and three-quarters. Because the treaty halted construction of new battleships and reduced the number of large naval vessels—indeed, the treaty was said to have sunk more British ships than the Germans did—it was hailed by pacifists as an important step toward disarmament.

Other agreements at the Washington Conference brought fewer cheers from pacifists. In the Four Power Treaty, the powers agreed to respect each other's interests (that is, colonial possessions) in Asia, which meant the Philippines for the United States and Taiwan and Korea for Japan. In the Nine Power agreement, all the main players in Asia accepted free access to Chinese markets, in effect internationalizing the U.S. Open Door policy. Yet no Chinese representatives were invited to sit at the conference table.

Nationalist engagement overseas points to the error of labeling postwar policy as isolationist. If isolationism is taken to mean disengagement from world affairs, then the United States was anything but isolationist. In pursuing its own interests in the international arena, the United States joined the nationalist trend that had produced the war in 1914.

CONCLUSION

The First World War took place in an age of revolution. Beginning before 1914, uneven development in agrarian societies brought upheaval to Mexico and China, followed by the overthrow of the tsar and the Bolshevik Revolution in Russia. In addition, Europe's ancient continental dynasties—the Hohenzollerns and the Habsburgs—were overthrown at the end of the war. Even in societies like the United States, where there was no possibility of overturning the established order, social movements were able to win victories, namely expanded labor rights during the war and women's suffrage starting in 1920.

In responding to revolution, American elites asserted changing ideas of liberalism. Emerging as a rival to Vladimir Lenin, Woodrow Wilson became a prophet of liberal revolution. When the Versailles Peace Conference convened outside Paris, liberals and nationalists greeted Wilson as a kind of messiah of political freedom and world peace. In this moment, Americans believed that they had the power to spread their version of liberty and free-market capitalism worldwide.

But as world events continued to spin out of control, the bulk of American elites came to regard any hint of revolution as a threat to liberal democracy. Believing that liberty was best preserved within the boundaries of the liberal nation, they suppressed radical ideas, rolled back several Progressive reforms, and sharply curtailed immigration. European elites were forced to concede more to the common people, but on both sides of the Atlantic, rulers were largely successful in reestablishing order and their own preeminence. By the mid-1920s, the revolutionary impulse Reed and Bryant first witnessed in 1917 seemed safely contained and the world entered a vexing yet calm interlude before the next great crisis of the 1930s.

FURTHER READING

Ewing, Adam. *The Age of Garvey: How a Jamaican Activist Created a Mass Movement and Changed Global Black Politics.* Princeton, NJ: Princeton University Press, 2014.

Jacobson, Matthew Frye. *Barbarian Virtues: The United States Encounters Foreign Peoples at Home and Abroad, 1876–1917.* New York: Hill and Wang, 2001.

Manela, Erez. *The Wilsonian Moment: Self-Determination and the International Origins of Anticolonial Nationalism.* Oxford: Oxford University Press, 2009.

Ngai, Mae. *Impossible Subjects: Illegal Aliens and the Making of Modern America.* Princeton, NJ: Princeton University Press, 2003.

Nichols, Christopher McKnight. *Promise and Peril: America at the Dawn of a Global Age.* Cambridge, MA: Harvard University Press, 2011.

Tyrell, Ian. *Reforming the World: The Creation of America's Moral Empire.* Princeton, NJ: Princeton University Press, 2010.

Vitalis, Robert. *White World Order, Black Power Politics: The Birth of American International Relations.* Ithaca, NY: Cornell University Press, 2015.

CHAPTER 6

DEMOCRACY FACES THE GREAT DEPRESSION, 1925–36

Ford Motor Company's iconic River Rouge plant, capable of generating 60 million pounds of steam per day from 2,500 tons of coal, became a symbol of American economic strength by the early 1940s. Photograph by Alfred T. Palmer. Library of Congress Prints and Photographs Division, Washington, DC.

1933: DEPRESSION JOURNEY

In February 1933, Walter Reuther lost his job as a tool and die maker at Henry Ford's River Rouge plant in Detroit, Michigan. It was the very bottom of the Great Depression, and Reuther had no job prospects. So he decided to head to the Soviet Union, where there was plenty of work for young idealists who wanted to build a new Socialist society. Cashing in his savings in the nick of time—his bank soon became one of the record number of failures that winter—he set sail across the Atlantic.

*Departing just as Franklin Roosevelt was about to launch the New Deal,
Reuther arrived in Germany in time to witness the Nazi seizure of power. Dock-
ing in Hamburg, he saw a city in the throes of a near civil war between Nazis
and Communists. Moving on to Berlin, he visited the smoldering ruins of the
Reichstag fire, in which the Nazis used the burning of the German parliament as
a pretext to crack down on Communists. When Nazi paramilitary forces came
in the dead of night, his Berlin host had to escape down a rope ladder.*

*Making a speedy exit from Fascist Germany, Reuther caught a train to
Russia. For the next few years, he worked at the sprawling automobile factory
being constructed in the city of Gorky deep in the Russian interior. Living with
one hundred other Americans in the American Village, he escaped the worst
of Russia's dreary housing conditions and poor food. Despite the hardships, he
reported, "I loved every minute."*

*Although Reuther later became staunchly anti-Communist as the head
of the United Autoworkers Union in the United States, he embraced the Soviet
experiment in the early 1930s because Soviet Communism seemed to be the
main bulwark against Fascism. It also stood out as a viable alternative to the
laissez-faire form of capitalism whose collapse in the Great Depression had sent
him on his pilgrimage in the first place.*

DEMOCRACY FACES THE GREAT DEPRESSION

Reuther's extraordinary journey made him an eyewitness to three of the key
developments in world history in the 1930s: New Deal liberalism, German Fascism, and Soviet Communism. These three systems represented alternative ways
of dealing with the Great Depression that began with the U.S. stock market crash
in 1929 and continued for nearly a decade.

Coming off a period of stability in the late 1920s, democracy fell on hard times
during the Depression. From central Europe to Latin America to Japan, one
country after another took an authoritarian turn in efforts to preserve capitalism and enforce social order. At the extreme, Nazi Germany under Adolf Hitler
imposed totalitarian controls over all forms of social life, from making money to
making babies. In Germany, Italy, and Japan, the authoritarian turn was accompanied by ferocious overseas conquests.

The rise of fascism posed a serious threat to democracy, which had seemed victorious in the First World War. Among the Western democracies, only the United States
devised a Progressive response to the Depression in the form of Franklin Roosevelt's
New Deal. Although the New Deal left much to be desired—it had only mixed results in repairing the failures of capitalism and it excluded most racial minorities
and women from its benefits—it had considerable success in revitalizing democracy.

PEACEFUL INTERLUDE, 1925–29

By the mid-1920s, the world war and wave of revolutions had stopped, counterrevolutionary forces relaxed, and the world entered a short period of relative

calm. Such peace allowed the growth of the world economy and political stability. Elites from both sides of the Atlantic reached international agreements on currency stabilization, arms control, and border security. British financial leaders in particular hoped to restore the lost world of Victorian preeminence and reestablish the gold standard. Other countries followed suit, hoping that stable currencies would promote increased trade, which would, in turn, underwrite political stability.

The American Role in Economic Stabilization

Americans played an important role in this search for stability. Despite the U.S. absence from the League of Nations, internationally minded financiers such as Thomas Lamont of the House of Morgan and Benjamin Strong of the New York branch of the Federal Reserve Bank sounded like Wilsonian internationalists in pointing out the American stake in a Europe prosperous enough to buy American exports and repay American war debts. Influential commerce secretary Herbert Hoover supported their position.

With this in mind, a U.S. delegation joined French, British, and German counterparts in negotiations to reschedule German reparations payments. The result was the Dawes Plan of 1924, named after the Chicago industrialist Charles Dawes, which sought to ease the burden on Germany by stretching out the repayment schedule. In addition, extensive American lending made it possible for Germany to pay in the first place. The result was a triangular flow of capital that began with U.S. loans to Germany, which underwrote German reparations payments to Britain and France, which were thereby able to repay their war debts to Americans. Everything depended on the capital flow from American banks. If U.S. loans dried up, the whole system would fail.

Americans also contributed to diplomatic stability. They took the lead in staging the Washington Naval Conference of 1921–22, which produced a series of treaties establishing limits on ships among the world's major navies with a five to five to three ratio among Britain, the United States, and Japan, respectively (see Chapter 5). Another boost came at the Locarno Conference of October 1925, which readmitted Germany to the family of civilized nations and guaranteed the Franco-German border.

The 1920s was also a period of relative calm in East Asia. After escalating tensions between China and Japan during the First World War, the engine of Japanese territorial expansion stalled, and the country settled into an uneasy period of rule by civilian political parties. Although militants assassinated a high commander with the aim of goading officials into restarting expansion, cooler heads later prevailed, and in 1928 the Tanaka government recognized Chang Kai-shek's Nanjing regime as the legitimate government of China, ending for the time being the threat of war between Japan and China.

International stability was good for the United States. Emerging relatively unscathed from the war, the United States went on to enjoy prosperity after a brief downturn in 1921. From 1922 to 1929, the gross national product increased from $149 billion to $227 billion. During the 1928 presidential campaign, Republican newspaper ads promised "a chicken in every pot, and a car in every backyard," while the president of the reputable American Economic Association foresaw "a permanently high plateau" of stock values. After the catastrophic events surrounding the First World War, the global move toward stability amounted to a peaceful interlude before the next catastrophe of the Great Depression.

New Woman at Bay

This period of relative calm and prosperity posed surprising new challenges for women, ranging from the glorification of motherhood to the retreat of feminist politics. The celebration of Mother's Day—instituted in 1914 by American reformers to honor women's labor—took on a conservative cast as florists, greeting card companies, and patriotic organizations exploited the holiday for their own purposes. In Europe, governments of all political stripes adopted pronatalist policies. Worried about the long-term decline in the French birth rate, the French government issued medals to the most fecund mothers: bronze for five children, gold for ten. While America's liberal traditions blocked direct federal aid to families, the Republican administrations of Harding, Coolidge, and Hoover in the 1920s promoted family formation through a ban on birth control information, which was deemed obscene, and ideological endorsement of self-reliant consumer families.

Yet, the renewed glorification of motherhood in the 1920s did not equal the empowerment of women. To the contrary, women lost autonomy to institutions beyond their control. Just as corporate advertising intruded into the private domain of the home, so the overwhelmingly male profession of obstetrics increasingly took over control of childbirth, another sphere where women had once predominated. Home births attended by a local midwife declined from more than 50 percent in 1900 to less than 15 percent in 1930, whereas hospital births with a physician in charge increased in inverse proportion, reaching 55 percent by 1940. The fact that Europe lagged behind on this medical path—only a quarter of British births took place in hospital in the late 1930s—made the United States seem all the more modern.

Feminism faced strong traditionalist opposition and was everywhere in retreat. In the United States, feminists settled into the privileges of women's suffrage and ceased to dream of revolution. Women activists narrowed their focus to such one-issue campaigns as the Equal Rights Amendment prohibiting sex discrimination, the Child Labor Amendment outlawing child labor, or the Sheppard–Towner Act, which provided federal assistance to mothers and infants. Although activists continued their quest for social justice, they faced resistance from the Supreme Court and political leaders in both Republican and Democratic parties. All this put the New Woman on hold.

With feminism in retreat and social reform blocked, many women activists turned their energies toward the international peace movement. Appalled by the carnage of the First World War, women activists led the largest peace movement in history. Women took the lead in organizing conferences on the "causes and cure of war" and campaigned for the "outlawry of war," gaining international support from pacifist counterparts in Britain and France through such groups as the Women's International League for Peace and Freedom. Reformers celebrated such diplomatic achievements as the Kellogg–Briand Pact (1928), in which the United States and more than a dozen other countries pledged not to use war as an instrument of foreign policy. Advances for the peace movement stood in stark contrast to the retreat from reform in other realms.

Romance of Consumption

Rather than reform the public sphere, many Americans were told to contribute to social progress through private consumption. The master of the assembly line, Henry Ford, had proclaimed, "Mass production requires mass consumption," and advertisers increasingly directed their sales pitch to women. As the queen of home consumption, the happy housewife smiled out from the pages of *The Saturday Evening Post* while pushing a Hoover vacuum cleaner or doing the laundry in a brand new General Electric washing machine. Where once free love was combined with revolutionary hope, now consumer citizens were expected to bestow their love on pop-up toasters and Packard motorcars. In a gentle criticism of the new materialism, F. Scott Fitzgerald gave the title character of *The Great Gatsby* a passion not only for the beautiful and elusive Daisy, but also for a bright yellow automobile. In short, Americans began to indulge in the romance of consumption.

The rise of consumption played on status competition, wish fulfillment, and what the U.S. economist Thorstein Veblen called *conspicuous consumption*. Leading advertising agencies located on New York's Madison Avenue hired psychologists such as Edward Bernays, the son-in-law of Sigmund Freud, to design their ads for maximum impact. Using seductive appeals to narcissism and psychic insecurity, one ad man noted of his mostly female customers, "she must like *herself* better for buying the product."

American Culture Overseas

Postwar American culture increasingly gained influence throughout the world. Wherever people aspired to modern ways of life, American culture appeared as an image of their own future. Especially in terms of popular culture, fun-loving American lifestyles set the standard for what was modern (or *cool* in today's parlance) in Western Europe. In Tokyo, the modern boy and modern girl dressed in casual, American-style clothes on their way to a performance of American jazz. In Latin America, too, U.S. popular culture made significant inroads. Although the Latin elite still looked to France and Spain, the masses were beginning to enjoy such Yankee imports as baseball, chewing gum, and Hollywood movies.

Jazz seemed to make its way everywhere. Combining Spanish, French, Irish, and African influences, the innovative musicians of New Orleans developed an improvisational style as a challenge to traditional musical forms. Dismayed by the bloody wars of their own traditional Western civilization, postwar Europeans were especially receptive to non-Western culture, including the jazz of African American master musicians such as trumpeter Louis Armstrong. Bored with their own hyperrefinement, the younger generation of Europeans embraced the banana-and-grass-skirt dances of Josephine Baker and treated her exotic performances as an art form that was somehow both primitive and modern. In the same vein, writers from abroad closely followed the Harlem Renaissance, a flowering of African American arts and letters with significant African and Caribbean influences exemplified by Alain Locke's *The New Negro* (1925).

Just as the Harlem Renaissance and American jazz reflected transatlantic cultural exchanges, so, too, did Hollywood movies. Europeans looked to Hollywood for a more freewheeling kind of modernity as a replacement for the failings of their own bourgeois and aristocratic traditions. Like Americans themselves, Europeans took to heart Charlie Chaplin, whose comic genius was displayed through his impish screen character, the Little Tramp. Another star with international appeal was Douglas Fairbanks, best known as the swashbuckling Robin Hood.

The fact that Chaplin and Robin Hood were both British imports showed how people, ideas, and cultures flowed in both directions across the Atlantic. The blending of European and U.S. influences was evident in the musical compositions of George Gershwin, the son of Russian Jewish immigrants, who paid homage to postwar Franco-American connections in *An American in Paris* (1928). Meanwhile American expatriate authors did some of their best writing in and about Europe, including Ernest Hemmingway, whose well-received antiwar novel *A Farewell to Arms* (1929) perfectly captured the spirit of postwar disillusionment. Many of the American expatriates who lived in Paris in the 1920s developed a new politics of social democracy that was shaped as much by their time abroad as by their experience of the Depression and the New Deal back in the United States.

At the same time, American culture did not always receive a warm welcome abroad. Prohibition and other forms of American moralism, such as the ban on teaching evolution made famous in the 1925 Scopes trial, had few overseas imitators. Moreover, racism, lynching, and race riots marred America's image abroad. Likewise, the conviction of Niccolo Sacco and Bartolomeo Vanzetti, two Italian anarchists accused by a prejudiced court of murdering a Massachusetts payroll guard, raised a global outcry from Buenos Aires to Rome against what many saw as a gross miscarriage of justice. Indeed, one of the largest of these protests took place not in Boston, but in Paris, where French- and Italian-born radicals mobilized protests outside the U.S. Embassy. To the partisans of this international cause, the 1927 execution of the good shoemaker and the poor fish-peddler, both dedicated revolutionaries, reinforced the image of America as a land of intolerance. By the end of the 1920s, this first red scare had all but erased the nineteenth-century image of America as a refuge for oppressed nationalities and political dissenters.

And yet, the competing image of the United States as a land of progress remained strong. That was clear in the enthusiastic reception given Charles Lindberg when he landed the single-engine *Spirit of St. Louis* in a field outside Paris after the first solo flight across the Atlantic in 1927. In the same year that crowds were demonstrating against the execution of Sacco and Vanzetti, exuberant Europeans flocked to embrace Lucky Lindy as a symbol of American individualism, technical modernity, and transatlantic unity. In fact, the spread of both sets of images—the one repressive and bigoted, the other modern and progressive—showed the varied impact of American culture in the 1920s.

American Model versus Soviet Model

American culture was not the only model competing for attention on the world stage. The Soviet Union also sought to influence people and societies throughout the world. With European prestige in steep decline as a result of the First World War, forward-looking people around the globe increasingly looked either to American market society or Soviet collectivism for ideas about how to organize their own societies.

On the surface, capitalist America and Communist Russia could not have been more different. "The business of America is business," declared President Calvin Coolidge (1923–29), and his blunt assertion was confirmed by the retreat from government regulation and the ascendancy of General Motors, General Electric, and other giant American corporations. Under the watchword of efficiency, large corporations rationalized their operations to boost productivity, while the American middle classes increasingly defined the pursuit of happiness in terms of consumption—on the installment plan. American values centered on equality of *opportunity* to move up the ladder of success. It did not matter how far apart the top rungs were from the bottom. Other peoples may have disapproved of inequality, but the high-production/high-consumption way of life in the United States set the standard for material aspirations around the world.

By contrast, business in the Soviet Union was under state ownership. After abandoning many of the revolutionary aspirations of 1917 and the market reforms of the early 1920s, Stalin imposed a *command economy* where large property was under the direct control of the state. The professed aim was to dismantle capitalist inequality, promote equality of *condition*, and build "Socialism in one country" as a model for others to follow.

In fact, Russia's collectivist social organization appealed to many modernizing elites around the globe who saw in the command economy a quick way to lift their countries out of economic backwardness. Moreover, Asian and

African nations found the Soviet prohibition on all forms of racism from white supremacy to anti-Semitism more appealing than the American system of Jim Crow segregation.

The two rivals had also developed different kinds of empires. It could hardly have been otherwise, given their different geographical positions and political traditions. Whereas the United States was a maritime empire, which preferred informal rule to formal colonialism, the Soviet Union was the heir of the great tsarist land empire, which preferred direct territorial rule. Russia's near neighbors trembled as a result, but more distant countries in Asia and Africa could afford to be friendlier.

Despite these many differences, there were also unexpected similarities between the United States and the Soviet Union. Both systems, for example, were obsessed with production as technocrats embraced the gospel of productivity. Soviet economic planners and U.S. corporate managers outdid one another in driving their engineering and industrial relations departments to ever-greater feats of output. Under the first of a series of five-year plans, Soviet bureaucrats rushed to transform their country from a backward, agrarian society into a modern industrial one. Asked for a definition of Communism, Lenin replied, "Communism is Soviet power plus the electrification of the entire country."

Soviet technocrats studied the time-and-motion techniques of American efficiency expert Frederick Winslow Taylor and imported the technological wonders of Henry Ford's vaunted assembly line. As far as Soviet planners were concerned, anyone with a little Socialist enthusiasm and experience at the Rouge plant, such as Walter Reuther, was welcome in Russia. For their part, U.S. engineers admired Soviet central planning and, especially after the capitalist economy went into free fall in 1929, there was a vogue for *technocracy*, the idea that production should be governed not by the pursuit of profit, but by social needs and the requirements of technical efficiency. In truth, the obsessive materialism in the United States and *dialectical materialism* in the Soviet Union, a Marxist concept that an economic system can develop its own sources of decay even as it expands, had more in common than either side cared to admit.

FROM BOOM TO BUST

After 1929, the stable interlude of the 1920s came to a crashing halt. The years on either side of the economic collapse appeared as different as day and night. Beforehand, economic prosperity underwrote political stability and world peace. Afterward came a global depression, political instability, and the menace of another world war. In retrospect, the 1920s appear out of step with the catastrophic series of events that shaped the first half of the twentieth century, from the start of a world war in 1914 to the bombing of Hiroshima in 1945. The Great Depression of 1929–39 was part of this tumultuous period.

With signs of trouble appearing as early as 1928, the world economy crashed in late 1929 in the worst crisis in the history of capitalism. In October of that year, billions in paper values disappeared onto the floor of the New York Stock Exchange in an avalanche of falling stock prices. By the winter of 1932–33, the economic wreckage could be seen everywhere: record bank failures, unprecedented levels of unemployment, and growing numbers of people hungry and desperate. Ironically, the crash hit hardest the very countries—the United States, Germany, and Japan—that had led the way toward rationalization and higher productivity in the boom years. Now, workers were being laid off in record numbers resulting in unemployment levels between 25 and 30 percent. No matter what the level of social protection for the destitute—higher in Germany, lower in Japan and in Hoover's America—relief agencies everywhere exhausted their resources, leaving starving workers to rummage through garbage cans for food.

Although stunned at first, disaffected workers recovered enough to mount protests by 1932. There were massive marches in Berlin, where Communist demonstrators fought pitched battles with Fascist gangs, and smaller demonstrations in Washington, DC, where thousands of veterans of the First World War camped out on public land demanding early payment of a promised bonus. Despite being peaceful, the Bonus March was rousted by the U.S. Army under orders from President Hoover.

Unemployed workers demonstrating in Columbus, Kansas, 1936. Arthur Rothstein, photographer. Library of Congress Prints and Photographs Division, Washington, DC.

Although economists of different stripes—monetarist, neoclassical, Marxist, Keynesian—disagree on the reasons for the economic collapse, it is clear that something as extensive as the Great Depression had deep-seated causes. Despite the appearance of prosperity, capitalism in the boom years was afflicted by a set of built-in imbalances. One of these lay between country and city. After experiencing a golden period during the First World War, agriculture resumed its long decline and large numbers of family farms lost out to agribusiness. Cash-crop agriculture operated in world markets, and increased efficiency resulting from mechanization and fertilizer drove small producers out of business, while tenants lost ground to large landlords. The impact was greatest in Western Europe and North America, but the Depression also affected market-oriented peasants from rural Mexico to the villages of China.

More important was the imbalance between the capacity to produce and the capacity to consume. In each of the three leading economies—the United States, Germany, and Japan—giant corporations, or corporate groupings called cartels in Germany and *zaibatsu* in Japan, accumulated the lion's share of the proceeds of the higher productivity of rationalized industry. That left workers with too little income to buy all the Model T's and home radios they were producing with ever-greater efficiency, and it left owners with more capital than they could profitably reinvest in new productive facilities. The successful assault on the union movement during the red scare weakened workers' ability to wrest higher wages from their corporate employers. Because Ford's aphorism was true—"mass production requires mass consumption"—that meant that if consumers lacked sufficient purchasing power, a certain portion of capital would stand idle or go into speculative investment. That is what the British economist John Maynard Keynes, the most prominent economist of the mid-twentieth century, had in mind when he said, "this is not a crisis of poverty, but a crisis of abundance."

In fact, the origins of the crisis in the late 1920s can be traced to the movement of capital, especially in the United States into what Herbert Hoover called "an orgy of speculation." The more stock prices rose, the more investors transferred their wealth from production to paper securities. Not only did this create a bubble on the New York Stock Exchange, but also it reduced the flow of U.S. loans to Europe. Given that American banks provided the loans, which German investment houses could use to offset reparations payments to Britain and France, when U.S. banks stopped lending, international capital markets dried up, and the ripple effect produced shutdowns and layoffs.

Similar Responses

One common response to the Depression was *economic nationalism*, where nations sought to secure what they could of the shrinking economic pie. Everyone seemed to have the same impulse toward self-sufficiency, or *autarky*, whether in the command economy of the Soviet Union, the state-controlled system of Nazi Germany, or the preferential trading systems of the British and French empires.

In Latin America, economic nationalism took the form of *import-substitution industrialization*. Responding to the collapse of commodity prices—coffee plummeted from twenty-two cents a pound to eight cents between 1929 and 1931—Latin countries in the bottom tier of the world economy tried to make a virtue of necessity by boosting domestic industry. Since the decline in exports of primary products made it hard for them to pay for industrial imports, leaders in Brazil, Mexico, and Argentina decided to manufacture their own. They achieved some success with economic growth rates higher than in the United States.

The United States moved in the same nationalist direction. Congress raised barriers to imports in the Smoot–Hawley Tariff of 1931, and President Roosevelt withdrew his support of the London Economic Conference, a 1933 gathering of finance ministers aimed at stabilizing international currency exchanges. Although some countries benefited from autarky—Germany, the Soviet Union, and several Latin American countries—the overall result of these policies was to further contract the world economy.

Along with economic nationalism, several nations engaged greater state control of society. Given the different starting points—for example, between liberal America and authoritarian Germany—there was a range of outcomes. Where states were already strong, they grew stronger. The Nazis went furthest in taking full command of social life, but Japanese militarists were not far behind. In Latin America, patriarchal and militarist traditions led to military rule either directly or through civilian "strong men" such as Anastasio Somoza in Nicaragua, Rafael Trujillo in the Dominican Republic, and Fulgencio Batista in Cuba. Even where liberal traditions kept the state relatively weak, as in the United States, the state grew stronger as well. Franklin Roosevelt greatly increased the capacity of the federal government to manage the affairs of business, labor markets, and even families, with programs such as the Agricultural Adjustment Act, the Tennessee Valley Authority, and the Home Owners' Loan Corporation.

Gender and Sexuality

Another broadly similar response to the Depression lay in the patriarchal reaction against women's equality. Efforts to bolster the nuclear family with its stay-at-home-mom intensified in the 1930s. These were partly a response to economic conditions, which left many men unable to fulfill the expectation of providing for their families. In the United States, there was a comparatively mild patriarchal reaction expressed, for example, in social policies that favored male breadwinners. On the faulty assumption that married women were not breadwinners themselves, business and government put severe pressure on women workers to leave the labor force, and many state governments fired women upon becoming married. Moreover, Social Security payments would be tied to previous earnings, and since discrimination normally kept women's wages below two-thirds that of men's, the result was lower payments to women.

Even in the midst of this patriarchal reaction in America, a number of women rose to challenge gender norms in the 1930s. Rosalind Russell, for instance, starred as Hildy Johnson in the Hollywood film *His Girl Friday*, a remake of the 1931 film *Front Page*, which originally featured a male lead. Babe Didrikson Zaharias established herself as one of the greatest athletes of the early twentieth century when she won three medals in the 1932 Olympics. Also in 1932, Amelia

Earhart became the first woman to fly solo across the Atlantic. Earhart remarked that her flight proved the equality of men and women in jobs requiring "intelligence, coordination, speed, coolness and willpower."

Amelia Earhart challenged gender norms on both sides of the Atlantic. In her public speeches, she called for moving beyond stereotypical views of what is considered feminine work. Instead, she argued women should be encouraged to pursue their individual talent. Photograph of Amelia Earhart, 1932. Harris and Ewing Collection, Library of Congress, Washington, DC.

In other nations, however, the patriarchal reaction was more severe. Mussolini had perfected a more aggressive kind of masculinity in the 1920s, and masculinity proved even more integral to German Fascism. After taking power, Nazi leaders did all they could to tie women's destiny to their biology by glorifying motherhood and discouraging employment outside the home. They also clamped down on all manner of sexual expression outside the nuclear family and suppressed the underground culture of sexual experimentation in Berlin. The Nazi campaign for sexual and racial purity went hand in hand with the burning of books by such prominent authors as Thomas Mann and the purging of what Nazi propaganda minister Joseph Goebbels deemed degenerate art, including the work of such modern masters as Pablo Picasso and Marc Chagall. The trend toward sexual inhibition gained ground in the Soviet Union, as well. Moscow and St. Petersburg, once home to a libertine form of Bolshevism, turned puritanical under Stalin, as reflected in the unbelievably wholesome peasants and workers portrayed in the propaganda posters of Socialist realism.

As part of the campaign against what was deemed sexual immorality, authorities also targeted birth control and abortion, hoping to raise birth rates in the process. In the 1920s, abortion was subject to ever more stringent prohibitions in both Catholic and Protestant Europe. A 1929 British statute, for example, turned abortion into a crime punishable by life imprisonment. The Soviet Union caught up with the trend in 1936 by making abortion a crime, which, according to a Soviet physician, "places a heavy burden on the state because it reduces women's contribution to production."

In the United States, abortions had been illegal for decades, although that did not mean women stopped having them. Abortion was one reason for the ongoing decline in birth rates, which fell to eighteen per one thousand people in the 1930s, the lowest on record up to that point. Most of the decline was the result of other methods of birth control, including the increased use of condoms. As measured by booming sales, condoms were on a marked upswing, despite official prohibitions on distributing information about such "artificial" means of birth control. As government officials quickly learned, it was almost as hard for the state and its moral police to control sexual behavior as it was to control the consumption of alcohol.

Different Responses: Fascist, Communist, Liberal

Alongside these developments there were also great differences in the responses of various nations to the Depression. Three major political economies in this period—Fascism, Communism, and liberalism—marked distinctive national responses. German Fascism and Soviet Communism were implacable enemies, and both were hostile to liberalism as exemplified in the United States. The question hanging over all three was what kind of future—if any—democracy would have.

The Fascist answer was clear: ordinary people would have no say in their own government. Fascism was a mortal threat to democracy because it sought the elimination of all centers of power not controlled by the one-party state; it imposed a "capitalism by violence" that eliminated freedoms for working people and sought unlimited overseas conquest.

As the Fascist pioneer, Mussolini's Italy had introduced corporatist forms of rule in the 1920s that incorporated functional interest groups—finance, agriculture, industry, labor—in the state and suppressed any political opposition. Japan, too, took an authoritarian turn away from fragile party government toward its own brand of Fascism. But the greatest threat to democracy came from Fascist Germany. Because of the size of its economy (second only to the United States), its strong, growing military, and its central place in Europe, Nazi Germany—with the goal of a Thousand Year Reich—posed an enormous historical challenge.

Although Fascism had roots in patriarchal and authoritarian traditions in Western society, it is doubtful it would have ever come to power in Germany without the Depression. Under increasingly desperate Depression conditions, many German citizens found elements of Nazism resonated with their own local culture and desire for economic and social change. Capitalizing on popular discontent, the National Socialist Workers Party rose from a gang of street-fighting thugs to win more than a third of the seats in the Reichstag (parliament) in the fall of 1932. Nazi ideology represented a bellicose form of German nationalism with its habits of obedience to authority and glorification of the state. As the sworn enemy of democracy and of the whole Enlightenment legacy of reason and tolerance, Nazism rallied the frightened "little guy" to the swastika banner, while also winning support from business, landed, and military elites for what amounted to a constitutional coup d'etat in January 1933. Having come to power under the Weimar Constitution, the Nazis immediately turned around and destroyed it, eliminating all semblance of democratic rule and imposing a brutal one-party dictatorship that jailed or killed its opponents, silenced press criticism, and destroyed all independent labor unions and political parties. As the leader of the Nazi Party, Adolf Hitler was a megalomaniac who took German love of order and authority in the virulent direction of the *fuhrerprinzip*, the idea that all authority culminated in the genius of one man.

In the name of *ein Volk, ein Reich* (one people, one empire), Nazis made war on anyone who dared oppose them, including labor organizers, religious dissenters, Communists, Jews, and Slavs. The tragic disunity among the victims of Nazi persecution is captured in a well-known passage from the Lutheran pastor Martin Niemoller: "In Germany they first came for the Communists, and I didn't speak up because I wasn't a Communist. Then they came for the Jews, and I didn't speak up because I wasn't a Jew. Then they came for the trade unionists, and I didn't speak up because I wasn't a trade unionist. Then they came for the Catholics, and I didn't speak up because I was a Protestant. Then they came for me—and by that time no one was left to speak up."

Soviet Communism took a decidedly different approach to the question of democracy. Soviets claimed to have established a people's democracy operating under the principle of *democratic centralism*, as opposed to the partisan squabbling in the bourgeois democracies of the West. Moreover, Communists embraced the egalitarian principles of the Enlightenment and rejected anything like the Nazi theory of Aryan superiority. Another difference lay in property relations. Instead of capitalism by violence, the Soviet Union had imposed socialism by violence in seizing ownership of private industry and finance and in collectivizing agriculture. Finally, foreign policies were different. Unlike Nazi Germany, Soviet ambitions were limited to restoring the tsar's empire, not conquering the rest of Europe. Although Stalin appeared to support revolutionary activity through the Communist International, in fact, he put the narrow national interests of the Soviet Union first.

At the same time, the Soviet system squeezed the lifeblood out of democratic practice. Under the control of the Communist Party, Lenin's idea of "the dictatorship of the proletariat" was construed to mean the dictatorship of one man, Josef Stalin. Stalin personified Soviet Communism while also embodying long-term aspects of Russian history. As the spiritual heir of the tsar, Stalin, shy in public but ruthless in private, perfected the centralization of power in himself, while his paranoid destruction of his enemies, real and imagined, went beyond anything his predecessors had imagined. Stalin employed the same kind of totalitarian methods as the Nazis. The Communist Party ruled with an iron fist through a secret police force, strict control of the media, and the criminalization of dissent.

That left the fate of democracy in the hands of the liberal regimes of the West, but even there, the initial response to the Depression gave little reason for hope. Neither President Herbert Hoover nor the leaders of Britain and France showed any ability to bring ordinary people into the process of finding solutions. In fact, several of Hoover's innovations, including the Reconstruction Finance Corporation, which gave government loans to big business, pointed toward a mild form of corporatism. John Dewey, America's most respected philosopher and a keen observer of the political scene, sensed that democracy was imperiled in the United States. In 1932 Dewey warned, "We have permitted business and financial autocracy to reach such a point that its logical political counterpart is a Mussolini, unless a violent revolution brings forth a Lenin."

As it turned out, the United States eventually did come to the rescue of democracy in the New Deal of Franklin Roosevelt. Roosevelt represented deep-seated aspects of the nation's history. Although a Yankee blueblood to the manor born, Roosevelt was a "traitor to his class" who personified the wheeler-dealer side of the American character. As a master politician, he skillfully maneuvered through dire straits of Depression politics. Crippled by polio and confined to his wheelchair, Roosevelt proved that charismatic leadership did not require the strutting masculinity of a dictator. The key was having the common touch. In his political rhetoric—"the only thing we have to fear is fear itself"—and in his friendly radio broadcasts known as fireside chats, Roosevelt connected with the hopes and fears of common people. His New Deal reforms were not the inevitable by-product of depression conditions, but, instead, the result of historical choices among a range of options in which popular forces played a leading role.

Depression as a War Emergency

Most Depression-era leaders had come of age during the First World War, so it is not surprising that they envisioned the Depression as a kind of military enemy. In his 1933 inaugural address, President Roosevelt asked for "broad Executive power to wage a war against the emergency, as great as the power that would be given to me if we were in fact invaded by a foreign foe." In creating new federal agencies, such as the National Recovery Administration, which oversaw business, Roosevelt drew directly on the War Industries Board and other agencies of the First World War in which he had held minor posts.

In the Roosevelt period, in fact, pacifism was at its historic peak in the United States and Britain. Most Americans came out of the First World War believing that war was a betrayal of American ideals: an exceptional episode, not the continuation of the prevailing politics. The 1920s saw the strongest peace movement in American history, and antiwar sentiment rose even higher in the 1930s. Pacifism was equally strong in Britain. Deeply shaken by the bloodletting of the trenches, Britons vowed never again, and flocked to take the Oxford Pledge in the mid-1930s affirming their refusal "to fight for King and country." In addition, having had a long experience with parliamentary government, the British public was accustomed to electoral transfers of power from one party to another and was not inclined to view politics as warfare.

The contrast with Germany and the Soviet Union could not be more striking. Both Fascists and Communists treated domestic politics as a kind of warfare. Take the case of Germany. From the moment of defeat in 1918, Germans harbored resentment over their ignominious defeat. Although the facts show that military leaders and aristocrats such as Paul von Hindenburg were responsible for accepting defeat, right-wing agitators like Hitler blamed liberal and Socialist politicians for the stab in the back. In *Mein Kampf,* Hitler talked of war as the normal state of affairs in the struggle for power both internationally and domestically.

As in Nazi Germany, politics in Stalinist Russia was conducted as a form of warfare. Russian Communists did not need a depression to be convinced of that point. During the First World War, Lenin had called on the lower classes to turn "imperialist war into class war," and under Stalin the state made war on the countryside. In pursuit of Stalin's order to "liquidate the *kulaks* (rich peasants) as a class," at least thirty thousand were shot outright and as many as ten million were forcibly removed to collective farms or other distant locations. Although some party members were appalled at this grotesque parody of the doctrine of class struggle, they toed the line. Stalin's paranoia was more pathological than ideological. Even after consolidating his power, he did not rest easy until the last enemy was eliminated. Beginning with the assassination of the Communist mayor of Leningrad, he conducted a series of purges, from 1934 to 1937, which decimated the army and wiped out many remaining old Bolsheviks, no matter how impeccable their revolutionary credentials. Prior to the purges, as part of his campaign to fund his industrialization program through the exportation of grain, Stalin imposed a famine on the Ukraine that killed several million of its inhabitants.

Responses to the Depression in Latin America provide additional examples of politics conducted as a form of warfare. Latin America joined the global trend away from democracy toward authoritarian rule. In the short span of 1929–33, a dozen governments fell; most were victims of military seizure of power. Inspired by Fascism in Italy and Spain, conservatives took power in Argentina and prepared the way for a military coup in 1943, just as the Brazilian military backed Getulio Vargas, who went from an elected president to dictator in 1937 ruling over what he dubbed the *Estado Novo,* or "new state." With his proclamation, Vargas joined everyone from Franklin Roosevelt with his New Deal to Adolf Hitler with his New Order in trying to capture the imagination of people who had all but abandoned hope.

Economic Planning

As the economic slump worsened after 1930, there was a widespread turn away from the free market toward government-led economic planning. The Soviet

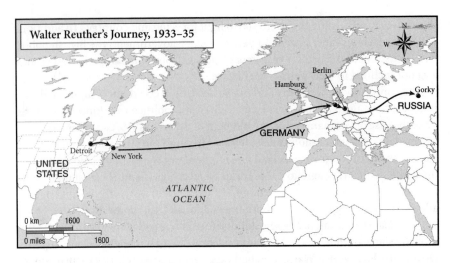

MAP 6.1

Union was already far down this path. Beginning in 1929, the Communist Party implemented its first five-year plan on the way to constructing a centrally controlled command economy where state planners, not private owners, set production targets and allocated resources. Soviet bureaucrats decreed the creation of vast new industrial complexes, including the largest steel mill in the world at Magnitogorsk and the auto plant at Gorky where Americans like Walter Reuther did their part to build Socialism.

To feed the cities, Stalin imposed collectivization of agriculture, a policy that held dire consequences for peasants. Russian cities were fed with state grain requisitions, which jumped from 15 percent of the total harvest in 1928 to 37 percent in 1937. But the Soviet countryside was convulsed by famine in 1932–33, which resulted from a violent struggle between Russian peasants seeking to maintain a measure of autonomy over their harvests and party officials insisting on the need to ship food from the rural areas to the cities. "A ruthless struggle is going on between the peasantry and our regime," wrote one higher official. "It has cost millions of lives, but the collective farm system is here to stay. We've won the war." American journalists reporting from Russia framed the famine as part of Russia's plan to "starve itself great," leading observers in the United States to emphasize Russia's impressive modernization over its brutality.

These episodes point to the moral complexity of the period. It was the atrocities of collectivization that made it possible to feed the mass of factory laborers who turned the Soviet Union into an industrial power. Economic might, in turn, made it possible for the Soviet Union to resist the German invasion of 1941 and make an essential contribution to Allied victory in the Second World War.

Nazi Germany was also part of the trend toward greater state control of the economy. Although the commanding heights of the German capital remained in private hands, the Nazis divided industry into thirteen compulsory cartels (a cartel is a group of cooperating companies) and subjected them to arbitrary government control, the Nazi version of corporatism. Driven by ferocious nationalism, Nazi economic planners began large investments in roads and weapons, flouting prohibitions in the Versailles treaty against remilitarization. State spending (although not the sort that Keynes preferred) on autobahns (superhighways), armaments, and associated industries (including the car maker Volkswagen) led the way toward restored prosperity by 1936.

The United States lagged far behind in imposing state control. Economic nationalism in the United States was accompanied by a vogue for planning, although the Soviet example was much more admired than the Nazi one. John Dewey wrote that state planning "is now the sole method of social action by which liberalism can realize its professed aims." Intellectuals like Dewey were attracted to the idea of technocracy where scientifically trained engineers, not profit-seeking businessmen, would control production. But government leaders were restrained by the folklore of the free market and business hostility to state regulation. Apart from the Tennessee Valley Authority, a public corporation that built dams for flood control and hydroelectric power, the New Deal implemented few actual examples of full-scale state planning.

Instead, President Roosevelt initially tried to coordinate private enterprise rather than command it. Instead of seizing the banking system—an unprecedented four thousand banks failed in one twelve-month period as depositors made desperate runs to withdraw their savings—the first act of Roosevelt's legendary First Hundred Days was to declare a Bank Holiday, closing all banks and allowing only sound institutions to reopen. That the bank runs stopped led one observer to remark, "Capitalism was saved in eight days."

Moving to shore up industry, Roosevelt pressed a compliant Congress to create the National Recovery Administration in 1933. The organization set up industry committees in steel, textiles, and other industries that were the equivalent of government-sponsored cartels. Agriculture came next, with the creation of the Agricultural Adjustment Administration in 1933, which set out to manage crop allotments and commodity pricing. Both reforms had their limits, notably the failure to address the needs of African Americans facing persistent workplace discrimination. Yet, at the end of the First Hundred Days, it appeared that this new administrative state might bring the United States in line with more robust forms of corporatism in Europe and Latin America.

But proponents of liberalism quickly checked America's move toward corporatism. Drawing on the ideology of laissez-faire, the justices of the Supreme Court threw out the National Recovery Administration in the *Schechter* decision of 1935 on two grounds: first, that it was an unconstitutional delegation of congressional authority to the executive branch, and, second, it violated the constitutional prohibition on federal regulation of internal commerce within a state.

In limiting the powers of the federal government, the Court unintentionally underwrote the pluralism of American politics. By sending Roosevelt back to the drawing board, it forced him back to the political arena of pluralist interest groups jockeying for influence through rival political factions. The Supreme Court's ruling served as a powerful obstacle to Fascism and allowed democracy some breathing room.

A New Deal to Save Democracy

By 1935, Roosevelt faced critics on both the right and the left. Conservatives claimed New Deal reforms amounted to Socialism, whereas leftists argued the New Deal did not do enough to support working-class and poor Americans. Among the most outspoken critics of Roosevelt was Huey Long, a radical governor of Louisiana who became a U.S. senator in 1932. As part of his Share Our Wealth plan, Long called for a tax on the wealthy that would provide a minimum income of $2,500 for impoverished Americans. In a similar vein, Francis Townsend, a physician in Long Beach, California, proposed a monthly pension for retirees that would be subsidized by a national sales tax. The proposals of Long, Townsend, and others, including the Socialist author and politician Upton Sinclair, met with growing popular support and pushed Roosevelt to do more in the White House.

Roosevelt and the New Deal Democrats responded to mounting pressure from the Left by passing a series of reforms in the mid-1930s. Political leaders of both parties had long courted labor votes through ethnic and religious appeals through local machine politics, but now, for the first time, the Democratic Party mobilized working-class votes through structural reforms that provided economic security and gave workers a share of power. On top of job-creation efforts, such as the Works Progress Administration of 1935, Roosevelt lent his support to the Wagner Act of 1935, named after its chief congressional sponsor, Senator Robert Wagner of New York. The Wagner Act encouraged wage earners to join "organizations of their own choosing" (i.e., trade unions) and barred employers from engaging in such unfair labor practices as firing employees for union activity. As the crowning piece of labor legislation, the Wagner Act reversed decades of antagonism to trade unions on the part of the federal government. Equally important was the fact that industrial workers became an essential part of the so-called New Deal coalition. As testimony to the pluralism of American politics, the coalition also included urban white ethnic groups, African Americans, middle-class liberals, and Southern whites, or Bourbon Democrats.

Roosevelt's leftward push was also reflected in New Deal social legislation epitomized by the pathbreaking Social Security Act of 1935. Legend has it that Secretary of Labor Francis Perkins, the first woman to hold a cabinet post, locked a group of legislators in a room with a bottle of whiskey and told them not to come out without a bill. Guided by experts in social insurance from Great Britain as well as the International Labour Organization in Geneva, Switzerland, Perkins designed the act to reduce chronic insecurity in the labor market and provide unemployment compensation, old-age assistance, and aid to families with dependent children. Although some of those in greatest need

President Roosevelt signing the Social Security Act in 1935 with Secretary of Labor Frances Perkins, the sole woman in his cabinet, looking on.
Franklin D. Roosevelt Presidential Library and Museum.

of social protection—including domestic servants and agricultural laborers, two occupational groups with high concentrations of African Americans and Latinos—were excluded at the behest of powerful Southern Democrats, Social Security provisions brought the United States in line with other industrial societies and laid the foundation for the U.S. welfare state. Equally important in overcoming insecurity was the 1938 Fair Labor Standards Act, which fulfilled the decades-long quest of progressive reformers for minimum wages, maximum hours, and the abolition of child labor.

Although the economic impact of these reforms was limited, the political impact was immediate. New Deal legislation shifted power from owners to workers, brought traditional American liberties into the workplace for the first time, and gave Italian, Polish, Jewish, and other ethnic Americans a stronger feeling of belonging to the national community than they had ever known. To be sure, elevating the weak caused the strong to protest. Raising the banner of liberty, privileged business and ethnic groups complained they were losing the cherished freedom to do whatever they wanted with their property, which in practice had meant firing union members, avoiding taxes, and suppressing dissent. Opponents of the New Deal coalesced in the Liberty League funded by the archconservative DuPont family. But most working people enjoyed their newfound sense of freedom and thanked Roosevelt in 1936 by giving him a landslide victory in the most class-polarized election in modern U.S. history.

By then, the New Deal was gaining international acclaim as democracy's answer to both Communism and Fascism. Western reformers could now boast that the needs of working people were being addressed under capitalism without the need for a workers' state like that in the Soviet Union. In a different way, New Deal reform was also an alternative to Fascist methods. Nazi labor policy was part of totalitarian rule. No independent labor organization—Socialist, Communist, Catholic, or otherwise—was tolerated. Instead there was a kind of nationwide company union called the National Labor Front. By 1938, German unemployment was a mere 3 percent and was fast disappearing at a time when unemployment remained at Depression levels in the United States (15 percent) and Britain (13 percent). But as New Dealers were quick to point out, what German workers lacked was democratic freedom.

By embracing the New Deal, Americans found themselves at the forefront of social progress. New Deal programs rewrote the social contract between the individual and society to include compromises between labor and capital that, together with regulations of business, pointed in the direction of the mixed economy of reformed capitalism that would emerge out of the Second World War. John Maynard Keynes proved the most vocal advocate of the mixed economy. In his landmark *General Theory of Money and Prices* (1936), Keynes laid out his argument that government spending, including deficit spending, was necessary to counter the cycle of depression. In an economy increasingly oriented toward mass consumption, if the market could not put money in consumers' pockets, then the government would have to step in with countercyclical spending, such as Social Security, and the encouragement of collective bargaining to raise worker's wages.

The redistribution of wealth and power to the working and middle classes in the 1930s was central to preserving democracy in the United States, which, in turn, was nothing less than the key to the survival of democracy in a world that seemed to be turning against it.

Race and Racism

Yet, American democracy was very much an experiment, marked by successes as well as limitations and imperfections. In the initial stages of the Depression, the belief in a strict hierarchy of races persisted. Racial segregation was the law of the land in the Southern United States. Racial hierarchy was upheld by strong barriers to interracial sex, as exemplified by U.S. statutes prohibiting interracial marriage. Southern white opponents to race mixing often justified their position with reference to Christianity, as in the case of one lower court judge, who wrote, "Almighty God created the races. . . . The fact that he separated the races shows that he did not intend for the races to mix." The statutes that grew out of this mentality remained on the books until it was declared unconstitutional in 1967. In the *Loving v. Virginia* decision, the Supreme Court invoked the Fourteenth Amendment's equal protection clause to reverse the lower court decisions and remove race as a barrier to marriage.

The most egregious examples of racism were found in Nazi Germany. According to Nazi theory, humanity was divided into superior groups known as *Ubermenschen*, with Germans themselves classified as *Uber Alles*, and various inferior groups known as *Untermenschen*, including Slavs, Jews, and Romany (Gypsies). Among the *herrenvolk* (ruling people), everyone was presumed equal, an idea that attracted many of the otherwise "forgotten men" of the postwar era. But it was a perverse form of equality in which the individual was first reduced to nothing and then exalted as part of the master Aryan race destined to rule over inferior peoples.

At the level of ideas, the Nazi ideology of racial hierarchies was disturbingly close to the Western mainstream. What put the Nazis in a class by themselves was their vicious treatment of those deemed inferior. Once the Second World War began, the Nazis either slaughtered or subjugated the conquered Polish, Russian, and other Slavic peoples. Those that were not killed were often shipped back to work as slave laborers in German factories. The worst treatment was reserved for Jews. The 1935 Nuremberg Laws enshrined anti-Semitism into law by stripping Jews of citizenship, prohibiting intermarriage (like laws in the Southern United States that prohibited marriage between blacks and whites), and specifically criminalizing interracial sex. The logical conclusion of Nazi race theory was mass murder. Hitler ordered tens of thousands of mental patients, deemed racially defective, to be put to death in 1939. Beginning in 1942, Hitler initiated the so-called Final Solution by embarking on the extermination of the entire Jewish people, history's most terrible case of genocide.

Revolted by Nazi extremes, a dissenting minority of Western intellectuals rejected the whole premise of racial classification. Drawing on research that debunked any association of blood groups or genetic ancestry with races, the British anthropologist Ashley Montague attacked "the fallacy of race" in his 1942 *Man's Most Dangerous Myth*. Likewise, while confirming the existence of ethnic groups, the British biologist Julian Huxley traced racism, a concept coined in the 1930s, to economic and political interests that required a virulent form of nationalism to justify their rule. With an eye on Hitler's Aryan myth, Huxley wrote, "Racialism is a myth and a dangerous myth at that."

Some in the West were influenced by Soviet science, which had already consigned racial explanations of human behavior to the junk heap of history. Soviets rejected racial determinism because it got in the way of their efforts to construct the New Man and New Woman by redesigning the natural environment. With Stalin's official sanction, Soviet biology came under the spell of Trofim Lysenko. Lysenko adopted the discredited Lamarckian theory of the inheritance of acquired characteristics, often illustrated with the dubious example of the giraffe supposedly developing a long neck over several generations by stretching to reach the higher leaves on trees. Although Lamarck's version of Darwinian evolution would have its critics in later decades, for now it reinforced the rejection of genetic, or racial, determinism.

Despite these attacks on race thinking, the world would have to wait until after the Second World War for Western officials to repudiate ideologies of racial inequality in both colonial and domestic settings.

INTERNATIONAL RELATIONS

Just as the Depression shaped national economies, polities, and cultures all around the world, it also had far-reaching effects on international relations. It divided the world into expansionist powers—Germany, Italy, and Japan—and status quo powers—Britain, France, the United States—with the Soviet Union somewhere in between. In the arena of foreign relations, the differences in responses to the Depression clearly outweighed any similarities.

Militarism in Japan and Germany

Among the most ominous responses to the Depression was Japan's return to the path of conquest. No country was hit harder by the Depression than Japan. As in Germany, Depression conditions discredited civilian leaders and fostered a climate of fear conducive to saber rattling against "foreign devils." Militarists traded on a legacy of belligerent expansion that went back to the new imperialism of the late nineteenth century in which victories over China in 1895 and Russia in 1905 led to the annexation of territory and only whetted the appetite of military leaders for more. But military impulses had been restrained in the 1920s by civilian political parties in the Diet, or parliament, and by diplomats and financiers who wanted to remain on good terms with Western business.

Those restraints were loosened by the collapse of international trade after 1929, which had a devastating effect on Japanese exports. Like their Nazi counterparts, Japanese leaders looked to foreign conquest rather than world markets to secure the resources vital to survival, and they dreamed of creating a self-sufficient empire under the flag of the Rising Sun. Seeking both economic resources and nationalist pride, they used a fabricated account of Chinese sabotage of a Japanese railway—the so-called Manchurian Incident—to send the Japanese army to conquer resource-rich Manchuria in October 1931.

The Diet proved unable to assert civilian authority over the military as liberal political parties lost ground. Instead, civilian politics was increasingly infused with a modern version of *bushido*, the code of the warrior. As in Germany, military rearmament brought Japan out of the Depression by 1934. Although the economist John Maynard Keynes had called for government spending to counteract market failure, he did not have military spending in mind.

Overseas expansion made Japan an active player in world politics. Having long regarded Russia as an imperial rival in Asia, Japanese leaders sought security through an alliance with Nazi Germany and Fascist Italy. Under the 1936 Anti-Comintern Pact, the three countries pledged to defend one another if attacked by the Soviet Union or its friends in the Communist International.

Increasingly in the mid-1930s, aggressive powers menaced world peace. In addition to Japanese marauding in Manchuria, Italian boots were tramping in Africa. In a display of conquest for conquest's sake, Mussolini invaded Ethiopia in 1935 while the League of Nations stood idly by. In a speech to the

Italian people, Mussolini justified the invasion in terms of a hierarchy of peoples, claiming Ethiopia was a country "without the slightest shadow of civilization." Mussolini also invaded to erase the shame of Italian defeat by Ethiopian forces in the 1896 Battle of Adwa, one of the few occasions when an army of color defeated a European colonial power.

Emboldened by the Japanese and Italian examples, Germany embarked on its own cycle of conquest. From the beginning, the Nazis won support at home by directing hatred outward at foreign foes, including the French and the Poles, as well as British bankers and Russian Bolsheviks. Dreaming of a Thousand Year Reich, they based their plan for economic recovery in the idea of *Lebensraum* (room to live), believing that the scarce resources that liberal systems like the United States sought to obtain through the market could only be won through foreign military conquest. They reached beyond the limits imposed in the Versailles Treaty by rearming, and they sent German troops into the Rhineland in 1936, the region bordering France that had been put off limits to German arms in the Paris Accords. In violating the terms of Versailles, Hitler made his expansionist intentions clear to all who cared to look.

The Spanish Civil War, 1936–39

Although Fascism and democracy would eventually collide in World War II, the two first came to blows in the Spanish Civil War of 1936–39. Civil war broke out in Spain when General Francisco Franco led a revolt with the backing of the Catholic hierarchy and the landlord class against a coalition government of republican and leftist parties that had come to power through a democratic election. Almost immediately, Spain became an international battleground between the Fascist right and democratic left. Using Spain as a kind of proving ground for their own air and ground forces, Fascist Italy and Germany sent arms to Franco, who used them in indiscriminate bombing of civilian targets, including the town of Guernica, whose destruction was immortalized in Pablo Picasso's painting of the same name.

Meanwhile, the Soviet Union sought to rally international support for the Spanish Republic through the Popular Front. The Popular Front was a genuine coalition of democratic forces—liberal, Progressive, Socialist, Communist—formed in 1935 to oppose the spread of Fascism. The crowning glory of the Popular Front was the International Brigades, volunteers who came to Spain from around the world to fight against Fascism. Nearly three thousand Americans in the Abraham Lincoln Battalion joined the total of some forty thousand international volunteers who stood behind courageous Spanish defenders of the Republic, such as the woman known as *La Passionaria*, who cried out "*No passaran!*" (They shall not pass!) in the Battle of Madrid.

For Communists serving in the brigades, associating with the Soviet Union presented no problem. After all, who but the Soviet Union stood up for the Republic? But for others on the left, linking arms with Stalin presented a troubling moral dilemma. The same leader who came to the defense of democracy in Spain was engaged in persecuting his enemies inside the Soviet Union. Stalin's Great Terror was a grotesque mockery of justice that led to the death of millions.

Given that democracy was on the line, the Western democracies—Britain, France, and the United States—might have been expected to come to the rescue of the embattled Spanish Republic. But they did not. Wanting to avoid a test of arms with Hitler and Mussolini, they stood by and watched Franco's Fascist forces gradually gain the upper hand. Madrid fell to Franco in late March 1939.

Thus, the first battle between Fascism and democracy ended with Fascism victorious. In the next battle, the Western democracies would join forces with Soviet Union, and the outcome would be different.

American Isolation

As international conflict intensified, Americans were determined to stay neutral. Taking the opposite turn as the Germans and the Japanese, Americans in the 1930s retreated from taking direct action on the world stage. The most they could muster was moral disapproval, as in the Stimson Doctrine denying the legitimacy of the 1931 Japanese conquest in Manchuria. Otherwise, they sought to remain neutral.

By 1935, the United States made neutrality official when Congress codified the policy in a series of neutrality laws. The first Neutrality Act imposed an embargo on loans and arms shipments to belligerents. The ostensible intent was to hurt Italy's ability to make war on Ethiopia. The effect, however, was the opposite because it prevented Ethiopia from obtaining the arms it needed, whereas Italy, which had plenty of arms of its own, was free to buy all the oil it needed from American suppliers. Another provision withdrew protection from any American citizens traveling on the ships of belligerent countries. Congress extended the laws to civil wars in 1936, effectively denying the democratic forces fighting for the Spanish Republic the assistance they needed to defeat Franco, who was receiving abundant aid from Fascist Germany and Italy. In 1937 Congress added a cash-and-carry provision further restricting trade with belligerent countries.

The neutrality laws responded to what Americans had learned about foreign entanglements during World War I. Had these laws been in place during the neutrality period of 1914–17, they may have stopped the United States from entering the First World War by banning the buildup of loans and munitions-based prosperity and preventing the loss of American life on the *Lusitania* and other British ocean liners that had inflamed American opinion against Germany. But by the 1930s times had changed. Now American disengagement was taken as a green light by powers bent on conquest. Although Americans cannot be blamed for the behavior of others, the consequence of their neutrality was to postpone conflict to a later date, when belligerent powers would be even more powerful. But preoccupied with their national economic crisis, Americans in the 1930s had little interest in overseas conflicts that seemed to be none of their business and posed no apparent threat to them.

Good Neighbors? *The United States and Latin America*

The United States' nonintervention had positive results in U.S.–Latin American relations where the Good Neighbor Policy replaced gunboat diplomacy. The roots of the Good Neighbor Policy go back to the postwar period. As the red scare died down and international politics stabilized, U.S. leaders felt they could safely address the demands of anti-imperialists for an end to military occupations in the Western Hemisphere. Just as U.S. troops had come home from Europe and Russia, so U.S. occupations ended successively in Cuba in 1922, the Dominican Republic in 1924, Nicaragua in 1933, and, finally, Haiti in 1934. Tensions with Mexico eased as well, when Mexican President Obregón signed the 1923 Bucareli agreement, promising to pay compensation for damages to American property during the revolution. Meanwhile, both North and South America benefited from high levels of trade as Yankee consumers increased their appetite for coffee, sugar, and other commodities exported from the tropics.

President Herbert Hoover, a Republican, promoted noninterventionist policy in Latin America. Seeking to distance himself from his interventionist predecessors—Republican and Democratic alike—Hoover went on a well-publicized goodwill tour of Latin America, proclaiming to countries that had become jaded by U.S. interventions, "True democracy is not and can not be imperialistic." Upon becoming president in 1929, Hoover officially repudiated the Roosevelt Corollary to the Monroe Doctrine, thus rejecting the role of regional policeman that the United States had exercised over the past quarter century.

The impact of the Depression only furthered this tendency toward nonintervention and inward-looking nationalism throughout the Western Hemisphere. The result was a loosening of Uncle Sam's strings at a time when Latin Americans were untying them. That was certainly the case with Mexico's dynamic new president Lázaro Cárdenas. Proclaiming a "Revolution of the Indians," Cárdenas was elected in 1934 as the candidate of the political establishment but soon angered defenders of the status quo by embracing reform. Picking up where the earlier generation of Mexican revolutionaries left off, he distributed millions of acres of land to poor peasants, mostly in the form of *ejidos*, or communal holdings. Seeking to fulfill the pledge of Article 27 in the Constitution of 1917, which asserted national ownership of mineral rights, Cárdenas stepped in to support workers on strike against foreign oil companies. Most dramatically, he went on to nationalize oil properties in 1938.

In earlier times, such threats typically resulted in military intervention to defend American property. Now, however, President Roosevelt refrained from sending troops into Mexico. Instead, he proclaimed the policy of the good neighbor in his 1933 inaugural address, and his secretary of state, Cordell Hull, reaffirmed it at a Pan-American conference in Montevideo, Uruguay, later that year. A key part of the Good Neighbor Policy was the formal abrogation of the Platt Amendment in 1934, which ended Cuba's status as a virtual protectorate. Regarding Panama in 1936, Roosevelt revised the infamous 1903 Hay–Bunau–Varilla

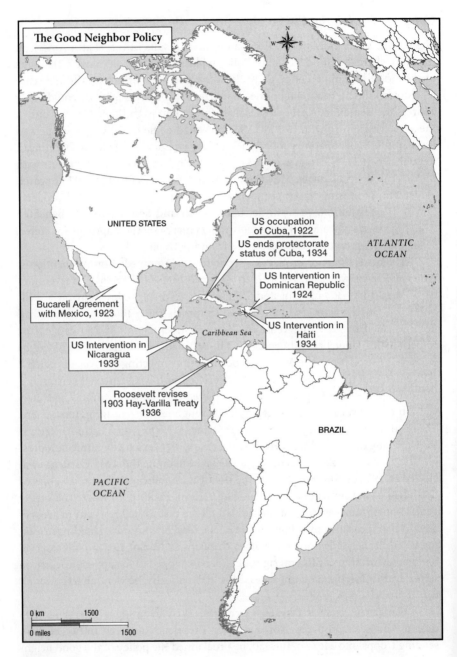

The Good Neighbor Policy

UNITED STATES

US occupation
of Cuba, 1922

US ends protectorate
status of Cuba, 1934

ATLANTIC
OCEAN

US Intervention in
Dominican Republic
1924

Bucareli Agreement
with Mexico, 1923

Caribbean Sea

US Intervention in
Haiti
1934

US Intervention in
Nicaragua
1933

Roosevelt revises
1903 Hay-Varilla Treaty
1936

BRAZIL

PACIFIC
OCEAN

0 km   1500

0 miles   1500

MAP 6.2

Treaty and renounced U.S. rights to unilateral intervention there, thus improving
relations and ensuring a more secure canal as war clouds gathered. In general, U.S.
foreign policy retreated from the imperial interventions of the past. Accompanying this diplomatic leveling was greater cultural exchange. For example, Diego

Rivera, the great Mexican artist, was invited to Detroit, San Francisco, and New York to paint murals of technology and progress, as pictured below.

Diego Rivera at work on his mural *Man at the Crossroads* (1934) in New York's Rockefeller Center. When building managers demanded that an image of the Soviet leader Vladimir Lenin be removed for fear it conveyed an anticapitalist message, Rivera refused and the mural was later destroyed. Rivera never returned to the United States for future commissions. Library of Congress Prints and Photographs Division, Washington, DC.

Although in the United States the benefits of nonintervention in Latin America were quickly overshadowed by the costs of nonintervention in Europe and East Asia, there was no doubt that Latin Americans of nearly all political views preferred the good neighbor to the gunboat diplomat of the past. This important turn in U.S. policy would pay big dividends during the Second World War when practically all of the Latin American republics allied with Washington and declared war on the Axis powers. The strategic raw materials and workforce south of the Rio Grande would significantly strengthen the anti-Fascist coalition.

At the same time, there were limits to this kind of Progressive internationalism. When John D. Rockefeller saw Lenin depicted in a Rivera mural that was commissioned to adorn Rockefeller Center in Manhattan, he ordered it destroyed. There was also a limit to the retreat from empire. Even with the Good Neighbor Policy in place, the U.S. supported dictators in Latin America, such as Fulgencio Batista, who seized power in Cuba in 1933 with American backing, and Anastasio Somoza, the U.S.-trained head of the National Guard in Nicaragua who led an attack on leftist opponents the following year, again with U.S. support. Opposition in Washington to the brutality of U.S.-backed dictators was overridden by pro-American and probusiness sentiments. The lesson of the long occupations of Nicaragua, the Dominican Republic, and Haiti was that neither stability nor democracy could be imposed by foreign guns. What followed in all three cases was the temporary stability of dictatorships, which were eventually overthrown after the Second World War.

The U.S. immigration policy toward Latin American migrants was another line of continuity in this period. Although New Deal Democrats advanced many liberal reforms in both domestic and foreign policy, they made no effort to repeal the restrictive immigration laws put in place by Republicans in the 1920s. As joblessness fueled ideas of nativism and xenophobia in the 1930s, some Americans called for even more restrictive measures along the U.S.–Mexico border. Beginning in 1932, new restrictions limited Mexican immigration to two thousand people per year. And over the course of the decade, as many as one million Mexican Americans and Mexican-born immigrants moved back to Mexico, either voluntarily or as part of stepped-up deportation campaigns to remove illegals.

CONCLUSION

The Depression of 1929 proved a challenge to not only capitalism but also democracy. Although democracy was extinguished in the Fascist and Communist regimes overseas, a bright spot remained in the United States where democracy was being transformed from an obsession with individual opportunity to an embrace of greater social solidarity and wartime collectivism. Although American liberalism did not extend to all in this period (notably Mexican migrants and African Americans, among others), the New Deal did help build the foundation for the postwar welfare state throughout the Western world.

FURTHER READING

Blower, Brooke. *Becoming Americans in Paris: Transatlantic Politics and Culture between the World Wars.* Oxford: Oxford University Press, 2011.

Ekbladh, David. *The Great American Mission: Modernization and the Construction of an American World Order.* Princeton, NJ: Princeton University Press, 2011.

Engerman, David C. *Modernization from the Other Shore: American Intellectuals and the Romance of Russian Development.* Cambridge, MA: Harvard University Press, 2004.

Gabaccia, Donna R. *Foreign Relations: American Immigration in Global Perspective.* Princeton, NJ: Princeton University Press, 2012.

Hsu, Madeline Y. *The Good Immigrants: How the Yellow Peril Became the Model Minority.* Princeton, NJ: Princeton University Press, 2015.

Katznelson, Ira. *Fear Itself: The New Deal and the Origins of Our Time.* New York: Liveright, 2014.

Lichtenstein, Nelson. *Walter Reuther: The Most Dangerous Man in Detroit.* Urbana: University of Illinois Press, 1997.

Patel, Kiran Klaus. *The New Deal: A Global History.* Princeton, NJ: Princeton University Press, 2016.

CHAPTER 7

GLOBAL WAR, 1937–45

A B-17 bomber conducting a bombing mission over Berlin, Germany, in 1944. After this plane was hit, it crashed to the ground, along with the entire crew. Franklin D. Roosevelt Presidential Library and Museum.

ESCAPE FROM NAZI-OCCUPIED EUROPE

On November 5, 1943, George Watt climbed aboard a B-17 Flying Fortress and took off on a bombing run to German rail yards in the Ruhr Valley. Because of their high losses, American GIs sarcastically dubbed Germany's well-defended industrial heartland the Happy Valley, and now it was Watt's turn to be shot down. When fate disabled one of the four engines, the crippled B-17 became a sitting duck for a German Folk-Wulf fighter plane. Lucky to be able to bail out as the plane went down, Watt landed in a farmer's field in German-occupied Belgium.

What followed was an extraordinary journey of escape from Nazi-occupied Europe. Sheltered initially by local villagers, Watt was fortunate to be picked up by members of the Belgian resistance who connected him to the underground group named the Comet Line. Risking their lives to help the American flyer, couriers on the Comet Line accompanied Watt to a safe house in Paris where they gave him false documents. He then boarded a train to Bordeaux in the south of France, where he was shepherded across the Pyrenees into neutral Spain.

When Watt climbed the Pyrenees, it was for the second time in his life. Six years earlier, he had traveled to Spain as a member of the Abraham Lincoln Brigade. As part of this group of American volunteers who went to Spain to support the democratically elected Republican government, Watt fought against General Francisco Franco, the leader of a right-wing revolt against the Republic who had the support of the Fascist governments of Italy and Germany.

The United States had been neutral in the Spanish Civil War, but now America was fighting to defeat the Germans in the world war. Back in New York, Watt's wife, Margie, was doing her part as a riveter on airplane tail sections in a Long Island defense plant. When he finally reached British Gibraltar at the southern tip of Spain, Watt was able to cable his beloved Margie that he was coming home.

GLOBAL CONFLICT AND TOTAL WAR

Watt's harrowing escape from Nazi-occupied Europe is but one small episode in the monumental story of global conflict between 1937 and 1945. This chapter explores how the Second World War mobilized whole societies for total war, transformed international relations, disrupted daily life around the world, and killed, directly or indirectly, perhaps sixty million people, 70 percent of whom were civilians. The war served to reinforce an ongoing shift in global power as the United States and the Soviet Union rose to superpower status and supplanted Europe as the world's prime power center.

The Second World War was both the outgrowth of deep historical continuities and a dramatic change in human affairs. The continuities reach back to the late nineteenth century when the Industrial Revolution and the new imperialism brought new conflicts onto the world stage. There were social conflicts among contending groups—upper and lower classes, rival ethnic and cultural groups, and different elites—for state power and cultural standing. These internal conflicts played out alongside international conflicts among nation-states and empires for dominance in Europe and Asia. These domestic and international conflicts led to the outbreak of the First World War, in which Germany's bid for dominance in Europe was checked but not destroyed. The continuity between the First and Second World Wars lay in the fact that the outcome on the battlefield and at the Versailles Peace Conference left the basic social and international conflicts unresolved.

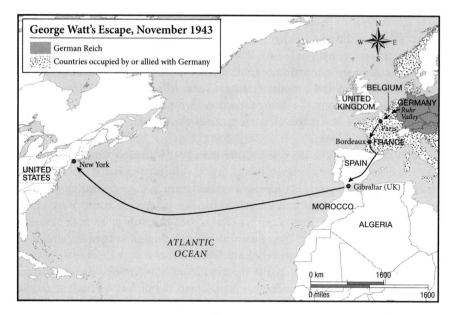

George Watt's Escape, November 1943

German Reich

Countries occupied by or allied with Germany

BELGIUM
UNITED KINGDOM
GERMANY
Ruhr Valley
Paris
Bordeaux FRANCE
New York
UNITED STATES
SPAIN
Gibraltar (UK)
MOROCCO
ALGERIA
ATLANTIC OCEAN

0 km   1600
0 miles   1600

MAP 7.1

But there was also change. Under the weight of the Great Depression in the 1930s, German and Japanese elites enlisted their respective populations in the superpatriotic, hypermasculine, racist ideology known as Fascism in Germany and militarism in Japan. Both nations became trapped in a vicious cycle in which foreign conquest was necessary to feed domestic industrial production, which, in turn, fueled further conquests abroad. Germany and Japan reached toward world dominance until they met their match in the wartime Grand Alliance of the United States, the Soviet Union, and Britain. In the end, it took the catastrophes of two world wars and one Great Depression to resolve the long-term conflicts over power, wealth, and identity that had led to war in the first place.

WAR IN ASIA

The history of the Second World War begins not in Germany, Britain, or the United States but in East Asia. Ever since the new imperialism of the late nineteenth century, East Asia had been a major arena of imperial rivalry, and Japan with some sixty-nine million people in 1935 was the rising power. In the context of the Great Depression, Japan sought to seize its neighbors' resources through force of arms to expand its military and imperial power. In 1936–37, military zealots animated by a modern version of *bushido*, the code of the warrior, brushed aside the restraining hand of political parties in the Diet (parliament) and called for overseas conquest. The army and its civilian supporters were divided into factions, which outdid one another in condemning liberal democratic and Socialist ideas as threats to national unity. While the Imperial Way faction espoused a mystical cult of the emperor, the Control Faction sought the long-range transformation of Japan into a modern military state. After a series of assassinations, arrests, and executions, the Control Faction eliminated its rival. With an ideology akin to Fascism—patriarchal, racist, and authoritarian—the militarists had finally seized full power.

After concluding the 1936 Anti-Comintern Pact with Germany and Italy, the Control Faction lost no time in launching full-scale war against China proper in 1937. To provide a pretext, Japanese soldiers went to the extraordinary length of donning Chinese uniforms and attacking Japanese units at the Marco Polo Bridge outside Beijing. This staged attack was used to justify a full-scale invasion to restore Japanese honor. Once again, as in 1931, foreign conquests reinforced the power of militarists back in the homeland.

China itself was in no position to fend off the invader. Unlike Japan, China had been slow to modernize, and four-fifths of its 505 million people in 1935 tilled the soil as they had done for centuries. Industrial centers such as Shanghai along the coast were no match for modern Japanese steel and armaments production, now abetted by the rapidly industrializing sectors under Japanese rule in Manchuria. Politically, China was deeply divided into three groups: a weak central government under Nationalist Premier Jiang Jieshi (Chiang Kai-shek), a group of Communist rebels in the interior province of Yan'an, and a faction of local warlords who often kept national taxes for themselves.

Although Chinese forces put up fierce resistance to the Japanese invader, one city after another was quickly overrun: Tianjin, Beijing, Canton. The assault on Shanghai involved the first deliberate aerial bombing of civilian targets in history, an act that would be repeated by both sides with appalling consequences when the war became a global conflict a few years later. Frustrated at meeting significant resistance, Japanese forces committed the rape of Nanjing, one of the worst atrocities in the history of war. Having subdued all military resistance in overrunning the Nationalist capital of Nanjing, soldiers went on a bloody rampage of murder, rape, and pillage. When it was over seven weeks later, as many as three hundred thousand defenseless Chinese had been killed.

Despite growing alarm about imperial Japan's threat to democratic values and liberal capitalism, Americans were in no greater mood to fight than they had been in the years before U.S. intervention in the First World War. When the Japanese sunk an American gunboat, *The Panay*, during the attack on Nanjing, the United States refused to be provoked, even by the loss of American life. Although President Roosevelt officially supported the Neutrality Acts (see Chapter 6), he would undermine this policy when he spoke of the need to "quarantine the aggressor."

WAR IN EUROPE

At the same time, Europeans were bracing for war for the second time in a generation. In explaining the causes of renewed violence, historians debate whether the two European wars should be understood as one thirty years' war lasting from 1914 to 1945. Despite many differences, the two phases of fighting were linked in an overarching pattern involving the struggle for dominance in Europe. In essence, Germany's bid for dominance provoked opposition from Britain, France, and Russia (the Soviet Union), whose combined force, along with the twice-delayed entry of the United States, was necessary to subdue German power. The outcome of round one (1914–18) was inconclusive because the Allies imposed a harsh settlement at Versailles that they were unwilling to enforce against the German desire for revenge, which led to a second round (1939–45) that brought significantly more destruction and much harsher peace terms, this time enforced by Allied occupation. Ironically, the struggle for dominance within Europe resulted in Europe's overall decline as power shifted to the United States and the Soviet Union.

Germany was the leading protagonist in both rounds of war. The launching of German attacks on Belgium in 1914 and Poland in 1939 ignited the wider wars by provoking British and French resistance. The roots of Germany's expansion, like Japan's, lie in social and economic forces that generated a cycle of military conquest. The cycle began with growing industrial power, which gave German elites both the means and the motive for external expansion. The means lay in the combination of German nationalism and war production, known as *Wehrmacht*, the most fearsome war machine in Europe, and the motive lay in the need to keep the machine humming by securing scarce resources abroad. In addition, elites believed that war would be a means to unify the nation under their rule. As Germans embraced *Wehrmacht*, Germany's neighbors had reason to tremble.

And tremble they did, as the Nazis grew increasingly bellicose. Embarking on full-scale rearmament in 1936 and driven by a virulent form of nationalism captured in the slogan *Deutschland uber alles* (Germany over all), Hitler demanded that all people of German descent be brought under the Nazi Swastika. He set his sights first on his native Austria. By coaxing some Austrian leaders and bullying others, he pressured Austria to join the Third Reich. Then he turned to the Sudetenland, a section of Czechoslovakia that abutted Germany and had a German majority. In the spring of 1938, he rattled embassies all over Europe with a peremptory demand for its annexation.

Diplomatic Surprises

Hitler's demands on Czechoslovakia led to a flurry of diplomatic activity that culminated in the Munich Crisis of September 1938. By this time, there was no mistaking Hitler's aggressive intentions. His bellicose demands on the Czechs made promises of peaceful intent ring hollow. In fact, he had already secretly informed his senior staff a year earlier that "Germany's problems could only be solved by means of force." Even so, whether another war broke out depended on how other countries responded. For their part, British and French diplomats recognized that Hitler could not be appeased but sought time to build their own nations' military strength. Settling for Hitler's promises of peace, they acquiesced to the annexation of the Sudetenland, enabling British Prime Minister Neville Chamberlain to fly home with the false promise of "peace in our time." The illusory hope was that appeasement would satisfy Hitler's appetite for expansion. Although there were few outright Fascists in Britain and France, many among the upper classes saw Nazism as a bulwark against Communism, and many others hoped the Nazis might be turned eastward against the Soviets.

Because of their hostility to the Soviet Union and distrust of its ruler, Joseph Stalin, Western diplomats ignored pleas from Soviet Foreign Minister M. Litvinov to join in collective security against Nazi aggression. Reminding the French of their defense pact with the Czechs, Litvinov warned in prophetic tones that failure to resist Hitler at this stage would only mean postponing the inevitable conflict. Whether collective promises to support the territorial integrity of Czechoslovakia would have deterred someone as rapacious as Hitler is by no means clear. But a serious plot by elements of the German army to overthrow Hitler was undone by the Munich accords. The failure of appeasement became even clearer when Hitler occupied most of Czechoslovakia in March 1939 and laid secret plans to invade Poland.

Given the horrible reality of the war that followed, much is made of the lost option to contain Hitler through collective security. Within a narrowing range of options, historical actors might have made different decisions in the late 1930s. The British and the French, for example, might have deterred Hitler by drawing a clear line sooner, especially if they had received support from the Americans.

Instead, Americans hunkered down behind the great moat of the Atlantic Ocean and tried to stay out of the conflict brewing in Europe, just as they had done in 1914. Although American sympathies lay overwhelmingly with their former First World War allies, isolationist sentiment was even stronger in the 1930s. The U.S. Neutrality Acts made it difficult for President Roosevelt to play a forceful role at Munich. And despite his own inclinations toward Wilsonian internationalism, Roosevelt was preoccupied with fending off Republican challenges to the New Deal, which had intensified after major Republican gains in the 1938 midterm elections. American isolation in the late 1930s abetted appeasement.

Appeasement made for a strengthened Nazi regime that could rule with tyranny over its own citizens. Shortly after Munich, the Nazis increased their persecution of German Jews by orchestrating a violent rampage of murder and vandalism aimed at Jewish shopkeepers. It was dubbed *Kristallnacht*, or the night of broken crystal, for the shattered windowpanes that littered the streets. Although Americans overwhelmingly condemned this brutality, they did not revise their own restrictive immigration laws, originally intended in part to deny entry to Europe's Jews. Under the National Origins Act, quotas remained an effective barrier, for example, to the desperate Jewish refugees aboard the *St. Louis*, a ship from Europe denied entry at American ports in 1939. Forced to return to Europe, many of the passengers later perished in the Holocaust.

If appeasement was expected to set Germany against the Soviet Union, it had the opposite effect. To everyone's astonishment, Hitler and Stalin signed a non-aggression pact in late August 1939. Placing power politics over ideology, the Hitler–Stalin Pact served the interests of both sides in dividing Poland between them and buying time to build up armaments for the day they might have to fight one another.

Blitzkrieg

Within days of signing the pact, Hitler launched the first round of *Blitzkrieg* (lightening war) against overpowered Poland. Panzer (armored) divisions reached the capital of Warsaw in a matter of weeks, and, as agreed, Stalin's forces grabbed the eastern sector of the country. Once again, as before the Napoleonic era, Poland was wiped off the map. The Nazi strategy of Blitzkrieg was developed initially as an answer to the stalemate of trench warfare in the First World War. It was a bold way of compensating for Germany's economic predicament of being required to go outside its borders for essential raw materials, since only coal was present in abundance. The hope was that lightning would shatter enemy forces before they had time to react.

Then after a lull lasting until June of 1940, the *Wehrmacht* launched the second round of Blitzkrieg to the west. Fast-moving German mechanized forces quickly outflanked France's supposedly impregnable Maginot Line, a vast complex of fortifications. Racing through Belgium, the Germans descended on Paris and within weeks received France's capitulation in the same railroad car where the Germans had themselves surrendered in the First World War.

The fall of France left Britain as the lone obstacle to German domination of Europe. In advance of a cross-channel invasion, Hitler unleashed the *Luftwaffe* (air force) on British civilian and military targets alike in the summer of 1940. The object of aerial terror bombing was to break civilian morale, but, in a pattern repeated whenever aerial bombardment has been used to terrorize civilians, the Blitz only increased Londoners' determination to fight on. The Royal Air Force won the desperate Battle of Britain, deterring a seaborne invasion, but German bombing of English cities persisted until May 1941.

The most significant diplomatic event of this phase was the signing of the Tripartite Pact on September 27, 1940. The Tripartite Pact was a full-scale military alliance among Germany, Italy, and Japan that marked the official creation of the Axis. For the moment, it was aimed at displacing the British and French empires around the world. The underlying impulse, however, pointed toward world domination. For that, it would also be necessary to subdue both the United States and the Soviet Union.

UNITED STATES RESPONSES BEFORE PEARL HARBOR

At first, Americans were slow to respond to the Axis threat. Convinced that their participation in the First World War had been a mistake, Americans were determined not to repeat it. Like British and French elites who had tried to appease Hitler at Munich in hopes he would turn against the Soviets, most American business and political elites were content to let Hitler run amok, so long as he did not directly threaten their interests. Indeed, leading U.S. corporations, including IBM and General Motors, did a brisk business in Nazi Germany. A small fringe of American Fascists, represented in the German–American Bund, and some prominent conservatives, notably Charles Lindbergh, the hero of the first solo flight across the Atlantic, sympathized with Hitler. Others praised Mussolini for imposing order on his otherwise unruly society.

Elite conservatives were the leading force behind America First, the most prominent isolationist voice in support of neutrality. But America First also attracted a motley collection of people from across the political spectrum. Like the coalition of conservative nationalists and Progressives who had defeated the Treaty of Versailles, opponents of U.S. overseas entanglements came forward in the late 1930s, including one-time Progressives from the West, such as the Montana senator Burton Wheeler, Socialists such as Norman Thomas, historian Charles A. Beard, and John L. Lewis, the leader of the United Mine Workers. Even American Communists, ever faithful to Soviet foreign policy during the period of the Hitler–Stalin Pact, joined the chorus crying out, "The Yanks are not coming!"

But after the fall of France in late spring 1940, the hearts of the great majority of the American people went out to England, standing almost alone against the German onslaught. Winston Churchill had replaced Chamberlain as prime minister, and he did all he could to reinforce the unity of what he liked to refer to as the English-speaking peoples. He ardently courted his American "cousins" (Churchill actually had cousins through his American mother) with increasingly urgent appeals for aid. Among the most gifted orators of his time, Churchill stood before Parliament and vowed in rhythmic cadences, "we shall fight on the beaches, we shall fight on the landing grounds, we shall fight in the fields and in the streets, we shall fight in the hills; we shall never surrender." Then he added his appeal to the Americans, "until in God's good time, the new world, with all its power and might, steps forth to the rescue and the liberation of the old."

At a time when Anglophilia still held sway among America's upper crust, a group of well-placed leaders, including Republican William Allen White, won Roosevelt's backing to set up the Committee to Defend America by Aiding the Allies, which effectively countered the arguments of America First. More important in the short run, a growing segment of the power elite decided their interests lay with a British victory, just as they had in 1917. Britain had to be kept afloat because the closed systems of Germany and Japan were antithetical to both the democratic spirit of the open society and the capitalist aims of open markets that had been the hallmarks of U.S. policy since Woodrow Wilson.

It was not necessary to persuade Franklin Roosevelt on that point. Using his considerable political skills to prepare for intervention, the president took the lead in a series of modifications of the Neutrality Acts. Beginning in late 1939, he persuaded Congress to lift the arms embargo and followed through in 1940 with a fivefold increase in military appropriations and the nation's first peacetime draft, which Congress passed in September by one vote. In the same month, Roosevelt arranged the Destroyers-for-Bases plan, which sent fifty aging ships to Britain in return for long-term leases on British bases in the Caribbean and Latin America. Although Churchill was loath to admit it, this marked another step in the decline of the British empire in the Western Hemisphere.

This plan also marked the effective end of U.S. neutrality, although Roosevelt could not say so in public. In the midst of the 1940 reelection campaign, he was afraid to get too far ahead of public opinion and promised the voters, "Your boys are not going to be sent into any foreign wars." The more American boys got involved, the less foreign the war was. Moreover, the public wanted to believe that aiding the Allies would somehow keep America out of German gunsights, instead of having the more likely opposite effect. With British orders helping to restart production lines, self-interest combined with sympathy for Britain to convince a majority of the American public that the destroyer deal was the right thing to do. According to one of the earliest Gallup polls, in fact, a full 70 percent of Americans supported the deal. In the 1940 election, Roosevelt was given political cover by his Republican challenger Wendell Willkie, who was even more of an internationalist. Handily defeating Willkie, Roosevelt felt free to proclaim in one of his most important fireside chats, "We must be the great arsenal of democracy." Although not legally at war, the United States was very much a participant in the Battle of the Atlantic by 1940.

Further steps toward participation came quickly in 1941. In March, Congress approved Lend–Lease, under which the United States began loaning all the supplies that could be mustered to Britain. The same deal was extended to the Soviet Union in October, four months after its invasion by the Nazis. To make sure supplies arrived, American merchant ships were armed against German U-boats, and by November 1941 ships were being convoyed across the Atlantic by the U.S. Navy. In one exchange with German U-boats, the United States lost 115 merchant seamen aboard the *Reuben James*. In other words, in the months prior to

Pearl Harbor, the United States was already fighting an undeclared naval war in the North Atlantic. Americans were engaging in combat elsewhere as well. Under the ruse of being volunteers, American pilots were sent to Britain, and the legendary Flying Tigers began flying missions in August 1941 in southwestern China against the Japanese.

Marketing the War

All this required justification. In some of his most memorable rhetoric, Roosevelt made the case for Lend–Lease in his third inaugural address of January 1941 with a homespun metaphor: when your neighbor's house is on fire, you lend him your hose to put it out, and you don't demand payment first. Roosevelt also had his speechwriter draft a section describing the Four Freedoms that he believed were at stake in the growing conflict with Nazi Germany. As later depicted in a popular series of Norman Rockwell paintings, they were Freedom of Speech, Freedom of Worship, Freedom from Want, and Freedom from Fear. Finally, in the Atlantic Charter of August 1941, four months before Pearl Harbor, Roosevelt and Churchill issued a joint declaration of war aims that recalled Wilson's core principles, including global democracy and an international body to keep the peace. Again, as in the First World War, the banners of messianic democracy were unfurled in the fight for freedom against dictatorship. Secretly, the two leaders also agreed to make defeat of Germany their first priority, with Japan second.

A World War II poster showing Norman Rockwell's painting of Freedom from Want originally published in the *Saturday Evening Post* in 1943. Roosevelt promoted the Four Freedoms (Freedom of Speech, Freedom of Worship, Freedom from Want, and Freedom from Fear) as the opposite of Nazi rule. Library of Congress Prints and Photographs Division, Washington, DC.

Hollywood enlisted in the battle for public opinion. *Casablanca*, one of the all-time greatest American films, was a sophisticated effort to persuade America to join the fight against the Nazis. The hero Rick is played with characteristic toughness by Humphrey Bogart, a seemingly cynical veteran of the Spanish Civil War washed up on the shores of Morocco as the operator of Rick's American Café. As a French colony, Morocco is nominally under the Vichy regime, which is collaborating with the Nazis, and Rick must walk a fine line to avoid offending the local French prefect of police. In the end, French patriotism (there is a stirring rendition of "*La Marseillaise*") and American justice triumph over the Nazis, and the two volunteer soldiers march off arm in arm "in a beautiful friendship" to fight Hitler.

Sergeant York, which opened in theaters in the summer of 1941, also contributed to the emerging prointerventionist sentiment. This film spoke directly to Americans disillusioned with war by portraying Alvin York as a World War I soldier who overcame his own reluctance to fight to become one of the most decorated soldiers of the war. According to a 1937 Gallup poll, two-thirds of Americans were inclined toward U.S. neutrality, believing U.S. entry into World War I had been a mistake. In the summer of 1941, however, when Hitler's armies seized increasing swaths of Europe and invaded the Soviet Union, many Americans watching *Sergeant York* were ready to reconsider their isolationist stance. Yet the fact that the U.S. Senate investigated Hollywood for allegedly producing prowar propaganda films suggests persistent support for neutrality in Congress.

Operation Barbarossa

Two critical events in 1941 brought the war in Europe and the war in Asia together in a single global conflict. The first was Germany's invasion of the Soviet Union in June. Hitler's decision to invade was the all-but-inevitable consequence of the Nazi logic of conquest. Determined to be the master of Europe, like Napoleon before him, Hitler knew that sooner or later he would have to strike against Russia. The only question was whether to wait until Britain was defeated in a cross-channel invasion or to put Britain on hold while concentrating his forces against the main territorial and ideological rival on the continent. After two successful years of Blitzkrieg in Europe, Hitler turned his attention to Russia.

Operation Barbarossa began on June 22, 1941. Three million German troops supported by 3,300 tanks in the feared Panzer Divisions supported by 7,000 pieces of artillery fanned out in a three-pronged assault aimed at Leningrad in the north, the Soviet capital of Moscow in the center, and Kiev, capital of Ukraine, in the south. One column of Hitler's troops set out from Brest–Litovsk, site of the treaty that had ended the First World War on the eastern front on humiliating terms for the Bolsheviks. Hitler trained his Blitzkrieg methods against the Soviet Union in a war of annihilation aimed at wiping the Communist state off the map. He told his generals, "The war against Russia will be such that it cannot be conducted in a knightly fashion; the struggle is one of ideologies and racial differences and will have to be conducted with unprecedented, unmerciful and unrelenting harshness."

But Hitler faced a stronger enemy than expected. It is true that the Red Army was debilitated by Stalin's purges of 1937–38, which killed a significant portion of the officer corps, and true, too, that the army was initially caught off guard because Stalin refused to believe his own or British intelligence reports on German preparations for an invasion. But under Stalin's dictatorial rule, the Soviet Union had built up a modern mechanized army, and what they lacked in technical quality they made up for in quantity, producing more tanks and aircraft than vaunted Germany. The greatest imbalance was in soldiers, with some 4.75 million soldiers of the Red Army fighting a German army of 3.3 million stretched thin over several fronts.

With the goal of defense in depth, retreating Russians followed a scorched-earth policy, burning factories, warehouses, and bridges to reduce the stock available for German plunder. Wherever possible, they dismantled whole factories and shipped them out of harm's way east of the Urals. They mobilized all the energies of Russian people, soldiers and civilians alike, in the Great Patriotic War for the defense of the motherland. In the siege of Leningrad, a form of warfare reminiscent of medieval times, perhaps one million people died, mostly from starvation. Even then, German armies failed to take the city. The same was true at the gates of Moscow, where all-out Russian defenses stopped German forces within sight of the city. Key to the Soviet success was information from Russian spy Richard Sorge that Japan planned on attacking south in the Pacific and not north into Siberia, enabling Stalin's transfer of vital reserves from Asiatic Russia to the Moscow front. Thus did Hitler's Blitzkrieg come to a halt.

Crimes against Humanity

Ironically, German brutality seemed to work against Hitler's aims. Hitler's war planners hoped to turn the black earth of Ukraine into a German garden worked by docile Slavs, but their thuggish methods of seizing crops, deporting labor, and exacting collective punishment for the slightest resistance had the opposite effect. It turned Ukrainians against the invader. Peasants simply stopped sending wheat to market, resulting in severe famine.

It was as part of Operation Barbarossa that the so-called Final Solution to the race problem emerged. As the elite troops of the *Schutzstaffel* under Heinrich Himmler moved into Russia, special units known as *Einsatzgruppen* began a systematic campaign of large-scale murder of the Judeo-Bolshevik foe. At the Wansee conference near Berlin in January 1942, this and other scattered efforts were brought under a single bureaucratic command with the task of coordinating the extermination of the entire Jewish population of Europe. Prior to Wansee, anyone deemed an enemy of the state had been herded into "labor camps" where they were often worked to death, as at Auschwitz in Poland, where the slogan *Arbeit Macht Frei* (work makes one free) was full of bitter irony. After Wansee, Auschwitz and other sites became death camps where innocent human beings were herded into Zyklon B gas chambers and killed by the hundreds of thousands using the most modern scientific methods available in the all-consuming fires of what came to be called the Holocaust.

The Holocaust defies moral comprehension. How could one group of human beings seek to exterminate another? Seeking rational explanation, military strategists have wondered why the German high command would divert resources to gratify the pathological impulses of a madman. Perhaps the most plausible answer is that pathology was built into Nazism. It rested on the premise that making war on enemies foreign and domestic was the normal state of affairs. Although some six million Jews were the single largest victims of genocide in world history, other victims of the Holocaust included Communists, Gypsies, "degenerates," and countless others killed in wanton disregard of universal moral teachings. So monstrous were the crimes that new terms were invented to describe them, including *genocide* and *crimes against humanity*.

Pearl Harbor

The second event of 1941 that turned two wars into one was the Japanese attack on the U.S. naval base at Pearl Harbor on December 7. Although Japanese civilian leaders were reluctant to make war on the United States, the Japanese military prepared to enter the war in support of Germany. On the American side, President Roosevelt was increasingly engaged in the Battle of the Atlantic and hoped to avoid a second front in the Pacific. Roosevelt's secretary of state Cordell Hull was particularly anxious not to provoke Japan and stalled for time to postpone what many saw as the inevitable clash.

Time began to run out, however, in the summer of 1941. Germany's invasion of the Soviet Union gave Japan the choice of striking northward against the Soviets, as Hitler interpreted the terms of the Tripartite Pact, or lunging southward toward the British and Dutch oil fields and risking war with the United States. Having concluded a neutrality agreement with the Soviets in April, Japan's Tojo government opted for the southern strategy. But if Russia could wait, oil could not. With only a sixty-day supply remaining, Japan was even more dependent on foreign supplies than Germany. Distrustful of world markets, militarists pressed the cabinet for war. In another illustration of the vicious cycle of conquest, an expanded war was deemed necessary to get the fuel needed to feed the war machine so it could get more fuel and revive its stalled conquest of China. With a green light from the Vichy government of France, Japan occupied southern Indochina in preparation for what everyone expected would be an attempt to seize the oil fields of Indonesia.

Roosevelt's response to the Japanese threat put the two countries on a collision course. The president increased aid to Chang Kai-shek and by September Roosevelt negotiated an international embargo on oil to Japan in hopes of using economic leverage to obtain withdrawal from China (although not Manchuria) and to forestall an invasion of Indonesia. From Thomas Jefferson's day forward, market-oriented Americans have tried to use economic levers short of war to advance their aims. In the days of dollar diplomacy early in the twentieth century, such a strategy often worked on countries too weak to defy U.S. gunboats. But in the 1940s, stronger foes like the Japanese were not so easily intimidated.

While diplomats engaged in a series of efforts to resolve the conflict, military leaders on both sides prepared for war. In early November 1941, the Joint Board of the U.S. Army and Navy (later the Joint Chiefs) decreed that any attack on British or Dutch colonies would be tantamount to an attack on the United States. This willingness to defend the general interest of market democracies foreshadowed the postwar U.S. role as the defender—what scholars call the hegemon—of the world capitalist system.

For their part, Japanese militarists decided to launch simultaneous attacks on several Allied targets in the Pacific Ocean, including the Philippines. The key strategic assault designed to knock out the U.S. Pacific Fleet from any interference in its multipronged offensive was the bombing of Pearl Harbor. On a brilliant Sunday morning, Japanese Zeros flying from aircraft carriers in the middle of the Pacific appeared without warning in the skies over Pearl Harbor, Hawaii (then a territory of the United States). Taking maximum advantage of surprise, they sank or crippled five of the eight U.S. battleships resting at anchor, destroyed 180 planes before they could scramble in defense, and killed some 2,300 seamen and others. Ironically, the U.S. Pacific Fleet had recently been sent to Pearl Harbor for the purpose of deterring just such an attack. In ringing tones of defiance, Roosevelt called December 7, 1941, "a date that will live in infamy." The next day, with virtually no debate, Congress declared war on Japan.

The United States and the Grand Alliance

In explaining the causes behind the U.S.–Japanese war, the role of cultural misjudgment should not be forgotten. The Japanese attack rested on a miscalculation that Americans were too self-indulgent to mobilize for full-scale war. Another contributing circumstance was American complacency in the face of warning signs. New radar installations picked up what later was recognized as Japanese planes. In retrospect, it might seem that American intelligence should have given forewarning of the attack. Some conservative friends of the military, embarrassed at being caught flat-footed on December 7, even concocted a story about Roosevelt conniving in the Japanese attack so he could get a full-scale declaration of war. Yet there is no evidence to substantiate this conspiracy theory because U.S. intelligence had cracked the diplomatic but not the crucial military codes of the Japanese at this juncture. The more plausible explanation was American disregard for the capabilities of the Japanese, augmented by racial prejudice against Asian peoples in general. If an attack did come, the American military assumed it would be against their vulnerable outpost in the Philippines and the Dutch East Indies, but never against the home port of their Pacific Fleet anchored thousands of miles from Tokyo in apparent safety. The Japanese also miscalculated on two vital fronts—first they assumed that the success of their surprise attack would stun the Americans into submission instead of enraging them into an epic quest for revenge. And second, they were sure that the Nazis would capture Moscow and knock the Soviets out of the war. Instead, the day before Pearl Harbor, the Russians launched their massive winter counteroffensive that flung the exhausted and freezing Germans back from their capital and transformed the European conflict into a long war of attrition that Germany could never win.

But the outbreak of war in the Pacific had deeper roots. The United States and Japan were two increasingly incompatible empires. From the Japanese side, the underlying logic of conquest meant subjecting much of Asia to Japanese control. From the American side, the United States was bound to resist Japanese imperialism because it meant the closing of access to markets, friendly harbors for refueling, naval bases, and sea lanes. A similar kind of logic underlay the conflict between America's open system and the closed system of the Third Reich. There was a deep-seated conflict between liberal and authoritarian values, between the Atlantic Charter and *Mein Kampf.* For American elites, as well as the common people, such values proved to be worth fighting for. Liberal values and America's informal empire were imperiled by Japanese conquest.

The events of 1941—Germany's invasion of the Soviet Union and Japan's attack on Pearl Harbor—launched the United States into the fighting and brought about the Grand Alliance that eventually prevailed over the Axis. Leaders of the United States, Britain, and the Soviet Union recognized the absolute necessity of joining forces with the others to defeat the Axis. Perhaps Churchill best explained the need for the alliance when he said, "If Hitler invaded hell, I would at least make some favorable references to the Devil in the House of Commons." The formation of the Grand Alliance altered the strategic balance of forces in ways that would ultimately be the undoing of the Axis. But with Britain overextended, the Soviet Union on the defensive, and the United States not yet fully mobilized, Axis Powers held the upper hand from 1937 through the end of 1942.

TOTAL WAR

The Second World War was a total war even more than the first. It mobilized whole societies to fight on economic, political, and cultural fronts. And it was even more a war of machines. In the past, it was said, armies fought on their stomachs. Now they fought on their internal combustion engines. The war of machines reached its peak at Kursk south of Moscow in July 1943 with the largest tank battle in history involving rival armadas of some 2,600 tanks on each side supported by 10,000 artillery pieces and 1,800 planes. Its counterpart in naval warfare was the Battle of Leyte Gulf in the Philippines in October 1944, which involved hundreds of naval vessels and hundreds of airplanes.

A war of machines was necessarily a war of production. Measuring the combined economic capacity of the Allies against the Axis, the ratio was almost two to one in favor of the Allies, and the ratio in arms production stood at an even more imbalanced three to one. Oil dictated strategies of the German High

Command in driving toward the Caucasus oil fields, and the same was true for Japan in its southern campaign to capture Dutch oil fields in Indonesia. Yet, the Allies far exceeded the Axis's manufacturing capacity. True to Roosevelt's pledge, the U.S. arsenal of democracy was the main producer of war machines for the Allied effort, producing three hundred thousand airplanes by 1945 and twenty-seven thousand Liberty Ships to ferry supplies. All this materiel came at a cost of over $100 billion annually, more than half of the total U.S. gross national product. As if to confirm Keynesian prescriptions for prosperity, the wartime economic boom in the United States combined with devastation in Europe and Asia to vault the United States so far ahead of other economies by 1945 that it was manufacturing as much as the rest of the world combined.

The war also had a major impact on technology. There were advances in radio and in cryptology on both sides. British efforts code-named Ultra had some success in breaking the German code Enigma, and the improvements in electronic calculations helped lay the foundation for postwar computers. Americans and Japanese also had some success in breaking each other's code. Another technological advance was radar. By the time of Pearl Harbor, primitive devices were in use, although inexperienced operators stationed in Hawaii misread incoming signals and failed to sound the alarm, with fatal results.

Total war also enlisted racial ideologies. Pearl Harbor engendered a spirit of revenge, which combined with racist attitudes toward Asians to produce savage

The view from a Japanese bomber above Pearl Harbor, December 7, 1941.
Franklin D. Roosevelt Presidential Library and Museum.

fighting in the Pacific. Hollywood films turned the war into a simple melodrama of good versus evil, freedom versus slavery, best exemplified in *Why We Fight*, a series of heavy-handed propaganda films directed by Frank Capra, already famous for sentimental films, such as *Mr. Smith Goes to Washington*. At the same time, the Japanese adhered to a belief in their ethnic superiority over other Asians, especially but not only the Chinese. These prejudices led to millions killed in atrocities, as did Nazi racism toward Slavs and Jews.

Class Relations and the Social Contract

Total war dramatically reshaped social relations, although with mostly opposite effects in the Axis Powers and Western democracies. In the Axis and in the Soviet Union, all of society was subordinated to military command and the one-party state. Obedience to hierarchy was the rule of the day from the army platoon to the munitions plant to the local school. By contrast, Western democracies allowed unions and political parties to make demands on elites. American and British authorities sought to win over the working population by expanding the social contract of economic benefits, sharing power, and recognizing claims of women and African Americans for higher status. All of this had a leveling effect in the West.

The same was true of efforts to secure labor peace by granting trade unions guarantees of union membership and a friendly attitude from federal agencies. In this favorable climate, union membership in the United States rose dramatically during the war from about 10.5 million to almost 15 million, on its way toward reaching almost 40 percent of eligible workers in the early 1950s. In a parallel effort to win popular support, social security benefits were boosted, including minimum wages, unemployment compensation, and retirement benefits, all of which pointed toward an expanded postwar welfare state. In Britain, the 1944 Beveridge Plan established an even more ambitious welfare system with socialized medicine and extensive investment in public housing. In short, the war expanded the social contract in the Western democracies.

The war also produced *mixed* economies in Western nations—that is, a combination of private enterprise and public regulation that preserved the profit motive at the heart of capitalism while incorporating aspects of Socialism. Pushing liberal restraints aside, the war emergency brought forth unprecedented state intervention in the market in the form of food rationing, price controls, and huge state investment in everything from aluminum plants to atomic research. To pay for this, income taxes were increased and rates were made more progressive—another leveling effect—but most of the bills were paid by patriotic citizens who loaned the government money through war bonds. All told, expansion of the social contract, power sharing with wage earners, extensive public investment, and close regulation combined to produce an increasingly mixed economy. The choice of powerful elites to address the needs of the working majority further strengthened the foundations of democracy.

Labor and Women Workers

For the warring nations, labor resources were of the utmost importance. Once Germany turned to total war, the need for fresh supplies of workers became more urgent. Technocrats in charge of production, such as Albert Speer, woke up to the fact that killing Russian prisoners of war (a total of three million died, mostly through starvation) deprived the Reich of much-needed labor. In a shift of policy, German armies rolling through Eastern Europe began to round up as many able hands as they could and ship them back to the Reich. All told, some eight million forced laborers constituted as much as one-third of the work force in arms factories and a quarter in other essential war industries, and an additional two million were under German discipline elsewhere. Here was another case of the cycle of conquest: nations at war expanding to seize the labor necessary for further expansion.

In contrast, the United States relied more heavily on labor markets than forced labor to meet growing labor needs. The relative strength of the market compared to the state was one of the main differences between the United States and Germany, although these differences narrowed substantially during the war. In the United States, the main method of mobilizing labor was to recruit from the reserve army of the unemployed, which as late as 1939 stood at 15 percent of the total labor force. With war orders coming in and military enlistments rapidly rising toward a peak of twelve million, unemployment virtually disappeared by 1943. In addition, new sources of labor were found in the countryside. In a reversal of Depression-era trends, rural laborers and sharecroppers, black and white, boarded trains and buses and headed north to war plants in Chicago and Detroit. Mexican and Puerto Rican agricultural workers poured onto U.S. farms and fields, replacing U.S. labor now in uniform. Women also answered the call. Like Rosie the Riveter, the symbolic poster figure with rolled-up sleeves and bulging biceps, women took jobs in industries where women had not been seen before. From 1939 to 1944, the proportion of employed women over the age of fourteen rose from 26 percent to 32 percent.

Britain followed a similar course, although with greater state direction. When unemployment was eliminated in 1941, British authorities resorted to conscripting unmarried women in certain age groups for work in defense plants, with the result that the proportion of employed women over the age of fourteen rose from 27 percent in 1939 to 37 percent in 1943, somewhat higher than in the United States. One result was to nearly eliminate the class of female domestic servants living "below stairs," a group that had been so important to class consciousness in prewar Britain. Even in this class-ridden society, the war had a leveling effect on social relations.

Women played an even greater role in the Soviet Union. In this Communist society, the servant class, at least in theory, had already been eliminated, and women fought on the front lines of the war from the beginning. Whereas there were only a handful of American women pilots trained to fly planes behind the lines, Soviet women piloted aircraft on combat missions. Moreover, already accustomed to working outside the home, Soviet women increased their already large share of the civilian labor market from 38 percent in 1940 to 53 percent by 1942.

Nothing better illustrates the difference gender ideology makes than the contrast between the roles of women on the two sides of the war. Under the Nazis' reactionary ideas of patriarchal order, women belonged with *Kinder, Kirche, und Kuche* (children, church, and kitchen), not in the workplace or in positions of authority, let alone in the supremely masculine world of battlefield combat. Nazi bureaucrats met increasingly desperate needs, not by recruiting women, but through the forced labor of foreigners, prisoners of war, and slaves. Women's employment outside the home barely changed during the war, and maids remained on duty. Nazi economic planners were able to say truthfully that by and large Aryan women remained at home in fulfillment of their "biological" duty. Much the same was true in Japan. Until the last desperate months of the war, Japanese authorities kept women in the home in an effort to preserve the kind of male dominance they had long been accustomed to.

Race Changes

The war had a major impact on racial attitudes. As with beliefs about gender, there was a contrast between Axis and Allied societies. For Nazi Germany, in particular, World War II was a race war. Since Hitler wrote *Mein Kampf* in the 1920s, the Nazi movement held Germans to be a master Aryan race destined to rule over various inferior groups known as *Untermenschen*, such as Poles, Russians, and other Slavic peoples. Such racism helps explain the staggering brutality the Nazis visited upon their victims, including, for example, measuring what happened as people were deliberately frozen to death. The utter dehumanization of Jews and Roma (Gypsies) was a precondition for the Holocaust that followed.

The imperial ambitions of Japan and Russia were infused with racial beliefs that were only somewhat less virulent. Reacting against European pretensions of white supremacy, the proud Japanese had been asserting racial equality since the Versailles Peace Conference of 1919, while at the same time propounding a vision of Pan-Asian racial unity. But this broad vision of Asian identity was overridden by a narrow Japanese nationalism. Japanese thinkers imitated social Darwinists by dividing humanity into a hierarchy of races, but then placed the Japanese—the Yamato Race—on top. As with the Nazis, the dehumanization of supposedly inferior races was a precondition of the violence that took place in the rape of Nanjing and in the medical experimentation on human subjects in the Japanese-conquered provinces of Manchuria and Korea. The Soviets carried out horrendous wartime atrocities against ethnic minorities in the Caucasus, the Ukraine, and the Crimea, among those suspected of collaboration with the Germans. Whole ethnic groups such as the Chechens, Kalmyks, Don Cossacks, Crimean Tatars, and Volga Germans were marched en masse to Siberia. Nearly

40 percent of them died from disease, malnutrition, and exposure during their resettlements.

Racism was also present in the Western democracies. Anti-Semitism played a role in the weak response to Nazi death camps, whose existence was known to Allied leaders as early as 1942. In 1943, Orthodox rabbis organized a march on Washington to demand that the United States do more to end the killing of Jews in Europe, but President Roosevelt declined to meet with them. In the summer and fall of 1944, John J. McCloy, the assistant secretary of war, rejected pleas to bomb the Nazi gas chambers and rail lines at Auschwitz. Whether such bombing would have significantly reduced the slaughter has been debated ever since.

Thus, despite revulsion against the Nazi theory of an Aryan master race, white supremacy continued to be the order of the day in the United States. Anti-Semitism persisted alongside antiblack and anti-Japanese sentiment during the war. From beginning to end, African Americans were forced to fight in segregated units. Racial hatred also played a role in the violence committed by American GIs against so-called Japs, and anti-Japanese prejudice contributed to the decision to intern all residents of Japanese descent, citizens and foreigners alike, living within two hundred miles of the Pacific Coast. Indeed, because the majority of those interned were born in the United States, the internment policy suspended the rights of some seventy thousand American citizens. American citizens of German and Italian descent were also subject to internment, although in much smaller

Photograph by Dorothea Lange of a grandfather and grandson at the War Relocation Authority Center. In contrast to the photos of her colleague, Ansel Adams, Lange's photographs captured the tragic dimension of internment.
Dorothea Lange Gallery, National Park Service, https://www.nps.gov/manz/learn/photos multimedia/dorothea-lange-gallery.htm

numbers. United States servicemen savagely beat Mexican American youths in Southern California and the Southwest during the infamous Zoot Suit riots of 1943, reflecting the racial tensions against the swelling population of Mexican braceros who came to the United States to work during the war.

At the same time, the war experience helped dismantle ideologies of white supremacy. An increasing number of Western scholars launched attacks on segregation. For example, the Swedish sociologist Gunnar Myrdal published an influential book in 1944 in which he appealed to Yankees to put an end to the "American dilemma" by resolving the contradiction between racism and democracy. African Americans had been highlighting that basic contradiction since the American Revolution, and now civil rights leaders waged a double-V campaign for victory over the Axis abroad alongside victory over racism at home. Official steps in this direction were few and far between, but the most important was Roosevelt's 1941 Executive Order 8802 prohibiting racial discrimination in federal contracts. Roosevelt issued the order to head off a threatened march on Washington led by A. Philip Randolph, head of the Brotherhood of Sleeping Car Porters. Randolph had called for urgent action, pointing to the similarity between American and German racism to advance the cause of racial equality in the United States: "Oppression of the Negroes in the United States, like suppression of the Jews in Germany, may open the way for a Fascist dictatorship." Nonetheless, a vicious race riot in Detroit in June 1943 raged for three days, claimed thirty-four lives, and necessitated the deployment of U.S. combat troops that might have better served in the fight against racist Nazis rather than against racist Americans.

Another challenge to ideas of white superiority came in the 1943 repeal of the 1882 Chinese Exclusion Act, which had barred the immigration of Chinese laborers to the United States. The World War II alliance between the United States and China helped challenge long-standing prejudices against the yellow races of Asia. Pearl S. Buck, the Pulitzer Prize–winning author of *The Good Earth* (1931), a novel about life in China, spoke publicly in support of the repeal during congressional hearings in 1943. Buck argued that the United States should repeal Chinese exclusion as a war measure. "The Japanese," she argued, "have not failed to taunt [the Chinese] with the friendliness of our words and the unfriendliness of our deeds." President Roosevelt signed the repeal in 1943, stating such an act would "silence the distorted Japanese propaganda."

World War II also helped to discredit the entire legacy of social Darwinism. The war undermined the belief in a strict hierarchy of races and cast doubt on the pseudoscience of eugenics. Desegregation efforts accelerated as African American veterans returned from the battleground to demand their civil rights. Colonial subjects also seized on the moment to advance the cause of freedom. The war gave Africans and Asians newfound strength to oppose their increasingly debilitated colonial masters. Finally, the defeat of the Axis Powers discredited master race theories and allowed the Enlightenment tradition of individual human rights to become enshrined in the 1948 Universal Declaration of Human Rights. Ironically, what began as a race war ended up undermining racism.

Allied Victory: The Russian Contribution

Militarily, the war unfolded in two phases. In the first, lasting from 1937 through the middle of 1942, victory belonged to the Axis. The Japanese won a string of unbroken conquests—China, Indochina, Indonesia, the Philippines, Pearl Harbor—that extended what was known as the Co-Prosperity Sphere throughout East Asia and the western Pacific. Meanwhile, the Germans and their Italian partners overran Europe from the shores of the Atlantic to the gates of Moscow. The Axis seemed poised for further victories that would enable the Germans moving from the west and the Japanese moving from the east to join forces in India and thereby capture all of Eurasia. Against such a colossal force, the peripheral powers of Britain and the United States would not likely have been able to hold out.

That the world did not come to live under Swastikas and Rising Suns was the consequence of two developments. The first was successful Russian resistance to the German advance. The heroic defenses of Moscow and Leningrad forced German war planners to abandon Blitzkrieg in early 1942 in favor of a long-term war of attrition. As soon as Germany was forced into such a war on the steppes of Russia, it was fighting a losing battle. With the joint resources of the Grand Alliance beginning to resist the Axis, Churchill took note of the shift in a speech on November 10, 1942, following the British decisive victory over the Afrika Korps at El Alamein: "This is not the end," he said. "It is not even the beginning of the end. But it is, perhaps, the end of the beginning."

Churchill's hunch was soon proven correct by German defeat at Stalingrad. Stymied in the Russian north and center, German forces turned south toward the oil fields of the Caucasus. Adjusting their strategy to a war of attrition, war planners in Berlin made obtaining oil the highest priority. To secure the approaches to the Caucasus, they needed to take the Soviet strongpoint at Stalingrad, the namesake of the Soviet dictator, which stretched out along the broad Volga River running south to the Caspian Sea. The Battle of Stalingrad witnessed some of the most horrendous fighting of what had already become the most destructive war in human history. A German officer described the grisly battle, street by street, house by house: "We have fought for fifteen days for a single house with mortars, grenades, machine-guns and bayonets. Already by the third day fifty-four German corpses are strewn in the cellars, on the landings, and the staircases." After six months of artillery barrages, which reduced Stalingrad to a rubble-strewn graveyard for perhaps one million soldiers and civilians, German Field Marshal Friedrich von Paulus finally capitulated. A Russian commander named Chuikov bade farewell to the ruined city: "Goodbye, our friends, lie in peace in the land soaked with the blood of our people. We are going west and our duty is to avenge your deaths." Two years later, he and his comrades marched into Berlin.

Had German armies succeeded in cutting through to the Caucasus, they might have moved on to the Middle East, linked up with Field Marshal Erwin Rommel's Afrika Korps advancing from Egypt, and continued toward India.

There, depending on fighting in Asia, they could have joined with the Japanese. Failure to capture the oil fields deprived the German war machine of its most essential resource and allowed Russia to rebuild its arms factories and then go on the offensive in 1943–44. That is why Americans followed the battle with close attention. They knew that their own fate hung on the outcome of the battle on the Volga. Mighty battles were yet to be fought on the eastern front at Kursk, Kiev, Belarus, and Warsaw before the Russian offensive succeeded in stopping the *Wehrmacht*. But Stalingrad was the turning point, after which the Allies advanced steadily toward final victory. Some 75 percent of all German casualties in the Second World War occurred on the eastern front.

Allied Victory: D-Day and the American Contribution

The second reason the tide turned against the Axis was Anglo-American industrial output and firepower. American might was first brought to bear in the Allied invasions of North Africa and Italy. Then on June 6, 1944, when American, British, and Canadian troops landed at Normandy (D-Day), the Germans were forced to fight on two fronts, the same disadvantage they faced in the First World War, while also contending with the Allies' strategic bombing campaign. Civilian populations of industrial cities were especially hard hit, although, as later revealed by the Allied Strategic Bombing Survey, the Germans were able to maintain a high level of military production. General Dwight Eisenhower, Supreme Allied Commander, wisely used the strengths of his subordinates, the cautious Bernard Montgomery, the top British field marshal, and the impetuous American general George Patton, to drive German forces across northern France and turn back the last German counterattack in December 1944 at the Battle of the Bulge.

It took six months of fierce combat to push German armies back across the Rhine River toward Berlin. In recognition of the leading role of Soviet forces in defeating the Germans, Eisenhower agreed to allow Russian armies the honor of taking the Nazi capital of Berlin. The possibility of ferocious resistance that in the end claimed half a million Red Army casualties may have played a role in his decision as well. Eisenhower was also aware that Berlin lay in the Soviet postwar occupational zone agreed on by the Allies at Yalta. By the time the Russians got there in April 1945, Hitler and his mistress, Eva Braun, had retreated to an underground bunker and taken cyanide, thus ending Nazi ambitions of the Thousand Year Reich.

When the Germans finally capitulated on May 8, 1945, fighting was still raging in Asia. Although the final outcome was not in doubt, it took superior American firepower to overcome Japanese ferocity. Under a modern version of the *bushido* code of the warrior, Japanese soldiers came forward on suicide missions, including *banzai* charges and the notorious *kamikaze* ("divine wind") pilots who crashed their planes into U.S. ships in defiance of defeat. Unlike Europe, where the Russians bore the brunt of the Allied effort, in the Pacific theater it was the

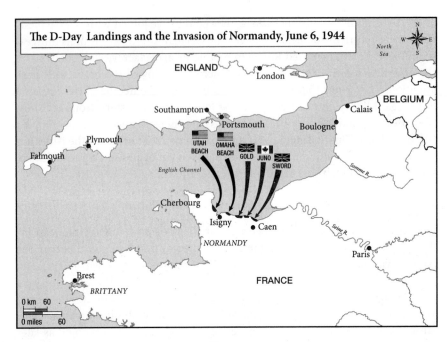

MAP 7.2

Americans who took the battle to the enemy in an island-hopping campaign against forces who had often been ordered to die rather than surrender.

In what became the largest naval battle in history, the naval forces of the two sides met at Leyte Gulf in the Philippines in late October 1944. In a battle spread over hundreds of miles, the Japanese had the advantage of the world's largest battleships, shrewd decoy maneuvers, and *kamikaze* missions. But American fleets under Admirals Halsey, Mitscher, and Kinkaid prevailed. The triumph of American sea power enabled General Douglas MacArthur, Allied commander in the Pacific, to make good on his pledge, "I shall return." MacArthur led his forces ashore to retake the Philippines, while other Americans recaptured the Mariana Islands, which in November 1944 became launching pads for B-29 bombing raids on Tokyo.

Even as the *bushido* code continued to drive the Japanese army, Japan faced severe shortages at home. At a time when American production of planes and ships was increasing, Japanese factories lacked the oil and other resources necessary to replenish dwindling war stocks. Already in 1942 the disparity in firepower was evident in the fact that for every American serving in the Pacific theater there were four tons of supplies, compared to a scant two pounds for every Japanese. The highly successful American submarine campaign in the Pacific cut Japan off from its far-flung imperial resources.

The two reasons for Allied victory—Russian resistance and American output and firepower—point to the future alignment of world power. By the late winter of 1945, it was becoming clear that war was hastening the shift of power away from Western Europe toward the United States and the Soviet Union, subordinating the once-dominant force in world affairs to what would soon be known as the two superpowers.

ENDGAME

Superpower strength became evident in Allied diplomacy at the end of the war. Although the press spoke of "the Big Three"—Roosevelt, Churchill, and Stalin—behind the scenes it was clear that American and Soviet aims counted the most. Although everyone wanted a postwar framework that would prevent a Third World war, there were underlying differences over how to achieve world peace, since each side's foreign policy was a projection of the inner conflicts of its own social system. For the Americans, that meant an open world of individual competition moderated by government regulation of the sort embodied in New Deal and wartime regulations, an ideal expressed in Roosevelt's call for the Four Freedoms.

For the Soviets, a closed system at home dictated centralized control over adjacent territory. As Soviet armies swept through Eastern Europe on the way to Berlin, Stalin was determined to reclaim the tsarist empire lost during the First World War—and more. As he put it, "Whoever occupies a territory also imposes on it his own social system," a lesson learned after the September 1943 Italian surrender from which the Western Allies excluded Stalin when they established a capitalist democracy there. Uppermost in his mind was denying Western powers who were hostile to Russia invasion routes into his nation as in 1812, 1914, and 1941. The Soviets had suffered an enormous loss of life and property from the Nazi invasion and were determined never to see this happen again. It would not be long, however, before the differences between an open liberal empire and a closed territorial empire would shape the conflict that became known as the Cold War.

But in 1945, the relationship between the Allies was still marked by cooperation. After a preliminary meeting in Tehran, Iran, the Big Three met in the Crimean resort of Yalta in February 1945 to draw up the outlines of the postwar world they knew they were going to dominate. As they rushed in from opposite sides to fill the power vacuum left by the total collapse of the Third Reich, Americans and Russians shared several goals. Uppermost was making sure that the *Wehrmacht* would never again be able to march across Europe as it had done twice in living memory. Unlike 1918, Germany would be forced to surrender unconditionally and would be divided into Allied zones of occupation, with Berlin under joint occupation. At Yalta, they also confirmed the intention of founding an international organization—the United Nations—to keep the peace in the postwar era.

The spirit of cooperation was also evident in agreements on Eastern Europe. Despite clashing aims and Churchill's suspicions that both Roosevelt and Stalin held imperial ambitions, the Big Three bowed to the reality of military control already on the ground. The British had control of Greece, and the Soviets had tens of thousands of Soviet tanks plus more than three million Soviet troops spread out from the Baltic Sea in the north to the Balkans in the south. In the case of Poland, twice Germany's invasion route into Russia, Stalin remarked, "Poland is not only a question of honor but of life and death for the Soviet Union." Just as the Western Powers at Versailles had established an independent Poland to hold back Bolshevik expansion, now Stalin was determined to do the same thing in reverse, that is, to establish a pro-Soviet regime as a barrier against another invasion from the West. Differences between the open system of the West and the closed system of the East were papered over by the Allied Declaration on Liberated Europe, which delivered Wilsonian-style pronouncements about self-determination. In another Yalta agreement, the Soviets promised to break their nonaggression pact and attack Japan within three months after the conclusion of the war in Europe.

The third and last Allied conference was held in July at Potsdam just outside Berlin. By this time, underlying tensions were coming to the surface, and Potsdam was as acrimonious as Yalta was harmonious. President Roosevelt had died of a brain aneurism in April, and his successor, Harry Truman, was not an experienced diplomat. Emboldened by the success of the first atom bomb test at Trinity and, therefore, less eager for Russian intervention against Japan, Truman gave a tongue lashing to Soviet Foreign Minister Molotov, prompting Molotov to complain, "I have never been talked to like that." In addition, disputes over borders and governments in Eastern Europe went unresolved. With Britain and France slipping into second rank, Potsdam revealed the potential for superpower conflict.

Hiroshima and Nagasaki

Only one superpower had developed an atomic bomb. Following an appeal by Albert Einstein to develop an atomic weapon before Germany did, President Roosevelt began what eventually became the Manhattan Project. Under the command of General Leslie Groves, physicist J. Robert Oppenheimer assembled the best available American and British scientific talent at facilities spread out from a converted football stadium at the University of Chicago to the top-secret installation at Los Alamos, New Mexico. By July 1945 at the Trinity test site in New Mexico, scientists proved that splitting atoms of uranium-235 in a chain reaction would convert small amounts of mass into huge amounts of energy as predicted by Einstein's equation $E = mc^2$ (energy equals mass times the speed of light squared). Groves informed President Truman during the Potsdam Conference in late July that two atom bombs were ready, and Truman immediately ordered them to be prepared for use against Japan.

On July 26, the Allies issued the Potsdam Declaration calling on Japan to surrender unconditionally or face "prompt and utter destruction." At this point, Japanese leaders were divided between die-hards prepared to go down in suicidal resistance and moderates who were trying to get the Russians to mediate peace terms. What the Japanese did not know is that Stalin had promised at Yalta to bring Russian forces into the fighting within three months of the end of war in Europe.

In response to Japanese delay, Truman ordered the first atom bomb be dropped on Hiroshima. Dropped by the B-29 *Enola Gay*, the single uranium-235 bomb destroyed the entire city center, killed some 78,000 people almost immediately, and took the lives of up to 140,000 within a year through the scourges of burns and infection, along with the strange new sickness of radiation poisoning. Three days later, a plutonium bomb was dropped on Nagasaki, bringing the combined death toll from both bombs to more than 200,000. The targets were chosen not for their military value—indeed, their insignificance had spared them from previous bombing—but as a demonstration of the utter destruction that awaited. Since there were no more atom bombs, this was something of a bluff, and planning continued to go forward for a possible U.S. land invasion slated for November.

Whether such an invasion would have been necessary without the atom bombs has been the subject of much dispute. On the one hand, the fierce *kamikaze* defense of outlying islands—fully 250,000 Japanese had died defending Okinawa—foretold a willingness to fight to the finish in the home islands. On the other hand, Japan had something else to worry about in early August. On August 8, between the two atomic bombs, Stalin made good on his Yalta promise and ordered Soviet troops to attack Japanese forces in Manchuria. Suddenly, the Japanese were faced with the strategic danger they had tried to avoid in 1941 when they had made peace with Russia on the north to have a free hand to advance toward the oil fields in the south. Now the Japanese were being overrun in Manchuria while they were in full retreat in the South Pacific.

In the emperor's radio message of surrender—the unprecedented sound of a voice many regarded as divine was almost as astonishing as what he said—he made no mention of Hiroshima or Nagasaki and instead referred to "the unfavorable balance of forces arrayed against us," seemingly a reference to the outbreak of war with Russia. In assessing Japan's decision to surrender on August 14, it seems likely that the two factors—American bombs and Russian ground attack—finally convinced the emperor that the war was over.

Sorrow of War

It would be hard to find a period in history that compares to the concentrated brutality of the Second World War. The fact that it killed more people—on the order of sixty million—than all the wars of the past three centuries combined does not even begin to express the degree of suffering. Unlike previous wars where most casualties were soldiers, perhaps 70 percent of those killed were civilians, victims of savage massacres, carpet-bombing, mass starvation, and genocide.

The worst atrocities were perpetrated by the Axis aggressors. Their crimes included the siege of Leningrad and Moscow, the attempt to exterminate the Jews, the rape of Nanjing, and the killing of defenseless prisoners of war in the Bataan death march in the Philippines. But it is important to remember that the Allies also committed atrocities. Having discovered early on that high-flying bombers often missed their military targets, the Allies resorted to carpet-bombing of whole cities, creating in cases like Dresden and Hamburg horrible firestorms that incinerated and asphyxiated those who were not hit directly by bombs. In Japan, the U.S. fire-bombed Tokyo in March 1945, killing tens of thousands of civilians and destroying fully one-quarter of the city. And in the Katyn Massacre near Smolensk, Russia, the Soviet Secret Police murdered 4,400 Polish officers who Stalin had classified as enemies of Soviet authority.

Of all those who fought in the war, it was the Russians who likely suffered the most, some twenty-seven million deaths, several million from Stalin himself. Russians suffered an untold level of destruction of cities and towns and accounted for approximately one-third of the war's entire death toll. The loss of life was also immense in China and Poland, with estimates of eleven to fourteen million in the former and four to five million in the later, including millions of Polish Jews. By comparison, Americans suffered the least. Apart from Pearl Harbor and the occasional Japanese air balloon or German submarine appearing off shore, American land was not ravaged and few civilians died. The loss of 417,000 U.S. soldiers, three times the level of the First World War, was awful enough, but paled in comparison to the losses of the other nations. America's relative good fortune in being spared the worst reinforced the sense of being a chosen people invulnerable to attack.

CONCLUSION

It would take decades for the consequences of the Second World War to become clear. Some of the most important results will be explored in subsequent chapters on the Cold War and the end of European colonialism. But some results were already apparent in 1945. Above all, there was no doubt that the Fascist path to the future, whether German, Italian, or Japanese, was closed off for good as a global, visionary ideology. In the future, ideological conflicts would largely take place within an Enlightenment framework of belief in scientific reason, social progress, and human rights.

Just as the horrors of the First World War had amplified the Geneva Conventions, so the greater atrocities of the Second World War led to expanded efforts to apply the Enlightenment framework to the conduct of war itself. In trials of two dozen German leaders at Nuremberg and similar trials for their Japanese counterparts, the victors drew up the Nuremberg Principles, which added three new criminal categories to international law in outlawing war crimes, crimes against humanity, and wars of aggression. Under these principles, eleven Germans and seven Japanese leaders were condemned to death. In local trials, the former occupied nations of Europe hung hundreds more or imprisoned them for long sentences.

Another consequence was to raise the standing of common people. In contrast to the outcome of the First World War, the second coming of total war served to institutionalize government regulation of business, collective bargaining, consumer controls, and the social contract of the welfare state. These measures went furthest under the Soviet command economy, but the war experience convinced even individualistic America to accept the New Deal as a permanent arrangement.

Not surprisingly, these outcomes were seen as a moral good among the victors. But even the vanquished soon came to accept the new framework as enshrined in the United Nations and its Universal Declaration of Human Rights. There was a widespread feeling that the outcome of the most ghastly war in human history had, nonetheless, been a triumph for the good. Moral philosophers were left to speculate about how it was that something filled with the evils of genocide, firestorms, and atomic bombing, among a long list of atrocities, could have yielded positive changes for society.

In terms of world affairs, it was clear that Western Europe would no longer be the preeminent center of world power. In a development replete with irony, the rulers of Germany had gone to war in an effort to expand their power, only to succeed in wiping out any possibility of a Thousand Year Reich. The same irony applied to Japan's doomed effort to create a Greater East Asia Co-Prosperity Sphere. Moreover, the war had so weakened even victorious Britain and France that the future of their colonial empires was in serious doubt.

The centers of world power were shifting toward the Soviet Union in the East and especially toward the United States in the West. No one had to persuade Stalin of the need to exercise world power, but unlike in the aftermath of the First World War, American elites were now ready to step forward as well. Americans had come a long way in the half-century since 1898. Although a handful of prophets had foreseen American ascendancy, few had imagined that the country would rise to the point where it was the single most powerful force in the world. Thus were the seeds sown for a new conflict between the two superpowers, one with even greater stakes now that nuclear weapons had been developed.

FURTHER READING

Azuma, Eiichiro. *Between Two Empires: Race, History and Transnationalism in Japanese America*. Oxford: Oxford University Press, 2005.

Borgwardt, Elizabeth. *A New Deal for the World: America's Vision for Human Rights*. Cambridge, MA: Harvard University Press, 2007.

Dower, John. *War without Mercy: Race and Power in the Pacific War*. New York: Pantheon Books, 1986.

Gerstle, Gary. *American Crucible: Race and Nation in the Twentieth Century*. Princeton, NJ: Princeton University Press, 2017.

Green, Michael Cullen. *Black Yanks in the Pacific: Race in the Making of American Military Empire after World War II.* Ithaca, NY: Cornell University Press, 2010.

Kitamura, Hiroshi. *Screening Enlightenment: Hollywood and the Cultural Reconstruction of Defeated Japan.* Ithaca, NY: Cornell University Press, 2010.

Ramírez, Catherine S. *The Woman in the Zoot Suit: Gender, Nationalism, and the Cultural Politics of Memory.* Durham, NC: Duke University Press, 2009.

Takaki, Ronald. *Double Victory: A Multicultural History of America in World War II.* Boston, Little, Brown, 2001.

Thompson, Michael. *For God and Globe: Christian Internationalism in the United States between the Great War and the Cold War.* Ithaca, NY: Cornell University Press, 2015.

Part 2

BURDENS OF THE COLOSSUS, 1945–2012

CHAPTER 8

AMERICA'S COLD WAR ASCENDANCY, 1945–54

When U.S. Army troops took this picture near the Pegnitz River in Germany on April 20, 1945, Allied forces had already discovered the horrors of the Bergen–Belsen and Buchenwald concentration camps and the brutal destruction of Dresden. The scars of battle, like the devastation of this industrial zone in Nuremberg, were a common feature of war-torn Europe. National Archives at College Park–Still Pictures (RDSS).

GEORGE MARSHALL IN MOSCOW: 1947

> *In March 1947, a high-level meeting of World War II victors took place in Moscow to settle the postwar world. The U.S. secretary of state, George C. Marshall, the soldier-statesman best known for the Marshall Plan, the recovery*

program that pumped $17 billion dollars of aid into Europe to rebuild its economy and avert political collapse roughly a year later, led the U.S. delegation. Born in a small, rural Pennsylvania town in 1880, distant from the expanding global economy, but quietly caught in its currents, Marshall's career exemplifies America's growing engagement with the world in the twentieth century. Marshall began his military career in 1902, when he helped suppress the Philippine resistance to U.S. occupation. Thereafter, he served in the First World War and gradually climbed through the ranks during World War II to become the army chief of staff. Marshall won praise as the organizer of victory for his sharp administrative mind and ability to rapidly mobilize eight million soldiers to fight in the war. His other defining qualities—good judgment and resolute leadership—prompted President Harry Truman to recruit Marshall to head the State Department at a time of increasing tensions with the Soviet Union in the spring of 1946.

In Moscow, Vyacheslav Mikhailovich Molotov, the Soviet foreign minister, welcomed Marshall to the postwar negotiations. Like his U.S. counterpart, Molotov embodied the Soviet Union's rise to global prominence in the twentieth century. Born one of ten children in a small Russian town under tsarist rule, he joined the movement that brought about the Bolshevik Revolution in 1917. Hardened by the brutal politics of revolution and the Soviet state, Molotov moved up the party ranks to become a member of the Politburo (the main governing body in the Soviet Union). Known as a loyalist to the Soviet premier Stalin and a headstrong negotiator, he became commissar of foreign affairs and in 1939 negotiated the Non-Aggression Pact with Nazi Germany. When the Soviet Union joined the Allies after the German invasion, Molotov became the chief Soviet representative in the Grand Alliance with Britain and the United States.

By the time these two seasoned diplomats faced one another in Moscow, hopes for continued cooperation in the postwar settlement process were in doubt and quickly fading. When Molotov demanded billions in reparations from a united Germany, Marshall firmly rebuffed him. Likewise, when Marshall demanded open access to Eastern Europe, Molotov dismissed the idea as "an opportunity for British and American industrialists to penetrate the area and establish economic empires." After five weeks of fruitless discussion, the negotiations ended in deadlock. Abandoning all prospects of working with the Soviets, Marshall headed home to begin work on the European Recovery Program that would bear his name: the Marshall Plan. Molotov would soon follow with his own trade system that would link Soviet bloc countries in a tight alliance called the Molotov Plan.

With the world divided ideologically, geographically, and economically between America's open system of liberal capitalism and constitutional democracy in the West and the Soviet Union's closed system of socialism in the East, the two largest powers had set the boundaries of the Cold War. And since British prime minister Winston Churchill had designated that dividing line the Iron Curtain one year before in a Fulton, Missouri, speech, it was a boundary that had been named before it was created. Yet, the appearances were deceptive, and it quickly became evident that the Cold War geographies were not as stable as they seemed.

AMERICAN ASCENDANCY IN THE COLD WAR

The story of America's rise during the early years of the Cold War marks a pivotal turning point in world history. Never before had one state ascended to such heights of wealth and power in world affairs. Great empires of the past—Rome, imperial China, Spain—had achieved preeminence in their own regions, but there was no precedent for one superpower that exercised such a broad spectrum of global dominance; not even Great Britain had that standing. The United States was on the verge of attaining true global supremacy for the way it combined military, political, and economic superiority with control over culture, media, and ideas under one flag.

Two world wars and the stark bipolar system of the Cold War had opened the door to U.S. power, but another key development in America's ascendancy was the appearance of new frontiers that emerged at the outer reaches or margins of the superpowers. The boundaries where the two powers met took on added meaning in the polarized politics of the Cold War. They defined zones of contact, or borderlands, where rivals competed for wealth, territory, and power. They shaped imagined spaces that transformed and erased preexisting loyalties and political identities and created new ones. The dividing lines running down and across places like Germany, Korea, and Vietnam dotted Cold War maps in a testament to the standing that borderlands held in the postwar reality. Yet, as negotiated spaces at the edge of American and Soviet power, these borderlands proved more dynamic and less predictable than either country anticipated. In the ungovernable interstices of the Cold War, borderland communities carved out some measure of self-determination, which frustrated the ambitions of the United States and the Soviet Union. Managing the borderlands quickly took center stage in global politics, and the superpowers look less like masters of the postwar world and more like servants to its impulses.

For all its power, therefore, the United States was by no means omnipotent, and neither was its counterpart, the Soviet Union. The need to carefully monitor and intervene on its borders checked the other's global reach; both committed atrocities on the borderlands in the name of security, although Soviet Union violence outdistanced the trauma the United States inflicted by a wide margin; but neither could contain the upstart powers on its borders or local people who sought to chart their own path. Conflict between the United States and the Soviet Union made world affairs bipolar and it shaped—some say disfigured—world history in myriad unpredictable ways.

The World in 1945

The power vacuum at the heart of Europe following the war made it possible for the United States and the Soviet Union to assume commanding positions once the fighting stopped. What had been the main power center of world history for the previous three centuries had torn itself apart in two cataclysmic world wars. The piles of rubble gathered throughout Europe seemed to be all that was left of its great civilization. Surveying the wreckage, American travelers were overwhelmed by the extent of the destruction. Many German cities had been leveled by Allied bombs. On a visit to Berlin, General Lucius Clay, no stranger to the destruction of war, was shaken by the sight of streets piled high with broken buildings: "It was like a city of the dead." Taking time off from the Potsdam Conference in July 1945, President Truman was awestruck when he toured bombed-out Berlin: "I was thankful that the United States had been spared the unbelievable devastation of this war." The images were equally shocking in Asia. American visitors to Japan described the fifteen-mile stretch from Tokyo to Yokohama as a wilderness of rubble. Worst of all was Hiroshima and Nagasaki, where the atomic bombs killed 230,000 unsuspecting people (100,000 instantaneously) and left lasting effects so tragic that the U.S. government suppressed newsreel footage of the bombs' wreckage for over a decade.

If the vanquished lay in shambles, the victors hardly fared better. The Soviet Union had suffered worst of all among the Allies, losing as many as twenty-seven million soldiers and civilians. Starvation ravaged the country, the result of infrastructural devastation that saw some thirty thousand industrial plants, forty thousand miles of railroad track, and ninety-eight thousand collective farms destroyed. Britain also felt the devastating effects of modern weaponry. The bombers of the Nazi *Luftwaffe* during the Blitz of 1940, and then the random destruction of V-1 and V-2 rockets hurled across the English Channel, hit London hard. Aside from the total war casualties that eclipsed four hundred thousand, the bombings destroyed over 116,000 buildings in London, not to mention British industry in places like Coventry and Birmingham.

Against this grim backdrop, Truman's gratitude for America being spared the war's devastation is easy to understand. Except for the bombing of Pearl Harbor, there had been no fighting on American soil, no cities were destroyed, food production continued without major disruption, and communities remained relatively stable save for the effects of the Great Depression and soldiers going off to war. Because the infrastructure of factories, mines, railroads, and communications was all intact, wartime orders produced an economic boom that gave the U.S. economy more than 40 percent of the world's manufacturing and the lion's share of the world's gold reserves. Equally comforting was the U.S. monopoly of nuclear weapons that, when deployed against the empire of Japan, seemed to signal a new era in modern warfare.

All were signs of America's ascendancy in the hierarchy of nations, but what made the United States stand out was the way it leveraged the softer side of its power. In terms of mass culture, commodities, and technological innovation, no other country could match American output, and that gave the United States international prestige. Having been welcomed in France and Italy as liberators and "invited" to take an active role in their redevelopment, Americans arrived with the historic baggage of would-be conquerors, but they did not behave as such. If the United States resembled an empire, it was an unusually friendly one to the devastated world and it was surely indifferent to the role. Because they had no ambition for territorial conquest beyond military bases in strategic locations and because they had made anticolonialism a condition for their participation in the war through the Atlantic Charter, it seemed that friend and foe alike, even Germany and Japan, welcomed American occupiers after the war. How could they not, when cheerful GIs were able to win people over with cigarettes, Coca-Cola, and the promise to depart once things improved?

Like the French woman offering a drink to an American soldier in this undated image, locals welcomed Allied forces throughout Europe. Experiences such as this one made America's new role as a global leader seem natural and justified.
National Archives at College Park–Still Pictures (RDSS).

Such a benign posture masked the harder side of the economic and cultural forces at play. For many, America's genial presence abroad—in the form of soft drinks, cigarettes, Hollywood films, and tourists—obscured the gravity of what it meant for the United States to be the only fortunate one standing amid the rubble.

Internationalism Reborn

Americans emerged from the Second World War with more than a sense of their own fortune. They also carried a determination to use their awesome power for good in the midst of a world hungry for leadership and access to resources. Indeed, the call for the United States to take the reins came from places far and wide, from the developed countries of Europe and Asia to old countries with histories that stretched back to the beginning of civilization and new states not yet fully formed. For the second time in the twentieth century, the world looked to the United States. The first American moment had occurred in 1918, when everyone from the Slavic peoples of Eastern Europe to colonial subjects in Southeast Asia embraced Wilsonian ideals of self-determination and the concept of a League of Nations. American leaders of that day, however, turned their backs on the mantle of world leadership and the entanglements it implied and eventually succumbed to a combination of isolationist and unilateralist sentiment that President Warren G. Harding depicted as a return to "normalcy. The post–World War II generation had lived with the consequences of isolation, however, and they revived the spirit of Wilsonian internationalism in 1945 as the foundation of a new era of cooperation among nations.

Cooperation, however, took multiple forms and followed many different pathways. One road led to Moscow where, despite the rising tensions that had been the backdrop of their relationship since the nineteenth century, Americans and the Soviets found many occasions to work together in 1945. From drawing postwar territorial boundaries in the Yalta agreements to Victory in Europe, or V-E Day on May 8, 1945, which divided Germany into four zones of occupation and partitioned the former German capital of Berlin in two, the United States and the Union of Soviet Socialist Republics (USSR) tacitly nodded to the other's military control on the ground. Although the tenor of diplomatic relations cooled with the death of Franklin Roosevelt on April 12, 1945, his replacement, Harry Truman, a machine-politician from Missouri with none of Roosevelt's elegance, charm, or political insight, initially sought cooperation. Even as late as Marshall's trip to Moscow in March 1947, there was some expectation of continued collaboration.

Yet another avenue of international cooperation led to the United Nations (UN). As their armies made the final assault on Berlin, representatives of the wartime Allies gathered in San Francisco to fulfill a worldwide call for world peace, freedom from foreign rule, and economic prosperity. Both the United States and the Soviet Union showed strong support for the UN by sending their foreign ministers, former General Motors vice president and New Dealer Edward Stettinius and V. M. Molotov. Three months of work produced the blueprint for the new world body by June 1945. In an address to the delegates, President Truman compared the UN Charter favorably to the U.S. Constitution and applauded the delegates' ability to apply the lessons of wartime "military and economic cooperation" in creating "a great instrument for peace and security and human progress in the world."

The delegates incorporated lessons from the past in designing the UN. Hoping to extend the Grand Alliance into peacetime, they set up a Security Council composed of five permanent members: the United States, the Soviet Union, Britain, and China (whom Roosevelt had called the four policemen), plus France. The hope was that the great powers would act together to dissuade any potential aggressor nation, although the fact that each permanent member was given veto power reduced the prospect of united action. To broaden the base of support for peacekeeping, ten other countries served as council members on a two-year rotating basis.

To get at the roots of conflict, delegates set up the UN General Assembly as a forum where nations could settle their differences without having to resort to force. The assembly made the idea of one state, one vote the global model for civil society and as such enshrined the liberal traditions of the Enlightenment, namely the assumption of representative government, in geopolitics. The world's peoples, as opposed to nation-states, were the benchmark for representation in the UN, so the founders decided to grant official status to nongovernmental organizations. These organizations included such venerable international institutions as the Red Cross, along with associations of international jurists and scientists. As the number of nongovernmental organizations mushroomed into the hundreds, social movements for world health, racial equality, economic justice, and groups interested in a new issue—human rights—became people's lobbies at the UN headquarters in New York. Their presence marked the triumph of progressive ideas in world opinion, as did the creation of the Economic and Social Council (ECOSOC), which the UN charged with remedying economic and social wrongs in the belief that a more just world would also be a more peaceable one.

Organizations such as the Women's International League for Peace and Freedom and prominent individuals such as the former first lady Eleanor Roosevelt, an influential voice for social justice in her own right, promoted the belief that world peace rested on social justice. America's premier black intellectual, W. E. B. Du Bois, and its chief civil rights organization, the NAACP, also raised the banner of social justice as a remedy to America's struggle with racism and the world's history of colonialism. Even President Truman embraced Progressive thinking in saying, "A just and lasting peace cannot be attained by diplomatic agreement alone, or by military cooperation alone. Experience has shown how deeply the seeds of war are planted by economic rivalry and social injustice."

The UN adopted the Universal Declaration of Human Rights in 1948, a statement that promoted free speech, freedom of association, and other civil liberties conceived in the Enlightenment tradition and the language of rights that defined Progressive movements stretching back to the nineteenth century. Going a step further, beyond even Franklin Roosevelt's four freedoms, the declaration also decried discrimination based on race or sex. As a compendium of an evolving concept of human rights, the declaration became a touchstone for activists in the developed world and local opposition in European colonies, just as the UN evolved into a locus of world opinion and moral legitimacy. Before World War II, when the reformers spoke of universal rights, they called it the rights of man; the UN, however, made human rights the lingua franca of social reform.

Some fifty-seven nations, great and small, joined the UN immediately, a number that eventually rose above 180. All this suggests that the Cold War was not preordained. Before it began, differences between the two social systems— American market democracy and Soviet socialism—and their respective forms of power were not necessarily irreconcilable.

ECONOMIC RECONSTRUCTION, 1944–47

As the rubble was cleared away, economic reconstruction offered more avenues of international cooperation. American architects of the postwar world were determined to avoid a recurrence of the Great Depression with its terrible political fallout. Although they set out to restore markets for trade and investment, Western countries accepted an unprecedented degree of public planning in restoring the private enterprise system. What emerged was still capitalist, at least insofar as it upheld private enterprise and competition in the marketplace. But it was also a kind of mixed economy whose guiding principles shared certain elements of the laissez-faire of Adam Smith and the collective ownership of Karl Marx. Called "the Mix" by some scholars for its ability to leverage public means to achieve private ends, the emerging order made closed, inflexible systems like Soviet Socialism increasingly irrelevant as open, flexible systems like democratic capitalism in the United States became hegemonic after the war.

Fears of a new global depression brought officials from forty-four nations to the Bretton Woods resort in New Hampshire in 1944 to map out a reconstruction plan. With Englishman John Maynard Keynes and his American counterpart Harry Dexter White playing the key roles, the conference designed a new international apparatus to maintain stable currencies, promote consumer demand, and relieve poverty. In recognition of America's towering economic supremacy, the agreements made the dollar "as good as gold" and the international standard against which the market would compare all other currencies. Thus, the *dollar standard* joined the nineteenth-century gold standard as the financial foundation of the world economy. The Bretton Woods system, as it was known, created new institutions as well: the International Monetary Fund (IMF) to maintain stable exchange rates and the International Bank for Reconstruction and Development (the World Bank) to supply much needed capital for European revitalization. Later, in 1949, it added the General Agreement on Tariffs and Trade with the aim of removing barriers to international trade. Altogether, these measures comprised the main gears in the machinery of the Mix, which remained in place until 1971.

Alongside these global developments, Western leaders were drawn into the reconstruction of regional economies. The big question for Western Europe was what to do with Germany. After briefly considering turning the economic powerhouse of Europe into a land of shepherds and dairy maids, Western leaders decided that German recovery was crucial to prosperity in the whole of Western Europe. Under a policy of encouraging reindustrialization, postwar leaders restored to prominence the same German companies—IG Farben, Volkswagen— that had supplied the Nazi war machine.

On the other side of the war-torn world, things were different in Japan, which was under the unilateral occupation of the United States. No one in the Truman administration was eager to rebuild the country. In fact, U.S. officials, led by General Douglas MacArthur, first sought to break the close relationship between the Japanese state and giant corporations, called *zaibatsus*, that had provided such lethal war machines for Japan's military as the Mitsubishi Zero fighter plane. Japan was MacArthur's dominion, and his decision to institute his own version of the New Deal, where unions could organize (to further undermine the *zaibatsus*) and women were granted equal rights, surprised nearly everyone. Still, MacArthur's newfound liberalism masked the destructive impact of U.S. occupation on Japan's business and social hierarchy.

The ongoing threat of economic depression brought the rest of the U.S. officials onboard by 1948. Japan was the gateway to East Asian capitalism, and American occupiers began to promote reindustrialization and overseas trade in a manner that, according to one Japanese observer, resembled Japan's own ill-fated push for the Greater East Asia Co-Prosperity Sphere. The Korean War would aid America's new direction and kick into high gear Japan's reconstruction. It was, in the intemperate words of Prime Minister Shigeru Yoshida, a "gift of the gods." Orders came pouring in and production skyrocketed. Toyota, for example, went from three hundred trucks per month to two thousand. The Korean War was what Japanese businessmen gleefully called "the blessed rain from heaven." The United States even reversed its stance on the giant industrial–financial conglomerates, now called *keiretsus*. Reconstruction was so rapid and successful that the United States closed the occupation in 1952.

THE CHALLENGE OF COOPERATION AT HOME

As they moved into managing the world economy, American corporate and political leaders became more accepting of a mixed economy at home. To those who had created the levers of international economic management at Bretton Woods, the idea of state intervention seemed a sensible antidote to the threat of market and social instability. With this change, the ascension of the Mix was almost complete. John Maynard Keynes, the architect behind the mixed economic approach, shaped the landscape for competitive capitalism with an eye toward Adam Smith, but American policy makers pushed welfare state benefits as the backdrop to an economy that required high consumer demand.

The mixed economy survived a strong challenge from conservative Republicans in the volatile period after the war. Reconversion to peacetime production was accompanied by the lifting of price controls, which led to rapid inflation as consumers threw away their wartime ration books and came storming into department stores looking for nylon stockings, refrigerators, and other goods unavailable during the war. America's new consuming class needed higher wages to offset high prices, and when employers balked at wage increases, a rash of strikes broke out among the United Automobile Workers, the United Mine Workers, and scores of other union workers. The large number of Americans who joined strikes in 1946 was equal in percentage to the great wave of strikes that followed the First World War.

Business owners and social conservatives fought back. They prevailed on Republicans in Congress to draft new legislation to curb the power of unions. In a sign of the coming political backlash, Congress abolished the closed shop (where union membership was a condition of employment) in the Taft–Hartley Act of 1947, limited trade-union political activity, fortified so-called right-to-work laws, and required union leaders to sign affidavits against membership in the Communist Party. In addition, conservatives attacked what they saw as the creeping socialism of the New Deal and the treasonous internationalism of the Democrats. The stage seemed set for a repeal of the compromise between capital and labor that stood since the Wagner Act and Social Security, signaling the potential for a replay of the troublesome 1920s.

But it did not. Instead, prolabor Progressives responded with a vigorous defense of New Deal liberalism. President Truman advanced his own liberal program, the Fair Deal, that built on New Deal policies with a call for national health insurance and full employment. Truman's Fair Deal also broke new ground in supporting a civil rights bill, which pitted Washington elites against Southern segregationists for the first time since the 1890s and seemed like regional betrayal since Truman was a fellow Southern Democrat.

South Carolina governor Strom Thurmond led a regional movement against President Truman's civil rights legislation. His calls to preserve racial segregation galvanized the Southern Democrats, who formed a splinter group within the party called the Dixiecrats. By the mid-1960s, Thurmond left the Democrats for the Republican Party, and many southerners followed his lead within a decade. Library of Congress Prints and Photographs Division, Washington, DC.

Truman's strong statement on civil rights triggered a walkout in protest from Southern Democrats in the 1948 election led by the South Carolina governor Strom Thurmond, an ardent segregationist, and the Dixiecrats, a newly formed third party dedicated to right of states, not the federal government, to decide social questions. Thurmond ran as a Dixiecrat in the election, siphoning off precious popular and electoral college votes in the white South and jeopardizing the chance Democrats might retain the White House in 1948. Equally troubling for Truman was a challenge from the Left in the form of Henry Wallace, his one-time secretary of commerce. As the nominee of the newly founded Progressive

Party, Wallace ran a protest campaign against Truman's Cold War policies and tepid support for labor.

The tension in the Democratic Party came to a dramatic end with most unions and African Americans going all out for "give-'em-hell-Harry" and Truman eking out a surprise victory over Republican Thomas Dewey in the 1948 election. The *Chicago Tribune*'s iconic, if incorrect, front-page declaration "Dewey Defeats Truman" and the pictures of Truman's broad smile captured the profound sense of irony at the moment. Truman convinced enough voters that New Deal liberalism would be safer in his care at the same moment he was reshaping it along the lines of the mixed economy. That conglomeration of capitalism and socialism was crucial in defining Cold War liberalism and culture.

SOCIAL ROOTS OF THE IMPERIAL RIVALRY BETWEEN THE SUPERPOWERS

By the time of Truman's election, the wartime alliance between the United States and the Soviet Union had been replaced by Cold War hostility. What accounts for the change from cooperation to conflict? One obvious factor was the absence of a common enemy. With the Axis defeated, the United States and the USSR were free to go their separate ways. But the two countries had never been comfortable allies. At bottom, the deep ideological differences between their respective social systems led to conflicting worldviews about the aims of global power. This was not so much a difference between capitalism and communism, because to some degree America's mixed economy marked a convergence between the two. Rather, the key difference was ideological, an outgrowth of America's open society, on the one hand, and the Soviet's closed society, on the other. Together, they offered competing visions of twentieth-century modernity, and the roots of imperial rivalry lay in the clash between these two systems.

United States: An Open System

Each side of the Cold War took a foreign policy approach that reflected the inner dynamics of its own social system, with all its internal conflicts and crises projected outward. For the Americans, that meant a liberal or open society, where everyone was free to reach for privileged positions if their talents and efforts allowed. That principle was enshrined in the Declaration of Independence and the U.S. Constitution as liberty and was an outgrowth of the Enlightenment tradition. By no means had America perfected its system of liberty. Millions of women and men had little, if any, access to the full measure of their citizenship, and the question of liberty was at the center of nearly every political crisis since the beginning of the Republic.

When extended abroad, however, America's liberal system offered decisive advantages over more traditional approaches, such as colonialism. Liberal idealism allowed Americans to gain open access to overseas markets without the knotty entanglements of territorial possession. The United States did control strategic military bases in foreign lands, but that was to protect its corporate holdings abroad and global trade routes.

Despite many twists and turns in U.S. foreign policy, this open approach was the underlying continuity in the search for opportunity overseas. Originating in the Open Door policy at the turn of the century, the quest for free access to other lands took American dollars and gunboats to Asia and fostered Woodrow Wilson's quest for a world safe for democracy. In Wilson's case, democracy was the staging ground for liberty and free trade. Later, when Roosevelt defined U.S. war aims in terms of four freedoms, he continued the tradition; Truman would eventually make the link between liberty and trade more direct when he added the right to freedom of enterprise. Believing that the world war had grown out of the collapse of world trade in the 1930s, Truman declared, "Peace, freedom, and world trade are indivisible."

In the immediate circumstances at the end of the war, *freedom* meant open borders in Europe. At Yalta, Roosevelt had secured Stalin's assent to a "declaration on liberated Europe" intended to pressure the Soviet leader to permit free elections in Poland. Free elections were thought to be good in their own right, and they were also thought to be a good sign that a country was open for business. As for Western Europe, Americans secretly spent millions to support anti-Communist trade unions and political parties in postwar France and Italy. They did the same among client regimes in Latin America from Argentina to the Dominican Republic. In the Middle East and North Africa, transnational corporations, such as the Arabian–American Oil Company, and former colonial powers reinstated as protectorates, such as the French Maghreb (Tunisia, Morocco, and Algeria), became the chosen instruments for U.S. access to those lands. Although the United States did not hold territorial ambitions in any of these places, it continually intervened in the internal affairs of other countries to promote its worldview.

By arranging pro-American governments and favorable trade conditions overseas, Americans hoped they would be protected from unwanted foreign influences at home, whether socialism or economic troubles. Ironically, security at home seemed to require an unprecedented level of intervention abroad. America's postwar operations abroad included ongoing occupations of Germany and Japan, a far-flung system of bases in the Atlantic and Pacific (some acquired in the prewar destroyer deal with Great Britain), military interventions in Latin America, support for anti-Communists from France to French Indochina with the aim of obtaining privileged access for American business, and support for autocratic and corrupt regimes in North Africa and the Middle East.

American imperialism, then, was filled with contradictions. Even as the United States deposed unfriendly regimes, Americans could say in all sincerity that they harbored no territorial ambitions. Even as policy makers and diplomats manipulated foreign elections, they could claim that the United States was nobly fostering democracy. Even as American corporations and political elites cozied up to brutal dictators, they could defend it with the need to preserve the American way of life. And, even when the nation in one breath compared its military, economic, and political might to that of the great world empires of the past, including Rome, Britain, and Spain, in the next breath they could take it all back. Whether because of innocence or ignorance, arrogance or self-deception, Americans had difficulty sorting out the contradictions that accompanied liberalism in an open system.

Soviet Union: A Closed System

As with the United States, many aspects of Soviet foreign policy grew out of the demands of its socioeconomic system. Like other Eurasian land empires, the Soviet Union maintained a strong central government that attempted to control dissent within its borders through its infamous secret police, the KGB. Joseph Stalin picked up where his tsarist predecessors left off, but added a *command economy* that placed the market firmly under the control of the state. Beginning in the late 1920s, Stalin instituted a series of five-year plans designed to rapidly industrialize Soviet society. It was a prescient move, without which the Soviets could not have stood up to the Germans during the war. But it came at the high cost of "liquidating" a whole class of peasant landowners and the deaths of millions of forced laborers in the Gulag and on large infrastructural projects. This set a horrific record of internal oppression that would become a hallmark of the USSR's closed system. After the war, the Soviets showed interest in a loan from the United States to rebuild their devastated economy; but, when state planners found out about all the strings attached, including a requirement to open the books to outsiders, they quickly reversed course.

The Soviet's closed system at home led to centralized control over its provinces. Despite an official ideology every bit as anti-imperialist as that of the United States, there was no disguising the reality of Soviet imperial rule in Eastern Europe and within the Soviet borders as well. And within the borders of the USSR itself, Soviet repression and the KGB kept dissent in line, although armed guerillas fought against Moscow in the Ukraine until 1954—nine years after the war had ended.

During the maneuvering for position at the end of the war, Stalin had declared, "Whoever occupies a territory also imposes on it his own social system." Behind that crude dictum, Stalin set out to reclaim the tsarist empire in Eastern Europe lost during the First World War. As part of the 1939 pact with Hitler, he had gained control over the Baltic states of Latvia, Lithuania, and Estonia and had no intention of relinquishing his rule. Although he was intent on establishing a Soviet sphere of influence, Stalin had an added motive—self-defense. Twice in living memory Germany had ravaged the Russian motherland and Stalin refused to see it happen again. The same considerations—imperial ambition and self-defense—made Stalin inflexible on controlling Eastern Europe. On the strength of thousands of Soviet tanks taken from areas near the Baltic Sea in the north

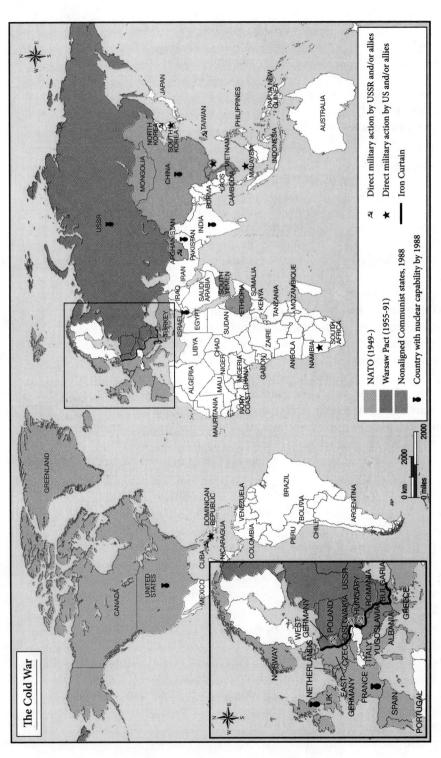

The Cold War

NORTH
AMERICA

GREENLAND

CANADA

UNITED
STATES

MEXICO

CUBA
DOMINICAN
REPUBLIC
NICARAGUA

VENEZUELA
COLOMBIA

BRAZIL
PERU
BOLIVIA

CHILE
ARGENTINA

0 km   2000
0 miles 2000

USSR

MONGOLIA

CHINA

NORTH
KOREA
SOUTH
KOREA
JAPAN
TAIWAN

AFGHANISTAN
PAKISTAN
INDIA
BURMA
LAOS
VIETNAM
CAMBODIA
PHILIPPINES
MALAYSIA
INDONESIA
PAPUA NEW
GUINEA

AUSTRALIA

IRAN
IRAQ
SAUDI
ARABIA
SOUTH
YEMEN
SOMALIA
ETHIOPIA
KENYA
TANZANIA
MOZAMBIQUE

TURKEY
ISRAEL
EGYPT
LIBYA
SUDAN
CHAD
ANGOLA
ZAIRE
NAMIBIA
SOUTH
AFRICA

ALGERIA
MALI
NIGER
NIGERIA
GHANA
GABON
IVORY
COAST
MAURITANIA

NORWAY
NETHERLANDS
UK
WEST
GERMANY
EAST
GERMANY
POLAND
CZECHOSLOVAKIA
USSR
HUNGARY
ROMANIA
BULGARIA
YUGOSLAVIA
ALBANIA
GREECE
ITALY
FRANCE
SPAIN
PORTUGAL

NATO (1949-)

Warsaw Pact (1955-91)

Nonaligned Communist states, 1988

Country with nuclear capability by 1988

Direct military action by USSR and/or allies

Direct military action by US and/or allies

Iron Curtain

MAP 8.1

216

and the Balkans in the south, plus more than three million Soviet troops, Stalin tightened his grip on the Soviet-occupied zone in Germany and quickly imposed pro-Soviet governments on Poland and Hungary. To strengthen the bond with supposedly willing Socialist republics and emphasize the command economy, Soviet allies shared access to the spoils of war, but only through a trading system closed to outsiders. Within the borders of the USSR, Stalin also used KGB agents to repress dissent and keep citizens in line. It largely worked, although armed guerillas, like the Organization of Ukrainian Nationalists and its controversial leader, Stepan Bandera, fought against Moscow well into 1953.

The West protested the expansion of the Soviet empire in Eastern Europe. With Truman by his side in 1946, the recently deposed British prime minister Winston Churchill angrily characterized Soviet aggression as the spread of an iron curtain from the Baltics to the Balkans. Despite his rhetoric, Churchill was in no position to object, having gone to Moscow in October 1944 and cut a deal that recognized essentially the same territorial division he opposed in his speech—that is, the Soviets would control Eastern Europe in exchange for British control in Greece and Turkey.

What the West saw as a reasonable demand for open borders, however, looked to the Soviets like *capitalist encirclement*. From the Soviet point of view, the existence of U.S.-occupied Germany on one side and U.S.-occupied Japan on the other put them between the jaws of a vice. Mutual suspicions produced similar reactions. At the same time that U.S. charge d'affaires, George Frost Kennan, was writing the "long telegram" to his superiors in Washington from Moscow warning of the Soviet threat, his Russian counterpart, Nikolai Novikov, sent a similar telegram to the Kremlin detailing what he perceived as the aggressive posture of the United States in its plans for maintaining over two hundred military bases in each of the Atlantic and Pacific Ocean basins.

COLD WAR CONFLICT, 1947–54

Although it is misleading, if not incorrect, to say the Cold War was inevitable, tensions between the superpowers were almost impossible to avoid. Unlike the mighty empires of the past, from the legendary struggles of Greeks and Persians, British and French, and Chinese and Japanese, whose epic battles have dominated the historical record over the centuries, the superpowers were rivals that often did not go head to head in battle. The Cold War was waged through proxies, whether at the geographic frontiers in contested borderlands or at the periphery of society in culture, technology, and commerce. America and the Soviet Union jousted in border zones—the Balkans, the Middle East, the Korean Peninsula, the Caribbean, Indochina—which had been arenas of imperial conflict for centuries. On one level, the Cold War represented the latest phase in the centuries-long contest between the Asian empires of the East and maritime empires of the West—between ancient Persia and Greece, Ottoman Turkey and Venice, and tsarist Russia and Britain battling one another in "the great game" played out in the mountains of nineteenth-century Afghanistan. On another level, the Cold War offered something original in its mobilization and deployment of technology, mass communication, and global commerce.

Consolidating Borders in Europe

The self-inflicted wounds of two world wars had temporarily reduced most of Europe to the status of frontier zones between the superpowers. By 1947, both the United States and the Soviet Union were moving rapidly to consolidate their control over territories they each deemed vital to their security. Reacting against Soviet reestablishment of the tsarist empire in Eastern Europe, an increasingly irate Harry Truman decided to draw the line of containment in the eastern Mediterranean.

Perhaps the most influential figure in formulating Truman's containment policy was George F. Kennan, a former diplomat in Moscow turned head of the policy-planning group in the State Department. In contrast to those calling for, in 1950s parlance, the rollback of Soviet power, Kennan was content to operate within the Yalta agreements that, in effect, divided Europe into spheres of influence. He believed that if the United States could provide an "unalterable counterforce at every point where they show signs of encroaching upon the interests of a peaceful and stable world," the Soviet system could be stopped from expanding and, thus, would be contained. Forced to live within its own closed system, Kennan believed eventually the Soviet Union would collapse, as Marxists would say, of its own internal contradictions.

When Truman decided to come to the aid of pro-Western regimes in Greece and Turkey in March 1947, however, containment lost its pretense of benign competition between the superpowers and became synonymous with direct, even violent, action. What triggered the crisis was Britain's decision, facing the collapse of its empire, to treat its former colonies more or less as equal members of the British Commonwealth. While handing over South Asia to its Indian and Pakistani indigenous leaders, Britain also announced it could no longer defend the pro-Western monarchy in Greece against a leftist revolt. The news came on the heels of a period of high Cold War tensions. The previous year, Stalin took a series of aggressive moves in the Mediterranean and Near East, beginning with his refusal to draw down the Russian troops that occupied the northern border of Iran and ending with pressure on Turkey to grant exclusive control over the Dardanelles Straits and, by extension, the Black Sea. Urged on by these events, Truman began sending military and economic aid to the Greek monarchy.

Truman and his advisors knew that intervention in Greece and Turkey would not be universally popular with the American people. The general expectation at the end of World War II was that U.S. soldiers would come home and the country would revert to its historic role of limited involvement. At the extreme, some like Robert Taft, a Republican senator from Ohio, called for diplomatic isolation. Mindful of this opposition, Michigan's Republican senator and chair

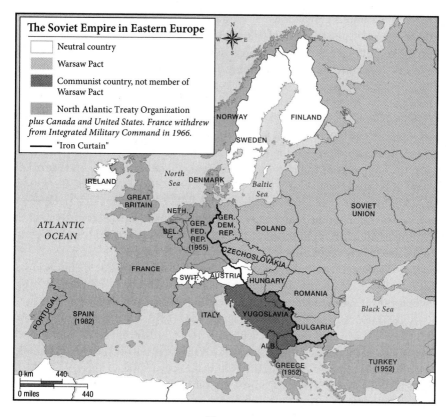

The Soviet Empire in Eastern Europe

☐ Neutral country
▨ Warsaw Pact
■ Communist country, not member of Warsaw Pact
▨ North Atlantic Treaty Organization *plus Canada and United States. France withdrew from Integrated Military Command in 1966.*
—— "Iron Curtain"

MAP 8.2

of the Foreign Relations Committee, Arthur Vandenberg, told Truman he would have to "scare hell out of the American people" if he wanted sell the idea of an active international role. And scare the hell out of the nation is what the president did. In his speech announcing the Truman Doctrine, he gave a ringing declaration of intent "to help free peoples to maintain their free institutions and their national integrity against aggressive movements that seek to impose upon them totalitarian regimes." It worked. Truman helped create a domestic climate of fear in which the Truman Doctrine could become the cornerstone of U.S. policy in the Cold War. The Truman Doctrine marked the globalization of the Monroe Doctrine. Just as a succession of American presidents had promised to defend the sister republics of Latin America against European colonialism, Americans now extended that promise to "free peoples" anywhere on the planet who were threatened by totalitarianism.

At about the same time, in April 1947, Secretary of State Marshall returned from his ill-fated trip to Moscow convinced that America had to defend against Soviet encroachment in Europe. "All the way back to Washington," reported an aide, "Marshall talked of the importance of finding some initiative to prevent the complete breakdown of Western Europe." Surrounded by a group of staunchly anti-Communist advisers, among them Dean Acheson and W. Averell Harriman, Marshall put them to work devising a plan of economic aid to help revive the wounded European economy. He announced the European Recovery Program, or the Marshall Plan, at a Harvard University commencement speech that June.

Praised for its altruism, the Marshall Plan was a good investment for U.S. business since it was tied to credits for buying U.S. exports, thus indirectly creating new customers in Europe. Hoping these benefits would translate into American jobs, the Congress of Industrial Organizations made support for the Marshall Plan a top legislative priority. The plan's passage in 1948 opened the floodgates of $13 billion (the equivalent of perhaps $305 billion in 2013 dollars) in outright grants. For Truman, the Marshall Plan and his doctrine on U.S. commitment to fighting totalitarian regimes were "two halves of the same walnut" intended to hold back Soviet encroachment.

If containment were to have a lasting effect, however, the United States would have to make fundamental domestic changes to meet the new global reality. Vigilance against Communism required a coordinated system of experts and institutions dedicated to meeting the Soviet challenge on a global scale. Over time, the Cold War cause would demand even more than Truman imagined—consensus on social questions, demonstrations of loyalty and patriotism, and systemic responses to perceived threats. The National Security Act of July 1947, which created the National Security Council, Joint Chiefs of Staff, Central Intelligence Agency (CIA), and a civilian-headed Department of Defense, represented the bureaucratic response to the Soviet threat. Big in scope, it was the centerpiece of the national security state, placing the tremendous power of containment in the hands of the presidency. With America's long history of liberal opposition to centralized authority, only a state of national hysteria—a people scared as hell—could pull off such a feat.

Responding to the challenge of containment, the Soviets tightened their hold on Eastern Europe. The Soviet ambassador to the UN complained in 1947 about U.S. efforts "to split Europe into two camps," making one side a servant to "the interests of American monopolies." In 1948, Russia installed a pro-Soviet regime in Czechoslovakia, an area outside the old tsarist empire, whose German takeover ten years before had helped ignite World War II. Stalin then provoked the first major East–West crisis by closing off Western access to Berlin. He did so partly to protest the Western Allies' plan to unify their occupation zones and create a new West German state, which Stalin regarded as threatening. But he also closed off Berlin to stop defections to the West.

Located deep inside the Soviet zone of occupation, Berlin was the former capital of the German Reich; the Cold War made it a constant flash point. To the Soviets, the presence of Western forces was like a cancer inside the body of Communism. To the West, Berlin was an outpost of freedom to be defended at all costs. With British support, the United States responded to the Soviet roadblock with the Berlin airlift, a sustained aviation resupply effort. Although tensions remained high, Russia's decision to spare the resupply planes, and hence not escalate the crisis further, averted World War III. It was certainly not détente, but the Berlin crisis provided a script for conducting the Cold War.

Mutual Containment

Instead of going into direct war with each other, the two powers locked themselves in mutual containment. Each consolidated control in its respective domain. Seeking economic aid and military shelter under the U.S. nuclear umbrella, Western Europeans responded eagerly to U.S. initiatives to cement together the Western Alliance, and in 1949 they created the North Atlantic Treaty Organization (NATO). The Soviet Union responded in kind a few years later with the Warsaw Pact in 1955 that corralled their east European satellites in a military pact. True to form, the Soviets tolerated no deviation. When dissent erupted in East Germany in 1953 and then in Hungary 1956, Soviet tanks rolled in to restore order. Although rebels hurled Molotov cocktails at the tanks, they were no match for the relentless columns of Soviet troops. The United States was no less active in preserving their sphere of influence. They were just far less heavy-handed, preferring to send aid to anti-Communist forces or conduct covert operations, such as the 1954 CIA-sponsored coup d'etat that toppled the nationalist government of Jacobo Árbenz in Guatemala. The previous year, the CIA overthrew a similar nationalist leader in Iran, Mohammad Mossadegh.

Key to mutual containment was the nuclear arms race. The Soviets exploded an atomic bomb in the August 1949, breaking the American nuclear monopoly. Three years later, the United States developed the first hydrogen bomb, and the Soviets responded the following year with a hydrogen bomb of their own. The nuclear arms race swung back and forth at such an increasingly rapid pace that it kept both sides at bay. But the rate of advancement only accounts for part of its neutralizing power. The shift from the atomic fission bomb, which got its energy by splitting uranium atoms, to the hydrogen fusion bomb, where energy was released by driving hydrogen atoms together to form helium, marked a quantum leap (a phrase taken from quantum mechanics) from kilotons (thousands) to megatons (millions) of TNT. Either way, the awesome amount of energy stored in the mass of an atomic nucleus was released to devastating, mindboggling effect.

By the mid-1950s, the nuclear arms race had raised the possibility that tens of millions of people on both sides would be killed in one devastating military exchange. Because of the enormous destructive capacity of even a Hiroshima-style kiloton bomb, a strategic nuclear exchange between the two superpowers had become unthinkable. It was precisely because nuclear weapons raised the cost of war to such unacceptably high levels—the annihilation of millions, the destruction of civilization—that they reduced the likelihood of war between the superpowers.

Hemmed in by their own destructive technology, the superpowers trapped themselves in mutual containment. American leaders had embarked on a policy of

Nuclear weapons changed the culture and politics of the Cold War. When the United States detonated atomic weapons over the Bikini Islands in July 1946 during Operation Crossroads, it reflected an escalation of tensions with the Union of Soviet Socialist Republics. By 1954, those tensions pushed America to hydrogen bombs in the Bikini Atoll, which were a thousand times more powerful than the weapons used on Nagasaki and Hiroshima. National Archives at College Park–Still Pictures (RDSS).

containment, not realizing that it would work both ways, holding the Americans in check as well as the Soviets. America was the most powerful nation the world had ever seen, but it was not all-powerful; supremacy did not mean omnipotence.

The Cold War Goes Global

The Cold War that had begun in Europe became a global contest by 1950. The United States was the first to go global with the Truman Doctrine. Then, with the formation of NATO, Americans for the first time in their history turned their backs on George Washington's warning against "entangling alliances" and entered an agreement to defend other people's territory as if it was their own. The shift to a global vision of national security took a further step in 1950 with the adoption of a global defense posture by the National Security Council, a product of the war that had become the key body for making U.S. foreign policy. In April 1950, policy planners issued NSC-68, a landmark statement of the new vision in which

America's total energies—economic, political, cultural—would be mobilized against the totalitarian enemy. With this leap from hemispheric to global ambition, the United States entered a new phase in its history, just as America's earnest participation in global competition marked a new phase in world history.

Following closely behind, the Soviets, too, shifted to become a global superpower by 1950. After four years of pulling back in Asia to concentrate on defending Soviet interests in Europe, Stalin was now ready to broaden his imperial frontier. Formerly lukewarm toward Chinese Communists, he now welcomed Mao Zedong's triumph in 1949. Once unwilling to stir up trouble in East Asia, he now gave a green light to North Korea to invade the South, providing its forces with Soviet tanks, artillery, and later MIG jet fighters.

By 1950, cooperation against the Axis and the harmonious mood at Yalta seemed distant memories. Leaders on both sides had come to regard their relationship as a zero-sum game where one's gain could only come at the other's expense, and the stakes had been raised by the beginnings of a nuclear arms race. Nevertheless, those same developments made it harder for the two superpowers to fight any direct battles. The testing of imperial borders in Berlin and the eastern Mediterranean had essentially reconfirmed the Yalta settlement as a bulwark against radical change.

This situation contrasts markedly with the time of the First World War when the fires of revolution were burning in Europe, with both Wilson and Lenin stoking them to their own advantage. Now Truman and Stalin tried to temper radicalism within the nucleus of their respective domains as they consolidated control. In border zones around the world, however, the two superpowers prepared to battle for influence.

Establishing Borders in Asia

With Europe already divided, the split between the capitalist and Communist camps spread to Asia with the 1949 Communist Revolution in China. After a protracted civil war, Communists under Mao Zedong finally defeated the corrupt Nationalists under Jiang Jieshi. For the first time in history, a major power was commanded by rulers who claimed to speak for the peasantry. While Stalinists championed the urban proletariat, Mao broke with orthodoxy. He based the social revolution in communities of small peasants and landless laborers of the countryside, where most of China's six hundred million people as of 1960 toiled as they had for centuries. Taking a page from the book of westernization, Mao accepted Western ideas—Marx, after all, was European—and adapted them to East Asian conditions. In this way, Mao rejected the reactionary path of Chinese nativists, such as the Boxers, and instead imitated the Japanese, who had adapted Western practices to improve their position.

Despite philosophic disagreement, the Soviets and Chinese agreed on one thing: the United States had become a threat. With the United States occupying Japan, the two Communist powers worried that it would act as the successor to

224 | PART 2   Burdens of the Colossus, 1945–2012

Japanese imperialism. Their fear was ill-founded. Truman had no ambition to follow the Japanese example and invade mainland China. With isolationists such as Robert Taft warning of the suicidal folly of fighting a land war against millions of Chinese ready to defend their homeland, any thought of an invasion of the Asian mainland to keep Mao from taking the Chinese capital at Beijing had been dismissed as foolhardy. Although right-wing Republicans would later blame Truman for losing China, it was not his to lose. He had sent General Marshall on a special mission to try to end the civil war, but neither side was willing to compromise, and there was nothing Americans could do to prevent Communists from seizing power, despite criticism from the powerful China Lobby.

Coming at almost the same time as the Soviet atomic bomb, the Chinese revolution raised the fear in U.S. circles that history was siding with the Communists. For Americans accustomed to getting their way in world affairs, this was too much to bear. Unable to shape the new reality, American officials refused to recognize it. They withheld diplomatic recognition of red China, insisting that the Nationalists who had retreated to the island of Taiwan off the Chinese coast were the legitimate rulers of the mainland. Americans successfully blocked the transfer of China's seat in the UN to the Communist government until the 1970s, when President Richard Nixon went to Beijing. Then, in a dramatic turn, the United States looked the other way as the UN voted to remove Nationalist China once the Communists came in.

Korean War

As in Europe, neither superpower was willing to bear the cost of a strategic conflict at their frontiers in Asia. Instead, they contested one another through proxies. The Korean Peninsula had long been just such a zone of imperial rivalry. The great Asian land empires of China and tsarist Russia had long meddled with the Hermit Kingdom until Japan claimed it at the beginning of the twentieth century. Korea was a formal colony of Japan until the end of the Second World War, when the Allies stripped Japan of all her colonies. At that point, Korea was divided at the thirty-eighth parallel into what were intended to be temporary Soviet and American zones of occupation.

But by the spring of 1950, the thirty-eighth parallel had hardened into a national border separating the Communist North Korea, backed by the Soviet Union, and the capitalist South Korea, backed by the United States. Having secured support from Stalin and Mao Zedong in China, North Korea's leader, Kim Il Sung, ordered his troops to cross the border shortly after dawn on June 25, 1950, and advance on South Korea's ill-prepared army toward the capital in Seoul. The attack triggered a quick response from the United States. American diplomats in New York sought, and received, the first of several UN Security Council resolutions authorizing military action to repel the invader. The Soviets failed to cast a veto because they were boycotting the UN over the refusal to allow Communist China a seat on the Security Council. In effect, mutual containment

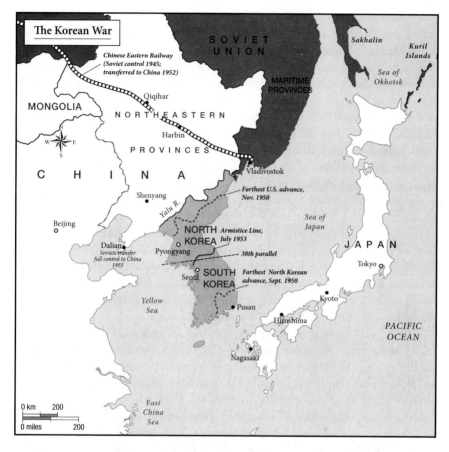

The Korean War

Chinese Eastern Railway
(Soviet control 1945;
transferred to China 1952)

SOVIET
UNION

Sakhalin

Kuril
Islands

Qiqihar

MONGOLIA

NORTHEASTERN

MARITIME
PROVINCES

Sea of
Okhotsk

Harbin

PROVINCES

CHINA

Vladivostok

Shenyang

Farthest U.S. advance,
Nov. 1950

Yalu R.

Sea of
Japan

Beijing

NORTH
KOREA

Armistice Line,
July 1953

JAPAN

Dalian
Soviets transfer
full control to China
1955

Pyongyang

38th parallel

Tokyo

Seoul

SOUTH
KOREA

Farthest North Korean
advance, Sept. 1950

Kyoto

Yellow
Sea

Pusan

Hiroshima

PACIFIC
OCEAN

Nagasaki

0 km   200

0 miles   200

East
China
Sea

MAP 8.3

allowed the United States to dominate the UN. But it would not be enough. In a mere three days since crossing into South Korea, the invaders captured Seoul.

Within three months, North Korea pushed south to Pusan, near the bottom of the peninsula. Facing the loss of the entire Korean Peninsula, Truman made the controversial decision—without congressional approval—to order U.S. air-strikes above the thirty-eighth parallel. Then, he granted the request of the commander of UN forces in the Pacific, General Douglas MacArthur, to unleash U.S. combat troops. The decision amounted to exercising war powers, but Truman never sought congressional approval and that put the legality of America's participation in the Korean conflict in doubt. Truman called America's role a police action, but questions remained.

In just five years after the worst killing in human history, Korea took center stage in world politics. The determining factors for the Korean War were framed in the same containment dynamics that brought the UN into the fight. For the Soviet side, Stalin was evidently alarmed that U.S. occupation forces might use

Korea as a staging ground for further assaults on the Asian mainland, just as Japan had. As heir to tsarist ambitions in East Asia, Stalin hoped to use his client, Kim Il Sung, to forestall that possibility.

But he misread U.S. intentions to defend its ally in South Korea. As an Open Door power, Americans had no ambitions for territory on the Asian mainland on the order of Japanese imperialism. All the same, the United States was ready to defend its client state at the south of the peninsula, especially since it was so close to another key ally in the region, Japan. Since the crisis in Berlin, Truman had come to think of international relations as a zero-sum game in which every loss of an American client was a gain for the Russians. He also felt genuine revulsion for Stalin's totalitarian methods of rule. Outraged at the North Korean attack, Truman blamed it directly on the Kremlin. While Stalin was comparing the United States to imperial Japan, Truman immediately drew a comparison between Stalin and Hitler. Confiding in his diary, the feisty American president wrote, "it was Munich and we must not appease him." What America failed to recognize was how the rapidly escalating showdown among superpowers concealed the civil war dynamics of the conflict. The rivalry between Kim Il Sung and Syngman Rhee over how to organize their divided people politically had inflamed guerrilla war and border skirmishes for years before the 1950 invasion.

For the next three grueling months, the war dragged on, with each side scoring victories and subsequent losses, that is, until General MacArthur decided on the strategy of coming in behind enemy lines with an amphibious landing at Inchon, near Seoul, and dividing North Korean forces. MacArthur drove the invader north in October 1950, far above the thirty-eighth parallel, until UN forces approached the Yalu River in late November. Fearing a threat to its border, and with last-minute assurances of support from Moscow, the Chinese sent three hundred thousand "volunteer troops" that Mao Zedong had put on China's border four months earlier across the Yalu, driving MacArthur's troops below Seoul once again. To prevent defeat, MacArthur requested authorization from the president to use no fewer than twenty-six atom bombs against the Chinese. Truman wisely rejected this reckless request; he also fired MacArthur on April 11, 1951, for publicly critiquing the decision to fight a limited war.

When North and South Korea signed a truce on July 27, 1953, the conflict had stalemated into a World War I trench-style battle not far from the very place it began—the thirty-eighth parallel. But the war had enormous consequences because it led to a major buildup of U.S. conventional and nuclear capabilities, not to mention a tripling of the U.S. defense budget by 1953 that further militarized the Cold War. At home, the war prompted a second red scare and exaggerated anxieties of Communist infiltration of U.S. society.

Cold War Culture

By the mid-1950s, the Cold War had become a deeply engrained state of mind. Like the two world wars, it was a total war in the sense that it engaged the whole of American society, not just diplomats and generals. Office secretaries were as deeply affected as secretaries of state. It was fought in women's fashion (frumpy Soviets versus stylish Westerners), children's games (good guys versus bad guys), and stereotypes (bureaucratic tyrants versus greedy capitalists). It infused popular culture with new technologies, concepts, and possibilities. For example, Americans took their fear of nuclear weapons and the anxieties of living in an atomic age and transformed them into an industry of consumable products that reshaped leisure, entertainment, style, and imagination. The U.S. nuclear testing in the Pacific inspired everything from the bikini bathing suit, named after the tiny Bikini Atoll where much of the testing took place, to the 1954 Japanese movie about Godzilla, a giant reptile with radioactive breath aroused from the depths by nuclear explosions. It even spread to music as Bill Haley and his Comets, one of the founding bands of Rock 'n' Roll, fantasized in a song about a pleasant aftermath of nuclear war when there would be "thirteen women and only one man in town."

Since the ideological battle between America's open system and the Soviet's closed system was, at its core, a conflict among societies rooted in the Enlightenment tradition, both sides used similar means to make their case. Americans and Soviets both rejected the irrationality of Nazi race theories and the belief that might makes right, and both appealed to the Enlightenment ideals of liberty and equality, as well as modern notions such as democracy. As with any ideology, Cold War visions of freedom shrouded many ugly realities. Soviet pretensions that it was a workers' state ignored the fact of its top-down control and the absence of independent trade unions to promote workers' interests. Likewise, the so-called German Democratic Republic, a Soviet client state, was a democracy in name only, since all the key decisions were made by a tiny ruling committee of the Communist Party subservient to Moscow.

The West was more strident in its rhetoric of democracy, but its actions overseas were hardly better. It was not only that the United States supported the dictatorships of Syngman Rhee in South Korea, Ferdinand Marcos in the Philippines, Anastasio Somoza in Nicaragua, and the Shah in Iran, but also that Cold War rhetoric pretended such dictators were, in fact, democrats. It did not matter that they routinely imprisoned, tortured, and killed their domestic political opponents. The fact that they were pro–United States was enough to put them on the side of democracy.

Constant international tension generated a climate of fear. Because the Soviet media reflected the Kremlin line, it is not easy for historians to gauge the state of public opinion in Russia. There was a deep reservoir of love for the motherland, rekindled in memories of the Great Patriotic War against the Germans, and patriotism was combined with a messianic view of Russia's mission to defend other Slavic peoples—Ukrainians, Serbs, Poles—on their western border. As tensions with the West increased, however, patriotism gave way to paranoia. In part, Russia's paranoia was a projection of Stalin's personal fears, which produced a succession of party purges. But irrational fear of encirclement, and the belligerence that went with it, seems to have been a product of the Soviet system, not just one man. Soviet citizens grew disillusioned and cynical as the promises of Marxist prosperity never materialized. Shortages, rationing, and meager living conditions plagued Soviet society, while the West boasted of a consumer paradise.

The United States, too, was caught up in its own paranoia—the red scare. As was the case after the First World War, many Americans could not understand why victory did not enable them to have everything their own way. Captivated by delusions of their own omnipotence, they could not accept the reality of limits. Although they had even less reason to fear encirclement, that did not prevent the spread of paranoid fantasies of a blood-red tide engulfing the land of liberty. Demagogue politicians, epitomized by Joseph McCarthy, a Republican senator from Wisconsin, fomented fears of subversion from within and grabbed media attention with completely unfounded claims of Communist infiltration of Truman's state department. One reason McCarthy's false claims received so much attention was that they offered a simple explanation of why the most powerful nation on earth had not been able to prevent Communist takeover in Eastern Europe, the loss of China, or a stalemate in Korea. There must be "enemies within," they reasoned.

No one did more to promote this climate of fear than J. Edgar Hoover, the virulent anti-Communist head of the Federal Bureau of Investigation. As Hoover's agents scoured the country for Communists, they sewed distrust of all nonconformists, including homosexuals, cultural critics, and civil rights activists. Hooverian anxiety even spread to popular culture, where it inspired the 1956 film *Invasion of the Body Snatchers*. Set in small-town America, the movie ominously told of hostile aliens who arrive in giant milkweed pods from outer space and gradually take over. Indeed, it seemed abduction was an apt metaphor to describe the reality in the 1950s as the Cold War induced a curious mass psychosis over Americans that required strict conformity to the dominant culture. The quest to be normal turned into an obsession for many.

COLONIAL INDEPENDENCE

The mass psychology of fear could not prevent change from taking place. One of the most far-reaching developments of the postwar era was colonial independence. After decades of captivity under European rule, a flock of new nations took wing in the aftermath of the Second World War. Struggles for self-determination were not new. They had begun almost as soon as the new imperialists of the late nineteenth century had arrived in Asia and Africa, and they gained strength with the rise of educated professional classes, trained in the Enlightenment tradition at the best universities in the United States and Western Europe, determined to run their own affairs. Whereas the outcome of the First World War had stifled dreams of independence, the outcome of the Second World War was the opposite: Asians and Africans were in revolt.

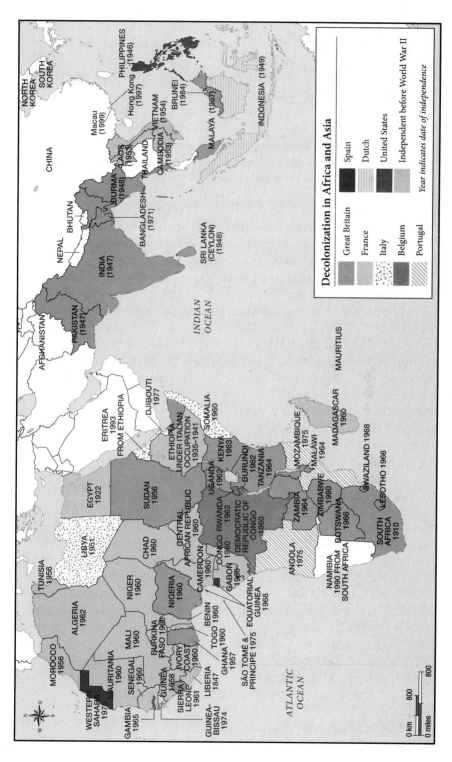

Decolonization in Africa and Asia

Great Britain		Spain	
France		Dutch	
Italy		United States	
Belgium		Independent before World War II	
Portugal			

Year indicates date of independence

NORTH KOREA
SOUTH KOREA
PHILIPPINES (1946)
Hong Kong (1997)
Macau (1999)
BRUNEI (1984)
VIETNAM (1954)
CAMBODIA (1953)
MALAYA (1967)
LAOS 1953
THAILAND
INDONESIA (1949)
CHINA
BURMA (1948)
NEPAL
BHUTAN
BANGLADESH (1971)
SRI LANKA (CEYLON) (1948)
INDIA (1947)
PAKISTAN (1947)
AFGHANISTAN

INDIAN OCEAN

MAURITIUS

ERITREA 1993 FROM ETHIOPIA
DJIBOUTI 1977
ETHIOPIA UNDER ITALIAN OCCUPATION 1935–1941
SOMALIA 1960
KENYA 1963
UGANDA 1962
BURUNDI 1962
TANZANIA 1964
RWANDA 1962
CONGO 1960
DEMOCRATIC REPUBLIC OF CONGO 1960
EGYPT 1922
SUDAN 1956
CENTRAL AFRICAN REPUBLIC 1960
CHAD 1960
LIBYA 1951
NIGER 1960
NIGERIA 1960
CAMEROON 1960
GABON 1960
EQUATORIAL GUINEA 1968
MOZAMBIQUE 1975
MADAGASCAR 1960
MALAWI 1964
ZAMBIA 1964
ZIMBABWE 1980
BOTSWANA 1966
SWAZILAND 1968
LESOTHO 1966
SOUTH AFRICA 1910
ANGOLA 1975
NAMIBIA 1990 FROM SOUTH AFRICA
TUNISIA 1956
ALGERIA 1962
MOROCCO 1956
MAURITANIA 1960
MALI 1960
SENEGAL 1960
BURKINA FASO 1960
IVORY COAST 1960
GHANA 1957
TOGO 1960
BENIN 1960
GUINEA 1958
SIERRA LEONE 1961
LIBERIA 1847
GUINEA-BISSAU 1974
GAMBIA 1965
WESTERN SAHARA 1975
SÃO TOMÉ & PRÍNCIPE 1975

ATLANTIC OCEAN

0 km 800
0 miles 800

MAP 8.4

229

Asians were the first to break free when India and Pakistan won independence from Britain in 1947, followed by Indonesia's break from the Dutch two years later. Africans were not far behind. Egyptians took command of their own affairs in 1954, followed by Sudan in 1956 and Ghana in 1957, the first independent country south of the Sahara desert other than South Africa (see Chapter 9). After that, the black, green, and yellow colors of African independence rapidly filled up the map of the once-subjugated continent. Exhausted by the bloodletting of two world wars and financially constrained, European empires simply lacked the will to hold on to peoples determined to break free of their grip.

As they watched these fledgling nations stretch their wings, Americans had conflicting feelings. Remembering their own anticolonial origins, they reached out in heartfelt sympathy to the newly liberated peoples. Hoping to reap a harvest of friendship among former subjects of colonialism, U.S. diplomats distanced themselves from European empires. At the same time, they worried about losing ground in frontier regions to their Communist adversaries.

Vietnam lay along just such a frontier. Once a tributary of China, Vietnam had been ruled by the French since the 1880s, until the Japanese kicked them out in World War II. In the subsequent struggle against Japanese colonialism, the United States was happy to collaborate with the Vietnamese independence movement led by Ho Chi Minh, a patriot who had become a Communist after earlier rebuffs from the West. At the end of the war, Truman initially considered supporting Ho's independent Vietnam, but quickly changed course to back a restoration of the French empire, fearing that a weakened France might fall prey to internal Communist forces and that an independent Vietnam might not be able to prevent China from reasserting its traditional sway in Indochina. By the early 1950s, Americans were paying three-quarters of the French cost for suppressing the Vietnamese revolution.

Truman was backing a losing horse in this race, however. Having underestimated their adversary's ability to drag artillery up seemingly insurmountable mountains, the French concentrated their forces in the remote highlands at Dien Bien Phu, where they suffered final defeat in 1954. Interested parties gathered in Switzerland and agreed to the Geneva Accords, which stipulated that the temporary dividing line between North and South Vietnam, established at the seventeenth parallel, would be erased within two years through national elections to unify the country. Although the French and the British accepted the Communist government in the North, the United States did not. John Foster Dulles, President Dwight Eisenhower's secretary of state, refused to sign the accords, and when it came time for ceremonial handshakes, he refused to grasp the hand of Communist China's foreign minister, Zhou Enlai. For the North Vietnamese, led by Ho Chi Minh, the United States was just another empire they would have to endure, as they had the French and Chinese before that, on the route to full independence.

The anticolonial revolts, however, carried a genuine impulse for social revolution. National independence was combined in some cases with deeper aspirations for social and economic change infused with Socialist ideals of equality and the elimination of poverty, along with the Enlightenment ideals enshrined in the UN's Universal Declaration of Human Rights. Notably, these were reactions to colonial relationships grounded in a complex mix of class and racial oppression, where dark-skinned laborers produced the crops and precious metals that enriched the lives of light-skinned European plantation and mine owners. Some independence leaders, such as Jawaharlal Nehru in India and Sukarno in Indonesia, aspired not to take the place of the white master class but to create new and more equitable relations as part of the move to independence. These dreams rarely came to fruition. It proved easier to get rid of the European *sahib* in India or *bwana* in East Africa than to undo the deeper history of class and racial inequality or economic dependency on Western nations.

Civil Rights Revival

In a parallel development, the quest for civil rights revived in the United States. Although African Americans were by no means colonial subjects, they were treated as third-class citizens, especially in the South, where they were denied basic civil rights and where cotton plantations resembled the rubber and banana plantations of the colonies. The Great Migration, the mass movement of African Americans out of Southern plantation districts to Northern cities that had begun as a trickle in the period around the First World War and grew to a torrent in the Second, hastened the civil rights revival. The Great Migration led to greater educational opportunities, which hastened demands for civil rights, just as in African colonies. So did the contradiction between the ideal of equality and the reality of racism, which deprived African Americans of good jobs and positions of authority in a system of class and racial oppression. The hardships African Americans faced in the U.S. South bore a striking resemblance to the predicament of colonial subjects.

International influences were also important to the resurgent movement for civil rights. Forging direct links across the Atlantic and even the Pacific, African American activists such as W. E. B. Du Bois and organizations such as the Council on African Affairs drew inspiration from postwar stirrings of African and south Asian liberation efforts. Black Americans explicitly drew the parallel in both racial and economic terms between anticolonial movements in Africa, transracial colorism in India, and the African American quest for freedom. Since the nineteenth century, African Americans had cultivated unique bonds with south Asian anticolonialists, such as Lala Lajpat Rai, around questions of development after domination by Western whites. The dialogue supported African Americans' interpretation of Nehru's 1955 Asian–African Conference in Bandung, where twenty-nine nations from the respective continents gathered, as the first meeting of the "World's Darker Peoples" (see Chapter 9). Black Americans also tried to internationalize America's race problem with appeals to the UN in the late 1940s to investigate American racism.

As the black community gained strength and determination, white supremacy grew weaker as a morally or politically defensible worldview. Discredited by association with Hitler's grotesque theories of Aryan supremacy, the whole system of racial segregation came to be seen as unjust, not simply because of the stigma it imposed on African Americans, but also because it violated the Enlightenment tradition's basic precept of human equality. In an influential book on "the American dilemma," the Swedish sociologist Gunnar Myrdal described racism as the central contradiction in American democracy. The fact that racism was explicitly condemned in the Universal Declaration of Human Rights suggests that the dilemma was by no means exclusively American, but applied wherever Enlightenment principles were embraced, which is to say almost everywhere, ironically, thanks to European imperialism itself.

Partly to avoid indictment in the court of world opinion, Washington elites began for the first time to embrace civil rights. Seeking to win goodwill in Africa and Asia in the unfolding Cold War, the Truman administration took unprecedented initiatives to promote civil rights. Part of these efforts was merely rhetorical. In 1947, the same year as India and Pakistan won their independence and the Truman Doctrine was issued, the national Commission on Civil Rights published a landmark document *To Secure These Rights*, which developed the key argument that America's sorry record of racial discrimination would undermine its efforts to attain leadership on the world stage. Other steps went beyond rhetoric. In 1948, Truman issued Executive Order 9981, desegregating the U.S. armed forces and mandating an end to racial discrimination in federal hiring. Although implementation was slow, they marked a decisive turn away from the decades of segregation. They helped pave the way for the Supreme Court's *Brown v. Board of Education* decision of 1954 outlawing segregation in public schools. By that time, liberals had grown accustomed to making the case that as long as the United States failed to rectify the wrongs of racism, the Soviet Union would be able to score propaganda points. That argument gained strength every time a new nation in Asia and Africa started looking around to determine its true friends.

Nonetheless, civil rights faltered because of conservative opposition under both the Democrat Truman and his Republican successor, Dwight Eisenhower. The Cold War cut two ways. On the one hand, it prompted Washington elites to support mild reform. On the other hand, the intensifying red scare had a chilling effect, narrowing the range of acceptable demands for equality. While accepting the end to legal segregation, Washington elites did not address the collision of class and racial oppression that trapped so many African Americans, North and South, in the bondage of the ghetto. Only the political Left called for any significant redistribution of economic resources, but they had been marginalized by the red scare. Nor did elites tolerate dissent in foreign policy. Those like Paul Robeson and Du Bois in the Council on African Affairs who continued on the path of the U.S–Soviet wartime alliance had their passports confiscated by the State Department and their speaking engagements canceled after their hosts were visited by the Federal Bureau of Investigation.

THE GOLDEN AGE

As the race problem gained national attention, class receded into the background. The postwar economic boom was a major reason. American levels of prosperity were so high, in fact, that later generations would call the 1950s a golden age. The average annual rate of growth in the world economy rose to 4.9 percent between 1950 and 1973, more than double the 2.3 percent that prevailed before 1950. After a decade of sacrifice during the Great Depression followed by wartime rationing, consumer capitalism came into its own. In the first-tier economies of the developed West, high growth rates translated into the good life for the growing ranks of middle-income consumers. Especially in the favored land of the United States, even well-paid, unionized workers were able to live in Levittown-style suburban developments. By the mid-1950s, observers talked about the affluent society as if the age-old dream of universal abundance had finally arrived.

What accounts for this exceptionally good fortune? Explanations vary. Some emphasize the cyclical aspect. From the early nineteenth century onward, capitalist development was accompanied by cycles of boom and bust. Those businesses that survived the dismal years of the 1930s were rewarded with a cyclical upturn in rates of investment, productivity, and profit. In the United States, war spending had restored profitability, and reconversion to peacetime production kept things on an upward curve, whereas in Europe (and somewhat later in Japan), the need to rebuild after the war provided profitable investment opportunities. The cyclical character was also evident at the other end when the world economy downshifted in the 1970s to annual growth rates of only 2.6 percent from 1973 to 1989.

Another part of the explanation has to do with deeper structural changes. After a false start earlier in the century, the postwar period ushered in the *American model*, a system pioneered by Henry Ford. The American model linked high levels of mass production and mass consumption through a series of feedback loops, where one factor influenced a second, which influenced a third, which in turn reacted back on the first with greater intensity and effect. Mass production in the postwar period led to a growth cycle where, for example, corporate investment in large-scale production facilities, such as General Motors factories in Detroit, led to increased productivity (output per worker per hour) of reasonably priced cars. High demand fostered strong sales, strong sales generated large profits, large profits spurred investment in new machinery, and new machinery fed increased production and renewed demand, thus starting the cycle again.

Americans led the way in the era of mass consumption. Chief among the discoveries was the role advertising played as an engine that increased demand for U.S. goods. As a trade, advertising had existed for decades, but the growing economy sent the industry into overdrive as marketers found new techniques for selling American products. They began to stratify markets by status, income, and taste—Chevrolets for workers, Buicks for dentists, and Cadillacs for executives. They refined their sales pitch to include everything from patriotism ("See the USA in your Chevrolet") to sex appeal (a gorgeous model draped over the hood).

They learned to segment markets by age group, such as golf clubs for the middle aged and hula hoops for the young; gender, as in home appliances for women; and even race, as Coca-Cola—"the real thing"—was originally reserved for whites, whereas blacks were relegated to no-name cola beverages.

Advertisers kept a close eye on demographics. The total U.S. population reached 152 million by 1950, more than double what it had been a half century earlier in 1900, when it stood at 76 million. Between 1945 and 1962 the United States witnessed a "baby boom" in which birth rates rebounded from the low of eighteen per thousand population in the 1930s and rose to twenty-five per thousand in the mid-1950s, multiplying the ranks of consumers by the millions. Consumer culture pivoted around the nuclear family, idealized as two parents of opposite sex living in a suburban ranch-style house stuffed with refrigerators, televisions, and an abundance of toys for the kids.

Another structural change was the transition from an urban-industrial to a suburban-service way of life. This was a global phenomenon where railroads had once concentrated people in cities and factories but now automobiles brought people into surrounding suburbs. As the space between urban centers started to fill with homes and office buildings, new terms were invented to describe these giant agglomerations of people, such as the *conurbation* that spread out from Birmingham, England, and the sprawling *megalopolis* that stretched from Tokyo to Yokohama, Japan, or another from Boston to Washington, DC.

One of the key features of postwar prosperity was a balance between labor and capital. The social compromise rested on the willingness of corporations to share the wealth with the workers who produced it. In contrast to the labor battles of the past, corporations now bought labor peace through union recognition and an increasing package of health benefits, vision care plans, and retirement pensions. General Motors, for example, settled a 1946 strike with a hefty increase to its benefits package that outstripped that of its counterparts in Europe. American workers also received Social Security and other public benefits, and the combination of private benefits and the *social wage* of public welfare added up to a decent social contract.

When relatively high wages were added in, the result was to make life more comfortable for American wage earners than ever before. The distribution of national income had become more equal during World War II, and shares going to different segments of society remained on a plateau of relative equality through the 1960s. Poverty all but ceased to be a fact of life for industrial workers. That did not mean poverty disappeared for those at the margins, including agricultural workers and the elderly, or that racial minorities and women did not suffer the economic disadvantages of discrimination. But unlike the 1920s, America's newfound affluence did not abrogate the social contract.

Role of the State

The final component of postwar prosperity was the onset of state regulation. After the period of economic nationalism from 1914 through 1939, world leaders shifted from autarky and self-sufficiency to economic internationalism and cooperation. Gone were the days when a handful of international bankers worked together to maintain stability. Now corporate and political elites on both sides of the Atlantic knit together another set of positive feedback loops. They forged links between the currency stabilization of the International Monetary Fund, increased lending through such channels as the Marshall Plan, and expanded trade through the reduction of trade barriers under the General Agreement on Tariffs and Trade. Where capitalists had retreated to their national bunkers in the 1930s, now the capitalist class became internationalized through transatlantic ties. Such an international system required the Mix, or state influence in capitalist enterprise, to be successful.

In short, Keynesianism became the received wisdom and government promoted consumer demand. For the most part, this was accomplished through the so-called transfer payments of unemployment compensation, old-age pensions, and the like, which also functioned as income stabilizers moderating against economic downturns. One special case of state promotion was military spending. In the United States, military spending never returned to pre–World War II levels. Instead, the Cold War increased budgets steadily year by year. Many aerospace corporations, such as General Electric and Boeing, came to depend on government contracts for bottom-line profits, just as university science departments counted on federal support for defense research. Because of the stimulating effect on private enterprise, the rise of what President Eisenhower called the military–industrial complex was an example of what others called military Keynesianism, or the state sponsorship of military spending and technology.

The state was also deeply involved in serving the needs of consumer capitalism through foreign policy. One striking example is the diplomacy of oil. The new suburban-service economy depended on an almost limitless supply of cheap oil. Where textile mills and railroads were once powered by coal, now assembly lines and automobiles were powered by petroleum. Oil companies such as Standard Oil, one of the wealthiest corporations in the world, benefitted politically from this strategic position and exercised tremendous influence over global markets. Because an increasing share of oil came in from overseas, oil companies gained special leverage in U.S. foreign policy, as well as tax credits at home. Petrodiplomacy in the Middle East began when Franklin Roosevelt stopped in Saudi Arabia on his way back from Yalta in 1945. Roosevelt committed the United States to support the House of Saud in return for a Saudi agreement to keep cheap oil from the Arabian–American Oil Company flowing at all times. The influence of Big Oil, as many called the petroleum lobby, was also evident in nearby Iran when the CIA organized the overthrow of the democratically elected government of Premier Mossadegh in 1953 after he nationalized Iranian oil fields. The leader reinstalled after the coup d'etat, Shah Mohammad Reza Pahlavi, proved more agreeable, restoring corporate profits and becoming a pillar of U.S. power in the Middle East until his overthrow in 1979. As a result of these favorable arrangements in the Middle East, plus the arrival of new supplies in the world market from Venezuela, Nigeria, and the North Sea, the price of oil went down from $1.71 per barrel in 1950 to $1.30 in 1970, giving an added boost to the postwar boom.

The Americanization of Western Europe

With Americans seemingly everywhere on the European continent, Western Europeans began to speak—not always favorably—about the *Americanization* of Europe. At one level they used the term to describe the tidal wave of American imports—Western movies, blue jeans, and Coca-Cola—that flowed in from across the Atlantic. Although U.S. imports were nothing new, they had never arrived on this scale and never with so many U.S. government strings attached. In addition to Marshall Plan aid, the State Department often made U.S. loans contingent on free-market access for U.S. firms.

The MGM movie *An American in Paris* was one of the highest-grossing films in 1951. It illustrated the influence and translatability of U.S. popular culture abroad, but also how Hollywood consciously sought to appeal to foreign audiences and markets.
Wikicommons, unknown source.

Flexing their political muscle, U.S. corporations made the most of their newfound opportunities. The Coca-Cola Company, for example, secured a contract to make Coke one of the items of *government issue* that gave the GI his name. At first confined to the military PX (postexchange), Coke increasingly found its way to civilian consumers. Germans, for example, put down their beer and slurped enough Coke to make their country the biggest overseas market for the hugely profitable Atlanta-based corporation. By 1950, fully one-third of the company's profits came from overseas. Having originated as an international drink that brought Caribbean sugar, Peruvian coca, and West African cola nuts to Americans, now Coke had come full circle to become a preferred drink of Latin Americans, Africans, and Europeans.

Hollywood movies tell a similar tale. Pulling on the same governmental strings, Hollywood studios took command of the European film market, accounting for more than 60 percent of film showings in the early 1950s. Looking beyond Europe, MGM, Paramount, and other Hollywood giants went on to conquer world markets, accounting for a low of 48 percent of film showings in the Far East to a high of 76 percent in Mexico and Central America. The only place where Hollywood did not dominate was where the Iron Curtain came down over the silver screen. The Soviet ban on Hollywood movies was an example of what made U.S. corporate executives so upset about command economies in the first place. By 1959, half of the profits of the U.S. entertainment industry came from overseas. Executives recoiled at the thought of losing overseas markets.

American products were subtle ambassadors of American power. When a German or a Pole put on a pair of Levi's, he (and increasingly she) also donned a symbol of the freewheeling lifestyle of the American West. Similarly, when young people in Rome or Amsterdam went to see a Donald Duck cartoon sponsored by the U.S. Information Service at the local U.S. consulate, how could they not feel affection for the culture that produced such an irascible but lovable little creature? In this way, the marketing of commodities "made in the U.S.A." underwrote U.S. geopolitical power. It may have been true, as Mao Zedong said, that "political power grows out of the barrel of a gun," but it was also true that the soft power of symbols and ideas could be as effective. Hollywood movies succeeded, as the president of the Motion Picture Association said in 1953, precisely "because they are not obvious propaganda," although many clearly promoted the American consumer lifestyle. Europeans who loved Coca-Cola and Mickey Mouse were more likely to welcome U.S. military bases on their soil. Thus, did the soft power of cultural imports reinforce the hard power of NATO.

If at first glance this appears to be cultural imperialism, closer inspection reveals a more complex relationship where many Western Europeans willingly courted access to the open and seemingly class-exempt aspects of the American way of life. After experiencing a generation of war rooted in their own culture, the younger generation, in particular, was hungry for a different set of values. They were especially repulsed by the grotesque excesses of Fascism, with its mindless patriotism and loathsome death camps, but they were also disenchanted with more mainstream German *Kultur* and French *haute civilisation*. Against this backdrop, American cultural icons were irresistible: the impish Mickey Mouse; the resolute individualism (and existential loneliness) of Gary Cooper in *High Noon*; the instant gratification of chocolate, cigarettes, and nylon stockings given out by ever-smiling GI's. Europeans selectively imported pieces of American culture to use in their own projects of inner transformation and satisfaction.

Not all reactions to American symbols were favorable because not all expressions of U.S. cultural imperialism were subtle. Resisting what they saw as an American invasion, the French, in particular, worried about *coca-colonization*. When Coke built a bottling plant in Marseilles in 1949, a coalition of wineries, soft drink producers, and the Communist Party tried unsuccessfully to have the sugary liquid banned. Similar anxiety about Hollywood was more pervasive. While young Europeans flocked to Hollywood westerns and gangster movies, the older generation complained about degraded standards of civilization.

At the deepest level, European anxiety was not so much about Americanization as it was about the process of *globalization*. In this period, Americanization was the name for the transition in upper-tier economies from the early stage of urban-industrial society to the American model of high production/high consumption of middlebrow culture and goods that prevailed in the middle decades of the twentieth century. Although the United States was the first to arrive at this destination (just as Britain had been the first to industrialize in the nineteenth century), the process was transforming all the countries of the developed world from Germany to Japan. With radios in most upper-tier homes by 1950 and automobiles becoming commonplace, modern telecommunications and transportation were relentless in their push against isolation and tradition. Since change brought dislocation and disruption, America also became a sign of change—sometimes welcome, sometimes not—that transcended national boundaries.

CONCLUSION

Only at rare moments in world history has one power arisen to as commanding a position as the United States occupied at the end of the Second World War. Contemporaries were on the mark in comparing American ascendancy to that of Rome in the first century, imperial China under the Qing, Spain in the sixteenth century, or Britain in the Victorian age. That Americans stubbornly refused to see themselves in imperial terms did not erase the realities of American power: the dollar's preeminence as the standard for the world economy; the American military's global reach in hundreds of foreign bases; the wide appeal to American virtues and its vices; the vastness of America's network of protectorates and clients, which included Western Europe, much of Latin America, and parts of Asia and Africa. No other state could boast such a global reach.

Because their power was so great and their self-proclaimed intentions so benevolent, Americans struggled to understand why they could not make history just as they pleased. Being powerful fostered the delusion of being all-powerful. They reacted to checks on their power as an affront to freedom, not an expression of other people's right to take control of their own destiny as they saw fit.

Despite the imbalance in power and purpose, the Cold War involved certain symmetries. From each side, it seemed to be a permanent battle between us and them, Western bloc and Eastern bloc, capitalists and Communists, good and evil (or the other way around). Each side rallied clients and allies to its side in great alliance systems and in bruising ideological combat and constructed an image of its own virtue against the others' imputed vice. Americans liked to contrast freedom and affluence to Soviet totalitarianism and privation. The Soviets, for their part, counterposed equality and industry to American racism and imperialism.

The real world never fully conformed to the Cold War's simple bipolar model. One complicating factor was the "Third World." Newly emerging countries in Asia and Africa often refused to join either the first world of the capitalist West or the second world of the Socialist East. Instead, they became an influential Third World of their own.

FURTHER READING

Cumings, Bruce. *The Korean War: A History*. New York: Modern Library, 2010.

Dukes, Paul. *The Superpowers: A Short History*. London: Routledge, 2000.

Jian, Chen. *Mao's China and the Cold War*. Chapel Hill: University of North Carolina Press, 2001.

Killick, John. *The United States and European Reconstruction, 1945–1960*. Edinburgh: Keele University Press, 1997.

Kwon, Heonik. *The Other Cold War*. New York: Columbia University Press, 2010.

Leffler, Melvyn. *A Preponderance of Power: National Security, the Truman Administration, and the Cold War*. Stanford, CA: Stanford University Press, 1992.

McMahon, Robert. *The Cold War in the Third World*. New York: Oxford University Press, 2013.

Schlesinger, Stephen. *Act of Creation: The Founding of the United Nations*. Boulder, CO, 2003.

Wagnleitner, Reinhold. *Coca-Colonization and the Cold War: The Cultural Mission of the United States in Austria after the Second World War*. Translated by Diana Wolf. Chapel Hill: University of North Carolina Press, 1994.

Zubok, Vladislav, and Constantine Pleshakov. *Inside the Kremlin's Cold War: From Stalin to Khrushchev*. Cambridge, MA: Harvard University Press, 1996.

CHAPTER 9

AMERICAN REFORM AND THE THIRD WORLD, 1955–65

The son of a prominent African American minister in Atlanta, Reverend Martin Luther King Jr. served as the voice of poor black Southerners who lived under Jim Crow segregation. By 1963, Dr. King took the civil rights movement to its pinnacle, but left an uncertain legacy for the young activist who followed his lead. National Archives at College Park–Still Pictures (RDSS).

JOURNEY TO FREEDOM: 1957

In 1957, Dr. Martin Luther King Jr. journeyed to West Africa to take part in the celebration of Ghana's independence. A former British colony known as the Gold Coast, Ghanaians had elected one of their own, Kwame Nkrumah, the first prime minister, and he invited King to attend what soon became the start of an independence wave in West Africa. Reverend King had already made his mark as a civil rights leader, and he went on to become a Nobel Prize winner, national hero, and martyr to the civil rights cause. For now, he was eager to witness Ghanaians lower the British flag and raise their own flag, and as they did, King was overcome with emotion. "Before I knew it," he wrote, "I started weeping. I was crying for joy." The streets of Accra, the capital city, filled with tears of joy that day. And as King listened to crowds chanting "Freedom!," echoes of the old Negro spiritual, "Free at last, free at last, Great God Almighty, I'm free at last," stirred in the back of his mind.

King's elation in Ghana stemmed from his recognition that African Americans were part of a larger quest for freedom spanning continents, oceans, if not history. The fate of Africa and America had been intertwined since the time of slavery, when Ghana was a major leg of the Atlantic slave trade. Over many generations, the transatlantic bond had been renewed in struggles against empire, slavery, and the brutal legacy of both—racism. Now those struggles were reaching a climax in parallel efforts to end racial segregation in the United States and European colonialism in Africa.

REFORM, THE THIRD WORLD, AND THE COLD WAR

The interlocking historical destinies of Africans and African Americans offer another example of the influence of people and events around the world on the United States. As an open system, the West placed crucial social and political questions—namely, race and empire—on the table for discussion in communities as well as between states. In the United States, civil rights laws and liberal reform efforts were part of a worldwide movement to upend old patterns of dominance and prejudice. Although circumstances differed from place to place, a sense of common purpose linked struggles against colonialism, segregation, and white supremacy. The quest for racial equality was more than a reaction to Western oppression; therefore, it was also bound up in beliefs about a more just society, whether African Socialist, Chinese Communist, or liberal capitalist. And although the range of possible responses was narrower for the United States, President Lyndon Johnson's Great Society was in line with the reform impulse sweeping through other nations at the time.

Looming over calls for global reform was the Cold War. Brandishing nuclear weapons at one another, the United States and the Soviet Union battled for advantage in border regions of the Third World. As they pushed and prodded each other from Cuba to Congo to Vietnam, the first world of Western capitalism and the second world of Eastern socialism each did its best to bring the non-aligned nations of the Third World into their orbit. For American leaders, the desire to win diplomatic favor in Third World countries was a strong motive to support domestic reform as a way of projecting a positive image overseas. If it was going to pose as champion of the free world and the enemy of totalitarianism, the United States could do no less. The mantra of reform, therefore, became an indispensable ideological weapon in the Cold War.

The Third World

To the chagrin of leaders in both the Western and the Eastern blocs, many newly independent nations refused to join either side and instead gravitated toward a loose grouping of *nonaligned* or neutralist nations that appropriated, but also reinterpreted, French demographer Alfred Sauvy's term *the Third World* to mark their stance. Under the slogan "neither West nor East," leaders from twenty-nine nonaligned African and Asian nations gathered in Bandung, Indonesia, in April 1955 for what was, in effect, the founding convention of the Third World. Marking the historic departure, Indonesia's President Sukarno proclaimed, "This is the first international conference of colored peoples in the history of mankind."

Initiative for the Bandung Conference—known officially as the Asian–African Conference—came largely from India. The second most populous nation in the world with some 431 million people in 1960, India was the most important of the nonaligned nations. The country's westernized elites, epitomized by its first prime minister, British-educated Jawaharlal Nehru, had cast aside British rule in 1947 and created a new regime based on democratic elections, mixed economy, and diplomatic nonalignment.

On the surface, the Bandung Conference accomplished little. No diplomatic alliance system on the order of NATO or the Warsaw Pact emerged—indeed, the very principle of nonalignment all but precluded it—nor did it solve regional disputes. Nevertheless, the conference was significant for placing key demands regarding race, empire, and equity on the world's agenda. The Egyptian president and Pan-Arab leader, Gamal Abdel Nasser, used the conference as a platform to continue his battle against Western imperialism, an effort he began in 1952 when he led the overthrow of British colonialism in Egypt. The language of nonalignment, which he characterized as positive neutralism, and the rhetoric of Afro-Asian solidarity put Cairo at the center of Middle East politics and elevated Nasser, along with Nehru and Sukarno, to the leadership of the Third World movement. As representatives of some of the poorest regions on earth, the delegates emphasized economic development, primarily through World Bank investment, plus greater cooperation in technology and trade. Embracing the UN's Universal Declaration of Human Rights, they tied the persistence of racism to economic inequality and social oppression, and in the most direct rebuke to the two superpowers, they called for an end to the dangerous and costly nuclear arms race siphoning off precious development aid that could go to poor nations.

The global landscape seemed to be changing, if not in strength then certainly in numbers. Representing a slight majority, there were fifty-three African and Asian nations in the UN General Assembly by 1961, in many ways following the clear majority Asians (56 percent in 1950) and Africans (9 percent) had in the world's population. As a symbol of the growing influence of non-Western

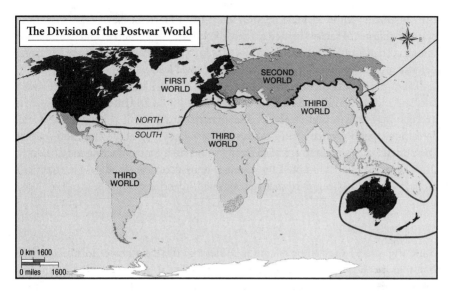

The Division of the Postwar World

FIRST WORLD

SECOND WORLD

THIRD WORLD

NORTH

SOUTH

THIRD WORLD

THIRD WORLD

0 km 1600

0 miles 1600

MAP 9.1

nations, U Thant, a former Burmese subject of the British Empire, was named UN general secretary in 1961.

American officials were of two minds about the Third World. On the one hand, the wave of Asian and African independence happened at a time of high tension in the Cold War, and President Dwight Eisenhower demanded unequivocal allegiance from the new regimes. The Third World movement's neutralist stance appalled Secretary of State John Foster Dulles. An ardent Cold Warrior, Dulles considered non-alignment an "immoral and short-sighted conception." Like Eisenhower, Dulles favored unquestioned fidelity and a clear political stance from Cold War allies and enemies. Drawing such a fine diplomatic line compelled the United States to seek closer ties with the Islamic government in Pakistan rather than the predominantly Hindu government in India, because Dulles characterized Hinduism as morally relative, socially passive, and thus vulnerable to Soviet influence. Dulles used similar logic to cast the South African as a conservative stalwart against Communism, rather than a racist holdover from the politics of the 1930s, when the Afrikaners adopted apartheid in 1948. On the other hand, the administration sympathized with the move toward independence, which is why Eisenhower sent his vice president, Richard Nixon, to stand alongside Prime Minister Kwame Nkrumah and Martin Luther King Jr. at Ghana's independence ceremony.

Bandung took place under the cloud of such concerns, and Dulles, unable to derail the nonaligned movement or obstruct Nasser's rise among Third World leaders, had to content himself with a two-pronged response. First, he denied passports to W. E. B. Du Bois and Paul Robeson, African American leaders sympathetic to Third World concerns, who wanted to attend the conference. At the same time, the State Department reluctantly gave a green light to Adam Clayton Powell, the outspoken, unpredictable congressman from Harlem, New York, mainly to counter charges of racism leveled at the United States by conferees and Communist nations. The gamble paid off when Powell went to Bandung and mounted a strong defense of America's racial progress and free world leadership.

The larger issue of race persisted, however, and much like gender, it became a wild card in Cold War politics, collapsing domestic conditions and international concerns and defying easy assumption about social dynamics in the United States or the world. By taking a public stance against racism and racial privilege at the very moment that the United States sought to establish clear ground rules for conducting the Cold War, Third World nations co-opted the message and set a new standard for America's global leadership— improved race relations within and without U.S. borders.

Sino-Soviet Split

Bandung caused another problem for Dulles and the Eisenhower administration, one tied directly to America's efforts to sway Third World people from Communist influence. China's shrewd foreign minister Zhou Enlai was at Bandung, too, and sought to claim outsider status for China on par with other Third World states. But because it was technically a Communist nation, and thus aligned with the Communist camp, China had difficulty selling its nonalignment credentials. Nevertheless, as the most populous nation on earth with approximately six hundred million people at the time, and as a result the largest Asian nation, no Asian–African conference could be complete without it.

China was emerging as India's rival for leadership of the Third World, and its split with the Soviet Union would soon enhance China's legitimacy as an independent actor in the Cold War. Tensions between the two Communist giants arose over ideological differences. Challenging the orthodox Soviet emphasis on the revolutionary leadership of the urban proletariat, Mao Zedong's version of Marxism emphasized the revolutionary role of the peasantry. Likewise, Mao rejected Soviet willingness to accept the stalemate of "peaceful coexistence" with Western capitalism. Like Leon Trotsky in the 1920s, Mao wanted permanent revolution, a position that had wide appeal to Asian radicals.

Perhaps the overriding difference lay in power politics, as both Russia under Nikita Khrushchev and China under Mao aspired to leadership of the Third World. By 1960, relations had cooled to the point of becoming a Cold War within the Cold War. The split could have been a golden opportunity for the West to drive the wedge in deeper, but America's fervid anti-Communist ideology prevented U.S. diplomats from conceptualizing anything outside the confines of containment until President Richard Nixon visited China in 1972.

The Lower Tier in the World Economy

Once the independence wave crested in the early 1960s, most countries of the Third World languished in the lower tier of the world economy. Euphoria gave way to the reality of economic dependency, and lacking essential capital for internal investment, the new countries had to turn to banks in the metropolitan centers of London, Paris, Frankfurt, and New York. Going ever deeper into debt, they became economically dependent on the same powers from which they had only recently won their political independence, a predicament called *neocolonialism*. As a result, the term Third World increasingly lost its original meaning and eventually became synonymous with the world's poor nations. The Third World's new definition was elastic enough to incorporate places left out of Bandung, such as Latin America. In the new definition of global poverty and dependence, however, the existence of destitute barrios in Caracas and São Paulo placed Latin America squarely in the impoverished ranks of the lower tier.

Escaping poverty would prove even more difficult in the long run than beating back colonialism, and that was not entirely the fault of the rich nations. Another aspect of neocolonialism was the self-interest of many Third World elites who often did well under existing arrangements. No Saudi oil prince or Indonesian banker was eager to jeopardize his own privileges to improve the lot of the suffering masses.

A handful, such as Ghana's Kwame Nkrumah, did make serious attempts to find their way out of neocolonialism. Returning from seminars at elite schools, such as the University of Pennsylvania, filled with enthusiasm for nationalization, they sought to use the powers of the nation-state to promote economic development. In the case of Guatemala, democratically elected President Jacobo Árbenz nationalized the estates of the United Fruit Company and other absentee corporations to break the cycle of dependence. Likewise, in Iran, Premiere Mohammad Mossadegh seized absentee oil corporations in an attempt to keep revenues at home for investment in domestic development instead of enriching multinational corporations, like the Anglo-Iranian Oil Corporation.

Since third-tier countries were overwhelmingly agrarian, development began with land reform and the highly contentious and usually short-lived redistribution of giant estates. Industry came next, often in the form of a grand mixed economy or socialized capitalism schemes, such as Nehru's use of public money to build an Indian steel industry, when private capital was not available. Success of mixed economy solutions varied because Third World development projects often succumbed to corruption, inefficiency, and the opposition of international adversaries. The Central Intelligence Agency (CIA) played a crucial role in the successful overthrow of Árbenz and Mossadegh and was instrumental in an ill-fated attempt on Castro's regime. The pretext for CIA involvement was Cold War containment, but multinational corporations stood to gain just as much as the cause of democracy.

When the mixed-economy approach failed to yield results, Third World nations resorted to the command economy of Communism. Whether in the form of Soviet-style centralized planning or Maoist mobilization of the peasantry, the command economy (although not Communist property ownership) held a strong attraction for many military and bureaucratic elites in underdeveloped countries. Yet neither model was effective at delivering on their promises. Soviet collective farms were so inefficient they were barely able to feed their own population, forcing the importation of grain, and China lost an estimated thirty million people to famine.

China's economic disaster was the product of a twelve-year development program embodied in what are called the little (1956–58) and Great Leap Forward (1958–62). In an answer to both Western capitalism and Soviet-style heavy industry, Mao decreed that all energies would be directed toward raising industrial output through backyard steel furnaces, agricultural communes, and similar grass-roots production. And because orders came from the state, but local communities carried them out, Mao created a version of societal development in which the Communist Party could claim decentralized power and give it back to the people. The result was devastating. Instead of making China self-sufficient, the leaps only swallowed up scarce resources, failed to produce enough food to feed the nation, and turned out steel of such poor quality that it was useless for modern industry. With Soviet advisors departing in disgust, it widened the Sino-Soviet split and proved a doubtful model for other struggling economies.

By contrast, American farms continued to be the most productive in the world. Favorable soils and climate made it so, as did heavy use of fertilizer and machinery, extensive government support, and the rise of agribusiness that reduced the number of rural producers to less than 10 percent of the U.S. workforce by 1960. Farmers in the United States were able to feed the country and still have huge quantities left over for export. But because the costly American model was not easily transferred to the Third World, American agronomists sought to artificially increase productivity through what they called the Green Revolution instead. The Green Revolution touted high-yield, hybrid seeds—the forerunner of genetically modified food—as a guaranteed way to raise nutritional levels in the Third World without going through the contentious process of land reform. Despite the appearance of benevolent guidance, U.S. corporate and political elites discouraged industrial development in the regions they did business in an effort to keep lower-tier states as a reserve for food and strategic resources, such as oil. Only later would that change with the coming of *globalization* in the 1980s.

AFRICA IN THE COLD WAR

As Third World countries struggled to get out of poverty, they had to reckon with the Cold War. No less than other regions, Africa was a Cold War battleground. Although not strategically located on the border of either superpower, African resources (oil, gold, copper) were important to the world economy, and the decisions of African leaders—whether to join the West, the East, or the Third World—were of considerable symbolic importance. Timing gave African nations added leverage. At roughly the same time the independence wave crested in 1960, celebrated as the Year of Africa for the seventeen new nations born that year, confrontations between the United States and Soviet Union that stretched from Berlin to Havana heightened Cold War tensions and placed Africa's transformation under greater global scrutiny.

Of all the African nations, Egypt was a special Cold War prize because it straddled the Suez Canal that linked the Mediterranean Sea and to the Indian Ocean. Egypt's leader, Gamal Abdel Nasser, was an army colonel who epitomized the role of military elites in using nationalization to promote economic development. A shrewd diplomat, in 1956 he nationalized the Suez Canal in a maneuver to play the two superpowers against each other for funding the Aswan Dam, a huge hydroelectric system that would stride the fabled Nile River. That touched off the Suez Crisis, which saw Britain and France mount a joint military operation to recapture the canal. They coordinated their invasion with Israel, which seized the Sinai Peninsula from Egypt. Angered by the preemptive attacks, Eisenhower acted in a bid to establish America's leadership in the Third World. Under the weight of U.S. criticism and local resistance, the Franco-British effort fell apart, leaving the United States looking like an opponent of old-style European imperialism.

Patrice Lumumba was the first democratically elected prime minister of the Democratic Republic of Congo following its independence from Belgium in 1960. Rifts within Congo and alienation from Western states because of perceived ties to the Soviet Union led to his murder by a rival faction. Library of Congress Prints and Photographs Division, Washington, DC.

The United States did not always look so pretty. Depending on circumstances, American diplomacy could just as easily come down on the side of empire. In Congo, for example, the CIA worked closely with former Belgian rulers to depose Patrice Lumumba, Congo's first democratically-elected prime minister, after only a few months in office. A strong nationalist, Lumumba was hostile to Western influence in the country's mineral-rich provinces. In his effort to end the pattern of Western meddling, he committed the unpardonable sin of turning to the Soviets for development aid. America's backlash was fatal. With CIA help, Lumumba was assassinated in short order and replaced by the more compliant, but brutally corrupt military leader, Joseph Mobutu.

Elsewhere in Africa, the United States showed similar support for decolonization, tempered by an insistence that the new states align with the West. Seeking to supplant the Europeans as the major Western player, the United States encouraged black majority rule in the vast geographic area from Ghana in the west to Kenya in the east and from Algeria in the north to Tanzania in the south. They drew the line, however, at South Africa. As the one country in the world that rejected the postwar trend toward racial equality, South Africa tightened the rules of apartheid (separation) to become the world's worst example of repressive white minority rule. Because it was also staunchly an anti-Communist nation, held significant U.S. corporate investment, and possessed a trove of strategic materials, the United States extended unswerving support for the apartheid regime.

Civil Rights Movement

Struggles against European colonialism had an analogue in the African American freedom movement. Like the changing tides and shifting channels of a river, the freedom movement rose and fell in response to its environment. Coming off a tactic of political pressure and gradual gains in the public sector, Cold War civil rights quickly shifted to the single aim of eliminating legal barriers to equal treatment. The legal strategy fit nicely within the postwar emphasis on pluralism in American society. Pluralism was salad-bowl Americanism—the harmonious mingling of ethnic, racial, and religious groups within the framework of common American identity. Rather than embracing separate Old World identities, second-generation Jewish and Catholic immigrants preferred to stress assimilation into American society. In similar fashion, African Americans began to play down African identity, fearing that too close an identification with Africa might impede integration and the quest for legal equality in America.

Operating within that pluralist framework, civil rights leaders developed brilliant strategies for challenging Jim Crow, first in the courtroom and then in the streets. In what turned out to be the catalyst for the revival of the freedom movement, black residents of Montgomery, Alabama, joined together in 1955 to boycott the segregated bus system. The boycott began with the refusal of Rosa Parks, an office secretary of the local NAACP, to give up her seat to a white man as Jim Crow custom demanded. Once word of her arrest reached the community, the local branch of the NAACP, which was eager to change the social structure, turned the jailing of Parks into the spark for an organized challenge to segregation. After months of carpooling or walking to work and failed negotiations with city officials and representatives of the Montgomery Bus Line, a Supreme Court decision requiring the bus system to end its discriminatory practices rewarded the black community's sacrifice and sent signals to the nation.

The figure who emerged at the head of the boycott was Dr. Martin Luther King Jr. At the start of his extraordinary pilgrimage that ended in martyrdom, King was an untested, twenty-six-year-old son of one of Atlanta's leading black ministers. With degrees from Morehouse College in Atlanta and Boston University's school of theology, the mesmerizing Baptist preacher seemed ready to take his assigned place as a member of the South's black elite.

But King was destined for greater things. He had a genius for braiding together many different religious traditions and theological themes, including the spiritual passions of Afro-Christianity, the cool-headed rationalism of Reinhold Niebuhr, and the social reform–minded teachings of the social gospel. King's intellectual pedigree made the philosophy of nonviolence, the belief that social change comes through peaceful confrontation with unjust authority, a natural fit. Rejecting both reliance on authority and violent revolution placed King in the rarified company of Mohandas Gandhi, the spiritual leader of Indian independence.

In his lifelong struggle against British rule, Gandhi had embraced *satyagraha*, a Hindu concept meaning "the force of truth," as the central tenet of nonviolence. Believing in the central truth of human equality even brought Gandhi to eventually reject the ancient Hindu caste system, a rigid social hierarchy with Brahmins on top and Dalits, or "untouchables," on the bottom. Dalits, in fact, were so debased that Indian society deemed them beneath even the lowest caste. Hence, they were *outcasts*. Gandhi also opposed religious intolerance, and his embrace of Muslim brothers made him the target of a fanatical Hindu assassin.

Although the two never met, King had a chance to see the fruits of Gandhi's legacy during a pilgrimage to Nehru's India in 1959. King found the official campaign to eradicate discrimination against untouchables particularly striking, and when introduced warmly to an Indian audience as "a fellow untouchable from the United States of America" later during his stay, the analogy reminded King of the ties between America's civil rights movement and the global quest for human rights and dignity. He was at first offended to think of himself as one of the wretched of the earth. But as the statement sank in, he realized the crushing effects of oppression were the same wherever you go. "Yes," he affirmed, "I am an untouchable."

The sense of change gripping Africa and Asia came to the United States with full force. The Montgomery bus boycott had broken down the status quo, and in 1960, the year of Africa, a handful of college students in Greensboro, North Carolina, waged a frontal assault on Jim Crow by sitting in at the lunch counter in the local Woolworth's Department Store as protest against its rule denying service to African Americans. The tactic energized the youth, who ached for a way to challenge the social injustices at odds with the promises of America and the rhetoric of the Cold War. The following year, blacks and whites, women and men, defied segregation and braved violent attacks by climbing aboard Greyhound buses on Freedom Rides through the South.

CONSUMER CULTURE

The simple act of seeking a cup of coffee, a bus ride, or a train ticket exposed the boundaries of segregation in the United States. Jim Crow had always rooted itself in commerce, tastes, and culture, but it was an unstable mix requiring constant attention and maintenance because segregation depended on a society of discriminate desires, bracketed by custom and access, if not a culture of consumption limited in its scope and appeal. Yet, consumption marked a broad quest of African Americans as the evolving Cold War made it a condition of living in the "free" world. Freedom Rides revealed the ironies of the tension between consumption and freedom in a segregated society, and the violence unleashed was so obscene that many Americans recoiled in horror. The contradictions could also be subtle. When blacks held up the mirror of magazine and television advertising and saw only white-skinned, blue-eyed models instead of anything close to their own image, this too would become a frontline in the civil rights movement.

On the positive side, consumption destabilized rigid notions of difference through the spread of popular culture and luxury goods. Blacks could not live in certain neighborhoods because of restrictive policies against home sales, but they could buy the latest fashion from mail-order catalogs and expensive cars and defy the appearance of their inferiority to whites. Popular culture's open door policy introduced white youth to black artists as the music industry drove a generational wedge into Jim Crow. There was a measure of pride in hearing the cry for freedom absorbed into mainstream culture through Louis Armstrong's popular Dixieland jazz, Chubby Checker's "The Twist," and Ray Charles's " What'd I Say." Elvis Presley, gyrating across the stage with songs about his hound dog and blue suede shoes, ironically became the top musical star of 1950s-segregated America by singing black rhythm and blues to a largely white audience. Popular culture demonstrated segregation's untenability, just as it suggested the vast reach of consumer culture and, by extension, the Cold War.

The shift of gears in the world economy that brought postwar prosperity also spread consumer culture throughout the upper tier of the world economy. Led by a vanguard of suburban shoppers in the United States, Westerners increasingly pursued *the good life*, defined in terms of bigger and better possessions—refrigerators, televisions, cars, and eventually homes—and creative uses of leisure time, such as travel, sports, and movies. Released from the privations of depression and war, the younger generation pursued happiness through drive-in movies, vacations at the beach, and rock 'n' roll music. Chasing after a more enjoyable way of life than their parents and grandparents had known, they added a fifth freedom to the four freedoms of the Second World War—freedom to shop.

Again, Americans were in the lead, as they had been in the 1920s. Resuming the romance of consumption that had been interrupted by depression and war, Americans fell in love all over again with movie star Marilyn Monroe and baseball hero Mickey Mantle, who chased Babe Ruth's record as home-run leader. At a time of political conformity, rebellious impulses among the younger generation were channeled into inaccessible entertainment outlets, such as Elvis Presley's winding hips, the irreverent lyrics of "Jailhouse Rock," and the impo-

For the youth of the 1950s, rock 'n' roll offered a way to defy their parents and the demands of the Cold War. No figure captured the spirit of rebellion more vividly than Elvis Presley. Crossing racial and class lines, Elvis brought the raw energy of lowbrow culture into the mainstream of middlebrow America. Library of Congress Prints and Photographs Division, Washington, DC.

tent protest of movie hero James Dean in the aptly titled *Rebel without a Cause* (1955). Even Allen Ginsberg and other so-called Beat poets, the most recognizable cultural rebels of the day, seemed to concede defeat. "America," wrote Ginsberg, "you are everything, and I am nothing."

Similarly, trends toward women's independence were contained within the world of the consumer household. Flattered by television programs like *Queen for a Day*, where the winning contestant was wrapped in a royal ermine robe, the stereotypical suburban housewife picked up shopping tips in women's magazines such as *Ladies Home Journal* and *House Beautiful*. Gathering up an unending supply of home products and kitchen gadgets in her supermarket shopping cart, the "rebel girl" of old turned into the queen of household consumption.

Sexuality also received the containment treatment. Just as consumer culture has revised the age-old image of the Madonna, so, too, it reworked her evil twin—the sexual vixen—into the sexually available girl next door. At least, that was the message encoded in glossy photos of bare-breasted women that proliferated in men's magazines like *Playboy*, where images of gorgeous stereo sets also competed for young men's attention. The move toward self-indulgence was an incredible reversal for a country built on Puritan self-denial, but it had the stabilizing effect of absorbing potentially unsettling trends into a lifestyle built around consumption.

By the early 1960s, the North Atlantic had become a two-way street for consumer culture. The premier European export was the Beatles. The four boys with the "mod" look from Liverpool, England, were an even bigger phenomenon than Elvis. Having bounced around the clubs of Hamburg, Germany, singing "Kom Gibst Mir Deiner Hand," they arrived for a triumphal tour of the United States in 1964 singing "I Want to Hold Your Hand." Their innocent invitation to romance could send masses of adolescent girls into a screaming frenzy. Seeing a huge teenage market in the Beatles craze, producers arranged an appearance on *The Ed Sullivan Show*, the leading television variety show of the day, where the stiff, suit-and-tie Sullivan played the role of cultural mediator between older and younger generations.

The Beatles' second tour in 1965 marked the advent of the giant rock concert as a tribal rite of the younger generation. The collective roar of the rock concert was an inchoate demand of the baby boom generation for freedom from the conformist atmosphere of the 1950s. Although rock culture demanded tribal conformity of its own, all the partying that went with rock music awakened a spirit of rebellion that would soon explode in demands for sexual freedom. At the same time, the commercialization of youth culture demonstrated the difficulty of gaining cultural freedom within consumer-driven capitalism. In *Understanding Media* (1964), philosophical guru Marshall McLuhan wrote that "the medium is the message." And commercial channels, the emerging medium, transformed everything, even rebellion, into a profit.

The Empire of Consumption

The spread of American pop culture played an important role as soft power in bonding Western Europe to the United States. Despite hostility toward materialism, Western Europe was fascinated by U.S. technology and the sheer abundance of goods and was thus moving in the same direction toward consumer culture. By 1960, European recovery was far enough along that its affluent population could indulge their desires and mimic U.S. patterns of consumption. Often this came in the form of buying Donald Duck comics, Elvis Presley records, and other American imports. Growing up in the late 1950s, the influence of American pop culture bombarded young Europeans. One Italian reminisced, "During our teen years we idolized James Dean and Marilyn Monroe, listened to Elvis Presley, Brenda Lee, and Jerry Lee Lewis. . . . Our food was Kentucky Fried Chicken, burgers, fries, and Cokes, and our clothes were T-shirts, sweatshirts, and jeans."

Europeans immersed in the "hip scene" learned the lingo of Beat poets—"groovy, crazy, cool, and heavy." Just half a century earlier, American imports were more likely to be physical commodities such as Kansas grain, Chicago beef, and Henry Ford's cheap automobiles. Now the imports were more likely to be cultural, whether fashion, music, food, or ideas. This shift to intangible commodities, the realm of ideas and symbols as some scholars note, reflects the larger transition from the urban-industrial to the suburban-service economy.

Consumer culture was also a weapon in the Cold War and a catalyst for U.S. hegemony. It showed that Western capitalism, with its emphasis on democratic choice and open access, could deliver in ways Soviet Communism's closed system could not. During a 1959 visit to a special American exhibition in Moscow, Vice President Richard Nixon squared off against Soviet Premier Nikita Khrushchev in a famous "kitchen debate." In a pure expression of what freedom meant in market terms, Nixon proclaimed that the most important difference between the two systems was the American consumer's right to choose. The ranch-style home at the U.S. exhibit brimmed with the most modern conveniences, the latest fashion, and the brightest colors. "We don't have one decision made at the top by one government official," Nixon said; "We have many different manufacturers and many different kinds of washing machines so that the housewives have a choice." Seeing an opening for rebuttal, Khrushchev outlined what would be the Soviet counterpoint to unbridled consumption in the West—rational consumption. It was a concept launched following Stalin's death to bring the Communist sphere closer to the emerging global mainstream without abandoning Communist morality or identity. Khrushchev countered that Soviet women were not confined to the home as mere consumers of commodities under the "capitalist attitude toward women" and boasted that, instead, they played a major role in factory production. Nor were they exploited as sex objects by Soviet media, which featured wholesome role models, not nude models, and edifying classical music, not decadent rock 'n' roll.

Each side would soon be surprised to find women in revolt against their assigned roles. Even as Nixon extolled the freedom of the American housewife, feelings were rising against what feminist Betty Friedan described as the prison of the suburban home. Friedan's landmark book, *The Feminine Mystique* (1963), called on women to break free so they, too, could experience the fulfillment of a professional career. Within a decade of the kitchen debate, feminists were in revolt against the patriarchal family model of husband-breadwinner/wife-homemaker. They demanded the right to choose their own destiny.

No matter how much Khrushchev boasted about surpassing the United States—"We will bury you," he said—the Soviet battle against Western decadence was doomed to defeat. Whether or not Western materialism was morally superior to Eastern stoicism—Beats and other cultural critics insisted it was not—there was no way the closed societies of the East could keep out Donald Duck, not to mention Elvis Presley and Marilyn Monroe. Sooner or later, the fortress would be breached by radio broadcasts and satellite communications that could never be totally jammed.

Although feminism would soon transform Western consumerism, it did not have the shock consumer culture itself delivered to the Soviet system. Once the Soviet people caught wind of Western prosperity, it shook their faith in the command economy. The demand of Soviet women (and men) for the very consumer goods that were in such abundance in the West contributed much to the eventual collapse of the Communist system. Slavenka Drakulic, a Croatian feminist, stated as much when she noted in the midst of the empire's dissolution Soviet women "sitting in their kitchens—because it was the warmest room in their apartments," thinking of "how they hoped to buy a new refrigerator or a new stove or a new car."

THE BALANCE OF POWER, CIRCA 1960

By 1960, the two Cold War superpowers had been locked in a deadly embrace for over a decade. In retrospect, considering the collapse of the Soviet Union, it is clear that they were not evenly matched at all. It was not only that the United States was winning on the culture front, but also that America had by far the bigger economy. Although its share of world trade and manufacturing had declined from its postwar peak to about 30 percent, the United States remained by far the world's biggest economy, with a gross national product two and a half times that of the Soviet Union, an imbalance that only increased when one includes their respective allies. Furthermore, international organizations such as the UN and the International Monetary Fund were generally favorable to the West.

What was more, the United States maintained a huge lead in the nuclear *balance of terror*. Eisenhower premised his approach to foreign policy on America's nuclear supremacy and the fact that the United States had a seventeen-to-one advantage over the Soviet Union in nuclear warheads. That did not stop Democrat John Kennedy from accusing Eisenhower of creating a "missile gap" between the two superpowers and threatening America's nuclear security. Indeed, there was a gap, but Kennedy had it backward. Although it had lost its nuclear monopoly in 1949, the United States never relinquished its lead in nuclear weapons. During the Eisenhower administration, the number of U.S. warheads available to support the doctrine of massive retaliation leaped from one thousand to eighteen thousand and increasingly shifted from high-flying B-52s to guided missiles, which were harder to defend against. With its sophisticated technology of high-flying U-2 spy planes and spy satellites, the United States could watch what the Soviets were doing, but the Soviets did not have the same technology. Not only did more U.S. nuclear submarines roam the seas, but also by 1960 the United States had land-based missiles pointed at the Soviet Union from bases in Britain, West Germany, Italy, the Netherlands, Greece, Belgium, and Spain. The biggest thorn in the Soviet's side was the presence of U.S. Jupiter missiles in Turkey on the border of the Soviet Union. When they surveyed the geopolitical terrain, the Soviets felt encircled, because they were.

At the same time, the Soviets had their own triumphs. With the 1957 launching of *Sputnik I*, the first space satellite to orbit the earth, the Soviets catapulted into

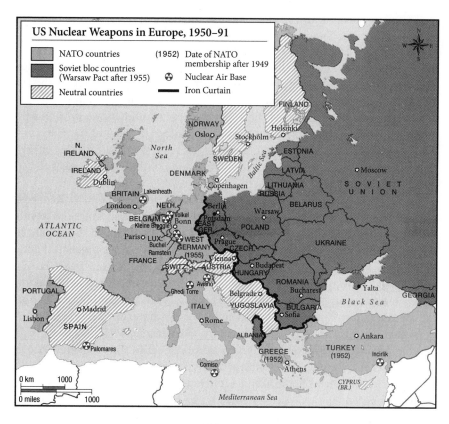

US Nuclear Weapons in Europe, 1950–91

	NATO countries	(1952)	Date of NATO
	Soviet bloc countries		membership after 1949
	(Warsaw Pact after 1955)	✪	Nuclear Air Base
	Neutral countries	▬	Iron Curtain

MAP 9.2

the lead in what immediately became a "space race." A year later, the Americans answered back with the satellite *Explorer I,* but the Soviets quickly countered in 1961 with Yuri Gagarin, the first human to orbit the earth. Although the American John Glenn followed close on Gagarin's heels and President Kennedy vowed to put a man on the moon before the end of the decade—a pledge fulfilled in 1969—for the time being it seemed to a watching world that the Soviets were beating the United States at its own technological game.

More ominously, early Soviet triumphs in space showed off monster rockets that could easily be converted to intercontinental ballistic missiles. Having acquired their own arsenal of H-bombs, the Soviets played catch-up in warheads and delivery systems, while maintaining larger conventional forces of the sort appropriate to a land empire. In addition, some historical trends seemed to favor the Eastern bloc, especially after the 1949 revolution in China boosted Communist prestige in Asia and Africa. To the children of Third World elites graduating from Western universities, the model of a command economy looked extremely attractive as they prepared to take the reins of power on returning to their newly independent homelands.

Berlin Crisis

In terms of the threat of war between the superpowers, the early 1960s were the worst years of the Cold War. Like two heavyweight boxers, leaders on both sides seemed almost eager to come out of their corners swinging. Nikita Khrushchev had prevailed in the Kremlin power struggle to succeed Joseph Stalin. Irascible and blustery, he once displayed the boorish manners of his peasant origins by pounding his shoe on the table during a speech at the UN. Having dared to condemn Stalin's crimes in a dramatic speech in 1956, he needed a capitalist enemy to maintain his power in the Soviet Politburo and bolster his credentials in the Third World.

In the opposite corner, the youthful American president, John F. Kennedy, seemed the antithesis of the crude Soviet leader. The heir to Irish American wealth exuded urbane sophistication. Kennedy had campaigned under the slogan of the New Frontier, a sweeping catchphrase intended to evoke the urgency of both Frederick Jackson Turner's thesis on the closing frontier and the New Deal. The imagery applied to everything from space exploration to economic growth to shaking off 1950s conformity. Overseas, the New Frontier updated the classic tradition of the open door in seeking to expand U.S. influence, but did so through concentrated development efforts. In fact, with plans on the table that included the Peace Corps and the Alliance for Progress, Kennedy's advisors dubbed the 1960s the Decade of Development. Despite the contrast with his Soviet counterpart, Kennedy was equally driven to prove his masculine toughness and consolidate his power at home. Having won the 1960 election by a hair, he, too, needed a foreign enemy.

He had no trouble finding one. The first confrontation between Kennedy and Khrushchev came along the imperial border between eastern and Western Europe in a crisis over Berlin. By the summer of 1961, East Germany was hemorrhaging resources and prestige as thousands fled to the West. To shore up a sagging regime and constant immigration to the West through Berlin, Soviet Premier Nikita Khrushchev proposed to make the division of Germany permanent, threatened to cut off Western access to Berlin, and issued thinly veiled warnings about enforcing his demands with nuclear weapons. No less a Cold Warrior, Kennedy vowed never to relinquish an inch of territory, and he, too, indicated he was ready to defend West Berlin with nuclear weapons.

In this tense climate, the two leaders tested each other's mettle at a summit conference in Vienna that failed to end the acrimony. Two months later, in August 1961, Khrushchev devised his own solution to the Berlin problem by constructing what grew into the twelve-foot-high concrete barrier known as the Berlin Wall. The wall immediately became a symbol of East–West division, although the moral symbolism was hardly symmetrical. Every time East German police shot someone trying to scale the wall to reach the other side, the West notched another propaganda victory. Two years later, in June 1963, President Kennedy made a triumphal visit to the divided city to say "Ich bin ein Berliner" to an electrified crowd. Kennedy's visit also marked how far the former allies had moved from the warm atmosphere of the Yalta Conference of 1945, where there was a chance they might share occupation of a united Germany.

Cuban Revolution

The Berlin crisis was the most dangerous moment of the nuclear era until the Cuban Missile Crisis roughly a year later. At several points during the four decades of East–West confrontation, decision makers on both sides contemplated unleashing nuclear destruction, but this moment brought them to the brink. The crisis had its origins in the rise of the Third World as a key arena in the Cold War exemplified by Cuba under Fidel Castro. Graced with great charm, personal courage, and exceptionally good luck, Castro had led a successful rebellion in 1959 against the corrupt dictator Fulgencio Batista. Unlike ordinary Latin American palace coups, Castro borrowed from Mohammad Mossadegh's notebook on Third World comeuppance and nationalized landed estates, sugar mills, and foreign banks in a revolutionary challenge to the oligarchy that had run the island for decades with close ties to the United States.

Although it is possible to debate whether the virtues of the Cuban Revolution (mass education, free health care) outweigh its vices (one-man rule, intolerance for dissent), it is hard to find another example of revolution on a small island that has had such a deep impact on modern world history. Following in the distant footsteps of the Mexican Revolution of 1910, Cubans refused to accept the hemispheric dominance of the United States. From the perspective of Washington, this would have been daring at any time, but at the height of the Cold War, it was as inconceivable as it was unpardonable. Land redistribution and bank seizures had barely begun before the CIA began drafting a plot to overthrow this experiment in public ownership. What confirmed Castro's pariah status was his acceptance of Communist Party members into his inner circle and his February 1960 agreement to trade five million tons of sugar with the Soviet Union over five years. By the time Kennedy was sworn in, CIA plotters had already created an exile army with its own air force operating from hidden bases in the jungles of Central America. Guatemala was especially important, both as a training site and as a model of how a regime had been toppled in the 1954 coup d'etat.

The CIA-organized invasion at the Bay of Pigs on Cuba's south coast was a disaster. Instead of inciting a popular uprising as predicted, the rag-tag army of Cuban exiles met fierce resistance, and not even air support (limited to disguise U.S. involvement) could rescue the doomed CIA army. The invasion also failed in both of its larger objectives. Kennedy wanted to prevent Castro from becoming a model of change in Latin American and to check Soviet ambitions in the U.S. sphere of influence. To Kennedy and America's chagrin, Castro—and his comrade in arms, Che Guevara—became a model to other revolutionaries, and the Soviet Union found its first ally in the Western Hemisphere. In retaliation, the United States initiated Operation Mongoose, a CIA plan of sabotage against the Cuban economy and assassination attempts against Castro.

Cuban Missile Crisis

The failed invasion and subsequent CIA sabotage campaign only stiffened Castro and Khrushchev's resolve to defend the Cuban revolution, a fateful decision that led to the missile crisis. The crisis began on October 16 when American U-2s photographed Soviet missiles capable of striking Washington, DC, on the island. Why would Khrushchev embark on such a provocative course? Although Soviet motives are not altogether clear, there seem to have been two objectives. First, Khrushchev was determined to support the Cuban Revolution. Whether or not he truly believed in Socialist revolution, he wanted to bolster his revolutionary credentials in the face of China's challenge for leadership of the Third World. Second, Khrushchev sought to redress the strategic imbalance of nuclear power. He seems to have hit on the risky idea of sending missiles to Cuba at the time of the deployment of American Jupiter missiles in Turkey in April 1962. Stationing Soviet missiles ninety miles from Florida, Khrushchev said, would give the Americans "a little taste of their own medicine."

Responding to unmistakable evidence of missiles, Kennedy convened the Executive Committee of the National Security Council and held it in almost continuous session. The president was under pressure from the Joint Chiefs of Staff for military action ranging from a strike against the missile sites to full-scale invasion of Cuba. General Curtis "Bomber" LeMay, an early advocate of immediate bombing against Cuba, even taunted Kennedy about his manhood, knowing this was a point of pride for Kennedy men.

Nonetheless, the president chose a more limited response. On October 18, two days after receiving the photographs, he announced a blockade (called a quarantine but technically still an act of war), sent American warships to stop all shipping bound for Cuba, and delivered an ultimatum calling for the dismantling of all offensive weapons in Cuba. Mounting a masterful media campaign, Kennedy also conducted diplomacy by television, appearing as an earnest, reasonable statesman, while also dispatching Ambassador Adlai Stevenson to the UN General Assembly to present the photographic evidence before the court of world opinion.

Kennedy's ultimatum sent a tsunami of fear around the planet. Gripping their seats, people wondered whether this was the eve of destruction. Everyone waited breathlessly to see what the Soviet response would be. It took ten days for the Soviets to back down. According to accounts released after the collapse of the Soviet Union in 1991, discussions in the Kremlin Politburo were as heated as those in the National Security Council, with Soviet generals engaging in the same kind of saber rattling as their American counterparts. Although Khrushchev's mood swung back and forth between bravado and panic, in the end, he decided nuclear war was too high a price to pay. After reading KGB reports from Washington that the military was pushing Kennedy toward a violent showdown, Khrushchev backed off and agreed to withdraw the missiles. Only much later did the world learn that a side deal had been cut in back-channel negotiations. In return for the removal of Soviet missiles from Cuba, the U.S. Jupiter missiles, a symbol of U.S. encirclement, would be removed from Turkey (and so they were), and the United States would pledge not to invade Cuba again.

In the aftermath, realizing how close they had come to nuclear war, both sides took a step back from the brink. Disarmament discussions were put on a faster track, leading to a nuclear Test Ban Treaty in 1963, which outlawed nuclear testing in the atmosphere. In terms of prestige, Kennedy's resolve defeated Khrushchev's recklessness. The media, which thrives on transparency, contrasted American openness favorably with Soviet secrecy. The fact that the United States was truthful in presenting accurate evidence also won high praise.

The United States in the Third World

That did not mean the Cold War was over. In an attempt to catch up, the Soviets accelerated development of deadly intercontinental ballistic missiles. But because nuclear weapons made head-to-head war unthinkable, the two superpowers jockeyed for position in other frontier zones of the Third World. As a maritime power, the United States sought to expand free or open access to markets—what was originally called the Open Door, now rechristened the New Frontier. For its part, the Soviet Union sought to expand its closed or command economy and control of territory as a continental land empire. When new nations came of age in Asia and Africa, each rushed to be the first suitor at the door, whether or not new countries asked to be courted.

Latin America had long been the proving ground of U.S. empire. Before there was a Soviet Union, the United States had taken on an imperial role, and now Cold War rivalry reshaped U.S.–Latin American relations. Kennedy knew that

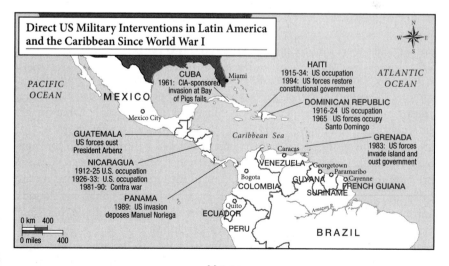

MAP 9.3

military action was not enough. The threat of revolution needed to be countered by reform. Tapping into the youthful idealism inspired by the New Frontier, he created the Peace Corps to send English teachers and agronomists to help poor countries advance. The cornerstone of his reform program was the Alliance for Progress. With the Bay of Pigs invasion only one month away, Kennedy laid out his plans to assist economic reform on March 13, 1961, with the intention of showing "to all the world that liberty and progress walk hand in hand." A year later, he uttered some of his most frequently quoted words: "Those who make peaceful revolution impossible will make violent revolution inevitable." Recognizing that alliance with tyrants hurt America's image, Kennedy sough to apply the same principles in the Middle East, pressuring the autocratic Shah of Iran to adopt constructive reforms, such as redistribution of land to peasants. Reluctantly bowing to pressure from his patron, the Shah announced a White Revolution aimed at thwarting Communist reds in the region. As it was, when the pressure from the United States eased, the program lapsed, as was the case with much of the Alliance for Progress.

In Kennedy's vision of the New Frontier, one of the main theaters of action lay in Southeast Asia. Since the end of the Korean War in 1953 and the partition of Vietnam the following year, the main frontier between capitalist and Communist blocs had not moved. With the increased activity of the Communist Viet Minh in South Vietnam, Kennedy was determined not to lose an inch of ground. His failure to dislodge Castro only toughened his resolve on the other side of the planet, and he expanded U.S. involvement in that faraway land from a few hundred advisors to some sixteen thousand by the time he was assassinated in November 1963. The U.S. client regime in the south, however, was no more enlightened than the Shah in Iran, and South Vietnam's eventual overthrow in 1975 seemed to confirm Kennedy's idea that failure of a peaceful revolution would only make a violent one inevitable.

PEACEFUL REVOLUTION FOR CIVIL RIGHTS

A peaceful revolution was the aim in the United States as well, only here, it came at the behest of civil rights activists in the South who undertook a nonviolent movement against segregation. Since 1960, civil rights became further entrenched in the domestic politics of the Cold War, with neither side giving ground. In the spring of 1963, the conflict reached a boiling point in Birmingham, Alabama, where thousands of demonstrators, braving the attack dogs and fire hoses of police chief Bull Connor, took to the streets in a sustained protest campaign against segregation in schools, parks, swimming pools, bus stations, and even the opera house. When Martin Luther King vowed to fill the jails, Chief Connor obliged by arresting hundreds, King included.

The civil rights movement, with its emphasis on the "beloved community" and peaceful change in the middle of a Cold War, was at a crossroads and, pilloried as troublemakers and outside agitators, it was losing the battle of public opinion. Responding to local white clergy who deplored the protests, Martin Luther King wrote what became the classic "Letter from a Birmingham Jail" on scraps of paper smuggled out of prison. Rejecting requests to go slow, King drew the connection to historic changes in Africa: "The nations of Asia and Africa are moving with jet-like speed toward gaining political independence, but we still creep at horse-and-buggy pace toward gaining a cup of coffee at a lunch counter." Holding up the vision of all peoples united in beloved community, King invited diverse people to work together in face-to-face relationships to build a just society. As he declared on many occasions, "Peace is not the absence of conflict. It is the presence of justice."

No one better understood the key role of the media in creating a virtual community of civil rights supporters. With the nightly television news showing well-dressed schoolchildren being knocked to the ground by powerful fire hoses and international journalists closely eyeing events, American opinion and President Kennedy turned against Bull Connor and his fellow segregationists. Overseas, the frightening images brought America's Cold War rhetoric of freedom and democracy into new focus, as the international community—aligned and non-aligned with the West—questioned whether the United States could ever overcome the ghosts of its past.

Africa, the Cold War, and Civil Rights

Beamed around the world, images of the awful spectacle in Birmingham hit home in Africa just as delegates from around the continent were gathering in Addis Ababa, the capital of Ethiopia, for the founding convention of the Organization of African Unity. Sickened by the water hoses and snarling dogs set on "our own kith and kin," delegates sent an open letter to Kennedy in May 1963 reminding the American president of the duty of "countries that hold themselves up as the leaders of that free world to see that all of their citizens, regardless of the colour of their skin are free." No less than American civil rights leaders, African diplomats knew how to play on Cold War dynamics in ways that divided Washington elites from Southern segregationists. They praised efforts of the federal government to end the "intolerable malpractices" of Southern officials, warning that failure to stop discrimination would lead to serious deterioration in diplomatic relations. The fact that so many African countries entered the world community during the most dangerous moment of the Cold War challenged leaders of the free world to do something about freedom for African Americans.

At first, Kennedy hesitated. He owed his political fate to the lily-white Southern wing of the Democratic Party, and it was not clear that African Americans and white liberals in the North could muster enough votes to offset votes that were sure to be lost in the white South if he came out against Jim Crow. What seems to have moved the administration off the fence were concerns about the international message. Kennedy was not only the leader of a divided United States, but also the leader of the free world. Secretary of State Dean Rusk, a Wall Street lawyer with

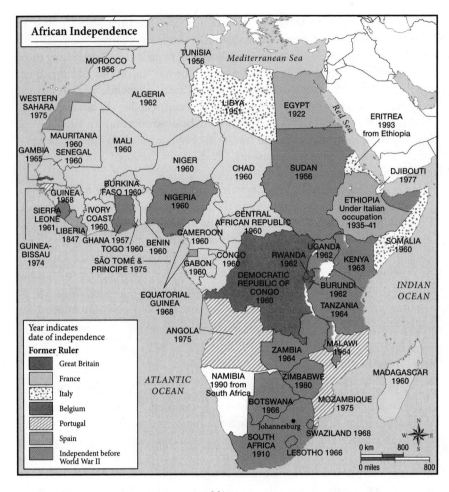

MAP 9.4

strong ties to the Rockefellers, put his finger on the essential linkage between civil rights and Cold War foreign policy. In congressional testimony on the civil rights bill, he highlighted the damage done to America's image abroad by racial discrimination at home. Reminding the senators of America's messianic mission—"we are expected to be the model"—Rusk pointed out that racial discrimination offended Asians and Africans, while handing the Soviets a propaganda weapon. "In their efforts to enhance their influence among the non-white peoples and to alienate them from us," Rusk observed, "the Communists clearly regard racial discrimination in the United States as one of their most valuable assets."

Driven by changing attitudes in the United States and changing diplomatic calculations, President Kennedy came out strongly for civil rights in the end. Sensing the shift in political tides, he declared in June 1963 that it was time to end the contradiction in a country that had "no class or caste system, no ghettos, no master race except with respect to Negroes." Putting political substance to his rhetoric, he gave his support to a bill that became the Civil Rights Act of 1964, outlawing segregation in public accommodations and other forms of racial discrimination. Sadly, Kennedy's assassination in Dallas on November 22, 1963, prevented him from seeing it through.

African Americans and the Colonial Analogy

Connections between the African American freedom movement and struggles for national independence on the African continent became more prevalent among critics of white supremacy in the early 1960s. Like new leaders in Africa and Asia, civil rights leaders in the United States threw Western ideals of freedom and equality back in the faces of privileged whites, asking them to "let freedom ring!" King spelled out the connections: "This determination of Negro Americans to win freedom from all forms of oppression springs from the same deep longing that motivates oppressed peoples all over the world. The rumblings of discontent in Asia and Africa are expressions of a quest for freedom and human dignity by people who have long been the victims of colonialism and imperialism. So, in a real sense, the racial crisis in America is part of the larger world crisis."

That much was clear. But the exact nature of the connection was in dispute. On the one hand, to the lawyers and teachers of the NAACP and the ministers of the Southern Christian Leadership Conference (SCLC), latent feelings of African kinship were set aside in favor of appeals to the American creed with its promise of equality in a pluralist society. Sincere in their convictions, they also knew that too close an association with African identity, let alone Third World revolution, risked alienating the white liberals on whom they increasingly depended for political and financial support.

On the other hand, to the black nationalists in groups like the Nation of Islam in the North and leaders like North Carolina's militant NAACP leader Robert Williams in the South, African Americans in the United States were colonial subjects as well. They saw little difference between blacks in the United States and the postcolonial states that attended Bandung. Under the colonial analogy, therefore, the struggle against white supremacy was the same in the United States and in Africa. Recalling the back-to-Africa message of the Garvey movement in the 1920s, Elijah Muhammad, the founder of the Nation of Islam NOI, adopted Islamic beliefs and customs, such as the prohibition on pork and alcohol, as a protest against what he deemed the "slave religion" of white, Western Christianity. Teachings about black pride, "white devils," and the unity of African peoples galvanized young men like Malcolm Little, a former street hustler known as Detroit Red who was reborn as Malcolm X (the X was a substitute for his "slave name"), to take a radical stance against white supremacy. An exceptionally dedicated and effective leader, Malcolm X won many followers among the urban poor—and attracted the attention of the Federal Bureau of Investigation—with his calls to act against racism "by any means necessary."

While activists protested in southern cities and marched on Washington, DC, for civil rights gains, Malcolm X, born Malcolm Little, became a powerful countervoice to the message of nonviolent direct action. Malcolm X promoted black nationalism and the individual's right to self-defense, which became an attractive message as the civil rights movement reached a stalemate and Third World nationalists looked for radical allies among first-tier economies.
Library of Congress Prints and Photographs Division, Washington, DC.

Robert Williams, a veteran of both the U.S. Army and the Marine Corps and leader of the Monroe, North Carolina, chapter of the NAACP, challenged the local Ku Klux Klan and called for armed self-defense against white supremacy. Like Malcolm X, who would become an ally, Williams traced a direct line between Jim Crow and colonialism, casting his lot with what some scholars call the Third World Left. Fidel Castro was a gravitational center for Williams and other radicals (black and white) who formed a group called the Fair Play for Cuba Committee that promoted the principles of the Cuban Revolution. In the pages of his periodical, *The Crusader*, Williams spoke passionately for solidarity throughout Africa, its diaspora, and the Third World, pitching a global version of black power before the idea took root in the United States.

No black leader in the South could last for long in violent defiance of Jim Crow. In 1961, Williams was forced into asylum on Cuba. There, he launched a radio campaign against the United States he called Radio Free Dixie, an adaptation that stood the Cold War's Radio Free Europe on its head and attempted to use popular culture—music, commentary, and the like—as weapons against America.

Beyond the differences in their political philosophy and approach to challenging racism, the Nation of Islam, Robert Williams, and the Southern Christian Leadership Conference represented class divisions within the African American community. The spread of militant black nationalism among poorly educated, jobless men on the streets of American cities was a measure of lower-class alienation, just as appeals to the American creed of equality represented middle-class yearnings for acceptance into the consumer society. In determining which stance would prevail, the growing ranks of black industrial workers played a crucial role. Having broken barriers of discrimination to enter auto factories and steel mills during the Second World War, black workers now challenged American business to provide both jobs and freedom within the framework of American capitalism.

Second Reconstruction

The combination of domestic and international pressures caused such strong federal action on civil rights that some call the response the Second Reconstruction. By 1965, Congress had enacted the most significant laws against racial discrimination since it added the Fourteenth and Fifteenth Amendments to the Constitution in the Reconstruction period after the Civil War. Domestically, the freedom movement reached high tide in August 1963 at the March on Washington. If ever there was a beloved community in action, it was the quarter-million who marched along the Washington Mall to stand at the feet of the Lincoln Memorial. More than a civil rights march, the gathering marked the rebirth of a broad coalition of African Americans, white liberals, and organized labor that had first come together in the 1930s around the New Deal. The influence of reform-minded trade unionists such as A. Philip Randolph, the venerable leader of the Sleeping Car Porters, and Walter Reuther, the energetic head of the United Auto Workers union, was especially important in building a coalition around the slogan "Jobs and Freedom." Speakers emphasized that redeeming the pledge of emancipation would require economic justice no less than the elimination of racial discrimination.

The best remembered part of that remarkable day was Martin Luther King Jr.'s eloquent "I Have a Dream" speech. Quoting Jefferson's credo—"We hold these truths to be self-evident, that all men are created equal," King did what Jefferson would not: apply the creed to all, regardless of race. In a crescendo of moving cadences, he called out to the crowd and to the watching world, "Let freedom ring" from the "prodigious hilltops of New Hampshire" to "every hill and molehill of Mississippi" until the day would come when "all of God's children, black men and white men, Jews and Gentiles, Protestants and Catholics—will be able to join hands and to sing in the words of the old Negro spiritual, 'Free at last! Free at last! Thank God Almighty, we are free at last!'"

For their part, diehard segregationists seemed almost eager to play their negative part. Just over a month before King's speech on the Washington Mall, George Wallace, the pugnacious governor of Alabama, had physically blocked the integration of the state university by standing in the door. In January 1963, Wallace had sealed his commitment to Jim Crow by vowing, "Segregation now! Segregation tomorrow! Segregation forever!" in his inaugural address. Although Wallace apologized years later for his obstructionism, in 1963 his pledge was a battle cry of segregationist resistance, and that summer the South saw a rise in racial violence, punctuated by the assassination of Mississippi's NAACP leader, Medgar Evers, in his driveway.

As the grass-roots movement gained strength in the United States, pressure on U.S. policy makers intensified. Movement leaders repeatedly called media attention to the violent actions of white racists. In Mississippi, the Student Non-Violent Coordinating Committee SNCC, the youth arm of the civil rights movement, devised the strategy of bringing northern white college students into the state for voter registration during Freedom Summer in 1964, knowing television cameras would not be far behind. The murder of three young Freedom Summer volunteers—James Chaney, Michael Schwerner, and Andrew Goodman—by a posse that included two sheriff's deputies confirmed Mississippi's reputation as the worst bastion of racism in the nation.

By the time the bodies of the three Mississippi workers were discovered in late summer 1964, Congress had enacted the most significant civil rights legislation since Reconstruction. Under Johnson's relentless pressure and with the shadow of slain President John F. Kennedy hanging overhead, the Civil Rights Act passed Congress. Only one thing slowed it down: sex. In an effort to subvert the bill by making it ridiculous, a Virginia senator proposed an amendment adding sex to the categories of prohibited discrimination. To his surprise, the amendment carried, laying the foundation for future litigation on behalf of gender equality. Otherwise, the bill emerged virtually unscathed from Congress. It prohibited discrimination in public accommodations based on race, religion, or sex and it established an Equal Employment Opportunity Commission to monitor discrimination. America was on the cusp of a new phase in the long women's rights movement. Peace activists from the 1950s and young women in the civil rights movement were gravitating toward a large-scale movement for women's rights, and the Civil Rights Act of 1964 provided the legal footing to launch a campaign against gender inequality.

With equal brilliance, movement leaders also exploited the split between state and federal authorities by putting thousands of demonstrators into the streets demanding the federal government intervene to defend its own Constitution. Chanting "Freedom now!" and singing "We Shall Overcome," demonstrators set out from Selma, Alabama, on their way to the state capital in Montgomery to demand voting rights. The Selma march garnered worldwide attention when Alabama state troopers clubbed the peaceful demonstrators on March 7, 1965, in a violent suppression that became known as Bloody Sunday.

After Bloody Sunday, public revulsion at the brutal treatment of peaceful demonstrators widened the political base of support for civil rights. Able to sense the political winds every bit as well as his fallen predecessor, President Johnson seized the moment to propose a voting rights bill that authorized the Justice Department to intervene in states with a pattern of racial discrimination in voting. Johnson even started singing in the movement choir when he went on national television to promote the bill, proclaiming in his Texas twang to astonished viewers, "We shall overcome."

Passage of the Voting Rights Act of 1965 marked the climax of civil rights. Few pieces of legislation have ever had such sweeping—and contradictory—consequences. Because of federal oversight, the number of black voters gradually advanced to the point where the South had more black elected officials and sent more African Americans to Congress than any other region. At the same time, as grateful blacks moved into the Democratic Party, resentful whites moved out to join a mostly white Republican Party. Within thirty years, the once solidly Democratic South would become just as solidly Republican.

In assessing the triumph of civil rights, it is necessary to seek out causes ranging from the grass roots to the high peaks of international diplomacy. Diplomatic concerns certainly pushed a broad range of national elites from the Supreme Court in the Earl Warren era to President Lyndon Johnson to become advocates of integration, resulting in a split between national liberals and Southern conservatives. That split, in turn, gave the freedom movement a once-in-a-generation opportunity to hammer home the wedge between these two sets of powerful elites. Like their predecessors in the First and Second World Wars, movement leaders threw the rhetoric of democracy back in the faces of the president and Congress. The difference was that with the Cold War in full force, Washington was sufficiently embarrassed over police dogs lunging at peaceful demonstrators in Birmingham and Selma to come down hard against segregation. In the end, what explains the Second Reconstruction was the ability of the movement itself, behind gifted strategists such as Martin Luther King, to exploit division among the powerful.

JOHNSON'S GREAT SOCIETY

The triumph of civil rights was only one of the major developments in this remarkable moment in 1965 when the country adopted the most significant social and economic reforms since the New Deal. Although Kennedy had been a popular president, his accomplishments were few. It was left to his successor, Vice President Lyndon Johnson, to use the country's grief over the loss of a president as a lever to move reforms through a compliant Congress. Running as a New Deal liberal and Kennedy's heir, Johnson won a landslide victory in the November 1964 election against Barry Goldwater, the libertarian conservative Arizona senator, who was painted as a reckless warmonger who would turn the clock back to the days before Social Security and the Wagner Act. In contrast, Johnson promised to extend the New Deal in a package of reforms he labeled the Great Society.

Johnson's resounding victory marked a moment of national consensus around reform. Support for progressive social and economic change had been building since the March on Washington brought together the interracial coalition for reform. In an unusual case of convergence among social movements, the separate movements for civil rights, labor, and peace coalesced for a short time in the mid-1960s into what was called simply the Movement. Inspired by the overthrow of European colonialism, movement activists rejected the narrow conformity of the 1950s and called on the country to live up to its pledges of freedom and equality. In a continual round of marches and demonstrations, they released a flood of energy that had been pent up by the domestic Cold War.

President Lyndon Johnson waged a War on Poverty for people like Mary Mallow, pictured above from Cumberland County, Maryland, under the belief that he could create a social safety net more expansive than the New Deal. The Vietnam War, civil rights activism, and youth counterculture undermined his efforts in the end. Library of Congress Prints and Photographs Division, Washington, DC.

The social engineers who designed the Great Society sought to bring the disinherited into the system. They took it for granted that industrial wage earners had already been taken care of in the social contract between large corporations and industrial workers that comprised America's unique public/private welfare state. Taking their cues from *The Other America* (1962), an influential book by socialist Michael Harrington, they sought to address the needs of those who had been left out of the comprise: the elderly, the chronically unemployed of the cities, the rural poor of Appalachia, and victims of racial and gender discrimination.

Capitalizing on his electoral mandate, Johnson showed why he was the most skilled politician since Franklin Roosevelt by rushing a raft of Great Society legislation through a normally slow-moving Congress. Hesitant legislators received the *Johnson treatment*, a combination of browbeating and cajoling from the overbearing man with the supersize ego who occupied the White House. Shamelessly vulgar, Johnson once lifted his shirt during a press conference to show off a scar from an appendix operation. But Johnson was also keenly intelligent and genuinely committed to creating opportunity for the kind of poor folk he had known as a young schoolteacher in Depression-era Texas.

Deploying all his political skills, Johnson prevailed on Congress to enact the most significant social legislation since the New Deal. The most far reaching came in health care with Medicare, a federal medical insurance program for retirees paid for with payroll taxes, and Medicaid, federal medical assistance to the poor. By eliminating the profit motive and bypassing insurance companies, Medicare and Medicaid were highly efficient—although increasingly expensive—federal programs that greatly improved the health of the elderly, while reducing the burden of care on their families and the disgrace of old-age poverty. In addition, the Great Society provided funding for grass-roots community development in the so-called War on Poverty, plus the first major federal aid to local education systems. These would have been enough to mark out the Great Society as a major moment of reform. But there was still more to come.

Cold War Liberalism

Where the Great Society broke new ground for American reform, and even moved ahead of countries in Europe, was in outlawing discrimination based on race and sex. Under statutory authority of the Equal Pay Act (1963) and the Civil Rights Act (1964), the Equal Employment Opportunity Commission shortly began to enforce prohibitions against discrimination. What later became known as affirmative action also got its start in the Johnson administration with an order to make every effort to seek out qualified minorities in hiring and promotion. At its inception, affirmative action was a hodgepodge of methods, with quotas serving as only one tool among many to achieve the goal. The Nixon administration would make the quota system a central feature of its perfunctory effort to address the symptoms of discrimination in work and the public sphere. Despite the uncertain path it would follow, the Equal Employment Opportunity Commission's affirmative action tack did challenge actual abuses and give substance to the rhetoric against discrimination.

In a parallel development, the long-dormant women's movement gained new life in the face of transformations in the civil rights movement and retrograde practices among the emerging New Left. None of the movements for social justice during the Cold War took place without the courageous and tireless efforts of women. Whether it was the black domestics who refused to ride the Montgomery City bus lines, the mothers who protested for a "sane" nuclear policy, or college-age women who sat in at lunch counters and went into the Deep South to register voters during Freedom Summer, women like Ella Baker, Fannie Lou Hamer, and Casey Hayden had always been conspicuous on the front lines of social activism.

With Betty Friedan at the helm, the National Organization for Women (NOW) was founded in 1966 to promote equal rights for women through education, lobbying, and legal action. Like the more moderate civil rights organizations, the National Organization for Women was part of the liberal consensus and operated under the belief that removing racial and gender barriers to opportunity was the key to realizing the promise of the open society.

The improved status of African Americans was linked to a reaffirmation of ethnic diversity as one of the great strengths of American society. In the optimistic mood of the day, pluralist faith in the ability to absorb newcomers was extended beyond European ethnic groups to embrace nonwhites for the first time. The 1965 Immigration Reform Act removed racial obstacles to Asian and African immigration that had been in force since the 1920s. This proved to be one of the most far-reaching pieces of Great Society legislation because it lifted a stigma on nonwhites and because it opened the doors to Chinese, Indians, and Ghanaians, among others, shifting the ethnic composition of the American population away from its historic combination of Europeans and Africans.

With the exception of the controversial War on Poverty, all of these reforms became permanent fixtures in American government. Taking their place alongside Social Security, they survived repeated conservative assaults because they provided individuals with significant benefits, reduced social problems, and thereby won enormous popularity. In comparative terms, Johnson's Great Society brought the United States closer to the mold of European social democracy, a mixed economy where private enterprise coexisted with significant government regulation. As in Europe, it was hoped that the incorporation of dispossessed groups would build support for the existing system and score propaganda points for the West.

In that sense, reform was central to Cold War liberalism. Until the end of this period in 1965, elites succeeded in containing reform within the Cold War framework. Conflict with the Soviet Union created conditions that pointed in the same direction of social compromise as the hot wars themselves. To mobilize civilian energies and win popular consent, a bargain was struck. Liberal elites would raise the social wage to support an increasingly suburban way of life and open the gates of opportunity for women and minorities. In return, housewives would use their kitchen appliances to wage ideological warfare against Communism; workers would accept management prerogatives on the shop floor; taxpayers would support an expensive military establishment; and African Americans would settle for a series of civil rights laws. Although something like the Great Society might have occurred under different circumstances, the presence of a Communist alternative was a goad to reform in the capitalist democracies, just as it had been in the 1930s. Reforms would answer Communist charges that Western capitalism oppressed racial minorities and dispossessed the poor. American leaders could argue that the West was far superior and getting more so every day. Indeed, they could hold up their very willingness to admit faults and redress grievances as proof of the superiority of the West over the rigid societies of the East.

Liberal Interventionism

While Johnson was building his Great Society at home, he was also conducting the most interventionist foreign policy since Woodrow Wilson. Caught in the same superpower stalemate as his predecessors, he fought the Cold War in the frontier zones of the Third World. Unexpectedly, Latin America was becoming just such a borderland between East and West. Once securely within the U.S. sphere of interest, the Cuban Revolution seemed to open the whole region to Soviet influence. Seeking to close it off again, Johnson gave clandestine support to the overthrow of Brazilian leader, João Goulart, in a 1964 military coup after Goulart took steps to limit the profits of foreign business. Following in Kennedy's footsteps at the Bay of Pigs, Johnson sent U.S. Marines into the Dominican Republic in 1965 after the CIA warned that Dominican nationalists seeking to reclaim their rightful leadership from a military junta might try to set up a Castro-type government. Determined to succeed where Kennedy failed, Johnson vowed that "we cannot, must not, and will not permit the establishment of another Communist government in the Western Hemisphere." This vow became known as the Johnson Doctrine. It reaffirmed a long-standing determination going back to the Spanish–American War of 1898 to treat Caribbean nations as planets in orbit around the sun of Washington. Not since Woodrow Wilson had Latin America seen so many American marines coming ashore.

Southeast Asia loomed even larger as a full-fledged frontier zone of imperial conflict. Having inherited Kennedy's commitment to a non-Communist South Vietnam, Johnson was obsessed with avoiding a humiliating defeat at the hands of what he once called a pissant country and embarked on a path of military escalation. Lacking an official congressional declaration of war as mandated by the Constitution, he took his authority from the Tonkin Gulf Resolution, passed hastily in October 1964 by a Congress still debating the evidence of unprovoked attacks on a U.S. ship in international waters off Vietnam. Despite private misgivings about the prospects of success, in February 1965 Johnson authorized a campaign of sustained bombing, code-named Rolling Thunder, in hopes of forcing the North to accept permanent partition with the South. When that failed to bring Ho Chi Minh to his knees, Johnson made the fateful decision in July to wage full-scale conventional war using U.S. troops.

CONCLUSION

The period between 1955 and 1965 saw the intertwining of domestic reform and international affairs on many fronts. Along the fault line of race, what King called a world crisis witnessed a transnational assault on white supremacy in parallel struggles for African independence and African American freedom. Feeding off one another, these twin struggles took a giant step toward overcoming what W. E. B. Du Bois had called "the problem of the color line." As African national movements became nation-states and, in some cases, threw in their lot with the nonaligned Third World, they changed the landscape of world affairs. Likewise, as American social movements coalesced in the Movement and pressed for broad-ranging social and economic reforms, they changed politics in the United States. In both cases, ordinary people shaped the historical agenda.

But they did not shape it exactly as they pleased. Powerful elites had their own list of agenda items, at the top of which was gaining advantage in the Cold War. The new states in Asia and Africa may not have been powerful enough in their own right to make American elites rush to overthrow segregation, but they were major prizes in the Cold War, and the need to win their favor helped convince American elites that it was time for segregation to go. Likewise, Great Society reforms were effective in head-to-head ideological competition with the Soviets. Thus did international factors help rebalance the domestic power equation.

For all the triumphs in this truly hopeful moment of social reform, by the end of 1965 there were many signs of trouble ahead. A bloody race riot in the Watts neighborhood of Los Angeles was a warning shot that something more than civil rights legislation was required to address the needs of the urban poor. Meanwhile, a backlash of diehard segregationists in the South and vested political interests in the North spelled trouble for the Great Society from the right, while critics of Cold War liberalism were emerging on the left as students mounted the first of many antiwar demonstrations and teach-ins on college campuses. Moreover, the war in Vietnam was not going well. As U.S. forces met increasing resistance in the rice paddies of Southeast Asia, the difficulties of fighting guerillas in their own homeland were becoming acutely apparent. The increasing cost of that war raised the question of whether it was possible to have both guns in Vietnam while offering butter at home through the Great Society. Just as Cold War liberalism reached the pinnacle of success, things were about to come apart.

FURTHER READING

Brown, Kate. *Plutopia: Nuclear Families, Atomic Cities, and the Great Soviet and American Plutonium Disasters*. New York: Oxford University Press, 2013.

Dudziak, Mary. *Cold War Civil Rights*. Princeton, NJ: Princeton University Press, 2000.

Ekbladh, David. *The Great American Mission: Modernization and the Construction of an American World Order*. Princeton, NJ: Princeton University Press, 2011.

Gaddis, John Lewis. *We Now Know: Rethinking Cold War History*. Oxford: Oxford University Press, 1997.

Garthoff, Raymond. *Reflections on the Cuban Missile Crisis*. Rev. ed. Washington, DC: Brookings Institution, 1989.

McDougall, Walter. *The Heavens and the Earth*. New York: Basic Books, 1985.

Slate, Nico. *Colored Cosmopolitanism: The Shared Struggle for Freedom in the United States and India*. Cambridge, MA: Harvard University Press, 2012.

Tyler May, Elaine. *Homeward Bound: American Families in the Cold War Era*. New York: Basic Books, 1988.

von Eschen, Penny. *Race against Empire: Black Americans and Anticolonialism, 1937–1957*. Ithaca, NY: Cornell University Press, 1997.

Young, Cynthia. *Soul Power: Culture, Radicalism, and the Making of the Third World Left*. Durham, NC: Duke University Press, 2006.

CHAPTER 10

CRISIS OF AUTHORITY, 1965-72

The Tet Offensive presented a spectacular, but misleading, image of South Vietnam to the West. Aside from the mounting losses for the North Vietnamese forces, Western depictions also obscured the role of locals like the women volunteers of the People's Self-Defense Force of Kien Dien in a hamlet north of Saigon, who played a vital role in support of the Government of Vietnam.
National Archives at College Park–Still Pictures (RDSS).

THE TET OFFENSIVE: 1968

On the night of Tet, the Lunar New Year in Vietnam, George Jacobson retired to his bed in the U.S. Embassy compound in Saigon. Jacobson was a former army colonel now working as a diplomat, and because of his outgoing personality—he had once been a magician and master of ceremonies—he encouraged everyone to call him by his nickname, Jake. Having first arrived in Saigon fourteen years earlier, he was regarded as an old hand in Indochina. But nothing prepared him for what was to happen that night. At about three o'clock in the morning, he was awakened by an explosion. It did not take him long to realize that the U.S. Embassy was under attack. With Viet Cong commandos rushing around embassy grounds, he took cover in his bedroom with only a hand grenade for defense. He spent the next several hours expecting to die.

Jacobson was one of a multitude of otherwise anonymous figures thrust onto the historical stage during the Tet Offensive of January 31, 1968. Others, like Hoang Thi Khanh, a woman who spied for the National Liberation Front (called the Viet Cong by the Americans), and Nguyen Van Sau, one of the many men who fought for the Communist Viet Cong that fateful day, took history into their own hands and orchestrated surprise attacks that stretched from one end of South Vietnam to the other. Khanh, the daughter of plantation workers from Cambodia, rose in the ranks of the Communist Party to become the vice president of North Vietnam's General Confederation of Labor. During the attack, she used her undercover identity to transport arms from the countryside to the city, and in its aftermath she led an insurgent force composed almost entirely of women who continued the fight. Sau, an illiterate farmer, became a squad leader for insurgents stationed near the Michelin Rubber Plantation north of Saigon. When the last firecrackers of the New Year had died down, Sau and eighteen other commandos went into action. After killing two marine guards, they blasted their way through the embassy's protective wall and controlled part of the compound. Whether they knew it or not, Khanh and Sau were on missions doomed to fail. In Saigon, U.S. forces quickly responded, and within six hours, Sau and his fighters were killed. Eventually, Khanh was captured and sent to Con Dao, one of South Vietnam's most brutal prisons.

Because U.S. forces eventually suppressed the Tet Offensive, General William Westmoreland, the commander of U.S. forces in South Vietnam, could declare victory, ignominious as it was. And by war's end, when all the data were in, Westmoreland declared that the Viet Cong had lost a generation of fighters in the offensive. But Tet was designed to sap America's confidence, and it did. Tet shattered the official claims of progress in the war at the outset of a crucial U.S. election year. The attack on the embassy, the symbolic heart of the U.S. presence in Vietnam, caused many Americans to wonder about the cost of victory in the name of Cold War peace.

CRISIS OF AUTHORITY, 1965–72

In 1964, when folk singer Bob Dylan's discordant voice announced, "The Times They Are A-Changing," he spoke to a generation of Americans who were increasingly discontented. It became an instant classic. By 1965, Dylan's ominous warning of a "rapidly fading" order took on global significance as Third World fighters inflicted major wounds on the world's main superpower. It was not just that the United States was struggling in Vietnam. The Cold War itself was beginning to break down. Economic recovery in Western Europe decreased political dependence on America. In the East, the deepening rift between the Soviet Union and

China splintered the Communist bloc, prompting a new contest for influence in the Third World. The world itself was undergoing change, as forces bubbled up from below and a new generation came of age in revolt against the Cold War orthodoxies of liberal capitalism and Soviet Socialism. Refusing to accept the world created by their parents, young rebels in the West and dissidents in Eastern Europe launched a series of protests that culminated in a worldwide revolt against authority in 1968.

The change was dramatic. In the early stages of the Cold War, there was a kind of symmetry and everything seemed to line up for the United States and the Soviet Union, like iron filings between the opposite poles of a magnet. But by the late 1950s, Third World (see Chapter 9) ascendance began to challenge the bipolar reality of the Cold War. Then, in the 1960s, new forces emerged—mass protest, European resurgence, Maoist diplomacy—each pulling in different directions that unraveled the Cold War's equilibrium and unleashed much more disorder by decade's end.

The most significant consequence of disorder was a crisis in authority. World leaders faced agonizing dilemmas. The more U.S. President Lyndon Johnson and Soviet Premiere Leonid Brezhnev pursued Cold War policies, the more opposition they aroused. That was especially true in the West where Johnson's escalation of the war in Vietnam stirred up angry mass protest. Johnson became so unpopular that he eventually gave up on a second term in office. Powerful reaction to Vietnam broke what was once the most powerful man in U.S. politics. Similarly, in the East, rising discontent among the peoples of Eastern Europe forced Soviet leaders to rewrite the script of global Communism. In a time of unrest, the United States and Soviet Union approached the 1970s as a period of recalibration. Without ever admitting it, the two superpowers fell back on their shared history in the Cold War and attempted to find new symmetry built on cooperation. Both saw cooperation, chiefly in the form of détente or a relaxing of tensions, as a way to reclaim the narrative of global authority from the malcontents in their respective spheres.

Disorder in the Cold War

By the middle of the 1960s, old patterns of the Cold War began to change. After two decades of U.S. economic dominance, Western Europe began to regain strength and push for greater independence from the American system. Even the U.S. nuclear umbrella began to fray, as Premier Charles de Gaulle took France and its nuclear weapons out of NATO in 1966. Europe was becoming less of a marchland and periphery between the two superpowers and more of a region looking toward its own destiny—and possible unification.

In the Eastern bloc, there were even deeper rifts. After 1960, the Soviet Union and China were no longer on friendly terms, and relations worsened when China acquired its own nuclear weapons in 1964. Mao Zedong and Zhou Enlai bristled at the thought of China serving a junior role to Russia and distrusted Soviet nuclear monopoly within the Communist sphere of influence. China's maneuver for autonomy reached a breaking point in 1969, when border disputes with the Soviet Union erupted into skirmishes and both sides took casualties. The fact that the two Communist giants also competed for leadership of the Third World added to their divisions, just as it further complicated the old East–West competition between capitalists and Communists. As the Communist bloc fell apart, Washington was too preoccupied to notice. Vietnam and social disruptions at home occupied all of America's attention and narrowed its sense of the Cold War.

GLOBAL CONFLICT IN VIETNAM

By the second half of the 1960s, the war in Southeast Asia became a flashpoint for many disorders around the world. The bitter conflict in the jungles and rice paddies of Vietnam, once called French Indochina, was a case where local events truly had global impact. Vietnam was a proxy war (a war where larger powers use substitutes to fight one another) fought in a frontier zone between rival global superpowers. It also represented a civil war and the site of the Third World's struggle for independence from colonization. Such far-reaching significance is what made the Vietnam War a pivotal event in world affairs and a symbol of an era.

Proxy War on the Frontier of Empire

From the earliest moments of the Cold War, nuclear weapons made direct combat irrational, if not impossible. Constrained by the horrible prospect of mutual assured destruction, the superpowers instead resorted to exerting power and defending their perimeters in a manner reminiscent of the old empires. Thus, the United States and Soviet Union focused on Eastern Europe, Korea, and Southeast Asia as imperial frontier zones.

Historically, imperial China had been the preponderant power in Southeast Asia, lording over the tributary states in the region, like Vietnam, in a contentious cycle of conquests and revolts. With their conversion to Communism, China had repudiated their imperial past. Yet, the Communist rulers of China were heirs to a great land empire and were determined to avoid the fate of the old imperial dynasty, which had crumbled under pressure from the West. In addition, Mao Zedong sought to unseat the Soviet Union as the leader of global revolutions by supporting Third World resistance to the West and the war of national liberation in Southeast Asia. In Vietnam, China supplied roughly three hundred thousand "volunteers" over the course of the war that guided construction projects and advised antiaircraft batteries.

The presence of Chinese advisors in the North, as well as the prospect of a Chinese attack on Western forces (as had occurred fifteen years earlier at the Yalu River during the Korean War), served as an effective firewall against an American invasion across the seventeenth parallel in Vietnam. The result was a bloody stalemate. In the South, nothing assuaged U.S. fears of Chinese retaliation, not even signs of internal turmoil in China by 1968. In the North, the Soviet Union was even more important in bolstering Vietnamese resolve against the United States. No less than Mao, Soviet leaders wanted to demonstrate their revolutionary credentials to an increasingly doubtful Third World. Although neither Communist power sent combat troops to North Vietnam, the Soviets, in particular, provided essential military hardware, technical assistance, and diplomatic support. The presence of Soviet ships and advisors was an implicit warning to the United States against attempts to conquer the North. Likewise, Soviet aid raised the possibility of nuclear weapons in the retaliatory equation. Facing such odds, the United States was compelled to fight a limited war in the South.

As far as the Americans were concerned, the main rival was not China but the Soviet Union. Like every administration since Truman, the Johnson administration drew an analogy between Soviet Communism and Nazi Germany. In a speech to the nation on April 7, 1965, President Johnson laid out his reasoning in terms that recalled the lessons of Munich. "We must say in Southeast Asia—as we did in Europe—in the words of the Bible: 'Hitherto shalt thou come, but no further.'" The zero-tolerance approach to communist advance in Asia was the bulwark of the Johnson Doctrine, and in setting the line of containment at the seventeenth parallel between North and South Vietnam, Johnson was intent on demonstrating U.S. credibility to allies in Europe and clients in Latin America.

The emphasis on credibility pointed to American insecurities, while suggesting the influence of gender ideologies on policy making. To be tough in defense of honor was seen as a masculine virtue. The difficult world of international politics was seen as a man's game, not for the supposedly feminine faint of heart. None of the five presidents who tried to keep South Vietnam in the U.S. orbit—Truman, Eisenhower, Kennedy, Johnson, or Nixon—wanted to suffer the damage to the masculine ego of being labeled soft on Communism. Nor did any want to endure the domestic political costs of being the one who lost Vietnam the way Truman had lost China, leading to his party's loss in the next election.

America's War for Empire

If post–World War II wealth, might, and influence brought the United States to the heady position of global hegemon, the Vietnam War snapped America back into the ranks of a struggling empire. The evidence of this reversal became increasingly apparent as the conflict progressed. The U.S. war in Vietnam was an imperial war fought to determine whether Vietnam would join the U.S. sphere of influence. Why Vietnam, however? What drew Americans to a country eight thousand miles across the Pacific? It could not have been the profit motive because U.S. investments in Southeast Asia, even the development of a Tennessee Valley Authority–style dam system in the Mekong River valley region, were miniscule. Nor was it an appetite for land. Not since 1900 had Americans seriously entertained the possibility of annexing new territory. What then explains U.S. action?

From the perspective of corporate and political leaders, the United States had a stake in spreading its open, market-driven system into new frontiers. The architects of Vietnam policy were the usual collection of intellectual and political elites, but a significant number of the top advisers came to political office from the corporate world, including Secretary of Defense Robert McNamara, the former chief executive officer at Ford Motor Company, and Secretary of State Dean Rusk, a Wall Street lawyer and head of the Rockefeller Foundation. They feared that the loss of access in one place in the world would edge out the United States elsewhere and cause a chain effect of successive losses that President Eisenhower called *the domino effect*—today Vietnam, tomorrow Thailand, the next day Indonesia, and then possibly the Philippines. Although the direct financial interest in Vietnam was small, no one was willing to risk all of Asia to global Communism. Guided by such fears, they chose Vietnam as the place to keep the dominoes from falling.

The choice to focus on Vietnam, however, was based on flawed assumptions. American officials—considered by some "the best and the brightest"—operated on the ideological and legal fiction that South Vietnam was an independent nation. South Vietnam did not exist until Washington and Paris conjured it up, but only after breaking international agreements guaranteeing Vietnam's

When the Buddhist monk, Thich Quang Duc, sitting calmly in the lotus position in a Saigon street, set himself on fire in protest of the South Vietnamese president Ngo Dinh Diem's religious intolerance, it exposed the realities of America's nation-building endeavor. As the scene played out on television and in pictures back in the United States, President Kennedy, like the public, began to doubt America's efforts. Library of Congress Prints and Photographs Division, Washington, DC.

independence. According to the 1954 Geneva Accords that ended French imperial rule, Vietnam was to be temporarily divided into northern and southern
sectors that would be reunited through national elections within two years. As
the Americans took over from the French, the counterfeit nation, as historian
Gabriel Kolko aptly called South Vietnam or the Government of Vietnam, owed
its existence to the U.S. officials who backed the leader they installed, President
Ngo Dinh Diem, when he canceled national elections rather than lose to Ho Chi
Minh, the North's Communist leader.

If the creation of South Vietnam was an imperial maneuver, it was a unique
blend of empire by imposition and empire by invitation. Between supporters in
the South's capital of Saigon and other urban areas along the southern coast who
wanted no part of a people's revolution and the commercial-minded elite eager
for access to America's enormous financial resources, the United States had many
friends in the South who looked to Washington. But the regime had a reputation
for corruption and carried little support in the general population. Buddhist opposition to the Government of Vietnam's largely Catholic leaders of the South was
expressed in the spectacular form when a monk named Thich Quang Duc, aided
by members of his order, doused himself with gasoline and set himself ablaze.
Even before the assassination of President Ngo Dinh Diem in 1963, internal troubles plagued the Government of Vietnam, primarily because of its relationship
with the United States. Contrary to the claims otherwise, South Vietnam was no
more than a client state of the United States, similar to the Eastern European satellites of the Soviet Union. When President Johnson offered a solemn pledge "to
help South Vietnam defend its independence," therefore, he was not just keeping
faith with Eisenhower and Kennedy, but also obscuring America's role as its architect and patron.

Revolutionary Nationalism

In choosing to support the fiction of an independent Vietnam, American officials
prepared the way for an uneven battle. On one side was an impoverished lower-
tier economy whose peasant soldiers walked on sandals through jungle terrain
carrying light rifles. On the other was the world's richest nation and premiere
nuclear power whose forces commanded the most advanced weaponry in human
history. Only a handful of Americans were wise enough to recognize that, despite
all appearances, the Vietnamese had the upper hand.

The reasons were many. First, the Vietnamese were fighting for their own
homeland on their own soil against a foreign foe. As Ho Chi Minh once told a
French official, "You will kill ten of our men and we will kill one of yours, and in
the end it is you who will tire of it." Resisting foreign domination was nothing
new to the Vietnamese. In their long quest for national independence, they had
defeated a succession of imperial rulers—Chinese, Japanese, and French (aided
by the Americans). The American War, as many Vietnamese called it, was but the
latest phase of the imperial struggle.

Second, Vietnam's resistance against Western power was part of a global trend toward nationalism in the postwar period. In the mid-twentieth century, the willingness of millions to die for their respective homelands culminated in two world wars and demonstrated the strength of nationalism in world politics before the Cold War. In the same way, colonial subjects in Asia and Africa proved they were willing to sacrifice their lives to win independence from foreign rule. The Vietnamese were no different in that respect.

But Vietnamese nationalism was also notable for being thoroughly entwined with the global quest for social justice. National Liberation Front (NLF) soldiers or Viet Cong—the insurgents permanently entrenched in the South—believed they were fighting what their leaders called a war of national liberation: a form of popular struggle that combined people's revolution against internal oppression with resistance to foreign domination. "If the French were colonialists," said Trinh Duc, a Vietnamese village chief, "the Americans were neocolonialists, financial exploiters who were out to force our people into their own kind of enslavement." The fact that NLF cadres often redistributed land from landlords to poorer peasants was a big factor in their rural popularity and political control of much of the countryside.

The close ties between the Viet Cong and the peasantry reflected the oft-quoted dictum of nineteenth-century military strategist Baron von Clausewitz, "War is politics by other means." Yet, because of the NLF's propensity for guerilla warfare tactics, a more apt association is Mao Zedong's contention that guerrilla warriors "swim like fish in the sea." The NLF cadres forged intimate links with members of rural society as a base from which they could launch small-scale surprise attacks from village hideaways and then melt back into the local population or jungle. Except when they changed to conventional tactics, as in the case of the Tet Offensive, Vietnamese guerrillas were increasingly successful in waging asymmetrical warfare against a far more powerful foe.

Americans had only to look to their own history to understand the politics of asymmetrical or guerrilla warfare. After all, their own nation was born out of struggle against the greatest empire of the day. A handful of critics in Vietnam and the United States drew comparisons to the American Revolution, with Vietnamese rebels in the role of American patriots and the United States cast as the oppressive British Empire. A few also pointed out that successful nations require organic connections to local soil and society, not the false designs of foreign rulers. Occasionally, such criticism could be heard within the administration. Undersecretary of State George Ball, for example, argued against the notion that "a white ground force of whatever size can win a guerrilla war—which is at the same time a civil war between Asians—in jungle terrain in the midst of a population that refuses cooperation." William J. Fulbright, an Arkansas senator and chair of the Foreign Relations Committee, surprised his colleagues by coming out as a critic of empire. Fulbright deemed the conflict in Vietnam a dangerous overextension of U.S. power and a threat to republican traditions of representative government at home.

In the early years of the war, only a small number of Americans cared or knew enough to raise objections. In fact, few noticed when fifteen thousand people showed up at the Washington Monument in April 1965. It was the first of what would be many antiwar demonstrations.

Escalation in Vietnam

At the beginning of 1965, the fateful year President Johnson decided to send in combat troops, few in the highest echelons of power paid attention to the conflict unfolding eight thousand miles away. Top officials exhibited what Senator Fulbright labeled "the arrogance of power" and simply refused to consider the possibility that the world's most powerful country could ever be defeated, least of all by a small, underdeveloped nation. Such overconfidence had dire political consequences, beginning with President Johnson's decision to escalate the war under the pretext of events like the Tonkin Gulf incident of 1964 and, later in February 1965, attacks on U.S. bases at Pleiku and Qui Nhon. The Tonkin incident, where the U.S. vessels *Maddox* and *Turner Joy* claimed to be fired on by North Vietnamese patrol boats (a claim that was never substantiated), convinced Congress to give Johnson open-ended power to wage combat in South Vietnam. Attacks on Pleiku and Qui Nhon led to Rolling Thunder, a massive bombing campaign against the North to dissuade further revolutionary activity in the South. Rather than shrink in fear, America's actions stiffened the North's resolve, leading to ominous U.S. intelligence reports of a likely Communist triumph by the spring of 1965.

Faced with the prospect of losing Vietnam, Johnson made the fateful decision on July 28 to commit ground forces. From that point, the Vietnam War would be Johnson's war. Under General William Westmorland, U.S. forces poured into coastal bases in South Vietnam, reaching almost 200,000 by the end of the year, a number that would grow to a peak of some 550,000 within three years. The direct costs of Vietnam exploded at the same time from about $5 billion in 1965 to some $33 billion in 1968. By that time, one journalist estimated that each Viet Cong corpse cost approximately $400,000.

Once on the ground, American soldiers were expected to adapt their training in conventional warfare to the conditions of a guerrilla war. Back home, the media promoted an image of an enlightened solider, equipped with the best technology in the world, and glamorized U.S. Special Forces, especially the Green Berets, who the military specifically created for counterinsurgency against guerrilla fighters. Unfortunately, meeting the guerilla challenge, which included gruesome acts of terrorism against enemies and civilian "collaborators," meant occasionally responding with an equal measure of brutality. The CIA's Operation Phoenix, which assassinated thousands of Vietcong civilian sympathizers, is especially illustrative. The violence was not restricted to the CIA, however. Some of the regular soldiers—self-described grunts—turned the Maoist adage about guerrillas swimming like fish in the peasant sea into a justification for committing atrocities against civilians. The most egregious example was the My Lai Massacre of 1968, where Lieutenant William Calley led his company in the indiscriminate slaughter of a whole village of mostly women and children, but there were also reports of casualties in other places such as the Quang Ngai province. To those with a long historical memory, it was reminiscent of the campaign against guerrilla fighters in the Philippines early in the twentieth century and the war against Indians still earlier.

While the moral costs of the war were mounting, American leaders began to question whether victory was possible. As the U.S. death toll rose to 19,562 by the end of 1967, Secretary of Defense Robert McNamara sent a memo to Johnson in May outlining the difficulties: "The picture of the world's greatest superpower killing or seriously injuring 1,000 non-combatants a week, while trying to pound a tiny backward nation into submission on an issue whose merits are hotly disputed, is not a pretty one." Years later, McNamara disclosed deep misgivings about the prospects of U.S. victory. President Johnson, too, was troubled by the long grind in the war, but kept his doubts hidden. Instead, at the end of 1967, Washington exuded confidence and boasted about seeing the light at the end of the tunnel to a public growing impatient with the casualties and costs.

America's Global Reach

Surveying the global situation at the end of 1967, U.S. officials had in fact many reasons for optimism. In the Caribbean and Latin American, they had succeeded in confining Communist power to the island of Cuba. Despite a U.S. attempt to dislodge the Communist regime there by slipping Fidel Castro a poison cigar, Cubans used Castro's comrade in arms, Che Guevara, to stoke revolutionary fires throughout in Latin America. Che, as he was affectionately known, was an idealistic Argentine-born physician-turned-guerrilla fighter. In 1965, he took his crusade to Central Africa to fight for Third World liberation in the Afro-Asian bloc, but returned to Latin America in 1967 to foment revolt among oppressed *campesinos* of the Bolivian highlands. Exiled from Cuba and Russia for questioning their commitment to Third World liberation, he was hunted down and killed by Green Beret–trained Bolivian troops. As a martyr to the cause, Che was more influential in death than in life. His image lived on, emblazoned on T-shirts and coffee mugs. Celebrated among radicals in the First World, in the Third World he was sanctified by revolutionary movements as a kind of secular Christ who had sacrificed his life for the poor.

Fearing a Castro-style revolution, the United States conducted an extensive counterrevolutionary campaign in Latin America. Many features of the effort involved constructive reforms that were consistent with John Kennedy's adage, "those who make peaceful revolution impossible will make violent revolution inevitable." Building on Kennedy's Alliance for Progress, the Agency for International Development provided funds and technical assistance to raise living standards in the Caribbean and Latin America through economic development.

Johnson's counterrevolutionary efforts had two faces, however. Along with the promise of economic and technical aid came repression from the agency's infamous Office of Public Safety and the threat of CIA subversion. Clandestine operatives, often working through labor-linked front groups such as the American Institute for Free Labor Development, inhabited U.S. embassies throughout the region. In addition, there were training schools for Latin America military officers, such as the Army School of the Americas at Fort Gulick in the Panama Canal Zone, dubbed the School of the Assassins by its critics for the violent methods its graduates learned and later used to eliminate their political opposition. The combination of reform and subversion proved highly effective at containing revolution in the region.

Across the Atlantic in Africa, however, those methods were much less effective. By the mid-1960s, the independence wave had crested and both superpowers were showing less interest in African affairs. Although each had offered its own international volunteer program at the beginning of the decade, which in the American case culminated in the Peace Corps, access to precious resources and the prospect of gaining the strategic upper hand soon edged out reform. Both sides actively sponsored dubious client regimes, often at the expense of their own professed principles. That was certainly true for U.S. support of the corrupt and brutal dictator Joseph Mobutu in Congo, as well as the apartheid regime in South Africa, whose violent enforcement of racial separation made it the most racially oppressive system in the world.

In the Middle East, U.S. policy rested squarely on a contradiction: Americans gave strong support to the Shah of Iran, the Saudi Sheiks and other autocratic Arab regimes, and the state of Israel, despite Arab hostility toward the Jewish state. As a major consumer of Arab oil, the United States could hardly do less. But Arab enmity toward the United States intensified after their defeat at Israel's hands in the Six-Day War of 1967 and the resulting loss of Palestinian control over the West Bank and Gaza, as well as Egypt and Syria's respective loss of the Sinai and Golan Heights. By being a friend to both sides, the United States believed it could be the "honest broker" between them, but a surge in nationalism and shifts in geopolitics began to unravel that role in the 1970s.

Despite the many frustrations, American leaders had reason to be optimistic at the end of 1967. They had succeeded in preventing a Communist takeover in South Vietnam; despite the rise of Castro, they prevented the spread of Communism in the Caribbean; in Africa, they held leftist insurgencies at bay; and they successfully navigated a delicate course in the Middle East. Although the Soviet Union and China posed a constant threat to America's global leadership, U.S. power still seemed to be on the rise, in no small part a result of its resources— the world's biggest corporations, the dollar standard, a favorable public image, and unparalleled capacity for both clandestine operations and overt military intervention—at its command. Taken together, America had reached the zenith of power as a global hegemon. Few credible observers could have predicted the rapid descent America would undergo over the next three years.

REVOLT AGAINST AUTHORITY, 1965–67

In the middle years of the 1960s, powerful elites around the world faced a mounting revolt against their authority. Raised on Cold War principles of freedom and equality, young rebels threw these ideals back in the face of their elders from Boston to Moscow. In the East, where the state towered over society, dissidents typically struck out against the centralized political authority. In the West, because of the decentered and elusive nature of authority, dissent took the form of challenges to the sources of power found in racial and gender privilege, demeaning advertisements and popular culture, and controlling university bureaucracies.

The Black Power Revolt

Beginning in the summer of 1965, America's urban ghettoes became a hotbed for revolt. Angry young men rioted against oppressive living and work conditions, as jobs and opportunity shifted out of the nation's cities into the suburbs, in what sociologists labeled *white flight*. As children of the Great Migration who came from the rural South to the urban North, young black men found that the well-paying industrial jobs that had attracted their parents to Detroit, Newark, and Los Angeles were fast disappearing in the new world economy.

The first in a series of riots took place in the Watts neighborhood of Los Angeles. Conditions there were sadly typical of the worst urban ghettoes. More than a third of adult men were unemployed, seven or eight times the rate among white men, and two-thirds of the residents received welfare. In a district whose residents were 98 percent black, there were frequent complaints about racist treatment at the hands of district police, 97 percent of whose officers were white. Unlike their Southern forbears, the new generation no longer deferred to white authority. When white police attempted to arrest a young black man for a traffic violation on a hot summer night, an unruly crowd gathered and showered police with rocks and bottles. This initial outburst triggered six days of arson, vandalism, shooting, and looting.

The riot meant many things to the residents of Watts. For some, it was a chance to finally obtain their piece of the consumer society and the fruits of living in the wealthiest nation on the planet. With stores going up in flames, rioters helped themselves to the television sets, liquor, and furniture promised by alluring advertisements but denied by poverty. For others, it was a political blow to racial oppression and class distinctions. For some, the chance to consume and strike back at their low social status gave way to opportunism . When a black journalist confronted a man making off with a living room sofa, he was told, "Don't bother me now. I've got to hurry back to get the matching chair." Finally, like the surge of nationalism taking place in Asia, Africa, and Latin America, some viewed the riot through the lens of anticolonialism where law enforcement represented the occupying troops. Restoring order took fourteen thousand national guardsmen plus thousands more local police. By the time it was over, the riot had destroyed

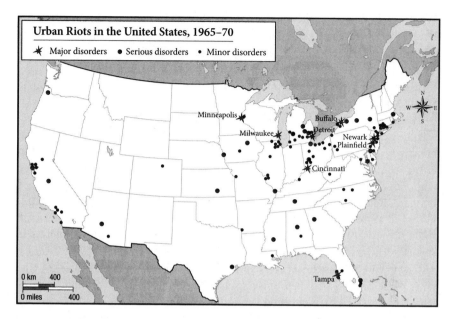

MAP 10.1

millions in property, displaced hundreds of people from their homes, and left thirty-four dead, most at the hands of the authorities.

The pattern repeated in scores of other cities from Newark, New Jersey, to Detroit, Michigan over the next three "long-hot summers" almost as if scripted: an incident involving white authority (typically the police) led to a mob response; ghettoes erupted in flames; police and firefighters were met with bricks and sniper fire; and then state leaders would call out the National Guard, whose untrained young soldiers sometimes shot rioters and bystanders alike, as in the case of Newark. Add crumbling houses, abusive landlords, de facto public segregation, broken school systems, and apathetic political leadership to these events and the results were explosive. All told, there were over 163 disturbances in this period and they proved the greatest civil disorders since the white rampages at the end of World War I.

The promise of racial harmony that had been cultivated since the civil rights legislation of 1964 and 1965 disintegrated rapidly. Almost before the ink was dry on the civil rights laws, it was clear that outlawing discrimination, worthy as that was, would not address the way racism and poverty were tangled together in the ghetto. Building on the legacy of Malcolm X, who was gunned down by his rivals in 1965, a new crop of militant leaders, notably Stokely Carmichael, began to demand Black Power. Although ghetto riots lacked any distinct political ideology, Black Power became a useful conceptual tool for equating what activists called ghetto rebellions to Third World revolution. As if borrowing a page from Fidel Castro's notes on revolution, Carmichael told an audience in Havana in 1967, "Black Power means that we see ourselves as part of the Third

World." Believing African Americans were victims of colonialism as much as any resident of Africa, militants like Carmichael saw the black "struggle as closely related to liberation struggles around the world." Under the colonial analogy, America—sometimes spelled *Amerikkka* to make a guilty association with the Ku Klux Klan—was not just imperial, but also an apartheid society similar to South Africa's Afrikaner regime.

Perhaps the most widely recognized symbol of Black Power around the world was the heavyweight boxing champion, Muhammad Ali. Known for his swagger, brash witticisms—"float like a butterfly, sting like a bee"—and having fists as fast as his insight, Ali became the most prominent critic of Western hegemony and white supremacy. Born Cassius Clay in Louisville, Kentucky, in 1942, he changed his name to Muhammad Ali after converting to Islam. In an expression of his faith and as an act of solidarity with the Vietnamese, Ali refused induction in the U.S. military under conscientious objector status. For his unwillingness to report because of his beliefs, he was stripped of his boxing title. Ali's steadfast refusal to compromise his beliefs, combined with his achievements in the boxing ring, made him a global hero, perhaps the single most recognized figure in the world. Few named their children Lyndon or Leonid during the Cold War, but all over the world, babies were named Muhammad, not only in honor of the Muslim prophet, but also for the defiant African American boxer.

New Left and the Antiwar Movement

Central to the rising global movement against the Cold War was the protest against America's involvement in the Vietnam War. Because Southeast Asia had become a focal point of global power struggles, opposition to the war took on global proportions as well. Reaction was particularly sharp in France, whose failures in Vietnam in the early 1950s had drawn the United States into the conflict. The French knew something about Vietnamese resistance to empire, and after being forced out of Algeria in 1962, the French had soured on imperialism altogether. Taking notes from Jean Paul Sartre, France's leading intellectual and a fierce critic of both French and U.S. imperialism, protesters condemned the United States for following their own government's path in trying to rule over a faraway Asian people. Alarmed at America's messianic self-image, a French journalist worried what would happen if the United States prevailed: "A nation holding a monopoly of power would look on imperialism as a kind of duty, and would take its own success as proof that the rest of the world should follow its example."

Such complaints did not stifle French enthusiasm for American popular culture, however. In almost equal measure to their outrage at U.S. fighting in Southeast Asia, they delighted in Hollywood westerns, the novels of Hemingway and Faulkner, and the protest songs of Joan Baez and Bob Dylan. The French were no different from other Europeans who had learned to distinguish between the freewheeling spirit of American culture, which they admired, and the policies of the American government, which they often opposed.

Antiwar protests were linked to the rise of the New Left. The New Left had been born in Britain in the late 1950s out of protests against NATO and its nuclear weapons. By the mid-1960s, Americans were building a New Left of their own. Typically, Americans preferred to express dissent through loosely organized social movements rather than tightly disciplined political parties, and so it was with the New Left. In what became known as the Movement, Americans braided together several different social movements, including the radical wing of the civil rights movement, the growing anti–Vietnam War movement, and campus rebellion against bureaucratic authority. Later, radical feminism joined the effort, bringing together three pillars of progressive activism at the close of the twentieth century: race, class, and gender.

The New Left energized students, like the antiwar protesters pictured here at Yale University, to challenge the authority of political, economic, and social leaders. Continuing the politics of dissent from the 1950s Beat Movement, the New Left youth challenged Western leaders to live up to the promises of democracy under the Cold War. National Archives at College Park–Boston.

Of the many groups that would be associated with the Movement, including Fair Play for Cuba, the Student Peace Union, the Free Speech Movement, the Student Nonviolent Coordinating Committee, and the Young Lords Party, it was Students for a Democratic Society (SDS) that proved the most critical. An outgrowth of the leftist trade union, League for Industrial Democracy, SDS took notes from the lunch counter sit-ins, Southern Freedom Rides, and radical thinkers like C. Wright Mills and Herbert Marcuse to proclaim in its 1962 manifesto *The Port Huron Statement* that the times required a New Left. Intended as a break from the dogmatic Marxist-Leninist efforts of the 1920s and 1930s, SDS rejected false claims of both the Western free world and the self-described people's democracies of the Communist East. Instead, it set its sights on a notion of liberalism that placed the individual at the center—humanist liberalism—and the goal of a genuine participatory democracy. Although created in 1960, SDS became nationally recognized in the spring of 1965 when it staged the nation's largest anti–Vietnam War rally. Later that year, Carl Ogelsby, one of its leaders, gave *the system* a face when he equated America's unjust war eight thousand miles away and social oppression at home with *corporate liberalism*, or government efforts to protect and advance big business. The movement reduced corporate liberalism to the shorthand of liberalism. Thereafter, SDS and the New Left waged war against liberalism and denounced liberals as the cause of America's betrayal of its principles.

As critics dug deeper, however, they discovered other sources of the war besides liberalism. Becoming increasingly radical, they began to argue that empire and capitalism were tangled at the roots. Martin Luther King, for example, began pointing to the economic causes of intervention. Later remembered as a moderate prophet of racial integration, King actually moving rapidly toward a more radical position in response to prodding from the New Left and advocates of Black Power. In a landmark speech at New York's Riverside Church on April 4, 1967, King came out against the war. Breaking with more moderate civil rights leaders, he criticized the Johnson administration for being "the greatest purveyor of violence in the world today." Challenging corporate power, he attributed U.S. intervention to a desire to preserve "the privileges and the pleasures that come from the immense profits of overseas investments." Quoting President Kennedy's plea to accept peaceful reform or face violent revolution, he chastised his own country for being on the wrong side of world revolution and pleaded for a "radical revolution of values" that would put things right.

Despite their momentum, opponents of the war were a relatively small minority at the end of 1967. Although doubts about the war were rising, most people supported Johnson's escalation, not the antiwar calls for withdrawal. In fact, public opinion surveys demonstrated that hawks outnumbered doves until well into 1970. What began to reverse this trend was the Tet Offensive.

The Tet Offensive

At the beginning of February 1968, the world tuned in to the chaotic drama unfolding in the Tet Offensive. In a major gamble, the NLF attempted an all-out coordinated assault from one end of South Vietnam to the other. With sixty-seven thousand troops committed to battle, the NLF counted on civilian uprisings in the cities to help topple the South's government. Having the advantage of total surprise, it appeared in the early hours that the gamble might pay off. The Viet Cong attacked Hue, Saigon, and over one hundred other cities. The insurgents even breached the outer wall of the U.S. Embassy in Saigon and were able to hold

MAP 10.2

it for a brief period of time. Never before had American forces been faced with
simultaneous conventional attacks on dozens of installations across such a wide
front from the Mekong River delta to the ancient imperial capital of Hue.

Although they were caught off guard, U.S. commanders recovered quickly. It
helped that they were defending fortified positions against lightly armed attackers.

The U.S. forces retained complete air control, provided by such devastating machinery as the AC-47, a gunship immortalized with the quirky nickname Puff the Magic Dragon. Deceptively named after a 1959 children's story and a hit song by Peter, Paul, and Mary in 1963, the AC-47 lit up the sky like a fierce mystical beast when it laid suppression cover. But superior firepower did not necessarily mean political wisdom. In a comment picked up by the antiwar movement that illustrated the absurdity of the war, one U.S. commander reported, "It became necessary to destroy the town in order to save it." Still, within thirty-six hours, U.S. forces had beaten back most of the attacks. Only in Hue were the Americans pinned down for more than a few days. In the end, rifles and sandals proved no match for helicopter gunships.

In purely military terms, the Tet Offensive was a spectacular failure for the North Vietnamese and the NLF. Completely outgunned, the Viet Cong suffered thirteen thousand killed, compared to a few hundred on the American side. In some sectors, the Viet Cong never regained strength. After years of eluding U.S. forces under the protective jungle canopy, they made the mistake of coming out into the open. In the accurate assessment of one U.S. official based in Vietnam, "They abandoned the countryside where they were doing very well, and boy did they get creamed in the cities." In its public pronouncements, Hanoi hailed the heroes who had delivered such a strong blow to the enemy. Beijing propaganda even went so far as to refer to the Tet Offensive as the spring victories. But internal documents disclosed later revealed that the Communist commanders were well aware that civilians had not risen up, nor had the Offensive been able to hold any of its military objectives.

In political terms, however, Tet was a great success for the NLF. Remembering that "war is politics by other means," the offensive rippled out from the epicenter in Southeast Asia and sent political shock waves to the entire world. In the Third World, Tet lifted the spirits of revolutionaries eager to believe the propaganda about Viet Cong victory. By putting U.S. forces on the defensive, Tet enabled Beijing propaganda mills to label the United States a *paper tiger*. In Europe, Tet swelled the ranks of war critics. In the United States, Tet jolted the public like nothing else, exposing the confident assessments of military progress as lies. Having gone to war to prove American credibility, Johnson was now descending into his own credibility gap.

Tet's global reverberations illustrate the importance of mass media to world politics. In the developed world, television made Vietnam the first living room war. Turning on their televisions to watch the evening news that night, American viewers heard reports within a few hours of the massive attack. Most shocking were Telestar satellite transmissions the next day of raw footage showing U.S. Embassy personnel pinned down by Viet Cong commandos. In one instance, an NBC camera operator filmed the horrifying spectacle of a South Vietnamese general as he summarily shot an insurgent in the head and then walked away unemotionally. Witnessing chaos on the ground in Vietnam on their own televisions, Americans were no longer prepared to trust official reports of progress.

The fact that wars have political causes means that they ultimately require political settlements. To his credit, Johnson immediately invited Ho Chi Minh to begin peace talks in the wake of Tet. The Russians—but not the Chinese—urged Ho to accept. Before the talks actually began, the parties wrangled over who would be invited to the table and where they would sit. In particular, the president of South Vietnam, Nguyen Van Thieu, balked at admitting the NLF as an equal party, fearing it would be the beginning of the end of his regime. In the end, four parties—the United States, South Vietnam, North Vietnam, and the NLF—faced each other around a square table. Although talks dragged on for five years, the fact that David had forced Goliath to come to the table suggested a major change had taken place in the global balance of power. If there was one moment when U.S. hegemony began to decline from its zenith, this was it.

1968

The worldwide revolt against authority culminated in a wave of rebellions in 1968. It was as if the Tet Offensive was a signal for protests to begin from East to West and everywhere in between. Under the watchful eyes of television cameras, crowds of mostly young demonstrators poured into the streets to demand changes in the status quo, whether an end to the war in Vietnam, changes in university social rules, or an end to state censorship. When images of authorities cracking down on demonstrators were projected around the world, they helped create a chain reaction. Just as telephones and radios had compressed time and space early in the twentieth century, so now television synchronized clocks around the world. There was the sense of a common struggle against oppression that made 1968 a pivotal moment in twentieth-century world history, or at least so it seemed at the time. In the end, however, the world did not change quite the way the protesters wanted.

One common characteristic was the prominence of the younger generation in rebel groups. In Europe, discontent among the rapidly rising numbers of university students was directed against an antiquated system of examinations and overblown professorial authority. In Berlin, students boycotted classes and persuaded dissident faculty to teach outside the walls. Students in La Plaza de las Tres Culturas at Tlatelolco, Mexico City, staged strikes to protest top-down control of the universities by the *Partido Revolutionario Instutional*, the long-time ruling Institutional Revolutionary Party, which they said needed to be more revolutionary and less institutional. Young people were also prominent in Czechoslovakia's Prague Spring, the temporary loosening of restrictions on freedoms of speech and assembly. In Japan, too, students were in the vanguard of radical action. The leading radical student organization known as *Zengakuren* tapped into widespread anger over the government's support for the U.S. war effort in Vietnam. After all, Japan was the only country in the world besides Switzerland whose constitution prohibited military intervention overseas. There was also popular opposition to U.S. air bases in Okinawa and to U.S. nuclear-powered ships.

In China, the Red Guards were the youth arm of the Great Proletarian or People's Cultural Revolution. A popular Red Guard who had volunteered to leave Beijing for the countryside in the summer of 1968 captured this generation's youthful idealism in a memoir. "I did this," she confided, "out of a conviction that it was not fair for some young people like my schoolmates and me to enjoy all the privileges China could offer. . . . In new China everybody should be equal." In harmony with the youth in Europe and the United States, she held the conviction that politics was personal. "If we wanted to reform society," she continued, "we ought to have the courage to let the change start from us."

Across the globe, the combustible mix of campus protests and a heavy-handed response from state authorities exploded into major political events. When truncheon-wielding police ended a student occupation of administration buildings at New York's Columbia University, the mostly white, middle-class students were astonished to see violence used against them. The fact was that a police bust in the United States was nothing compared to violent repression elsewhere. One of the worst cases was in Mexico, where military authorities massacred hundreds—the exact number remains unknown—of peaceful demonstrators in Mexico City's La Plaza de las Tres Culturas.

Days before the 1968 Olympics in Mexico City, where African American athletes Tommie Smith and John Carlos raised their fists against oppression in the United States, the government of President Gustavo Díaz Ordaz killed over 350 students protesting his rigid policies. Mexico and the United States blamed the uprising on the "international left," but that was never confirmed. It was part of a greater revolt among the youth, however, that touched open and closed societies alike. Marcel·lí Perelló, Wikicommons.

The most serious political crisis of the West in 1968 erupted in France. Tapping into France's great revolutionary tradition, self-described *enrages* at the University of Paris seized control of buildings and spray-painted graffiti such as "take your desires for reality." When Charles de Gaulle's government ordered troops to retake the buildings, the resulting violence won sympathy for the protesters and in some instances converted the student revolt into a genuine revolutionary threat as the French working class joined in the dissent. Workers had their own grievances against de Gaulle's government for cutting back social insurance payments. Massive strikes of industrial workers brought the Communist and other leftist parties into the fray, and by the time transport workers walked off the job in May, they had paralyzed the entire country.

At the other end of the spectrum, the United States was nowhere near a revolution. The social contract between business and labor, which made working-class Americans partial to the kind of gradual reform embodied in the Great Society, gave workers faith in the status quo. Forgetting about the strikes and sit-ins that had been necessary to force their employers to compromise in the 1930s and 1940s, the working class often looked on university building occupations as the tantrums of privileged rich kids. All the same, antiwar demonstrations, student sit-ins, urban riots, and the beginnings of women's protest seemed to split America at the seams, inspiring hope for radical change in some quarters and fears of chaos in others.

Liberal Dilemmas

Radical unrest posed agonizing dilemmas for liberals. On the one hand, President Lyndon Johnson sympathized with the calls for change and could point to a string of reforms aimed at redressing past wrongs and leveling the playing field. Had not his Great Society provided aid to education and enacted the most important civil rights bills in one hundred years? And, had not his War on Poverty attempted to include everyone in the American Dream? On the other hand, pushing such changes risked alienating powerful interests vested in the existing order. For instance, when the Community Action Program, a Great Society initiative, encouraged "maximum feasible participation" by counseling the poor to advocate for themselves against local government agencies, they riled political machines in the urban North, whose support was essential to Democratic victory. A similar pattern unfolded in the South. Tough enforcement of antidiscrimination laws chafed white southerners, whose support the Democrats had depended on since before the Civil War.

Johnson's dilemma grew out of the fact that the Great Society had been designed for those left out of the social contract. The options before him were as treacherous as a minefield: If Johnson gave in to increasingly radical demands of the very poor, who were disproportionately African American and Hispanic, he risked alienating another part of his base—white, industrial workers, who were mostly of European descent. Additionally, industrial workers were willing to have a portion of their tax dollars go to fund the health care of the poor (Medicaid) and the elderly (Medicare), but once jobs began to disappear and taxes started to increase, white industrial workers thought twice about subsidizing the poor they deemed undeserving.

On top of these inner contradictions, there was a growing conflict between the Great Society and the war in Vietnam. Johnson had hoped to avoid a choice between "guns and butter," but in choosing war, as historian Fredrik Logevall has noted, he had reduced the Great Society to a beggar state by 1968. As war expenses mounted, funds to combat poverty slowed to a trickle, and as Johnson related to his biographer, he had to wake to a bitter reality: "If I left the woman I really loved—the Great Society—in order to get involved with that bitch of a war on the other side of the world (Vietnam), then I would lose everything at home." Nonetheless, knowing the risk, Johnson continued to escalate the war, fearing that a loss overseas would result in "an endless national debate—a mean and destructive debate—that would shatter my presidency, kill my administration, and damage our democracy." Johnson's foresight was accurate, but impaired. His presidency was shattered not because he left the war but because he remained wedded to it. Trapped by his decisions, Johnson startled the nation by announcing in March 1968 that he would not run for reelection.

Even more damaging to political authority were repeated assassinations of respected leaders. John Kennedy had fallen first in 1963, followed by Malcolm X in 1965. In April 1968, an assassin gunned down Martin Luther King Jr. while he was standing on the balcony of a motel in Memphis, Tennessee, where he had gone to support a sanitation workers strike. King's death was an incalculable loss that removed the one global figure whose vision of a world without war, poverty, or racism held the most promise for resolving ongoing national dilemmas. His assassination touched off a new round of riots in cities like Baltimore, Maryland, where six people died and seven hundred more were injured in the mayhem. Another visionary leader was Robert Kennedy, the former president's younger brother. After winning the California primary of the Democratic Party in June, he, too, fell to an assassin's bullet. Never before had the country endured serial assassinations of prominent public figures on this scale. The crisis of authority deepened. As these leaders were buried, the liberal consensus behind the Great Society was interred along with them.

Conservative Counterrevolt

Meanwhile, a conservative counterrevolt was under way that was every bit as global as the initial revolt against authority. Reacting to challenges from below, authorities attempted to reassert control from above. The crackdown was most severe in Eastern Europe, where Leonid Brezhnev rolled Soviet tanks into Czechoslovakia to put an end to the Prague Spring. The youth and intellectuals in Prague pressed the Czech government to liberalize its policies on personal freedom. Stifled under Communist rule, Prague protesters forced a change in Czech leadership who promised to implement reforms. Fearful that change might come too quickly, Brezhnev doused the flames of reform and reestablished the status quo. Likewise, Mao Zedong decided that the cultural revolution had gone too far. After the Wuhan incident in which Red Guards mobbed an emissary from Beijing, Mao unleashed the People's Liberation Army to quell any future disturbances. Although the cultural revolution continued in name, its radical phase had ended. Before long, both Brezhnev and Mao independently sought stability though contacts with the West.

In Western Europe, de Gaulle fought back against student and worker protests in France with a June referendum that divided his opposition. Offering improved wages and working conditions to laborers, he garnered the necessary support to shore up his position in government among the students. That action shifted the perception of events, making the impending revolution in May look more like a continuation of the status quo by June, when worker solidarity with the students splintered. De Gaulle only lasted one more year before resigning from office in frustration. The French, however, were not the only ones to have second thoughts about rebellion. Large sectors of public opinion in Japan turned against the students, who shut down college campuses in 1968–69.

Conservatives made headway in the United States as well. Culture wars broke out between defenders of conventional values and the irreverent *hippies* of the counterculture. Likewise, against the backdrop of escalating violence in Vietnam, political battles between hawks and doves grew more intense. Many whites reacted in horror as they watched urban ghettos erupt in flames, fueling a white backlash against Black Power. Demagogic politicians, such as George Wallace, fomented racial tensions and disaffection with diatribes against "anarchists and revolutionaries out to destroy our country." A new political narrative emerged amid the turbulence, one that called for the reestablishment of law and order.

The call for order shaped how the public reacted to the protests at the 1968 Democratic convention in Chicago. In many respects, the drama was the culminating event of the revolt against authority in the United States. No less than ten thousand mostly young demonstrators came to the Windy City to call for an immediate end to the war in Vietnam. A small army of well-armed Chicago police under orders from Mayor Richard Daley, Chicago's political boss and an ally of President Johnson, put down the demonstrators. Four days of running battles ensued over who controlled the streets and city parks. To those watching television images of the violence, it was reminiscent of the fighting in Vietnam. Chanting "The whole world is watching," the demonstrators wanted to convey the idea that the Chicago police were brutalizing American citizens the way the U.S. military was brutalizing Vietnamese peasants. Yet most of the American public read it the other way. Although there was concern about what a Democratic senator denounced as Daley's "Gestapo tactics," surveys showed that most Americans identified with the police, not the demonstrators, many of whom had college draft exemptions.

America at Impasse

Given liberal failures to resolve the twin dilemmas of domestic inequality and conflict overseas, it is not surprising that conservatives gained strength. Against the backdrop of disorder at home and frustration abroad, the fall 1968 election revealed a close balance between declining liberals and rising conservatives. Johnson's heir apparent was Vice President Hubert Humphrey, who probably lost the fall election because of voter disenchantment over violence in the streets at the Chicago Democratic Convention and Humphrey's association with the failed presidency of Lyndon Johnson.

The winner by a hair was a veteran of Cold War politics, Republican Richard Milhous Nixon. Known to his enemies as Tricky Dick, Nixon was not so much a conservative true believer as a wily political opportunist. Having built his early career as a staunch anti-Communist, he would become the first president to cut deals with the Communists. Nixon campaigned on the promise that he had a plan to end the Vietnam War and bring "peace with honor." There was no such plan. With George Wallace running from the right, Nixon took the opportunity to appear as a centrist candidate promising to restore law and order. Unlike Wallace, Nixon was no race-baiter, but he knew how to play a more subtle game of racial politics using law and order to appeal to whites in the so-called Southern strategy.

Nixon's narrow margin in popular votes (almost as close as his loss to Kennedy in 1960) was more a sign of internal polarization than the triumph of conservatism. During the campaign, he had promised to "bring us together." Instead, what the election showed was that the country remained divided among liberals, conservatives, and radicals. At the end of 1968, the mood was as rancorous as it had been harmonious just three short years earlier. Liberal consensus had come undone and America was at an impasse.

CONSERVATIVE DILEMMA IN VIETNAM

Just as liberals faced difficult dilemmas, so conservatives confronted similar problems from the other side of the political spectrum. Nowhere was America's impasse more painfully apparent than in Vietnam. Nixon and his chief advisor Henry Kissinger had contradictory goals. On the one hand, they wanted stability. They hoped to restore law and order at home through a policy of *Vietnamization*, or turning the fighting over to the South Vietnamese, abroad. They knew that discontent at home was undermining U.S. world leadership. As Kissinger later wrote, "The consensus that had sustained our postwar foreign policy had evaporated." To rebuild consensus, the two moved away from the sharp polarities of the Cold War and promulgated a new Nixon Doctrine: "We shall look to the nation directly threatened to assume the primary responsibility of providing the manpower for its defense." Like Rome inducting barbarians into its legions, the United States attempted to change "the color of the corpses." Under Vietnamization, Nixon began a slow withdrawal of U.S. forces in 1969, reducing the number to 335,000 in 1970 and ending U.S. ground combat by August 1972.

In addressing the key demand for U.S. withdrawal, Vietnamization, along with ending the draft lottery, was largely successful in deflating the antiwar movement whose demonstrations dropped following the troop reductions. But

Nixon had another goal. He was determined to win the war. Yet the goal of victory would prove incompatible with the goal of stability. At the outset Nixon had vowed, "I will not be the first American president to lose a war." Following the same logic as all of his predecessors since Truman, he declared that U.S. credibility was at stake. If the United States reneged on its pledge to maintain an independent South Vietnam, he warned, "we would not be worthy of the trust of other nations and would not receive it." Even as he pursued disengagement on the ground, he escalated the air war, dropping more bomb tonnage than all of his predecessors, targeting Hanoi and its harbor Haiphong for the first time in the Christmas bombing of 1972 and risking a bigger war by bombing Russian ships.

As dangerous as the bombings in North Vietnam were, Nixon went further and expanded the ground war into Cambodia in the spring of 1970 (and Laos in 1971). The expressed intent was to block movement of enemy troops and supplies down the Ho Chi Minh trail, a supply line through Laos and Cambodia, while proving to an increasingly doubtful world that the United States was not "a pitiful, helpless giant." But it had the opposite effect. The Cambodia invasion deepened global opposition and set in motion a chain of destabilizing events that would bring to power the Khmer Rouge in Cambodia, one of the most murderous regimes in history. In the United States, the invasion sparked massive protests that shut down scores of college campuses. Even what Nixon called the silent majority was turning against him on the war. By 1970, the majority of the U.S. public told pollsters they favored withdrawal, although the reason had more to do with military failure than any sense of moral outrage.

Nor did Nixon's victory strategy work. Although the NLF had suffered huge losses in the Tet Offensive, the North Vietnamese stepped up their supply of troops and returned to the more successful strategy of guerrilla war in the countryside. They proved capable of absorbing seemingly endless punishment of air strikes, while remaining at the peace table in Paris with Soviet support and Chinese opposition. In fact, even as the Chinese were cutting back their own support as part of a tacit understanding with the United States around Nixon's visit to China in 1972 (see Chapter 11), they were urging their Communist brethren to fight to the last Vietnamese. After recovering from the Tet Offensive, Communist forces fought on successfully against the poorly motivated troops of the South and launched a major offensive in the spring of 1972 that the United States just barely checked with a massive airpower response. Clearly, Vietnamization could not win the war.

Trapped between the competing imperatives of stability and victory, Nixon and Kissinger finally reached agreement at the Paris peace talks in January 1973. Although South Vietnam retained its nominal independence as a client of the United States, the most important part of the agreement was the U.S. commitment to withdraw all of its ground troops and end its attacks in exchange for the return of American prisoners or war. Whatever lingering impulse to continue there might have been in the White House, Congress shut off the funds in 1973 and prohibited the reintroduction of U.S. ground troops. To recover some of its power following the Gulf of Tonkin crisis, the Congress curtailed the president's use of U.S. troops abroad in the War Powers Act. Without the presence of the U.S. military, South Vietnam, a fictional nation to begin with, was doomed to disappear. The next offensive in 1975 would succeed in uniting Vietnam under one flag where Tet had failed, but it was not the flag U.S. officials would have chosen.

Cultural Revolutions in the East

One of the major legacies of the 1960s was an ongoing clash of values between old and new. Societies around the world experienced the clash in different ways. In the Third World, modernity faced off against tradition. Modern values of secularism, gender equality, and consumerism were pitted against traditional values of religiosity, patriarchy, and kinship. In the oil-rich Middle East, for example, there was a deep gulf between Western-oriented secular leaders such as the Shah of Iran and ordinary people bending in prayer in the Mosque. A different kind of conflict beset Eastern Europe. In the Soviet Union and other so-called people's democracies, cultural dissidents rejected official Marxist ideology. Chafing under police-state controls and demanding the material comforts promised by their leaders, dissidents often expressed their view in underground publications called *samizdat*.

Much of the world's attention focused on the Chinese variant of the clash between old and new. Beginning in 1966, the Great Proletarian Cultural Revolution played out as a melodramatic struggle between the supposedly good values of the new China and the evil ways of the old. It was at the same time a power struggle at the top between Mao Zedong and his enemies that opened a fault line all the way to the bottom of Chinese society. Raised on the heroic ideals of egalitarian Communism, the younger generation was especially eager to enlist in the struggle to overturn both Soviet-style bureaucracy and Western-oriented "capitalist roaders" within the Communist Party. Toting Mao's *Little Red Book* of pithy writings, volunteer battalions of Red Guards combated authority wherever possible. They denounced their teachers for having retrograde ideas, condemned Confucian tradition with its Four Olds, and threw ancient treasures on the bonfires of revolution. In an effort to root out moral corruption, they adopted an extreme code of sexual abstinence that ruled out extramarital sex.

Cultural Revolutions in the West

Western society provided yet another variation on the theme of cultural conflict. In the consumer society, new values of abundance ate away at the old values of scarcity. The older generation that had experienced the hardships of depression and war clung to the sturdy virtues of hard work and self-sacrifice. The motto around the family dinner table was "finish everything on your plate." By contrast, the baby boom generation that was born in the postwar abundance and came of age in the 1960s adopted the values of entertainment and entitlement. Abandoning the family dinner table for a burger at McDonalds and the thrill of a rock concert, they embraced the mottos of rock star Mick Jagger, "too much is never enough" and "I can't get no satisfaction."

As a trend among the youth, cultural rebellion in the United States rode the demographic wave of the postwar baby boom into the expanding service economy. The shift toward a service economy prolonged youth, the phase of life before entrance into the job market, by keeping people in school, where they could acquire the skills necessary to work in hospitals, schools, and corporate offices. As always, the United States led the world in mass education. By 1970, more than three-quarters of all American seventeen-year-olds had a high school diploma, up from 57 percent twenty years earlier, while university enrollments doubled over the same period to almost one-third of the eighteen- to twenty-four-year age group. Feeling ready to be adults, college students bristled under forms of authority designed for children, such as *in loco parentis* (administrators acting as parents) and parietals (restrictive social rules that prohibited men from visiting women in dorm rooms). Western Europeans followed their American counterparts on the same path toward mass higher education. Starting at much lower levels, university enrollments quadrupled in West Germany and doubled in Britain in the two decades before 1970.

On both sides of the Atlantic, college campuses became hotbeds of youth revolt. In some respects, student protests at the Berkeley campus of the University of California were the catalyst for more student uprisings. Berkeley students defied university restrictions on public speaking and launched a free-speech

Students at the Berkeley campus of the University of California protested against university policy that curtailed student conduct. It grew into a movement against the conformity of the Cold War and America's presence in Vietnam. Crowd around and atop the police car in Sproul Plaza holding Jack Weinberg, Free Speech Movement photographs [graphic], BANC PIC 2000.002—NEG Strip 7:10, Steven MArcus Photograph. © The Regents of the University of California, The Bancroft Library, University of California, Berkeley.

movement in 1964. Following the script of antiwar protests, university administrators summoned police, whose arrest of peaceful demonstrators only increased support for student protesters.

Counterculture

The young were especially attracted to the counterculture. Raised on ideals of the free world, cultural rebels turned against Cold War conformity to expand the boundaries of artistic and sensual freedom. The roots of cultural rebellion lay among Beat poets, who had crafted irreverent verses in the bohemian coffee shops of San Francisco and New York in the 1950s. Following in the footsteps of the Beats, the counterculture came of age in the 1967 summer of love in San Francisco's Haight–Ashbury neighborhood, where hippies and bare-footed flower children roamed the streets. The motto was "don't trust anybody over thirty." The counterculture hit a high note in the 1968 musical *Hair*, which hailed the dawning of the "age of Aquarius," where men's hair was long, women's skirts were short, and nudity was in. It reached its apotheosis in August 1969 at the rock concert in Woodstock, New York, a huge gathering of young people enjoying three days of music, marijuana, and love-making, sometimes in public.

As the over-thirty generation watched these hedonistic celebrations, they could not help but wonder what had become of the old values of Depression-era scarcity and Cold War security. Outside the urban capitals of bohemia, many young people joined their elders in recoiling against the let-it-all-hang-out exhibitionism of the counterculture and embraced what came to be called *traditional values* of church, family, and restrictive sexuality.

For all its rebel edge, the counterculture was at the same time part of the very consumer culture it professed to reject. While repudiating the old values of scarcity, the battle cry of "sex, drugs, and rock 'n' roll" was also a call to uninhibited consumption. The Beatles would have gone nowhere without the channels of commercial entertainment. The new music took a turn toward hard rock after 1965, evident in the growing transatlantic popularity of the Rolling Stones, the bad boys of English rock. Even the Beatles moved from being loveable mop-tops to dabblers in drugs and harder-edged, political rock 'n' roll. But the music industry was big business. Likewise, advertisers capitalized on youth identity in selling soft drinks to the Pepsi generation.

As the children of Hollywood and Coca-Cola, young Americans had grown accustomed to gratifying their desires. The turn to hedonism had actually begun in the 1950s when the pursuit of happiness became identified with stereo sets and flashy cars. The ambivalence built into rebel conformity is illustrated in the film *The Graduate*, the biggest box office draw of 1967. In this brilliant satire of suburban alienation, a young couple struggles against the seductions of the backyard swimming pool, the corporate career, and the extramarital affair. At the end, the hero smashes a church window and rescues his heart's desire from the altar of a loveless marriage. It would seem that love conquers all. But in the final scene, the couple rides off to an uncertain future where they may well wind up in the same trap where they began. As with the cultural rebels of the early twentieth century, once again, what began as rebellion was eventually absorbed into the new mainstream of mass consumption.

Collapse of the New Left

As the counterculture receded, the New Left collapsed. Never cohesive to begin with, the movement for radical change suffered from internal sectarianism, racial conflict, and youthful impatience. After 1968, increasing segments were caught up in the delusion that Third World revolution could be imported to the United States. Inspired by Frantz Fanon's *The Wretched of the Earth*, radicals sought to adapt the national liberation struggles in Algeria and Vietnam to American society. Pouring over the *Little Red Book* of Mao's quotations, some looked to the cultural revolution in China for lessons on how to transform the United States, despite the fact that China was a peasant society under a dictatorship, whereas the United States was fast becoming a postindustrial society with constitutional liberties, democratic rights, and relatively affluent suburbs that contained over a third of its citizens. Impoverished villagers in the Third World could barely imagine what was the norm in the United States, and the New Left refused to acknowledge this reality.

The fact that the larger antiwar movement was gaining strength did not seem to matter. By 1970, a majority of the American public had swung around to an antiwar position. President Nixon had begun to withdraw U.S. forces from ground combat in Vietnam and, in an effort to deflate student protest, he eliminated the draft lottery. Leftists chose this moment to abandon the highly successful mass mobilization that had brought hundreds of thousands of demonstrators to Washington in 1969 and to embrace, instead, violent tactics intended to "bring the war home."

Despite the absence of revolutionary conditions in the United States, the Weathermen, a splinter group from SDS, adopted the tactics of revolution. Impatient with the pace of disengagement from Vietnam, disdainful of a white majority complicit in racism, and goaded by black radicals, the Weathermen picked street fights with police and set off a spate of bombs at corporate offices, the Pentagon, university labs, and the U.S. Capitol. Reminiscent of Russian nihilist's *propaganda of the deed* at the beginning of the century, the bombs marked a turn to violent protest that seemed incongruous in democratic America. They became self-destructive when five Weathermen unintentionally blew themselves up in a lower Manhattan townhouse in March 1970. The self-destructive impulse also afflicted the counterculture. At a 1969 concert in California, the Rolling Stones hired thugs from the Hell's Angels motorcycle gang and the Angels beat a gun-carrying concert-goer to death. By 1971, leading icons of the rock music scene, including Janis Joplin, Jimi Hendrix, and Jim Morrison, were dead of drug or alcohol overdose.

An example of the collapse of the New Left was the meteoric rise and fall of the Black Panther Party. The self-proclaimed revolutionary Black Panther Party took form in 1966 out of the inchoate notion of Black Power. Inspired by national liberation struggles in Algeria and Vietnam, the party's founders imported Marxism-Leninism from the Third World and set out to end what they regarded as the imperialist occupation of America's black communities. Critics found it hard to see how national liberation would do anything to free economically depressed ghettoes from the grips of poverty.

Nonetheless, the Panthers won much support in the black community, with free breakfast programs for children and militant defiance of white authority. In Oakland, California, and a few other places, the Panthers won a slice of political power. At the same time, they trapped themselves in their own calls to "off the pig" (kill the cops), to which big-city police were only too eager to respond with arrests, raids, and late-night shoot-outs that left far more Panthers than police dead.

The Panthers, as well as other leftists, were targeted by secret counterintelligence units of the Federal Bureau of Investigation and local "red squads" as part of Operation COINTELPRO. Agents used provocation, surveillance, and manipulation designed to disrupt and destroy militant opposition. Although America's homegrown revolutionaries made their own choice to metaphorically jump off a cliff, the Federal Bureau of Investigation was there pushing them to the edge. Nor were moderates immune from attack. Even the altogether nonviolent Martin Luther King was the target of a vicious campaign, which included threatening letters and suggestions of suicide.

Changing Patterns of Social Reproduction

One part of the Movement that survived the sixties was feminism. The feminist revival took place amid important changes in social reproduction (defined as the handing down of a way of life from one generation to the next) linked to the rise of consumer capitalism. Keeping up with the Joneses required spending money—the more the better—on everything from new cars to children's education. Having fewer children was considered an antidote to the cost of raising children. The baby boom of the 1950s was followed by a baby bust in the 1960s, when U.S. birth rates fell to sixteen per thousand women, about the level they had been in the Depression years of the 1930s. Although there was a slight rebound in later years, birth rates eventually hovered just above the threshold necessary to replace population in the United States and fell below that threshold in Europe. Although declining birth rates were made possible by widespread distribution of the birth control pill, the drop in population was more the result of changing attitudes that favored fewer children.

The shrinking family size dovetailed with another approach to bolster family finances, namely, sending wives out to work. In earlier times of large families, wives had their hands full taking care of the household. As late as 1930, only 25 percent of adult women in the United States were in the labor force. But by 1980,

Birth Rates in U.S. and Europe

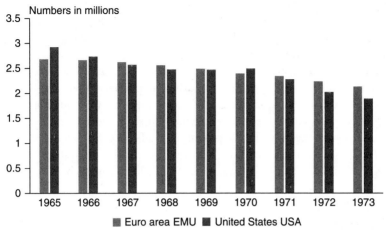

Source: Census Bureau

Number of Full-Time, Year-Round Workers with
Earnings by Sex: 1967 to 2009

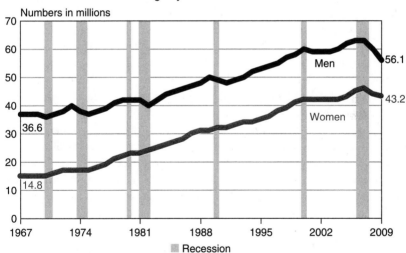

Source: US Census Bureau

the number had doubled to 50 percent. Meanwhile, marriage itself was changing from lifelong monogamy to a set of more varied practices. Divorce became
more common, affecting almost half of all marriages by 1970, and female-headed
households increased in number as well.

These changes in social reproduction raised basic questions about sexuality. If couples were having fewer children, what was the purpose of sex? Was it procreation or pleasure? From the first Kinsey Report of 1948 through the studies of human sexuality by Masters and Johnson in the 1960s, researchers found evidence of a sexual revolution involving the ever-increasing frequency and variety of sexual behavior among both heterosexuals and homosexuals. They took careful note of the widespread practice of masturbation, premarital sex, and extramarital sex. Increasing public acceptance of sex for pleasure was evident in ever more explicit depictions of love scenes in television soap operas and in Hollywood movies. Under the prevailing legal definition of obscenity—any depiction of sex without "redeeming social value"—courts were loosening restrictions to permit explicit material in mainstream films. Even adult films, such as the 1972 pornographic sensation *Deep Throat*, evaded censorship.

Feminism and Its Enemies

The same changes in social reproduction raised questions about gender. Was motherhood women's destiny? Was women's place in the home or in the workplace? Who ruled the home in two-earner families? These questions challenged the entire Western world, but societies answered them in different ways. Gender equality advanced furthest in Scandinavia. Having been the first in Europe to grant women's suffrage, Scandinavian countries went on to build the most extensive welfare states in the world. They provided public child care, medical care, family leave, and other social supports that not only freed married women to join the labor force but also enabled working wives to escape the "double burden" of doing housework after a day of paid labor outside the home. Moreover, the door to women's political leadership was open widest in Scandinavia, and women were elected in large numbers to legislative and executive positions.

The United States started down a similar path toward gender equality but did not complete the journey. The first steps came in the late 1960s with the emergence of the largest feminist movement since the 1910s. Picking up where the suffragists and radicals of the first wave left off early in the century, feminists of the second wave resumed the quest for equality. With the formation of the National Organization for Women in 1966, liberal feminists such as Betty Friedan launched a campaign of public education and legislative lobbying aimed at turning the language of the 1964 Civil Rights Act prohibiting discrimination based on sex into reality. Sporting buttons that read "59 cents," feminists challenged the practices that gave women wage earners fifty-nine cents to every dollar men earned. Liberals took the lead in pushing for adoption of the Equal Rights Amendment (ERA) that proposed to outlaw all forms of discrimination based on sex. After the National Organization for Women's successful lobbying effort, the ERA easily garnered the required two-thirds vote in Congress necessary to go out to the states for ratification in 1972. As a sign of broad consensus for women's rights, within a year the majority of state legislatures endorsed the ERA, and it looked like it would gain the necessary three-quarters to be added to the Constitution. Building on the welfare state provisions of the Great Society, the country seemed headed in the same direction as Scandinavia toward a more equal future.

In their own way, another more radical group of feminists was heading there, too. The impulse behind women's liberation began with women's mixed experience in the Movement. Even as they were part of a principled struggle for racial equality, women were typically consigned to typing and making coffee. Realizing that "the personal is political," they launched a full-scale assault on male privileges and prerogatives in everyday life, demanding that men do their share of typing, dishwashing, and childrearing. They also called for a new form of masculinity that did not include violence against women. Radical feminists did not oppose liberal demands for equal pay and equal opportunity; they just believed that achieving equality required nothing less than overturning male dominance in all facets of life.

As philosophical daughters of Emma Goldman, the rebel advocate of free love early in the century, radical feminists made their mark as partisans of sexual freedom. Seeking to turn the sexual revolution in a feminist direction, they promoted new scientific insights on "the myth of the vaginal orgasm," hoping to find a more fulfilling sexual experience with or without a man. In an effort to combat male violence, they set up rape-crisis centers and battered women's shelters. Among feminists, a minority even proclaimed the logical conclusion of women's liberation was lesbianism.

Liberals and radicals alike advocated freer access to birth control and abortion. The goals were to make it easier to have sex without also having children and to relieve women of the burdens of unwanted pregnancy. Feminists cheered when the birth control pill and other contraceptives became legally available to married couples in the *Griswold* Supreme Court decision of 1965 and to single people in the *Baird* decision of 1972. The biggest celebrations came after the landmark 1973 decision in *Roe v. Wade*, which upheld a woman's prerogative to have an abortion in the first six months of pregnancy. A close look at the decision showed that the Court's argument was based not on women's rights, but on the right to privacy under the due process clause of the Fourteenth Amendment. Even so, it seemed that the United States was on the path to greater equality. Even Catholic Europe was moving in the same direction, as Italy and France, two largely Catholic countries, liberalized their abortion laws.

But then the second wave seemed to crash. By the late 1970s, a conservative backlash against feminism was in full swing. Having gotten tantalizingly close to ratification, the ERA never made it. Alarmed at what they saw as gross moral decay, antifeminist activists like Phyllis Schlafly, the Catholic Legion of Decency, and various conservative Protestant groups, such as the Moral Majority, mounted a counterrevolution against the sexual revolution. Religious opposition did not seem to stop either Catholics or Protestants from using birth control, seeking abortions, having out-of-wedlock births, or practicing

Women's rights evolved into a movement that would bring activists together from all over world. In 1971, Vancouver and Toronto, Canada, hosted one of the largest conferences on women's liberation and solidarity that reached across racial, ethnic, class, and cultural lines. The United Nations designated 1975 the International Year of the Women and U.S. activists held a National Women's Conference in Houston two years later. These meetings raised the stakes of women's rights, but they also exposed internal divisions among activists and energized a fierce conservative backlash. National Archives at College Park–Still Pictures (RDSS).

homosexuality. But partly because they were losing control over their flocks, religious conservatives entered the public arena to oppose sex education in the schools and to campaign for laws restricting sexual expression and abortion. All this became standard fare in fierce culture wars between liberals and conservatives (see Chapter 12).

CONCLUSION: MIXED LEGACY

By the early 1970s, the crisis in authority was unresolved. The revolt of 1968 had failed to overturn deeper structures of power. Elites remained ensconced in power. Talk of revolution—sexual, cultural, Third World—fell to the fringe corners of the sectarian Left. The moment passed without either restoring the old or bringing in the new. It appeared to be a turning point at which history failed to turn. The ground was littered with broken sexual taboos, shattered assumptions about gender roles, and weakened racial barriers, and radicals were in disorderly retreat. Although the welfare-state reforms of the Great Society and their overseas counterparts were deeply implanted, liberals, too, were in disarray. And although conservatives rode a growing backlash against radical and liberal changes, they were unable to repeal liberal social reforms or recapture the culture they imagined. Simply put, America was in flux. Political dilemmas were unresolved. Economic troubles foretold the end of the golden age. The Vietnam War ended in stalemate, at best. The United States and the world at large were at an impasse.

FURTHER READING

Anderson, David L., and John Ernst. *The War That Never Ends: New Perspectives on the Vietnam War.* Lexington: University Press of Kentucky, 2007.

Bloom, Joshua, and Waldo Martin. *Black against Empire: The History and Politics of the Black Panther Party.* Berkeley: University of California Press, 2013.

Carson, Clayborn. *In Struggle: SNCC and the Black Awakening of the 1960s.* Cambridge, MA: Harvard University Press, 1981.

Caute, David. *The Year of the Barricades: A Journey through 1968.* New York: Harper & Row, 1988.

Gilbert, Marc Jason. *Why the North Won the Vietnam War.* New York: Palgrave, 2002.

Herring, George. *America's Longest War.* New York: McGraw–Hill, 1986.

Isserman, Maurice, and Michael Kazin. *America Divided: The Civil War of the 1960s.* New York: Oxford University Press, 2000.

Klimke, Martin. *The Other Alliance: Student Protests in West Germany and the United States in the Global Sixties.* Princeton, NJ: Princeton University Press, 2010.

Logevall, Fredrik. *Embers of War, The Fall of Empire and the Making of America's Vietnam.* New York: Random House, 2012.

Rosen, Ruth. *The World Split Open: How the Modern Women's Movement Changed America.* New York: Penguin, 2003.

Yang, Rae. *Spider Eaters: A Memoir.* Berkeley: University of California Press, 1997.

Young, Marilyn. *The Vietnam Wars.* New York: Harper, 1991.

CHAPTER 11

IMPERIAL IMPASSE, 1972–80

As Richard Nixon looked for ways to reshape the Cold War and America's position in the Vietnam War, he found unlikely opportunities to steer the conversation and public perception. Few would have guessed that the game of table tennis would be a conduit for improving more than twenty years of tension between the United States and Mainland China, but it was. And Nixon leveraged this small incident into a larger Cold War strategy that linked the United States, China, and the Union of Soviet Socialist Republics. National Archives at College Park–Still Pictures (RDSS).

1972: NIXON MEETS MAO

On February 21, 1972, Richard Nixon arrived in Beijing on an extraordinary mission aimed at bridging the deep gulf between the People's Republic of China and the United States. After handshakes at the airport, the American president was taken straight to the Forbidden City to meet Mao Zedong, the leader of the Chinese Communist revolution who was frequently referred to as the Great Helmsman. Despite decades of mutual rancor and vituperation, the two leaders conducted the historic dialogue with surprising good humor. When Nixon attempted to flatter Mao by saying he had "changed the world," Mao replied modestly, "I have only been able to change a few places in the vicinity of Beijing." Mao even jested, "I voted for you during your election," and explained that he liked rightists like Nixon because he knew where they stood. Parading before an astonished world, the rightist American president and the leftist chairman of the Communist Party behaved like old friends.

Nine months before Nixon and Mao shook hands in Beijing and one year after Nixon ordered U.S. troops into Cambodia, fifteen Americans of varied backgrounds—including college students, an immigrant to the United States, a housewife, a college professor, and a self-described hippie—ended two decades of acrimonious detachment with a symbolic game of Ping-Pong (table tennis) in China. The currents of rapprochement were already in motion before the Chinese decision to attend the World Table Tennis Championship in Nagoya, Japan, and before U.S. Ping-Pong player Glenn Cowan broke decorum to sit on the Chinese team's bus. Cowan, a countercultural nonconformist who would become known for sporting a t-shirt with the Beatles lyric, "Let It Be," soon found himself standing before Chinese Premier Zhou Enlai on April 15, 1971. Audaciously, Cowan asked Zhou his thoughts on American hippies, and the revolutionary leader replied, "Youth must seek out the truth, and out of this search various forms of change are bound to come." He added, "This is a transitional period. . . . When we were young, it was the same, too." Zhou's avuncular response suggested that radicalism is for the young and that eventually everyone has to grow up.

Ping-Pong diplomacy made clear for the public, in the United States and in China, what was already in play at the highest levels of government. Secretly, Nixon and National Security Advisor Henry Kissinger had been testing the waters of rapprochement for nearly two years. The spectacle of the American Ping-Pong team's visit announced a historic rapprochement in the midst of the Cold War. It also gave the appearance that such cooperation reflected the will of the people. In truth, two revolutionary moments were passing each other—the radicalism of the sixties and the conservatism of the seventies—and Mao and Zhou skillfully used the former to usher in the latter.

AMERICA AT IMPASSE

The Cold War Left and Right were heading for a new vital center as the disorders of the late 1960s resulted in a search for order in the early 1970s. Both China and the United States recognized that the simple bipolarity of the Cold War could no longer contain world affairs. For proof they had to look no further than their own borders, as the rebel sixties exploded in the United States and the cultural revolution crested in China. And so, national leaders reached out to their adversaries—be it Nixon's visit to China, new relations between China and France, or renewed interest in détente in the United States and Soviet Union—in an effort to establish a new multipolar world order that could quiet discontent at home.

For Americans, the new multipolar arrangements represented an acknowledgment of their own limits. After a generation of ascendancy in world affairs, they were forced to take account of the economic resurgence of Western Europe and Japan, the stubborn endurance of Soviet power, and the rise of China. What was more, Americans had to reckon with a succession of international setbacks—the Arab oil embargo, defeat in Vietnam, Marxist regimes in Africa, and Americans held hostage in Iran—all of which had the sting of being bullied by foreigners.

And there were internal limits. The crisis of authority in the late 1960s led to an impasse among liberals, radicals, and conservatives. And after three golden decades of growth, American capitalism ran into trouble in an unprecedented combination of economic and employment stagnation and inflation known as *stagflation*.

Reactions to these shifts varied. Some Americans welcomed the relaxation of Cold War tensions and accepted economic and imperial limits as the natural outgrowth of historical change. Repudiating the excesses of the past, they learned to live within limits and followed President Carter's advice during the energy crisis of the 1970s to put on a sweater and turn down the heat.

Others, however, objected to a world governed by restrictions as it defied their understanding of American history and rights. Had not America, they reasoned, claimed its place among the world's nations through ceaseless expansion, whether on the Western plains or in Latin American markets? Had not John Kennedy only recently promised a new frontier? Were not unfettered consumption and bold innovation keys to winning the Cold War? Echoing Ayn Rand's *Virtue of Selfishness*, individualism was neither incidental to this emerging group's outlook nor symbolic. Instead, it was a way of life. Outraged at being challenged overseas by Communists, oil sheiks, and radical Muslims and resentful of being told to accept limits at home, they swung behind the conservative revolt that resulted in Ronald Reagan's election in 1980.

Adjusting to Economic Limits

An early sign of limits stemmed from America's waning position in the world economy. After decades of being in the driver's seat because of its productive capabilities, the United States was beginning to depend on other nations for the resources that fueled its prosperity. One area of newfound weakness was the deficit in balance of payments. Just as individuals must balance their checkbooks, so must countries balance revenues and expenditures to avoid going bankrupt. America faced the problem of paying out more than it took in. Dollars flowed out through several channels. Some went to pay for Saudi Arabian oil, Japanese televisions, and other imports. This would not have been a problem if U.S. exports, a primary source of income, had kept pace with the expenditures (because dollars would have come back in equal numbers). But exports did not keep pace, and the year 1971 became a crucial tipping point. For the first time since 1894, Americans imported more merchandise than they exported, amassing a trade deficit that topped $1.3 billion. With that change, the United States marked a major shift from a country of producers to a consumer nation.

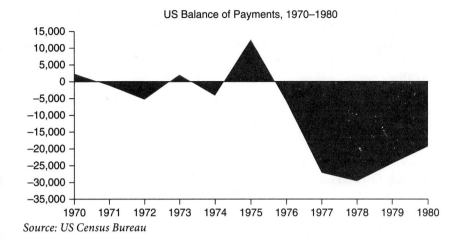

US Balance of Payments, 1970–1980

Source: US Census Bureau

Additional dollars went out to pay the costs of U.S. military operations over-seas. Just after the Gulf of Tonkin incident in South Vietnam, military expenditures stood at $70.6 billion (adjusted to $533 billion in 2015 dollars) in 1965. By 1971, military outlays would grow to $97.9 billion (or $575 billion). That not only increased the balance-of-payments deficit but also reduced the value of U.S. currency and contributed to inflation. Although military spending, on balance, was a stimulus to the economy, which some called military Keynesianism, all those dollars for bombs and bases tended to drive up prices. After years of pretending it was possible to have prosperity at home and a formidable defense of U.S. interests abroad, commonly referred to as having both guns and butter, it was becoming clear that America would have to cut back somewhere.

Responding to these troubles, President Nixon adopted a series of actions to regain economic balance. The most far reaching was his 1971 decision to remove the dollar from the gold standard and let it "float" among the other international currencies, including the German marks, English pounds, and Japanese yen. By separating the dollar from its golden safety net, Nixon terminated the Bretton Woods system that had been in place since the end of the Second World War. His aim was to devalue the dollar and thereby make U.S. exports cheaper. It was a protectionist gamble designed to give the United States an advantage in the world market. Yet, it also came with the risk of further weakening America's position relative to the world economy, as Nixon and the country would learn.

Meanwhile, to keep inflation under control, Nixon imposed federal controls on wages and prices. Hoping to keep consumers happy with price controls, Nixon admitted, "We are all Keynesians now," by which he meant that even center-right politicians like himself accepted the necessity of extensive government intervention to promote mass consumption. In another Keynesian stratagem, Nixon presided over a significant increase in total federal expenditures for the welfare state, which jumped from $27 billion in 1969 ($175 billion in 2015) to almost $65 billion in 1975 ($119.4 billion in 2015). He even proposed a plan (although it was never adopted) for a guaranteed minimum income to put an income floor under the poor.

As these measures show, Nixon worked within the basic framework of domestic political economy that had been in place since the New Deal, like all his postwar predecessors, Republican and Democratic alike. What was different was that Nixon could no longer count on America's unquestioned dominance in the world economy.

TOWARD A MULTIPOLAR WORLD

Partly because of its weakening economic position, the United States also saw its predominant position in world affairs diminished. In fact, both superpowers were slipping free of their Cold War moorings and sailing out into uncharted waters of new international arrangements. What had been a simple bipolar face-off at the height of the Cold War was turning into a set of multipolar alignments by the beginning of the 1970s. On the Communist side, the Sino-Soviet split, now over ten years old, had become irreparable. On the capitalist side, Western Europe and Japan completed their postwar reconstruction and were once again becoming powerhouses of their own. Recognizing these new realities, President Nixon and National Security Advisor Henry Kissinger foresaw a world of "five great economic superpowers": the United States, Western Europe, Japan, the Soviet Union, and China. In such a fluid environment, what was required was not the ideological rigidity of us versus them, but the recognition of a more sophisticated balance of power. To take advantage of such conditions, the president emphasized the politics of realism, which accepted the world on its own terms— including the dark possibility of aligning with illiberal states—and stressed national interest in decision making over idealism and ideology. As Nixon himself proclaimed, "What is important is not a nation's internal political philosophy. What is important is its policy toward the rest of the world and toward us." The Nixon Doctrine reflected this way of thinking. Since the United States could no longer absorb the costs of war, the realist solution was to redirect the burden (and risk) onto America's allies.

The new diplomatic realism had another dimension as well. American leaders were motivated to reach accommodations with former enemies by their desire to quiet the discontent that had been growing since 1968. Dissent was not just an American problem. For similar reasons, Soviet leaders were eager to join hands with their American counterparts in hopes of quieting disorders in Eastern Europe, just as Chinese authorities were looking for international respectability while they curbed the excesses of the cultural revolution. This convergence of interests among global elites, with the objective of reasserting control over restive populations, helped produce a set of dramatic diplomatic breakthroughs.

China Beckons

The most spectacular breakthrough was the rapprochement between the United States and China. From the side of the People's Republic of China, the opening to the United States was the product of mounting difficulties, both internal and external. Aspiring to leadership of world Communism, Maoist China had long been denouncing Soviet *revisionists* for betraying the cause of Third World revolution. In March 1969, relations between the two Communist rivals degenerated to the point of an exchange of gunfire around Zhenbao Island near the Ussuri River. The conflict spread out along their shared border and lasted into August. Seeking a counterbalance to the Soviets, the Chinese decided to break out of diplomatic isolation and play "the American card."

Economic troubles provided a second impetus to open up to the West. While still suffering from the self-inflicted blow of the Great Leap Forward (1959–61), China had plunged headlong into another period of upheaval in the cultural revolution (1966–76). Hoping to repair the earlier economic damage, the so-called Petroleum Group, Chinese experts from the influential Ministry of Petroleum which Mao Zedong recognized as a model for national development, were eager to lay their hands on Western technology.

These diplomatic and economic pressures led to a new realism in foreign policy in the People's Republic of China. Leading the move toward realism was Premier Zhou Enlai, one of the key players on the stage of twentieth-century world history. Born to an elite family, Zhou had studied and worked in Europe after the First World War. Like Ho Chi Minh in Vietnam and so many other Asian students, he was initially attracted to Wilson's promise of self-determination, but when Wilson abandoned China, he turned to Lenin's brand of Communism. Returning home a traitor to his class, Zhou participated in the Long March, fought in the Second World War, and rose to the post of premier after the Communist Revolution. He impressed all he met with his elegant self-possession. As Henry Kissinger observed, "He moved gracefully and with dignity, filling a room not by his physical dominance (as did Mao or de Gaulle) but by his air of controlled tension, steely discipline and self-control, as if he were a coiled spring." Although unswerving in his political beliefs, he was a pragmatist ready to change course to serve Chinese interests.

Even Mao Zedong, the Great Helmsman of Communist revolution, was ready to shake hands with the capitalists. For over a decade, the Chinese countryside had rung with Mao's inspiring exhortations: "The whole world should unite and defeat imperialism, revisionism, and all reactionaries, and establish socialism." These slogans would continue as useful rhetoric for public consumption, but in private, Mao mocked the very revolutionary slogans he propagated. The aging leader confessed, "I think that, generally speaking, people like me sound like a lot of big cannons!"

In internal debates over whether to befriend the West, it helped that the political zeal of the cultural revolution was receding. Flagging ideological intensity reduced the risk of criticism against leaders as "capitalist roaders" for inviting the imperialist enemy into Communist China. In fact, the leading opponent of Western ties, Lin Piao, died in a plane crash while fleeing China, eliminating the main obstacle to improved relations.

Rapprochement started slowly. In the spring of 1971, the realists persuaded Mao to bring an American table-tennis team to China, setting off Ping-Pong diplomacy. Meanwhile, arrangements were made for Kissinger to come to Beijing for secret talks (kept secret even from the secretary of state). Out of these talks came the invitation for Nixon to visit in February 1972.

The United States Responds

President Nixon had his own reasons for accepting. Hoping to go down in history as a master of grand strategy, Nixon sought recognition as the Western statesman who could transcend Cold War divisions and foster a new multipolar framework of diplomacy. The irony was that Nixon himself, whether out of sincere conviction or political opportunism, was one of the architects of the red, or Communist, menace fears he now sought to change. Perhaps Nixon's past inoculated his administration against possible fallout from such a move. Whereas a Lyndon Johnson or a Hubert Humphrey would worry about being pilloried for being soft on Communism, few conservatives openly criticized Nixon for cozying up to Communists because his anti-Communist credentials spoke for themselves. As he told Mao, "Those on the right can do what those on the left can only talk about." Perhaps the conditions at the time—the war in Vietnam, social protest and violence in America's streets, and a cultural revolution among the nation's youth—diverted the public's attention away from such detached and outmoded concerns.

Another motive for going to China was to fend off economic troubles. In the uncertain environment after the abandonment of Bretton Woods and its special protection for the U.S. dollar, American businesses dreamed once again of China's fabled market, which had been closed since Mao and the Communists captured mainland China in 1949. Nixon hoped that the opening to China would serve the larger interests of Western capitalism while promoting the narrower interests of American business. Just as with the Open Door policy at the beginning of the century, U.S. diplomats sought equal access to Chinese markets for foreign capitalists. Then, as now, American corporations believed they could beat the competition if only they could get in the door.

After their initial meeting, Mao kept out of sight. Suffering from congestive heart failure, he had difficulty speaking and left Zhou Enlai to conduct the historic dialogue. At the welcome banquet, Zhou raised a prosaic toast to the establishment of "normal state relations," while Nixon, a normally an awkward speaker, tried to wax eloquent: "This is the day for our two peoples to rise to the heights of greatness which can build a better world." Music accompanied the toasts, a homage to diplomacy and cooperation that featured *America the*

Beautiful followed by a Chinese Communist anthem "Sailing the Seas Depends on the Helmsman."

By the visit's end a week later, it was clear that the theme songs announced a newfound harmony. To be sure, deep divisions remained. The propaganda machines on both sides did not immediately go out of business, and the Shanghai communiqué issued on the eve of Nixon's departure stated their differences on a number of issues. And there was still the thorny issue of compensation for U.S. assets totaling $196 million seized by the People's Republic of China between 1949 and 1950 and the danger mainland China posed for Taiwan, an American protectorate. Nonetheless, it was an astonishing moment, as Nixon observed metaphorically when asked about the progress while visiting the Great Wall: "We have begun the long process of removing the wall between us." To be sure, walls would remain, but from that day forward they would not be as great.

The challenges of the Vietnam War compelled the Nixon administration to seek out new ways to conduct the Cold War. China, in the waning years of Mao Zedong's leadership and the ascension of Zhou Enlai, offered Nixon a way to refashion the Cold War along great power lines and put pressure on North Vietnam to negotiate an end to the Vietnam conflict. Nixon Presidential Library.

The new rapprochement did not please everyone. The North Vietnamese had reason to be upset. The Chinese had repeatedly rebuked them for negotiating with the United States, and here were the Chinese doing exactly that. What made the betrayal especially bitter was the intensification of U.S. bombing campaigns in the weeks before the toasts in Beijing. American B-52s conducted some of the most merciless raids of the war, with bombs that threatened Chinese ships and even struck vessels stationed in North Vietnam. Despite the withdrawal of U.S. ground forces under the policy of Vietnamization, even at this late date Nixon held out hope of defeating the Vietnamese militarily. Now, the North Vietnamese feared that the Chinese would sell them out as they had done twenty years earlier at Geneva. Chagrinned, the North Vietnamese soon learned they were correct.

The Vietnamese were not the only ones betrayed by the new Sino-American relationship. Nixon's gambit also left the Taiwanese twisting in the wind. Despite a public stand against the expulsion of Taiwan from the United Nations, the United States did nothing to prevent the mainland government from reclaiming China's seat on the Security Council. Moreover, everyone knew that Nixon's meeting with Mao ended forever the fantasy of the Nationalists ever ruling again in Beijing. Beyond that, both sides betrayed their own ideological principles by dealing with their leftist (Maoist) and rightist (Nixon) enemies, respectively. That was why so much of the preliminary diplomacy had to be conducted in secret.

Yet, who can say that these betrayals troubled either side? To the contrary, the Chinese ended a dangerous period of isolation, whereas the Nixon administration's opening to China was the high point of an administration that would culminate in his disgrace. In the longer term, the consequences of China's opening to the West were enormous. It was the first crack in the dam that would burst open in the 1980s, allowing China to emerge as one of the key sites of world economic development.

Soviet–American Détente

Simultaneous with the Sino-American breakthrough, the United States and the Soviet Union were scaling back tensions in what world leaders called *détente*. The leaders of the two sides were fit partners to come to grips with changing world realities. Soviet Premiere Leonid Brezhnev was, if anything, even more of a cautious pragmatist than Richard Nixon and Zhou Enlai. An unimaginative leader, he had never even dreamed of world revolution, for which he was reviled as a revisionist by the more ardent Maoists. Reacting angrily to the new Sino-American ties, Moscow issued pro forma denunciations of China's hypocrisy in betraying the Vietnamese. But such fulminations did not reverse the move toward détente. There was too much at stake. The Soviets were out to win Western acceptance of its control over Eastern Europe, stabilize the costly nuclear arms race, and obtain enough food to make up for potentially catastrophic shortfalls in Soviet agriculture.

Putting aside the resentment of having the Chinese upstage the Soviets, Brezhnev hosted President Nixon in Moscow at a summit meeting in May 1972, three months after Nixon's historic visit to Beijing. In a virtual replay of 1921, when Herbert Hoover facilitated a deal that allowed America's highly productive farms to help feed starving Russians, the summit produced a wheat deal in which the Soviets contracted to buy a quarter of the U.S. wheat crop at below-market prices. This time, the deal was far less one sided. The sale helped reduce the U.S. balance-of-payments deficit while also filling depleted Soviet granaries.

The meeting's most recognized diplomatic accomplishment was the signing of the first Strategic Arms Limitation Talks (SALT I), under which the two superpowers agreed to set a ceiling on the number of nuclear missiles and terminate efforts to develop an antiballistic missile defense system. Instead of trying to protect themselves from a nuclear first strike, they agreed to rely on mutual assured destruction, which took the unsettling acronym MAD, to deter a full-scale strategic exchange of nuclear missiles. The policy of deterrence relied on neither side being willing to strike first because the consequences would be suicidal—the immediate death of millions on both sides, the collapse of both civilizations, and a prolonged nuclear winter leading to the extinction of many species and possibly even the death of humankind.

Disarmament and peace activists, such as the Committee for a SANE Nuclear Policy, protested MAD's dangerous reasoning and the irrationality of a nuclear arms race. The only rational course, they maintained, was disarmament and disarmament alone. And when the superpowers immediately resumed the arms race by making more powerful weapons, such as multiple independently targeted reentry vehicle (MIRVs) technology that put multiple warheads on each missile, and then strategically omitted that technology from SALT I, these objections, viewed as alarmist by some, gained currency. For the sake of parity between the superpowers, the Soviets were allowed more missiles (1,600) than the United States (1,054), but Americans enjoying a two-to-one lead in warheads. Essentially, multiple independently targeted reentry vehicles took back with one hand what SALT I had given with the other.

Even so, MAD lent an air of stability to superpower relations. Another move toward easing tension came in the Helsinki Accords of 1975. The United States won a commitment from the Soviets to respect human rights and, in return, the West accepted the borders in Eastern Europe, including the division of Germany into East and West. The fruits of détente were many. As each superpower got what it wanted, a sense of stability stretched across the globe. And both Brezhnev and the Nixon/Ford administrations ignored the cries for human rights in the Communist bloc for the sake of stability.

By the mid-1970s, powerful interests within the superpowers had succeeded in rearranging world affairs to their liking. Responding to popular protests of the late 1960s, American, Soviet, and Chinese leaders had adjusted to new realities and gained something for themselves in the process. By entering into forced friendship with the United States, the Chinese acquired a counterbalance to Russia. By accepting permanent coexistence with the capitalist adversary under the policy of détente and paying lip service to human rights, the Soviets helped contain discontent in Eastern Europe and stabilize the costly arms race. By accepting coexistence with Communist adversaries, the Americans gained a more predictable international environment and some relief from the criticism of liberals at home. Conservative critics, however, deemed limits on American power unacceptable, setting the stage for a conservative resurgence in the 1980s.

SHOCKS FROM THE MIDDLE EAST

As the West became dependent on ever-increasing supplies of oil, the Middle East acquired unprecedented strategic importance. As the location of almost two-thirds of the world's oil reserves, the Persian Gulf region had become the world economy's leading supplier of petroleum. What worried the West was the volatility of this Third World region. Since its independence from European powers in the decades after World War II, the Middle East had become a land of contrasts where modern oil derricks rose up among Bedouin camels. Torn between tradition and modernity, the region was also polarized between rich and poor. Especially as oil prices, whose profits were called derisively *petrodollars*, poured into Middle Eastern countries to fund a sudden explosion of conspicuous consumption at the top in the form of marble palaces and luxury yachts while the vast majority lived in cramped hovels.

The Middle East had long occupied a pivotal role in world history. It was the cradle of three world religions—Judaism, Christianity, and Islam—and a crossroads of East–West trade and cultural contact from Hellenistic times to the present. Although most of the region's inhabitants were Muslims, sectarian division between majority Sunnis and minority Shiites was another source of tension, as were ethnic differences between Arabs at the core and Egyptians, Iranians, Kurds, and Turkmen, among others, at the peripheries. In a special case of ethnoreligious tension, Israeli Jews were a modern island in an often hostile Muslim sea. Both Jews and Muslims, like the smattering of Christians in the region, traced their origins to the same patriarch Abraham and worshiped essentially the same One God. In that sense, the Arab–Israeli conflict was a family quarrel—and a heated land dispute. Like other family quarrels, that did not make it any less intense.

In the 1970s, the West found out just how pivotal the Middle East was in the age of oil. A decade before, Saudi Arabia, Iran, Kuwait, Venezuela, and Iraq—five of the prime oil-producing states in the Third World—met in Baghdad and created an intergovernmental organization, the Organization of the Petroleum Exporting Countries (OPEC), to control the flow of oil to industrialized countries. Europe and Japan got almost all of their oil from the Middle East—80 percent and 90 percent, respectively. Even the United States, which got 12 percent, was vulnerable to price increases in the world market. Until 1973, supplies of cheap oil were guaranteed by the special relationship between the United States and its local clients, of whom the most important were the Royal House of Saudi Arabia and the Iranian dictator Shah Reza Pahlavi.

What complicated the picture was the fact that Israel was another client state of the United States. Many of its neighbors, the Saudis in particular, regarded Israel as an illegitimate occupier of Arab land. And after the Six-Day War of 1967, when Israel defeated Egypt and Syria, seized Palestinian territory in the West Bank and Gaza, and began decades of occupation deemed illegal under a series of UN resolutions, Arab opposition only intensified. In an effort to reassert Arab strength, Egypt and

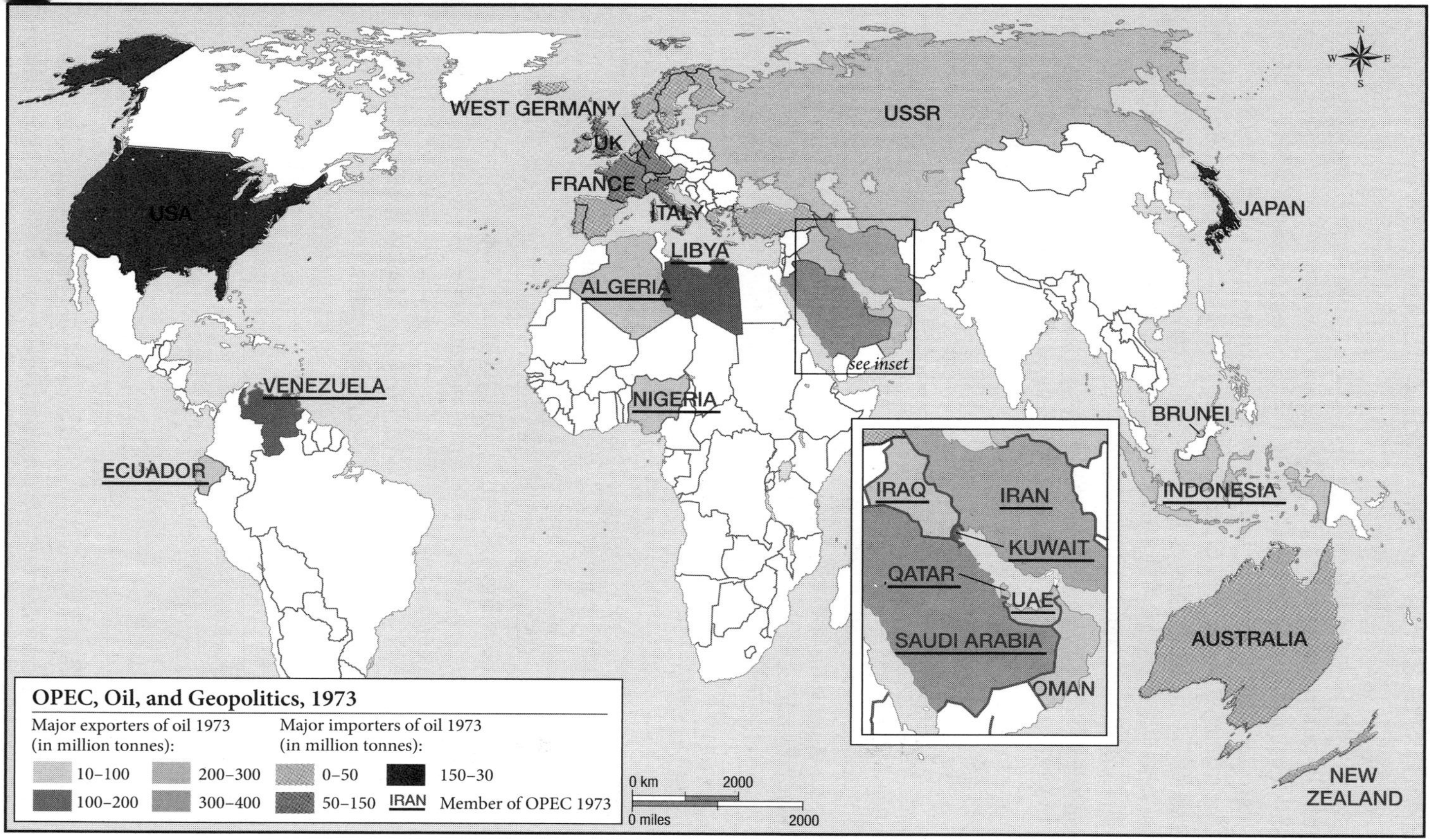

OPEC, Oil, and Geopolitics, 1973

Major exporters of oil 1973 (in million tonnes):
10–100
100–200
200–300
300–400

Major importers of oil 1973 (in million tonnes):
0–50
50–150
150–30

IRAN Member of OPEC 1973

MAP 11.1

NEW ZEALAND

AUSTRALIA

JAPAN

BRUNEI

INDONESIA

USSR

IRAN
KUWAIT
UAE
OMAN
IRAQ
QATAR
SAUDI ARABIA

see inset

WEST GERMANY
UK
FRANCE
ITALY
LIBYA
ALGERIA
NIGERIA

VENEZUELA
ECUADOR

USA

0 km   2000
0 miles   2000

319

Syria attacked Israel in the Yom Kippur War of 1973. Arab leaders were motivated not so much to liberate the Palestinians as to avenge their own loss of prestige and territory in the Golan and the Sinai six years earlier. And when Israel successfully launched counterattacks that affirmed its military dominance in the region, Arab leaders retaliated against Israel's supporters in the West, especially U.S. arms shipments to Tel Aviv, by imposing an oil embargo aimed mainly at the United States.

For five months, the OPEC cartel limited the export of oil, creating the first "oil shock" in the United States. Rationing and increased prices produced brownouts, school closings, and the terrible choice for the poor between "heating and eating." Americans could be found across the country waiting long hours in line for gas only to be told the pump was dry.

To people who equated freedom with automobility and cringed at the thought of shortages, the embargo was more than just a nuisance. Growing consumer anger was directed mostly at OPEC, but there were also charges of profiteering directed at Exxon, Texaco, and other oil corporations. Although the idea of cleaning up the environment appealed to Americans who were moving to the suburbs and vacationing in national parks, it was hard for them to accept any restraints on household consumption. After decades of getting to choose their heart's desire, they now felt jilted in their romance of consumption and it took a devastating toll on the national confidence. America did not suffer the shortages alone, however, as the pain spread throughout what scholars would later designate the global North. Many developing countries of the South that had no oil reserves also had to pay painfully high prices for energy.

One unintended consequence of the oil shock was the first serious effort toward conservation of energy since the advent of cheap oil. The U.S. federal government stepped in with new regulations and soon shoppers discovered comparative energy use labels on their refrigerators and air conditioners and improved fuel efficiency in their cars. High prices in the marketplace and state regulation combined to conserve energy. Even as the U.S. gross domestic product rose by about 45 percent between 1973 and 1986, total energy use remained about steady. Noteworthy as this was, Japan's response to the oil shock was even more impressive. As a result of conservation and improvements in efficiency, Japanese oil imports declined by 25 percent between 1973 and 1987, even as the Japanese economy doubled in size.

The energy crisis, however, revealed an apparent vulnerability in the West and troubling signs of weakness in America's ability to lead the free world. Proud notions of U.S. hegemony that opened the Cold War were giving way to the realization that America was subject to the will of smaller nations. The disorder and loss of control that had played out in America's streets seemed to be taking on global proportions that reshaped the language and alignment of domestic politics.

Nixon's Fall

President Nixon's political troubles and forced resignation in August 1974 comprised one of the most stunning developments of the period. The roots of perhaps the worst presidential crisis in U.S. history lay in Nixon's effort to silence critics of his Vietnam policy. Seeking to plug press leaks about Vietnam, he authorized the creation of a secret domestic espionage team appropriately nicknamed the Plumbers. During his reelection campaign in 1972, the Plumbers, probably without the president's direct authorization, conducted what Nixon called a third-rate burglary at the Watergate offices of the Democratic Party. When the burglars were caught, the president publicly denied any connection to the White House, but privately began a cover-up by ordering the Central Intelligence Agency (CIA) to tell the Federal Bureau of Investigation not to pursue the case and by paying hush money to the defendants.

Such illegal methods were not as rare as they should have been. Stung by the depth of popular opposition to the war in Southeast Asia, the Federal Bureau of Investigation had secretly begun domestic surveillance of antiwar critics, both liberal and radical leftists. Until they were exposed in congressional investigations conducted by Senator Frank Church, the counterintelligence programs, code-named COINTELPRO, sought to disrupt the work of antiwar critics, Black Panthers, and the Socialist Workers Party, among others. These covert operations echoed the Justice Department's campaign to root out and destroy the Communist Party in the 1950s and the still earlier persecution of the Industrial Workers of the World in the 1910s. Like the earlier red scares, these domestic spying operations caused considerable controversy. Defenders said they were necessary to protect national security from internal subversives, whereas critics countered that police-state methods violated constitutional protections of civil liberty. Between these two poles, the Bill of Rights hung in the balance, especially the First (free speech), Fourth (no unreasonable searches), and Fifth (due process) Amendments.

Given the serious nature of Nixon's reaction, the House Judiciary Committee began a televised investigation of whether the president had committed impeachable offenses. Under the Constitution, removing a president from office for "high crimes and misdemeanors" is a two-step process that begins with impeachment (indictment) in the House of Representative and moves to a trial in the Senate. The high point of impeachment hearings came with the disclosure that President Nixon had secretly taped his order to have the CIA intervene in the election of 1974; it was a smoking gun that sealed his fate. Anticipating inevitable impeachment by the full House for obstruction of justice and abuse of power, as well as likely conviction in the Senate, Nixon resigned in 1974.

With Richard Nixon's fall, the Vietnam War had claimed its second president. As with Lyndon Johnson, Nixon succumbed to his own flaws and insecurities. Nixon was a lonely outsider who built his political career as an embattled survivor against a host of enemies, real or imagined. That approach worked until there were no friends left. The irony was that the president had snared himself in his own web of secrecy and deception.

Nixon's foibles aside, however, the downfall of two successive presidents exposed the dangerous overreaching of what has been called *the imperial presidency*. An imperial president employs unchecked power over his own people, if not the larger world, in the unwarranted pursuit of power. Both Johnson and

Nixon fit this description. They defied democratic accountability and tried to rule outside the constitutional system of checks and balances by repeatedly deceiving Congress and the public about the Vietnam War. Having lost the trust of the people, Johnson withdrew from the presidential nominating process. If Nixon's violations were more egregious, they nonetheless stemmed from a similar impulse to conduct foreign policy free from domestic restraints.

For critics of both administrations, the downfalls marked twin victories for constitutional law and the efficacy of democratic rule. In Nixon's case, congressional action was a ringing affirmation of the system of checks and balances, under which even the commander in chief of the most powerful country on earth was subject to the law. Likewise, the War Powers Act of 1973 returned to Congress the war-making powers that had been conceded to the president in the Gulf of Tonkin Resolution, while the Church Commission investigation revealed the unseemly practices of the CIA and led to restrictions on covert operations.

Defeat in Vietnam

In the most glaring illustration of America's waning power, the United States suffered defeat in Southeast Asia. Communist forces took control of Saigon at the

The Nixon–Ford administrations looked for a way to achieve peace with honor in South Vietnam, believing that it was possible to salvage the meaning of over twenty years of U.S. intervention in their civil war. When the last helicopters departed in 1975 and the sad images of the United States leaving behind South Vietnamese supporters became public, it was evident that there was little honor in the peace America forged. National Archives at College Park–Still Pictures (RDSS).

end of April 1975, and the images of U.S. diplomats kicking terrified Vietnamese off the runners of helicopters evacuating people from the roof of the U.S. Embassy as panicked Americans scrambled to flee transfixed and shocked television viewers in the United States. What was the longest war to that point in American history, and the first one it ever lost, was over.

In long-term historical perspective, American defeat was not so surprising. The postwar period had brought a string of defeats for European colonial powers. What the French could not do in Vietnam and Algeria, the Belgians could not do in the Congo, and the British could not do in South Asia it was unlikely the Americans could do in Indochina. The handwriting was also on the wall for the Soviet empire. In what would soon become "Russia's Vietnam," the Soviets invaded Afghanistan in 1979, only to be forced into an embarrassing retreat ten years later, by which time they had to relinquish their empire in Eastern Europe as well.

Vietnam was viewed differently across the political spectrum in America. To some hawkish conservatives, defeat was a self-inflicted wound. The United States fought, they said, with "one hand tied behind its back." It is true that compared to the Second World War, Vietnam was a limited war. The use of nuclear weapons was never on the table because of the threat of Soviet retaliation, nor was a land invasion of North Vietnam because of the possibility, at least until 1968, that masses of Chinese troops would come pouring across the border, as they had in Korea.

Nevertheless, within those limits, the United States had unleashed immense military force. Beginning with Rolling Thunder in 1965, high-flying B-52s rained down death and destruction almost at will in the South, since the National Liberation Front had virtually no air defenses. They also wreaked havoc in the North despite Soviet-supplied MIG jet fighters and antiaircraft batteries. The scale of this air war is staggering. In the most extensive bombing campaign in world history, U.S. forces dropped on Southeast Asia three times the tonnage used by all combatants in all the theaters of the Second World War.

Some Americans began to feel the effects of *Vietnam syndrome*, the deep wound in national psyche concerning U.S. ability to wage war that hung over Americans like a cloud for decades. To Colin Powell, a young military officer who served in Vietnam, the lesson was to ensure there was strong public support for intervention, then go in with overwhelming force, and make sure to have a strategy for getting out. This became known as the Powell Doctrine, and when he became national security advisor to President George H. W. Bush, Powell implemented it during the Gulf War of 1991.

For others, the lesson was not to intervene in the first place, except in defense of vital interests under direct attack. This was the position of those in the peace movement who agreed with Daniel Ellsberg, a former Pentagon advisor and leading war critic, when he said, "We were not *on* the wrong side. We *were* the wrong side." In the years to come, Americans would argue over the correct lesson of Vietnam every time they sent troops overseas.

However traumatized Americans were in defeat, their experience paled in comparison to the sufferings of the victorious Vietnamese. Looking out from napalm-scorched hamlets, they saw a countryside pockmarked with bomb craters and poisoned by defoliants like Agent Orange. The two million or more dead Vietnamese bore mute testimony to the fact that, from their side, it was a total war. Ultimately, it was their willingness to absorb endless punishment that enabled them to hold out until the Americans tired of fighting. Although Ho Chi Minh died six years before the war ended, one of his poems captured the feeling of the moment: "What could be more natural? / After great sorrow comes joy."

In the end, the Vietnamese were able to take pride in a long string of victories against more powerful enemies. Centuries earlier they had held off imperial China, then the French, and finally the Americans. "Do you realize," a taxi driver said to an American historian visiting Ho Chi Minh City, "we are the only nation on earth that's defeated three out of the five permanent members of the United Nations Security Council?"

DOWNSHIFT IN THE WORLD ECONOMY

The 1970s also witnessed major changes in the world economy and America's place within it. The golden decades came to an end with a worldwide slowdown that would last almost to the end of the century. The world economy downshifted to slower annual rates of growth on the order of 2.6 percent, compared to almost 5 percent during the golden years of 1950–73. Although the command economy of the Soviet Union was seemingly beyond the reach of capitalist economics, it, too, entered an era of stagnation. It seemed that nothing worked. Transportation broke down, industry sputtered, shortages appeared, and harvests failed. The fact that the Soviet Union was forced to become the world's largest food importer, some of it in the wheat deal with the United States, was a damning indictment of the command economy. Stagnation became a prime cause of the eventual demise of the Soviet Union.

In the market economy of the United States, the worldwide slowdown was reflected in flat profits and stagnant wages. Slower growth led to unemployment, which tended to keep wages more or less even in real terms from the 1970s through the late 1990s. To a generation that had experienced the seemingly limitless growth of the postwar years, this was an unpalatable reversal of fortune. The burden of the slowdown fell most heavily on the northern Rust Belt, which stretched from the brass factories of New England to the steel mills of Midwest. The loss of high-paid unionized jobs in once-mighty industrial centers like Detroit, the motor capital of the world, and Pittsburgh, bastion of the steel industry, undermined overall wage levels. The growth of jobs in boomtowns throughout the South and Southwest, in places like Phoenix, the fastest-growing city in America, failed to make up the difference because wages were lower in the southern and western Sun Belt. The global economic slowdown was accompanied by an internal demographic and economic shift from Rust Belt to Sun Belt.

The problems did not end there. In Adam Smith's classical theory of supply and demand, low wages—and thus low demand for goods and services—were supposed to keep prices down. In fact, prices were also rising faster than ever before. Economists invented the term of stagflation to name the new phenomenon. In effect, Americans were caught between inescapable economic pincers: stagnant wages and rising prices. Inflation was the consequence of many factors: including increased spending for guns and butter under both Johnson and Nixon without corresponding tax increases, and Nixon's decision to let the dollar float in world currency markets, which diminished its value.

Economic troubles were also linked to the skyrocketing price of energy. The first OPEC oil shock of 1973–74 had temporarily driven the price of gasoline at the pump from thirty-four cents to one dollar a gallon and spread inflationary pressure throughout the economy. Not long thereafter, the rate of inflation crossed over into double digits, far surpassing President Ford's ineffective Whip Inflation Now campaign. The inflation rate took another leap with the second OPEC oil shock of 1978–79 when the price of a barrel of oil doubled within six months. By 1981, the world market price was close to forty dollars a barrel, more than ten times the level before 1973. All told, by the end of the decade, inflation in the United States was running at an annual rate of 11 percent.

Yet not everyone felt the effects of stagflation equally. Debtors love inflation because it makes it easier to acquire dollars to pay back loans at fixed interest with cheaper currency in the future. For that reason, populist farmers had agitated for "cheap money" at the end of the nineteenth century, transforming the social condition and the culture of politics. But since then, the United States had become a nation of consumers, and consumers hate inflation. Everything from hamburgers to haircuts cost more. The biggest outcry came at the gas pump during the second oil shock. For the second time in the decade, frustrated drivers had to wait in long lines, at times only to find that high-priced gasoline was not even available.

Another set of frustrated consumers were first-time homebuyers. In a country where over 60 percent of households owned their own homes in 1980, homebuyers were a special kind of consumer. Unlike farmers, whose property was income-generating capital, single-family homes were big-ticket consumer goods that soaked up income in the form of mortgage payments and

The "Whip Inflation Now," or WIN campaign, was President Gerald Ford's effort to build grass-roots support for stopping inflation at the local level. Buttons like the one pictured are all that remain of Ford's national campaign. Wikicommons, Gerald R. Ford Presidential Museum.

maintenance costs (at least until resale). Whereas holders of low-rate home mortgages made out like bandits, soaring mortgage rates that reached 18 percent in 1981 priced many aspiring homeowners out of the market, where they joined the growing wail of protest against inflation.

Caught in the economic pincers of stagflation, irate voters looked to President Jimmy Carter, who had beaten Gerald Ford in the 1976 election. In what might stand as a motto for the era of limits, Carter told the disgruntled electorate in his first inaugural address, "We have learned that 'more' is not necessarily 'better,' that even our great Nation has its recognized limits." America, riding the crest of nationalism and celebration in its bicentennial year, recoiled at such advice, especially from its commander in chief. Having witnessed defeat in South Vietnam, chaos in America's streets, and instability in the global economy, many considered Carter's solution another surrender of the founding generation's ideals. Such complaints would prove Carter's undoing and usher in a new muscular political mood and economic stance focused on the promotion of individual rights and consumption.

Roots of Globalization

The internal migration of industry from North to South was part of a larger shift in the world economy well underway in the 1970s that would eventually come to be called globalization. Manufacturing gradually moved out of highly industrialized regions of the upper tier—the United States, Western Europe, and Japan—and into middle-tier countries such as Brazil and Mexico. What appeared in the United States as deindustrialization was actually relocation of industry to new sites overseas. This global dispersion of capital and industrial production fundamentally changed the geography of wealth and poverty.

The effects could be seen in industrial America. As overseas producers began exporting manufactured goods, the market share of U.S. corporations began to fall. Between 1960 and 1979, the share of the U.S. market held by American corporations fell from 96 percent to 79 percent in autos and from nearly 100 percent to 80 percent in electrical components, with similar declines in everything from shoes to machine tools. To look at it another way, manufacturing imports rose as a share of total U.S. manufacturing outputs from 4 percent in 1960 to 22 percent by 1980. Despite pleas to "buy American," consumers in the United States were buying less and less from factories located within its borders.

Corporations in the United States were also buying fewer American goods. The U.S. giants such as General Motors, the biggest industrial corporation in the world, were fast becoming multinational corporations. In the previous era of national economies, businesses rooted in one country normally traded with businesses in other countries. But in the age of the multinational corporation, businesses operated in many countries simultaneously. Doing an end run around high wages and growing government regulations in the United States, they began to outsource their production to overseas facilities, while failing to invest in more efficient production methods at home. The result was to hasten deindustrialization in the upper tier, leaving once-thriving industrial cities such as Detroit, Pittsburgh, and Camden to rust.

Deindustrialization led to the relative decline of the U.S. economy. Although different measures yielded different results, the U.S. share of total world product declined from a peak of 32 percent in 1950 to about 26 percent in 1970 and continued to fall to about 22 percent in 1980. An even clearer indicator of decline was the fall in the share of world manufacturing from a peak of 45 percent in 1953 to 32 percent in 1973. In part, these trends reflect a return to normal conditions after the distorting effects of World War II. The U.S. share was bound to rise as Europeans and Asians lost productive facilities in the war and then was equally bound to fall again as they rebuilt after the war. Even so, American economic strength was not what it used to be.

CHALLENGES FROM THE THIRD WORLD

The two superpowers also faced challenges arising in the Third World. As the exhilaration of independence wore off, the countries of Africa, Asia, and Latin America were faced with the grim realities of poverty and dependency known as *neocolonialism*. Several countries implemented strategies of economic development borrowed from the storehouse of Western Socialist or nationalist ideas in an attempt to build modern industrial societies. Whereas these modernizing projects did little to alleviate the poverty of the masses, they exacerbated tensions between modernity and tradition. Just as the advent of the capitalist market had led to social upheaval in nineteenth-century Europe and the United States, so now a similar process saw the reassertion of custom and tradition against change. These tensions gave rise to two different kinds of politics, one focused on economic development and the other based on cultural identity. Both posed challenges to the United States.

In the politics of development, Third World leaders objected to the maldistribution of wealth. They condemned the fact that 5 percent of the world's population living in the United States was privileged to consume on the order of 25 percent of the world product. Far from accepting this gap as proof of Western superiority, they denounced it as Western neocolonialism.

Latin America posed a particular challenge for U.S. foreign relations. In Chile, for example, Salvador Allende came to power through a democratic election in 1970, the first avowed Socialist to do so in the postwar period, and Marxist Sandinistas took power in Nicaragua in 1979. Both regimes began to expropriate foreign holdings with the intention of keeping profits for domestic development. Not surprisingly, corporate interests in the United States did not stand idly by. With International Telephone and Telegraph taking the lead in demanding Allende's ouster, President Nixon and National Security Advisor Henry Kissinger authorized the 1973 overthrow of Allende in a CIA-backed coup.

MAP 11.2

There was a similar pattern in Africa, where Angola and Mozambique both emerged from Portuguese rule in the mid-1970s as independent nations with Marxist governments. In response to their vows to nationalize foreign holdings, the CIA sought to destabilize the new regimes by training and financing opposition movements, the National Front for Liberation of Angola and the National Union for the Total Independence of Angola, each with dismal records on human rights. Henry Kissinger, then serving as President Gerald Ford's secretary of state and looking to demonstrate his Cold War resolve following the Vietnam War, even called for direct intervention in Angola and gave South Africa's apartheid regime a nod when it launched covert operations.

Initially, the Islamic world also pursued the politics of development. As they broke free of European rule, most of the new secular regimes adopted what had originated as a Western idea: separation of mosque and state. Although few went as far as Turkey in proscribing all signs of religious observance, including the veil, most tried to bury any nostalgia for the caliphates of the past to modernize.

Such a turn toward modernization, however, rarely included democracy. Most secular regimes, including Nasser in Egypt, Assad in Syria, and Saddam Hussein in Iraq, ruled with an iron fist. They censored the press, outlawed opposition factions, tortured and killed dissidents, and otherwise attempted to eliminate their critics. One result was that the only safe place for dissent was in the mosque. One important unintended consequence was that these repressive secular regimes created religious opposition seething with resentment against affronts to Islam.

That was evident in the increasing turn to cultural politics in the Islamic world. With growing intensity in the 1960s and 1970s, keepers of tradition fought against the inroads of modernization. They defended customs and traditions of village life, reasserted the supremacy of religion, and championed traditional clan and family values. The battle between modernity and tradition was often fought over the place of women. Would women be able to take a place beside men in the public realm as voters, workers, and diplomats? Or would they be confined to the private sphere behind the veil in Saudi Arabia and sequestered in family compounds in Afghanistan? Hostile to Western ideas of gender equality and the indiscriminate mixing of the sexes, traditionalists reaffirmed the patriarchal subordination of women and the segregation of the sexes. At the most glaring extremes, modern ideas confronted ancient practices such as female circumcision in Sudan.

Whether developmental or traditional, Third World politics often put up resistance to the influence of the United States and globalization. Although the United States remained a potent force, defeat in Vietnam, the triumph of Marxist regimes in Africa, and the advent of Islamist movements in the Middle East suggested that the American imperium, like first-century Rome, might have reached its apogee.

Crisis in Iran

Nothing brought home that sense of limits more than the 1979 revolution in Iran. Especially after the seizure of the U.S. Embassy in Teheran by militant Islamic students, the stunning picture of the Carter administration paralyzed by Islamic militants was emblematic of Third World curbs on American power. As the most significant popular revolution since the 1960s, the impact of the Iranian Revolution reached far beyond Iran's borders, marking a turning point in the Third World from developmental to cultural politics.

The revolution originated in discontent with the rule of Shah Reza Pahlavi. The Shah (king) owed his crown to the CIA, which had fostered a coup that overthrew the democratically chosen Premiere Mossadegh in 1953. Showing his gratitude, the Shah went on to become a major supplier of Western oil and the main pillar of U.S. policy in the Middle East. As the largest recipient of U.S. military assistance in the world in the 1970s under the Nixon Doctrine, he became one of the most important clients in America's informal empire. He set out to modernize Iranian society by building roads and hospitals and by promoting women's equality with the strong support of his westernized wife and sister. But he also earned a reputation as a tyrant for stamping out opposition with the brutal methods of SAVAK, the notorious secret police. By putting secular opposition in jail, if not in the graveyard, he eliminated the moderates and unintentionally drove discontent into the mosque, where it increasingly took on Islamist views.

Islamist radicalism was personified by Ayatollah Khomeini. A revered senior cleric, or Imam, Khomeini had been expelled for criticizing the Shah's secular rule. Whereas most of the world's Muslims are Sunni, Khomeini was a Shiite, along with the majority of Muslims in Iran, and he was determined to restore the unity of mosque and state that had once prevailed in the caliphates of old.

Radical Islamists were the main current in the Iranian Revolution. They rallied the petty merchants of the bazaar, the urban poor, and the ulama (low-level clerics) to oppose the Shah as an Islamic apostate. Because SAVAK's repression had been so effective, secular currents were not as strong. There was a middle-class remnant of Nationalists who had once supported Mossadegh, plus students who had returned from Western universities as Marxists to join a weak Tudeh (Communist) Party or various Maoist factions. What drove the final nail into the Shah's coffin was the rise of working-class opposition in the form of strikes by electrical and oil workers. With so many sectors of Iranian society in revolt, protests attracted millions. At their peak, a demonstration could mobilize as many as a quarter of Iran's thirty-one million people, earning the distinction of being the largest protest demonstrations in world history. Whatever else, the Iranian revolution was a people's revolution. With the Iranian military divided and his U.S. backers giving contradictory signals, the ailing Shah fled the country in January 1979.

But unswerving support for the Shah came back to haunt the United States. Everyone with a grievance against the Shah blamed the United States for foisting the dictator on them. They intermingled their chants of "Marg bar Shah!" (death to the Shah) with chants of "Marg bar Amrika." At the same time, Iranians drew a distinction between the American people and their government. Although they were typically friendly toward American visitors, like others around the world, they were angry at U.S. policy.

In this explosive crisis, President Carter admitted the deposed monarch into the United States for cancer treatment. Although Carter's motive had to do with loyalty to a long-time client who had friends in high places, David Rockefeller and Henry Kissinger among them, it appeared to many Iranians that the CIA might be plotting another coup to return the Shah to power as in 1953. Moreover, support for the Shah led to charges of hypocrisy against President Carter. Determined to restore America's good name after the Vietnam debacle, Carter

The Iranian Revolution came on suddenly to most Americans and seemed like the latest illustration of how far the United States had fallen subsequent to Vietnam. To many in the developing world and second-tier economies, the Ayatollah Khomeini represented blowback for decades of support for brutal, authoritarian leaders for the sake of Cold War stability. Wikicommons.

had come to office with a pledge of support for human rights, a pledge that was inconsistent with favorable treatment of a dictator.

Within two weeks of the Shah's arrival in New York, Islamist militants seized the U.S. Embassy on November 4, 1979. While Iranian police looked on passively, women in chador withdrew giant chain cutters from their dark robes, cut through the embassy locks, and led Muslim students following the line of the Imam through the gate onto embassy grounds. As CIA officials quickly shredded sensitive documents, the militants began rounding up embassy personnel. Intending only to stage a short sit-in, the exhilaration of occupying what they saw as a den of spies led to a hostage-taking that lasted all of 444 days.

The seizure of hostages outraged most Americans. Not only was it a flagrant breach of international law, diplomatic immunity, and the right to personal liberty, but also it seemed to have no rational basis. Believing in their own good intentions and knowing little about their own government's support for the dictatorial Shah, many Americans saw it as the work of crazed religious fanatics driven by irrational hatred. Television networks stoked the fires of patriotic anger, as in the case of ABC's nightly news show *America Held Hostage*. If Khomeini was going to call the United States the Great Satan, then a few American fanatics responded, "Nuke the Ayatollah."

Tempers flared, but not everyone lost their heads. Some of the television and press coverage did educate the public about the forces involved, while some of the hostages released as a goodwill gesture—only women and African Americans—seemed to sympathize with the Shah's overthrow. But the overriding American response was a feeling of wounded national pride. Especially when Carter's attempt at rescuing the hostages by helicopter ended in failure in April 1980, Americans felt frustrated and helpless. Once again, as in Vietnam, a Third World country had humiliated the great superpower.

CONCLUSION

After three decades of almost uninterrupted expansion, Americans faced obstacles to the open society everywhere they turned in the 1970s. They came up against economic stagflation, defeat in Vietnam, the downfall of a president, failed attempts at human rights, the collapse of Cold War liberalism, and, at the end of the decade, the agonizing spectacle of Americans held hostage in Iran. Accustomed to living with open frontiers, many Americans viewed these events as setting unwelcome limits on their freedom.

In the 1960s, freedom had been associated with liberation for African Americans and women or else the freedom to experiment with sexual pleasures and mind-expanding drugs. By the end of the 1970s, however, Americans associated freedom with the liberty of property owners to do whatever they wanted with their business and belongings. The Movement to liberate freedom from the control of the few—men, whites, Protestants, heterosexuals, the wealthy—and extend it to the many quickly turned inward as the libertarian ethos of personal freedom and choice took its place. Many searched for tradition, stability, and order after a decade of pondering the inchoate meaning of being and purpose. Frustrated with the bigness of U.S. aims, minimalism gained a new chic not seen since the 1920s.

President Carter seemed helpless in the face of the shifting national mood, and his "Crisis of Confidence" speech, delivered to the nation on July 15, 1979, seemed to illustrate just how far he was from the public. He intended to give America a dose of realism that would snap the country back into focus and break the malaise. But instead, Jimmy Carter's discouraging words fell hard on the nation, and they took him to task for weak responses to the impasse of the decade. Americans never gave up on the benefits that came with and from globalization, however, and they were ready to respond to voices promising to advance the frontiers of this new kind of freedom.

FURTHER READING

Berman, Larry. *No Peace, No Honor: Nixon, Kissinger, and the Betrayal in Vietnam*. New York: Simon & Schuster, 2001.

Farber, David. *Taken Hostage: The Iranian Hostage Crisis and America's First Encounter with Radical Islam*. Princeton, NJ: Princeton University Press, 2005.

Frieden, Jeffrey. *Global Capitalism: Its Fall and Rise in the Twentieth Century*. New York: Norton, 2006.

Gleijeses, Piero. *Conflicting Missions: Havana, Washington, and Africa, 1959–1976.* Chapel Hill: University of North Carolina Press, 2002.

Jenkins, Philip. *Decade of Nightmares: The End of the Sixties and the Making of Eighties America.* New York: Oxford University Press, 2006.

Keys, Barbara. *Reclaiming American Virtue: The Human Rights Revolution of the 1970s.* Cambridge, MA: Harvard University Press, 2014.

McMahon, Robert. *The Cold War and the Third World.* New York: Oxford University Press, 2013.

Suri, Jeremi. *Power and Protest: Global Revolution and the Rise of Détente.* Cambridge, MA: Harvard University Press, 2003.

Weiner, Tim. *One Man against the World: The Tragedy of Richard Nixon.* New York: St. Martin's Press, 2015.

Westad, Odd Arne. *The Global Cold War: Third World Interventions and the Making of Our Times.* New York: Cambridge University Press, 2005.

CHAPTER 12

CONVERGING GLOBAL TRENDS, 1980–91

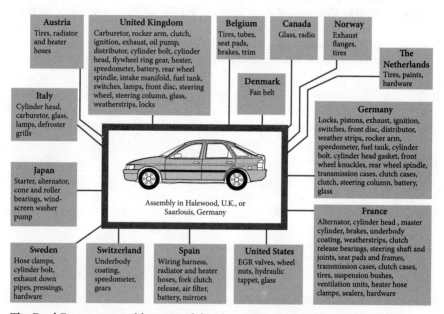

Austria
Tires, radiator and heater hoses

United Kingdom
Carburetor, rocker arm, clutch, ignition, exhaust, oil pump, distributor, cylinder bolt, cylinder head, flywheel ring gear, heater, speedometer, battery, rear wheel spindle, intake manifold, fuel tank, switches, lamps, front disc, steering wheel, steering column, glass, weatherstrips, locks

Belgium
Tires, tubes, seat pads, brakes, trim

Canada
Glass, radio

Norway
Exhaust flanges, tires

The Netherlands
Tires, paints, hardware

Italy
Cylinder head, carburetor, glass, lamps, defroster grills

Denmark
Fan belt

Germany
Locks, pistons, exhaust, ignition, switches, front disc, distributor, weather strips, rocker arm, speedometer, fuel tank, cylinder bolt, cylinder head gasket, front wheel knuckles, rear wheel spindle, transmission cases, clutch cases, clutch, steering column, battery, glass

Japan
Starter, alternator, cone and roller bearings, windscreen washer pump

Assembly in Halewood, U.K., or Saarlouis, Germany

France
Alternator, cylinder head , master cylinder, brakes, underbody coating, weatherstrips, clutch release bearings, steering shaft and joints, seat pads and frames, transmission cases, clutch cases, tires, suspension bushes, ventilation units, heater hose clamps, sealers, hardware

Sweden
Hose clamps, cylinder bolt, exhaust down pipes, pressings, hardware

Switzerland
Underbody coating, speedometer, gears

Spain
Wiring harness, radiator and heater hoses, fork clutch release, air filter, battery, mirrors

United States
EGR valves, wheel nuts, hydraulic tappet, glass

The Ford Escort was emblematic of the changes in America's economy as it became more global and moved manufacturing offshore. As America outsourced production, which was a natural consequence of its century-long effort to create an expansive and integrative economy, U.S. cities faced a rapid decline in blue-collar jobs.

THE WORLD CAR, 1980

> When Ford Motor Company announced the launch of its new car, code-named
> Erika, in early 1980, it was an admission the times had changed. For much
> of the century, the automobile held a special place in U.S. culture as a symbol
> of American style, affluence, and independence, as well as technological in-
> novation and manufacturing muscle. The city of Detroit rose as an industrial
> powerhouse responsible for the hardware of America's global dominance, from
> tanks and planes during World War II to cars in the postwar period. Among the
> Titans of Detroit, no brand carried more weight than Ford, the common man's
> car. When Henry Ford introduced the Model T, Tin Lizzy, in 1908 and built a

revolutionary factory system that transformed manufacturing and corporate culture through innovations like the moving assembly line, eight-hour work day, and a five-dollar-a-day wage, he made access to what he called "God's great open spaces" available to everyone. By the 1970s, the mythology of Ford's rise as one of America's most storied brands seemed to make it impervious to change, even when Ford produced what the American Motors Corporation president and would-be Michigan governor, George Romney, coined gas guzzlers.

A decade of falling sales, driven by global events such as the Vietnam War, the 1973 oil embargo by the Organization of the Petroleum Exporting Countries, foreign competition, and a downward turn in the U.S. economy, not to mention bad press from its rear-exploding Pinto model, however, compelled Ford to revive its spirit of innovation and Populist rhetoric. Project Erika went into production as the Ford Escort, the company's first world car; the Escort announced Detroit's return to its roots as a world leader. Ford had long since expanded from its home base in Detroit to various sites in Europe and become a fixture in the global auto market. The Escort, however, was not merely another international product; it was the embodiment of the globalization process itself, a combination of parts from around the world. As Philip Caldwell, Ford's chair, explained, "It was designed by Germans and Americans and Englishmen and Swiss and Spaniards, and will have components from a chain of countries—from Japan to Yugoslavia."

As batteries, gearboxes, and antilock brakes shuttled from one country to another and Ford assembled all the parts following the unified logic of a central-ized design, whether in Michigan, Germany, or Japan, the integrative process that some would call the global factory was complete. Yet this global factory gave rise to several new realities: increased interdependence between the constituent parts of production, expanded international trade, and a never-ending search for cheaper production costs and workers. Although Detroit and other Rust Belt cities in the North felt the pain of multisourcing, as multinational corporations pushed their most sophisticated and expensive technology into more pliable, but less developed regions of the world—first in the Sun Belt of the U.S. South and then to second- and third-tier economies in Latin America and Asia—the loss of jobs would be one of the many consequences global convergence would bring to the upper tier of the world economy.

GLOBAL CONVERGENCE

The Ford Escort points to the trend toward global convergence unfolding in the late 1980s. The most striking instance of this new convergence was the end of the Cold War, but it could also be seen in more subtle form in markets, religion, politics, labor, technology, and foreign affairs. The drive to find equilibrium after nearly four decades of hostility fostered convergence and even cooperation between global antagonists. Tensions still mounted, which did little to end suffering and injustice in second- and third-tier economies, but a new reality set in that assumed an integrated world over a divided one.

Among Cold Warriors, the reality of an integrated world took hold when both sides concluded the conflict had become an unbearable burden. Although the 1980s began in a mood of fierce animosity, the pressure of living under economic strain and the constant threat of nuclear war fostered a growing undercurrent of fatigue on both sides of the Cold War that hastened convergence. World leaders astonished even themselves by the end of the decade in adopting nuclear disarmament, regional settlements, and official declarations of mutual friendship. To the chagrin of hardliners like Margaret Thatcher, Soviet loyalists, and Cold War hawks in the United States, by the end of 1989 nearly everyone agreed that the Cold War was over.

Another aspect of convergence was the centrality of conservative beliefs in economic globalization. In the West, the 1980s saw the opening of a new era focused on global markets and presided over by conservatives. Riding to power on a wave of frustration with the limits of the 1970s, conservative champions of the free market—Margaret Thatcher in Britain and Ronald Reagan in the United States—set out to liberate business from what they saw as the chains of government regulation. If the rise of New Deal liberalism defined the post–World War II moment and the dawn of the Cold War, heterogeneous conservatism was its successor.

What was more surprising was that the convergence of economic and political ideas blurred the line between conservative and liberal, particularly in the East. China's Deng Xiaoping, who succeeded Prime Minister Zhou Enlai in 1977, embarked on an open door, or economic liberalization, policy of market reforms aimed at speeding the country's lagging development. Similarly, the Soviets gained newfound interest in the markets that took shape when General Secretary Mikhail Gorbachev introduced restructuring (*perestroika*) aimed at lifting the country out of stagnation. As these reforms gained momentum, they brought the command economies of the East and the mixed economies of the West closer together in a global economy controlled not by governments but by multinational corporations.

The rise of multinational corporations points to the paradox of globalization: each player was both independent and dependent. The ligaments, or binds, of the Cold War and a mixed economy blurred the line between autonomy and dependency, which fostered multiple illusions of control and mastery. Because of its far-reaching effects and its ability to obscure the sources of power, understanding the full complexity of global convergence requires separate discussions of globalization's two overlapping tracts: the origins of globalization in the 1980s and America's ability to influence globalization at the end of the twentieth century.

ECONOMIC GLOBALIZATION

Underlying the conservative turn in the West was the shift in the world economy from national markets to an integrated, global capitalist system. Beset by a squeeze on profits during the stagflation of the 1970s, chief executive officers of banks and major corporations came to regard the outgrowth of the mixed economy of the postwar years—a tangle of taxes, regulations, union contracts, and social benefits—as chains that shackled American creativity and constricted what they considered capitalism's natural potential for growth. In another round of "creative destruction" that had characterized capitalism since it came into existence five centuries earlier, business leaders tried to escape these restraints on profit making by going global, in many ways reasserting the ethic of laissez-faire from a century earlier.

The Global Factory

Going global reshaped the world economy in many ways. One was the development of the *global factory*. Under the watchword of *flexibility*, multinational corporations (large companies operating in several different countries simultaneously) sought to reduce supply costs by outsourcing or transferring the production of their component parts to less developed regions of the world. In its early stages, the global factory was located in the developed regions.

The Ford Escort might be the global factory's best illustration. But as time went on, multinationals moved production to the agrarian regions of the underdeveloped bottom tier for cheap labor and lower production costs, a shift any American consumer comparing the labels on blouses, shoes, or television sets between 1970 and 2000 could confirm. The shift from "Made in the USA" to "Made in Bangladesh" and a host of other foreign locations marked an epochal change

Owned and operated by the United States, *maquiladoras*, like the one pictured here in Tijuana in the early twenty-first century, sprang up throughout Mexico in the 1980s. Paying low wages, sometimes as little as five dollars a day, *maquiladoras* provided the cheap exports that fueled mass consumption in the United States. Wikicommons, Guldhammer.

in commerce and culture. Multinational corporations built factories in Mexico (where they were called *maquiladoras*), Brazil, and other Latin American countries, as well as in the East Asian "tigers" of Hong Kong, Taiwan, South Korea, and Singapore. What attracted capital to the bottom tier were cheap labor, weak unions, and soft government regulation, all of which lowered the cost of doing business and eased the pressures on profitability that had been the incentive to go global in the first place.

With the acceleration of overseas investment beginning in the 1970s, the outlines of the new global economy began to take shape. Reduced to its essentials, the world economy began to divide into two levels: the global North and the global South. On the one hand, the global North was a region of high consumption, which contained the main centers of wealth, finance and investment capital, and trade. These were places like the United States and Great Britain. On the other hand, the global South, where most of humanity lived, was a region of low consumption that contained a multitude of sites of commodity production. These tended to be states in Asia, Africa, and Latin America. This emerging geography of polarization cut across the old three-tier division of the world economy and defied the logic of a simple North–South geographic division at the root of their designation. It brought industrialization to many regions that had been in the bottom tier and geographic South (Asia, Latin America) and simultaneous deindustrialization to what had been the top tier and geographic North (Western Europe, North America, Japan). It created a new set of relations between labor and capital and new relations between low-wage industrial producers of the global South and more affluent consumers of the global North.

Social Dislocations

The turn to a global economy disrupted existing ways of life and virtually everyone on the planet had to adapt their social practices to the new conditions. Given different starting points around the world, however, there was no uniform pattern. A middle-age male autoworker losing a job in Detroit had a different experience than a Korean teenager leaving her village to stitch garments in Seoul. Yet in both cases, the rupture with the past made it difficult to pass on deep-rooted customs and traditions to the next generation.

The greatest dislocations occurred in the global South. To be sure, there were palpable economic gains for peasants moving from the rural countryside to the city. But these improvements often did not make up for the cultural losses that followed broken family ties, urban isolation, and loss of contact with ancestors, an important point among cultures where dead ancestors were an honored part of everyday life. The resulting demoralization sometimes plunged wayward migrants into the underside of city life where a young woman might fall prey to the sex trade, while a young man might join a gang or turn to drugs and crime.

Residents of the global North experienced dislocation of a different sort. The shift from urban manufacturing to a suburban-based service economy had a wrenching effect on families poorly positioned to make the transition. Aging industrial workers, housewives without marketable skills, and victims of racial and sexual discrimination were all left behind. For a place like Detroit, Michigan, where the link between the automobile industry and city was so strong that Americans dubbed it the Motor City, the transformation was as deadly as it was depressing. Between 1980 and 1981 alone, the city lost seven hundred thousand jobs in companies directly or indirectly related to the automobile industry, which forced one in every three residents into public assistance. The tax base collapsed, schools deteriorated, and public health declined. Infant mortality rose to four times the rate of Michigan's suburbs, as did the pollution that causes respiratory illness. Crime and drug use skyrocketed as the youth, mainly African Americans, turned to the underground economy when legitimate avenues for income closed, and its residents, again predominantly African American, existed in isolation under conditions that resembled the worst of any developing country. Detroit's sad condition represented a larger change happening in many of America's cities along its northern corridor.

These new stresses added to long-term social pressures that had been undermining family cohesion for decades. Although marriage remained the preferred form of family life, divorce rates shot up to the point where half of all marriages ended in divorce on both sides of the Atlantic by the early 1980s, leading to a rapid increase of blended and single-parent families. Meanwhile, birth rates declined sharply, falling below the level of reproduction in some places (primarily Eastern Europe and Italy) because of the widespread availability of birth control and freer access to abortion. At the same time, the proportion of births out of wedlock doubled or tripled in many countries between 1970 and 1990.

Dislocations resulting from globalization added another dimension to the crisis of authority that had been unfolding since the late 1960s: the proliferation of therapeutic solutions and authoritarian cults that replaced mainline churches as a balm for spiritual anxieties. Sometimes the two combined, as in the intense if not abusive psychotherapy group known as est, or Erhard Seminar Training, and in doing so revealed the scope of the crisis, not to mention the desperate efforts to reimpose order. But, another example of the response to the crisis of authority, one that received more publicity and reflected the darkest manifestations of the anxieties of the time, was the utopia-turned-death camp in Jonestown, Guyana. Jim Jones, father figure to Americans who abandoned the United States to live communally in the settlement, suffered from paranoid fears of a takeover by the Central Intelligence Agency (CIA), and in 1978 he killed 914 of his own followers with cyanide-laced Kool-Aid in a mass murder–suicide.

Because liberals had been unable to resolve the crisis in authority and the New Left had burned itself out, the conditions were ripe for a new approach. Presenting themselves as the responsible, sober, and patriotic alternative to a society spinning out of control, conservatives took charge. To correct the course, conservatives called for a retreat from the liberal politics of the previous decades and the recovery of all that had been lost in the indulgences of the 1960s. Few could have guessed, however, that an escape from one social malady—the 1960s culture of permissiveness—would pave the way for others: the profligate worship of individualism, consumption, and national strength in the 1980s.

RISE OF CONSERVATISM

By the late 1970s, residents of the United States and several other countries—notably, Britain—began moving to the right. Having passed through the crisis of authority in the late 1960s only to land in a frustrating era of limits in the 1970s, many in the global North were ready to follow conservative promises of a brighter future by returning to a golden past. Three main strands formed this new push for conservatism: cultural conservatism, which focused on restoration of patriarchal authority in the family; economic conservatism, which demanded a return to the supposed free market of yesteryear; and foreign policy conservatives, also called neoconservatives, who sought to restore the national greatness lost in the aftermath of Vietnam. Although tension riddled the three main strands of conservatism, opposition to sixties radicalism, New Deal liberalism, and America's retreat from foreign affairs knit them together.

The election of 1980 was the crucial turning point for conservatives to overtake the old New Deal coalition. When Ronald Reagan took the presidency and his party captured the Senate that year, conservatives celebrated these victories as the start of a new era of Cold War militancy, free-market economics, and Christian values. And as long as things went well overseas with no more fiascos like Vietnam, the conservative coalition remained intact.

The Politics of Religion

Like each contour of the new conservatism, cultural conservatism was part of a world-historical transformation. The prime vehicle for the restoration of patriarchal authority was a global religious revival that took place after 1975. In the face of scientific uncertainty and unsettling social change, fundamentalist clerics from all major faiths reasserted the absolute moral authority of scripture, whether the Koran, the Torah, or the Bible. Because of local circumstances, the worldwide trend of reclaiming traditional faith and customs took different forms. In the Islamic world, strong reactions against the forces of modernization could be found everywhere from Saudi Arabia, where Wahhabi authorities presided over the spiritual center of Mecca, to Indonesia, home of the world's largest Muslim population. Fundamentalist clerics preached a doctrine of purification from the toxic influences of Hollywood and Western consumerism and women's freedom, sometimes requiring women to cloak themselves in the veil (*hijab*) in Islamic communities.

Struggles for political power accompanied the religious revival, especially in the Islamic world where centuries of tradition had linked the mosque and state. But no place was immune to this shift because it was becoming increasingly difficult to separate religion from politics throughout the world, including the United States. Moreover, the efforts of secular leaders such as Nasser in Egypt and the Shah of Iran to keep religion and politics apart had the opposite effect and drove political opposition deeper into the mosque and church. One result was the Islamic Revolution in Iran (see Chapter 11), which produced a theocracy where Ayatollah Khomeini and his successors ruled under Islamic law known as *Sharia*. In Europe, after losing campaigns against the legalization of birth control and abortion in such nominally Catholic countries such as Italy and France and its struggle with Communists in Poland, Pope John Paul II, a native of Poland, brought a new militancy to the Catholic Church's role in the world.

Fundamentalist revival also reshaped politics in the United States. Since the arrival of the Puritans, American Protestantism has gone through cycles of slumbering and awakening. Now evangelicals were awakening again with renewed fervor. Reacting against the relativism and uncertainty built into modern life, the new evangelicals sought refuge in the certainty of moral absolutes. Despite the constitutional separation of church and state as enshrined in the First Amendment, religious conservatives ardently believed that religion belonged in the public square. They burst on the scene in the late 1970s, not as Holy Rollers harvesting souls for eternal salvation as they had in the past, but as the Religious Right determined to save a Christian nation from its sinful ways. In a departure from the narrowness of evangelical Protestants of the past, the Religious Right was willing to work with Roman Catholics.

Cultural Conservatives and Family Values

Armed with Christian conviction, conservatives waged cultural war against what they saw as the permissiveness of the 1960s. The war raged most acutely on the battlefield of sex and the family. Ever since the sexual revolution of the sixties, conservatives had mounted a counterrevolution against the rhetoric of free love, gay rights, and women's liberation in an attempt to restore the traditional family. Although the ideal of the 1950s nuclear family—husband-breadwinner, stay-at-home mom, and two kids—had not existed much before that decade and although demographic and economic trends made it a distinct minority (no more than 20 percent of all families resembled this Rockwellian image by the 1980s), conservatives believed that restoring the patriarchy was the solution to all manner of social ills. To them, this was not misty nostalgia, and the answer was simple: by putting the father back in charge and keeping the mother at home to raise the kids, the United States could reduce immorality, teenage pregnancy, drug use, and even street crime. In this respect, cultural conservatism represented a patriarchal reaction against the dislocations in social relations engendered by the ongoing processes of modern capitalist development and globalization.

Calls for a return to patriarchy revealed an undercurrent in conservative responses to societal ills that sought to gain control over what they saw as anarchy in relations between the sexes. Reverend Jerry Falwell founded the Moral

Majority in 1979, for example, as a movement to fight the Supreme Court's 1973 decision of *Roe v. Wade* upholding abortion. Falwell drew inspiration, in part, from opposition to abortion among Catholic bishops. However, for evangelical Protestants and conservative Catholics alike, feminism was the real enemy.

The greatest political victory of the Religious Right was the defeat of the Equal Rights Amendment (ERA) to the U.S. Constitution by 1979, which would have prohibited all discrimination based on gender. The most articulate leader of the anti-ERA movement was Phyllis Schlafly. A wife, mother, and professional, Schlafly convinced many women that the ERA would wipe out legal protections for housewives and prevent divorced mothers from collecting alimony from ex-husbands. Lawyers argued to the contrary, but Schlafly and the Religious Right effectively subverted the feminist critique of American society by putting a woman's role in the patriarchy at the center of politics. Tradition, masquerading as liberal individualism, became a new political identity, and for Americans fed up with encroachments on their way of life, the conservative message offered a return to the natural ordering of things.

Despite the growing strength of cultural conservatives, rebuilding patriarchal authority was an arduous task. Restoring the *paterfamilias*, or the male, to his place at the head of the family was harder in America's individualistic society than in other places in the world, such as the Bedouin camps of Arabia or the Islamic villages of Iran. Moreover, secular influences remained strong, not least among religious folk themselves. Far from being otherworldly or backward looking, evangelical Christians were very much at home in modern consumer culture. Their Christian theme parks imitated Disneyland, and televangelists such as Falwell, Pat Robertson, and D. James Kennedy could match their late-night talk-show rivals in the hallmarks of mass communication: spectacle and emotion.

Beginning in the 1970s, conservative women like Phyllis Schlafly mounted vigorous opposition to second wave feminism and the Equal Rights Amendment. By the 1980s, the battle against abortion rights caused their numbers to swell and brought together a diverse coalition on the Right that included cultural conservatives, religious traditionalists, and women who rejected the political assumptions of feminism. Library of Congress Prints and Photographs Division, Washington, DC.

Another obstacle to success came from within. In the mid-1980s, the Religious Right almost imploded as the result of moral scandal. Charges of hypocrisy were easy to level against the enterprising Jim and Tammy Faye Bakker, who practiced the very greed they condemned in their sermons, and televangelist Jimmy Swaggart, who gained unwanted notoriety when he was caught in a cheap motel with a prostitute. Like the New Left of the late 1960s, the Religious Right sometimes resembled the very things it opposed.

Although it was plagued by scandals and inconsistencies, the New Right maintained its appeal and popularity. And the extreme rhetoric of true believers such as Pat Robertson, who characterized support for the ERA as "a movement that encourages women to leave their husbands, kill their children, practice witchcraft, destroy capitalism, and become lesbians," proved a powerful driving force for the surging anger. A few zealots even went beyond rhetoric by bombing abortion clinics under the belief it was their mission to save unborn babies.

Yet the Religious Right was not a radical fringe. Like the New Left, it expressed widespread discontent, staked out a strong position in the culture wars, and by comparison to the radicals of the 1960s was far more effective in politics. By 1980, it constituted a key portion of the mass electoral base and led to the triumph of conservative Republicans.

Science and Religion

Large areas of U.S. culture resisted the tide of Christian fundamentalism. Despite the resurgence of religious and spiritual explanations for ultimate reality, secular and scientific thought remained strong in the 1980s. When fundamentalist religion began to challenge Darwinian ideas about evolution and offered creationism or intelligent design as an alternative, there was a strong reaction in favor of Darwin. Although some local schools included the Biblical story of a seven-day creation in elementary science classes, by far the majority of students learned about the Big Bang some fourteen billion years ago. And despite the challenge of religion, the consensus on the scientific method—the testing of hypotheses against observable evidence in repeatable experiments—as the standard for research suggested the underlying strength of secular habits of thought.

The fact that in the 1980s physics was undergoing the most significant new thinking about the nature of the universe since the 1930s also gave science an upper hand. The new turn in physics revolved around the quest for a unified field theory, the holy grail of physics that became Albert Einstein's preoccupation in the last years of his life. The goal was to uncover natural laws that governed both the infinitesimally small world of subatomic forces and the unimaginably large world of an ever-expanding universe. In the 1980s, physicists offered a new *string theory* that purportedly united the tiny realm of quantum mechanics, which relied on Heisenberg's uncertainty principle, and the huge realm of universal time-space that followed from Einstein's theory of relativity (see Chapter 3). Strings, they argued, were loops of shimmering energy that constituted reality itself at both the micro and the macro levels. As if Einstein's theory was not esoteric enough, theorists maintained one could only understand string theory through mathematical equations and not by the traditional means of scientific experiment.

In contrast to Einstein's theory that produced the atom bomb, the concept of strings remained merely a curiosity to the average American. But without any practical application for string theory, even scientists such as Stephen Hawking, who tried to explain mysteries such as why time can only go in one direction toward the future, could not peak popular imagination. Contrary to its dynamism in the first half of the century of the twentieth century, physics at the end of the century was largely meaningful only for physicists.

FREE-MARKET CONSERVATIVES

The second main thread in the conservative surge was a renewed commitment to the free market. Reacting against New Deal liberalism, free-market conservatives promised to liberate private property from the restraints of state regulation and union rules. In what was cleverly dubbed *the revolt of the haves*, corporate leaders and small taxpayers alike rose up at the end of the 1970s in the United States and Britain to demand new policies that would reduce government regulation, cut taxes, and shrink the welfare state. It was odd to see free-market conservatives furious at the system that had made them so wealthy, but their anger spoke to deeply held beliefs that reached back to classical theories about capitalism, ownership, and the meaning of value.

In fact, it was somewhat of a misnomer to call them conservative, because their hostility to the state mirrored the laissez-faire liberalism of the nineteenth century. Properly, then, the new free-market conservatives were actually *neoliberals*. But because they invoked traditional values and sought to preserve the privileges of the wealthy and powerful under the auspices of merit and ownership, they were also properly described as conservatives. The fact that in the 1980s conservatives were neoliberals might be confusing in terminology, since most today consider *conservative* and *liberal* polar opposites. To avoid such discrepancy, it is best to use the term *free-market conservatives*.

For decades at think tanks and universities on both sides of the Atlantic, free-market ideas developed out of intellectual debates about the nature of the economy. Borrowing ideas from Austrian philosopher Friedrich Hayek, economists such as Milton Friedman at the University of Chicago argued against Keynesianism to wage ideological warfare on behalf of monetarism. Under the doctrine of monetarism, the prime economic role of the state is to regulate the money supply and otherwise leave the market to its own devices. Whereas Keynesians believed government should manage consumer demand, monetarists preferred to restrict the supply of money, reduce taxes, deregulate business, and let the market dictate growth through its prices. That was the natural behavior of capitalism, monetarists contended, in a nod to laissez-faire capitalists a century before. Because they worked from the conditions that drive supply in the economy—capital accumulation, technological innovation, improvements in the labor force, and regulatory independence, among other factors—they were lumped together under the label *supply-side economics*. For opponents, the notion was reminiscent of Herbert

Hoover's trickle-down philosophy that served the United States so poorly during the Great Depression.

As elites developed the neoliberal ideas of free-market conservatism, a tax revolt along with calls to end affirmative action rose up from the "crabgrass" roots of suburban America. Responding to oil shocks, stagflation, and tax increases in the 1970s, small property owners grew frustrated with the status quo and turned their anger against government. Invoking the antitax symbols of the American Revolution, California conservatives in 1978 campaigned successfully for a ballot initiative called Proposition 13, limiting tax increases and preventing government spending from rising faster than revenues. Similarly, instead of blaming multinational corporations, disgruntled voters around the country were ready to listen to conservative politicians who blamed government for their troubles. Because many of the beneficiaries of government social programs were African American or Latino, the tax revolt's language of merit, favoritism, and handouts, along with its calls to end affirmative action, concealed distinct racial undertones. In the realm of politics, the economic condition played out in deep-seated cultural animosities held over from the 1970s.

Breakthrough to Power

The trend toward conservatism arrived at roughly the same time in different places. Perhaps the most notable illustration is the 1979 election of Margaret Thatcher as the British prime minister just a year before Ronald Reagan took the U.S. presidency. When Queen Elizabeth asked Thatcher to form a government,

President Ronald Reagan and British Prime Minister Margaret Thatcher ushered in a new era of conservative politics that challenged the assumptions of the post–World War II order of global liberalism. Wikicommons, Ronald Reagan Presidential Library.

Thatcher made history as the first woman to hold the office of prime minister, although she pointedly refused to identify with modern feminism. Instead, to the applause of the media, Thatcher proudly wore the label of Iron Lady and presented herself as a tougher leader than the vacillating men of the Labour Party. As a new breed of uncompromising conservatives, she led Britain's Conservative Party away from the social contract of the welfare state toward laissez-faire. Challenged on her opposition to legislation aimed at a more just society, she unabashedly remarked, "There is no society." Asked what she thought about alternatives to the free market, she flatly replied, "There is no alternative."

Ronald Reagan agreed. One of his favorite one-liners was, "Government is not the solution. It is the problem." Although miles apart in personality—Thatcher was a stern, Methodist grocer's daughter, whereas Reagan was an affable, storytelling former sportscaster and actor—they shared key beliefs about the free market and the evils of Communism, and each played on the cultural symbols of their respective countries. Whereas Thatcher evoked old-fashioned, stiff-upper-lip British tradition, Reagan represented Hollywood illusion (he had gotten his start in radio and gone on to star in B movies), often appearing with the stars and stripes of the U.S. flag breezily waving as a backdrop. If Jimmy Carter's folksy cardigan sweater had represented limits in the 1970s, Nancy Reagan's lavish White House redecoration, complete with a gold-rimmed china set, characterized the symbolic breakthrough to a new limitless frontier. In an era of *infotainment*, where image was reality, Reagan's expert image-makers made him seem the very personification of patriotism.

Conservatism was not confined to Anglo-America. The free-market tide also swept over Western Europe. In France, for example, even the Socialist premier Francois Mitterrand bowed to international pressures and cut back on business regulations and social welfare. Mitterrand, like much of the continental conservatism, however, was less extreme than his Anglo-American counterparts. With the dark memory of Fascism looming overhead, conservative leaders were not prepared to go all the way to laissez-faire. Germany's Helmut Kohl, for example, came to power in 1982 as the leader of the traditionally conservative Christian Democratic Union. But Kohl embraced the Catholic tradition of social solidarity, and as unemployment rose he refused to cut back benefits for fear of encouraging neo-Nazism.

Conservatism in Action

Once in power, conservatives launched a two-prong attack on *big government*. The first arm involved getting rid of what they considered burdensome regulations on business. As Prime Minister Thatcher began to privatize British telecom and other public-owned companies, conservatives in the Carter administration, who had little to sell off, began to deregulate the airline and trucking industries. Similar efforts sprang up in Latin America, where leaders like Chile's Augusto Pinochet, the military leaders who overthrew Salvador

Allende in 1973, and Mexico's president Miguel de la Madrid embraced privatization and deregulation to address economic ills. Meanwhile, monetarists seized the key command post of economic policy in 1979 with Carter's appointment of Paul Volcker as the chair of the Federal Reserve Board. By raising the *discount rate* (the interest rate charged to member banks), Volcker initiated a *tight money* policy that hurt President Carter's reelection bid in 1980, but eventually lowered inflation for his successor. Soon double-digit inflation subsided to a 3–5 percent annual level, allowing bankers and consumers—both of whom hate inflation—much-needed relief.

Taking a giant step forward with Ronald Reagan's election in 1980, conservatives moved quickly to cut taxes. Embracing supply-side theory against the Keynesian demand side, conservatives won approval for a huge cut in corporate and personal income tax rates in the 1981 Tax Act. Included were a series of detailed provisions that transferred the tax burden from corporations to individuals and at the same time reduced tax rates for upper-income individuals from 70 percent to 39 percent, which shifted the burden a second time from the upper ranks to middle- and lower-income earners. Many highly profitable corporations, such as General Electric, paid less in income taxes than their employees because of these changes—some actually received rebates.

Supporters of the supply-side approach alleged that tax cuts would raise revenues by generating new economic activity, a theory that Vice President George Bush had earlier dismissed as *voodoo economics*. In fact, the opposite happened as tax cuts caused the deficit to balloon. Topping $200 billion in 1983, the Reagan administration racked up the largest peacetime deficit to that point in American history. Huge deficits required huge debts, and the United States went deep into credit with overseas lenders. Tax revenues were being collected from ordinary taxpayers and handed over to holders of Treasury bonds, who were typically the kind of affluent investor living in the wealthy suburbs of New York or overseas in Tokyo or Riyadh. Even conservative columnist George Will recognized that the consequence of huge interest payments on the national debt amounted to "a transfer of wealth from labor to capital unprecedented in American history."

Foreign indebtedness was another key factor in America's transfer of wealth. Not since the nineteenth century had Americans borrowed more from foreigners than they loaned out overseas. But by 1985, the United States had become a debtor nation, in fact the world's biggest debtor nation. This was a remarkable reversal of fortune for a country that had emerged from the First World War as the world's biggest creditor nation.

These changes in the flow of capital signaled a power shift to global investors and multinational corporations. Indeed, corporate power rivaled that of national governments. It is true that General Motors and Exxon did not have F-16s (although critics mused that they could hire the U.S. military if they wanted to), but about half of the world's largest economic entities were corporations, whereas the other half were national economies. The shift to free-market conservatism and the removal of many government regulations, environmental standards, and labor guarantees beginning in the Reagan administration revealed corporate influence over the government.

Attack on the Welfare State

Conservatives directed their second arm of attack against the welfare state. As the state grew in size over the twentieth century, it became a kind of system for redistributing wealth, taking from some in the form of taxes and giving to others in the form of spending. Generations of social reformers—Populists, Progressives, New Dealers, and Great Society liberals—had tried to make the system redistribute wealth downward to foster a more equal society, with some success. Now the tide turned against equality. Believing that equality led to inefficiency and stifled innovation, conservatives sought to reverse the reforms and instead promoted policies that favored individual liberty. The main beneficiaries, however, were corporations and the wealthy.

In other words, the Reagan administration threw the redistribution system into reverse. On the taxing side, it shifted the tax burden from corporations and the wealthy to less affluent individuals. On the spending side, it cut the budgets of numerous Great Society programs, including food stamps, housing assistance, and grants to cities (where the bulk of the poor lived). The assault on the working class and the poor happened in both Thatcher's Britain and Reagan's America. Both places were particularly successful in reducing government subsidies for housing assistance and grants to cities (where most of the poor lived), as well as taxed unemployment benefits. Both also witnessed a predictable increase in the population of homeless men and women sleeping in city streets. Outraged at the cruelty toward the most vulnerable members of society, critics lambasted this as "Robin Hood in reverse."

Despite such changes, the basic structure of the welfare state remained intact. Although the conservative assault began dismantling programs aimed at groups deemed "undeserving" after the 1970s, it failed to undo the core elements of the welfare state: Social Security, Medicare, and Medicaid. Likewise, state pensions and the National Health Service in Britain remained intact. It came as a surprise to both sides in the battle over the welfare state when government welfare expenditures held steady through the 1980s at about 11–12 percent of the gross domestic product (GDP) in the United States and twice that level, or 24–27 percent, in Britain. Defenders of the welfare state pointed to a reduction of suffering and its consequent popularity among the general public, whereas critics complained about the demoralizing habit of dependency. Either way, the social safety net, which Americans call the third rail of politics, proved too dangerous for most politicians to touch.

The persistence of the welfare state helps explain why there was so little discontent from the working class, despite facing one of the worst economic conditions since the depression of the 1930s. Although unemployment levels in the

United States briefly reached double digits in 1983 (unemployment was even higher in many parts of continental Europe), there was little sustained protest. Although the American Federation of Labor–Congress of Industrial Organizations mounted the largest protest in its history on Solidarity Day in November 1981, they essentially fell silent thereafter.

Another conservative theme that helped undercut public disaffection was the emphasis on law and order. Because of the passage of laws increasing punishments and requiring mandatory sentences, the rate of incarceration rose in both the United States and Western Europe. Lengthy jail terms were far more common in the United States, where incarceration rates rose from 139 to 297 prisoners per 100,000 between 1980 and 1990. In what some called the age of punishment and others would refer to as the prison–industrial complex, imprisonment was the principle method of containing disorder in the streets and gratifying the conservative need to get tough on crime.

Culture Wars

When added together, all of these changes—reduced government regulation, tax cuts, welfare cuts, and law and order—gave economic conservatives many reasons to feel triumphant in the first Reagan administration. Cultural conservatives, however, had less to cheer about. After their success in blocking the ERA, they were either defeated or stalemated on several fronts, including the one that would stir their most passionate opposition: abortion. Although President Reagan lent the prestige of his office to the antiabortion cause, his heart was clearly not with the moral crusaders. Despite limitations on access enacted in several state legislatures, the original *Roe v. Wade* decision upheld the basic right to an abortion in the first three months of pregnancy, which rankled cultural conservatives.

Sexuality was another contentious issue. Despite objections from the Religious Right to teaching about sexuality in the schools, the extent and frankness of sex education remained well above where it had been in the 1950s. The same was true of pornography. With Attorney General Edwin Meese prodding them on with his 1986 report on obscenity and pornography, moral crusaders sought to remove what they regarded as obscenity from sex magazines and X-rated movies. But their efforts were checked by advocates of free speech and even more effectively by commercial interests that capitalized on sexual desire through the new technology of video tapes (later the Internet) for big profits. Although it outraged cultural conservatives, sex sold well and salacious entertainment blossomed in the age of mass consumption.

Conservatives also failed to stem the tide on the question of America's acceptance of homosexuality. As far back as 1973, the American Psychiatric Association concluded that homosexuality was not a "diagnosable mental disorder," a position officially reaffirmed in 1998 when it faced another round of challenges from the Religious Right. With more and more lesbians and gays coming out, or "out of the closet," as the phrase went, several state legislatures prohibited discrimination on grounds of sexual orientation, and soon positive gay characters began to appear in films and television sitcoms. When some cultural conservatives characterized AIDS as the gay plague and used it as another argument for sexual abstinence before marriage, cultural liberals condemned homophobia and retorted with an emphasis on safe sex.

With losses mounting, the cultural conservative response sometimes looked as futile as if they were trying to stop the advancement of time itself. And when the saxophone-playing Bill Clinton was elected president in 1992, it seemed as if conservatives were losing the culture wars.

RESTORING NATIONAL GREATNESS

The successful rise of conservatism also had to do with their promotion of national greatness and U.S. exceptionalism. Here conservatives enjoyed considerable success, both in launching the largest peacetime military buildup in American history and in renewing enthusiasm for the flag and other patriotic symbols. After the psychologically deflating experience of seeing their countrymen held hostage by Iranian militants in 1979, American voters were eager to restore a sense of American power. In the 1980 election, many embraced Ronald Reagan because he promised to return the United States to Cold War prominence. Reagan used his skills as a master communicator to tap into a set of deep-seated myths that appealed to U.S. pride. His catchphrase "morning in America" touched on the notion of United States as the land of opportunity; his cowboy regalia brought to mind the myth of the frontier; his missionary rhetoric in opposing the "evil empire" of the Soviet Union evoked the messianic image of America as the world savior.

Reagan was not alone in his use of nationalism and imagery. Prime Minister Margaret Thatcher also knew a thing or two about evoking myths of national greatness. In her case, it was the matter of imperial nostalgia that played out in the 1982 Falklands War with Argentina after its military dictatorship made an aggressive play for the island. Fought against the inept and inferior Argentine forces over the strategically insignificant Falkland (Malvinas) Islands in the South Atlantic, British victory rescued Thatcher from possible defeat in the 1983 election. Reagan would have a similar imperial nostalgic victory that year against a Marxist regime in the tiny Caribbean country of Grenada.

Of greater importance was the revival of tensions between the superpowers. Since 1947, there had been several cycles of tension and relaxation in the Cold War. The easing of tensions in the Test Ban Treaty of 1963 had followed the Cuban Missile Crisis of 1961. Then détente followed a growing conflict over Vietnam in the 1970s. Now a new cycle started with rising tension in the early 1980s. The source of America's new hardline stance was a fledgling group of thinkers and policy makers called *neoconservatives*, who were often former liberals or socialists still seething about defeat in Vietnam and the presence of totalitarian regimes, chief among them the Soviet Union. The early 1980s saw a streak of neoconservative anti-Communist saber rattling so pronounced that few at the time could imagine another round of détente after 1985, let alone the end of the Cold War itself.

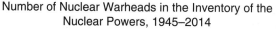

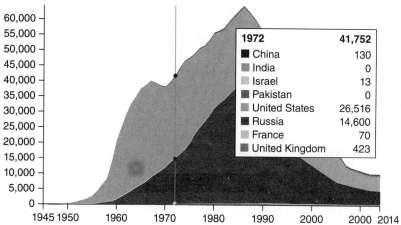

Number of Nuclear Warheads in the Inventory of the
Nuclear Powers, 1945–2014

1972	41,752
■ China	130
▨ India	0
▦ Israel	13
■ Pakistan	0
▨ United States	26,516
■ Russia	14,600
▧ France	70
■ United Kingdom	423

Source: https://ourworldindata.org/nuclear-weapons/

Cold War II

What triggered the latest cycle of Cold War tensions was the 1979 Soviet invasion of Afghanistan. In an effort to maintain its hold on the Soviet sphere of influence in Central Asia and ward off Islamic fundamentalism among his own growing Muslim population, Premier Leonid Brezhnev sent troops to prop up a fragile pro-Soviet regime in Kabul. Meanwhile, to bolster the Soviet position in Europe, Brezhnev introduced a new generation of medium-range, nuclear-tipped SS-20 missiles. President Reagan immediately construed these missiles as Cold War provocations and upped the rhetorical ante. In reality, Reagan needed no prodding to raise the banners of anti-Communism. Having launched his public career in the 1950s on the anti-Communist lecture circuit, Cold War sentiment dividing the forces of good from the forces of evil was natural to him. Now he called the Soviet Union an evil empire and accused them of carrying out "the greatest military buildup in the history of man."

But the words backfired because America's arms buildup under Reagan was bigger than the Soviets'. Indeed, it was the biggest in American peacetime history. What stood out were big-ticket items like the MX missile, cruise missiles, Pershing II intermediate-range missiles (to counter Soviet SS-20s), B-1 bombers, and Trident submarines (technology begun under Carter). Moreover, in 1983 Reagan announced a new Strategic Defense Initiative (SDI), instantly dubbed Star Wars for its proposal to use laser beams as a defensive shield. The Star Wars plan met stark criticism. Arms experts and diplomats outside the administration bashed SDI as Hollywood fantasy and lamented the absence of a sound disarmament program. Some went further and said that even if SDI could become operational, it would violate the 1972 Anti-Ballistic Missile Treaty.

The decision to replace détente with a renewed arms race centered on the power of vested military establishments on both sides. This was especially so as the Soviet economy stagnated. There the military absorbed a huge share of resources, accounting for approximately 12 percent of GDP. For many Soviet citizens, the military was second only to the Communist Party as a path for career advancement. The United States spent handsomely on its military as well. But because America's $4.2 trillion economy was about two and a half times larger than the Soviet economy, its military spending required less of the GDP, roughly 6 percent, and caused fewer visible effects.

There was no doubt that the buildup was a windfall for military industries on both sides of the Cold War. The *military–industrial complex* that President Eisenhower had warned about in his 1961 Farewell Address had greatly expanded in the United States as corporate and state power fused with the arms industry. A long list of major U.S. corporations, including General Electric, Boeing, and McDonnell Douglas, maintained powerful lobbies in Congress and sustained large profits through a steady stream of government contracts. Moreover, numerous corporate executives went through a "revolving door" into government service and back again, including such Reagan-era cabinet officials as Caspar Weinberger and George Shultz, both from Bechtel, a leading construction company with huge military contracts.

Spending for weapons was a notable exception to the rule of monetarism. Leading intellectuals and critics sometimes called the flow of federal funds to private enterprise *military Keynesianism* because deficit spending helped create prosperity by pumping money into the economy that would not otherwise have been in circulation. Some critics pointed out that spending for F-16s and Trident submarines was wasteful and inefficient in comparison to civilian spending, because it produced fewer jobs dollar for dollar and did nothing to raise the standard of living or augment the stock of productive capital. Others also complained that it far exceeded the budget, starting the largest peacetime deficits in the history of the country (until the second Bush and Obama administrations broke the record). Although Keynesians preferred to increase consumer purchasing power through social spending, the fact was that deficits were one of the main tools of Keynesian economics.

COLD WAR IN THE THIRD WORLD

Despite rising tensions, mutual assured destruction barred the two nuclear superpowers from engaging in direct combat. Instead, they continued to confront one another indirectly on Third World battlegrounds. The United States fought its losing battle for empire in Vietnam, and in 1979 it was the Soviet Union's turn in the rugged mountains of Afghanistan.

When the Soviet Union invaded Afghanistan to support its pro-Soviet regime, it triggered a guerrilla war led by Islamic militants known as *mujahideen*, many of whom received their training in Pakistan's *madrassas*, Islamic religious schools. Saudi oil money financed much of the *madrassas*, but the *mujahideen* also received funding from the CIA, which sought to use Islamic militants as proxy soldiers against the Soviets in Central Asia. In hindsight, it is particularly noteworthy that the *mujahideen* included many Arab Afghans, one of whom was the renegade member of the Saudi royal family named Osama bin Laden. Later, that same man, Osama bin Laden, would turn his wrath on the United States and launch a series of strikes that culminated in the September 11, 2001, attacks on the World Trade Center and the Pentagon.

Africa was another Third World battleground of the Cold War. After the demise of European colonialism, several Socialist or Marxist regimes had come to power in the 1970s while the United States was preoccupied in Vietnam. Now, the Reagan administration provided clandestine assistance to counterrevolutionary movements, such as the National Union for the Total Independence of Angola forces led by Jonas Savimbi. In addition, the Reagan administration supported the white supremacist Afrikaner regime in South Africa, while the Soviets aided the armed struggle of the African National Congress, whose aim was to overthrow apartheid and institute a nonracial democracy.

Central America was also the scene of violent conflict exacerbated by the Cold War policies of both sides. In Guatemala, a ruthless dictatorship, successor to the regime installed by the 1954 CIA-backed coup, waged bloody war against its own people, especially the indigenous population of Quiche Indians. In nearby El Salvador, another U.S.-backed regime relied on "death squads" to suppress leftist guerrillas, the Farabundo Martí National Liberation Front, through a campaign of assassination that swept up Catholic priests and nuns as collateral casualties.

In Nicaragua, leftist rebels turned the tables on U.S.-backed leaders after the 1979 revolution threw out the brutal Somoza dictatorship and brought the leftist

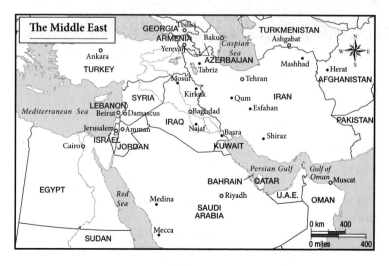

MAP 12.1

Sandinistas to power. Like Lyndon Johnson in the Dominican Republic and Richard Nixon in Chile, high officials in the Reagan administration refused to accept "another Castro" in the Western Hemisphere, and soon the CIA was mobilizing disgruntled supporters of the Somoza regime to become counterrevolutionaries, or *Contras*. This provoked a battle with Congress, which recoiled from the idea of subverting a freely elected foreign government, and in response the Congress passed the Boland Amendment in 1984 cutting off funds for the Contras. Faced with a law it did not like, the Reagan administration simply broke the law by securing funding from conservative U.S. allies in the developing world. Reagan's secret support for the Contras was one aspect of the complicated tangle of events that later played out publicly as the Iran–Contra scandal.

The Iran–Contra Scandal

The Iran–Contra scandal was an incredible story of secrecy and intrigue on the part of an imperial presidency unwilling to accept the limits of the law or the Constitution. The scandal connected the two Third World nations of Iran and Nicaragua on opposite sides of the globe. Beginning with U.S. policy in the Middle East, the scandal led to Reagan's secret support for the Contras in Nicaragua. Since the 1979 Islamic Revolution, Americans had been unwelcome in Iran, and militant Islamic groups took several Americans hostage in Lebanon in protest against U.S. support for Israel. Nonetheless, the National Security Council and the CIA created a plan to provide arms to the Iranians, believing that the Iranian mullahs could influence their friends in Lebanon and win the release of American hostages. The original suggestion for the bizarre scheme came from Israel's secret intelligence agency, Mossad. The first shipment of arms to Iran, in fact, came from Israel in August 1985. Subsequent sales of Hawk and TOW missiles came directly from Pentagon stocks.

Reagan faced a significant problem, however, because the arms sale was illegal. Moreover, the State Department had designated Ayatollah Khomeini's Iran a state sponsor of terrorism, placing any dealings with the mullahs clearly outside the law. Thus, the Reagan administration had to keep the arms-for-hostages deal secret, even from the normal supervisors of CIA covert operations.

This secret arms deal took place in the context of a full-scale war between Iran and Iraq in which the United States gave aid to both sides. The war began when Iraq's dictator, Saddam Hussein, invaded neighboring Iran in an effort to take advantage of turmoil in the Islamic Republic, gain control of the strategic Shatt al-Arab waterway, and expand his power in the region. Other conservative Arab states and U.S. allies in the region, such as Saudi Arabia, feared the Islamic revolution in Iran and encouraged Saddam's invasion. In this conflict, the Reagan administration supplied arms to Ayatollah Khomeini, while also providing intelligence and logistical support to Saddam Hussein. Like the Israelis, Reagan officials apparently wanted to use each side as a check on the other in hopes of maintaining access to Persian Gulf oil.

The two parts of the story came together when a lower-level National Security Office lieutenant, Colonel Oliver North, arrived at the clever idea to use the profits from the Iranian arms sales to fund the Contras in Nicaragua. Here was a way to swindle the Iranians and circumvent the will of Congress at the same time.

The tangled web of deception finally began to unravel in the fall of 1986 when Nicaraguans shot down a CIA operative's plane and stories of the arms deals began to appear in the Arabic press. Despite early denials and further deception, a combination of separate efforts that included a Senate investigation, press reporting, and a Justice Department probe gradually exposed the truth. As matters unfolded, a story that seemed pure fiction or conspiracy turned out to be shockingly true.

The Iran–Contra affair resulted in the conviction of over a dozen Reagan administration officials, although few actually served prison terms. The courts reversed some convictions on technicalities, and George H. W. Bush pardoned several others, including Secretary of Defense Caspar Weinberger in 1989 when he moved into the White House. Evidently, the age of punishment did not extend to high officials of the government. Nor was the president himself brought to justice. Although a bevy of legal opinions held that Reagan's infractions of the law and his breach of constitutional checks and balances were more serious than anything that compelled Richard Nixon to resign, Reagan escaped censure and impeachment.

Why? The answer probably has to do with the mood among policy makers and political leaders. Conservatives were on a mission to restore authority, not undermine it, and neither Republicans nor Democrats had the stomach for another wrenching blow to presidential leadership. Unlike the paranoid and vengeful Nixon, Reagan's affable personality spared him the popular outrage prevalent in the 1970s. Reagan's ability to avoid criticism caused some to call him the Teflon president, after DuPont's popular synthetic coating that boasted similar nonstick properties. In any event, Reagan's escape from accountability signaled the return of the imperial presidency, that is, an executive with a free hand in foreign policy.

Liberal Response to Conservative Ascendancy

Increasingly driven from the center of power, liberals fought from behind against the conservative advances. After the initial shock of seeing a Hollywood actor become president, liberals and radicals regrouped to mount vigorous protests. Labor also briefly came back to life. When Reagan fired the striking Professional Air Traffic Controllers in 1981, the American Federation of Labor–Congress of Industrial Organizations woke from its long slumber to organize America's all-time biggest labor march, some four hundred thousand strong, on Solidarity Day in the fall of 1981. But these kinds of popular rallies had little effect on the growing militarization and rise of corporate power in the Reagan years.

Critics of U.S. foreign policy were nonetheless active on several fronts. Strong reaction against U.S. intervention overseas led to a national movement in solidarity with popular movements in Central America, a spirit reflected in congressional passage of the Boland Amendment. Likewise, in the face of Reagan's constructive engagement with the Afrikaner regime in South Africa, a vibrant antiapartheid and divestment movement developed. Joining forces with European allies, the coalition scored a victory reminiscent of the civil rights period with the release of Nelson Mandela, the leader of the African National Congress, in 1990 after more than two decades in prison.

Popular discontent made its way into politics in the United States coalescing around the 1984 and 1988 campaigns of Jesse Jackson for president. As a Baptist minister and former aid to Dr. Martin Luther King Jr., Jackson represented a progressive religious alternative to the Religious Right. Especially in his second "Run, Jesse, Run" campaign of 1988, Jackson rallied what he called "the democratic wing of the Democratic Party" into a rainbow coalition that included Progressive labor, feminists, and other social activists. Although his voting base lay among African Americans, Jackson's protest message appealed to many Rust Belt workers and hard-pressed farmers, who surprised everyone by handing victories to Jackson in Democratic Party primaries in Michigan and Iowa before he went on to lose the nomination to Michael Dukakis, the liberal governor of Massachusetts. Jackson's coalition was a sign that Progressive ideas were still very much alive in the Reagan era.

PEACE MOVEMENT AND RENEWAL OF DÉTENTE

The one area where popular movements did gain traction in the higher circles was nuclear disarmament. The renewal of Cold War tension produced an opposing reaction from supporters of disarmament. Alarmed by Reagan's nuclear saber rattling, perhaps one million peaceful protesters poured into the streets of New York on June 12, 1982. This stands as the single largest mass demonstration in U.S. history, bigger even than massive marches of the Vietnam era. Meanwhile, across the Atlantic, the European nuclear disarmament movement mobilized large protests against medium-range Soviet SS-20s and U.S. Pershing missiles stationed on European soil. The aim of both events was to get the superpowers to drop all plans for new weapons with the hopes it would lead to actual arms reduction. That did not materialize in 1982, but the transatlantic nuclear freeze movement, as it was called, demonstrated that peace activism was still viable in the West.

Especially in Europe, peace campaigners were out to dismantle not only nuclear missiles but also the whole apparatus of the Cold War. Toward that end, they reached into the Soviet sphere of influence to forge links with east European dissidents. Andrei Sakharov, a renowned Soviet physicist who turned against the Kremlin for both its nuclear and its repressive social policies, embodied these alliances. In fact, dissension was rising in East Germany, where Democracy Now would soon mobilize mass protests against Soviet occupation, and in Czechoslovakia, where the Charter of 77 cracked open the door of free speech that a Soviet backlash had closed since the 1968 Prague Spring.

Nearly one million people crammed themselves into New York City's Central Park in 1982 to protest nuclear weapons. The nuclear freeze movement, as one its organizers, Dr. Randall Caroline Forsberg, called it, revived the antinuke and peace protests of the late 1940s and 1950s and directed its critique at Reagan's aggressive Cold War politics.

Although far from the levers of power, these political movements helped shaped the political climate for disarmament. Ronald Reagan and his top national security officials had entered office talking glibly of fighting and winning a nuclear war. But Reagan was eager to please his audience, and as crowds of antinuclear demonstrators grew larger, he began proclaiming publicly that "a nuclear war cannot be won and must never be fought." He even went so far as to declare, "To those who protest against nuclear war, I can only say: 'I'm with you!'"

Gorbachev and Reagan

Yet, it was not Reagan who took the initiative in reversing the nuclear arms race, but his Soviet counterpart, Mikhail Gorbachev. Born in 1931 and baptized in the Russian Orthodox Church, Gorbachev was educated at Moscow State University, where he became familiar with the whole tradition of Western philosophy, not just orthodox Marxism. When three predecessors died in rapid succession, Gorbachev unexpectedly emerged as the youngest premier in Soviet history and soon began to impress everyone with his calls for new thinking. Like John Kennedy's New Frontier, Gorbachev's new thinking aimed at breaking free of the status quo, in this case the Brezhnev era of stagnation. In one of the favorite metaphors of Soviet ideologues, the Soviet Union was supposed to be the locomotive of history.

If so, it was clear the locomotive was running out of steam in the 1980s. As economic stagnation worsened, a joke went around Polish shipyards and Russian factories: "We pretend to work and they pretend to pay us." Determined to overcome stagnation, Gorbachev sought to revitalize the Soviet economy through a combination of *perestroika* (restructuring) and *glasnost* (openness).

To find breathing room at home, Gorbachev began to push for a revival of détente. Echoing the main message of the peace movement going back to the First World War, he summed up the urgency of global interdependence with a vivid mountain-climber metaphor: "All peoples are similar to climbers roped together on the mountainside. They either can climb together to the summit or fall together into the abyss." For supporting arguments, he turned to the international scientific community. Among the many groups of scientists that provided expert testimony on both sides of the Atlantic, two were rewarded with Nobel Prizes, the International Physicians for the Prevention of Nuclear War in 1985 and a group with the homely name of Pugwash in 1995.

Reagan surprised everyone, perhaps even himself, by responding positively to Gorbachev's initiatives. Part of the reason involved concern among fiscal conservatives in his administration about unprecedented budget deficits. The other part had to do with repairing a reputation damaged by the unfolding Iran–Contra scandal and revelations of administration corruption. Thinking of his historical legacy in the second term, the arch–Cold Warrior reversed himself and decided to see Gorbachev not as a mortal enemy, but as a partner for peace.

The two leaders met in Geneva in November 1985 for the first in a series of summits that marked the renewal of détente. At Geneva, the two sides agreed in principle on a 50 percent reduction in strategic forces. In an aside to the Soviet premier, Reagan whispered, "I bet the hardliners in both our countries are squirming." Hardliners may have squirmed, but the rest of the world sat transfixed over the next few years as the unexpectedly convivial mood launched the détente phase in the by-now familiar cycle of tension and relaxation in superpower relations.

End of the Cold War

No one at the time imagined this was the beginning of the end of the Cold War, but it was. Even more stunning developments were in store at the next summit in Reykjavik, Iceland, in October 1986. Under different conditions, the meeting of the United States and Soviet Union in Iceland to discuss their frigid Cold War relations might have been the basis of a terrific pun. But when Reagan journeyed to meet Gorbachev, it was no laughing matter.

After dismissing their respective expert advisers, the two leaders huddled for private discussion on how to get beyond the doctrine of mutual assured destruction. As they talked, the answer seemed obvious: a zero option on the total elimination of nuclear weapons. For one moment, the two most powerful leaders in the world gravitated toward the peace movement's utopian vision of a world free from the menace of nuclear annihilation.

The moment did not last long. Negotiations stalled over Reagan's unshakable commitment to SDI. Reagan and Gorbachev hesitated just long enough for their respective advisors to jump in with reminders that deterrence, not elimination, was what maintained the Cold War order. Yet, although the press judged the summit a failure, there was an ironic effect: it was in the land of ice that the Cold War began to warm.

Although the grand vision of the zero option quickly disappeared, détente moved forward with a landmark agreement eliminating U.S. Pershings, Soviet SS-20s, and other intermediate-range missiles. Momentum continued at the next summit in Washington in December 1987. Having grown comfortable in each other's company (unlike their wives, Nancy and Raisa, who like the United States and the USSR remained distant), the two leaders beamed while putting their signatures on a historic pact eliminating the entire class of medium- and short-range missiles. Since Europe was the most likely battleground for these Hiroshima-size bombs, Europeans celebrated the agreement as the beginning of a new era. And more was on the way. In an increasingly desperate effort to revive the Soviet economy, Gorbachev implemented *perestroika* by redirecting military resources toward civilian needs. At their last summit in Washington in 1988, Gorbachev announced the unilateral decision to reduce Soviet troop strength by five hundred thousand, mostly in Eastern Europe, with corresponding reductions in tanks and artillery over the next two years. He coupled this with the withdrawal of troops from Afghanistan and decreases in aid to Marxist regimes in Cuba and Angola. By this time, it was becoming clear that new thinking signaled a retreat for Soviet empire.

Some in the United States refused to believe what they were witnessing. Cold War hardliners or hawks, like Robert Gates and Richard "Dick" Chaney, rejected the notion that America could trust Gorbachev and Russia's new thinking, calling Gorbachev's actions a ploy. Bush, however, was convinced otherwise. "Look," he told his advisers, "this guy *is* perestroika." The world would witness just how far Gorbachev was willing to go with his new thinking on self-determination within the Soviet sphere in Germany.

One of the final acts of the Cold War drama took place on the island of Malta in the Mediterranean. In early December 1989, Gorbachev and Reagan's successor, George H. W. Bush, confirmed what was increasingly evident to the world:

The February 1987 Washington Summit between Ronald Reagan and Mikhail Gorbachev resulted in one of the visible signs that the Cold War was coming to an end—the Intermediate-Range Nuclear Forces Treaty.
National Archives at College Park–Still Pictures (RDSS).

the threat of nuclear war was diminishing because the United States and the Soviet Union no longer regarded each other as mortal enemies. At Malta, they struck a gentlemen's (meaning informal) agreement that the United States would not intervene in the independence efforts cropping up throughout central Europe if Russia ruled out the use of force in its response. The Malta agreement only affirmed what Bush already thought about Russia's new leader. Although economic troubles and fears of dislocation eroded Gorbachev's popularity at home, he ascended to the pinnacle of world esteem. On a visit to China in the midst of Chinese students' campaign for democracy in June 1989, the Soviet leader was greeted as a patron of democracy. Hailed by *Time* magazine as the man of the decade, he was awarded the Nobel Prize for peace in 1990. Not since Woodrow Wilson had a single figure come to symbolize hope for a better world the way Gorbachev captured the world's imagination as the Cold War came to an end.

Assessing the Cold War

What can be said in assessment of the Cold War? First, there is no doubt the Cold War had a major impact on world history. During the long period of tension between the two superpowers lasting from 1947 to 1989, the Cold War triggered several "hot" wars, took millions of lives, cost trillions of dollars, and otherwise shaped life for everyone on the planet. From the perspective of both sides, the world seemed to be a permanent battle between West and East, us and them, capitalists and Communists. Each imperial center rallied clients and allies to its side in great alliance systems—NATO and the Warsaw Pact—and each side engaged in bruising ideological combat, constructing an image of its own virtue against the others' imputed vice. While the Americans counterposed their freedom and affluence to Soviet totalitarianism and privation, the Soviets, for their part, compared their equality and industry against American imperialism and racism. The mentality of each side resembled the Manichaean vision in ancient Christianity of a world divided between good and evil.

The real world never conformed to this simple bipolar model. For one thing, the relation was not symmetrical. The West's economic superiority more than offset the greater land mass and raw numbers in the East. Another complicating factor was the Third World. Newly emerging countries in Asia and Africa often refused to join either the first world of the capitalist West or the second world of the Socialist East and instead became an influential third force of their own. Nor were the blocs themselves monolithic. By the early 1960s, the Chinese had split from their Russian comrades and were competing for leadership of the Third World. Finally, relations between the Cold War empires cycled through periods of confrontation and relaxation, reaching their most dangerous point in the early 1960s in frightening confrontations over Berlin and Cuba, only to move in and out of relaxation in the decades that followed.

What brought about the end of the Cold War? Some attribute it to Reagan's military buildup in the early 1980s, which gave the Soviets a choice of further bankrupting their economy in a futile effort to match the West's superior technology or throwing in the towel. But it seems just as likely that when relations soured between the United States and the USSR, effectively halting détente in the 1970s, Reagan's buildup and muscular Cold War rhetoric might have forced the two sides back to the negotiation table. Others, however, highlight problems internal to the Soviet system itself. A rapid succession of leaders following the death of Leonid Brezhnev, a disastrously inefficient bureaucracy, a failing economy, and a generational shift that welcomed the innovations of the West and the chance to participate in the globalization trend all undermined the relevance and credibility of the Soviet system. Still other observers pointed to the risky strategy of Mikhail Gorbachev. His symbiosis with the changes already unfolding in the Soviet Union challenged the idea that Reagan and Bush won the Cold War. Social movements also played an important role. Dissidents in the Soviet bloc, like the Polish trade union federation, Solidarity; environmentalists who wanted to save the world, East and West; Pope John Paul II and the Catholic Church, who called for an end to the wasteful arms race; and countercultural movements worldwide who preferred Hollywood and rock 'n' roll to militarism—all helped bring about change. The influence of social movements goes back even further than that, however. In protesting the U.S. war in Vietnam, the Soviets in Afghanistan, and the nuclear arms race, peace movements on both sides set limits on elites and created a popular base of support for ending the conflict.

End of Soviet Empire

The end of the Cold War was bound up with the collapse of the Soviet empire. Even as late as the beginning of the fateful year of 1989, no one saw this coming. Nowhere did the boundary between East and West seem more permanent than in Eastern Europe. Along what Churchill had first dubbed the Iron Curtain in 1946, the Soviets had built the Berlin Wall, suppressed a series of popular rebellions (East Germany in 1953, Hungary in 1956, Czechoslovakia in 1968), and cut off trade and cultural exchange with the West, all in the name of building a self-contained Communist system. Cowed by the secret police epitomized by the notorious Stasi in East Germany, the peoples of Eastern Europe had fallen into a mood of sullen resignation. Yet resignation to the status quo was not the same as consent. Moscow's suppression of the forces of liberalization only drove east Europeans into deeper opposition. Like most people under foreign rule, they withheld their consent to a system they deemed illegitimate.

For their part, leaders in the West had also come to accept a divided Europe. They abandoned the idea of a rollback of Communism with the 1975 Helsinki Accords and even went so far as to prop up satellite regimes with loans totaling $66 billion by 1980. Although Ronald Reagan revived the rhetoric of rollback in pointing to Berlin and calling on the Soviets to "tear down that wall!" no one expected him to do any more than his Cold War predecessors to actually tear down the wall or the Soviet system.

But history is littered with the rubble of seemingly permanent arrangements. Eastern Europe under the Soviets was like a tree that was solid on the outside but rotting at the core. Economic stagnation was pervasive. The global economic slowdown that began in the early 1970s was especially severe in the Eastern bloc, where annual GDP growth rates plummeted from nearly 5 percent in the early 1970s to 1.4 percent in the early 1980s. In the West, the slowdown was accompanied by inflation, but since prices were controlled by the state in the East, Soviet and neighboring consumers faced shortages instead. The frustration of waiting in an occasional gas line in the West was nothing compared to the daily frustration of lining up for hours to get the meat and soap that was often gone from the shelves by the time the customer reached the counter.

When mass discontent finally erupted in 1989, it went far beyond anything that had happened in 1968, the last moment of worldwide upheaval. A foretaste of popular protest came with the outbreak of shipyard strikes in Poland in 1980 led by the trade union known as *Solidarnosc* (Solidarity), which garnered strong support from the Polish-born Pope John Paul II. Despite martial law and other setbacks, the Polish movement succeeded in 1989 in bringing the first non-Communist government to Eastern Europe since the late 1940s. By that time, popular movements were knocking down the Iron Curtain everywhere from the Baltics to the Balkans.

Key to the success of the movements from below was a change in Moscow. Unlike his predecessors in 1968, Gorbachev adopted a policy of nonintervention. Wishing to avoid what scholars call the Khrushchev dilemma, after Khrushchev's use of Soviet troops to halt liberalization in Hungary in 1956, and China's massacre of a thousand protestors at Tiananmen Square in June 1989, Gorbachev took a softer approach. In the absence of Soviet tanks, communist regimes fell like a string of dominoes, with the Velvet Revolution in Czechoslovakia and the spectacular breaching of the Berlin Wall in November 1989 that led to the collapse of the East German government. There were bloody exceptions to this peaceful transit, however. One happened within the Soviet Union in April, when the military crushed mass demonstrations in Tbilisi, killing nineteen people. The other occurred when the Nicolae Ceausescu government in Romania collapsed in December 1989, following his attempts to put down protesters who defied his regime. The tragic scene played out in a hail of bullets from battles that pitted Ceausescu security forces against the army and Romanian citizens. His government came to a violent end, and the new Romanian leadership summarily executed Ceausescu and his wife on Christmas Day.

When the dust settled, the Soviet empire ended. Along with the loss of Eastern Europe, Gorbachev bowed to the inevitable and withdrew the last Soviet troops in 1989 from further humiliation in the mountains of Afghanistan. In truth, empire had been an anachronism all along. The empire of the hammer and sickle was a doomed effort to recreate the tsarist empire of the black eagle at a time when the tides of world history were running strongly against colonial rule. Not even the rulers believed in empire any longer. And so the Soviets joined the

Habsburgs, Hohenzollerns, Ottomans, British, French, Spanish, and Portuguese in the list of fallen empires. One question remained: What would be the fate of the United States, which shifted from empire to hegemony and back during the Cold War? (See Chapter 14.)

Collapse of the Soviet Union

Following the collapse of the Soviet empire, even more astonishing things were in store for the Soviet Union itself. Gorbachev had introduced *perestroika* and *glasnost* in the mid-1980s with the intention of reforming, not overthrowing, the Communist system. But events slipped out of control, and after bidding farewell to empire in Eastern Europe, Gorbachev was unable to prevent the disintegration of the Soviet Union itself at the end of 1991. Top heavy, overcentralized, and unable to deliver the goods, the closed system ultimately fell apart because it lacked a popular base of support. Following the example of Poles and Hungarians, most of the ethnic groups that comprised the USSR—Lithuanians, Ukrainians, Kazaks, and Georgians—wanted out. By the end of 1991, about the only ones left in the new Russian Federation were ethnic Russians.

The collapse of Communism marked the conclusion of a failed experiment in alternatives to capitalism. Because history is usually written by the victors, it becomes increasingly difficult to remember the central role that Communism played in all the major events of the twentieth century. Beginning with the Bolshevik Revolution in 1917, Communists staked out a position to which everyone had to react, whether positively or negatively. In the 1930s and 1940s, the Communist alternative was a goad to Western leaders to reform capitalism before it was too late. As a polarizing presence, Communism drew fire from Socialists and liberals, and anti-Communism was at the heart of German Fascism. At its height in the early 1950s, perhaps a third of humanity lived under Communist rule, and the presence of powerful Communist regimes in the Soviet Union and China divided the world into the Communist and capitalist camps of the Cold War.

Because it played such a pivotal role, some observers thought the collapse of Communism marked the end of history. Inverting the Marxist dialectic in which capitalism was supposed to evolve into Communism, they cheered when it went the other way. The counterrevolution to overthrow the Bolsheviks that had begun in 1917 had finally triumphed. Crowing over the victory of capitalist democracy, Anglo-American conservatives argued that the search for a more egalitarian alternative to capitalist democracy was over and that the liberal, free-market side of the Enlightenment was now the only game in town.

CONCLUSION

As in every major moment of change, the end of the Cold War resolved old conflicts and disclosed new ones. The forty-five-year contest between the two superpowers was resolved very much in favor of the United States and its allies and

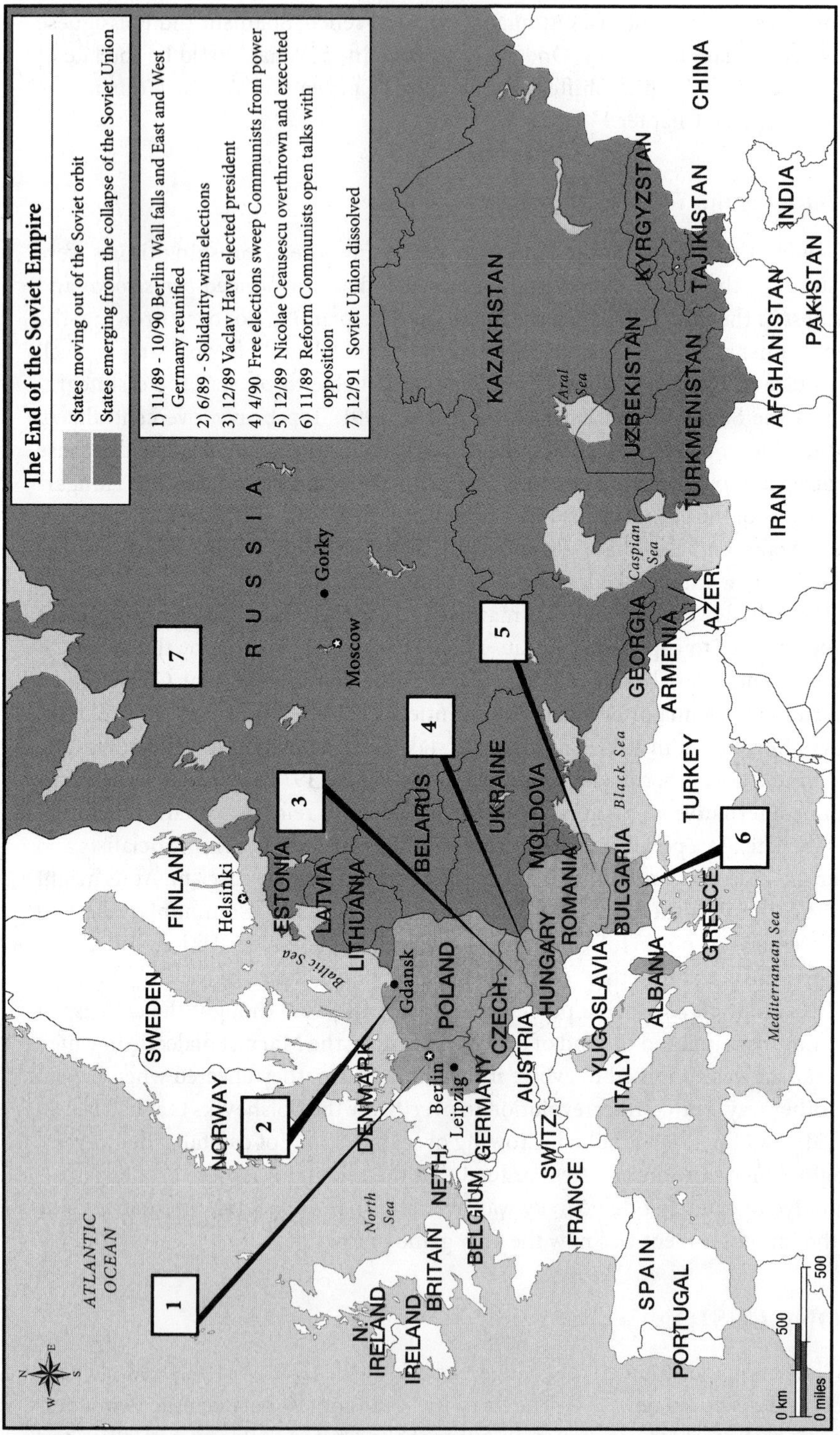
The End of the Soviet Empire
States moving out of the Soviet orbit
States emerging from the collapse of the Soviet Union
1) 11/89 - 10/90 Berlin Wall falls and East and West Germany reunified
2) 6/89 - Solidarity wins elections
3) 12/89 Vaclav Havel elected president
4) 4/90 Free elections sweep Communists from power
5) 12/89 Nicolae Ceausescu overthrown and executed
6) 11/89 Reform Communists open talks with opposition
7) 12/91 Soviet Union dissolved
ATLANTIC OCEAN
North Sea
Baltic Sea
Black Sea
Caspian Sea
Aral Sea
Mediterranean Sea
R U S S I A
Moscow
Gorky
KAZAKHSTAN
UZBEKISTAN
TURKMENISTAN
KYRGYZSTAN
TAJIKISTAN
CHINA
INDIA
PAKISTAN
AFGHANISTAN
IRAN
AZER.
ARMENIA
GEORGIA
TURKEY
UKRAINE
MOLDOVA
BELARUS
ESTONIA
LATVIA
LITHUANIA
FINLAND
Helsinki
SWEDEN
NORWAY
DENMARK
POLAND
Gdansk
Berlin
Leipzig
GERMANY
CZECH.
HUNGARY
ROMANIA
BULGARIA
YUGOSLAVIA
ALBANIA
GREECE
AUSTRIA
SWITZ.
ITALY
FRANCE
BELGIUM
NETH.
BRITAIN
N. IRELAND
IRELAND
SPAIN
PORTUGAL
0 km
500
0 miles
500
1
2
3
4
5
6
7

MAP 12.2

clients. Conservative triumph removed from the historical agenda any thought of abolishing capitalist property in the name of the proletariat along the lines of the Communist workers states of the East. In the West, conservatism reversed decades of social democratic efforts to incorporate modern industrial workers into the machinery of state through a social contract involving union recognition and the welfare state.

But as the quest for equality gave way to the celebration of liberty, both individual and corporate, actual inequalities of wealth and power became more extreme. Once obscured by the Cold War, globalization and its discontents came into view. As the clash between East and West dissipated, tensions only increased between the global North and the global South, between rich societies and poor societies. The central place of the United States in the process of globalization is the topic of the next chapter.

FURTHER READING

Bacevich, Andrew. *American Empire: The Realities and Consequences of US Diplomacy.* Cambridge, MA: Harvard University Press, 2002.

Cannon, Lou. *President Reagan: The Role of a Lifetime.* New York: PublicAffairs, 2000.

Cooper, Barry, Allan Kornberg, and William Mishler, eds. *The Resurgence of Conservatism in Anglo-American Democracies.* (Durham, NC: Duke University Press, 1988.

Cowie, Jefferson. *Capital Moves: RCA's Seventy-Year Quest for Cheap Labor.* Ithaca, NY: Cornell University Press, 1999.

Evangelista, Matthew. *Unarmed Forces: The Transnational Movement to End the Cold War.* Ithaca, NY: Cornell University Press, 1999.

Garthoff, Raymond. *The Great Transition: American–Soviet Relations and the End of the Cold War.* Washington, DC: Brookings Institution, 1994.

Grandin, Greg. *Empire's Workshop: Latin America, the United States, and the Rise of New Imperialism.* New York: Holt, 2006.

Mazower, Mark. *Dark Continent: Europe's Twentieth Century.* New York: Knopf, 1999.

Rodgers, Daniel T. *Age of Fracture.* Cambridge, MA: Harvard University Press, 2011.

Zubok, Vladislav. *A Failed Empire: The Soviet Union in the Cold War from Stalin to Gorbachev.* Chapel Hill: University of North Carolina Press, 2007.

CHAPTER 13

THE UNITED STATES AS GLOBAL LEADER, 1990–99

Michael Jackson played fourteen concerts in Japan on his way to a world tour that took him to fifteen countries over the span of a year and four months. The tour was so successful it would set Guinness World Records and establish pop—both the music and the soft drink—in the global mainstream. Getty Pictures.

MICHAEL JACKSON IN JAPAN

> *In September 1987, the American pop singer Michael Jackson arrived at Narita airport outside Tokyo to kick off his first solo world tour for his album, Bad. Japanese media hyped his visit with the headlines, "Michael Typhoon Lands*

Today," and some three hundred thousand fans—many of them screaming teenage girls who paid scalpers as much as seven hundred dollars for a ticket—welcomed Jackson. Pepsi-Cola and Nippon Telephone and Telegraph, which intended to cash in on the performer's all-time best-selling record album, *Thriller*, underwrote the tour, and as expected, it sold out. The Jackson effect was widespread. Lured by his phenomenal success, in fact, Japan's Sony Corporation purchased the American company CBS Records the following year in a deal worth $2 billion.

By the time he arrived in Japan, Jackson was probably the world's best-known entertainer. As the Elvis Presley of his era, Michael Jackson attracted fans with his trademark dance steps, most notably his gravity-defying move, the moonwalk, his sparkling rhinestone glove, and his eccentric lifestyle. Trained in the Motown music system, where owner Berry Gordy combined the raw emotion of the black Jim Crow South experience with the driving rhythms of Detroit's northern industrial condition, Jackson was a childhood prodigy who mastered the stage and art before the age of fifteen. Along with four of his brothers (including his youngest brother, Randy, in some cases), Michael Jackson defined mainstream American music for generations that passed from R&B in the 1960s to disco in the 1970s to pop in the 1980s.

As his career took off in the 1980s, Jackson built the lavish Peter Pan–esque compound, Neverland, just as Presley had built Graceland as a glitzy monument to himself. And like Elvis, who became addicted to drugs, Jackson went into a tailspin after his hit 1991 album *Dangerous*. His finances grew shaky. He settled a child molestation suit out of court, only to face a similar charge later. And, to draw the unusual connection to Elvis even tighter, he married (and soon divorced) Presley's daughter, Lisa Marie.

All along, Jackson remained an enigma. Raised as an African American, he kept changing his image by bleaching his skin, straightening his hair, and shrinking his nose. He was a confection of images: neither black nor white, male nor female, American nor anything else. Despite the socially tinged titles of some of his biggest hits, like "Black or White" and "Heal the World," his body seemed a deliberate evasion of the main public issues of the day: corporate power, racial difference, and world poverty.

Since his death on June 25, 2009, at the age of fifty, Jackson's popularity and mystery have only grown. Tens of millions worldwide gathered around the television for three hours to watch the spectacle of his memorial and burial, and Nielsen reported that eighteen channels simulcast the event. Record companies rushed to release a sketchy collection of studio recordings as his last album, and video games, such as *Michael Jackson: The Experience*, immortalized him as an interactive avatar. In death as in life, Jackson continues to raise profound questions about the modern condition, most notably for the United States and globalization: Does his life, and even his death, represent the epitome of the new global citizen and identity? Was Jackson's celebrity and ubiquity a form of power? As national borders dissolve and technologies bind strangers closer together, could everyone expect to tap into some measure of Jackson's experience?

THE U.S. ROLE IN GLOBALIZATION

Few things illustrate the interconnection between Americanization and globalization better than the worldwide popularity of American entertainers. By century's end, the Internet, digitization, and virtualization made worldwide interconnectedness a shorthand for globalization, and the circuits of world history tied in everyone on the planet, except for a handful of Amazonian tribes, New Guinea hunter-gatherers, and Siberian herders. At the same time, greater awareness that everyone shared in a common human destiny did not mean everyone was the same. Divisions heightened even as global trends brought distant peoples into close contact. The convergence of societies around the world produced a single global system, but one internally divided in multiple ways by class, region, and culture, among other things.

The United States played a key role. Emerging after the Cold War as the lone superpower—in fact, a hyperpower "that is dominant or predominant in all categories," as the French foreign minister Hubert Vedrine once charged—the United States led the world toward a consensus, called, in fact, the Washington Consensus, on the free market, free trade, and unabashed consumption, all in the name of individual liberty. Meanwhile, Coca-Cola and Mickey Mouse turned up in ever more remote villages around the globe, in some cases followed by F-16s. Yet as Americanization wended its way to a dominant place in the world, globalization had a simultaneous impact on America. The ironic undercurrent of U.S. wealth and cultural influence was its dependence on the rest of the world for loans, food, manufactured goods—such as the iconic American cultural symbol, blue jeans, that had been outsourced to China and Mexico—television sets, and even pop culture itself.

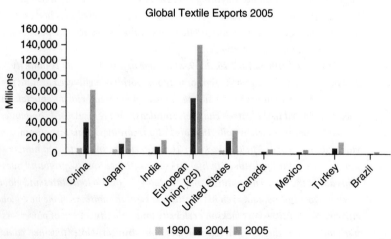

Source: WTO 2006

ECONOMIC GLOBALIZATION

The origins of the global era and America's complex role in it date back to the 1970s, when American businesses took a leading role in the global economy. Information technology and multinational corporations reached into everyday life from Boston to Bangladesh. Promising universal prosperity, global elites used existing institutions, such as the International Monetary Fund (IMF) and the World Bank, to reduce tariffs and other barriers to free trade. Elites also created new institutions to develop strategies for global development, including the Trilateral Commission, a nongovernmental organization formed in 1973 by leaders from the United States, Western Europe, and Japan (thus trilateral), and the World Economic Forum, begun in 1982 as a gathering of global leaders at a ski resort in the Swiss town of Davos. Where *stability* had been the hallmark of industrial giants in the older mixed economy, the new watchword of world capitalism was *flexibility*.

What made the world economy truly global for the first time since before the First World War was the dramatic opening of the former Communist East to capitalist businesses. The collapse of the Soviet Empire in Eastern Europe in 1989 and the subsequent disappearance of the Soviet Union in 1991 conjured visions of an abundance of untapped markets in these formerly closed societies. The same was true of China. As the world's most populous society, and still nominally Communist, China began to open its doors to foreign investors in the 1980s. When Chinese leader Deng Xiaoping proclaimed, "To get rich is glorious," it seemed as if he fulfilled five hundred years of capitalist expansion.

Information Technology and Interconnectedness

The greatest source of global interconnectedness, and the nerve center of the third industrial revolution, was an explosion of new communications technologies. As in earlier phases of rapid technological change, innovations reinforced one another in another round of feedback loops (see Chapter 1). A good illustration is the way in which the personal computer and the Internet leapfrogged one another. The development of semiconductors, electronic circuits that could be squeezed onto microchips, enabled the computer to shrink from a room-size mammoth of a machine named ENIAC in the late 1940s to ubiquitous desktop personal computers by the mid-1980s. As time went on, computers continued to shrink, giving way to handheld devices with cute and disarming names like Walkman, BlackBerry, and iPod.

Building on this microtechnology, companies were developing the Internet. Beginning in 1969, a handful of universities linked their computers together in a communication network called ARPANET. Further advances in data switching in the 1970s allowed the network to expand to a multitude of university and military users, and by 1985, when millions of personal computer users were coming online, the Internet was up and running just in time to connect them.

The U.S. Department of Defense funded most of the early advances in Internet technology, but Europe's CERN Laboratories made a vital contribution with the development of software that created the World Wide Web in 1992.

By the time the Web launched publicly, the Internet had found a multitude of commercial uses. No one was more adept at commercializing information technology than Bill Gates, whiz kid and founder of Microsoft. Although he was ahead of his time, Gates was also a throwback to an older breed of entrepreneur-inventor and mirrored his predecessors in striking ways. For some, he was the Thomas Edison of his day, and like the Wizard of Menlo Park, Gates was as much a business promoter as he was a scientific inventor. For others, he resembled John D. Rockefeller, founder of Standard Oil, because Microsoft had monopolized the software industry. Just as Standard Oil was prosecuted under the 1910 Sherman Antitrust Act, the antitrust division of the U.S. Justice Department attempted to break up Microsoft in the late 1990s.

In a sign of the shift in power across the twentieth century toward large corporations, Microsoft won in court. The trend continued in other markets as well. The Justice Department's 1998 decision to allow the creation of ExxonMobil, the world's largest oil company, to go unchallenged, for example, reunited two of the offspring of John D. Rockefeller's Standard Oil Company in an eerie reminder of the Gilded Age.

The proliferation of an increasingly dense network of information technology added up to the third industrial revolution. If the foundation of the first industrial revolution lay in the steam engine, the railroad, and the telegraph and the foundation of the second rested with the automobile and the electric dynamo, the foundation of the third belonged to the combination of microchip processing and Internet communications. Each of these three revolutions altered the social geography of human habitation. The first industrial revolution had concentrated population in cities, and then the second had dispersed people to the suburbs. Now, the web of communications in the Internet age facilitated further dispersion of service jobs beyond the suburbs to affluent *exurbs*, or *edge cities*.

Like their predecessors, the new technologies also altered time and space. It was not so much that human bodies could travel faster and further through space—indeed, all the way to the moon—as that people could transmit images and words at the speed of light almost everywhere on the planet. To enter cyberspace was to follow Alice down the rabbit hole into Wonderland, where one could seem to be everywhere and nowhere at the same time. Cyberspace also complicated the clear lines of division between the global North and South and obscured the distinct power relations at work.

Finance Capitalism

Globalization placed finance at the center of the economy because its scale required truly massive sums of capital. The saying that capitalism is a system designed for the making of money rather than the making of things was never more true than in the last quarter of the twentieth century. Under the watchword of flexibility, financiers took hold of the levers of economic power. Alongside blue chip banking institutions, such as New York's Citicorp, Tokyo's Matsui, and Lloyd's of London, the 1980s produced a new breed of entrepreneur risk takers who treated multi-million-dollar industrial corporations as if they were cheap commodities or trinkets they could buy and sell with little consequence. Deal-makers like Donald Trump (who would win the U.S. presidency in 2016) ran up huge debts in mergers and acquisitions, while corporate raiders such as T. Boone Pickens devoured vulnerable companies in hostile takeovers. Sometimes reckless disregard of the rules landed bond traders in jail, as in the case of America's junk-bond king Michael Milken. Under the pressure of corporate raiding, a number of well-established corporate giants, including Eastern Airlines and Transworld Airlines, became victims of flexibility and went out of business.

Another aspect of the rise of finance was an explosion in international money trading. Operating in cyberspace, currency traders bought and sold intangible money values to the tune of some $2 trillion a day by the 1990s. Although super-star traders such as Hungarian-born billionaire George Soros could operate from anywhere, financial services tended to settle in cities associated with specialized functions, including Tokyo as the world's prime lender, New York the prime bor-rower, and London the prime transfer point.

Factories Move East

Globalization also altered the geography of world manufacturing. Since the first industrial revolution, making things had been concentrated in the top tier of the world economy. Now, in a spectacular reversal, the rich nations of the devel-oped world underwent deindustrialization as manufacturing moved into what had been the underdeveloped agrarian regions of the bottom tier, and the places where finance and manufacturing settled created the basic framework for the global North and South.

In the startling downfall of the once-powerful United States Steel Corpora-tion, the world witnessed an illustration of the trend toward deindustrialization. Founded in 1901 as the world's first billion-dollar corporation, US Steel epito-mized the age when heavy industry reigned supreme in both war and peace. Steel employment peaked in the 1940s, and when the steelworkers union struck in 1949, almost five hundred thousand people went on strike. By the 1980s, how-ever, American steel was losing market share to imports, steel itself was giving way to aluminum and plastic, and employment at US Steel fell behind that of the McDonalds food chain. Cannibalizing itself, US Steel dismantled whole facto-ries and shipped them to Korea, invested in oil companies and real estate, and changed its name to USX.

As manufacturing jobs disappeared in the developed societies, factory jobs resurfaced in many parts of East Asia. Riding the wave of postwar prosperity, Japan's "economic miracle" had already made it the world's third largest economy as early as 1966, and by 1988 Japan ($2.1 trillion gross domestic product [GDP]) surpassed the Soviet Union ($2 trillion) to move into second place behind the United States ($5.3 trillion). In the process, Japanese banks became predominant in world finance, displacing American banks (just as New York had displaced London after the First World War). By the late 1980s, Japan had the advantage of being the world's largest creditor, with no less than seven of the world's ten biggest banks. None of the top ten was in the United States.

Japanese finance underwrote the modernization of Asian manufacturing, first in Japan itself and then elsewhere in the region. Unlike the detached relation between American business and the state, Japanese capitalism developed through financial–industrial groupings called *keiretsu*, which had close ties to government bureaucracies, such as the Ministry of Industry and Trade. Where Japan had once imitated the West, now the reverse was true. Detroit automakers and Bremen shipbuilders made pilgrimages to Yokohama to study the techniques of *just-in-time* inventory and learn about employee pep sessions that seemed to be the secret of astounding Japanese advances in cost savings, labor productivity, and product quality. By the late 1980s, as labor costs rose in the Japanese homeland, investors fanned out in search of cheaper labor and helped develop Asia's four "Little Tigers"—South Korea, Taiwan, Hong Kong, and Singapore— into centers of export manufacturing. Somewhat later, the same would be true of Japanese investment in China.

Japan's success bred not only imitation but also hostility in the United States. When displaced Detroit autoworkers looked for someone to blame for being out of work, instead of pointing the finger at the inefficiency and lack of innovation at General Motors, many turned their ire on the "Japanese invasion" of U.S. markets. The media sensationalized this sentiment in 1981, for instance, when Detroit workers took sledgehammers to a Toyota Corolla.

With Japanese investors buying up Manhattan real estate, including Mitsubishi's 1989 acquisition of such iconic symbols of American capitalism as New York's Rockefeller Center, speculation ran wild about Japan surpassing the United States as the dominant force in the world economy. In the early 1990s, a saying circulated that captured Japan's ascent: "The Cold War is over and Japan won." As it turned out, the worry was misplaced. The Japanese stock market bubble burst in 1990, leading to a decade of stagnation in which, among other liquidations, Mitsubishi sold Rockefeller Center in 1995.

THE UNITED STATES IN THE GLOBAL ORDER

Although globalization by definition did not belong to any one country, the United States played the leading role. Especially in the aftermath of the Cold War, no other country was in a position to compete for world leadership, or *hegemony*. The irony was that precisely because of its deep involvement, forces beyond its control shaped the United States like no other country. That was evident in all three areas essential to world power. Economically, the United States was the world's largest market, and for just that reason, everybody—Japanese automakers, German music makers, and Saudi investors—wanted a piece of it. Culturally, American influences were more pervasive than any other and were therefore the frequent target of Yankee-go-home resentment. Militarily, the lone superpower was expected to act as the global sheriff, especially after the collapse of Communism, but that resulted in unwanted episodes of *blowback*, where Americans became targets of attack. In the long run, there was no escaping the backlash to America's large global footprint.

Americanizing the World Economy

In the global economy, the United States took the lead primarily through multinational corporations. American preeminence is reflected in data from 1999 showing eighty-two of the world's biggest two hundred corporations (41 percent) headquartered in the United States, with Japanese firms in second place, with 21 percent. Operating on a world scale, American megacorporations epitomized by the top three—General Motors, Walmart, and ExxonMobil—all had annual sales bigger than the GDP of many countries in which they did business, including Poland, Indonesia, and South Africa.

An increasing number of U.S. multinationals received the major share of their profits from overseas sales, including Atlanta's Coca-Cola, Seattle's Boeing, and the ubiquitous McDonalds. The very structure and composition of multinationals challenge whether it is fitting to characterize them as American, especially when they showed little national loyalty in making economic decisions. Corporate chief executive officers had little patriotic guilt when abandoning local communities in moving plants overseas, *outsourcing* supplies from the global factory, and setting

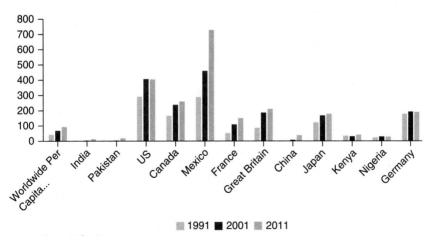

Per Capita Consumption of an 8 oz Beverage

■ 1991 ■ 2001 ■ 2011

Source: Coca Cola Company

up headquarters offshore to evade U.S. taxes. As the domestic content of U.S. products declined, the slogan "Buy American" became less and less exact.

One reason Americans assumed the mantle of leadership in the global economy is that U.S. multinationals were able to sell American culture. By closely monitoring market trends, innovative businesses such as Apple computers and Amazon books were able to develop new ways of making money in services and entertainment. Mass culture, as leading intellectuals deemed this trend, offset the steep decline in manufacturing. However, mass culture relied on a cult of celebrity and companies like Time Warner that turned pop star Madonna into the biggest-selling female vocalist of all time, just as Nike made millions by hiring superstar Michael Jordan of the world champion Chicago Bulls basketball team to peddle sneakers. Because of the international popularity of such American idols, U.S. businesses reaped a double reward, first in the massive home market and then again in world markets. When it came to mass culture, no other country could compete with the land of Coca-Cola and Levi's.

Paradoxically, the more world culture absorbed American culture, the less American it became. The Disney empire proved a fitting illustration. Following the original Disneyland constructed outside Los Angeles in 1955, an expanded Walt Disney World opened in Orlando, Florida, in the 1970s, and by 1990, Walt Disney World was receiving more than twenty-eight million visitors a year, more than all the tourist sites in Britain. Meanwhile, Disney went global with Tokyo Disneyland in 1983, followed in 1992 by the Euro Disney Resort outside Paris. Critics, especially in France, condemned what they saw as American cultural imperialism embodied in Disney's cute, small-town fantasy of the American Dream.

But Disney's aesthetic appeal and cozy nostalgia had more to do with an emerging global commercial culture than with specifically American styles. Similar trends developed in British rock, Japanese anime cartoons, and African music. Only in these cases, U.S. multinational corporations also turned them into vehicles for the emergence of a global consumer culture that rapidly outgrew their various national origins.

Still, American leadership was apparent in the institutional framework of the world economy. From the time of Reagan and Thatcher, Anglo-American elites had been enamored with free-market conservatism. United States officials such as Alan Greenspan, head of the Federal Reserve Bank, and Robert Rubin, secretary of the Treasury, preached the gospel of globalization to a growing flock of faithful adherents in elite circles, such as the annual gathering of the rich and powerful for the World Economic Forum at Davos in the Swiss Alps. By the early 1990s, most of the architects and prime movers of the world's economy joined in the Washington Consensus belief that trade liberalization would benefit everyone.

But free markets did not spread automatically. Many countries protected their own businesses and consumers, and in some cases, particularly among poorer countries, multinationals had to force markets open. That was where the IMF and the World Bank came in. As the most prominent enforcement officers of the Washington Consensus, the IMF and the World Bank insisted on liberalization as a condition of receiving a loan. Under *structural adjustment programs*, the IMF demanded privatization of publicly owned railroads and communications systems, the removal of food subsidies, and reduced spending on social programs. The main beneficiaries were not the world's poor, but foreign investors.

WORLD POLITICS AFTER THE COLD WAR

American leadership was also evident in world politics. With the end of the Cold War in 1989, everyone waited to see what would come next. Would there be a warm or a cold peace among the powers? Would the lone superpower dominate a unipolar world? Would the alliance of Western Europe, North America, and Japan control world politics? Would there be a clash of cultures pitting West against East, Christians against Muslims? As it turned out, all these tendencies came into play as elites in various regions tried to bend the elusive forces of globalization to their own end.

At first, the end of the Cold War seemed to promise a new era of international cooperation orchestrated by the United States. An early sign of U.S. leadership came in the near unanimity of its role in the opposition to Iraq's unprovoked invasion of neighboring Kuwait in August 1990. Because the Middle East contained two-thirds of the world's oil reserves, outsiders were understandably concerned when violence threatened to inflame the region. Vowing to drive Iraqi dictator Saddam Hussein out of Kuwait, President George H. W. Bush drew a line in the sand. When Hussein refused to retreat across the line, Bush launched Desert Storm in January 1991. A punishing bombing campaign was followed by a land invasion of some five hundred thousand coalition forces, mostly American.

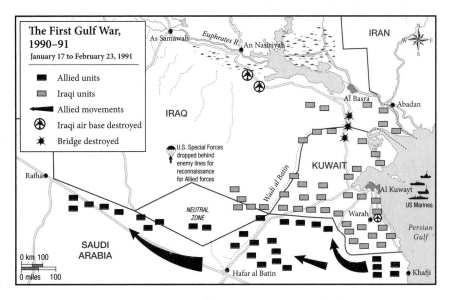

MAP 13.1

Pentagon strategy followed the lines of the Powell Doctrine, named after General Colin Powell, former national security advisor and then chairman of the Joint Chiefs of Staff. The Powell Doctrine called for the application of overwhelming force in pursuit of quick victory, which military planners hoped would overcome the lingering *Vietnam syndrome*, that is, the reluctance to send U.S. forces overseas. Indeed, coalition forces had little trouble driving the completely outgunned Iraqi army back across the border. At that point, President Bush called a halt, leaving Hussein in control in the Iraqi capital of Baghdad. Instead of toppling the regime, as the president's son, George W. Bush, would do a dozen years later with Powell as his secretary of state, the coalition powers preferred to keep Hussein in power as a check on the Islamic Republic next door in Iran.

Although a wise move for regional stability, the decision proved to be Bush's political undoing. Instead of coming clean about the central purpose of maintaining international control over Persian Gulf oil, President Bush had tried to win public support by painting Saddam not only as an aggressor—which he clearly was—but also as another Hitler bent on world domination, which he certainly was not. Having trapped himself in this outlandish comparison, Bush soon paid the price for failing to finish the job. Plummeting poll ratings, which were also driven by economic recession, preceded eventual defeat in his 1992 reelection bid.

The Gulf War represented a high-water mark for American world leadership. Perhaps the most striking thing about the war was the degree of international support for the U.S. invasion. It is not surprising that European powers and Japan—both highly dependent on Middle Eastern oil—joined the multinational coalition and ended up paying much of the bill. What was unexpected was the support from the Middle East. Setting aside long-standing opposition to outside intervention, Egypt, Saudi Arabia, and other Arab states threatened by Iraq's unprovoked aggression joined the Gulf War coalition. Most remarkable of all, the Soviet Union turned its back on its one-time Iraqi friend and backed the effort to bring Hussein to heel. By winning support from America's former Cold War enemy, which faced having American troops only a few hundred miles from the Russian border, it appeared Bush had become the global sheriff to whom everyone turned for the restoration of law and order. In this sense, the Gulf War was the embodiment of the post–Cold War drift toward a world organized around the American superpower.

When William Jefferson Clinton, known as Bill to the public, defeated Bush in the 1992 presidential election, the change in political party from Republican to Democratic did not mean a change in the policy of containment. Clinton maintained *no-fly* zones and occasional bombing of Hussein's military installations, and he also won UN approval for sanctions and weapons inspections in a successful effort to keep Hussein from developing nuclear and other weapons of mass destruction. In maintaining broad support in world opinion for containment, both Bush and Clinton won consent from the international community for American hegemony. But there was something more. The first Gulf War and subsequent containment of Iraq stood as one of the rare moments of collective security in twentieth-century history. In assembling a grand coalition against aggression, they built on the legacy of Woodrow Wilson, the father of collective security.

After Communism

Another development that pointed toward convergence was the collapse of Communism. By the time the Soviet Union joined the Gulf War coalition, the wheels were coming off what Communists once regarded as the locomotive of history. Instead of representing the epochal change from capitalism to Communism, the Soviet Union was destined to lead history in the opposite direction, from Communism to capitalism. When the Soviet Union ceased to exist at the end of December 1991, there was a sense of a new dawn in Russia, the largest of the successor republics, as well as in Kazakhstan, Ukraine, Georgia, and others. The contagion of independence was equally exhilarating in the former Soviet empire in Eastern Europe. Peoples who had once been forced to bow to decrees from Moscow soon found themselves reading a free press, demonstrating freely in the streets, and voting in multiparty elections.

But the thrill did not last long. Former Soviet citizens abandoned the doldrums of Communist stagnation only to come face to face with capitalist depression. As bad as the situation had been under the command economy of the Soviet system, things turned decidedly worse in the initial transition to the market economy. Once-protected steel and auto industries could not compete and had to be shut down. Privatization of public assets at fire-sale prices created a new class of super-rich *oligarchs* steeped in corruption. Overnight conversion to market pricing led to a precipitous decline in GDP. In 1950, per capita GDP in the Soviet Union had been 30 percent of that in the United States; by 1998 it fell to 13 percent for Russia.

Deterioration in Russian social conditions seemed to mock free-market ideals. Alcoholism, suicide, and violent crime all went up. Ugly nativism and xenophobia returned. Although the number of political prisoners shrank, the number imprisoned for crime skyrocketed until Russia shared the dubious distinction of having the world's highest incarceration rates with the United States. In 2000, the Russian incarceration rate (699/100,000 population) was about equal to that of the United States (702), far above that of other industrial countries such as Britain (125), Germany (95), France (90), and Japan (40). Disinherited and demoralized, the Russian people plunged into despair. Communism was gone, but there was no new moral economy to take its place.

The economic situation in Eastern Europe was not much better. Cut adrift from the Soviet empire, east Europeans crashed into the global economy with devastating results. Inefficient factories could not compete with cheaper goods from the West, with the result of massive unemployment in the former East Germany. Things got so bad in Poland and Hungary that the once-despised Communist parties made something of a comeback by the late 1990s. All the same, given a choice, few wanted to turn the clock back to the Soviet era. For better and for worse, East and West were converging.

Regional Settlements

One-time frontier zones of the East–West conflict in many parts of the Third World underwent a similar trend. What had been Cold War battlegrounds fell silent and former enemies remade ties, or so it seemed. In Central America, for example, opposing forces in Nicaragua and El Salvador reached accommodations that ended guerilla uprisings in both places. Something similar happened in war-torn Africa, where the United States and Russia stopped funding opposing forces that had brought so much misery to Angola, Mozambique, and Ethiopia.

The most astounding reversal came in South Africa. In the absence of the Communist threat, the white supremacist regime could no longer count on the backing of the United States and other Western governments, which had come under intense pressure from the global antiapartheid movement. The movement, which included a large contingent of American activists, played a major role in securing the 1990 release of Nelson Mandela, leader of the African National Congress who the Afrikaner regime had imprisoned for almost thirty years for his opposition to apartheid. An even greater triumph came in the official dismantling of apartheid in 1991 and its replacement by the *nonracial democracy* that was the congress's lifelong goal. The crowning glory came in 1994 in the democratic election that made Mandela president. Almost no one had predicted such a peaceful transition of power, and there was an outpouring of joy around the world.

Another hopeful sign of harmony was the 1993 agreement between Israelis and Palestinians known as the Oslo Accords. From secret Norway meetings in August 1993, Palestinian Liberation Organization leader Yasser Arafat and Israeli Prime Minister Yitzhak Rabin agreed to recognize the legitimacy of each other's government, share occupation of the West Bank, and work toward a five-year plan that would bring permanent peace. Although underlying issues remained unresolved, including Israeli occupation of Palestinian land, both sides believed they were taking the first steps toward a resolution of their differences.

The clustering of so many agreements in the short span at the beginning of the 1990s added to the sense that humanity was finally giving in to its better instincts and a better future was in store. The surprising transformation of groups and leaders who seemed very much entrenched in their politics of conflict and division seemed to fulfill the hopeful assumptions of a world without the Cold War. And Westerners, certainly people in the United States, were particularly attuned to the message of optimism about the future that rung loudly through the air.

Clinton and Blair

It was the good fortune of William Jefferson Clinton to win the American presidency in this moment of hope. As chance would have it, Clinton had been born in Hope, Arkansas, and "the man from Hope" overcame family troubles of an alcoholic father to become a high achiever with an extraordinary resume of accomplishments: Yale Law School student, Rhodes Scholar, governor of Arkansas, and one of the youngest presidents in American history. He won the White House in the 1992 election, first because his opponent George Bush was caught in a recession and had failed to finish the job in the Gulf War, and second because Ross Perot captured 19 percent of the vote in the largest third-party showing since Teddy Roosevelt's Bull Moose Party of 1912. Bill Clinton and First Lady Hillary Rodham Clinton were cultural liberals who supported abortion rights and acceptance of gays in the military and elsewhere. Because of his "I-feel-your-pain" understanding of racism and his appointment of African Americans to high positions, some intellectuals and social critics called Clinton the first black president (a phrase that would lose meaning after the election of Barack Obama in 2008).

But upon coming to power, Clinton was content to operate within the framework of free-market conservatism. Especially after an early attempt to institute national health insurance failed spectacularly, Clinton became adept at borrowing issues from the conservatives. A prime example was welfare reform. Vowing to "end welfare as we know it," Clinton put his weight behind a coalition of Republicans and conservative Democrats that prevailed on Congress in 1995 to end the lifelong entitlement to public assistance that had evolved since the introduction of the Social Security system in the 1930s.

In 1996, Clinton became the first Democrat to be reelected president since Franklin Roosevelt, thanks to a strong economy, cooptation of Republican issues, and his inspirational message of building a "bridge to the future." To Clinton, that bridge ran straight through liberalized global markets. He urged Americans to "embrace the inexorable logic of globalization that everything, from the strength of our economy to the safety of our cities to the health of our people, depends on events not only within our borders but half a world away."

In promoting globalization, Clinton had a partner in British Prime Minister Tony Blair. Born in 1953, the British Labour Party chose Blair as its head in 1994 on the strength of his ideas for *new Labour*, which involved jettisoning any lingering ties to Socialism and embracing the free market. Elected in 1997, Blair became the youngest prime minister of the century and immediately embraced a close alliance with his U.S. counterpart.

In an earlier era, Clinton and Blair might have been social democrats. But they recognized that the political spectrum had moved to the right and they were opportunistic enough to move with it. Global free markets had no more enthusiastic supporters than Clinton and Blair, who dwelled in the shadow of Reagan and Thatcher, an earlier duo of Anglo-American conservatives.

In cultural terms, the United States continued to ride the long wave of favorable opinion that had gathered during the Second World War. Since 1945 (outside the Eastern bloc), the United States had been seen as a good giant, especially in comparison to the bad giants of Nazi Germany and militarist Japan. Likewise, compared to the direct rule of European empires, America's indirect empire felt more benign. Even when foreigners condemned America for its oversized ambition and behavior, as in Vietnam, they tended to distinguish between the policy of the American government, which they did not like, and the American people, whom they generally did. As late as 2000, world opinion as reported in the Pew Survey made this distinction, one that was essential to maintaining the soft power essential to world leadership.

United States as Global Sheriff

When it came to military hard power, the United States was unequaled. No other country came close to matching its high-tech weaponry, such as the flying AWACS radar system or its vast network of 750 overseas military installations strewn around the globe, from the giant Ramstein Air Base in Germany, a legacy of the U.S. postwar occupation, to Diego Garcia, an island base in the Indian Ocean inherited from the British empire. In fact, with annual military budgets hovering around $400 billion, the United States spent almost as much on its military as the rest of the world combined.

Military spending trended downward everywhere after the Cold War. With the abandonment of empire following World War II, European members of NATO had dropped their military budgets to an average of 3.4 percent of gross national product by the 1980s, and the decline continued after 1989 for both Western Europe (Britain and France were partial exceptions) and the Russian Federation, successor to the defunct Soviet Union. Following this trend, military spending in the United States declined as a percentage of GDP from about 5 percent in 1950 to about 3 percent in 2000 (excluding veteran's benefits and that portion of interest on the national debt attributable to the military). What permitted America to be so much more heavily armed than everyone else was the absolute increase in the size of the U.S. economy, from $1.5 trillion in 1950 to $5.5 trillion in 1990. With global military spending down, if there was going to be a global sheriff to keep the peace, there was only one candidate for the job.

In the first post–Cold War intervention outside the Middle East, President George H. W. Bush sent U.S. forces into the faction-ridden country of Somalia on the horn of East Africa in December 1992. After a chaotic occupation, President Clinton, still new to the White House, withdrew U.S. forces less than a year later. By 1994, when Rwanda devolved into Hutu genocide against the Tutsi minority and the UN refused to act, even when Tutsi were killed in the safe zone, the United States showed no inclination to step in, beyond labeling the killings genocide. Having the big gun does not always guarantee success, and the Somalian episode was a dire example of when a superpower fails.

However, there were times when the U.S. military did help stabilize war-torn regions. When Yugoslavia disintegrated shortly after the end of the Cold War and ethnic tension degenerated into efforts to separate peoples of the Balkans through ethnic cleansing, European powers were reluctant to intervene. Instead, they

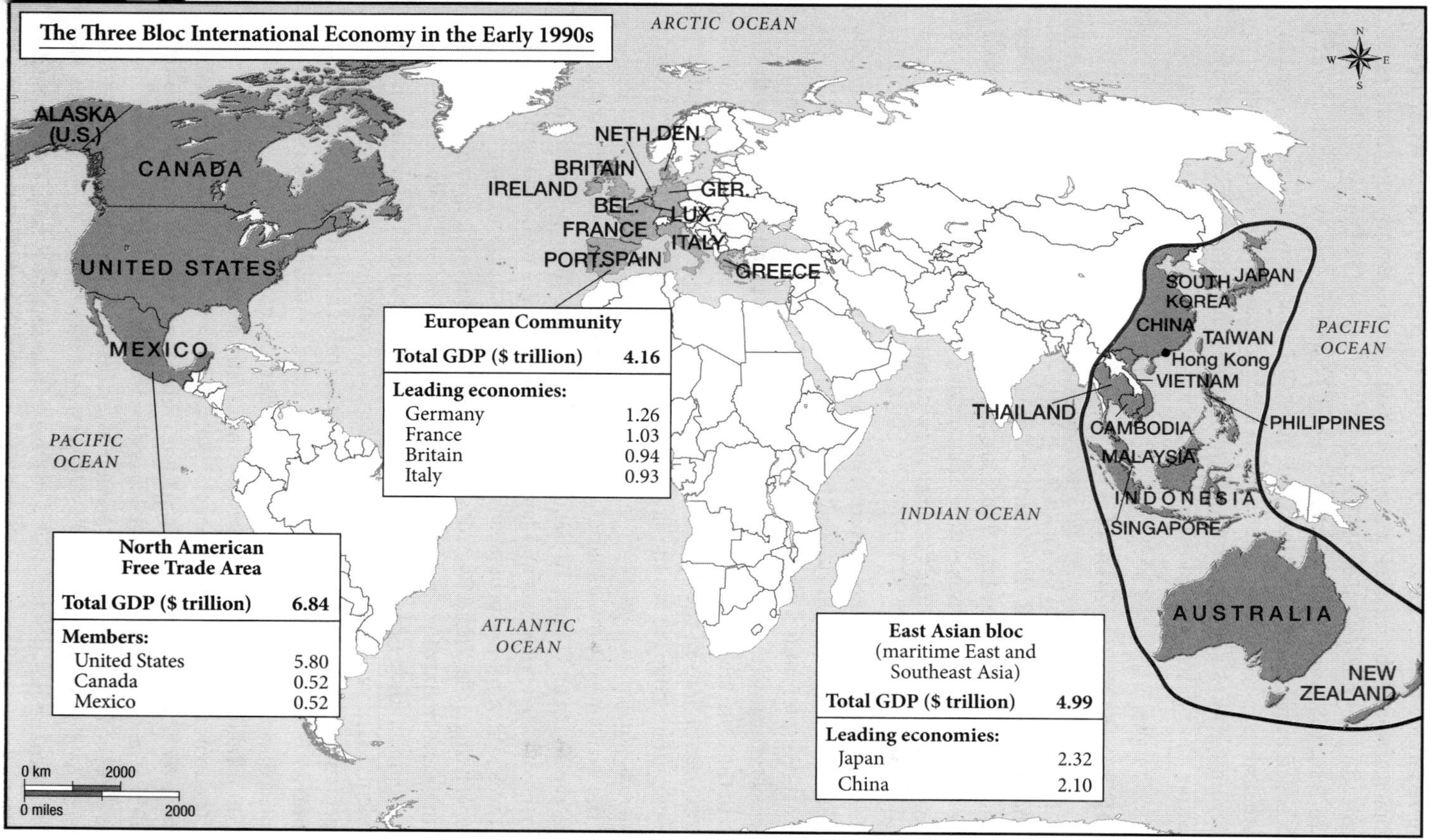
The Three Bloc International Economy in the Early 1990s
ARCTIC OCEAN
ALASKA (U.S.)
CANADA
UNITED STATES
MEXICO
PACIFIC OCEAN
ATLANTIC OCEAN
INDIAN OCEAN
PACIFIC OCEAN
NETH. DEN.
BRITAIN
IRELAND
GER.
BEL.
LUX.
FRANCE
ITALY
PORT. SPAIN
GREECE
SOUTH KOREA
JAPAN
CHINA
TAIWAN
Hong Kong
VIETNAM
THAILAND
PHILIPPINES
CAMBODIA
MALAYSIA
INDONESIA
SINGAPORE
AUSTRALIA
NEW ZEALAND
European Community
Total GDP ($ trillion) 4.16
Leading economies:
Germany 1.26
France 1.03
Britain 0.94
Italy 0.93
North American Free Trade Area
Total GDP ($ trillion) 6.84
Members:
United States 5.80
Canada 0.52
Mexico 0.52
East Asian bloc (maritime East and Southeast Asia)
Total GDP ($ trillion) 4.99
Leading economies:
Japan 2.32
China 2.10
0 km 2000
0 miles 2000

MAP 13.2

deferred to the United States, which prevailed on NATO to launch its first-ever military action in the form of bombing in Belgrade, followed by diplomatic pressure leading to the November 1995 Peace Accords signed in Dayton, Ohio.

In Iraq, U.S. low-intensity warfare, plus UN-sponsored economic sanctions, succeeded in containing the Hussein regime. The strategy worked just as well in southeastern Europe. Key ingredients to success in both the Balkans and Iraq were limited aims and support from the international community. To be truly effective, hard power needed the moral legitimacy that came with soft power.

NORTH–SOUTH DIVIDE

The trend toward global convergence under U.S. leadership in the aftermath of the Cold War seemed to be traveling on a fixed course. But history is never a simple linear flow of events. There are always counterflows, back eddies, and errant trends; and so it was with globalization. While the main current moved toward convergence, other currents moved in the opposite direction toward divergence.

One of the strongest countercurrents was the growing split between the rich countries of the global North and the poor countries of the global South. Even as East–West tensions subsided, North–South conflicts gained in relevance and intensity. Because the term Third World had become an anachronism with the end of the Cold War, observers increasingly spoke of the global South to describe the poorer nations of the world, which often lay in the tropics or the Southern Hemisphere, as opposed to the rich nations mostly located in Europe and North America, plus Japan.

The growing gap in material standards of living reflected the divergence between North and South. At the upside, perhaps one billion people living in the North could take new cars and laptop computers for granted. On the downside, in the South, a billion people lacked safe drinking water, and over two billion people living on less than two dollars a day were without modern sanitation. One of the most frequently cited ways of measuring quality of life was the Human Development Index compiled by statisticians at the UN. The Human Development Index ranked countries according to a composite score based on life expectancy, education, and real income. Not surprisingly, fifteen of the top twenty countries in 2003 were in Europe (Norway rated first), and others included the United States at seventh, Canada, and the European offshoots of Australia and New Zealand. None of the top twenty was in Africa, Asia, or Latin America.

The one billion inhabitants of the global North were truly the world's most fortunate. The main centers of capital accumulation, political decision making, and high-end consumption were located in the triad of Japan, Western Europe, and North America. Even the poorest layers of these privileged societies were able to help themselves to plastic toys and television sets produced by low-wage workers in the global South and sold at bargain-basement prices. Indeed, the disparity in television sets, of all things, became a stark measure for gaps in wealth and income, not to mention influence, between the North and South. In 1997, the United States topped the list with eighty sets for every one hundred people (astoundingly, Americans reported watching an average of eight hours per day). At the opposite extreme, African countries were lucky to have one or two televisions per one hundred people.

There was an ongoing debate about the impact of globalization on the wealth gap. On the one hand, free-market conservatives took a win–win position, arguing that each country had its own comparative advantage and that the invisible hand of the market allocated resources and rewards in ways that benefited everyone. Indeed, there was evidence that the industrialization of former agrarian countries like China and India was lifting incomes of ex-peasants and reducing the gap between the developed and underdeveloped countries.

On the other hand, liberals and progressives saw a division between winners and losers in the growing polarization between the superrich and the superpoor. The gap between countries was evident in many measures. One illustration was the fact that the assets of the three richest billionaires of the late 1990s, including Microsoft's Bill Gates, the world's richest person, were equal to the combined gross national product of the world's poorest forty-eight countries, which accounted for some six hundred million people. The disparity was not mere coincidence. Some were rich because others were poor. Michael Eisner, the chairman of Disney Corporation, enjoyed the biggest payday in history to that point when he collected $565 million in 1997 in salary, bonuses, and stock options. Meanwhile, U.S. investigators in Mexico found workers making Disney logo-line clothes for fifty-seven cents an hour.

Whatever the precise intrinsic effect of economic globalization, the long-standing gap between the richest and the poorest continued to widen in the global era. Measurement of wealth and income on a global scale is inevitably imperfect, but scholars are certain about the overall trend toward greater inequality. Dividing the world's population into five groups according to income, it is possible to track the ratio between the top group and the bottom group. Estimates put the ratio at about eleven to one on the eve of World War I in 1913. By 1960, the ratio had climbed to thirty to one in the midst of high-growth years of the postwar period. Slower growth in the last quarter of the century, however, did not make for equality, and the gap continued to widen to sixty to one by 1990 and then grew rapidly to seventy-five to one by 2000.

Conditions in the Global South

The global South felt globalization's impact most acutely. In a shift of world-historical proportions, the last quarter of the twentieth century saw the beginning of the end of the peasantry. Since the turn to agriculture in the Neolithic Revolution some ten thousand years ago, peasants had comprised the largest segment of humanity. Now, Asian and Latin American peasants were following in the footsteps of their European predecessors a century earlier and migrating from country to city, swelling the mass of marginal women and men seeking work in Mexican *maquiladoras* and Hong Kong sweat shops. By 1980, five of the ten largest urban agglomerations were in Asia (Tokyo was the world's largest, at 28.5 million), three were in Latin America (with Mexico City the largest), and two were in the United States (New York and Los Angeles). None was in Europe.

As in the past, migrants to the city encountered the proverbial best of times and worst of times. On the one hand, they enjoyed unprecedented opportunities to improve their lot. Although factories in Mexico City or Guangdong paid what would have been starvation wages in the developed world, the fact was that assembly-line workers could earn many times the income of an agricultural laborer. Although the proliferation of subcontractors led to labor abuses, including slave-like conditions, rapid development created entirely new sectors of managerial and entrepreneurial employment. In the face of terrible overcrowding, poverty, and cultural dislocation, there was also the excitement and adventure of city life.

On the other hand, inequality became more glaring. Emerging classes of superrich businessmen in Shanghai and Bangalore looked down from high-rise office towers on slum dwellers below forced to live without clean water, public sanitation, or decent housing under conditions that made the wretched experience of European or U.S. industrialization look almost pleasant. Brazil earned the dubious distinction of being the world's leader in inequality, with the top 20 percent receiving two-thirds of national income, while the bottom 20 percent received a mere 2.5 percent.

The worst social catastrophe took place in regions abandoned altogether by the world economy. In what some have called the Fourth World, perhaps a billion people lived on one dollar day or less at the end of the century. While some countries of the former bottom tier of the world economy were weighing anchor and sailing out with engines humming onto the high seas of the global economy, others were cast adrift in lifeboats without the engines of trade or investment, leaving whole regions trapped in abysmal poverty. In the absence of the global factory in sub-Saharan Africa, real GDP per capita declined from 14 percent of the industrial countries to 8 percent between 1960 and 1987. With no bridge to the future, famine and the combination of natural and human disaster—drought, poverty, warfare, and corruption—stalked many Africans, but it rendered the Darfur region of Sudan, Ethiopia, Congo, and the Sahel some of the least hospitable places on earth.

In the Middle East, North Africa, and Central Asia, countries without oil or gas to sell in world markets were in scarcely better shape. The same went for residents of the Caribbean and the rural hinterlands of South America. The desperate plight of the Fourth World lent a kernel of truth to the saying, "The only thing worse than working for a multinational corporation is *not* working for a multinational corporation."

Backlash against the Global North

Although privileged residents of the global North often tried to ignore the ongoing humanitarian crisis in the global South, the crisis grew too large. Chronic

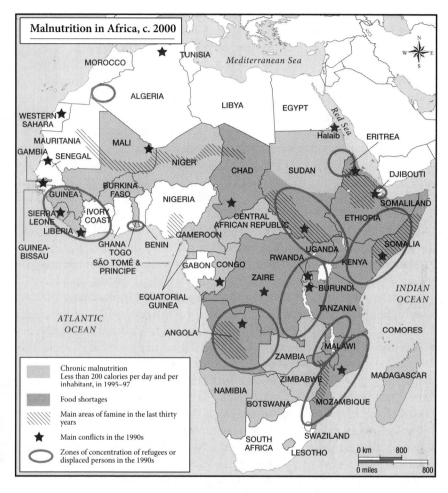

MAP 13.3

poverty and festering resentment combined to cause instability around the world. Disease, like the HIV/AIDS epidemic in the 1980s and 1990s, spread like wildfire because of poor sanitation and health practices.

In many places, the countereffects of globalization were self-evident. The decaying carcasses of shuttered factories littered the landscape of inner cities, forming the Rust Belt that stretched from Birmingham to Chicago. As steel mills and textile factories shut down, formerly well-paid, unionized workers suffered pay cuts and job loss. Stark forms of class polarization began to emerge throughout the global North, especially in Britain and the United States.

The growing gap between wage earners and employers was particularly severe in the United States, where in 2000 the ratio of chief executive officer pay to workers' pay was in the range of five hundred to one, compared to a ratio of about forty to one in 1980. The change was not the result of idleness among Americans, nor did they work fewer hours. To the contrary, American workers spent more hours on the job than workers in any other developed country. In 2000, for example, they worked three and a half weeks more than the Japanese, six and a half weeks more than the British, and twelve and a half weeks more than the Germans.

Often the most exploited workers were immigrant workers displaced from the global South, which highlights another backlash of globalization. As multinational corporations drove ever more deeply into the global South, displaced villagers headed north. Often their route ran along the old pathways of empire, as one-time Algerian subjects of French rule flocked to the vertical slums of suburban Paris, former British subjects in India and Pakistan filled up whole sections of London, and Indonesians headed for the old imperial capital of Amsterdam. Along with Turkish guest workers in Germany, the newcomers in Europe were overwhelmingly Muslim, with the result that majority-Christian Europe acquired a significant Muslim minority for the first time since the Spanish expelled them in 1492. Uprooted by global forces, these millions of migrants were subjected to low wages, substandard education, and ethnic discrimination.

It is striking how much the same pattern applied to the United States. As U.S. corporations made their way south, the uprooted villagers who left home originally to work for agribusiness and *maquiladoras* in Mexico and the Caribbean crossed the U.S. border, sometimes without the required documentation. The influx of one-time imperial subjects from the Philippines and Puerto Rico, as well as the rest of the Caribbean and Latin America, reached such proportions that by 2004, Latinos of all national backgrounds, immigrant and native combined, accounted for an estimated 14 percent of the total U.S. population.

Carlos Fuentes, noted author and Mexican diplomat, summed up the overall situation: "How do we deal with the Other: North Africans in France; Turks in Germany; Vietnamese in Czechoslovakia; Pakistanis in Britain; black Africans in Italy; Japanese, Koreans, Chinese, and Latin Americans in the United States. Instant communications and economic interdependence have transformed what was once an isolated situation into a universal, defining, all-embracing reality of the twenty-first century."

Blowback

The most severe backlash appeared in attacks on U.S. service personnel overseas. Deployed in 750 overseas installations, U.S. forces could not avoid becoming targets of hostile forces. For example, militants believed to be associated with Hezbollah, a Lebanon-based Islamist guerilla group with links to the Islamic Republic of Iran, killed nineteen Air Force personnel in the 1996 bombing of the Khobar Towers in Saudi Arabia. Two years later, on August 7, 1998, U.S. embassies in the African capitals of Nairobi, Kenya, and Dar es Salaam, Tanzania, were severely damaged by car bombs that killed more than two hundred people, all but a dozen of them African civilians. In retaliation, President Clinton ordered a cruise missile attack from U.S. warships in the Red Sea on a pharmaceutical plant in Dar es Salaam, erroneously believed to be a chemical weapons facility, and on al-Qaeda training camps in Khost, Afghanistan.

Afghanistan proved a critical site of counteractions. The reason Americans had no trouble determining the bombing coordinates of the Afghan training camps is that the United States had built some of these same facilities in the late 1980s when the CIA was supporting the struggle of the Afghan *mujahideen* to expel the Soviets from Afghanistan. At that time, the CIA was working with Arab Afghans, including Osama bin Laden, the renegade member of the Saudi royal family who sought the overthrow of the Saudi regime. Bin Laden was the mastermind behind al-Qaeda believed to be responsible for the series of attacks on American targets that began with a failed bombing at New York's World Trade Towers in 1995 and led to the African Embassy attacks, an attack in 2000 on the USS *Cole* in a harbor in Yemen, and, finally, the spectacular destruction of the World Trade Towers on September 11, 2001 (see Chapter 14). In their published statements, bin Laden and his co-conspirators said that the presence of U.S. troops in Saudi Arabia after the Gulf War—considered a desecration of Islam's holiest territory in their view and a pretense for propping up the despised Saudi regime—motivated their violent campaign. This terrible example of blowback, the CIA's term for unwanted repercussions of a covert operation, illustrates the inescapability of the past. Although it is impossible to foresee such consequences, it is possible to trace them back through the chain of causation to their root causes.

Globalization of America: The Open Door in Reverse

One of the most striking consequences of globalization was the way it made Americans dependent on other peoples. In everything from children's toys to food to the foreign loans that kept the government solvent, Americans relied on the kindness of strangers.

Although American popular culture continued to be a bonanza for Coca-Cola, Disney, and other U.S. multinational corporations, the irony was that globalization opened American culture to foreign influences. One Japanese craze after another—Nintendo, Power Rangers, Pokemon, anime, and Hello Kitty—swept up American children. Major League Baseball, the classic American pastime, opened its 2001 season with a quarter of the roster foreign born. When Japan's Ichiro Suzuki of the Mariners became rookie of the year, thousands of Japanese fans flew to Seattle to see the team owned by none other than the Japanese president of Nintendo.

The importation of so many foreign-made goods into the United States amounted to America's Open Door policy in reverse. Japanese automakers, German media giants, and Saudi oil exporters rubbed their hands together with the same kind of glee over the American market as U.S. business had always done in looking to foreign markets. The same was true for another special kind of import: capital. In a stunning turnabout in world finance, the United States moved almost overnight from being the world's largest creditor to the largest debtor by 1985. As it became a net importer of capital, the United States slid from the top of the banking establishment. By the late 1980s, American banks accounted for only one of the world's biggest twenty-five banks (Citicorp), a remarkable shift for American finance, which in 1965 had held fifteen of the top twenty-five slots.

The cause for the reversal was Americans who spent beyond their means and had to borrow to pay for it. They overspent in both public and private markets, leading to the emergence of the *double deficit* in the 1980s. The first was the federal budget deficit. Because the Reagan administration cut taxes at the same time as it ran up the largest peacetime military budget in history, there were not enough revenues coming in to pay all of America's bills. To cover the gap, the government sold bonds, and most of the big buyers came from overseas. Although the federal deficit was eliminated under President Clinton, it later returned with a vengeance under the second President George Bush, leading to renewed dependence on foreign loans.

Americans also depended on foreigners to bail them out of private consumer debt. To satisfy their insatiable consumer appetites, they imported things no longer produced in the United States. Normally, a country balances its books by selling abroad, but Americans no longer produced many of the things the rest of the world wanted to buy. Thus, foreign loans were necessary to balance the books so Americans could continue shopping in the global department store. Not since the Spanish Empire of the eighteenth century had an economic giant been so dependent on foreign capital. Historical experience gave cause for worry on this point. In the cases of Spain, Russia, and other great powers trapped in this situation, dependency was the prelude to decline.

Decline of the United States?

America's perilous situation compelled many to wonder whether it had run its course as a superpower. Although the end of the Cold War appeared to leave the United States the sole world power, it was also true that the disappearance of the Soviet threat eliminated the need for U.S. protection. Meanwhile, the disturbing proliferation of nuclear weapons—India and Pakistan joined the nuclear club in 1998—suggested a diffused structure of world power.

One sign of diffusion was the rise of regional groupings. Western Europe, for example, rallied behind the new European Union. Originating in a postwar vision of a united states of Europe, the European Union had evolved from a common market anchored in the two largest countries, France and Germany, to a regional network of institutions that included a parliament and an administrative commission based in Brussels. Although not a state in the traditional sense—the European Union lacked an army or independent taxing power—it increasingly set common standards for people who thought of themselves as Europeans first and Germans or Italians second. Under the Treaty of Maastricht, member countries opened their borders to unrestricted flow of people and trade.

A further step toward regional union came with the adoption of the Euro in 1999 as common currency in a dozen countries. Economic integration under the Euro brought the European economy as a whole slightly above the level of the United

States. Before the Euro, American currency and its valuation standards—dollars, gallons, and pounds—provided a safety net for corporations that wanted to sell in international markets. Now the European Union was setting the pace in Euros, liters, and kilos.

Lured by the promise of prosperity, former provinces of the Soviet empire, including Poland, the Baltic states, the Czech Republic, Hungary, and Bulgaria, flocked to join the European Union, which by 2004 had expanded eastward even into parts of the former Soviet Union. Although many disgruntled citizens objected to the loss of national identity, the tide was clearly running toward European regionalism. The paradox of American power in a global age was that the lone superpower could not force others to do its bidding. It had to rely on consent of friends and bystanders, if not borrow from them outright.

China Rising

Another indication of the spread of power lay in the rise of East Asia. Japan and the Little Tigers—South Korea, Taiwan, Hong Kong, and Singapore—had made their mark in the 1980s. Now, in the 1990s, it was China's turn. Beginning with the open door reforms initiated by Deng Xiaoping in 1979, China embarked on a path of capitalist development whose pace and scale were historically unprecedented. Neither Britain in the take-off period of the first industrial revolution nor the United States in the spectacular growth of the second industrial revolution could match China's sustained annual growth rates of 8–9 percent over a quarter century. Only Japan had come close during its own postwar "miracle." Everyone who visited Shanghai or Guangdong in those boom years came away impressed with the constant din of jackhammers and the ubiquitous presence of construction cranes.

Although the face of Chairman Mao continued to shine down on Beijing's Tiananmen Square like an emperor of old, China's new profit-oriented development belied the image of the great Communist Helmsman. Under Mao, the slogan had been "The East Is Red." Under Deng Xiaoping, the saying went, "The East Is Green." And with its admission to the World Trade Organization (WTO) in 2001, China's full membership in the club of capitalist nations was complete.

China's extraordinary growth rested first on the backs of cheap labor. With a total population in 2000 of some 1.2 billion, the Chinese countryside was a vast reserve of untapped industrial labor. At a time when the average hourly wage for U.S. private-sector workers was around fourteen dollars per hour, Chinese factory workers were paid less than a dollar per hour. In scenes reminiscent of the early phases of the Industrial Revolution in Britain, workers toiled for twelve hours a day in sweatshop conditions. The wretched conditions of Chinese labor lay behind the *China price,* the benchmark wholesale price, which is what made it possible for global retailers like Walmart to offer their "everyday low prices" to American consumers.

A second part of the explanation for China's rise centers on government policy. As in Japan, Chinese business operated under the strict control of the state. What Communist Party leaders euphemistically called Socialism with

From its start as a local shop to its rise as a global conglomerate, Walmart distinguished itself from the competition by offering a great variety at bargain prices. Cost and convenience had universal appeal, which allowed Walmart to spread its business model to the world, even to former Communist states like China. Daniel Ng, Walmart Beijing.

Chinese characteristics was in reality a form of state capitalism. Through joint ventures between Chinese and foreign firms plus other controls on foreign capital, Chinese officials supervised the accumulation of private wealth. Departing from the Anglo-American model of limited state intervention, China combined a controlled market with top-down rule. That was also the case in politics. When student demonstrators in 1989 took over Tiananmen Square, the symbolic center of authority in the heart of Beijing, and erected a statue of the Goddess of Democracy that closely resembled America's Statue of Liberty, the authorities eventually imposed a violent crackdown.

By the turn of the century, globalization had altered the hierarchy of world economic power. The induction of agrarian economies like China and the Little Tigers into the ranks of industrial producers fundamentally changed the structure of the world economy. As one-time exporters of food and raw materials to the developed world began to export sweatshirts, auto parts, and other manufactured goods, the old three-tier system that had prevailed since the end of the nineteenth century evolved into a new set of relations.

The United States and Western Europe were ceding ground to East Asia. By some measures, East Asia (China, Japan, the Little Tigers) surpassed both the United States and Europe as the heavyweight in the world economy by the end of the century. Using *purchasing power parity* to compare what local currencies could buy in 2001, Asia (excluding India) weighed in at around 32 percent of the world GDP, while the United States and the other Americas together accounted for just under 30 percent, with Western Europe trailing at a little over 20 percent.

GLOBALIZATION ON TRIAL

By the late 1990s, globalization was coming under fire from several directions at once. Advocates for the global South raised objections to what they saw as unfair distribution of wealth and the vulnerability of open markets to the whims of investors. Victims of deindustrialization in the global North objected to the loss of well-paying jobs as corporations moved to overseas low-wage havens in a race to the bottom. The fact that the United States was the chief financial promoter, ideological cheerleader, and military enforcer of globalization meant that U.S. policy was a target as well. In short, beginning around 1995, globalization was on trial.

Culture Clash

One of the heaviest ironies of global interconnectedness was the sharpening of cultural divides. In the early stages of globalization, scholars and social critics predicted that having instant access to information would homogenize world culture. Everyone would inhabit a *global village* (Marshall McLuhan's term) in which tastes would become universal. In some ways, that turned out to be true. Especially in the realm of pop culture, intangible commodities like Michael Jackson's *Thriller* and American TV shows like *Baywatch* and *Dallas* could be seen in dubbed versions from Rio to Hong Kong.

But that is only part of the story. Differences that were once tolerated, or even celebrated, hardened into what some called a clash of civilizations. As the conflict between Communism and capitalism faded into the shadows, the difference between East and West was redefined to mean a sense of opposition between modern, Judeo-Christian, Western civilization and the more traditional Buddhist, Islamic, and Confucian cultures of the East. As in Kipling's day a century earlier, many came to believe "East is East, and West is West, and never the twain shall meet."

People in far-flung places may have been in closer touch, but that did not make them alike. Perhaps 25 percent of the world's peoples in the 1990s spoke English as a first or second language. When the remaining 75 percent connected to the World Wide Web, they looked for websites in Chinese, Hindi, or Russian, and advertisers increasingly catered to their diverse tastes.

Nor did living closer together make people like each other. In many places, the intrusion of global influences and foreign immigrants, in particular, provoked reassertion of local cultural traditions. Waves of nativist hostility to immigrants periodically washed across Europe and North America. Politicians like America's Pat Buchanan and France's Jean-Marie Le Pen won prominent places in public life by fomenting religious and ethnic prejudice.

In many places, cultural revival took the form of religious fundamentalism. In India, for example, Hindu fundamentalists in the BJP Party called for a return to strict ancestral ways (*hindavut*), partly in reaction to the rise of militant Islam. There was an equally deep fault line between the Islamic world and the Judeo-Christian West. Reacting against the spread of secularism, Islamist radicals waged cultural warfare in the name of Islam against what they saw as the polluting influences of the West. In regular Friday prayers and lectures in Islamic schools called *madrassas*, Islamists traced the vices of the open society—moral laxity, sexual exploitation of women, family breakdown, and pornography—back to the virtues of individual freedom, women's independence, and freedom of expression. To these radicals, the virtues of the West were inseparable from the vices. The sense of Islamic culture under siege fueled resentment of Western economic and military intrusion in Islamic lands and helped motivate violent attacks of al-Qaeda and other radical groups on U.S. targets.

In the end, information technology cut in opposite directions. In some ways it homogenized world communications, whereas in other ways it reinforced cultural divisions. It turned out that when everybody could talk to one another, they sometimes got into fierce arguments.

Debt Crises

Another kind of clash came about in countries that experienced the downside of open financial markets. In Latin America, for example, critics compared the influx of foreign capital to the flow of natural resources out of what one called "the open veins of Latin America." Indeed, the debt burden became too heavy to bear. One Latin country after another teetered on the brink of default—Bolivia in the 1980s and Brazil in the 1990s.

Mexico, too, went through a punishing financial crisis. The Mexican welcome to North American capitalists was capped in the North American Free Trade Agreement implemented on January 1, 1994. The agreement allowed foreign corporations to export products to *El Norte* (the United States) duty free. Yet, the arrival of giant agribusiness, such as Birds Eye and the Archer Daniels Midland Company, had a dire impact on the already declining Mexican small holders, whose production of corn, the basic staple first domesticated in Mexico some nine thousand years earlier, declined to the point where the country became a net importer of corn. Added pressure to earn foreign exchange came from the IMF, leading to Mexican subsidies for export-oriented agriculture to earn the dollars to pay the debt to U.S. and other foreign investors. But it was not enough. Only a last-minute, multi-million-dollar bailout by the Clinton administration in 1995 saved the day for U.S. banks and other holders of Mexican debt.

Economic troubles engendered agrarian protest. The most dramatic was the eruption of a peasants' revolt in the southern Mexican state of Chiapas on the day the North American Free Trade Agreement went into effect. Led by the enigmatic Subcommandante Marcos, the Zapatistas represented local resistance to global processes that dispossessed the poor. In Brazil, a similar movement of landless agricultural workers called *movimiento sin tierra* took over unused lands. In fact, throughout Latin America in the 1990s, an incipient revolt against free-market conservatism laid the foundation for political changes that would eventually bring a new raft of antiglobalization populists, such as Venezuela's Hugo Chávez, to power after the turn of the century.

The burden of debt was especially heavy in the Fourth World. Several African countries were paying out more to the wealthy foreign holders of debt than they were spending on the social needs of their own impoverished citizens. Denouncing the immorality of this situation, activists and some political leaders joined to call for debt relief. For example, a group called Jubilee 2000 proposed a moratorium or halt on debt payments for the world's most impoverished countries.

Debt was a major problem for even the more prosperous developing countries. In Southeast Asia, financial markets collapsed in the "Asian meltdown" of 1997 with devastating political consequences. Under neoliberal rules imposed by the IMF, Indonesia and Thailand had given foreigners more or less free access to their financial markets. The click of a computer key unleashed an "electronic herd" of currency traders who rushed in to these emerging markets, only to stampede out again at the first sign of strain. With the collapse of the Thai currency, speculators made a run on the currencies of Indonesia, Hong Kong, and South Korea, after which the Little Tigers no longer looked so fierce. Similarly, under the IMF demand for austerity, Indonesia's dictator Suharto withdrew food subsidies, leading to massive riots in the streets that ultimately brought down the Suharto government. Critics complained that the role of the IMF was to ride into a scene of economic disaster and shoot the wounded.

The conditions even affected the Russian ruble because of falling prices for Russian exports. In a move that would have been inconceivable only a few years earlier, Russia accepted a multi-billion-dollar bailout from the IMF, not that it did much good. Under Russia's *crony capitalism*, money coming in the front door merely disappeared through corruption out the back.

It is important to note that China was not subject to meltdown. What made the difference was the extent of state control. Unlike the victims of the electronic herd, China kept foreign capital under strict control, as did Japan. The lesson for developing countries was that state-guided capitalism, not the free market, was the safest route to control one's economic destiny.

Unsustainable Development

Whereas globalization supporters brushed off instability as the growing pains of economic development, they had a harder time dismissing the mounting evidence of environmental degradation. Nongovernmental organizations, such as Greenpeace, warned that humans were fouling their own nest to the point where it could become uninhabitable. Something had to be done to stop the buildup of toxic wastes, greenhouse gases, and industrial pollutants. Some environmentalists worried about whether the earth could sustain rapid growth at all. James Lovelock, for example, attracted widespread attention in the 1990s for the *Gaia hypothesis*, the idea that the biosphere was a self-regulating ecosystem that would rid itself of the danger of human civilization before it would allow itself to succumb to pollution.

Partly as a result of pressure from the environmental movement, the UN sponsored a number of international agreements to control toxic waste. In the 1987 Montreal Protocol, many countries agreed to reduce ozone-destroying chlorofluorocarbons. The global movement for *sustainable development* crystallized at the 1992 UN conference in Rio de Janeiro. This was followed in 1997 by the Kyoto Protocol, under which an eventual total of 175 countries committed themselves to specific targets for the reduction of so-called greenhouse gases, that is, CO_2 and other products of burning carbon that contributed to global warming. The United States, however, was not among them. In characteristic odd-man-out fashion, the U.S. Senate refused to ratify the Kyoto agreement.

Mass Protests: Seattle, 1999

Global elites ran into head-on opposition in the form of a grass-roots antiglobalization movement. Opposition bubbled up from many quarters. Concerned about the loss of manufacturing jobs in the global North, the American Federation of Labor–Congress of Industrial Organizations revived the tradition of American labor activism and agitated for the inclusion of labor and environmental standards in international trade and lending agreements. Pursuing *globalization from below* as an alternative to corporate globalization, more utopian sides of the movement set out to break the World Bank, eliminate the IMF, provide debt relief to Africa, and get rid of multinational corporations. Movement heroes emerged, including the Zapatistas in Mexico and a French farmer named José Bové, who drove his tractor through the front of a MacDonald's in protest of the fast-food component in corporate globalization. Even as some intellectuals were proclaiming the end of history in the triumph of liberal capitalism, movement thinkers were declaring, "Another world is possible."

All these forces converged on Seattle, Washington, at the end of November 1999 with the intention of disrupting the annual meeting of the WTO. In what became known as the Battle of Seattle, protesters delayed the kickoff session of the WTO and went on to stage a constant round of rallies, peaceful demonstrations, and occasional window breaking. After three days of disruption, WTO leaders called it quits and adjourned without agreement.

In its overall impact, the antiglobalization movement produced mixed results. Clearly, it failed to achieve its larger goals. It did not break the World Bank, send the IMF packing, or get the WTO to incorporate labor and environmental standards in a new global social contract. At the same time, it did help to shatter the Washington Consensus, give birth to a new kind of socially responsible global citizen, and instill a vision that another world is possible.

CONCLUSION

For a brief moment in the early 1990s, the world seemed poised to enter a new age of global harmony. With the end of the Cold War, the gruesome prospect of nuclear annihilation receded, the division of Europe was overcome, and hatchets were buried in many Third World battlegrounds. The bloody period that opened in 1914 with its world wars, civil wars, revolutions, colonial rebellions, and proxy wars now seemed, finally, to close. And despite the many great achievements of this period—triumphs over the scourge of ancient diseases, rising living standards, space exploration—they had to be measured against finally bidding farewell to so much death and destruction.

Moreover, for a brief moment, a new global era seemed to dawn in which the free exchange of goods and information would tie the world ever closer together. Long-term trends toward global convergence overrode all efforts at economic self-sufficiency, from the economic nationalism of the Western democracies in the 1930s through the Fascist Third Reich to the closed system of the Soviet Union. With the collapse of Communism and the spread of markets everywhere, it seemed the triumph of capitalism and, indeed, of the specifically American form of Open Door, free-market capitalism was complete.

Yet in the end, it proved to be a false dawn. The growing gap between rich and poor, tensions between East and West, environmental degradation, health crises, and a host of other problems bedeviled the world at the end of the twentieth century. The triumph of free-market capitalism was by no means an unmitigated blessing. To the contrary, there was growing polarization between global North and global South and deeper division between rich and poor. The rising economic tide failed to lift all boats. Even as one set of tensions was resolved, other conflicts came to the fore. The twentieth century left a deeply divided legacy to the twenty-first century.

FURTHER READING

Agnew, John. *Hegemony: The New Shape of Global Power.* Philadelphia: Temple University Press, 2005.

Barber, Benjamin. *Jihad vs. McWorld: How Globalism and Tribalism Are Reshaping the World.* New York: Ballantyne Books, 1995.

Barnet, Richard, and John Cavanagh. *Global Dreams: Imperial Corporations and the New World Order.* New York: Simon & Schuster, 1994.

Campbell-Kelly, Martin, and William Aspray. *Computer: A History of the Information Machine.* Boulder, CO: Westview Press, 2004.

Chan, Steve. *East Asian Dynamism: Growth, Order, and Security in the Pacific Region.* Boulder, CO: Westview Press, 1993.

Enloe, Cynthia. *Bananas, Beaches, and Bases: Making Feminist Sense of International Politics.* Berkeley: University of California Press, 1989.

Judt, Tony. *Postwar: A History of Europe since 1945.* New York: Penguin, 2005.

McGirr, Lisa. *Suburban Warriors: The Origins of the New American Right.* Princeton, NJ: Princeton University Press, 2001.

Moreton, Bethany. *To Serve God and Wal-Mart: The Making of Christian Free Enterprise.* Cambridge, MA: Harvard University Press, 2010.

Prashad, Vijay. *The Poorer Nations: A Possible History of the Global South.* New York: Verso, 2014.

CHAPTER 14

GLOBAL DIVERGENCE: THE POST-9/11 WORLD, 1999–2012

The Iraqi Armed Forces Band plays in a premier performance at the Presidential Republican Palace in Baghdad, Iraq, during Operation Iraqi Freedom. It was one of the many ways the United States sought to normalize the experience within the Green Zone. National Archives at College Park–Still Pictures (RDSS).

AMERICA ON THE TIGRIS

On March 19, 2003, U.S. military forces, leading a coalition of thirty-one nations—the Coalition of the Willing—began a fierce aerial attack on Iraq's capital city, Baghdad, as part of the George W. Bush administration's strategy of "shock and awe." It was the initial phase in a larger campaign that took the grand title Operation Iraqi Freedom, and a fast-moving land invasion soon followed that brought Americans to the Iraqi capital for what they expected would be a friendly occupation. "You will be welcomed as liberators," Secretary of Defense Donald Rumsfeld told American troops.

Confident of their ability to remake Iraq according to an American design, as the United States had with Japan after World War II, officials of the Coalition Provisional Authority set up headquarters on the banks of the fabled Tigris River in the huge walled compound known as the Republican Palace that once belonged to deposed dictator Saddam Hussein. In the next several months, the Halliburton Corporation and other U.S. contractors transformed the seventeen-square-mile compound into the Green Zone, a secured space where Americans could go about their business without armed escort and indulge in a little slice of home.

Being inside the walls of the Green Zone was like being back in the United States. Halliburton supplied the workers and troops with food that could be found in any hotel chain in America, including pork sausage for breakfast, pork chops for dinner, and plenty of alcohol, although this was an Islamic country where pork and alcohol were taboo. Inside the zone, no one thought it strange to see women in jogging shorts (another taboo) or to have Hollywood movies and dance hall music on demand. These were just the kind of amenities that had accompanied American forces overseas since the occupations of Germany and Japan after the Second World War.

But the occupation of Iraq turned out to be different from that of Germany and Japan. Outside the walls of the Green Zone, a mounting insurgency turned Baghdad into a red zone of roadside bombs, sniper attacks, and suicide bombers. Much of Iraq descended into chaos, with oil wells going up in flames, ancient art treasures looted, and daily life reduced to misery. Given the harsh realities outside the walls, life inside the Green Zone seemed as surreal as the Emerald City in L. Frank Baum's tribute to twentieth-century modernity and consumption, The Wonderful Wizard of Oz. Yet, rising guerrilla resistance outside the walls reminded many of the agonies of the Vietnam War.

GLOBAL DIVERGENCE

The Green Zone symbolized a larger trend of American isolation against hostile forces. After years of relative freedom to move about the channels of globalization, now American power met increasing resistance overseas. There was hostility from the Islamic world, exemplified by the violent Iraqi insurgency. The great powers of Russia and China increasingly challenged U.S. influence in the councils of world affairs, while Latin Americans elected a raft of leaders who sometimes defied U.S. authority.

After 2003 there was the sense of the open world closing down. A dozen years after the fall of the Berlin Wall, new walls were being built on troubled borders between the United States and Mexico, as well as between Israelis and Palestinians. Meanwhile, nativists and religious extremists increasingly policed cultural and geographic borders. After a period when the centripetal forces of globalization brought distant economies together, now centrifugal forces were driving rich and poor further apart, both within and between countries. The global convergence of the twentieth century seemed a distant memory from the vantage point of the twenty-first century, as world societies witnessed the increasing movement toward global divergence.

POWER SURGE

In the absence of any serious rival, the U.S. superpower expanded its influence across the globe. Shaken by the terrorist attacks of September 11, 2001, on New York's World Trade Towers and the Pentagon in Washington, DC, the United States exacted its revenge first on Afghanistan, who had actual ties to the terrorists, and then on the oil-rich country Iraq in 2003. The attack on Afghanistan seemed like an obvious choice, since its leaders, the Taliban, sponsored al-Qaeda and the terrorists who turned commercial airplanes into missiles. Iraq, however, which had no direct ties to the terrorists, was not so clear. Meanwhile, the sense of vulnerability wrought by 9/11 revived old Cold War fears about the intentions of its former adversary, Russia. In response, the United States pressed for expansion of NATO, itself a legacy of the Cold War, into the one-time Russian sphere of influence in Eastern Europe.

America's aggressive overseas posture developed alongside an expansion of executive power within the United States. After 9/11, those calling for the smallest possible government—neoconservatives and the political right—pressed for the largest expansion of the state and presidential powers since the late 1940s. Republicans drew on the old Reagan coalition of free-market conservatives, the Religious Right, and foreign policy hardliners to rally behind George W. Bush, the son of the former president George H. W. Bush, in the election of 2000. After the 9/11 attacks, Bush moved to concentrate power in the executive branch by expanding the military, ignoring the will of Congress, and infringing on civil liberties.

Republican Power

Republicans gained strength after the election of 1996 in a revolt against Bill Clinton, whom they refused to accept as a legitimate president. They objected not so much to Clinton's policies, since he governed from the center with support for free trade and deficit reduction, but rather what he represented. As a Democrat, Clinton was the heir to the politics that produced the New Deal of the 1930s and the counterculture of the 1960s, and conservatives were ideologically opposed to both. Unwilling to wait until 2000, they set out to reverse the results of the 1996 election through impeachment. In the House of Representatives, Republicans seized on Clinton's sexual indiscretions to bring the president before a grand jury, where his testimony regarding sex with a White House intern led to formal impeachment proceedings on the grounds of perjury and obstruction of justice. House conservatives, who had resisted Clinton's administration since

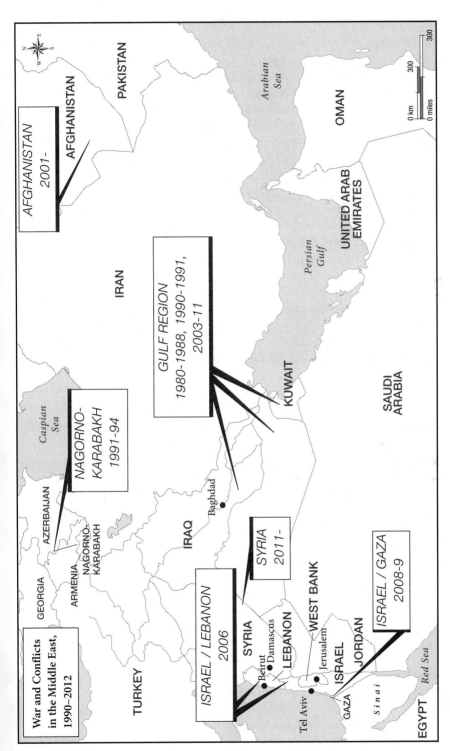

MAP 14.1

1994, believed that they had scored a victory against more than the president. Like the Alger Hiss trial of 1948, House Republicans saw Clinton's charge as an indictment of a corrupt, amoral welfare state under Democratic leadership. The outcome was different in the Senate, however, where Democrats were more powerful and where the president was found not guilty. Weary of political partisanship, the public opposed impeachment and punished its backers by dealing Republicans a loss in the 1998 midterm elections.

Emboldened by their ability to embarrass the president and the Democratic Party, however, the political Right regrouped in the election of 2000, which pitted Texas governor George W. Bush against Clinton's vice president and heir apparent, Democrat Al Gore. This was one of the most extraordinary elections in American history. Although Gore won the popular vote by a margin of 540,000, the outcome in the Electoral College, where the president is formally selected, was in doubt because of a dispute over the vote in Florida. On first count, Bush won by a razor-thin margin of 537 votes of almost 6 million cast, but Gore demanded a partial recount. Shortly after the recount began, the Supreme Court took the unprecedented step of intervening in the electoral process with a five-to-four vote that stopped the Florida recount and handed the victory to Bush. This highly controversial decision left the public bitterly divided and introduced new terms into the vocabulary, such as *hanging chads*, a reference to disputed ballot cards with inconclusive punch holes. It also left the new president without a clear mandate for governing.

Instead of acknowledging the division in the country and moving to the center, President Bush ruled from the right. Taking a cue from the Reagan era, he pushed through a series of tax cuts beginning in 2001 that he claimed freed the wealthy of an undue burden, including a rollback of Clinton's top marginal income tax rate. But within months of taking office, the Bush administration was beset by a host of economic troubles, the consequences of what the business page of the *New York Times* called "a near endless amount of greed and criminality" that took hold in the late 1990s. Bush's prowealthy, or in his parlance "earner," economic plan received a boost from congressional repeal of the law intended to prevent commercial banks from engaging in speculative investment. Free of such regulations, reckless investors created a stock market bubble by buying shares of virtually any company in the business of information technology. The burst of the *dot-com bubble* in 2001 undermined America's economy and proved an omen of economic crises to come.

More serious was a bevy of financial scandals at corporations with close ties to the Washington elite. Having cheated shareholders out of untold billions, several large corporations were buried under an avalanche of fraud and mismanagement that led to some of the biggest bankruptcies in American business history. The most spectacular was the December 2001 collapse of Enron, a once-booming energy-trading firm based in Houston, Texas. Enron chief executive officer (CEO) Kenneth Lay was prosecuted for false statements and insider trading. Although Lay died before sentencing, many of his corporate counterparts served jail time. Revelations of corporate corruption tarnished the era of freewheeling capitalism that began with government deregulation in the late 1970s and continued through Reagan and Clinton.

September 11, 2001

The whole world felt the consequences of corporate malfeasance in the United States, but this drama soon became the backdrop to a much larger crisis that resulted from attacks on American soil. On the morning of September 11, 2001, al-Qaeda, a shadowy organization of Islamic extremists led by Osama bin Laden, hijacked four commercial airliners and used them as missiles to attack major symbols of American wealth and power. With suicide pilots at the controls, two of the planes flew into the World Trade Towers in New York, giant monuments of capitalism and Western economic power. In the ensuing fire and building collapse, nearly three thousand people were killed, including dozens of heroic police and firefighters who selflessly rushed into the towering infernos to save others. A third plane gouged a huge hole in the Pentagon, an iconic symbol of U.S. military might. A fourth crashed in a Pennsylvania field after a brave struggle by passengers to wrest control from the terrorists and steer the plane away from major cities.

These vicious terrorist attacks did not appear out of thin air. United States intelligence had credited Islamic extremists with several attacks on American targets, including a first attempt on the World Trade Towers in 1993, the spectacular 1998 bombings of U.S. embassies in Nairobi, Kenya, and Das es Salaam, Tanzania, and more recently the 2000 attack on the USS *Cole* in a harbor in Yemen. In the months before 9/11, U.S. intelligence received information of another imminent attack, but poor coordination among immigration authorities, the Central Intelligence Agency (CIA), and the Federal Bureau of Investigation left America's defenses down. Even so, anticipating attacks is not the same as preventing them, as the world would discover when further terrorist actions killed dozens of innocent citizens in the Madrid train station (March 2004) and a London subway (July 2005).

The immediate roots of 9/11 lay in Saudi Arabia, homeland of fifteen of the nineteen hijackers. Bin Laden, a renegade member of the Saudi elite, had long opposed the United States for stationing troops near Islamic holy sites in support of a regime he sought to destroy. The irony was that bin Laden and the United States had once fought on the same side against the Soviet occupation of Afghanistan. During the Cold War, the CIA had sponsored Islamic warriors known as *mujahideen*, including so-called Arab Afghans, one of whom was Osama bin Laden (see Chapter 12). As a one-time conduit for CIA funds, bin Laden may have believed that having expelled the Soviet empire from Islamic lands, he was now strong enough to do the same to the United States. This effect, the violent reaction from friendly or neutral parties who suffered collateral damage as the result of U.S. activities in their land, happened frequently enough that the CIA coined the term *blowback* to describe the phenomenon.

Most Americans knew little, if any, of this history, and their leaders took few steps to enlighten them. Unwilling to acknowledge that the 9/11 attacks had anything to do with U.S. policy in the Islamic world, President Bush attributed the attacks to a pathological hatred of American values. "Why do they hate us?," he asked rhetorically in his September 20 address to the nation, and he answered simply, "They hate our freedoms—our freedom of religion, our freedom of speech, our freedom to vote and assemble and disagree with each other."

There was a kernel of truth in Bush's argument. Fanatical followers of al-Qaeda drew no distinction between Western vices and Western virtues. In his "Letter to America" of November 2002, for example, bin Laden wrote, "You are a nation that permits acts of immorality, and you consider them to be pillars of personal freedom." Among the supposed immoral acts he listed were "fornication, homosexuality, intoxicants, gambling, and trading with interest," along with the use of women as "advertising tools."

Whether the attacks occurred because of what America was or because of what it did—or both—they evoked a giant wave of sympathy around the world. "We are all Americans now," wrote a leading French newspaper *Le Monde*. Within the Islamic world, hostility was temporarily set aside in many quarters as governments awaited the inevitable U.S. retaliation. Retribution came with an attack on the Taliban regime in Afghanistan. Proclaiming a *war on terror* against both actual terrorists and "the governments that harbor them," President Bush began bombing Afghanistan on October 7, 2001, with the intention of overthrowing the arch-Islamist Taliban government in Kabul that was known to provide safe haven for al-Qaeda.

Tapping a deep reservoir of sympathy, the United States won considerable international support for military operations in Afghanistan. Only Britain sent troops, but Russia raised no objection to the stationing of U.S. troops at bases in the former Soviet republics of Uzbekistan and Kyrgyzstan, something that would have been inconceivable during the Cold War. Surprisingly, Pakistan's dictator, General Pervez Musharraf, turned against the Taliban, which was supported by Pakistan's secret intelligence services, and came out in support of the United States. Even Iran, home of the 1979 Shiite revolution, cooperated in defeating its Sunni rival, the Taliban.

Given the success of Afghan resistance to the ten-year Soviet occupation, most expected a long, hard fight for U.S. and British troops and their Afghan allies, the Northern Alliance. To everyone's surprise, the Northern Alliance swept into Kabul on November 12, 2001, only a month after the bombing began, sending the remnants of the Taliban into mountain hideouts, where they regrouped and continued to harass Western forces for years to come. In ways that resembled the international coalition of the first Gulf War against Iraq, the United States initially acted in Afghanistan as a kind of global sheriff with multilateral backing that continued when military command was turned over to NATO in August 2003.

BORDER CLOSINGS

It was not long, however, before the world that came together to denounce terrorism quickly began to split apart. Some of the reasons for growing global divergence after 2001 had to do with forces beyond American control. Globalization had its own homogenizing tendencies that, paradoxically, heightened cultural differences. The more different groups were brought together, the more they insisted on their own parochial identities as fundamentalist Christians, militant Islamists, or staunch Hindus. Another aspect at play was the deepening inequalities in the global economy that set class against class and local interests against global interests in complex struggles over the fruits of economic development. In addition, geopolitical differences produced rising tensions between the United States and China, which sometimes acted in conjunction with the other great Asian land empire, Russia. At the same time, rapid expansion of the global economy threatened the environment and future frontiers of development.

Beginning in 2002, American diplomacy abandoned the twentieth-century tradition of multilateralism and reverted to the nineteenth-century practice of unilateralism, often forging ahead without regard to the interests or wishes of other powers. Standing alone, the Bush administration rejected the Kyoto treaty intended to curb global warming, while angering America's sometime partner Russia in December 2001 by unilaterally renouncing the Anti-Ballistic Missile Treaty that went back to the years of détente under Nixon. The clearest manifestation of unilateralism was the 2003 invasion of Iraq, which was opposed by all the major powers except Britain. Even the so-called Coalition of the Willing looked less multilateral and more unilateral, considering the United States provided over 80 percent of the troops (the number rose to 92 percent by 2007)

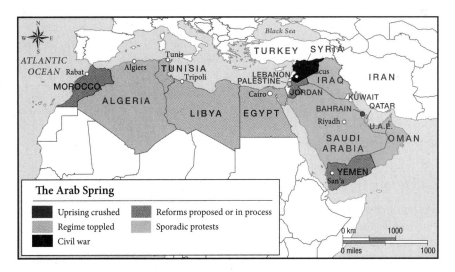

MAP 14.2

and nearly all of the financing for the invasion and occupation (in the range of $53 billion in 2003). Some critics like the senator and 2004 Democratic presidential candidate John Kerry mocked the idea as the "coalition of the coerced and bribed." As a result of these trends toward divergence, the United States lost the position of world leader it had held only a few years earlier.

Opening the Middle East

American unilateralism was most apparent in efforts to open the Middle East. Before the attacks of 9/11, Iraq and Iran were of special interest to the Bush administration. From the point of view of the president and his hawkish advisors, including Vice President Richard "Dick" Cheney and Secretary of Defense Donald Rumsfeld, the problem with these two countries was that they remained defiantly closed off to Western influence. Although the secular Baathist regime in Iraq and the theocratic Islamist government in Iran were ideological enemies, they both relied on family networks and top-down bureaucracies that formed a nearly impenetrable barrier to foreign commerce.

Driven by the ideology of free-market conservatism, however, the Bush administration was determined to break them open. The administration laid out its general goal in the National Security Strategy (NSS) report of September 2002, in which the administration proclaimed "freedom, democracy, and free enterprise" as the universal model. Explaining further, the NSS promised to press foreign governments to adopt policies that would "encourage business investment" and "lower marginal tax rates." If there was resistance, the NSS warned, "We will not hesitate to act alone" and act preemptively. In what many read as the declaration of a lone superpower, the NSS vowed to prevent any potential adversary from ever "equaling the power of the United States."

When this sweeping blueprint for changing the world was applied to the Middle East, it immediately became entangled in the politics of oil. Although rarely admitted by top U.S. officials, the fact that Iraq and Iran each sat atop roughly 20 percent of the world's proven oil reserves heightened their geopolitical significance, especially at a time of peak oil, when many feared that oil production would soon decline. Although the United States received less than 10 percent of its supply from the Middle East, for Europe and Japan the number was closer to 80 percent. Whoever controlled these vast reserves would have tremendous leverage in world affairs.

Call to War

Determined to assert U.S. control over Persian Gulf oil and, more generally, open the Middle East, President Bush went on the rhetorical offensive in his State of the Union address in January 2002. He portrayed Iran and Iraq as part of an Axis of Evil that sought weapons of mass destruction for use against the United States and its allies, notably, Israel. North Korea was designated the third member of the

Axis of Evil because it had an advanced nuclear weapons program. The bellicose tone marked a departure from previous administrations. President Reagan and the elder George Bush had found Iraq's dictator Saddam Hussein a useful antagonist to the Islamic regime in Iran, and Bill Clinton had continued this containment policy with sanctions and occasional bombs. None made such forward steps toward confrontation.

Bush's belligerent speech was the opening salvo in a campaign to convince the world of the need for regime change in all three countries, starting with Iraq. Yet nothing in international law allowed one government to overthrow another or to launch an unprovoked attack. Since the Nuremberg Principles after the Second World War, such an attack was seen as a war of aggression and, as such, had been explicitly outlawed by UN and Geneva conventions. The only exception was self-defense against imminent attack under the doctrine of preemption.

Was Saddam Hussein preparing to make war on the United States? Any attack on U.S. soil was out of the question, but opinion was divided at the time on whether he might have made trouble for U.S. allies in the region. He had done so before, when he invaded Kuwait and sent Scud missiles into Israel. Did he have weapons of mass destruction, as alleged by Bush spokespersons? Although UN weapons inspectors had found nothing in Iraq, Hussein had used chemical weapons in the war with Iran in the 1980s and had tried to develop nuclear weapons in the early 1990s.

The jury was still out on these questions when the Bush administration began a campaign for action in the fall of 2002. Vice President Dick Cheney was especially adamant in proclaiming that Iraq had nuclear, chemical, and biological weapons capability. In an attempt to sell the idea of regime change to a skeptical public, the administration did its best to link Hussein with bin Laden as common enemies of the U.S. war on terror. The day after the attacks of 9/11, the president ordered his counterintelligence advisor to "see if Saddam did this; see if he's linked in any way." By repeating the accusation often enough, administration officials convinced a credulous majority. Opinion polls in the United States reported that significant numbers of Americans believed Hussein, contrary to all evidence, was involved in the 9/11 attacks.

The fact that no links existed did not prevent the Bush administration from going forward with plans for preventive war. (In the absence of an imminent threat, the preemption doctrine did not apply.) Bush capitalized on the climate of fear engendered by the 9/11 attacks to win congressional approval for military action against Iraq. With Democrats divided, Republicans pushed through a resolution on October 11, 2002, authorizing the use of force. Then, in November, the administration prevailed on the UN Security Council to call for rigorous international inspections of Iraqi weapons programs, and three months later, Secretary of State Colin Powell returned to the UN seeking a tougher resolution authorizing the use of force. Behind a well-orchestrated media blitz, Powell declared on February 6, 2003, with professions of absolute certainty that Hussein possessed mobile biological weapons labs and had sought uranium and aluminum centrifuges necessary to produce a nuclear bomb.

Sitting before the United Nations in 2003, with the United States still on edge following the attacks of September 11 two years earlier, Secretary of State Colin Powell urged the Security Council to take action against Iraq's ruler, Saddam Hussein, for producing weapons of mass destruction. Unable to move the council, Powell and the United States cobbled together an alliance—the Coalition of the Willing—to act without the United Nations. Getty.

These claims were false. Whether they were knowingly false—in other words, lies—has been debated since. But a large segment of world opinion at the time refused to believe them. In the Downing Street memo of July 23, 2002, only later released to the public, a British intelligence officer reported after a visit to Washington that "the intelligence and the facts were being fixed around the policy." Not surprisingly, Russia and China, America's one-time Cold War adversaries, opposed the second UN resolution, but it was noteworthy that France, too, threatened a veto in the UN Security Council. In the end, the resolution never came to a vote, thus depriving the subsequent U.S. invasion of international approval. Even Germany, normally one of America's most reliable allies, refused to go along after an election that unexpectedly brought victory to an antiwar candidate.

The exception that proved the rule was Britain. Prime Minister Tony Blair was the only major head of state to stand with Bush. The Bush–Blair partnership was the latest case in the long tradition of Anglo-American cooperation going back through Clinton and Blair, Reagan and Thatcher, Roosevelt and Churchill, Wilson and Lloyd George, all the way to the Monroe Doctrine. Otherwise, world leaders opposed the Anglo-American invasion.

Heads of state opposed to the war were in step with street protesters. The most significant antiwar movement since the Vietnam era mobilized the largest peace protest in world history on February 15, a week after Powell's UN speech. Even the conservative journal the *Economist* was impressed enough with the ten million demonstrators around the globe to dub the peace movement *the other superpower*. The biggest crowds were in Europe, but over one hundred thousand (some estimated three hundred thousand) demonstrated in a frigid New York City.

Invasion and Occupation of Iraq

But neither diplomatic opposition nor popular protest convinced the Bush administration to change course. On March 19, 2003, U.S. forces began bombing Baghdad in a punishing barrage. The land invasion that followed quickly overwhelmed Iraqi troops, and three short weeks after the bombing began, U.S. forces occupied the capital Baghdad. It was the latest example of how the Open Door policy that had been in place since 1898 led to America kicking in doors when weaker countries did not cooperate.

Civil government during the ensuing U.S. occupation came under the Coalition Provisional Authority. The Coalition Provisional Authority set up headquarters in Saddam Hussein's Republican Palace and was led by L. Paul Bremer, a former associate of Henry Kissinger. Bremer was a man on a mission to ensure Iraq was open for business. Early on, he boasted, "We're going to create the first real free market economy in the Arab world." With utopian zeal, Republican political operatives flew in to assist Bremer in transforming Iraq's command economy into a model of laissez-faire capitalism by privatizing public assets, ending food subsidies, and removing restrictions on foreign ownership. One of the first U.S. companies to arrive was the Halliburton Corporation. With Vice President Cheney as its former CEO, Halliburton was in a good position to win the no-bid contract worth $1.7 billion to provide construction and logistical support for the occupation.

But it proved easier to enter Iraq than to occupy it. Contrary to Rumsfeld's optimistic prediction that Americans would be welcomed as liberators, occupying forces were greeted with sniper fire, improvised explosive devices, and suicide bombs. Insurgent attacks on U.S. forces and Iraqi militias mounted to a peak of 180 a day by the fall of 2006. Insurgents were a disunited group that included remnants of Hussein's Baath Party, disgruntled soldiers of the disbanded Iraqi army, and militant fighters for Islam. Indeed, the U.S. occupation transformed Iraq from a place that persecuted radical Islamists before the invasion to a proving ground for foreign fighters eager to wage *jihad* against the Christian occupier of Islamic land. In a bitter irony, prewar claims that Iraq harbored Islamic terrorists finally came true.

By contrast, prewar promises of democracy did not take root. Instead of switching from dictatorship to democracy, Iraq descended into anarchy. As the peace movement had predicted, toppling a repressive dictator was easier than ruling in his place. Efforts to construct a stable client regime foundered on religious divisions between majority Shiites and minority Sunnis, ethnic divisions between Arabs and Kurds, and multiple tribal divisions, all of which undermined the kind of overarching nationalism that had sustained the former Baathist regime. Ordinary Iraqis suffered civilian killings, electricity outages, food shortages, and polluted drinking water.

The Lonely Superpower

The struggling occupation of Iraq helped push the sole superpower into lonely isolation. Only recently recognized as *the* world leader, the United States quickly lost much of its following. The consequence of U.S. isolation was revealed most graphically in the cost comparison between the two Gulf Wars. The estimated $60 billion cost of the first Gulf War was born mostly by other states, either those directly in the line of fire, primarily Kuwait and Saudi Arabia, or those dependent on Persian Gulf oil, such as Japan and Germany. Conversely, the much greater cost of the second Gulf War—an estimated $822 billion as of 2013—was borne almost entirely by the taxpayers of the United States, who also picked up the tabs of several smaller countries that contributed troops.

The occupation of Iraq also exposed deeper fault lines between the United States and other world powers. The presence of Anglo-American armies in the Middle East renewed a centuries-old conflict between maritime empires on the periphery and continental land empires in the interior. Heirs to ancient centers of empire, Russia and China both pushed back against Anglo-American incursions. China needed Middle Eastern oil, while Russia, an oil-rich country itself, had long sought strategic influence in the region.

Great power interests collided in Iran. Since the Axis of Evil speech, the Bush administration insisted Iran was seeking nuclear weapons, but both China and Russia used diplomatic influence to deflect U.S. demands for ironclad sanctions. In October 2007, Bush raised the specter of World War III to win support for tougher sanctions in the face of Russian President Vladimir Putin's denials of an active Iranian nuclear program.

But then, in a surprising development, the threat of military action against Iran ran aground when U.S. intelligence agencies declared in November 2007 that Iran had given up its nuclear program four years earlier. This startling reversal of previous intelligence estimates effectively eliminated for the time being what the Bush administration had been using as a justification for another preventive war with Iran.

Tensions were heightened in Eastern Europe, as well, when NATO expanded eastward to include Poland and other former satellites of the Russian empire. Putin bristled at the U.S. announcement that it intended to deploy missiles in Poland and the Czech Republic. Raising the specter of a renewed Cold War in February 2007, Putin threatened to retarget Russian missiles on Western Europe, and in October he compared the situation to the Cuban Missile Crisis of 1962, with Bush playing the role of Nikita Khrushchev by installing threatening missiles so close to Russia.

The nuclear balance of terror had changed a great deal since 1962. In some ways, things had taken a turn for the worse. Although 95 percent of the world's nuclear bombs were in U.S. and Russian arsenals in 2007, the awesome destructive capacity of nuclear weapons meant there was reason to worry about the remaining 5 percent. Nuclear proliferation had expanded the nuclear fraternity beyond its older members—the United States, Russia, Britain, France, and China—to include Israel, India, and Pakistan. There was some comfort in the fact that many countries gave up their nuclear weapons programs, generally under outside pressure, including all three members of the so-called Axis of Evil. Even before Bush began to target Hussein, Iraq had given up its weapons program in the wake of the first Gulf War, and Iran had done so in 2003, according to U.S. intelligence agencies. Finally, North Korea agreed to end its nuclear weapons program in 2007.

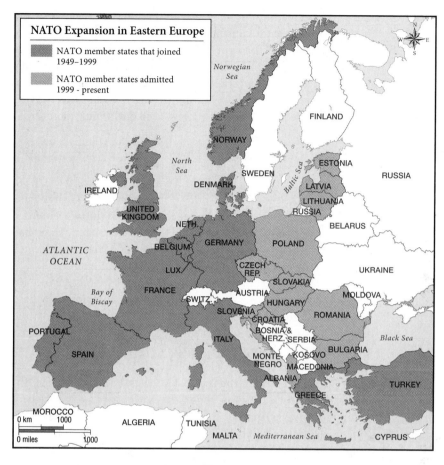

NATO Expansion in Eastern Europe

◼ NATO member states that joined 1949–1999

▨ NATO member states admitted 1999 - present

MAP 14.3

Closing Cultural Borders

Growing geopolitical tensions were accompanied by growing frictions among world cultures. At bottom, the reassertion of cultural difference was a paradoxical consequence of the homogenizing tendencies of globalization. The more everyone felt the pressure to be the same, the more they insisted on their right to be different. Even as consumer culture was welcomed in places like Japan and China, the openness epitomized by the American way of life was rejected as alien to tight-knit, family-based traditions.

Having been raised on the high ideals of the open society, including equality before the law, freedom of movement, and civil liberty, Americans were shocked by criticism of its excesses: the vulgarity of reality television, the immorality of poverty amid affluence, the selfishness of unfettered individualism, and disdain for the common good. In treasuring their own freedom, Americans failed to see how others could feel oppressed by their actions.

The cultural rift appeared most dramatically in the clash between Islam and the West. The spread of Western consumer values epitomized by McDonald's and Coca-Cola, along with freer forms of sexual expression and gender equality, met stiff resistance in cultures still defined by patriarchal values and the marriage of religion and everyday life. In contrast to the secular rhythms of Western society—five days of work and church on Sunday—it was the obligation of every Muslim to bow toward Mecca and pray five times each day, which complicated the Western model of work during the business day.

Especially with NATO bombs causing "collateral damage" to villagers in Iraq and Afghanistan, Muslim attitudes grew decidedly hostile toward the West. As measured by successive Pew surveys after 2001, favorable ratings of the U.S. fell precipitously everywhere in the Islamic world to the point where George Bush was far less popular than Osama bin Laden in many places. If the two had faced off in Pakistan, Egypt, or Sudan—that is, if any of these undemocratic states had held free elections—bin Laden would have won in a landslide. Yet even educated Americans were generally unable to comprehend the roots of this animosity.

Another kind of ideological rift ran through the Western Hemisphere. Latin Americans increasingly rejected the free-market ideology championed by both Clinton liberals and Bush conservatives. Having struggled to free themselves from right-wing dictatorships, Latin American voters elected a number of strong critics of the free market to power between 2003 and 2007, including Nestor Kirchner, followed by his wife, Cristina Fernandez de Kirchner, in Argentina, Evo Morales in Bolivia, Rafael Correa in Ecuador, and socialist Michelle Bachelet in Chile. The most vociferous of these new leftists was Hugo Chavez, whose control of the largest oil reserves in the Western Hemisphere gave him the confidence to defy U.S. power. Not since Fidel Castro's Cuban Revolution in the early 1960s had there been such strong opposition to the United States in the region.

Even Western Europe, the region with the strongest cultural bonds to the United States, felt estranged from its longtime ally. Having grown disillusioned with militarism after two world wars, Europeans instead settled comfortably into the peaceable pursuit of the good life. Seeing a growing breach between American militarism and European pacifism, one commentator drew a tongue-in-cheek distinction between the two societies based on the Roman gods of war and of love: "Americans are from Mars, and Europeans are from Venus." With their own colonialism safely in the past, European citizens and most political leaders rejected the Anglo-American war in Iraq.

Closings in the Open Society

The attempt to impose the open society by force in the Middle East was accompanied by efforts to close off channels of the open society in the United States. Posing a choice between freedom and security, the Bush administration initially won strong congressional support for a series of infringements on cherished civil liberties. In the emergency atmosphere after 9/11, Congress adopted the

USA Patriot Act, expanding domestic spying in a variety of ways, including the requirement that libraries and phone companies turn over patron records without their knowledge. In the months and years that followed, the president capitalized on the climate of fear to take a series of actions whose constitutionality was in question. These included the imprisonment without trial of thousands of men of Middle Eastern origin; the torture of prisoners at Abu Ghraib, a prison in Iraq; abuse of so-called enemy combatants at Guantánamo, a detention camp at the U.S. naval base in Cuba; the kidnapping of suspected enemy agents and their "extraordinary rendition" to countries known to practice torture; the creation of supersecret CIA prisons in Europe; and eavesdropping on phone conversations of U.S. citizens through warrantless wiretaps.

Some of these measures were struck down by the Supreme Court. A majority of the justices, for example, held that detainees at Guantánamo were entitled to such standard legal protections as the Geneva Conventions. But on the whole, the tradition of constitutional checks and balances did little to restrain the expansion of what some said was arbitrary executive power. Even the will of Congress was thwarted, often through an unprecedented number of presidential *signing statements*, or extraneous comments delivered at the bill's signing, that were contrary to congressional intent. Indeed, the imperial presidency made a remarkable return.

Nor did the American public initially do much to restrain centralized power. In ways reminiscent of McCarthyism in the early stages of the Cold War, political leaders fomented a climate of fear for their own electoral advantage. Drawing a false connection between terrorists and illegal immigrants, right-wing leaders campaigned for the erection of a giant fence between the United States and Mexico in an attempt to seal the border against foreign influences. Although President Bush himself refused to engage in immigrant bashing, he often spoke of an America under siege by foreign terrorists. As in the red scares after the two world wars, the terror scare proved to be effective at alienating political opponents.

That was demonstrated in the 2004 election. With unsurpassed skill at mobilizing the electorate, Karl Rove, a key White House political advisor, revitalized the Reagan coalition by rallying economic conservatives and the Religious Right around the flag. With the politics of fear riding high in 2004, George Bush was elected to a second term. The election of a bellicose free-market conservative seemed to exemplify America's inward turn and confirmed for many the distance between America and the rest of the world.

Power Failures

Not long after the election, however, the Republicans experienced a series of setbacks. An early sign of trouble came with congressional defeat of the administration's effort to begin privatizing Social Security. Because Social Security provided benefits for everyone from children to elderly retirees, it was the single most popular federal social program, and even free-market ideology was unable to dislodge it. Another sign of mounting difficulty came with the Bush administration's response to Hurricane Katrina in August 2005. Despite prior warning of a possible breach in the levees protecting New Orleans, the Federal Emergency Management Agency was unable to mount an effective rescue operation of thousands of poor people, many of whom were African American, stranded on rooftops and bridges. Race and poverty collided in media commentaries that frequently contrasted the Bush administration's neglect of the poor with the many favors granted to the rich.

A perfect storm of institutional and political failures, New Orleans produced images that shocked Americans. Hurricane Katrina's wrath went far beyond New Orleans, as this image taken during Secretary of the Interior Gale Norton's visit to the region shows, to the entire Gulf Coast. National Archives at College Park–Still Pictures (RDSS).

Yet another obstacle to Republican aims was continued resistance in Iraq, coupled with growing antiwar sentiment at home. As in Vietnam, Iraqi guerilla forces fighting for their homeland were able to hold off the mighty superpower. As the situation in Iraq continued to deteriorate and the number of U.S. deaths approached three thousand, the message of antiwar protesters began to take hold with the public. As early as June 2004, a narrow majority declared the war a mistake, and, more significantly, by the summer of 2006, a majority was calling for withdrawal.

It did not help that the administration kept changing its rationale for the occupation. When the initial justification of seizing weapons of mass destruction proved false, the message was changed to spreading democracy, then to fighting terrorism, and finally to bringing stability. In the end, none of the goals was achieved. Once again, as in Vietnam, public support could not be sustained for a small war in a faraway place that went so poorly on the ground. Opposition to the war in Iraq spilled over into criticism of the domestic war on terror. Even established, centrist newspapers such as the *New York Times* began to raise alarms about the threat of a "totalitarian system" overturning the open society from within.

Another force rising against conservative power was immigrant labor. Uprooted by the harsh impact of globalization on local economies, immigrants were on the move in unprecedented numbers around the world. From nearby Latin America came a steady stream of Latino migrants in search of work no longer available in Mexico or Central America. Counting both immigrants and their descendants, Latinos of all national origins swelled to about 14 percent of the U.S. population, surpassing African Americans sometime in 2005 to become the nation's largest ethnic and racial minority, a change with profound long-term consequences for American politics and the economy.

Although grateful for jobs, immigrants compiled a long list of grievances against substandard wages, racial prejudice, and harassment by local officials. The last straw was an effort led by Republicans in the House of Representatives to criminalize undocumented workers and anyone who employed, housed, fed, or otherwise helped ease their plight, including Catholic priests running soup kitchens for the hungry poor. Demanding social justice, immigrants and their supporters poured into the streets on May Day 2006—four hundred thousand strong in Chicago, perhaps five hundred thousand in Los Angeles, and well over a million in total—in what was the largest protest demonstration in U.S. history.

Electoral Reversals, 2006–8

The combined impact of these forces of opposition—civil libertarians, social justice advocates, antiwar critics, immigrant sympathizers—was registered in the mid-term elections of 2006. The power shift to Democrats was expected in the House, but not in the Senate, where Jim Webb, a strong critic of the war, eked out a victory in the Virginia Senate race that tipped the balance to the Democrats by just one vote. Declining electoral fortunes were accompanied by disarray in the normally disciplined ranks of Republican leadership. Tom DeLay, the House majority leader from 2002 to 2005, resigned his seat in disgrace in June 2006 after conviction on an ethics violation related to illegal fundraising, a victim of his own partisan excess. Meanwhile, leading Pentagon architects of the war also left office, notably, Under-Secretary of Defense Paul Wolfowitz in 2004 and his boss, Secretary of Defense Donald Rumsfeld, in 2006. Finally, Karl Rove, the political mastermind of the Republican rise to power since 2000, resigned in August 2007.

Sensing opportunity, Democratic hopefuls began campaigning for the presidential nomination earlier than ever before. Although Senator Hillary Clinton of New York, former first lady to President Bill Clinton, jumped out to an early lead,

Senator Barack Obama (2008–16) of Illinois eventually won both the Democratic Party's nomination and the White House in 2008. A talented law professor of mixed black and white parentage, Obama spoke eloquently of the need for a new direction in Washington and pointed to his vote in the Senate against the Iraq War as evidence of his ability to bring about the "change we need." In one of the most striking examples of the interconnections between foreign and domestic affairs, America elected its first black president in part because of opposition to the Iraq War.

PROBLEMS OF THE TWENTY-FIRST CENTURY

In the early twenty-first century, it was possible to see what had changed since the late nineteenth century and what had remained the same. The contrasts and continuities were particularly revealing in four major areas: the world economy, social and cultural developments, political power, and the relationship between human society and the natural environment.

The United States in the World Economy

First to note was the amazing growth of the world economy compared to the late nineteenth century. Measured in terms of gross domestic product, modern societies were more than fourteen times richer in 2000 than they were in 1900. This unprecedented growth required an exponential increase in energy consumption. It has been estimated that human beings employed more energy between 1900 and 2000 in all forms, including fossil fuels and nuclear power, than in the entire course of human history up to 1900.

For the people of more affluent countries, growth exceeded all expectations. Utopian dreamers of the late nineteenth century would have been dazzled by today's wide-screen televisions, giant sport utility vehicles, omnipresent cell phones, and tablet computers. One such dreamer was Edward Bellamy, author of the 1886 utopian novel *Looking Backward*. The novel's main character was a resident of Boston who awakens in the year 2000 after a prolonged slumber to a world of universal abundance where everyone uses a kind of credit card to shop in a giant warehouse, not unlike today's big-box stores.

Bellamy may not have been surprised by a visit to Walmart or Costco, but he would have been confounded to hear that most of the products on the shelves came from outside the United States. In his day, the United States and Europe were at the top of the three-tiered world economy. That was where clothes, streetcars, and steam engines were manufactured and where the main centers of capital accumulation were located. People of the top tier were the fortunate recipients of raw materials, tropical commodities, and agricultural products shipped in from the impoverished agrarian societies of Asia and Latin America in the bottom tier.

All that changed with globalization in the last quarter of the twentieth century. Were Bellamy to awaken in the actual Boston of 2000, he would have found virtually none of the apparel factories and machine shops so common in his own day. Instead, the heavy hardware of industrial production had moved overseas to former third-tier countries such as Mexico and China. By 2007, China had surpassed the United States and Germany to become the world's largest steel producer, often dismantling entire steel complexes and reassembling them in China's fast-growing industrial regions. By exploiting large numbers of young female workers, Asian factories recapitulated the early history of the industrial revolution in Europe and North America. Once Britain had been the workshop of the world, followed by the United States. Now it was China's turn.

The same shift was increasingly true of many services. The Internet made possible the transfer of many kinds of service work to poor countries. A customer in the real Boston of 2000 who called the telephone company with a problem was likely to wind up speaking to a technical-support person in Bangalore, Manila, or another Asian city where histories of colonialism left behind a legacy of English speakers.

What may have surprised Bellamy the most was the changing geography of capital. In 2000, the centers of capital accumulation were much more widely dispersed than they were in Bellamy's day. Instead of being concentrated primarily in Europe, capital was now found in Asia and the Middle East, from whence it flowed into developed societies of Europe and North America. One result was to turn the United States from a net exporter of capital after 1917 into a debtor nation beginning in 1985 and eventually into the world's biggest debtor. Chinese and Japanese banks owned a large part of the U.S. national debt in the form of Treasury bills and other securities. In addition, Persian Gulf petrodollars flowed back into the United States in the form of finance capital. For example, in November 2007, a *sovereign wealth fund* controlled by government authorities in Abu Dhabi bought a $7.5 billion piece of Citigroup, making the largest American financial corporation somewhat less American.

With manufacturing relocating to Asia and capital more dispersed, the relatively affluent societies of Europe and North America became increasingly centered around consumption. The decades-long American romance with consumption—the search for personal fulfillment through buying commodities—increasingly revolved around information technology. People connected with each other through the thickening web of mobile communications—mobile camera phones, MP3 players for music downloads, and multipurpose iPads and iPhones, with most of the electronic equipment coming from Asian factories. In addition, the Internet fostered the spread of do-it-yourself media, as amateur videos appeared on Internet sites with clever names such as YouTube, MySpace, and Facebook, shrinking the viewer audience for network television. Social critics wondered whether all this communication bound otherwise rootless people together in a virtual community or merely contributed to their sense of being lost in cyberspace.

In any case, the world economy in 2000 had changed significantly since 1900. Perhaps the most important change was the rise of Asia. Using purchasing power parity to compare what local currencies could buy, East Asia (China, Japan, the Little Tigers) weighed in at around 32 percent of world gross domestic product. Europe, on the other hand, had lost ground. At the beginning of the twentieth century, the first site of industrial capitalism and world empire had produced fully a third of world gross domestic product; now, after decades of internecine warfare, loss of empire, and industrial decline, Europe stood at just over 20 percent.

The long-range fortunes of the United States were mixed. To be sure, the United States remained by far the biggest single national economy, accounting for about 21 percent of the world's wealth in 2001. But control of America's economic destiny increasingly lay in the hands of outsiders. Americans depended on workers in Sri Lanka to make their clothes, Hispanic immigrants to make their hospital beds, and bankers in China to make good on their debts. If they were happy in their role as the world's leading consumers, they also had reason to worry about their dependence on foreigners. With the shrinking of the manufacturing sector, America produced fewer high-value goods that the rest of the world wanted to buy. That meant a diminished ability to pay for consumer spending and government expenditures. Concerned about the inability of Americans to pay their debts, private and public, the conservative British journal *The Economist* observed in 2005 that American finances "now look more like those of a banana republic than an economic superpower."

Walmart, the Global Department Store

The relation between Asian production and U.S. consumption is illustrated by the rise of Walmart. Starting out in the 1950s with a little retail chain in small-town Arkansas, Walmart founder Sam Walton expanded nationally through the strategy embodied in the advertising slogan "everyday low prices." Bargain basement prices were made possible in part by efficiencies in tracking inventory through barcodes developed in the 1980s and in part by relentless pressure on manufacturers to reduce prices.

Production for profit had always been the defining feature of capitalism, but what was new was the shift in power from manufacturers to retailers, factories to shopping malls, General Motors to Walmart. In the old system, giant factories with huge fixed capital costs had to find sales outlets. As Henry Ford said, "Mass production requires mass consumption." Boosting consumption was the goal of everything from Keynesian policies to Madison Avenue advertising. The drive for consumption succeeded so well, however, that it led to a new system where retailers directed production. Relying on an ever more elaborate web of fiber-optic cables, big retailers like Walmart relayed huge bundles of consumer wants back to manufacturers with the demand to keep the price low.

Contracting with Chinese and other cheap-labor producers enabled Walmart to increase pressure in the 1990s on U.S. manufacturers. Acting as a bridge between low-wage producers in the global South and relatively affluent consumers

Walmart relied on factories like this candle factory in China to produce the goods that fed America's vast appetite for consumption. Library of Congress Prints and Photographs Division, Washington, DC.

in the North, Walmart was on its way to becoming the world's largest employer, with 1.8 million workers and the largest corporation, surpassing General Motors and ExxonMobil by 2005 and going on to rack up almost $300 billion in sales by 2007. As a counterpart to the global factory introduced in the 1980s, consumers could now shop in the global department store.

Inequality

Another major problem of the early twenty-first century was inequality, as the global economy widened the gap between rich and poor and altered the geography of poverty. Especially under the impact of free-market ideology, restraints came off the accumulation of capital, allowing multinational corporations headquartered in London, New York, or Shanghai to advance at the expense of others.

Again, if Bellamy had awakened in the real world of 2000, he would have been dismayed to see the persistence of plenty for a privileged minority set against privation for the poor. Confounding his utopian dream of economic equality, the fortunes of the few exceeded even those of the fabled Gilded Age. For those in the upper ranks of the economic system, huge sums could be made in manipulations of hedge funds, futures markets, and other exotic financial instruments. There were nearly 1,426 billionaires in 2013 worth a total of $5.4 trillion. Although Americans Bill Gates (Microsoft), Warren Buffett (investments), and Larry Ellison (Oracle) occupied three of the top five spots, the list included representatives of countries absent a quarter century earlier, such as Russia, India,

Mexico, and China. The wealth of this elite one thousand was equal to the combined incomes of billions of people at the opposite end of the scale.

In another measure of the turn-of-the-century wealth gap, the rich countries of the United States, Western Europe, and Japan consumed roughly thirty-two times more resources and produced thirty-two times more waste than the inhabitants of poor countries. At the extreme, the average resident of the United States used about seventy-five times the amount of energy as the average resident of Bangladesh. Fossil fuels reinforced this gap because farmers in rich countries were able to buy oil to run expensive farm machinery and fertilize their fields, whereas poor farmers could not. Instead, the poor were forced off the land; in a dreadfully ironic twist, regions that once saw plentiful harvests such as corn in Mexico, sugar in Cuba, or grain in West Africa were replaced by imports.

Inequality also increased within countries. In the United States, average wages rose only slightly in the four decades after 1970, while CEO compensation skyrocketed. By 2000, the ratio of CEO salaries to hourly compensation stood at about 500:1, up from 40:1 in 1980. When the CEO of ExxonMobil retired in 2006, he had been paid a total of $686 million in earnings over thirteen years, or the equivalent of $144,000 per day. By 2011, the ratio would decline to 182:1, but as in the Gilded Age of the late nineteenth century, liberty for private enterprises was still at odds with economic equality.

Meanwhile, the geography of inequality shifted. Economic development in the formerly agrarian societies of Asia raised per capita incomes to the point where China, at least, followed Japan and the Little Tigers (Hong Kong, Taiwan, South Korea, Singapore) out of the bottom tier. At the same time, economic stagnation and crushing debt caused the poor of Latin America and especially that of Africa to fall further behind. In the end, the gap was not so much between rich and poor countries as between transnational classes and groups occupying different rungs on the ladder of global inequality.

The gender dimensions of inequality also became clear as women were often relegated to the bottom rungs of the economic ladder. As global corporations searched for ever-cheaper labor, many added a large number of young women to their payrolls. Subject to abusive treatment by foremen and patriarchal families alike, young women were deemed fit for labor precisely because they lacked the status—and in many cases even the legal rights—that conferred the kind of social power needed to stand up to the boss.

The bottom rungs were also occupied by dispossessed rural migrants living in the wretched conditions of urban slums. Although attracted to the city by the prospect of relatively well-paid factory work, there were not enough jobs to go around, and these marginal men and women were left to eke out a meager existence in the informal economy of street sellers, rickshaw drivers, and petty criminals. Cities such as Mexico City, home to the world's largest concentration of people with twenty-one million, offered little opportunity. Although Bellamy was no stranger to urban slums, he would have been aghast at social misery on such a gargantuan scale and appalled that his utopian dreams had turned into dystopia for so many people.

The Search for Global Justice

The problem of inequality engendered movements for social justice. In opposition to corporate globalization, an amorphous movement called for *globalization from below*. Having coalesced in the 1999 Seattle protests against the World Trade Organization, the movement went on to contest global elites at a series of confrontations over the next several years, including meetings of the International Monetary Fund and the World Bank in Washington in April 2000 and the World Trade Organization in Genoa, Italy, in July 2001, where the first fatality occurred when a protestor was shot by police. Spirited protests greeted global moguls at the yearly World Economic Forum meeting at a ski resort in Davos, Switzerland. Out of protests like these grew an alternative organization known as the World Social Forum, which brought together tens of thousands of activists for huge rallies in Mumbai, India, and Porto Alegre, Brazil.

Protest movements also developed in the wake of the 2008 global economic crisis. The crisis that began in Wall Street in 2008 soon became the most severe economic downturn since the Great Depression. Deregulation of financial instruments known as derivatives under the Clinton administration had allowed Wall Street banks to engage in increasingly risky speculation in the early 2000s. But when major banks such as Bear Stearns and insurance companies such as AIG failed, the government bailed them out. Growing frustration among the unemployed and homeowners facing foreclosure gave rise to the Occupy Wall Street movement in 2011. Galvanized by an apparent double standard in Washington, where the government bailed out banks and corporations but did little to support those struggling in the middle and working class, and the Middle East uprisings against corrupt and oppressive regimes in late 2010 called the Arab Spring, thousands of Americans took to the streets chanting, "We are the 99 percent." Beginning with a single protest outside Wall Street in New York, the movement used live-feed streaming and social media platforms, such as Twitter and Facebook, to spread to almost every state in the United States, as well as Mexico, Canada, Australia, and twelve nations in Europe.

These movements pointed to the contemporary disjuncture between state and society. Just as the laissez-faire governments of Bellamy's day failed to address the needs of urban workers, so renewed laissez-faire policies at the beginning of the twenty-first century failed to address the needs of the working poor. Some believed that the new social movements might eventually play a role similar to the movements that had brought about New Deal liberalism, European social democracy, or Asian Communism. But the prospects were uncertain, at best, for reforms such as these at the global level. Because globalization skillfully evaded the welfare state, social movements were barely able to defend existing national regulations, let alone subject global corporations to worldwide capital controls, labor standards, and environmental protections.

At a time when national governments seemed neither willing nor able to enforce the UN's Universal Declaration of Human Rights, there was no global authority capable of filling the breach—not the UN itself, nor regional structures like the European Union, nor the multitude of nongovernmental organizations, least of all the managers of international finance and trade. To the contrary, the International Monetary Fund, the World Bank, and the World Trade Organization often undermined welfare states without offering credible alternatives to the system of social protections.

At the same time, some forms of inequality underwent dramatic change. Overt racism, for example, declined as a pillar of social hierarchy around the world. To be sure, racism evolved new and more subtle forms with enough urgency to spark a major UN conference on the subject in Durban, South Africa, in early September 2001, which was boycotted by the United States. But because of the changing geography of exploitation, racism was not as central to the twenty-first century as it was in the twentieth. Since the liberation of African and Asian peoples from European colonialism, along with the winning of civil rights for African Americans, the myth of white supremacy had lost much of its force and all of its legitimacy. Now, with Chinese employers exploiting Chinese laborers and Indians exploiting Indians, the myth lost a prime reason for its existence, namely, keeping nonwhite workers in subordination.

In the United States, the influx of Latino and Asian immigrants further undercut notions of an exclusively *white man's country*. Racism was still a potent force in American social relations, however, as some U.S. whites felt estranged from the country in the midst of profound change. A resurgence of white nationalist sentiment that played out in complaints about affirmative action; politically correct, or race-neutral, language; and charges that immigrants were taking opportunity from more deserving blue-collar whites echoed the past, but was not comparable to it.

End of Empire?

A major question at the dawn of the twenty-first century centered on the structure of world power: Was there a unipolar world under American dominance, or was power more broadly diffused through the channels of globalization? Answers to this question varied along the political spectrum. Some saw the United States standing at the apex of a pyramid of power. They pointed to the fact that the United States remained the lone superpower two decades after the end of the Cold War with the world's largest economy and a military budget nearly as great as the rest of the world's combined. Proponents of this view included so-called neoconservatives who echoed Henry Luce's 1941 declaration of an American century in designing their Project for the New American Century. Neoconservatives saw the United States as the rightful heir to the legacy of Western dominance.

Others argued that the world was less susceptible to American influence than at any time since the 1970s. Just as American power had been unable to subdue Vietnam, so the lone superpower was unable to work its will in the Middle East. Iraq was a study in frustration where the U.S.-backed client regime failed to establish civil or political order in the face of collapsed infrastructure, sectarian violence, and anti-foreign insurgency. Nor was Afghanistan stable. Instead, another client regime struggled against a resurgent Taliban. President Obama would officially end the War in Iraq in 2011 and the U.S. House of Representatives would vote in 2013 to accelerate the end of the War in Afghanistan.

The U.S. prestige was at its lowest ebb since the Vietnam era. Opposition to the Iraq invasion came not only from the Islamic world, but also from European allies. There was disenchantment with messianic Americanism, the desire to save the world whether or not it wanted to be saved. In addition, America's growing parochialism undermined the ability of the United States to lead by example. During the Cold War, openness of all sorts—economic opportunity, free expression, a welcome for immigrants—had given the United States the moral advantage over the closed society of the Soviet Union, an advantage that persisted in the age of globalization that followed. But post-9/11, instead of offering an open model, America's unilateral foreign policy and nativist attitude toward foreigners seemed increasingly self-centered and parochial. America's soft power, as well as its moral and social authority, proved the casualty of this turn of events.

Finally, American empire was out of step with history. A time traveler from 1900 transported to the early 2000s would have been startled to discover that the age of empire was over. Europe had been displaced from the center of world power, and in the aftermath of the Second World War, the great European empires had collapsed as their colonies won national independence. Out went racial ideology as a justification for the right of white people to rule over others. The last of the great European empire fell in the 1980s, when the Soviet Union gave up control of Eastern Europe. That left the United States as the last empire in a postimperial age. For all its might, the lone superpower appeared like a giant aircraft carrier stranded on the ground after the tide went out.

Environmental Consequences of Economic Growth

Perhaps the overriding problem at the dawn of the twenty-first century was the relationship between human society and the natural environment. Could the planet support an increasingly lavish standard of living for billions of people? When Bellamy projected a future of universal abundance, he did not reckon with the possibility that abundance could reach a point where it would exhaust the natural resources on which it was based.

The onrush of economic growth—fourteenfold from 1900 to 2000—would have been enough to cause environmental damage by itself. What made the threat worse was unprecedented growth in the world population. The population rose four times across the twentieth century, from 1.6 billion people in 1900 to 6 billion in 2000. Moreover, there was a historic shift of humanity from low levels of subsistence in the country to higher levels in the city. After millennia of living in the countryside, the majority were estimated for the first time to be city dwellers around 2005. Because businesses distributed food more efficiently, the cities could manage the massive rise in consumers, undercutting the idea of a Malthusian crisis where population outstripped food supply. The only places that struggled with population increases were the ones cut off from the world economy, like part of Africa, where recurrent famines produced the kind of starvation once common to all humankind. Even so, the combined impact of population growth and economic growth placed unprecedented stress on planetary ecology.

The science of ecology focuses on the balance of nature. Living organisms, humans included, coexist within cycles of interdependence. Wheat becomes food for humans, whose waste becomes food for bacteria, which produce nitrogen, which becomes food for wheat, thus completing the circle. A stable relation between predators and prey is maintained through feedback loops, which uphold the balance between population and resources. If resources are not replenished, the ecosystem will collapse and lakes will die, forests will wither, and, ultimately, human communities will not survive.

As in the 1970s, there was a growing awareness of the limits to growth, a sense that unlimited consumption of nonrenewable resources was simply unsustainable in the long run. What was of greatest concern to many ecologists was the imperative for unlimited expansion built into the capitalist world economy where prosperity depended on ever-increasing consumption of ever-scarcer resources. In fact, human populations in many places have engaged in overfishing, overgrazing, and overcutting of forests, generating negative feedback loops that choke off the resource base necessary to sustain a healthy economy. The concern was that the consumer-oriented global economy would amplify local strains on a planetary scale.

Environmental degradation was inseparable from the problem of inequality. Inequality guaranteed that the worst effects would be felt by the people trapped in squalid shantytowns who were more exposed to air pollution, unsafe water, and diseases such as malaria and who could not defend themselves for lack of health care. But the problem was as much about overconsumption as it was underconsumption. What would happen if the poor were able to raise their living standards to the level they saw on television in the affluent West? It has been estimated that if the world's poor lived at the same level as the world's rich, the environmental impact would increase by a factor of twelve. The high standard of living of the richer countries already puts an unsustainable strain on ecosystems. Increasing that by a factor of twelve would surely produce a general collapse. Ecologists insist that hard choices must be made about whether the rich will share their wealth or retreat to gated communities, where they would merely be the last to watch the lights flicker out as unsustainable economies succumbed to environmental collapse.

Global Warming

The most pressing environmental concern was global warming. Scientists discovered that the discharge of carbon dioxide and other greenhouse gases into the atmosphere from the burning of fossil fuels tended to trap heat near the earth's surface. Alarming proof of that fact came in the occurrence of the hottest years on record between 1990 and 2012. In 1998, the highest temperature was 1 degree Fahrenheit above average, according to the National Climatic Data Center. Then, in 2012, temperatures in the United States were 3.3 degrees Fahrenheit higher than at any other point in recorded history. The most troubling measure to date came in 2013, when the U.S. National Oceanic and Atmospheric Administration reported that carbon dioxide had reached an average daily level of four hundred parts per million, a level not seen in millions of years. The effects of global warming could be seen in the rise of mean ocean temperatures, the dramatic melting of polar ice caps, and the disruption in planetary ecology. Residents of low-lying cities such as Calcutta, Shanghai, New Orleans, and Manhattan grew increasingly concerned that rising ocean levels would one day inundate their neighborhoods.

As data accumulated, the scientific community came to accept the fact of global warming. Business and political leaders were slower to come around, but under the prompting of scientists and environmentalists, UN representatives signed the landmark Kyoto treaty in 1997, calling for significant reduction of greenhouse gases. With Russia's ratification in 2004, the treaty went into effect. Momentum to act before it was too late intensified with the award of the 2007 Nobel Peace Prize to two recipients, the UN's Intergovernmental Panel on Climate Change, for its work building a scientific consensus around the need for urgent action, and Al Gore, the former U.S. vice-president, for his work promoting public awareness.

The only industrial country that refused to take action against global warming was the United States. Responding to the laissez-faire attitudes of U.S. business and libertarian principles of independence, Congress refused to ratify the 1997 Kyoto Protocol and other international agreements to safeguard the environment, and the Bush administration blocked mandatory emission controls on industry. That was despite or perhaps because of the fact that the United States was the single largest producer of greenhouse gases, accounting for a full 30 percent of the world's emissions in the 1990s. Worldwide hopes for U.S. leadership in combatting climate change were again frustrated at the 2009 UN Conference in Copenhagen, where President Obama failed to commit the United States to significant carbon reductions. Climate change marked another arena where the United States forfeited world leadership in the early twenty-first century.

By the end of 2007, China surpassed the United States as the world's leading producer of carbon emissions. In their rush to industrialize, the Chinese were as heedless of environmental damage as Western countries had been a century earlier. With little or no regulation, the Chinese purchased highly noxious steel mills and coke plants from the West and reassembled them in booming, soot-covered

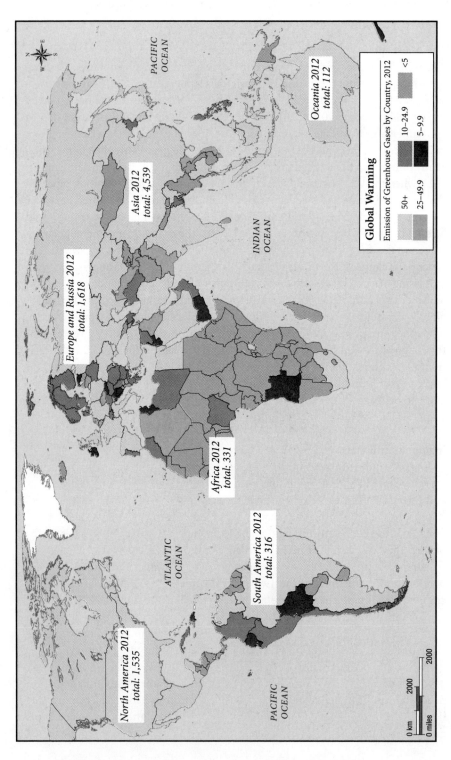

MAP 14.4

Global Warming

Emission of Greenhouse Gases by Country, 2012

50+   10–24.9   <5

25–49.9   5–9.9

Asia 2012
total: 4,539

Europe and Russia 2012
total: 1,618

North America 2012
total: 1,535

Africa 2012
total: 331

South America 2012
total: 316

Oceania 2012
total: 112

PACIFIC
OCEAN

INDIAN
OCEAN

ATLANTIC
OCEAN

PACIFIC
OCEAN

0 km   2000

0 miles   2000

cities that resembled nineteenth-century coal towns. Then they exported steel and other goods to satisfy consumer demand in the United States and Europe. The effect was to shift the environmental cost of manufacturing from relatively affluent Americans and Europeans, who had the means to remediate them, to Chinese workers and urban residents, who did not.

The lesson was that in a global economy, global warming was an international problem requiring international solutions. Luckily, the effort was not without precedent. Nearly three decades before, nations mounted a successful effort to reduce ozone depletion. By filtering out lethal ultraviolet rays, the layer of ozone high in the earth's atmosphere made life possible on earth. The use of chlorofluorocarbons as refrigerants and aerosol sprays had depleted the ozone layer and raised the incidence of skin cancer. Fortunately, the banning of chlorofluorocarbons in the late 1980s cut their use by 80 percent within just a few years.

Some small signs of willingness to build on this precedent appeared both in China, where officials promised to reduce pollution in advance of the 2008 Beijing Olympics, and in the United States, where President Obama acted in 2012 to raise mileage standards for automobiles and encourage a switch to renewable forms of energy, such as ethanol from plants. Another reason for a change in attitude was *peak oil*, the growing belief that petroleum production was reaching its peak and other energy sources would have to be found, no matter what. Extreme weather further alerted Americans to the need to address climate change. Hurricane Sandy barreled into New York and New Jersey in October 2012, leaving billions of dollars in damage in flooded subway tunnels and large-scale power outages in Manhattan, as well as widespread destruction along New Jersey's shore. Linking Sandy to climate change, Michael Bloomberg, the mayor of New York City and a political independent, endorsed President Obama in the Fall 2012 election, claiming the president was more likely to combat climate change than his Republican rival, Mitt Romney. Even so, growing development in China and unrestrained consumption in the United States did not bode well for a major reversal, despite the warnings of scientists that the hour was late—some said too late—to undo global warming.

CONCLUSION

As the world confronted the problems of the twenty-first century, human societies were bound to one another and to nature in a web of mutual dependence. Reacting against the boundless world of Internet-based globalization, local peoples turn inward in an attempt to reestablish cultural and political boundaries they felt were disappearing. Americans were no different. They attempted to fashion their own destiny within given conditions inherited from the past. Like others caught up in the historical process, they were forced to choose among limited options, but at the same time, they were free to make the choices they wanted. They could choose between unlimited consumption and environmental health, unregulated opportunity and economic equality, unilateralism and international cooperation.

Choosing wisely depended on accepting both sides of the equation, the limits of necessity as well as the creativity of freedom. To a people steeped in the values of the open society, freedom came naturally. It was harder for Americans to embrace restraint. But both were essential to making wise choices in a complex world.

FURTHER READING

Bergen, Peter L. *Holy War Inc.: Inside the Secret World of Osama bin Laden.* New York: Touchstone Books, 2001.

Chandrasekaran, Rajiv. *Imperial Life in the Emerald City.* New York: Vintage Books, 2006.

Eisenberg, Lee. *Shoptimism: Why American Consumers Will Keep on Buying No Matter What.* New York: Free Press, 2009.

Ghonim, Wael. *Revolution 2.0: The Power of People Is Greater Than the People in Power: A Memoir.* Boston: Mariner Books, 2012.

Gitlin, Todd. *Occupy Nation: The Roots, The Spirit, and Promise of Occupy Wall Street.* New York: Itbooks, 2012.

Hobsbawm, Eric. *The Age of Extremes: A History of the World, 1914–1991.* New York: Vintage Books, 1994.

Kagan, Robert. *Of Paradise and Power.* New York: Vintage Books, 2003.

MacKinnon, Rebecca. *Consent of the Networked: The World Wide Struggle for Internet Freedom.* New York: Basic Books, 2012.

McNeill, J. R. *Something New under the Sun: An Environmental History of the Twentieth-Century World.* New York: Penguin, 2000.

van Dijck, Jose. *The Culture of Connectivity: A Critical History of Social Media.* New York: Oxford University Press, 2013.

INDEX